Please return or renew this item before the date below

IMAGI...   ...EDGE

RSA

WITHDRAWN

Bright Pen

Visit us online at www.authorsonline.co.uk

D1447633

A Bright Pen Book

ISBN 978 07552 1196 8

British Library Cataloguing Publication Data.
A catalogue record for this book is available from the British Library

Authors OnLine Ltd
19 The Cinques
Gamlingay, Sandy
Bedfordshire SG19 3NU
England

This book is also available in e-book format, details of which are available at
www.authorsonline.co.uk

To my parents

Douglas and Mary H Cormack

and uncle John L McHarg

Douglas Cormack

We classify writers as expressing opinions more or less acceptable to ourselves, Yet, even as a schoolboy (1944-57) 1 noted that all were exposed to the same reality, and I concluded that opinions were mixtures of belief and subjectively selected knowledge; that science was objective, ever-expanding and internally consistent knowledge; that languages were comparatively static; and that everything else was opinion, though in those days teachers were dismissed for expressing political opinions. Thus, while I preferred knowledge to recycled opinions, and while I sought to analyse the latter into their knowledge and belief contents, I had not yet differentiated the one from the other with sufficient clarity for such general use.

Thus, while pursuing knowledge at the University of Glasgow through a 1st class honours B.Sc. in chemistry with subsidiary maths, physics, and microbiology and a Ph.D. in catalytic mechanism, followed by a postdoctoral appointment in oceanography and marine geochemistry in the USA, I continued my quest for knowledge belief differentiation by comparing the presence of direct observation and experimentation in the physicochemical earth sciences, astronomy, cosmology and cellular biology with their absence in the beliefs of pseudo-science. Meanwhile, I continued to analyse the undifferentiated mixtures of belief and knowledge which constitute history, literature, philosophy, religion and the so-called social-sciences.

Subsequently, I joined the UK Scientific Civil Service to experience belief-based socio-political policy at its interface with chemical engineering, catalysis and computerised process control, mineral processing and metal extraction, and the mechanical handling of viscous fluids, pastes, powders and phase separations; and with air pollution abatement and atmospheric monitoring, marine pollution prevention and response, materials recycling, contaminated land reclamation and waste disposal. On this experience from the levels of senior scientific officer to director/chief executive (Grade 3) including a knowledge-implementation posting to the Department's Marine Division HQ, I converted Warren Spring Laboratory to the DTI's Environmental Laboratory Agency in response to the Department's proposal to close the industrial support side of the Laboratory. Nonetheless, despite my subsequent profit-revealing annual reports having attracted venture capital interest in a management buyout, the Department closed the Agency in an apparently unconscious preference for reality-rejecting belief over knowledge.

Again, having encountered this same preference while acting as a private consultant, I have now written *The Rational Trinity: Imagination, Belief and Knowledge* to differentiate knowledge from belief, science from pseudo-science and commonsense from nonsense; to exemplify the necessity for such differentiation; and to commend *Change* from belief- to knowledge-based socio-political policies as incontestably preferable to continual change from one set of arbitrary beliefs to another in a continuing rejection of reality

Periodic table

hydrogen 1 H 1.0079																	helium 2 He 4.0026
lithium 3 Li 6.941	beryllium 4 Be 9.0122											boron 5 B 10.811	carbon 6 C 12.011	nitrogen 7 N 14.007	oxygen 8 O 15.999	fluorine 9 F 18.998	neon 10 Ne 20.180
sodium 11 Na 22.990	magnesium 12 Mg 24.305											aluminium 13 Al 26.982	silicon 14 Si 28.086	phosphorus 15 P 30.974	sulfur 16 S 32.065	chlorine 17 Cl 35.453	argon 18 Ar 39.948
potassium 19 K 39.098	calcium 20 Ca 40.078	scandium 21 Sc 44.956	titanium 22 Ti 47.867	vanadium 23 V 50.942	chromium 24 Cr 51.996	manganese 25 Mn 54.938	iron 26 Fe 55.845	cobalt 27 Co 58.933	nickel 28 Ni 58.693	copper 29 Cu 63.546	zinc 30 Zn 65.39	gallium 31 Ga 69.723	germanium 32 Ge 72.61	arsenic 33 As 74.922	selenium 34 Se 78.96	bromine 35 Br 79.904	krypton 36 Kr 83.80
rubidium 37 Rb 85.468	strontium 38 Sr 87.62	yttrium 39 Y 88.906	zirconium 40 Zr 91.224	niobium 41 Nb 92.906	molybdenum 42 Mo 95.94	technetium 43 Tc [98]	ruthenium 44 Ru 101.07	rhodium 45 Rh 102.91	palladium 46 Pd 106.42	silver 47 Ag 107.87	cadmium 48 Cd 112.41	indium 49 In 114.82	tin 50 Sn 118.71	antimony 51 Sb 121.76	tellurium 52 Te 127.60	iodine 53 I 126.90	xenon 54 Xe 131.29
caesium 55 Cs 132.91	barium 56 Ba 137.33	57-70 *	lutetium 71 Lu 174.97	hafnium 72 Hf 178.49	tantalum 73 Ta 180.95	tungsten 74 W 183.84	rhenium 75 Re 186.21	osmium 76 Os 190.23	iridium 77 Ir 192.22	platinum 78 Pt 195.08	gold 79 Au 196.97	mercury 80 Hg 200.59	thallium 81 Tl 204.38	lead 82 Pb 207.2	bismuth 83 Bi 208.98	polonium 84 Po [209]	astatine 85 At [210]	radon 86 Rn [222]
francium 87 Fr [223]	radium 88 Ra [226]	actinium 89 Ac [227]	thorium 90 Th 232.04	protactinium 91 Pa 231.04	uranium 92 U 238.03												

*Lanthanide series

lanthanum 57 La 138.91	cerium 58 Ce 140.12	praseodymium 59 Pr 140.91	neodymium 60 Nd 144.24	promethium 61 Pm [145]	samarium 62 Sm 150.36	europium 63 Eu 151.96	gadolinium 64 Gd 157.25	terbium 65 Tb 158.93	dysprosium 66 Dy 162.50	holmium 67 Ho 164.93	erbium 68 Er 167.26	thulium 69 Tm 168.93	ytterbium 70 Yb 173.04

TABLE OF CONTENTS

FOREWORD

This Book has had a life-long gestation. My father started me off by naming artefacts and their uses before I could talk and though he never sought to reduce my mother's Presbyterian influence with his agnosticism, I have been contrasting belief with knowledge since my earliest years. Thus, in primary school, I contrasted the creation myth as recounted in *Genesis* with *'How Things Began'* as broadcast on *Scottish Radio for Schools*, and I pursued such contrasts by reading widely. However, while attracted to the Enlightenment through discovering *The Free Thinker* while in senior school, I rejected secular dismissal of religion as 'irrational', by noting that rationality is common to both. Again, while secularists used Darwin's *Theory of Evolution* to reject religious belief, I discerned the theory itself to be belief in its failure to explain species-diversity as securely as the *Atomic Theory* explained my school chemistry. Yet again, while secularists rejected traditional behaviour codes as religious belief, I accepted them as knowledge-based attempts to reconcile our selfishness with the social cohesion essential to our group-species survival. Thus, I concluded that 'knowledge' and 'belief' needed clear differentiation, and that a start might be made by associating knowledge with social cohesion and progress and belief with social chaos or its totalitarian alternative.

Thus, I sought this differentiation of knowledge from belief in literature, philosophy, anthropology, history, economics and politics, while focussing on the knowledge provided by scientific method through a first in chemistry with subsidiary mathematics, physics and microbiology and a doctorate in physical chemistry at the University of Glasgow. In addition, during my post-doctoral sojourn in the USA, I extended my scientific knowledge to include oceanography, geology, meteorology and astronomy, while seeking differentiation of knowledge from belief in US history and politics. Thereafter, I joined the UK Scientific Civil Service to experience at first hand the interaction of scientific knowledge with government policy in chemical engineering, catalysis and computerised process control, mineral processing, metal extraction and the mechanical handling of viscous fluids, pastes, powders and phase separations; and in air pollution abatement and atmospheric monitoring, marine pollution prevention and response, materials recycling, contaminated land reclamation and waste disposal. On this experience, to Civil Service Grade 3 level, I concluded that humanity exhibits an unconscious preference for undifferentiated belief over knowledge in socio-political decision-making and indeed, in everyday life; and that differentiation could be based on the consistency of knowledge with reality and the inconsistency or neutrality of belief with reality.

Thus, having hypothesised that the difference between knowledge and belief is *reality-evaluation*, and having defined three categories of belief in Chapter 1, I provide evidence in Chapters 2 and 3 that our rational capacity to imagine, believe, act and observe, has been constant since the inception of our species; that reality-evaluation by observation of the consequences of imaginative belief-based action in the social sphere and on the external world produced the self-knowledge, craftsmanship and mathematics which progressed our social and physical welfare from that of hunter-gatherers to that of the city states and empires of the Iron Age; that imaginative attempts to gain knowledge of the underlying nature of our world gave rise to beliefs in the embodiment of Spirits, Essences and Forms from the Beyond, none of which were accessible to reality-evaluation; and that rational development of mathematics from its reality-validated axioms was thwarted by the number systems then available. As to beliefs incapable of resolution by reality-evaluation, Chapters 4 to 6 show that 'orthodox' Neo-Platonic Christianity sought resolution of conflicting beliefs by a series of Imperial Edicts designed to suppress all 'heretical' beliefs in the Beyond and all speculative beliefs on the underlying nature of our world; that irrespective of Pagan, Christian or Islamic beliefs, craft knowledge on the utility of the world continued to accrue, enhanced from as far east as China and by the Hindu number system, prior to re-absorption in Dark Age Christian Europe; and that Islamic beliefs opposed speculative beliefs on the nature of the world as did Christian belief.

However, counter to accusations that religion opposes knowledge, Chapters 1 to 6 show that religions had incorporated knowledge of human nature in their behaviour codes and in personifying their metaphorical deities, that they accepted all knowledge beneficial to human welfare, and that they opposed only the beliefs they chose to disbelieve. In contrast, however, Chapters 1 to 6 and 10 to 12 show that secularism opposes knowledge in promoting its own beliefs over those of religion; and that while religious-religious, secular-religious and secular-secular conflicts have usually been catastrophic to human welfare, all could have been avoided had knowledge and belief categories been sufficiently differentiated to permit those concerning human nature to be reality-evaluated against our need for social-cohesion while permitting those beyond reality-evaluation to be accepted, suspended or rejected as matters of personal preference. On the other hand, Chapters 7 to 9 show that the extension of reality-evaluation to beliefs concerning the underlying nature of our world produced the scientific method of experimentation which coupled to mathematics displaced belief in Spirits, Essences and Forms with knowledge of our world and cosmos in terms of its constituent atoms and energy; that this scientific method transformed earlier descriptive knowledge in astronomy, earth sciences and biology to the physicochemical sciences and associated welfare supporting technologies of today; and that while we may now be approaching our imaginative limits for production of beliefs (hypotheses) for further reality-evaluation, analysis of the applications and products of scientific method from its inception to our current knowledge of the wave-particle duality, relativity and quanta as provided in Chapters 5 to 9, fully describe the nature of this experimentation method of knowledge-acquisition while confirming reality-evaluation as the difference between knowledge and belief in general.

Thus, Chapters 10 to 12 show that we have nothing but belief, when reality-evaluation is absent; that secularism ignores reality-evaluation in dismissing the knowledge-content of traditional behaviour codes while promoting its own arbitrary interpretations of beliefs in equality, freedom and rights without reality-evaluating any of them against our requirements for social cohesion; that it claims spurious credit for science and technology as products of its rationality, while corrupting existing knowledge and scientific method to produce pseudo-science to protect its beliefs from commonsense challenge; and that having thus corrupted the social-sciences, the physicochemical sciences are now being corrupted by belief in the incompatibility of technology with biosphere welfare. Thus, despite the innateness of human nature and the knowledge-content of traditional behaviour codes from time immemorial, and despite the development of knowledge-based materials recycling and health, safety and environmental protection from hunter-gathering to the present, the beliefs of secularism and environmentalism are now more damaging to social and physical welfare than religious belief ever was, the religious never having resorted to pseudo-science.

Thus, despite reality-evaluation being the difference between knowledge and belief, and despite all social and physical welfare improvements having been knowledge-based, Chapters 10 to 12 show that arbitrary beliefs are now displacing knowledge because scientists, pseudo-scientists and the general public now support 'politically correct' beliefs when seeking socio-political preferment; that while the preference for belief over undifferentiated knowledge caused previous socio-political catastrophes, such preference is now aided and abetted by pseudo-science; that modernist democracies are now more belief-driven than were earlier social systems, though the beliefs are now secular rather than religious; and that while our condition is not yet catastrophic, social breakdown and damage to our physical, environmental and economic welfare are already observable though still moderated by innate commonsense despite the ubiquitous efforts of proselytising believers. However, these chapters also show that our socio-political affairs could become knowledge-based by public insistence that policy be implemented only after reality-validation, that all failures of previously implemented policies be treated as reality-refutations of their initiating beliefs; and that this change from belief to knowledge is the Change we need above all others.

This Book is, therefore, intended to expand public understanding of science to these ends, by showing how beliefs about the usefulness of our world were transformed to our traditional knowledge of craftsmanship and human nature by reality-evaluation through trial and error; by showing how beliefs about the underlying nature of our world were transformed to knowledge by the scientific method of reality-evaluation by experimentation; and by providing enough examples of use, non-use and misuse of this scientific method to permit public differentiation of science from pseudo-science, knowledge from belief and commonsense from nonsense. Further to these ends, this Book is also intended to show that while our species-specific capacities may limit further acquisition of physicochemical knowledge, there is much to be gained from conducting our socio-political affairs on the basis of commonsense, knowledge and scientific method rather than on belief, pseudo-science and nonsense; and that while the Beyond will certainly remain Unknowable, there is much inspiration, motivation and encouragement to be drawn from accepting or suspending beliefs beyond reality-evaluation, so long as we reject all beliefs which cannot be reality-validated as conducive to the social cohesion and physical welfare on which our group-species survival will always depend.

D. Cormack
November 2009

CHAPTER 1: INTRODUCTION

In my Foreword, I defined the difference between knowledge and belief as reality-evaluation. I now describe the process by which we convert belief to knowledge or otherwise stop at belief. My contention is that the external world interacts with our senses to stimulate our imagination to create belief as to the stimuli; that this becomes knowledge only when reality-evaluated for consistency with other stimuli; that even when knowledge stimulates imaginative belief, further knowledge requires further reality-evaluation; that rationality is the linkage whether the process stops at belief or completes to knowledge; and that without this rationality we could not share belief or knowledge in conversation or act cooperatively on either. Thus, the complete process is the *Rational Trinity* and its non-completion is the *Rational Duality*.

Thus, the tool-making of our hominid ancestors and our subsequent development of craftsmanship, science and technology are products of the Trinity, religion and philosophy are products of the Duality, and our traditional behaviour-codes, ethics, literature and political philosophy are undifferentiated mixtures of both, with imagination being the source of all. Thus, I compare the respective products of knowledge and belief to clarify their differentiation and I maintain this clarification by avoiding all common-speech 'synonyms' for 'knowledge' and 'belief'. In addition, my differentiation in terms of the completeness or incompleteness of a single rational process shows that both knowledge and belief are rational, that preferment of belief over knowledge is nonetheless mistaken, and that adherence to reality-refuted belief is the reality-rejection of madness.

Thus, not all beliefs can be transposed to positive or negative knowledge by reality-evaluation. Accordingly, I allocate to Category A, the purposeful beliefs (hypotheses) which on reality-evaluation produce the knowledge which is craftsmanship, science and technology together with *proto-knowledge* defined as belief unrecognised as knowledge though in conformity with commonsense; to Category B, beliefs which are inaccessible to reality-evaluation either in principle or *pro tem*; and to Category C, those which persist despite reality-refutation. Further to Category A, I define the *Ur-belief in knowledge* as that which believes ourselves and our surroundings to be knowable and which gives rise to the hypotheses of Category A while itself remaining suspended belief. Again, as to Category B, I define the *Ur-belief of religion* as our unformulated awareness of the Unknowable, the specific derivatives of which can only be accepted, rejected or suspended, or if touching on the reality of human nature can be submitted to reality-evaluation as hypotheses of Category A or to Category C as already reality-refuted; and the *Ur-belief in rationality* which must itself be rejected as believing knowledge to be available without reality-evaluation, though its derivatives may be submitted to reality-evaluation as hypotheses of Category A or to Category C as reality-refuted, while rationality develops mathematics from reality-validated axioms.

On this basis, my reviews of the Rational Trinity in action on Category A beliefs show that it produced not only the knowledge which is craftsmanship, science and technology, but also the self-knowledge of human nature which is the knowledge component of traditional behaviour codes, ethics, literature and political philosophy. Thus, I show that this knowledge of human nature arose from having to reconcile our innate selfishness with our innate interdependence as required for our survival and social cohesion as a group-species; that derivatives of the religious Ur-belief itself are reflections of this self-knowledge as confirmed by their ability to provide emotional support and to inspire motivate and encourage compliance with the required behaviour; and that such knowledge is accepted as belief by the religious and rejected as such by the anti-religious in a joint failure to accept reality as its source. Again, these reviews show that our concepts of good and bad and of right and wrong reflect knowledge of what works or not in craftsmanship and of what is beneficial or not to our collective survival; and that our conscience and sense of fairness express our innate acceptance of responsibility for this survival.

Nonetheless, my reviews of philosophy and religion show that the non- and anti-religious now rely on the rational Ur-belief in substituting their own beliefs for the self-knowledge component (empiricism) of traditional behaviour codes, ethics and political philosophy; that these secular beliefs should have been submitted to reality-evaluation as Category A hypotheses to confirm or develop our self-knowledge; and that in moulding social policy to these beliefs without reality-evaluation, secularists have shown themselves not only anti-religious but also anti-knowledge in their retention of beliefs consignable to Category C by their failure on implementation as social policy.

However, I show that this self-knowledge guides analysis of literary and dramatic works for the *Truth* of their content as judged by their capacity to inspire, motivate and encourage and by their capacity to provide emotional satisfaction through their artistry; that religious texts and dramatic ceremonials are not analysed in this way; and that denial of the self-knowledge of religion perpetuates the belief-based debate between the secular and religious despite its being resolvable by knowledge recognition and agreement to accept, reject or suspend belief. Thus, I show that both humanist and religious texts are mixtures of self-knowledge and belief, no matter how much the contestants respectively deny it; that the knowledge-content of religion relieves loneliness and improves behaviour, even when belief is suspended; that secularism bereft of this knowledge does neither, even when its beliefs are accepted; and that the belief-driven conflicts of both religion and secularism are equally bloodthirsty in their irrationality.

As to rejection of the Ur-belief in rationality as a source of knowledge, my reviews of craftsmanship, science and philosophy from the Dark Age to 1800 show that philosophers who had failed to recognise the reality-evaluation implicit in craftsmanship's use of reality, now failed to recognise it in the scientific method of experimentation which had begun to investigate the nature of reality. Thus, while reality-evaluation by direct observation had been the unconscious *sine qua non* of craftsmanship over millennia and while some in the Renaissance had welcomed experimentation, Enlightenment humanists maintained their mistaken reliance on rationality. Thus, whether failure to recognise reality-evaluation as the only means of transforming belief (philosophy) to knowledge (science) was due to ignorance or self-interest, I show that philosophy remained stalled on the Rational Duality, and that association of the term 'enlightenment' with eighteenth century secular humanism was mistaken then and since. However, as to progress by the Rational Trinity, my review of craftsmanship, science, technology and philosophy from the eighteenth century to the present day shows that science for its own sake went from strength to strength, transformed craftsmanship to self-supporting technology and brought about the abandonment of philosophy as a knowledge-source, though not as a source of belief. Indeed, scientists are as attracted to belief as anyone when in socio-political mode and especially when seeking public funds.

However, professional exponents of the Duality being incapable of any knowledge-based progress, began to categorise the humanities and science as distinct cultures, the former being civilising, liberalising and humanising and the latter de-humanising, illiberal and war-mongering. Now, while some such self-justification was to be expected, I show that the true dichotomy is

2

belief and knowledge, not art and science; and that science, technology, craft and art are sub-divisions of the knowledge continuum within which disputes, let alone wars do not arise. In addition, my reviews of religion and of the separate branches of philosophy show that consensus of belief is at best only a temporary stabilisation in an otherwise perpetual ferment with socio-political implementation of such consensual stabilisations being the source of the ills mistakenly attributed to science; and that even when differences in belief are peacefully containable within public debate, the ballot-box never provides conclusive stabilisation, reality-evaluation being absent from socio-politics. Indeed, stabilisations achieved by violence are only temporary, though they may be prolonged by further violence or its threat.

Thus, my review of social-political systems shows that while differences in belief can cause internal violence, knowledge brings peaceful resolution; and that while belief-based debate cannot avoid warfare over territory and resources relating to survival, all such can be aggravated by differences in cultural and religious beliefs quite unrelated to reality. Thus, I show that internal differences in belief destroyed the Roman Empire while inter-group differences perpetuated violence through the ensuing Dark Age, the religious wars of the counter-Reformation and all secular revolutions and wars thereafter; and that conflict resolution has always required knowledge-based action or direct contact with reality in the end. Thus, I show that whether belief or avarice be the cause, differentiation of knowledge from belief and preference for the former reduces the scope for conflict in all such cases; and that while physical force can be unavoidable, knowledge-based negotiation is more successful than its belief-based alternative.

As to whether there need ever be conflict between knowledge and belief, I show that none need arise between knowledge and category A beliefs (hypotheses), these being destined to become knowledge by reality-evaluation. Nor can conflict rationally arise between knowledge and category C beliefs, these having already been reality-refuted. Again, as to the religious Ur-belief of category B, there should be no dispute with knowledge let alone life-or-death conflict, such belief and its derivatives being beyond reality-evaluation in principle. Furthermore, with respect to derivatives of the religious Ur-belief and secular interpretations of the rational Ur-belief which touch on reality, my sub-division into belief category A (for reality-evaluation), category B (pending possible hypothesis formulation) and category C (already reality-refuted) can rationally prevent conflict with knowledge in every case. Thus, I show that such derivative beliefs, having no intrinsic value other than as hypotheses with respect to reality, provide no grounds for conflict with knowledge, and that believers have so far avoided this no-contest defeat by knowledge only because belief and knowledge have not been differentiated in my terms. Indeed, I show that religious and secular believers maintain a semblance of consequence for their respective beliefs only through their on-going struggle for control of human behaviour irrespective of our need for knowledge-based social cohesion; and that it is this mutually supportive obfuscation alone which avoids confrontation with knowledge and inevitable defeat for reality-refuted belief.

Thus, I show that conflict is not between belief and knowledge: it is between belief and belief. Again, as to claims that secular (belief-based) proposals for social improvement are opposed by religious belief in continuance of its earlier opposition to knowledge, I show that secular belief is not knowledge; that craft- knowledge has been acceptable to religious belief since time immemorial; that while prayer and sacrifice were believed to influence crop yield, they were never believed to be substitutes for the sowing of seed, survival related knowledge trumping belief in agriculture as it had in the maintenance of group cohesion. Again, in classical times, craft knowledge was accepted without question while the speculations of natural philosophy were co-extensive with religion, speculators and believers accepting or rejecting speculations as they did beliefs. Indeed, my review of early Christianity shows that orthodoxy opposed speculation as it did

3

heresy while craftsmanship developed unmolested through the Dark Age. Again, craftsmanship and natural philosophy were accepted by Islam until speculation conflicted with orthodoxy. Later, it was speculation with some undifferentiated (craft-like) knowledge of reality which might have been rejected had Thomas Aquinas not argued for its acceptance, while in any case, craftsmanship progressed to the end of the seventeenth century without knowing anything about the underlying nature of its materials and processes. Thus, I show that knowledge was rarely if ever opposed by the religious; that speculation was opposed as is one belief by another; that Christians became as tolerant of scientific knowledge as they had been of craft knowledge; and that the more pressing issue now is whether secular belief can tolerate knowledge in the socio-political sphere other than as a misapplied weapon against religion.

In fact, my reviews from the Renaissance onwards show that the possibility of dispute between Christian belief and knowledge evaporated into peaceful coexistence, this being particularly so with the Reformed Churches in which belief in a one-to-one relationship between the self and God, permitted more freedom in general. However, this religious freedom with its interest in self-improvement led to secular socio-political systems as shown by my review of developments in political philosophy from the sixteenth century to the present day. However, coexistence of scientific knowledge with religious belief was entirely possible. Thus, whether believing themselves to be revealing the mysteries of God's creation or whether indifferent to religious belief, there is little evidence of active campaigning against religion by scientists. On the other hand, I show that secularists used rationality/irrationality as a surrogate for secular/religious in promoting belief-based socio-political change; that rather than differentiating belief from knowledge, they conflated their rationality with knowledge to decry as irrational the knowledge-based codes of religion; and that in doing so they exhibited more desire to destroy religion than did any scientist other than Darwinists then and since, though their campaign is one of belief against belief.

Thus, I show that in touting rationality to discredit religion, the secular produced no new knowledge, though they did produce belief spectra as irresolvable as the heresy spectra with which orthodoxy had contended, reality-evaluation being shunned by believers as damaging to their respective beliefs. Indeed, so prevalent and multifarious is secular socio-political belief today that it is scarcely possible to identify a knowledge-based policy implementation to compare its success with the plethora of belief-based failures, none of which are accepted as a reality-refutation of belief or an opportunity to implement a knowledge-based alternative. Thus, while voter apathy is attributed to loss of trust in the personal probity of politicians, I show that unfulfilled promises, the persistence of inconclusive debate and the rejection of commonsense are the more likely causes; and that while voters have yet to articulate their disquiet in terms of knowledge differentiated from belief, replacement of the latter by the former would transform failure to success and voter apathy to enthusiasm.

Meanwhile, uncritical acceptance of secular belief permits one interpretation to defend another without limit while reality is rejected. Thus, knowledge-based behaviour codes have been set aside by optimistic juggling of beliefs in equality, freedom and rights, while Utopia's absence is attributed to the continuing presence of the religious authoritarianism mistakenly believed to have opposed 'rationality' all along. However, having shown this to be a fallacy, I also show that secular authoritarianism has no vestige of reality-evaluation; that its preference for belief over knowledge is irrational; that it treats its 'self-evident truths' as justifying suppression of counter-evidence and citation of partial supporting evidence where it deems such necessary to convince an otherwise sceptical public; that the ambience of belief thus created turns social-science to pseudo-science detrimental to social welfare, and physicochemical science from knowledge-based concern

4

for environment, recycling, health and safety to belief-based counter-productive alternatives to the detriment of physical welfare; and that all such misdirection could have been avoided had knowledge been differentiated from belief in what would then have been a real Enlightenment.

Thus, I show that those who believe technology to be heading for environmental disaster have no more regard for reality-evaluation than those who seek a belief-based social Utopia; that current interpretations of beliefs in equality, freedom and rights lack the reality-validation (empiricism) without which no socio-political system can be justified; that other arbitrary interpretations of these same beliefs have already led to dictatorships and to the most damaging conflicts in human history; that such arbitrariness of interpretation is the unrecognised source of national and international conflict; that secular beliefs are now a greater barrier to socio-political progress than religious beliefs ever were, the behaviour codes of the latter having a knowledge-content lacking in the former; and that reversal of the current preference for belief over knowledge requires the voting public to rely on its commonsense in insisting on policy failures being recognised as reality-refutations of belief, and in calling for knowledge-based alternatives.

As to the likelihood of this reversal being achieved by commonsense, I show that our innate Rational Trinity interacts with our surroundings from birth to provide the knowledge necessary for our immediate and early survival; that this process is subconscious before it is conscious as with all species within their species-specific limits; and that it has been operative since the inception of *Homo sapiens* as the basis of our inadvertent copying of our elders, of our trial and error learning and of our absorption of knowledge during upbringing and general education. Thus, commonsense is what we have innately learnt as a species and with others in our culture as non-specialist experiential knowledge for use and augmentation in all new situations including the acquisition of specialist knowledge. Thus, the latter is a further manifestation of the commonsense which secured our natural survival in the first place through our innate differentiation of good from bad, right from wrong and success from failure by reference to reality. Again, while we sometimes have to act on incomplete knowledge, on a mixture of knowledge and belief, or on belief alone, with mistakes being thus made at individual, national and international levels, we should recall that our individual commonsense is supplemented by that of our species as preserved in the knowledge-content of our behaviour-codes, cultural practices and historical records; that in relying on these we are relying as we would on a wise and experienced friend; and that commonsense should thus be adequate to differentiate knowledge from belief by noting the presence or absence of reality-evaluation.

Thus, with this expansion of my Foreword, I have introduced my history of science as a subset of knowledge contrasted with belief, the objective of which is to engage commonsense in changing belief-based democracy to knowledge-based democracy to avoid its destruction by rejected-reality, this *Change* being overdue, imperative and possible for the first time, knowledge having now been differentiated from belief and science from pseudo-science as defined and exemplified herein.

CHAPTER 2: FROM PRE-HISTORY TO THE IRON AGE

I start by establishing the commonality and continuity of our human inheritance, by comparing the innate abilities and behaviour patterns of other group-species with those of our apelike and hominid precursors, and by tracing the (DNA-related) evolutionary changes revealed through the developing craftsmanship and social arrangements of these precursors prior to the inception of our own *Homo sapiens*. Thereafter, I trace the manner in which our then stabilised species-specific capacities for the Rational Trinity and Duality were used from hunter-gatherer migrations through our earliest agricultural settlements to the city states and empires of the Iron Age, citing knowledge of geology, biology, archaeology, anthropology, history and physicochemical measurements of time and temperature.

These citations suggest that the imaginations of our earliest apelike and hominid ancestors were producing beliefs concerning day-to-day survival and social interaction while transforming some of them to proto-knowledge by unconscious reality-evaluation at the point of imaginative conception; that knowledge at the level of commonsense was later produced from unconscious reality-evaluation of beliefs as opportunity arose; and that later still, the imagination acted on this knowledge to produce hypotheses for reality-validation to more knowledge. The evidence also suggests that imagination would have produced beliefs beyond reality-evaluation either in practice or in principle; that such knowledge and un-validated beliefs were shared in social groupings at distinct locations; that these were bequeathed to successive generations as cultural acquisitions; and that all change would have been cultural henceforth, our innate brain/body capabilities having by then stabilised at the level characteristic of *Homo sapiens*.

2. 1 THE INHERITANCE OF HUMANKIND

Our earliest known inheritance has been traced back to the first ape-like fossils found in Kenya (circa 26 million years ago) *via* the more modern ape-like Afropithecines and other such fossils of Europe and Asia (c. 18 million years ago) though there is a gap in the fossil record coinciding with the up-lift of the Tibetan Plateau to a height of several kilometres over an area of several million square kilometres by the tectonic northwards movement of India, an event which altered the monsoon wind pattern sufficient to turn east African rainforest to the savannah (grassland) into which previously tree-dwelling apes moved about 5 million years ago (c.f. Sections 9.4.2 and 9.4.3). Thereafter, *Australopithecus afarensis* with a hip-structure similar to our own and a height of about 1m is found in Ethiopia, (c. 3 million years ago) followed by several other species with (volcanic) rock-piece tools and cave-dwelling habits at Olduvai, Tanzania (c. 2 million years ago), by *Homo habilis* with enlargement of the brain region (Broca's Area) associated with speech (ibid c. 1.7 million years), and by *Homo erectus* showing further development and a height of 1.8m in Africa, Europe and Asia (between 1.0 - 1.5 million years ago). As to tool-making, however, more recent finds in Ethiopia have pushed the earliest evidence back to 2.5 million years ago.

Over the last million years or so oscillations in ambient temperature (c.f. Section 9.4.3) are likely to have driven tool and artefact development towards greater levels of comfort provision and may have driven less adaptable hominids to extinction. Nonetheless, sharp flint tools have been found at Parkestone, Suffolk, (700,000 years ago) and there is evidence for the butchering of horse, deer and rhino by *Homo heidelbergensis* in Europe including Boxgrove, Sussex, (500,000 years ago). Later, in Europe (200,000-35,000 years ago) *Homo neanderthalensis* shows further brain development, evidence of speech, significant tool and artefact development and burial of the dead. Again, though his precursors seem to have been widely distributed, the earliest finds of *Homo sapiens* were once more in Ethiopia (c. 195,000 years ago) from whence he is supposed to have migrated northwards as temperatures permitted, as evidenced by a find in Israel (c.100,000 years ago).

Though finds do not prove location of origin, these fossilised remains from the earliest hominid to *Homo sapiens* indicate that the dexterity and knowledge to produce tools and artefacts was developing in step with changes in physical structure and increased brain-size and brain/body coordination, such changes being more likely due to step-changes in molecular DNA, than to natural variation and selection of the fittest individuals of an otherwise invariant species, though there is no direct evidence for either possibility (c.f. Sections 8.3.3, 9.2.4, 9.2.5 and 9.5.4). In any event, the structure and brain-size of *Homo sapiens* has not changed since first appearance, strongly indicating that brain/body coordination and intellectual capacity have not changed either; and that such climate changes as have occurred have been within our capacity to survive through tool and artefact development and/or migration to more congenial climes.

The available record also suggests that we inherited our capacity for group-living from our arboreal and ground dwelling precursors, these being similar to that of the other group-species of today, such as apes, monkeys, wolves, horses, reindeer, elephants *etc*. From this we may conclude that our social capacities are innate; that these involve mutual benefits and obligations between individual and group; that our care and regard for the living extends to mourning for the dead; and that we accept internal group hierarchy. Thus, our earliest cooperative hunting bands and work teams would have arisen from our innate social bonding, as would leaders capable of balancing self and group interests as required for social cohesion and the projection of unified force in defence of group territory. Such group activity is exemplified by Meerkats in taking direction from leaders to the benefit of the group, in exiling miscreants and in fighting other groups over territory; and by chimpanzees in competing for internal resources without destroying group cohesion under the leader and in engaging in inter-group conflict which can result in deaths on both sides in a manner reminiscent of human encouragement of warrior prowess directed outside the group and its discouragement inside. Thus, self-sacrifice may also be taken as innate to group-species, such sacrifice being without survival value unless of benefit to the group.

As to development, we may conclude that hominid behaviour initially similar to precursor apes, would have diverged as evolution proceeded towards *Homo sapiens*. Thus, the more or less equal male and female roles in hunting and gathering would have diverged with increasing male focus on hunting and female focus on the rearing of offspring as the period of dependency on parents lengthened with increasing brain-size and lengthening periods of post-natal development. Later, this sex-based division would have lent itself to successive elaboration in which males and females would have been required to commit to partnerships of sufficient duration to bring offspring to independent adulthood, within which females developed a full domestic role while males hunted and generally roistered about. Later, this male free-time was allocated to constructive roles beyond direct food provision in which males either initiated plans for the employment of other males or took orders from initiators within generally acceptable limits of hierarchical control and group cohesion. In contrast domestic females would have been comparatively independent of other females, except perhaps for shared supervision of offspring. Of course, contentment with this demarcation might have been less than general, but the reality to

7

which it is a response has only recently been challenged, though more on the basis of changing belief than of knowledge (c.f. Section 11.2.3). Nonetheless, life-long male/female partnerships must have been essential to overall social cohesion and to ensuring the proper nurturing of consecutive generations in the interests of group survival.

As to craftsmanship, we may conclude that the innate abilities of early hominids would have been similar to those of modern apes. Chimpanzees use straws to extract edible ants from their nests without damaging nests or angering ants. Again, monkeys also use stones as hammer or anvil to crack nuts, the young showing great motivation and persistence until their initially limited dexterity proves equal to the task. The reported observation that some geographically isolated groups are unaware of this technique shows that individuals are not all equally innovative and that cultural transmission of such individually-acquired knowledge is not limited to humans. Again, crows are capable of bending lengths of wire to hook and remove desirable objects not otherwise extractable from transparent jars. We may also suppose that the shelter-building ability of early hominids would have been comparable to that of modern chimpanzees and thus markedly inferior to that of birds such as tits and martins, and that cave use by hominids and early man must have been similar to that of bears. As to the development of manual dexterity, evidence suggests that the vertical gait which confers height advantage for predator and prey detection on grasslands in the absence of climbable trees, would also have freed the hands for ever-divergent purposes, while the grassland game-diet would have sustained the increased brain development and the increased brain/hand coordination which facilitated the making of an ever-diversifying range of tools for an ever-diversifying range of uses as Rational Trinity capacity developed to that of *Homo sapiens*.

As to the development of social hierarchy, observation of ground-hunters such as wolves and the hounds bred from them, show that individual differences in hunting ability depend more on sense-perception than on physical strength and that pack members defer to individuals possessing higher levels of the former in the emergence of leaders. Thus, it seems reasonable to suppose that hominids and early man would have become increasingly aware of attributes other than brute strength; that this would have extended beyond hunting to other activities; and that this, in turn, would have led to a division of labour in tool and artefact production and eventually to recognition of the need for leadership in the direction and management of both labour and defence deployments. Thus, we can discern the emergence of chiefs, innovators and craftsmen, and surely by now, shaman priests and/or medicine men. In passing, we might suppose that the inducement to urination provided by running water led to belief in rainmaking by the symbolic scattering of water and thus to all other forms of *Sympathetic Magic*.

It may be concluded that archaeological and anthropological comparisons support this assessment that early man was sociable and co-operative; that he progressively used the materials to hand to increase his survival chances and subsequent welfare whatever his habitat; that he increased the efficiency of his hunting weapons and extended the range of animals corporately hunted; and that he consequently extended his range of workable materials beyond the initial stone, wood, creeper, leaves *etc*, to bone, horn, sinew, skin, fur and feather which, in turn, extended his range of tools, uses and artefacts. Thus, the rate and extent to which needs were satisfied by weapons and tools, by clothing and shelter and by domestic utensils for collection and storage of food and water can be traced reasonably accurately from finds in bone, ivory, stone and earthenware which are stable over archaeological timescales, while the use of the more degradable materials such as skins, *etc* can often be deduced from finds of the more stable tools used to work them, such as needles, knives, and scrapers, all such finds being directly comparable with equivalents in use today by people with the inherited capacities of *Homo sapiens* who yet continue to follow the Palaeolithic lifestyle (c.f. below). Thus, it may be concluded that the innately inherited and unchanging capacities of *Homo sapiens* are our Rational Trinity and Duality which combined with our brain/body coordination have produced all of the social structure, craftsmanship, art, religion, philosophy, literature, law, science and technology which are to be reviewed in this book, starting now with the social arrangements, craftsmanship and group-migrations of the Palaeolithic Age.

2. 2 CRAFTSMANSHIP AND MIGRATION IN THE PALAEOLITHIC AGE

Having reviewed our innately inherited capacities for tool making and social living over some 5 million years, I now turn to their use in developing the hunter-gatherer lifestyle of the Palaeolithic Age of *Homo sapiens* which over some 200,000 years brought him to the agricultural lifestyle of the Mesolithic by about 10,000 BC. As with our ape-like and hominid precursors, the evidence I draw upon is from archaeology and anthropology supported by physicochemical dating and climatic evidence (c.f. Section 9.4.3), the achievements now reviewed being largely those of our own species.

2. 2. 1 The Birth of Tools, Artefacts, and Art

We have all had the experience of reaching for something handy to deliver a blow to something else in order to achieve a desired outcome, of noticing that the implement in hand is not as effective as it might be, and of looking for something more suitable. Again, we have all had the experience of believing that greater suitability might be achieved by modifying the original implement or by using it in a different way for this or that related task to achieve the same or a different outcome. Early hominids and man in the act of surviving, must have had such experiences repeatedly in daily efforts to perform basic tasks such as hitting, piercing, cutting, scraping, digging *etc*. Relating these experiences to my Rational Trinity, we see that the first step is the sense stimulation of an imagined need for action and outcome leading to a belief that use of the object to hand might achieve the imagined outcome; that the second step is implementation of this belief through appropriate brain/body coordination; and that the third is registration of the sensed stimuli which reveal the belief to be valid or not, thus transforming the belief to knowledge of cause and effect in respect of action and outcome. Such knowledge once acquired is of course available for repeated application and as a basis for any imagined modification of implement or use which through reiteration of the Rational Trinity will provide further knowledge from reality-validation of further belief, and so on. Again, though such innovations are due to individuals, maximum benefit requires social dissemination while their accumulation produces distinct cultural groupings.

For *Homo habilis* the objects to hand were small pieces of volcanic rock and there is no archaeological evidence that he progressed any further than acquiring knowledge that such could be put to use as found. For subsequent hominids and for *Homo sapiens*, however, the archaeological evidence reveals that my Rational Trinity identified other naturally available items which could be used as tools, such as hand sized stones (hammers), sharp-edged stones (axes), pointed stones and antlers (picks) and shoulder blades (shovels). If, however, the stone chosen as a hammer happened to be flint, its shattering on impact would have produced some sharp-edged fragments the cutting ability of which might have been immediately evidenced by a hand in contact with an edge. This knowledge acquisition by accident, would have amounted to the Rational Trinity in a flash. From there, step-wise application of the Trinity by suitably controlled impacts would have caused flint to exhibit its characteristic shell-like (conchoidal) fracture to produce flakes with cutting edges of various desired sizes for a range of uses, thus creating new tools for different tasks and all with an attractively smooth and shiny finish. Similarly, other materials were found to exhibit conchoidal fracture as alternatives to flint such as those now known as the similarly siliceous, obsidian and chert.

Once these initial observations had been made and appreciated, those with the necessary dexterity were fully able to develop production techniques while others developed user skills and yet others developed trade with those without ready access to sources of flint or acceptable substitutes, and all on application of the Rational Trinity as appropriate. As to modification of the initial technique, two distinct approaches were developed. In one, small flakes were chipped off as waste in the formation of core tools, such as axe, arrow - or spear-head. In the other, larger flakes were themselves the desired cutting blades or scrapers, these being produced by holding the source flint in one hand and striking it with a non-flaking pebble held in the other. In yet another, the flint was itself struck against a larger stone used as an anvil, or the flakes were struck from the side of a tortoise-shaped flint in an early example of more-or-less uniform mass production. Current flint knappers use a further modification known as pressure flaking in which a sharp piece of wood or bone is pressed hard against the work piece to produce the desired edge by controlled detachment of small flakes. By the late Stone Age, demand had created major centres of flint mining and knapping and well-established trade routes, the latter having been mapped by finds of flint products from single major sources. One such source is Grimes Graves in Norfolk, with its radiating galleries from shafts up to 10m deep and annual production rates estimated at thousands of tonnes. Where flint was unavailable or when its tendency to flake was a disadvantage in heavy work such as tree-felling, igneous rock such as basalt was used. Here process modification involved rough shaping by impaction with harder stone and finishing by grinding on sandstone or on a harder surface with sand and water. Clearly all such process modifications were achieved by successive applications of the Rational Trinity.

I will not attempt thus to account for the development of all Palaeolithic tools, fish hooks, traps, weapons, utensils, clothes, shelters and so on, though Rational Trinity chains similar to those outlined above apply *mutatis mutandis* to all of them. The general approach involves imaginative identification of need and opportunity, followed by belief in a hypothetical means of satisfying the need or opportunity, belief-driven action to create a prototype and observation of its effectiveness in use, with the whole process creating knowledge through the continuous application of rationality and reality-evaluation. Once a useable prototype has been produced, the imagination to recognise the scope for improvement will lead to development of the Mark II by the same process as previously led to the Mark I, and so on. The same process, *mutatis mutandis*, leads to distribution of the products and to the means of producing them fast enough to satisfy market demand.

It has already been noted that the keenness of basalt axe-edges was increased by sandstone or sand-grain and water grinding. Fine finishing as decoration, however, shows expenditure of effort beyond utilitarian need to the satisfaction of emotional need. Thus, axe heads were polished, perhaps by burnishing with leather and powdered clays of the fuller's earth type while the handle-finish on some daggers shows as much expenditure of time as does the sharpness of the blade. Earlier examples of time expenditure to conceptual ends are the female figures often carved from ivory and only a few cm in height found widely in Italy, France and Russia (c. 25,000 BC). Again, from as early as 40,000 BC paintings on cave walls may have been widespread, the best known examples being located at Altamira in Spain and at Chauvet and Lascaux in France, though similar less well executed examples have been found in the Urals. Taken together these depict animal and human activities and artefacts for which archaeological finds have otherwise suggested much later dates. In addition, these works reveal knowledge of natural pigments and drawing abilities as commendable as the best modern offerings, though some non-pigmented outline engravings of

10

somewhat less recognisable animals have also been found in North Africa. These efforts being well beyond the needs of survival must have had conceptual significance, though as always their existence is explained by their creators having imagined such to be creatable, having believed the means to be at hand, and having tested the belief by doing and by reality-evaluating the result.

2. 2. 2 Habitat Related Migration

Though temperature trends and oscillations caused no evolutionary change on *Homo sapiens*, they would have been sufficient to encourage development and adaptation of tools, artefacts and practices to enhance the comfort of living with such changes, while migration would have been a less technically demanding alternative. Again, as with everything else, migration would initially have been an imagined solution, believed to be possible, evaluated by implementation and transformed to the knowledge that it was beneficial in practice. I now consider these climatic threats and the migratory option in more detail.

As previously indicated, the Earth was experiencing a relatively warm and dry period when, 5 million years ago our ancient ape-like ancestors began life on the expanding savannah. However, temperatures were falling and by 2.5 million years ago the ice-free northern hemisphere began to glaciate. Nonetheless, as previously noted there were temperature oscillations within the last million years which might have had a forcing effect in regions inhabited by hominids. Indeed, they were sufficient to have rendered northern regions such as the British Isles uninhabitable for about seven distinct periods over the last 700,000 years. Thus, for example, the southwards advance of ice around 380,000 years ago would have wiped out hominids or caused them to migrate south, while another would have similarly affected Neanderthals who are known to have been in these Isles between 60,000 and 30,000 years ago. Indeed, temperatures were low enough for their oscillations to have encouraged both Neanderthals and *Homo sapiens* in their progressive craft based developments over the last 0.25 million years. Again, though there was a gradual warming from about 18,000 years ago, another notably cold interval occurred between 13,000 and 11,500 BC and it is unclear whether *Homo sapiens* could have survived this Younger Dryas Event without migrating south to Europe, such migration entailing a trek across what is now the English Channel, the thickness and extent of the northern icecap and consequent lowering of sea level making such pedestrian migration possible (c.f. Section 9.4.3 and 9.4.4).

Indeed, earlier in the current ice age, sea levels were between 100 and 200m lower than now, the warming which started 18,000 years ago gradually melting the then ice-cover and flooding what had previously been wide coastal plains as sea level rose. Nonetheless, after the temperature rise of some 7° C in about 50 years which ended the Younger Dryas Event some 11,500 years ago, this higher temperature with its smaller oscillations has remained substantially constant to the present, though the underlying trend is likely to be upwards until the present residual glaciation ends. It seems likely that memories of the earlier flooding have come down to us through the *Book of Genesis*, the *Epic of Gilgamesh*, songs and dances of the aboriginal inhabitants of Australia and the folklore of Celtic Britain. Prior to the current warming period, however, lowered sea levels had caused 'land bridges' to join Siberia to Alaska, the British Isles to Europe, Japan to China and Australia to the Indonesian Islands and to the Malay Peninsula, all of which facilitated the migration of animals and people. Though archaeological finds do not identify locations of origin, they reveal migrations consistent with temperature, sea-level and land-bridge data which account for human presence in Europe, Asia including Japan and Australia some 50,000 years ago, and in North America around 20,000 years ago. It should be noted that these global-temperature and sea-level changes will continue to occur and recur regardless of any inconvenience to us or of our attempts to stop them.

Though 'land-bridge' migration from Asia to the Americas has been supported by genetic studies of the native peoples of both continents, a complementary transatlantic route has recently been proposed. As to the latter, flint weapon finds in Siberia are reported dissimilar to those of North America, while the spear and harpoon heads of the latter are similar to those of south-western France while DNA analysis of the Ajibwa Tribe of the Great Lakes suggests transatlantic migration some 18,000 years ago. Thus we may visualise migration in latitudes of the Bay of Biscay and the Great Lakes along the southern edge of the northern sea-ice by people with water-proof stitched caribou clothing and *en route* kayak-borne hunting techniques similar to those of the current Inuit (Eskimo) at a time when the population of Europe would have been limited to the Mediterranean coast and Iberian Peninsula before following the retreating ice to the north as the climate became more favourable particularly from 11,500 BC onwards. Whatever the entry to North America, however, settlement at Monte Verde in Chile dates from about 11,000 BC.

At this point, it may be concluded that our innate capacities satisfied our welfare requirements more or less automatically in all habitats in which we have survived through application of the Rational Trinity; that all living organisms owe their survival to their species-specific versions of the Rational Trinity, just as our own hominid precursors did; that beyond these minimal requirements for habitat related crafts, artefacts and social arrangements, Palaeolithic man went on to create decorative effects, representations of human and animal form, oral traditions of past events, the beliefs of shamanism, and even hypotheses as to the nature of the physical world without which complex inventions such as the bow and arrow, slingshot, boomerang and fishhook would not have been possible; and that in doing so he had demonstrated the power of his innate capacities and indicated something of their then unrealised potential.

2. 3 CRAFTSMANSHIP IN THE CREATION OF AGRICULTURE AND URBAN LIVING

Here, I review how Palaeolithic man took advantage of the temperature rise of 7° C (c. 11,500 BC) to leave his migratory hunter-gatherer lifestyle best suited to the previous temperature regime, for the settled livestock and crop rearing lifestyle which would later make possible urban living and its development of literacy, numeracy and calendar, water-engineering, inland transport, building, water transport and shipbuilding. Here again, archaeology and anthropology reveal our innate ability to imagine opportunity, to believe in means, and to reality-validate their practicality though the Rational Trinity.

2. 3. 1 Animal Domestication and Early Settlement
Initially, the seasonal migration of wild herds would have caused some hunter-gatherers to know the convenience of distinct summer and winter quarters, thus rendering them semi-nomadic. Others would have chosen to remain close to a single location of permanently available fish and shellfish, say in a sheltered and productive estuary if ambient temperatures no longer required seasonal north-south migrations. Again, co-existence with herd species would have led to domestication. Thus, by 15,000-10,000 BC the Magdalenians were focussing on reindeer as evidenced by their midden contents and as observable in current Lapp practice. Again, midden evidence suggests domestication of wild animals and plants on a wider basis by 10,000 BC, thus confirming at least some degree of settlement. Nonetheless, the existence of towns and cities provides the strongest such evidence while the magnitude of their food requirements provides the strongest evidence for the domestication of plants and animals which we now call agriculture. Such evidence is supplied by the walled city of

Jericho which covered 4 hectares by 8,000BC and by Catal Huyuk in Anatolia which covered 13 hectares by 5,000BC.

Before such levels of settlement were reached, however, seed-remains show that early Mesolithic Man was gathering wild grasses. Thus, he would soon have learned through application of my Rational Trinity that a cutting-tool would facilitate the gathering while threshing and winnowing would best separate seeds from stems *etc*; that pre-drying would secure seed storage for long periods; and that grinding to flour would enable best use to be made of seeds as a food source. These deductions are supported by finds of flints mounted on wood and bone and showing the edge-blunting characteristic of stem cutting; and of paired stones, the smaller hand-held (quern) being used against the larger (saddle) to grind grain. Accidental spillage and sprouting of such wild grain would inevitably have led to active sowing and to increased yield in locations more convenient for harvesting: knowledge acquisition by accident. As Louis Pasteur said, "accident favours the prepared mind". I would say, the Rational Trinity brain.

It appears that the sources of wild seed suitable for such sowing were the mountains of Anatolia and those of Zagros and Elburz south of the Caspian Sea; and that the locations favoured by soil and climate for wheat cultivation were the eponymous *Fertile Crescent*, later known as the *Cradle of Civilisation* when its productivity became sufficient to support the urban lifestyle. This Crescent extended from around the Dead Sea and Jericho northwards along the coastal strip of the Eastern Mediterranean and the Jordan Valley, and then south-eastwards between the Tigris and Euphrates, across the land later to be known as Mesopotamia. The two most important crops of the Crescent were wheat and barley, both introduced at about the same time, with emmer wheat at about 6,000 BC and einkorn some thousand years later. Later again, irrigation became necessary for the sustenance of increasing urban populations.

However, in pre-pottery times, (before c. 11,000 BC) crop cultivation and harvesting consisted of little more than a superficial scratching of the soil, the scattering and perhaps tramping in of seed, and hand-gathering and winnowing of crops to separate grain for food and sowing, from straw for thatching. Again, even in these early times flax was grown as a source of edible oil and textile fibre, though low population densities, movement to fresh locations and later the droppings from domesticated animals disguised the soil impoverishment which would otherwise have become apparent from successive cropping in the same location. Later, seasonal flooding most notably in the Nile Valley or deliberate irrigation elsewhere, satisfied this unrecognised need for soil nutrients in satisfying the more obvious need for water.

Further to animal domestication, recent genetic studies have suggested that this was achieved with the wolf in east Asia about 15,000 years ago and that all the world's dogs derive from those particular wolves rather than separately from local wolves elsewhere. On the other hand the hierarchical behaviour of wolves suggests that feeding would probably be enough to form a relationship from which domestication would follow to mutual benefit wherever it was attempted. Either way, dog-bones have been dated from 12,000 BC in Germany, from 10,000 BC in Israel and Iraq and from 8,500 BC in North America. Dogs are companionable animals with uses apart from hunting such as the protection of other domesticated animals, the consumption of food residues and wastes, and as a food source. The pig was also domesticated early perhaps because it too is a scavenger of wastes and is widely eaten. Again, the advantages of domesticating the bovine species must have been obvious at an early stage as a continuous source of milk, as a power source for ploughing, load-carrying and carting; and as meat and pelts at the end of life. Again, though sheep and goats are smaller, they also supply wool on a repetitive basis. However, while cattle may have been domesticated *in situ* in Europe, sheep and goats, being native to south-east Asia, must have reached Europe after domestication.

As to the possibility of separate development in non-communicating centres, the French botanist Alphonse de Candolle identified China, south-west Asia including Egypt, and inter-tropic America, as such isolated centres and this identification has been broadly supported by later investigations including those based on genetics. Thus, the earliest evidence for agriculture in China dates the cultivation of wheat and millet on river terraces in the west and north-west at around 5,000 BC and wet-grown rice in the south somewhat later. The available evidence for Central American dates maize cultivation from around 2,500 BC and identifies quinoa and canihua cultivation in the Andes to which area these two crops are still unique. On the other hand where travel is a matter of walking, the sustained separation of China, south-west Asia and Egypt seems highly unlikely, knowledge being readily portable.

Thus, in general, information spread fairly freely and though cereals were the most important crops, other wild plants were cultivated from earliest times, such being the various pulses (peas beans and lentils), green and root vegetables together with fruits such as apples, pears, grapes, dates, figs and pomegranates. In addition, the date-palm supplied wood, fibre and leaves for various uses, the artificial fertilisation of this unisexual plant appearing to have been early known, while fermentation of soft fruits to produce alcohol seems to have been practiced even earlier. Indeed, the causative yeast being present on the skins, hunter-gatherers must have known of this spontaneous process in stored fruit and of the effects of alcohol: knowledge acquisition by accident. Again, the olive was important in southern Europe as a source of edible and lamp oil, though not in Mesopotamia where sesame seed was the oil source, nor in Egypt which imported olive oil from the eastern Mediterranean from around 2,500 BC. Yet again, flax was cultivated in south-east Asia (c. 7,000 BC) and in Babylonia and Egypt (c. 3,000 BC) while cotton first appeared in the Indus Valley (c. 3000 BC) from whence it spread west to Mesopotamia and Egypt and east to China. Again, hemp seems to have been the first vegetable fibre in China, having arrived from the Dnieper area of Russia. Such transfer of plants and of knowledge thereof, is recorded by Tiglath-Pileser I (1115-1102 BC) who introduced garden fruits, cedar, boxwood and possibly oak trees from conquered lands to Assyria. Similarly, the Ebers Papyrus (c. 1,600 BC) is a collection of some 700 (believed or known) herbal treatments from then ancient and widespread sources.

As with earlier hunting and gathering, the requirements of agriculture caused the appropriate implements to be imagined, designed, manufactured and progressively improved by steady application of the Rational Trinity. Thus, straight flint sickles were replaced by crescent-shaped copper and bronze versions by the second millennium BC as is clearly represented on Egyptian murals. Again, while the sowing of seed in the Nile Valley could be direct to post-flood mud before it dried, and while hand-hoes and clod-hammers were sufficient for pre-sowing preparation of small areas of light dry soils, the breaking of soil in larger areas elsewhere in the Middle East and Egypt required development of the plough. Though this was initially steered by one man while another pulled or pushed (breast-plough) against a cross-piece, the heavier and wetter soils of Europe led to development of the ox-drawn plough by the fourth millennium BC, though it may have appeared even earlier in Mesopotamia. Early ploughs were entirely of wood, hard varieties such as holm-oak being chosen for the share, though this was progressively shod with copper, bronze and iron as these became available. Again, when sowing in rows was known to facilitate weeding, seed-drills were developed as shown on Babylonian seals of the third millennium BC.

2. 3. 2 Agriculture, Irrigation and Urbanisation

Agriculturalists would quickly have recognised the need to compensate for deficiencies in rainfall and the potential use of natural bodies of water would have become apparent. The shaduf which enables a man to raise 3 tonnes of water a day, first appeared around 1500 BC and is still in use. This consists of a pole pivoted between two shear-legs (c.f. Section 2.3.5) about 2m high with a bucket at one end and a counter-weight at the other to facilitate lifting the full bucket for emptying into a delivery channel or storage cistern. Thereafter, continual use of the Rational Trinity produced the endless-chain of buckets which emptied on passing over its top pulley-cylinder, such being used to water the hanging gardens of Babylon by about 600 BC, and the screw-pump which appeared about the same time. Later, two different wheel-based designs for raising water were described by Vitruvius (first century AD) the first having external rim-cleats to be trod to turn the wheel to raise the water, the second having extended cleats by which the wheel was itself turned by the water-flow in the supply stream. In the light of the benefits conferred by small-scale additions of water, it would readily have been imagined that larger-scale operations would create food surpluses large enough to sustain non-food producing craftsmen, general labourers and soldiers in numbers sufficient for what would later be called city states. Such labour-intensive socio-political projects would have had to be conducted within the innate capacities for cooperation of all concerned and such cooperation might have been the more readily secured if the climate change of 11,500 BC was already causing drier conditions detrimental to agriculture as previously practiced.

One might suppose that the account of the *Expulsion from Eden* in *The Book of Genesis* refers to a climate induced transition from the leisurely and relatively free existence of hunter-gatherer and subsistence farmer to one of more continuous labour in the agriculture and civil-engineering projects of the hierarchical urban state. Whatever the reason, the problems of managing large volumes and high flow-rates of water and seasonal fluctuations in water-level were mastered for such rivers as the Tigris, Euphrates, Nile and Indus, and the construction and maintenance of major irrigation systems comprising channels, dykes, sluices and water-lifting devices were undertaken over huge areas, the whole being planned, designed, and executed through application of the Rational Trinity. Theophrastus in the third century BC, records that these developments were producing a 300-fold increase on grain sown and two to three harvests a year around Babylon in the Fertile Crescent. The fertility of the Nile Valley also became legendary, though being dependent on the flooding of the Nile between July and October, only one harvest per year was possible. As to the extent of these undertakings, the flood plain of the Nile was divided into areas of up to several thousand hectares to which the flood water was admitted through sluices to a depth of about 1m and held for several weeks to saturate the land and deposit its burden of (fertilising) silt. Though considerable skill and judgement were needed even at the best of times, abnormal conditions necessitated early-warning for which a system of water-level gauges was progressively extended up-steam as far as Nubia. In the Indus Valley the irrigated area associated with Harappan and Mohenjo-Dara is estimated at some 1.25 million square kilometres.

Just as the craftsmanship of the Palaeolithic hunter-gatherer continues to the present day, so too does that of the early Neolithic agriculturalist where that too suffices. However, the control of large river systems for irrigation required not only the development of appropriate craftsmanship and its application at ever-larger scale but also greater levels of opportunity recognition coupled with the ability to assemble ever-higher levels of deployable resources and to manage them towards the realisation of such opportunities. Thus, agricultural and urban developments continued in a parallel and mutually sustaining way, with an advance in the one permitting an advance in the other through the recognition of needs and opportunities coupled with the ability to respond to both through craft developments in one or the other. It seems clear also that the conception, creation and management of such major projects would require the emergence of leading figures, who would also control the deployment of resources both material and human, the latter being augmented by slavery as opportunity and deployable food resources permitted. One such leading figure is Hammurabi, King of Babylon (1792-1750 BC) remembered for his eponymous Code which survives as inscribed on a 2.5 m high tablet setting out *inter alia* the requirements for business transactions to be witnessed and sealed and the levels of fines to be imposed for specified derelictions of duty in the maintenance and operation of the irrigation system.

Such leading figures also protected their resources from predatory attack by envious neighbours whom they themselves would view as possessors of resources for the taking as opportunity arose. Such activities would give rise to soldiery and leading military figures while other specialists would predict the onset of dates relevant to the agricultural year. Others again, would possess knowledge relevant to the direction and management of agricultural and urban work-forces while others would formulate public policy and ensure that it was executed. In respect of all of this, we see the gradual emergence of the specialist roles of ruler, warrior, astronomer-priest, public administrator and executive, craftsman, free-worker and slave. As to slavery, we should note that prior to the introduction of the steam engine, the prime mover in all work was human or animal muscle fuelled by food; that there was a shortage of labour capacity both human and animal; and that, therefore, there was little incentive to keep prisoners of war, debtors and criminals in idle captivity, even though their work output was lower than for freemen, while their subsistence and other maintenance costs were often higher. Even in eighteenth century England, convicts might expect to 'climb' 10,000 feet per day on a treadmill, though now we sustain them in idleness.

2.3.3 Writing, Numerals, and the Calendar
Written records would have become essential with increasing complexity of life and once again the recognition of need would produce the desired result through the Rational Trinity. Writing was thus introduced around 4,000 BC and progressed from pictograms through the representation of phonetic syllables to alphabets. Egyptian hieroglyphs were widely used by 3,000 BC as were Sumerian wedge syllables (cuneiform) by about the same time. The wedges were made by applying a diagonally cut reed-point to clay tablets which were later fired to ensure durability. As a result, we have a wealth of written records covering agriculture and irrigation, military activities and even household accounts from that time. From about 2,000 BC, the Egyptians wrote on leather (parchment and vellum), but by 1,500 BC they were using the much cheaper papyrus sheets woven from pealed strips and sized with gum to produce a surface suitable for inked writing with a brush. Written numerals may have been introduced even earlier. Thus, the Sumerians and Babylonians were using numerals from at least 10,000 BC and tablets have been found from about 3,000 BC showing tables for multiplication and for the extraction of square and cube roots to assist in the application of arithmetic to business transactions and other computations. Long before that, however, *Homo sapiens* would have counted by pairing individual items with his fingers, would have added and subtracted groups of items in the same manner and would quickly have learned that the rules which applied to numbers of antelope or sacks of grain would apply to the numbers themselves, at which point the numbers would become generalisations or abstractions.

Thus, the Sumerians and Babylonians used the base-10 for their number system as we do, but because this base has only two factors, 2 and 5 (apart from itself and unity), they also introduced the base-60 (with factors 2, 3 and 5) which we still use for seconds and minutes in sub-dividing the hour and the angular degree of turning. The more factors the chosen base has, the more of its fractions turn out to be whole numbers. This is why, even after decimalisation it is convenient to retain the 24 hour day and its sub-divisions together with the dozen and the gross on the base-12. Thus, one can only pack ten uniform items as a line of 10 or as a rectangle of dimensions 5 by 2, whereas one can pack twelve such items as a cuboid of dimensions 2 by 2 by 3 which is more compact than the options based on ten or the corresponding linear or rectangular options based on ten or on twelve. Similarly, simple fractions of the base twelve are whole

16

numbers to a greater extent than are those of the base ten. Thus, a half, a third, a quarter, and a sixth of twelve are whole numbers, whereas only a half and a fifth of ten are. Thus, the base-60, of which 12 and 10 are factors was a facilitator of arithmetical computation. There is also evidence that the value of a Babylonian cuneiform numeral was denoted by its position in the sequence of numerals, but the need for a symbol to represent zero had not been imagined.

The use of a symbol for zero is accepted as natural nowadays and it seems obvious that such would have been introduced as soon as its need had been imagined. Just so, but it took a long time for this to happen. Even when the Greeks were using counting boards, they did not imagine a need to symbolise zero. However, consideration of these boards illustrates the difficulties which arose from this failure of the imagination. Early counting-boards had columns for units and successive powers of five (base-5), but later this changed to the base-10. Thus, on the latter base, the columns from right to left represented units, tens, hundreds, thousands and so on up to the millions with the number of units, tens, *etc*, being represented by that number of stones in the appropriate column. Addition of two numbers using the columns was just like modern column arithmetic and where we carry to the next column so did they. When addition within a column results in nothing in that column we enter a zero in the result line and carry to the next column to the left whereas in these circumstances they simply had a column with no stones in the result position. The absence of a symbol for zero did not detract from the utility of the board or from the ability of speech to express the result, but it caused problems in writing it down. Again, the Romans subsequently invented the abacus which consisted of movable beads strung on wires to replace the stones of their earlier counting boards, but they still did not imagine the need for a symbol for zero.

In its absence, the Greeks used alphabetical letters to denote numbers in writing, but the inadequacies of this system are illustrated by using the Roman alphabet for convenience. Thus, the numbers 1 to 10 were denoted by the letters *a* to *j* in alphabetical order, the subsequent multiples of ten, 20 to 90, were denoted by continuing the alphabetical order *k* to *r* (for example, 20 is *k,* 50 is *n,* 70 is *p* and 90 is *r*). As to the hundreds, the alphabetic order continued with *s* for 100, *t* for 200 and so on up to *z* for 800. In this way the number 234 would be written, *tld* and the number 111 would be written *sja*. The Roman system involved fewer symbols, with 1, 5, 10, 50, 100, 1000 being I, V, X, L, C and M as the basic system. This was supplemented by repetition whereby 2, 3 and 4 were written II, III, IIII, and 20, 30 and 40 were XX, XXX and XXXX; and by positioning, whereby a symbol was subtracted from the next and added to the previous, with 4, 9, and 40 being IV, IX, XL, and 6, 7, 8 being VI, VII, VIII. Thus, where we would write the number 641,792 on reading the stones or beads on counting-frame or abacus, the Romans would write it CCCCCCXLIMVIICLXXXXII. Clearly these systems are limited in scope and do not facilitate computation in written form.

All of the difficulties faced by earlier arithmeticians are eliminated by the later Hindu number system which we use, because it includes a symbol for zero (0) and thus requires only ten symbols in all for the base-10 system. A base-12 system would require two more symbols to designate 10 and 11 with twelve (the base) being 10, while on the binary system only two are required, one being 1, two being 10, (the base) three being 11 and four (the base squared) being 100. To revert to the base-ten, we denote numbers as they appear in sequence on a counting-frame or abacus using the symbol for zero (0) in any position where there are no stones or beads and where the other nine symbols always denote the same number of stones or beads whichever column or wire is represented in the place-order. Thus the Hindu system distinguishes between the numbers 11, 110 and 101 for example, and removes all earlier computational problems. Alas, this Hindu innovation did arise until between 100-150 AD (c.f. Section 5.2.2).

It seems that the earliest attempts to schedule the various activities of the year were based on observation of the rising and setting of certain constellations such as those of the zodiac, the signs of which appear on Mesopotamian boundary markers, perhaps in reference to their time of establishment. However, the creation of an accurate calendar requires detailed observations of solstices and equinoxes and of the phases of the moon. We now know that the number of lunar months (29.5 days) in the year (365.25 days) is 12.38, and that 12 x 29.5 gives a mismatch from year to year of 11.25 days. Therefore, calendar development involves measuring this mismatch as accurately as possible and deciding how to avoid accumulated slippage of any specified day as year succeeds year. By 3,500 BC, the Egyptians had a tolerably effective calendar for the purpose of anticipating the onset of Nile flooding, but it was not until the leap year was introduced by Ptolomey III of Egypt (in 238 BC) that the annual overrun of six hours (0.25 days) was accommodated. Meanwhile, by 3000 BC, the Babylonians had accounted for that mismatch by inserting extra (intercalary) months over a period of nineteen years. In China, apart from the scheduling of the activities of the agricultural year, anticipation of the annual snow melt and of the rainy season were also required, and again the intercalary solution was adopted.

2. 3. 4 Urban Water Supplies

Growing populations required reliable water supplies beyond the needs of agriculture, the satisfaction of which provides further evidence of the problem solving capacity of the Rational Trinity. Thus, around 2,500 BC the Egyptians built a dam across the Wadi Gerrawi in the eastern desert and about a thousand years later, Egyptians built a larger dam across the Orontes Valley in Syria to form the Lake of Homs over an area of some 50 square kilometres. However, sites suitable for dams are not always the most convenient for water users, necessitating conveyance of stored water by canals, the construction and grading of which across irregular topography presents further problems for solution. For example, that constructed by Sennacherib to bring water 80 kilometres from Bavian to Nineveh, crossed a valley on a five-arch aqueduct 300m in length and 20m wide, the whole being lined with stone and sealed with bitumen, the stone quarried at Bavian having been transported to the advancing work-site along the roadway provided by the canal-bed itself. Apart from these examples, thousands of other dams and water-conveyance systems were built at various places and times, the Nabataeans of the Negev and southern Jordan having constructed nearly 20,000 small dams of average length 50m in an area of some 130 square kilometres around Ovdat, in a 200 year effort to conserve flash floods from showers.

These Nabataeans avoided the high evaporative loss otherwise due to their high ambient temperature and low humidity by using underground conduits constructed by covering surface ducts or by tunnelling. Another tunnel example is that driven 1,100m through a 300m high hill by Eupalinos of Samos in the sixth century BC. The common practice was to sight and mark the tunnel-line on the surface with a series of posts, sink vertical shafts using the plumb-line at the marked positions, and connect the shaft-bottoms by tunnelling in opposite linear directions at the same time. The crossing of narrow valleys was achieved by carrying the water channel on a masonry faced embankment up to a height of about 2m and on arched aqueducts for greater heights. For heights up to 20m stable structures could be built from massive pillars provided the arches were narrow. If the height requirement was greater than 20 m a smaller second tier system of pillars and arches could be built on the first, and sometimes even a third on top of the second. The best known example is the three-tiered 55m high Pont du Gard near Nimes which was built in the first century AD and is still functional. Nowadays valleys are negotiated by carrying the water down one side and up the other, the pipe acting as an inverted-siphon. Although the Greeks and Romans understood this principle the internal pressures involved made its realisation difficult for
18

them. Nonetheless, a few were built such as that at Pergamum in 200 BC, though it was replaced by an arched aqueduct around 100 BC.

2. 3. 5 Inland Transport, Building and Mechanical Advantage

Water in open channels (canals) can be used to transport heavy goods many times more efficiently than land transport, provided suitable craft are available. Thus, the Persian Emperor Darius linked the Nile to the Red Sea in 510 BC, the Romans linked some of the rivers of Europe by canal for both transport and flood control, and in 133 BC the Han capital of Ch'ang-an was linked to the Yellow River by a 150 kilometre canal. Early canals used slipways for raising and lowering boats to cope with changes in topographical levels, the chamber-lock being a Medieval development.

Nonetheless, overland transport being necessary, a Mesopotamian bas-relief shows men carrying back-loads with the aid of forehead straps. Single and double shoulder yokes were also common as was suspension of a load from a pole carried on the shoulder of each of two men, or from two poles by using both shoulders of two men. Use of the ass as a pack-animal, effective with loads up to 60 kg, is first recorded around 3,500 BC, and of the closely related onager from central Asia which was domesticated in Mesopotamia by 3000 BC. Though the camel, also of Asian origin, is depicted on an Egyptian mural dated about 3000 BC, its use as a pack animal for loads of 300-500 kg cannot be established before the first millennium BC, again in Mesopotamia. Heavier loads had to be dragged and pushed, and again the Rational Trinity would have shown that the use of rollers or the construction of a sledge with runners makes the task easier and in sub-zero temperatures this latter solution is still in use. A Mesopotamian pictograph from Uruk of around 3,000 BC shows a device similar to the North American travois and Mesolithic rock carvings in Scandinavia clearly depict the use of skis.

Though much has been made of the invention of the wheel, it is just another incremental step in the process of meeting a need with the appropriate development. In addition to the travois, the Uruk pictograph shows a sledge and an identical vehicle fitted with wheels, and from about 3,000 BC evidence for the wheel is widespread in carvings, murals and vase paintings, models found in tombs and the remains of wheeled-vehicles themselves. Once imagined, development proceeded as with everything else through the Rational Trinity. Thus, in progression we have the wheel and axle turning together, the wheel rotating on a fixed axle to permit differential wheel speed when turning corners, two wheels per vehicle, then four with the front pair mounted on a swivelling bogie for cornering purposes, though the one-wheeled wagon (wheelbarrow) does not appear till the first century AD in China, and not in Europe till the Middle Ages. Similarly, wheels underwent development, the earliest being a three plank disc held together by two crosspieces or in Northern Europe where larger trees were available, a single plank disc. However, these were not cut from the end of cylindrical logs, heart-wood being soft and known to split radially. Later, from 3,000 BC wheels were strengthened by a rim of wooden felloes, later studded with nails or bound with metal. Again, solid wheels being clumsy even when only 2.5cm thick, four spokes were being used to connect rim to hub by 2,000 BC in Mesopotamia, this number increasing to six or eight in the West, and to sixteen in China by 1,000 BC.

Initially, vehicles were drawn exclusively by oxen harnessed on either side of a centre-line shaft, horse-drawn vehicles being first depicted at about 2,500 BC in Sumeria. The broad-shouldered ox pushed against a collared wooden yoke to which the comparatively narrow-shouldered horse was unsuited. Early attempts to overcome this horse-limitation by use of breast-bands were unsuccessful because they interfered with breathing and restricted blood supply to the brain even at loadings otherwise within the power of the horse. Draught vehicles themselves came in a wide range of designs for various purposes, from two-wheeled versions for personal and light local work to four-wheeled covered wagons in which the Romans carried fare-paying passengers over staged distances up to a total of 150km a day. Otherwise, load capacity was not great, the Theodosian Code limiting the lightest, the birota, to 70kg and the heaviest, the angaria, to 500kg. Thus, the heavy blocks of stone required by building design could only be moved short distances on rollers by pulling from the front and pushing and levering from behind as depicted on both Assyrian and Egyptian wall paintings of around 2,000BC, though by the first century BC Vitruvius (c.f. Section 3.2.1) was describing the movement of cylindrical stone columns by inserting short axles into their ends and into an over-frame and shaft, enabling them to be pulled by oxen in the manner of garden rollers. Later, his son Metagenes moved square-sectioned blocks by mounting a wheel and side- axle on a pair of opposite ends or by building a wooden cylinder or end-cylinders round them.

Building materials were generally sourced locally, though with much of the Middle East being flat alluvial plain with little access to stone and a scarcity of wood, sun-dried brick was the material most readily available. Even in Egypt where good building stone was plentiful, sun-dried brick remained the economic choice for everyday purposes. In China, on the other hand, wood was the main material with tile for roofs and brick for terraces and boundary walls only. High clay soils produced the best sun-dried brick, though it was preferable to add chaff and chopped straw to the mix before transferring to the open-frame wooden moulds which had been used from earliest times. Brick sizes were standardised early in several distinct regions and drying times were regulated to ensure product reliability. The kiln fired bricks which appeared in the fourth millennium BC required clay rather than earth-clay mixtures, but were much more durable than their sun-dried precursors. Cobwork was made by ramming the brick-material between parallel boards (shuttering) to form a continuous wall, the boards being subsequently removed and the dried wall plastered to assist the shedding of water. The Egyptians used gypsum (plaster of Paris) mortar to bond individual bricks while the Greeks and Romans used slaked lime and sand as we still do. Vitruvius specified sharp sand for greater cohesion and rejected the round smooth grains of river-bed or shore sand, the latter having too much salt in any case. The Romans also developed concrete by mixing pozzolana from the Alban Hills with slaked lime (roasted chalk) and sand and pouring the mixture into coarse aggregate held within shuttering as in cob-work.

The Egyptians began to use stone for permanent buildings from the middle of the third millennium BC, limestone being preferred to granite (mostly from Aswan) because the former could be worked relatively easily with picks, saws and chisels while the latter had to be shaped by pounding with 5 kg boulders held in both hands. Limestone, available to the north of Nineveh, was used in building from the eighth century BC and gypsum, being easier to work was used for sculpture in spite of its poor weathering-properties. Greece, on the other hand, consists largely of limestone, much of it occurring as marble of various types. Early masons were aware of the need to select stone with care and to leave it to weather in the open to detect defects prior to selection for use. Massive stone blocks could be accurately shaped for dry-jointing, though gypsum mortar is found in some Egyptian stonework and metals were also used for clamps and dowels to secure masonry. There was also a substantial trade in timber from earliest times to supply basic local deficiencies and to satisfy luxury requirements as, for example, in furniture making. As to local woods, cedar was common south of the Alps and oak to the north. Theophrastus, early in the third century BC records the best seasons for the felling of different species of tree and both merchants and users were aware of the need for seasoning before use. Where wood was available it was used in the construction of quite massive structures, as for example at Hambledon Hill in Wiltshire where some 10,000 oak posts were employed in the defensive ramparts at about 3,400 BC. Even when brick and stone were used for walls, wood tended to be used for roof members, the Greeks fireproofing their wooden building materials by treatment with alum (c.f. Section 7.2.4).

Where stone was not available, important civil or ceremonial buildings such as the ziggurats of the cities of Mesopotamia were constructed of brick and the dimensions of that in Ur of the Chaldees were 75 x 54 x 26metres. Spanning the space between the walls or columns of large buildings presented problems, however, because limestone beams are limited to spans of about 3m, and even those of the best Egyptian sandstone could not be relied upon beyond 10m. A further difficulty is the outward thrust of pitched roofs on their supporting walls which increases with the angle of pitch and which is compounded by the weight of stone beams and of stone or earthenware roofing slabs or tiles. Flat roofs were therefore preferred, though the Greeks managed to sustain pitch angles of up to 30° on occasion. The only solution to beam weakness, however, was to use internal column supports so numerously as to severely limit the usable space within the building, the columns themselves being massive enough to bear the loading imposed by the mitred ends of four orthogonal beams resting on their tops. This solution resulted in rectangular structures consisting of four rows of external columns topped by lintels, parallel rows of internal columns topped by beams and (usually) flat roofs such as that at Thebes, begun by Seti I, in 1293 BC, or the Parthenon, built in the time of Pericles (447-432 BC). Columns were usually built in drum-sections each prefabricated, adjusted for gradual tapering, and provided with inter-locking pin and socket pairs on the top and bottom of each, those in the Parthenon consisting of eleven 8 tonne drums to a height of 10m.

Later, the arch was introduced as an alternative to the lintel. In the earliest examples each successive course of masonry extended inwards until the space to be bridged was closed in what is known as a corbelled arch. When extended, such arching is known as barrel vaulting as in construction of the sewers at Ur. Domes may also be constructed in this way, early examples being the small burial chambers at Ur and the 'Tomb of Agamemnon' at Mycenae (circa 1450 BC). Roman arch construction, as in bridges, was based on tapered blocks and keystone, supported until completion by temporary wooden structures. Although such arches exerted enormous lateral thrusts, very considerable spans were achieved, that of the vaulted roof at Diocletian's Palace at Split being 35m and that of the dome at the Pantheon (started 120 AD) being 50m. Brick and Roman concrete being lighter than stone, there is evidence that the four or five storied residential blocks constructed at Ostia (the port of Rome) in the second century AD, had walls of brick with a concrete core and wooden stairways. In addition, the Romans installed heating systems (hypocausts) and cavity-walls to reduce dampness in Britain, Gaul, and the German Provinces.

The original step pyramid of Djoser at Saggara (c.2650 BC) consists of stones of manually manageable size, though the three pyramids at Giza (about the same time) were constructed from blocks of more than 100 tonnes and the Great Pyramid of Cheops, 146 m in height, contains some even larger blocks. Thus, though we know how the lifting problems associated with the stone construction units referenced in the previous section were solved (c.f. below) we only know that earlier and greater problems must have been solved for the completions to exist; and that while the kilometre long causeway constructed for the movement of blocks from quarry to work-site was described by Herodotus some 2000 years later, he could only suppose the principles of the roller and lever to have been applied together with sufficient pulling power as in the horizontal movement of the very large blocks depicted in murals.

On the other hand, the mechanical advantage of the inclined plane was understood quite early. That is to say, the force required to move a weight upwards on a ramp or slipway is less than that to lift it vertically. The wedge is an application of this principle in that insertion of the pointed-end beneath an object on the ground and delivery of blows to the vertical-end, raises the object vertically even though the force of each blow is less than the weight of the object. The axe is yet another application of this principle in that it enables greater lateral force to be applied to the splitting of material than the forces required to drive the cutting edge into it. The screw-press or jack described by Hero of Alexandria (c.f. Section 3.1.4) in the first century AD is an inclined plane wound into a spiral which permits the application of greater vertical forces than is required to turn the thread by means of a crank, the problem of cutting the moving and stationary thread-pair having been solved. The crank itself provides the means of applying a small force, moving round the circumference of a large-radius circle to apply a larger force to the circumference of a smaller-radius circle concentric with the larger. This benefit was perhaps first noticed by potters who poked the circumference of a larger fly-wheel to turn a smaller circular table on which the clay was worked (c.f. Section 2.4.1). The lever itself is another manifestation of the underlying principle of all of these machines, namely, that a large load can be moved by a smaller effort provided arrangements can be made for the effort to move further than the load in the same interval of time. The fulcrum of the lever (the point about which turning occurs) is placed closer to the point of loading than to that of the applied effort to ensure that the former moves in the arc of a smaller circle than does the latter.

A further example of this principle is the two-pulley system. The simplest use of a pulley is to pass a rope over it, to attach a load (a block of stone, say) to one end and a team of men to the other so that by pulling the rope, the load is lifted. This simple device already has two advantages. It enables more men to be applied to the task than could get their hands on the stone and it enables it to be lifted to any height by suitable positioning of the pulley. The Assyrians had this system. The Greeks and Romans went on to develop two-pulley systems of multiple wheel (sheave) pulleys (blocks). With these the rope is attached to the body of one pulley and is then rove through a sheave of the other then back through a sheave of the first and so on in succession. If one block is fixed to a strong-point (the standing part), the other is attached to the load, and the free-end of the rope (the fall of the running-part) is pulled, the two blocks come closer to each other more slowly than the fall is pulled away by those tailing onto it. Once again the effort is moving further than the load and so the effort can be smaller than the load. If, for example, the top block has 3 sheaves and the lower one has two, the ratio of these movements in the same time is 1:5 which confers the advantage that 200 kg of effort will lift 1,000 kg (1 tonne) and *pro rata*.

Shear-legs were introduced to position the top block. As the name implies these consist of a bi-pod system of poles the feet of which are splayed and the tops of which are fastened together to form the apex from which the top block is hung. This system is supported by adjustable guys which enable the position of the apex to be moved by altering the angle which the plane of the shear-legs makes with the horizontal. To facilitate this procedure the feet of the shear-legs could be hinged to load-bearing plates which in any case might be placed beneath the feet to prevent them sinking into the ground. It was also found beneficial to wind the fall of the two-block pulley system onto a spool which could be turned by a crank (the windlass) or by bars to which more men could apply their strength and weight (the capstan). To make sure that the load did not take charge or that those pulling could rest with the load secured at any stage during the lift, the pawl and ratchet system was introduced at least as early as the fifth century BC.

An essential step was to devise methods of attaching the stones to the lifting gear described above. The most direct solution was to pass rope slings under the stone and over the lifting hook. However, to avoid the obvious difficulty of passing ropes beneath a heavy stone, a U-shaped groove could be cut in each of a pair of its opposite vertical faces into which the lifting slings could be fitted. This, and other means involving insertion into the stone of dove-tailed or L-shaped metal hangers followed by rotation through 90 degrees to lock them in the load were described by Hero of Alexandria. Once the lifting equipments described above had been devised, however, there would have been every incentive to cut stones to sizes compatible with their associated weight limits. It may, therefore, be concluded that the very largest stones of the pyramids must have been raised by ramps (inclined planes) and levers, prior to the introduction of pulleys, shear-legs, capstans *etc*, otherwise these stones would also have been cut to those same weight-limits, unless, of course, the larger sizes had been chosen for reasons of prestige despite the handling difficulties involved.

2. 3. 6 Water transport and Shipbuilding

Leaving aside speculations on the use by early man of adventitious floating logs and perhaps of assemblages of logs (rafts), the earliest evidence of boat building is provided by a dugout canoe, the Pesse boat (4 m in length) excavated in Holland and dated at about 6,400 BC. This early approach to boat building reflects the availability of suitable timber sizes, the use of stone tools, and possibly of fire, whereas the reed boats of the Nile reflect the abundance of papyrus. Another early and more widespread approach was to stretch skins over a wooden or bone frame as exemplified by the Mesopotamian quffa, the Welsh coracle, the Irish curagh, and the Eskimo kayak. In addition, a relief from Nineveh of the seventh century BC, clearly shows inflated skins (implying the existence of bellows) lashed to wooden frames in the construction of rafts for the carriage of heavy loads.

The orientation of the Nile is kind to water-borne transport in that the current assists the north-bound journey while the prevailing winds assist the south-bound. These observations must have led to the advent of sails and depictions on pottery are evidence of sail-powered reed-boats being in use by 3,100 BC which were probably of well-established design by then, those depicted being equipped with square sails, bipod (shear-leg) masts placed well forward, back stays for mast support, halyards for hoisting and lowering sail and broad-bladed twin steering paddles aft. The surviving funeral ship of Cheops shows that by 2530 BC substantial wooden boats were in service. This particular craft was constructed from 1224 separate pieces of wood, mostly cedar, laterally fastened by tenons and thongs and extended longitudinally by both butt and scarf joints. It has no true keel, while outward (lateral) sagging of the hull planking is prevented by the decking which carries a cabin displaying some fine-workmanship. It is a 10-oared 43m long vessel, with two steering oars and rowing oars attached to tholepins by leather thongs, in which the oarsmen would have stood rather than sat at their work.

Egyptian wooden sailing ships with a length : beam ratio (block coefficient) of 4 : 1 were already trading in the Mediterranean by 3,000 BC. Though they were of planked construction, the deck beams were the only source of lateral strength there being no hull-framing. Again, there was no keel, the only longitudinal strength being conferred by a truss which prevented the hull from hogging (drooping) at the ends. This truss was a bight (loop) of rope which connected the topmost strong points at stem and stern and which could be shortened to increase anti-hogging tension by rotating a lever passed through it in the manner of the so-called Spanish windlass. Rock carvings at Thebes show that by 1,500 BC cargo ships still retained oars (30 in all) though the larger sail now had a spar at head and foot and the mast was now a single spar placed amidships rather than forward as formerly. This last development brought the centre of effort of the sail plan closer to the centre of lateral resistance of the hull, which would have increased the possibility of windward sailing. In addition, deck beams now increase lateral strength by being fastened to the outer side of the upper planking after passing through it, and the hogging truss is now tensioned by drawing its mid-point downwards towards the deck by means of a smaller Spanish windlass.

War galleys also relied on oars for wind independence and were equipped with a ram, but a block coefficient, of about 8 : 1 gave them speeds much higher than those attained by merchant ships. Such warships continued to be used in the Mediterranean up to and somewhat beyond the Battle of Lepanto in 1571. Various depictions show an Assyrian ship with ram and two banks of oars (bireme) of around 700 BC and sundry Greek triremes with rams at around 500 BC. The latter vessels would typically have been some 45 m in length and about 5 to 6 m in beam. The oar is another application of the lever in which the fulcrum is at the blade, the effort is applied by the oarsman at the other end of the oar, and the load is moved at the tholepin which thus causes the vessel to move by a smaller amount per stroke than does the effort at the loom. It has been calculated and recently demonstrated with a replica that oar-powered Greek war galleys were capable of sustaining about 8 knots in calm conditions. Merchant ships on the other hand, were more dependent on wind direction and strength, but at an average size of perhaps 20-25m long and 6 or 7m in beam they had a cargo capacity of perhaps 150 tonnes and a speed of some 3 to 4 knots under the most favourable conditions. Such speeds and carrying capacities compare favourably with land transport for which a system of staged pack-asses would move a 60 kg load a distance of 80 km per day.

At this point, it may be concluded that the innate ability of *Homo sapiens* to operate the Rational Trinity *i.e.* to imagine opportunities, to believe how they might be realised, and to validate or reject these beliefs by reality-evaluation through sense-experience in the real world, had enabled him to progress through his hunter-gatherer stage to animal and crop husbandry supported where necessary by substantial irrigation schemes which, in turn, provided urban water supplies, sewage disposal and transportation sufficient to support urban living at City State and Empire levels. It may also be concluded that such requirements were further satisfied by the same Rational Trinity which provided writing, numerals, computation and calendar; water management by sluices, counter-weight buckets, and tread-wheel pumps; water storage by dam and cistern; water conveyance by pipe-line, canal, tunnel, and aqueduct; building by wood-working, brick-making and stone-cutting; architectural engineering by columns, lintels, arches, barrel vaults and domes; mechanical load management by rollers, inclined planes, wedges, screws, levers, pulleys, windlasses, capstans and sheer legs; road transportation on human bearers, pack-animals, wheeled carts and bridges; and water transport by rivers, canals and sea, on rafts, boats and ships propelled by paddles, oars and sails. It may further be concluded that in step with the increasing demands for direction and control of the above, the Rational Trinity also provided the appropriate cooperative hierarchies for the long-term planning, project management and provision of human resources and raw materials, without which the Palaeolithic lifestyle would have continued everywhere without any of the above developments ever having been imagined, let alone achieved in reality.

2. 4 CRAFTSMANSHIP DERIVING FROM AGRICULTURE AND URBAN LIVING

Having reviewed the achievements of craftsmanship in the development of agriculture and urban living, I now return to the early Mesolithic to review the various crafts which derived from these developments and which made life more comfortable and convenient within them. These include the crafts of pottery and glass making; skin-tanning and the spinning, weaving and finishing of plant and animal fibres; cooking and other forms of food preservation; mining and the refining and working of metals.

2. 4. 1 Pottery and Glass

Pottery is yet another example of using materials to hand to make something to satisfy a need. In this case clay is used to make containers. The potter first kneads clay and water to a consistency soft enough to work to the desired shape, yet firm enough to retain this shape until he can convert it from the plastic to the rigid condition by heat-treatment. There are three methods of shaping such a container. The work-piece can be roughly hollowed to form a base and sides by progressive thinning between fingers and thumbs as the potter progresses repeatedly round the work-piece; the sides can be built up by coiling a 'rope' of rolled clay round and round from base to lip; or shorter rolls of clay can be used to build up one course at a time until the desired height is reached. It is but one small step from these processes to imagine that having the work-piece turn continuously towards ones fingers would be helpful, and but another to imagine that setting it on a rotating table (horizontally rotating wheel) would deliver this help. In Mesopotamia from about 3,000 BC clay was being 'thrown' on to a small wheel co-axial with a larger fly-wheel which maintained the momentum conferred on it by the operator by means of intermittent kicks or jabs with a stick (c.f. Section 2.3.5).

Early sun-dried pottery would set hard enough for use, though inadvertent observation of the effects of fires built on clay bases might have suggested deliberate firing at a relatively early stage in pottery development. The oldest examples of fired pottery are considered to date from about 11,000 BC and the technique seems to have progressed from building a fire above the pots which would attain temperatures of 450-700° C, through vertical kilns introduced at around 3 - 4,000 BC to the horizontal kilns of Roman times which would have provided about 1,000° C. Though extremely hard vitrified stoneware requires temperatures of around 1600° C for most clays, (too high for early potters) the Chinese were using kaolin clay to produce hard non-porous pots at lower temperatures by about 1,500 BC. Pottery lends itself to decoration and finish beyond the level of pure need and consequently there are many artificial replications of the appearance of wood, basketry, leather and even metal, as for example, with Minoan pots from around 2,500 BC. Over time, however, decoration developed from simple indented patterns to accurate depictions of everyday life and the pre-firing application of slips containing organic and inorganic colouring agents such as charcoal, oil, iron oxide or the ferruginous earths such as sienna, umber and ochre produced increasingly fine finishes while additional colouring effects could be achieved by excluding air and thus oxidative loss of colour during firing.

Glass was made by fusing sand and limestone with naturally occurring or plant-ash soda, and colours could be achieved by adding iron for a greenish tint and cobalt for a deep blue. Though glass objects appear from about 2,500 BC in Egypt, glass containers are not evidenced until about 1,500 BC and though Chinese glass is not found earlier than about 600 BC, it is notable for the brilliance due to its lead content, whether inadvertently or intentionally added. Large objects, such as the headrest from the tomb of Tutankhamun (circa 1,350 BC) were carved and ground from blocks of glass and more intricate small objects such as figurines were made in clay moulds, while containers were initially made by dipping a cloth bag of sand into the molten glass, followed by rolling the work-piece on a flat stone, the sand being removed after cooling. Glass-blowing was a later development probably just prior to the Christian era, and glass windows were available to wealthy Romans of the Empire.

2. 4. 2 Leatherworking, Spinning, and Weaving

In the production of buckskin, as traditionally practised by the natives of North America, the heated brains of the animal were rubbed into the scraped skin to produce a leather through which air could pass, but not water, while in tawing the prepared skin is treated with alum (c.f. Section 7.2.4) to produce white leather. Tanning involves prolonged soaking in contact with tannin-rich barks or oak galls according to availability, followed by softening and waterproofing with oil or fat. Other treatments with various offensive mixtures were even more unpleasant, the basic process being varied to produce a range of properties from the soft and supple for clothing to the hard and tough for the soles of foot-ware. Leather was also used to make water containers into which red-hot stones could be dropped to boil the contained water; to make harness for oxen and horses, tyres for chariot wheels, and sheaths for weapons; for covering the frames of canoes and boats; for laces, lashings, sails and tents; and as parchment or vellum for writing. It was decorated by blind punch indentation or excision, dyed or boned to a high polish.

Nonetheless, woven textiles could replace leather in some of the above applications, weaving being similar to basket and mat making. The weaving of reeds, grasses, flax stems and cereal straw was well established by 5,000 BC in the Middle East and Egypt while in China split bamboo was also used and in Europe, osiers. However, the constituent fibres of these materials can be obtained by prolonged soaking and subsequent beating in a process known as retting. This process can also be applied to hemp, another oil-seed crop from which the Chinese were making rope by about 2,000 BC; to jute available in the valleys of the Ganges and Brahmaputra; and to nettles in Europe. Again, the much finer fibres of the cotton plant appear to have been in use by 2,000 BC at Mohenjo-Daro in the Indus valley and in Egypt and China by 500 BC. The two animal fibres of importance are wool and silk, the former is available from sheep, goats and lamas, the latter from the cocoon of the silk worm cultivated in China on mulberry trees. Legend has it, that the wife of Emperor Huang-ti learned how to unwind the continuous filament at about 2,700 BC. These continuous silk filaments can immediately be twisted together to make a thread strong enough for weaving, but plant fibres and wool are collected as tangled skeins which must be drawn out in alignment as they are twisted into thread. This twisting or spinning process can be carried out by rolling the teased-out fibres between the hands or between the hand and thigh as is still done to this day, though more usually a spinning device is used to facilitate and speed up the process.

In simple weaving the vertical (warp) threads hang from a fixed horizontal top bar and are tensioned by individual weights which pass alternately in front or behind a lower horizontal fixed beam. The horizontal (weft) thread can thus be passed in front and behind alternate warp threads with a needle as in darning. The first stage of development was to attach alternate warp threads to a horizontal pole (the heddle) at a vertical position just above the lower fixed beam. The heddle is moved forward and backward by the operator so that the weft thread can now be passed straight through the two sets of alternate warp threads by means of the shuttle to which it is attached. In other words, the forward and backward movement of the darning needle with respect to the warp threads has now been replaced by a forward and backward movement of all the warp threads with respect to the straight path of the shuttle thus greatly speeding up the process. After each pass, the weft thread is pressed up close to the edge of the ever-growing cloth by means of a comb or sley.

This alternate crossing of single threads of warp and weft is known as tabby weave, though there are many other possibilities. If, for example, two weft threads are passed alternately over two warps we have canvas weave. Again, coloured threads could be used to produce patterns using such dyes as could be obtained from insects, plants and shellfish. For example, red could be obtained from an oak parasite, violet from lichens, yellow from the crocus, blue from woad, and Tyrian (Imperial) purple from a marine mollusc. Double weaving which produced a pattern on both sides by using duplicate warp threads was in use by 2,000 BC. Imperfections were obliterated by subjecting the woven cloth to fulling by trampling or beating in baths to which soda, soapwort or fullers earth was added. To give a softer finish to woollens the surface fibres were raised by brushing with teasels and hedgehog skins followed by shearing the resulting nap. Linen was sun-bleached and woollens by exposure to the fumes from burning sulphur.

2. 4. 3 Food Preservation and Cooking

Early hunter-gatherers must have eaten their food uncooked, though they would have become aware of the benefits of preserving meat, fish, and fruit by sun-drying or by exposure to cold low-humidity air as practiced by the native peoples of North America. Later, the use of fire would have revealed the benefits of cooking. Later still the advent of agriculture would have required preservation of other foods surplus to immediate need. Cereal grains if harvested ripe and stored dry do not spoil, but they do attract vermin which would have led to duties for the cat and further duties for the dog. Root vegetables also store well, but green vegetables would have been eaten as cropped, as would fruits in the main. Other fruits, with high sugar-content, however, such as dates, figs and grapes could again be preserved by drying, while grapes could also be used to make wine, and cereals to make beer. Both meat and fish in addition to drying, would later be treated with salt obtained by mining or from the evaporation of sea-water or saline spring-water. Milk has to be used quickly because it rapidly turns sour and the curd which deposits will not beneficially ripen in storage, though it can be eaten fresh. Cheese making requires an enzyme, rennet, available from calves stomachs and this process could have been discovered from attempted milk storage in a bag made from such a stomach, while butter is made simply by agitating milk in a churn and separating the resulting fat globules. The operations of the dairy are depicted in a Babylonian bas-relief showing that such practices were well established by then.

The simplest approach to cooking would have been to roast by an open fire which gives good results with both meat and the dough of cereals. A further development was to build the fire under a clay or stone oven, examples of which are found from earliest times at Jericho. There is also evidence of community bakeries in Sumeria, in Egypt, and of course throughout the Roman Empire. Pottery and metal vessels could be suspended above or placed directly on fires to permit stewing and by 1,500 BC the Chinese had introduced the Li, a squat cooking pot with three hollow legs which permitted greater contact with the heat source, and with a perforated platform above boiling water, *i.e.* as a steamer, it was used to make bread.

It would seem that the processes of food preservation and cooking could have resulted from accidental observations or from the reality-evaluation of imagined beliefs. As far as the heat treatments are concerned, however, they could have been readily extended to the extraction of metals from their ores as will be discussed below as further examples of the Rational Trinity in action.

2. 4. 4 Metal Extraction, Refining, and Alloying

During the period now under review mankind became aware of metals, namely, copper, silver, gold, tin, zinc lead, mercury and iron. The first three occur recognisably as metals in their natural state while the other four (with the exception of iron as meteorites) occur unrecognisably in the form of ores in which (as we now know) they are bound to non-metals, usually oxygen (as oxides), sulphur (as sulphides), or carbon and oxygen (as carbonates).

Generally speaking, roasting in air will simplify the metal-carbon-oxygen combinations to metal-oxygen only, with loss of carbon dioxide gas to the atmosphere, while metal-sulphur combinations can be transformed to metal-oxygen combinations with release of gaseous sulphur dioxide by roasting in air, and metal-oxygen combinations naturally occurring or produced from the sulphides or carbonates, can be transformed to free metal by combining the oxygen with carbonaceous materials under the influence of heat to release it as carbon dioxide to the atmosphere. We may suppose therefore, that heat from the combustion of wood (carbon) in a fire could have produced metal from an ore adventitiously present: knowledge acquisition by accident. We may also suppose that familiarity with other heat treatments such as those associated with cooking or with pottery or later glass production might subsequently have been modified to exploit this chance observation, especially if the observer was already familiar with the naturally occurring metal. Once again we may suppose that the systematic development process as previously described, would have led quickly to a reliable process for the routine production of the desired metal from the identified and recognisable pre-cursor through the Rational Trinity. One can also readily suppose that subsequently a range of likely looking minerals would have been heat-treated in expectation of metal release in a reality-evaluation of belief arising from knowledge with success making more metals available for use.

Whatever the experiences of heat treatment, however, copper appears to have been put to use as early as 5,000 BC. In its natural state it requires no metallurgical treatment and as such would have been directly usable. It occurs in this state most dramatically on the shores of Lake Superior, but also in smaller amounts in Cornwall, Siberia and the Urals, for example. In Greek it was referred to as chalcos and in Latin it was cuprum. It also occurs as the oxide (cuprite or ruby ore), as the sulphide (chalcocite), mixed with iron sulphide as chalcopyrite and as the carbonates (malachite and azurite). It appears that the metal was first extracted from its ores sometime in the fourth millennium BC and it may be concluded that the copper-oxygen, copper-sulphur and copper-carbon-oxygen bonds would have been dealt with as discussed above, without anything being known about oxygen, sulphur or carbon *per se*. Malachite (copper-carbon-oxygen) appears to have been the ore exploited under the reign Solomon (c. 1,000 BC).

A complication arises, however, with the mixed copper-iron sulphide (chalcopyrite) which appears to have been processed around 1,700 BC, one source of this ore being the eastern Alps. Here again the first step would have been to roast the ore. This operation preferentially converts the iron sulphide (with release of sulphur dioxide gas) to iron oxide which floats on the melted copper sulphide from where it can be skimmed off as a slag. Air is then blown through the melt by means of leather bellows to convert some of the copper sulphide to oxide with a release of more sulphur dioxide to the point where this copper oxide reacts with the remaining copper sulphide to produce metallic copper and a further release of sulphur dioxide. When the molten copper cools at this stage the further release of dissolved sulphur dioxide gives it a blistered appearance. To refine this copper, it is re-melted in a stream of air to remove any remaining sulphur as the dioxide, any arsenic as the trioxide, and any remaining iron as the floating oxide slag. It may at this stage, however, still contain a very small amount of copper oxide which makes it somewhat brittle. The Romans introduced the practice of stirring the melt with a log of green wood (retained into modern times) when the released hydrocarbons reduced any remaining oxide to copper. This product, containing about 99.5% copper, is known today as tough pitch copper. It cannot be improved upon without recourse to electrolysis (c.f. Section 7.2.5) which of course was not known to the ancients. Nowadays silver and gold are recovered from the 'anode mud' produced in electrolytic refining of copper to purity levels of 99.96 - 99.99%.

A date for the earliest use of tin has not been proposed, but its occurrence in Egyptian tombs is sufficient evidence for its antiquity in metallic form for our purposes, and there are reports of its natural occurrence as metallic tin in Bohemia, for example. The Greeks referred to it as cassiteros and to the Romans it was stannum, though the Sanskrit word castira, has been cited in support of an eastern origin for the tin of the Middle East and Mediterranean Region. The ore occurs mainly as the oxide (cassiterite) which can either be found as primary deposits of lode or vein tin or as stream tin in rounded lumps from secondary alluvial deposits. Pliny refers to Phoenician tin as coming from Insulae Cassiterides by which is meant the Scilly Isles as the source of Cornish tin. It can also occur comparatively rarely as a complex tin-iron sulphide, tin pyrites (stannite) or as other complex sulphides containing tin, copper, iron and sometimes zinc. Again, as for copper ores, the oxide is transformed to the metal with release of carbon dioxide by heat treatment in the presence of some carbonaceous material such as wood or charcoal and if the sulphide is present, the first stage of the roast will convert it to the oxide with the release of sulphur dioxide gas from which point the process will proceed as for the oxide.

Bronze is the name given to copper-tin alloys. It is known that bronze items were not uncommon in Mesopotamia even before 3,000 BC and that they subsequently become rarer for several centuries thereafter. This suggests that the early bronze may have resulted from processing the complex (copper-tin) sulphide ore, stannite, rather than from intentional addition of tin to copper after separate processing of their respective ores, and that the initial source of stannite became exhausted. In this connection it is interesting to note that although stannite is rare, there were two potential sources of this mixed ore fairly readily to hand in the Taurus Mountains of southern Turkey and at Ertzebirge in Bohemia. It would also have been possible to produce bronze by processing stannite with crude copper and there is evidence that this was done also. It appears that the technique of melting the separate metals to make bronze dates from around 1,500 BC when it was known that 10% tin greatly improves the properties of copper for weapon use, for example. Later, the Chinese *Artificers' Record* of the fifth century BC lists six compositions, three of which were 17%, 40%, and 50% tin for bells and pots, arrow-heads, and mirrors respectively. Zinc bracelets have been reported from the ruins of Cameros which was destroyed around 500 BC. The principal ore is the sulphide, zinc blende, but the carbonate, zinc spar (calamine) is also used. Once again, roasting of the sulphide releases sulphur dioxide and that of the carbonate releases carbon dioxide to produce the metal oxide in both cases, continued heating of which with charcoal produces the metal. Brass is the name given to copper-zinc alloys

Lead was known to the Egyptians, is mentioned in the *Old Testament*, and was used by the Romans to make water-pipes. The principal ore is again the sulphide, galena, and again the process is the roasting to the oxide and conversion to the metal by reaction with charcoal. At this point the lead is usually hard and brittle because of the presence of small amounts of antimony, tin, copper and silver. These can be removed by further heating when they are oxidised in preference to the lead, and rise to the surface as a scum (slag) which can be skimmed off. Mercury was mentioned by Theophrastus around 300 BC as liquid-silver or quick-silver. The principal ore is again the sulphide, cinnabar, in which small amounts of free mercury are disseminated. In this case, roasting of the ore liberates the metal directly with release of sulphur dioxide, without requiring the oxide-carbon reaction stage. The cinnabar mine at Almaden in Spain appears to have been worked at least as far back as 415 BC, and Pliny (circa 77 AD) reported that 10,000 lb of cinnabar were being brought annually to Rome in his day, (c.f. gold extraction below).

Iron is perhaps the most significant metal of all in that we would feel its loss more acutely than that of any other. The principal ores are the oxides (magnetite and haematite) and the carbonates. Once again the approach would have been to roast and react with charcoal. However, it should be noted that the conversion temperature of the oxide to the metal is lower for iron ($750°$ C) than for copper ($1100°$ C) and that iron, being to this extent the more accessible, might have come into use prior to copper and bronze. On the other hand, the melting point of metallic iron is higher than that of metallic copper to such an extent that even the use of bellows would have been insufficient to melt the iron in early furnaces and so slag could not have been separated by the process of flotation and skimming. Nevertheless, the slag can be hammered out of lumps of crude iron, the process being repeated until judged satisfactory. Thus, while the difficulty of purification by slag-skimming could account for the copper and bronze ages pre-dating the iron age, we should also consider the comparative corrosion rates of iron and of copper and its alloys as reducing the likelihood of finding iron objects in the earlier archaeological record. Iron implements have certainly been found in the Great Pyramid at Gizeh (circa 5000 BC) and the scarcity of copper in India makes it possible that the iron age did indeed precede the bronze age there.

Be that as it may, it appears that the first people of the west to use iron extensively at around 1,400 BC were the Chalybes, a people of the Black Sea region after whom the Greeks referred to iron as chalybs, when they were not calling it sideros from its presence in meteorites. The Chalybes were a subject people of the Hittites who played a part in distributing the iron-craft through the Middle East and who may have had it from further east still. The early Vedic poets mention iron as an ancient inheritance much used by artisans in the fashioning of tools and so this knowledge may have entered Europe through Aryan migration. The Etruscans were of Aryan stock and had a reputation for the working of iron. Our purpose, however, is not to establish dates and places of origin, but to show how much was achieved by Rational Trinity craftsmanship long before science revealed the nature of the processes involved.

Further to this latter purpose, I will now look at early successes in steel making. As produced above, early iron would inevitably have had variable properties. Thus, depending on the proportions of ore and charcoal, it would have contained variable amounts of dissolved carbon, *i.e.* steels of various types would have been produced inadvertently (c.f. Section 8.1.9). It is interesting that carbon will dissolve only in iron and it is now known that heating low carbon-content malleable iron surrounded by charcoal for long periods causes more carbon to diffuse into the iron to give a hard coating of steel around a softer core in a process known as case-hardening. Such solution would have occurred inadvertently in earlier times when it was found that repeated folding and hammering (forging) improved the product through achieving a more uniform distribution of the dissolved carbon, such hammering being a prolongation of that required to remove the slag. A Chinese knife of 112 AD is inscribed as having been forged 30 times and the best Chinese steel is known to have been forged 100 times. After the fall of Rome the production of iron and steel continued to develop in Spain where the Catalan forge became as famous as the Toledo blade.

Gold must have come to the attention of early man because it naturally occurs as the free metal, is attractive, and readily noticeable. It is generally found in quartz veins as reef gold and in river gravels as alluvial gold. Large nuggets are occasionally found, such as one from California weighing 190 lb. Gold is never found pure though specimens of 99% purity are sometimes found and one from Colorado was reported to be 99.9% pure. Quartz veins are crushed to release the gold, the associated dross washed away and the gold retained as in the panning of alluvial gravels. After crushing at the mines in Nubia (the land of gold), the Egyptians appear to have collected the resulting fine particle-size gold on sponges. The use of sheep-fleeces instead of sponges in the Caucasus is described by Strabo (c.f. Section 3.2.1) and may have been the source of *Jason and the Golden Fleece.* The natural impurities in gold such as silver or copper affect its colour, a feature used by early goldsmiths to achieve contrast patterns in ornamental work. Such impurities can be removed as we have seen above by melting the impure metal and skimming off the floating oxidised impurities, and Agartharcides describes such cupellation in clay crucibles in Egypt in the second century BC, though it was probably of much greater antiquity even then. The Romans dissolved the gold in mercury (from Almaden) to form an amalgam which separated it from impurities in the crushed ore, the gold then being recovered by distilling the mercury.

Silver too has been known since earliest times in native form, though it also occurs as the sulphide, silver glance (argentite) or mixed with several other sulphides such as those of antimony, arsenic, and copper; as silver chloride horn silver (kerargyrite) and in association with lead in

30

galena from whence it was extracted by the ancients. In the latter case, the lead-silver alloy (preferably rich in silver) is heated in a crucible (cupellation) to convert the lead to lead oxide (litharge) which can be removed from the surface leaving at the end of the process the clear surface of the pure molten silver. One of the earliest silver-ornament finds is that from the tomb of Queen Shub-ad of Ur (third millennium BC) while the Hittites appear to have had a monopoly in silver production from about the third millennium and may have been the first to introduce silver coins. However, by the first millennium silver was relatively cheap and in common use throughout the Middle East with the exception of Egypt where imported silver had twice the value of home produced gold, though by Hellenist times it was one-thirteenth that of gold. Because of their scarcity-related values, silver and gold were early and widely used in coinage, though copper was also thus used by the Romans. It is interesting to note that the timely emergence of a seam of silver in the lead mines at Soumis enabled Athens to build the fleet which defeated that of Persia at Salamis.

2. 4. 5 Metalworking

Techniques for working the above metals developed so rapidly that by 2,500 BC almost all today's techniques were in use with skills which have never been exceeded, except for centrifugal casting and electrochemical techniques. We may suppose that those metals which occur in the natural state would have been shaped by hammering (forging) and that once it was found they could be melted, it would have been obvious they would solidify again in conformity with the shape of their container, from which it would have been a short step to imagine desired shapes being achieved by moulding. It would also have become obvious that thin sheet metal (gold can be beaten into leaf as thin as paper) could be formed into containers of various kinds to improve on skins and pottery for various purposes; and that three dimensional objects would require less metal than moulding were appropriately shaped sheet-metal to be attached to wooden frames as for the statue of Pepi I of Egypt, circa 2,300 BC.

Altering the shape of metals by hammering after softening them by heating was much practiced in the ancient world. Even nails were hand forged, whereas nowadays they are mechanically drawn from wire. It would therefore have quickly become apparent that properties could also be altered in that process, an observation which led to the achievement of hard cutting-edges on copper and bronze tools and weapons by hammering the metal when cold. Again, copper, bronze, and iron can be softened by heating and gradual subsequent cooling, while iron and steel harden to extents depending on the rate of cooling. The highest rate was achieved by plunging the red-hot work-piece into cold water, the slowest by allowing it to cool in the air and an intermediate rate by immersion in oil. In very early sheet metal working, the edges of separate sheets were folded over and sewn together with wire, though soldering and welding were available in Ur for gold and bronze by 2,500 BC. Very delicate designs were produced by hammering the reverse side of metal sheets (repousse work) and again from earliest times designs were worked by means of hammer and punch. Again, though cold-hammering would eventually harden the metal to unworkable brittleness, it was found that malleability could be restored by heating and gradual cooling (annealing).

Early stone or clay moulds would have resulted in castings with one flat side whereas two-piece paired moulds were in use throughout the Middle East by 1,300 BC. Such moulds could produce axe heads and similar tools with cores inserted to provide sockets for wooden handles. It would have been but another small step to imagine that sand-bag cores could be removed after solidification to provide hollow castings to reduce metal usage. A variation on the core approach is the lost wax or *cire-perdue* process which involves shaping a model in wax, enclosing it in soft clay which is fired to cure the clay and melt the wax which runs out through pre-formed drainage holes. The cavity-mould thus created is then filled with molten metal and finally the clay is broken to reveal the desired artefact after the molten metal has solidified. For large castings, more than one inlet for the molten metal would be required to avoid premature solidification and blockage. A wall painting at Thebes of around 1,500 BC depicts the casting of a bronze door with the metal being poured through at least 20 inlets. Again, multi-piece moulds were assembled for large complicated castings.

Early craftsmen were also familiar with processes now known to depend on differences in electrical potential between metals. Thus, for example, the Romans were aware that iron objects can be coated with a thin film of copper by immersion in a solution of a copper salt such as copper sulphate (c.f. Section 7.2.5). Again, the Moche Indians of the Andes were aware that repeated hammering and annealing of the copper-silver-gold alloy known as tumbaga causes a surface enrichment to give the appearance of pure silver, this being said to have surprised the Conquistadors on melting such plunder.

As to the quantities of metal in circulation and use, the weight of standard copper ingots was about 70 kg in Roman times, while the waste-tip volumes of early copper mines in the eastern Alps suggest the production of this area alone to have been some 20,000 tonnes of copper between 1,300 and 800 BC, and those at Tarshish suggest the extraction of some 2 million tonnes of copper by pre-Roman and Roman workers between 1000 and 400 BC. In addition, the bronze bowl made for King Solomon's Temple, if properly described in the *First Book of Kings*, must have weighed around 200 tonnes. Again, excavation of the palace of Sargon II (722-705 BC) has yielded about 150 tonnes of iron bars while archaeological work for third century BC China provides evidence of mass-production of metal products based on a system of interchangeable moulds which could be stacked for simultaneous casting. It is clear that early mining operations must have been substantial and as always problems were solved as they were encountered. At the earliest stages the relevant minerals would have been on or very near the surface, otherwise they would not have been found at all. This would have given rise to open-cast operations in the first instance leading to the pursuit of ore veins underground in what would now be called drift mines, and it appears that timber roof-supports were in use by about 2,000 BC. Later, vertical shafts connected one level with another as operations went deeper as they had earlier in the flint mining at Grimes Graves.

At some point water would have become a problem in mining and where surface topography was suitable, drainage tunnels are known to have been constructed to convey water clear of work locations. One such system was driven through rock for a distance of 1.5 km by the Romans at La Zarza in Spain. Where water had to be lifted to the surface, tread-operated wheels and pumps such as those already developed for irrigation purposes, were used in mines. Thus, at Rio Tinto in Spain, the Romans used a series of tread-operated wheels to raise water from one level to another and finally to the surface over a total vertical height of 30 m. In addition, Archimedean screw pumps and even piston pumps in wood and bronze were used, not only in mine drainage but also in fire fighting in towns.

Thus, once again, it may be concluded that the development of all of the above crafts arose from application of the Rational Trinity whereby need, opportunity and means are imagined from which beliefs (hypotheses) as to practical implementations arise for reality-validation in operation, and from whence further problems are identified at the next stage for reiterative application of this same Rational Trinity and so on over many such reiterations over an ever-widening front. Thus, craftsmanship is the knowledge acquired by application of the Rational Trinity in specified areas of activity. Nonetheless, the full benefits of all such craftsmanship can only be realised fully through division of labour, apprenticeship-training, resource acquisition and deployment, distribution of products by trade and appropriate use of products by recipients, all of which also require the Rational Trinity to produce the necessary organisational hierarchy, law and order, peace and tranquillity for their full accomplishment.

2.5 WARFARE

I have noted that intra-group disputes arising from category A beliefs are resolvable by reality-evaluation; that those arising from category B beliefs touching on human nature may be resolved by reference to knowledge of the selfishness and mutual dependence which are inseparable from intra-group cooperation; that inter-group conflict over territory and resources often intensified by differences in the derivatives of the religious Ur-belief is not so easily resolved; that such may lead to armed conflict as the only way of acquiring or retaining the territory and resources in question; and that a willingness to fight over Ur-belief differences alone or even over the reality-refuted beliefs of category C cannot be discounted even to-day. As to these possibilities, archaeological, historical and current anthropological evidence of the behaviour of Palaeolithic societies shows that hunter-gatherer groups have always had intra-group disputes to settle by negotiation, and inter-group negotiations to conduct, with force being the innate default mode with *Homo sapiens* as with other group-species; and that the weapons of the hunt are handy and immediately serviceable. On the other hand, these same sources of evidence show that shared knowledge-based interests intensified by shared beliefs have often led to the creation of larger groups when the advantages of such unification were believed or known to outweigh the disadvantages.

It may be concluded, therefore, that such considerations would have led to the growth of large enough groupings to constitute cities and empires, though force or the threat of force would have been part of the inducement to growth. However, the wealth and power of one city or empire could excite the envy of another to the point of having to defend its interests by force. Thus the ever-present prospect of attack and the need for defence would cause the Rational Trinity to be applied by all such groupings and the knowledge thus acquired would be the craftsmanship of this activity as of all others. Accordingly, in this section, I review the adaptation of earlier hunting weapons for use in warfare, the construction of defensive camps, city walls and frontier defences, and the rise and fall of city states and empires up to and including those of Greece and Rome. Once again this review will show that all relevant knowledge was achieved through application of the Rational Trinity.

2.5.1 Weapons
In early man-to-man fights of a more or less casual nature opponents might have been armed with a knife or an axe. Later, hunting weapons such as the spear and bow and arrow would have suggested themselves because of the advantage of maintaining a distance from the enemy. In more organised and determined conflict, however, the advantages of close combat would become recognised when sufficient force could be applied. At this stage, the advantage of acquiring better weapons than those of one's opponents for both close and distanced combat would have been recognised, leading to use and development of swords, shields, thrusting-spears, javelins and bows and arrows, with progression from wood through copper and bronze to iron for improved penetration-tips and cutting-edges. Bronze (with 10% tin) and careful work-hardening by hammering on an anvil took better edges than did pure copper, but it was iron carburised to steel and tempered by hammering and quenching which gave the greatest advance in keenness, hardness and toughness for the manufacture of swords. Such high quality iron (steel) swords are first

associated with the Hallstatt (Celtic) culture of Austria around 1,000 BC. From around 400 BC the Roman javelin (pilum) used about 2 kg of iron and from 100 BC two light pins were used to attach the hard sharp iron tip to the soft iron shaft to allow the tip to detach on impact with the target and the shaft to bend on ground contact, both being intended to avoid a transfer of usable weapons to the enemy by attacking him.

Bows are clearly depicted on cave walls from at least 30,000 BC though they were substantially developed thereafter. The first stage concentrated on increasing the length and stiffness of the bow, an endeavour limited by the stature and physique of the bowman to a length of 2 m, a draw-distance of about 1 m and a draw-force of about 45 kg; by the availability of suitable materials; and by the mode of use by foot or mounted archers. Though the ultimate performance in these terms may have been achieved by the medieval English longbow of yew, powerful composite bows of wood, horn and sinew, were in use by 1,300 BC. However, further development permitted the use of both arms (90 kg draw-force) to pull and locate the string behind a hook while the weapon itself was held between the ground and body of the archer. In this gastrophetes (belly-shooter) of the Greeks (circa 400 BC) the bolt (arrow) was placed in a groove in contact with the drawn string and discharged by a trigger mechanism which released the string from its retaining hook. The next step was to use a winch, ratchet and pawl mechanism to produce the crossbow as we now know it, though the early Greek version could discharge a 2m long, 4 cm diameter bolt which could not only penetrate any contemporary armour, but also wooden fortifications. Biton (240 BC) describes a further development consisting of a 5 m long bow capable of projecting 20 kg stone balls some of which appear to have been found at Pergamum, and Philo in the second century BC refers to multi-shot devices which could be rapidly reloaded from a magazine. The Romans also developed a modification in which two separate arms were drawn back to store energy in twisting skeins of fibrous materials which on release returned to their rest positions in ejecting the shot.

Although chariots and horses appear from Asia around the middle of the second millennium BC and cavalry a little later, the Greeks mainly relied on heavily armoured infantry, the hoplites, supported by more mobile peltasts armed with javelins, together with small numbers of archers and slingers. Again, examples of full tunics of shaped plates and helmets of Greek bronze have been found. Thus, when Alexander the Great crossed the Hellespont in 334 BC with a joint Macedonian/Greek army of 40,000 men he had 8,000 cavalry to 25,000 heavy infantry, the latter traditionally deploying in phalanx formation to present tiered rows of spears to the enemy which were difficult if not impossible to break even by opposing cavalry. Initially, the Roman army was equipped on the Greek model with spear (hasta), sword, shield and body armour and was organised in legions of up to 6,000 men with some 300 cavalry. From about 400 BC some of the infantry were armed with the javelin (pilum), while in the first century BC, Marius disbanded the cavalry. Yet, the Parthian force which defeated Crassus in 53 BC at Carrhae consisted of 1000 cavalrymen equipped with lance, bow and heavy mailing for horse and rider, together with 10,000 mounted archers. Clearly there was considerable scope for potentially successful variants, though the Roman army was hugely successful and must be acclaimed the finest fighting and campaigning force of its time. From around 400 BC according to Polybius, the army of Rome and her Italian allies totalled some 800,000 men. It also had varying numbers of non-citizen auxiliaries at times.

2. 5. 2 Fortifications

Having already reviewed building capabilities by reference to cities, civic buildings and monuments, I now consider the development of fortifications over time. The earliest defensive structures of which we have knowledge are earth works in which material excavated in the digging

34

of a ditch was thrown up as a rampart sufficiently far behind the ditch to prevent subsidence into it and permitting friendly access through a narrow defendable rampart passage opposite a narrow element of uncut ditch. Some of these early structures may also have been used to protect cattle from marauders and the earth and wood defences later set up by the Roman army at night-halts on campaign in hostile territory may be thought of as temporary versions of these earlier permanent fortifications. Early development strengthened the outer rampart-face with wood revetments making it vertical and more difficult to climb, and later the rampart itself was constructed over a core of stone making it stronger and more permanent.

Where excavation was difficult, brick and stone were used to build defensive structures with the natural terrain being incorporated to save labour and materials. Later, design effort was devoted to placing attackers at a disadvantage by forcing their approach to expose their non-shield sides to the defenders and by around 1,500 BC very substantial and well-designed fortress-palaces had been built in Middle Eastern and Mediterranean areas as at Tiryns and at Mycenae for example. By 1,200 BC Rameses II had built a double-walled fortress at Medinet Habu with the outer wall crenulated to protect defending archers and at Sinjerli about 640 BC a fortress was constructed of three concentric walls surrounding the central strong-point, the citadel. Again, for the protection of the population at large, defensive walls were thrown round the city itself as for example at Troy by about 1.500 BC. Rome itself provides examples of progressive development in city defence with earthworks raised in the fifth century BC, which though breached in 386 BC, were replaced by 378 BC with the stone Servian Wall fronted by a ditch 10 m deep which deterred Hannibal in 211 BC. Again in 270 AD, Marcus Aurelius started a ten-year project to build new walls some 20 km long, 7 m high and 4 m thick which incorporated 13 defended gateways and nearly 400 defensive towers. Later still, these walls were strengthened and their height increased by Diocletian.

Frontier defence provides yet another expression of building capacity. The Assyrians built the 80 km Medean Wall between the Tigris and Euphrates to protect Nineveh, and the Great Wall of China finally stretched a distance of 2,400 km. From the time of Tiberius the Romans were under more or less constant pressure from the Germanic tribes on their northern frontier in response to which they constructed a fortified line over some 500 km between the Rhine and the Danube. In addition, the 120 km Hadrian's Wall was constructed (122-128 AD) from Wallsend to Bowness, initially earthen at the western end finally all in stone, reinforced with small mile-forts and by 17 larger ones along its length and supported by a garrison of 15,000 men during its most active period.

Of course, the creation of defences introduces the problem of overcoming them and here again we see the Rational Trinity at work as always. Though an obvious tactic for overcoming defenders within a fortified position was to subject them to thirst and starvation, this often took longer than the attackers could afford to wait. Thus, there are many examples of prolonged yet unsuccessful sieges, a notable one being Tyre's survival of a 13 year investment by Nebuchadnezzar in the sixth century BC by withdrawal to its island fortress and destruction of its access causeway. However, in less than a year, it fell to Alexander the Great who built his own approach to the island in 332 BC. To reduce the time required to come to grips with defenders, however, attackers could consider going over, through, or under defensive walls. Though the first option involved scaling the walls, the use of ladders had serious shortcomings in providing no protection to the attackers while climbing and in failing to deliver a significant weight of attack on reaching the top. These failings led to on-site construction of wheeled siege towers which could be filled with protected attackers on internal floors and on their internal connecting ladders to deliver a localised strength of attack more equal (even superior) to that of the defence at the top of the attacked wall-element. The second option was to gain access through gates by use of the testudo which consisted of a heavy iron-tipped battering ram suspended by ropes and swung by attackers protected within a roofed and wheeled structure. The third approach was to mine the walls by tunnelling under them and by burning the timber supports to bring down an element of wall by its own weight.

2. 5. 3 The Rise and Fall of Cities and Empires

Having reviewed the development of craftsmanship and socio-political organisation from the Palaeolithic to the Iron Age and having noted the transformation of hunting weaponry and building techniques to military purposes, I now review relations between cities and empires as further examples of the Rational Trinity applied to military and political power.

Our earliest records show the Sumerians to have arrived in the Middle East perhaps from Central Asia *via* Persia and to have been living in organised cities sustained by agriculture, irrigation and all other relevant crafts together with a calendar, a number system, a written language and a knowledge of metals by about 3,500 BC. However, about a thousand years later they were displaced by the Akkadians who in turn were displaced by the Amorites, both of whom were Semitic peoples from the Syrian region. Meanwhile in Egypt the agricultural communities of the Nile Valley with similar crafts to the Sumerians were creating the Old Kingdom around 2,700 BC which would endure for about 500 years and see the building of the pyramids, while further east the communities of the Indus Valley were establishing their agriculture and cities on the basis of similar craftsmanship. Again, by the second millennium BC, the Bronze Age Syrian and Babylonian Empires of Sargon I and Hammurabi respectively had command and control over very substantial resources. Nonetheless, the iron-working Hittites having invaded Asia Minor from the north, expanded yet further south to conquer much of Syria, to sack Babylon in 1595 BC and subsequently to conquer Egypt and Nubia. In turn, they were overthrown by other ironworkers, the Kassites from the Zagros Mountains who ruled the Syrian-Babylonian region for 400 years and by the horse-riding nomadic Hyksos from western Asia who took over Egypt as far as Nubia only to be thrown out after about 100 years by formation of the Egyptian New Kingdom which having experienced occupation, now expanded north into Syria and Palestine to confront the Hittites on the Euphrates and south to the fourth cataract on the Nile. Further west the Minoan civilisation developed on Crete between 3,400 and 1,100 BC, influencing the Aegean as far as Troy, Mycenae and Tiryns before falling to the Achaeans, while in the Indus Valley, the Harrapans fell to the Aryans.

The early successes of the nomadic peoples of the Central Asian Steppe and of the Ukraine depended on the light war chariot which appeared in Sumeria around 2,500 BC. Progressive improvement of this war machine by wheelwright, harness-maker and smith in bronze and iron, gave rise to a warrior aristocracy of charioteers of increasing potency and by about 1,200 BC the Hittite capital Bogazkoy in Asia Minor was more impressive than Babylon had been before it fell to them. Nonetheless, the increasing pressure which the Hittites experienced from other iron-working peoples finally enabled the Medes, Chalybes and Persians to bring into being the Assyrian Empire which at its height stretched from the Persian Gulf, north through Mesopotamia to Tarsus on the Mediterranean and from south of the Euphrates through Damascus to northern Egypt. However, in the seventh century BC the Cimmerians and Scythians, nomadic steppe-dwellers from the north, this time in cavalry formations armed with sword, bow and arrow, so weakened the chariot-based Assyrians as to enable their subject peoples to revolt and in 621 BC Nineveh fell to the combined assault of Scythians, Medes and Babylonians, the Assyrian Empire thus being broken up.

Further to the west, the Dorians took over what is now Greece and the Ionians what is now western Turkey, again from the north with the establishment of city states from about 750 BC. Further west still, the Etruscans entered northern Italy, though the Romans who had founded their city in 753 BC subsequently subdued them, established their Republic in 509 BC and went on to establish the greatest Empire of them all. The Greeks in contrast did not create an empire, Greek colonies overseas being independent city states, though Alexander the Great changed much of that. In contrast, the Roman Empire eventually encompassed much of the Middle East, Egypt including the north coast of Africa, most of Europe and most of Britain, though it was strongly influenced by Greek thinking, the joint legacy of which survives to this day.

While Greece and Rome were starting their respective careers in the west, the Medes and Chaldeans were creating a new Persian Empire in the east following their success at Nineveh and the new capital, Persepolis, became widely famed for its buildings, some having columns 20 m high and roofs of cedar, and for its extensive gardens (paridaiza). Under the leadership of Cyrus and Darius this Empire extended from the Hindu Kush to the Mediterranean and from the Persian Gulf to the Caspian Sea, though their plans to push further west were thwarted by the Scythians in the Ukraine and by the Greeks at Marathon in 490 BC. Again, during this period a Mid-European people known to the Greeks as the Hyperboreans or Celts were allied with them against the Persians and Carthaginians. The defeat of Xerxes at Salamis and of Hamilcar by Gelon in Sicily took place in the same year and just after that (c. 500 BC) Celts drove the Carthaginians from Spain, thus opening to the Greeks that overland tin trade with Britain for which the Phoenicians (Carthaginians) had founded the port of Marseilles in 600BC. A century later, we find Celts from Cisalpine Gaul contesting North Italy with Etruscans and Romans, during which struggle Roman mediators took up arms against them at their siege of Clusium in 391 BC, for which transgression of customary behaviour the Celts occupied Rome for almost a year (from July 390) and exacted a fine before withdrawing. Later, while the Celtic Empire was breaking up and losing its dominance over the Germanic tribes, the Cisalpine Celts were in alliance with the Etruscans in the third Sammite War with Rome.

Before this happened, however, the Thracians and Illyrians overwhelmed Macedon driving King Amyntas II into exile and killing his son Perdiccas II in battle. Pressure on his younger son Philip was greatly relieved, however, by Celtic successes against the Illyrians in the valleys of the Danube and Po. Later, the Greeks fell under the control of Philip and it was his son Alexander the Great who spread Greek influence throughout the Middle East and beyond. Having been assured by the Celts on oath that they would not take advantage of his absence, Alexander crossed into Asia Minor in 334 BC, marched successfully through Syria and Egypt, defeated Darius at Issus and again at Gaugamela in Mesopotamia and destroyed the cities of Tyre and Persepolis among others. His travels and conquests had taken him as far east as the Indus Valley, but he died in Babylon in 323 BC without fully consolidating his new territories, these passing separately to four of his generals. Thus, Egypt passed to Ptolemy and the city which he named Alexandria went on to become the cultural centre of the western world.

Though Athenians and Cretans had maintained substantial navies, the great sea-trading people from 2000 BC to 350 BC had been the Phoenicians (originally from Tyre, Biblos and Sidon), the founders of Carthage and subsequent controllers of much of North Africa, together with Sicily, Spain, the Balearics and Sardinia, and though the Greeks and Celts had successes against them, it was Rome which caused their final downfall. During these Punic Wars, in which Carthage and Rome contended for control of the Mediterranean world, Rome was almost defeated by Hannibal (son of Hamilcar) before Gaius Publius Scipio defeated him at the battle of Zama in 202 BC and destroyed Carthage. Again, around 200BC the Emperor of the state of Chin, having conquered all neighbouring states, became the first Emperor of China behind his Great Wall. Later the Kushans of central Asia, in moving into India through the Khyber Pass secured the Silk Road. However, in the west, the Seleucid Empire (named after another of Alexander's generals) in Asia Minor was taken over by Rome in 188 BC, Greece became a Roman colony in 146 BC, Egypt was brought within the Roman Empire after the battle of Actium in 50 BC, Julius Caesar conquered the Celts in Gaul in the first century AD, all of Alexander's previously conquered territories passed to Rome under Trajan and Severus in the second century AD; and campaigns were fought beyond the Rhine, the Danube and the English Channel under such as Hadrian and Marcus Aurelius.

It is generally considered that those who lived as Roman Citizens during the second century AD, say from Domitian to Commodus, enjoyed what Gibbon called a "Golden Age" in respect of physical well-being and security. In those days luxury goods were being traded from as far away as Kerala *via* the Red Sea on the reliable southwest-northeast winds of the monsoon. In contrast, by the third century AD, barbarian incursions and internal problems caused Diocletian to divide the army into four commands, to place the administration under two emperors (the Augusti) each with an alternate (the Caesars) and though taxes increased, incursions continued despite all efforts, while internal peace was beset by factional conflicts not least among Christians. Again, the fourth century AD saw civil war and though Constantine emerged as the victor in 324 AD and negotiated the establishment of Christianity as the state religion, neither he or his successors were able to halt the decline towards demise (c.f. Chapter 4). Thus, though the Germanic tribes of what had been Celtic Europe had only been mentioned briefly by the Greek geographer Pytheas around 300 BC, and had been defeated by Marius when they entered Italy as the Cimbri and Teutones at the end of second century BC, the Germanic peoples subsequently wrested the Rhine and Danube region from the previously dominant Celts and began to threaten Rome. Today, many German words in law, government, and war reveal Celtic origin as do many place-names over the rest of Europe while the designations of social position preserved until recently in Celtic culture are still extant in the Hindu caste system suggesting an Indo-European or even more universal origin.

Thus, as the incursions of Germanic and Slav peoples driven on by Huns from further east made even Roman Gaul increasingly untenable, Constantine founded his new city of Constantinople on the old Greek trading post of Byzantium, the withdrawal of Rome from Western Europe having already begun. Thus though in 395 AD the two sons of Theodosius had become respective rulers of the Eastern and Western Empires, the former continued for another thousand years despite the destructive efforts of Persians, Slavs, Arabs, and Turks, while the latter succumbed quickly to intra-Christian strife, and to incursions by Germanic Tribes of one heresy or another. Thus, with Alaric the Visigoth having sacked Rome in 410 AD, the western Pax Romana was effectively at an end with the last Emperor being deposed at Ravenna in 476 AD and with the Dark Age already begun (c.f. Chapter 5).

2. 5. 4 Transfer of Knowledge and Belief

It is clear from the above that the hunter-gatherer propensity to migrate had not been entirely abated by settlement; that the above movements involved peoples at more or less comparable stages of craft and social development, knowledge and beliefs having been distributed by travel and inter-community trade; that advances in craftsmanship would also have been transferred to the less advanced by invasive movement while adoption or rejection of religious and socio-political beliefs would have depended on the relative acceptance of donor and receiver beliefs, such in any case having a common source in the innate Ur-beliefs of the earliest days of *Homo sapiens*. Thus, leaving aside interim beliefs in shamanism and sympathetic magic of Palaeolithic peoples and the superstitions described in *The Golden Bough* of J. G. Frazer (1854-1941) we can proceed to the

38

oral origins of current religious beliefs through their documentation from about 2000 BC onwards by which time they would have been reliably available to the interested through the fluid and open nature of socio-political boundaries.

Thus, the oldest (eighth-ninth century BC) books of the Judaic *Old Testament*, take us back to Abraham at around 1900 BC in the Sumerian City of Ur, itself dating archaeologically from about 3500BC. Again, the *Iliad* and *Odyssey* of Homer (eighth century) take us back to Mycenaean Greece and Troy of 1400 -1300BC. Yet again, the earliest texts of the Hindu *Vedas* were first written between 2000-1500BC, the more philosophical *Upanishads* in the period 800-200 BC and the *Mahabharata* and *Ramayama* epics around 300BC, while the *Zend-Avesta* of Zoroastrianism takes us back to its founder in the sixth century BC. In addition we have the *Eightfold Path* of the sixth century BC Indian Siddharta Gautama, the Buddha, though this was not written until the first century BC, and the *Tao* (Way or Path) of the Chinese, many of the texts of which were written from the fifth to third centuries BC, the most significant being the Tao Te Ching of Lao Tzu and the teachings of Kung Fu Tzu (Confusius). In all of these religious and philosophical writings we have mixtures of belief and knowledge concerning human nature expressed through guidance on individual and social life and based on the concept of Good and Evil. In fact, to emphasise the difference between these two, the Persian Zoroaster (sixth century BC) speaks of Ahura Mazda (the Good God) and Ahriman (the Evil God) and assures of the final supremacy of the former.

Though all religions gather accretions to their common Ur-belief to promote cohesion of believers and their distinction from others, it is always possible to discern their core knowledge of what is good and bad for survival and social cohesion, all else being largely superfluous though replete with the potential to create conflict where none need arise. Thus, for example, strict adherence to rules on what to eat and how to kill and cook it, prevents those with differing rules from participating in the socially significant act of sharing food, this having the intentional or unintentional consequence of reducing social cooperation and increasing antagonism between groupings by emphasising otherwise absent differences. Nonetheless, whether accepted or suspended, the religious Ur-belief provides a metaphorical antidote to our individual loneliness in an infinitely mysterious universe and supports our group-species compliance with our species-specific knowledge-based ethical codes whatever their cultural belief-based presentations.

2. 6 CONCLUSIONS

At this point, it may be concluded that the Rational Trinity produced the craftsmanship, the self-knowledge and the hierarchical social cohesion necessary to provide food and materials for a widening division of labour and for exchange of commodities and products through internal and external trade; that this led to expressions of individual and socio-political group power at village, town, city and empire levels; that the most successful hierarchies were those whose Rational Trinity most effectively reconciled the innate selfishness and cooperativeness of *Homo sapiens* and most effectively integrated such reconciliation with derivatives of the religious Ur-belief in respect of purposeful cultural cohesion and enterprise at individual, family, social, commercial and military levels whether consciously or unconsciously; and that failure to achieve the necessary cohesion by these means would inevitably cause internal disruption and/or subjugation by more socially coherent, better equipped and more highly motivated invaders.

It may further be concluded that all social life was now alterable for good or ill by victory or defeat in armed conflict; that attack was the expression of desire to extend one cultural combination of knowledge and belief over more peoples, territory and resources; that defence was the expression of desire to preserve the integrity of the attacked culture, territory and resources against encroachment and overrun; that such conflict would best be avoided by knowledge-based diplomacy backed by the threat of credible force; and that otherwise the outcome would be victory to the more effective and submission by the less effective. It may be noted, by way of example, that the Celts in seeking to expand to the detriment of the Etruscans told Roman intermediaries that they were doing no more than the Romans had previously done; and that the normal usages of diplomacy and war were to do what could be done when co-existence and trade were believed to produce less advantage than conquest.

It may also be concluded that religious Ur-belief derivatives can only have meaning for a culture to the extent that they reflect its collective self-knowledge of human nature; that beliefs concerning the behaviour required of us by God are derived from such cultural self-knowledge; and that regardless of cultural differences an innate species-specific behaviour pattern has been confirmed and reinforced since time immemorial by progressive reality-validation of the requirements for social-group cohesion. Again, with respect to the Ur-belief in rationality, it may be concluded that growing awareness of the applicability of abstract number to the Real world encouraged belief in the Beyond and Real as a continuum; and that this encouraged belief in knowledge of the latter being accessible to rationality applied to the former, the imagination being the interface and Rational Duality belief concerning the Beyond being undifferentiated from Rational Trinity knowledge of craftsmanship and human nature in the Real (c.f. Chapters 1 and 3).

CHAPTER 3: THE SEARCH FOR UNDERSTANDING

Having seen how *Homo sapiens* applied his innate Rational Trinity to satisfy his survival needs and later to create agriculture, cities and empires through his increasing knowledge of craftsmanship and of human nature we should note that all might have been attributed to commonsense, craftsmen having learned how to use the world without having any specific knowledge of its nature while human behaviour was a matter of self-knowledge, even proto-knowledge (c.f. Chapter 1).

Thus, before considering our earliest speculations as to the nature of the world and of humanity, we should note that our animal and earliest hominid precursors would have accepted the world and themselves without any need to know the nature of either. In contrast, however, we should also note that the Rational Trinity capacity of such as *Homo neanderthalensis* would have been closer to that which caused *Homo sapiens* to address the Unknown and Unknowable for the first time. Again, given that apes, elephant, dolphin and other species exhibit concern for the dying and reluctance to abandon the dead, there seems no cause for surprise that *Homo neanderthalensis* buried his dead, that *Homo sapiens* believed in reincarnation of the spirit or soul in this world by analogy with winter death and spring rebirth or in an after-life in the Beyond as evidenced by burying artefacts with the dead for their later use. Yet again, his early belief in birth from (apparently) nothing would have stimulated belief in initial creation from nothing, as evidenced by the account of *Genesis* in the *Old Testament* and by the Greek creation myths, man himself being a creator of new life, tools and artefacts. Again, as a group-species believing in a creator, he would have distinguished social and anti-social behaviour as being compliant and non-compliant with the creator's intentions as evidenced again by the Greek myths and the behaviour codes of the *Old Testament*, such beliefs being of some 200,000 years' accumulation.

As to self-knowledge, we see that our creation myths support adherence to our behaviour codes these being further supported by more specific myths, fables and nursery rhymes; that while creation myths may be accepted rejected or suspended, the knowledge-content of our behaviour codes is consistent with our self-knowledge of human nature; that this is confirmed by our discerning meaning in behaviour said to be required of us by the Old Testament God and in the deeds of honour and dishonour exemplified by the lesser gods of Greek mythology for our emulation and avoidance, such discernment of meaning being impossible without the said self-knowledge. Nonetheless, at a practical level there was a need to avoid the civil disorder which arises when the innate selfishness of hierarchical direction overwhelms the innate cooperation of the directed. Thus, the need for behaviour conducive to maintenance of family, social and commercial life was a concern of the *Old Testament* writers as it was for those who sought to resolve civil conflict between sub-group interests of the directing and directed in the Greece in the seventh and sixth centuries BC, this latter causing sixth century Athenians to introduce a frame-work of Civil Law and a public prosecutor, and those of the fifth century to introduce a democratically elected ruling assembly, jury service and public administration to achieve the widest possible male consensus on public policy formulation and to reduce reliance on oracular assistance, this having been unhelpful compared to the codification and commentary of the *Old Testament*.

It is against this belief in the Beyond and the Real being a continuum that I now assess Greek attempts to maintain social cohesion through an understanding of human nature and to understand the nature of the physical world at a deeper level than is required for craftsmanship which in any case was taken for granted or as a gift from the gods. Thus, I now review Greek efforts to maintain social cohesion through Rational Trinity self-knowledge, to obtain knowledge on the underlying nature of the world through the Duality, and to acquire craft-like knowledge of the world through the Trinity, in contrast to Roman contentment with humanity and world as they were known or believed to be.

3.1 THE GREEKS

Though much is made of the Greeks as initiators of knowledge-based problem solving by rational thought, it is clear from our evolution, early craftsmanship and earliest oral and written traditions regarding human behaviour, that our rationality is innate and predates the Greeks, and from my differentiation of knowledge from belief by reality-evaluation, it is clear that rationality of itself cannot produce knowledge and thus cannot solve problems in reality (c.f. Chapters 1 and 2).

Thus, we see that Solon (the Law-giver) was acting on knowledge of humanity when in response to social-upheaval early in the sixth century BC, he stated that it is men, not the gods who must bring peace and order (eunomie) to their cities, though he invoked the assistance of Eunomie (a daughter of Zeus) "under whom all men's actions are fitting and wise, if directed towards peace and harmony". Thus, in making a clear statement that humans must solve their own problems and in invoking a Deity (a metaphor) to assist them, Solon reveals that to him the gods are metaphors for the responsibilities which humans must take upon themselves through knowing themselves, if peace and harmony are ever to be achieved and maintained among them (c.f. Section 3.1.2). Thus, Solon's invocation of a goddess for a purpose, is much like creating a tool for a purpose, though unlike a knapped-flint, the goddess does not exist in the real world of reality-evaluation, nor need she be claimed to exist in the world beyond such evaluation. Nonetheless, her usefulness as metaphor can be reality-evaluated to the extent of its contribution to the achievement of Solon's objective, provided she is believed to exist by others, or becomes a matter of suspended belief or indeed of metaphor to them. Again, though secularism has long dismissed the Greek deities as primitive precursors of a monotheism it wishes to destroy, we can see that while Poseidon may have been initially imagined as a supernatural human-like entity in control of the sea, he had become, at least for some in Solon's time, a metaphor for the 'moods' of the sea as observed in reality; that without this cultural background invocation of Eunomie would not have influenced society at large; and that imagination inspires, motivates and encourages by metaphor or suspended belief short of actual belief.

As to scepticism, we find Xenophanes asking whether the gods of horses are horse-shaped, ours being human-shaped; Socrates denying the existence of gods; Protagoras wondering whether their nature could be grasped by us were they to exist; and Aristotle recognising the very real benefit of myths to humanity. Thus, while there was scepticism on the existence of gods, there was influential support for their value as myth. Indeed, Homer (eighth century BC) has the gods playing an interactive part with humans in his mythical epics, the *Iliad* (on the Trojan War) and the *Odyssey* (on the homeward journey of Odysseus) and we see this tradition continuing in the *Dramatic Tragedies* of later Greek literature (c.f. Section 3.1.2) the purpose of which as stated by Aristotle (384-322 BC) in his *Poetics*, is to arouse the emotions of pity and fear in the audience and thus to extend its experience of what it means to be human in the best possible sense. Thus we may see the stories and plays of classical Greece as metaphors for the real lives of those in the audience, presented as the interplay of human personae with influences personified as deities. This is not to claim, however, that everyone accepted the metaphorical nature of the gods. Indeed, it is entirely possible that even those who did, could still retain some measure of belief in their actual existence whatever that might mean. Greeks after all, continued to observe their rituals and to consult their oracles while outright expressions of atheism continued to be relatively rare and to be viewed with unease. Indeed, Socrates was accused of "not acknowledging the gods the city acknowledges, of introducing other new powers, and of corrupting the young," for which he was condemned to death. Those who condemned him however, were aware of their recent defeat in the Peloponnesian War (431-404 BC), and may have believed offence to the gods inadvisable whether they existed or not.

We may, nonetheless, see that the Greeks were reaching an understanding of their gods as metaphors sufficient to have opened their imaginations to further consideration of the nature of humanity, and to speculative conjecture and observation as to the nature of the world, such attitudes and their consequences influencing Romans, Neo-Platonic Christianity and European culture from the Renaissance onwards. Against this background, I now review Greek thinking on humanity and on the natural world.

3. 1. 1 Greek Thinking: 600 BC-500 BC

The names of the individuals responsible for the craftsmanship and social innovations previously described, are largely unknown to us. Thus, apart from those known through earlier religious texts, it is only with the Greeks, such as Homer and Solon, that we begin to associate individuals with particular innovations, though we can be sure that many attributed innovations were derived from earlier unnamed initiators external to Greece. In this connection, we should note that the earliest named innovators first arise among the Ionians of western Asia Minor whose traditional contact with the knowledge and beliefs of Persia, Mesopotamia, Egypt and Phoenicia is well established.

Thus, Thales of Miletus (c. 624-565 BC) had visited both Egypt and Mesopotamia where he gained first-hand knowledge of the land-survey methods of the former and of the latter's Saronic cycle of solar eclipses, the recurrence-interval of which (eighteen years and eleven days) enabled him to acquire renown on returning home by predicting an eclipse which duly occurred in 585 BC. Again, the Egyptians had identified some empirical relationships involving triangles, rectangles, pyramids and spheres in the course of their post-flood surveys in the Nile valley and in their construction projects. Thus, they knew as perhaps others did before them, that specific triangles with sides of length 3, 4 and 5 or of 5, 12, and 13 units contained a right angle, though the extent to which they had reached general conclusions remains questionable. Be that as it may, the demonstration of a number of general relationships is attributed to Thales, such as that any angle at the circumference of a circle subtended by a diameter is a right angle; that the sum of the angles of any triangle is equal to two right angles; that two intersecting straight lines produce opposite angles which are always equal; that the angles at the base of an isosceles triangle are always equal; and that the corresponding sides of any two correspondingly equal-angled triangles are in constant proportion. These relationships, deriving from the surveying and building craftsmanship reviewed in Chapter 2, can be used to solve practical problems by using quantities which can be measured to calculate those which cannot be accessed for direct measurement. In addition, however, the generalisations attributed to Thales represent an abstraction (generalisation) of mathematics from the specifics of the real world which parallels the abstraction of number from identifiable items which gave rise to the arithmetic of the Sumerians and Babylonians (c.f. Sections 2.3.3 and 2.6).

It being natural that the survey work of the Egyptians would be recorded in plans and maps, we see that by 1400 BC depictions of the relative positions of houses, temples and gold mines of the New kingdom had been drawn up, and that all such could have been available to Thales during his visit to Egypt. Be that as it may, the Miletan pupil of Thales, Anaximander (611-547) attempted a map of the world as a whole which already shows a wider interest than local surveying. In addition, he worked on the Babylonian sun-dial from which accurate measurement of shadow lengths determined the dates of solstices and equinoxes, and he appears to have been the first to speculate on the sizes and distances from Earth of the celestial bodies, though he believed the former to be a flat disc at the centre of everything. Others contributing to knowledge of the world by direct observation with or without measurement at this time were such as Hercataeus, also of Miletus (c. 540 BC), who travelled to Egypt, to provinces of the Persian Empire, to Thrace, Lydia and the coasts of the Black Sea, to the Gulf of Genoa and to Spain as far as Gibraltar; and who also produced a map at around 500 BC. Another was Herodotus of Halicarnassus (c. 484-425 BC) who travelled widely in Greece and Asia Minor; to Susa, the Persian capital and to Babylon; to the Black Sea coasts, Scythia and Thrace; to Syria, Tyre, Palestine, Egypt and Sicily before settling in Italy where he wrote his *History* which records geographical details and the nature and habits of peoples.

Apart from his abstraction of generalisations from the empirical survey-rules of craftsmen to produce geometry, Thales shows awareness of a need to explain the physical world of experience. To this end, he proposed that the basic element of all things was water by which he meant some water-like essence of the Beyond which cycled from sky to earth through plants and animals, and back to sky. Later, Anaximenes his fellow Miletan, proposed that air (pneuma) by which he meant breath or soul, was the basic element or spirit which pervades and sustains the whole Universe including ourselves. Later still, Heracleitus (c. 540-475) in reviewing these proposals, concluded that everything being in a state of flux, the only reality was change; and that, therefore, the origin and image of all things animate and inanimate was the great transformer, the spirit of fire, everything being formed of the changing essences of which real fire, air, and water are particular manifestations. A wholly different view was taken by Democritus (c. 470-c.400 BC) who proposed that nothing existed except solid atoms and the void between them; that they were eternal, uncaused, invisibly small, homogeneous, incompressible and indivisible (hence the name); that they differed only in form, size and arrangement; that the qualities which we distinguish in things are caused by movement and re-arrangement of these atoms, such motion being as eternal and uncaused as the atoms themselves; and that all things, including ourselves, are but temporary atomic aggregations which separate in time and re-aggregate to form other things and other beings.

Though these speculations are believed by some to be the earliest steps in science, such is to misunderstand science and knowledge in general by conflating both with rationality (c.f. Sections 6.1, 6.3.4, 6.4, 8.3.4, 11.2.1and 12.1). Thus, while knowledge requires reality-evaluation of hypotheses to this end, the above speculations are pure belief impossible to reality-evaluate. Thus, we see that while *real* water might appear to transform to 'air' on evaporation, to condense and fall again as rainwater and to transform to earth (sand and silt) in river sand-bars and deltas; that while *real* air is essential to life; and that while *real* fire is a transformer; the nature of the essences themselves could not be submitted to reality-evaluations nor were they intended to be. Thus, while the Atomic Theory would later be reality-validated (c.f. Sections 7.1-7.3 and 9.1) through a succession of ever more focussed hypotheses, the speculative belief of Democritus was far short of being a scientific hypothesis, and though such beliefs have been termed theories, conjectures and speculations, they are simply beliefs, their limitations having been recognised by some contemporaries. Thus, Heracataeus, the geographer, had expressed the view (c. 540 BC) that "the stories of the Greeks are no less absurd than they are numerous" and Socrates, an exact contemporary of Democritus, is quoted by his pupil Xenophon (430-350 BC) as saying that "speculators on the Universe and on the laws of the heavenly

44

bodies are no better than madmen". Still, it should be noted that there was now an interest in the nature of the world; that this was producing imaginative beliefs and critical responses to them; and that despite the absence of science, craft knowledge on the uses of the world was progressing independent of all such beliefs (c.f. Chapter 2).

However, by this time, there were Greek colonies in southern Italy and Sicily, which consequently became additional centres of intellectual activity. Thus, Pythagoras, an Ionian of Samos (born c. 582 BC) settled in the Dorian colony at Croton around 530 BC, and established his school. The general proof of the theorem that the square on the hypotenuse of a right-angled triangle is equal to the sum of the squares on the other two sides, is attributed to Pythagoras though he left nothing in writing. It is the generalisation underlying the 3, 4 ,5 and other specific right-angled triangles of the Egyptians as noted above. The Pythagoreans revealed many other theorems of plane geometry concerning triangles, quadrilaterals and regular polygons, and by considering equilateral triangles and squares arranged in three dimensions, they discerned the 'existence' of four regular solids having all their edges equal. These solids are the 4-sided tetrahedron (double square-based pyramid), the 6-sided cube, the 8-sided octahedron (double square pyramid with all external faces equilateral triangles) and the 20-sided icosahedron (all faces equilateral triangles), to which they later added the 12-sided dodecahedron (all faces regular pentagons). They also identified a variety of number series and relationships, such as the series 1, 3 (*i.e.* 1+2), 6 (1+2+3), 10 (1+2+3+4) . . . , noted that the bracketed subsets form triangles when arranged as rows of contiguous beads, called these series members triangular numbers, and noted that the sum of any two consecutive members is a square number i.e. 1+3 = 4, 3+6 = 9, 6+10 = 16 . . . In addition, they recognised arithmetic, geometric, harmonic and musical proportions and the occurrence of irrational numbers. Again, they showed that the square of two numbers added together was equal to the sum of their individual squares plus twice their product, *i.e.*, $(a + b)^2 = a^2 + b^2 + 2ab$. This they did by drawing a square of side-length (a + b) within which they drew a square of side-length *a* and another of side-length *b* to show that the remaining internal area consisted of two rectangles each of area *a* times *b*, which together is 2*ab*.

The shortcomings of the mathematical notation of the time, however, did not allow progress in algebra beyond the level which could be visualised geometrically, and so the Pythagoreans took to seeking significance where none existed. Thus, Philolaus of Tarentum (c. 480- 400 BC) wrote the first book on Pythagorean doctrine in which, to the Sun, Moon, the five known planets and the sphere of the stars, he added an invisible counter-earth in order to achieve a total of ten items, the number sacred to the Pythagoreans. By similar reasoning, they took their first four regular solid objects to represent the elements water, air, and fire to which they were confident in adding earth as the fourth element, and later having identified the dodecahedron as their fifth solid, they used it to represent the Universe, there being no obvious candidate for fifth element. Again, having identified the pentagon and noting that a five-pointed star, the pentagram, could be formed by a continuous line joining its alternate vertices, they attributed mysterious significance to it and adopted it as their secret sign of recognition. Though all of the mathematical findings of the Pythagoreans proved useful, they attributed spurious meaning to numbers beyond their designation of quantity, thus demonstrating that even the gifted can engage in belief-driven endeavour when difficulties in hypotheses formulation, number-system *etc*, preclude any other activity.

As to medical matters, Democedes (born c. 540 BC) formerly medical attendant to the Persian Emperor Darius I, became associated with the earliest recorded medical School on the Cnidus peninsula in Asia Minor, and Alcmacon of Croton (c. 500 BC) a pupil of Pythagoras discovered by dissection, the nerves which connect the brain to the eyes and the passages which connect mouth and ear, the latter now called after Eustachi who investigated them some twenty-two centuries later in Italy. Again, Empedocles of Agrigentum (c.500-430 BC) who was also known to Pythagoras, believed the heart to be at the centre of the blood-vessel system which distributed the essential factor of life, innate heat as he called it, to all parts of the body. This in turn led Diogenes of Apollonia in Crete (c. 430 BC) to describe the system of blood vessels throughout the body and to distinguish between arteries and veins in terms of form, function and distribution. As to speculation, however, Empedocles, believing love and strife to hold sway over all things including the four elements and believing the latter to be in alliance or in opposition to one another, now associated pairs of the four allied or opposed qualities, wet, hot, dry and cold with each of the four elements, such that water is cold and wet, air is wet and hot, fire is hot and dry and earth is dry and cold. On this model, all the substances of experience were believed to consist of combinations of these four elements (essences) and qualities, so that, for example, the water of our experience was believed not to be wholly of the element water and its qualities, but an embodiment with contributions from the other three elements and their qualities in appropriate though unknown proportions.

At this point, we should note that the gods, having been imagined and believed in, were now becoming mythical and useful as metaphors in the development of law as a guarantor of civil peace; that mythical epics were being used to explain man to himself for the purpose of instilling individual responsibility for socially acceptable behaviour; that geometry was being abstracted from the craft of surveying as number had been abstracted from the craft of commercial accounting; that the world was being actively explored with map-making being developed from surveying; and that anatomy and physiology were being addressed through the craftsmanship of dissection. Again, we should note that attention was being given to the celestial bodies in respect of size and distance from earth, and to the nature of the Earth and universe in general. Nonetheless, as to the underlying nature of the world, there was only imaginative speculation (belief), there being no reality-validated knowledge other than of the observational craft-type.

3. 1. 2 Athenian Thinking: 500 BC-300BC

Following its naval victory over the Persians at the Battle of Salamis in 480 BC, Athens became the leader of a Greek defensive alliance against Persia and the centre of Greek intellectual life, being to these extents less provincial than the other Greek cities of Ionia, Sicily and southern Italy. In politics, Cleisthenes had espoused democracy in pursuit of personal power and Pericles had come to the fore as an esteemed statesman within this system, though the Peloponnesian War (431-404) could well have been avoided by more knowledge-based diplomacy on his part. Indeed, its continuation owed much to the unscrupulous self-proclaimed brilliance of Alcibiades and its disastrous outcome to the inability of the honourable and well-meaning Nicias to convey unpalatable truths (knowledge) to the demos. Thus, in his timelessly applicable descriptions of internal city-state politics and inter state negotiations before, during and after this war, Thucydides (c. 460-c. 399) identifies leadership-character as critical to the survival of democracy (c.f. Section 11.2.2 and Chapter 12).

As to Athenian intellectual life, we see a growing knowledge of humanity being expressed by the dramas of Aeschylus, Euripedes and Sophocles, by the comedy of Aristophanes; and by the eloquent educators who propounded the benefits of the examined life to a wider public. The seating capacity of the Theatre of Dionysus was approximately 17,000 and though performances were held there on only two annual religious festivals, productions also went on tour. Aeschylus (525-455), who fought at Salamis, is known to have written ninety-odd plays, only seven of which survive, though these are sufficient to show how he used human affairs to illuminate religious and theological questions. In contrast, Euripides (c. 482-406) concentrates more on human problems at

46

the human level, on analysis of human strengths and weaknesses, on ethical questions and on possibilities for their resolution, writing about ninety-two plays of which he produced eighty-eight, and while finding less immediate public favour, was posthumously the most popular of the three tragedians whose plays have come down to us. Again, Sophocles (c. 495-407) who served in public office on several occasions, wrote about one hundred and twenty-five plays of which only seven are extant. These assert the dignity and worth of man even in the face of inevitable death, and proclaim belief in a force behind the universe which ordains eternal laws while remaining ultimately incomprehensible to man. Again, the comic drama of Aristophanes (c. 445-after 387) expresses the belief that no person, institution or god should enjoy any immunity from criticism and derision.

As to the cultural background at this time, the Greek audience believed that in their mythical beginning, Ouranus (the sky) was king of the gods and Gaia (the earth) was his wife; that certain other deities such as the Furies (vengeance) were already established in their respective roles; and that gradually this arrangement was replaced by that of Cronos (son of Ouranus) under whom the number of deities increased as did their involvement with humanity as created also at that time. The reign of Cronos was the time of anarchy which preceded the institution of property, the establishment of cities and the framing of laws, in which the gods sought to impose certain principles of behaviour and response on man while he deployed his ingenuity to influence the gods and the powers of nature to favour his own enterprises. Here we have the notion of initial chaos, similar to being "without form and void" as the *Old Testament* has it, but we also see the Greek view that man stands erect, is ingenious, pro-active and capable of avenging injuries and slights, unless he judges it appropriate to be supplicatory, reverential and devotional. Eventually, according to the myth, mankind grew tired of anarchy as nature itself was moving from chaos, with Prometheus (a son of Gaia) becoming allied to humanity and to a profusion of new gods and goddesses as agents for the spread of imagination and knowledge, laughter and feeling, order and control in a universe which had previously lacked those human and now newly godlike capacities. At this time, also, Zeus (also meaning sky) who claimed descent from Ouranus, defeated the old forces of chaos and anarchy to establish reason and law under his new Olympian Dynasty. Thus, we see the gods evolving in compliance with man's sense of worth at his own achievements in civilised living under reason and law.

However as to the myth, on being invited to dine with the new Olympians as a reward for his contribution to their victory over the old gods, Prometheus took the opportunity to steal a spark of the divine fire for the benefit of mankind, a theft and intent which provoked the wrath of Zeus who considered human possession of the knowledge and uses of fire to be detrimental to divine supremacy. He, therefore, demanded repentance and complete submission from Prometheus and when he proved defiant had him chained to a rocky peak in the Caucasus. Prometheus responded by declaring that his mother (Gaia) had revealed to him that the ultimate downfall of Zeus was threatened unless he could be specifically warned in time. Zeus then resorted to torture to force Pometheus to reveal the warning, but Prometheus resisted for a thousand years until Zeus turned from violence to reason, offering Prometheus release and pardon in exchange for the warning. The revelation thus extracted was that a sea nymph, Thetis, was fated to bear a son who would be greater than his father. For Zeus, having in the meantime become enamoured of this nymph and in danger of fathering her son, this was a timely warning and he avoided his destruction by choosing a mortal husband for Thetis.

Now we see human characteristics, attitudes and value-judgements reflected in the gods through concepts of gratitude for gifts, understandable resentment, the desire for retribution, the inappropriateness of unreasonable anger and vengeful violence, and the benefits of reasonably negotiated agreement. We also see that even Zeus can be unknowing until informed by others, and is therefore not omniscient; nor can he simply reverse or obliterate actions taken, or cancel or negate consequences. He can only move forward, making the best of the new circumstances presented to him in a manner familiar to humans. We see too, that the gods interact with humans in humanlike ways.

Thus, the familiarity of these mythical humanlike gods was used by the dramatists to bring audiences to a deeper understanding of their humanity than would have resulted from the depiction of omnipotent and omniscient gods and thus to the development of ideas of justice, punishment and the rule of law in human life (c.f. Section 3.1.1). Aeschylus develops the Prometheus myth in these ways in *Prometheus Bound*. In *The Oresteian Trilogy*, of *Agamemnon, The Choephori*, and *The Eumenides* he pursues these ideas more at the level of human freewill and the evaluation of the right or wrong of actions taken by humans, even when at the instigation of the gods; and suggests that humans do best when they follow the new gods rather than the old, the latter still being there though now more under the control of the former as the baser instincts of man are now more controlled by the higher. The nature of man and his nobleness of standing in relation to the gods is further analysed, developed and presented to audiences by Euripides and Sophocles, particularly by the latter in his *Oedipus The King,* and *Antigone*. And, of course, we have the irreverent humour of Aristophanes putting the gods and everyone else in his place including, in his *Frogs,* Aeschylus and Euripides. Thus, we can see that very considerable progress has been made in what I refer to as reality-evaluated self-knowledge of human nature.

As to the celestial bodies and the rule of law, the Ionian, Anaxagoras of Clazomenae (488-428 BC) arrived in Athens in 464 BC, where he attracted the attention and friendship of the statesman, Pericles (490-429 BC) and the poet and dramatist Euripides (480-406 BC) by being perhaps the first to suggest that the heavenly bodies consisted of materials known here on Earth, the Sun being incandescent metal, the Moon reflecting light from its cold stone, and the other heavenly bodies shining by virtue of being white-hot stones. For this, he was accused of impiety and although defended successfully by Pericles, he judged it prudent to return to Asia Minor. This episode has been presented in the history of science as the first persecution of a scientist by religious dogmatists and as an introduction to later and supposedly worse examples. It was in fact, merely a dispute between two beliefs, no evidence (reality-evaluation) being available either way for the Sun and stars, though the phases of the Moon do show that it emits no light of its own and only reflects that of the Sun. (c.f. Section 3.1.3). Thus, overall, the significance of the incident lies in the commendable result that no official action was taken against Anaxagoras.

Again, we have Hippocrates of Cos (born c. 460) who has had an enduring association with medicine even as far as our own time. He was from a family of physicians of that island just off the Cnidus peninsula which had been a medical centre since the time of Democedes of Cnidus (c.f. Section 3.1.1), and after practicing his profession on extensive travels in Thrace, around the Sea of Marmora and on Thasos, came to Athens where his numerous pupils included his sons and sons-in-law. His reputation is based on his rejection of the belief that illness was an affliction from the gods and on his careful observation of the results of prescribed treatments. At a time when health was believed to be further evidence of the order demonstrated by the regular movement of the heavenly bodies, it is highly commendable that the Hippocratic writers continued to seek cause and effect relationships in such a difficult field as medicine. When one recalls the difficulty of detecting clear examples of cause and effect in later physiology (c.f. Section 8.2.5) and the disregard for it among their contemporary religious believers and speculators, the efforts of Hippocrates and his followers must be judged more than doubly commendable in proceeding to general conclusions only when supported by observation, this being much more like science than anything earlier. It is certainly more craftsmanship than speculation. *Munchausen's Syndrome by Proxy* would not have got far, had Hippocrates and his colleagues been referees.

Also in Athens at that time was Hippocrates of Chios (c. 430 BC) the mathematician who first attempted to compile the *Elements of Geometry*, a subject and a title which were later to make Euclid famous. He was a businessman who came to Athens to pursue a law-suit and stayed to become the first mathematical specialist to be recorded as such. He proved the theorem that the areas of circles are to one another as the squares of their diameters. On this basis he was able to determine the areas of crescents (lunes), *i.e.* figures bounded by circular curves, by showing them to be equal to triangles, the areas of which are easily determined. Thus he demonstrated that a lune formed by two curves, one of which is a 90° arc of a circle and the other is the 180° arc of a second circle constructed on the 90 degree chord of the first, is equal in area to the triangle subtended by the 90° chord with its apex at the centre of the first circle. He went on to discover two other lunes whose areas could be similarly determined and he showed that the area of a particular lune when added to that of a circle can be represented as a square.

In addition, mention must be made of Parmenides of Elea in Southern Italy (c. 425) who sought a means for the establishment of first principles where observation or the statement of axioms (as in geometry), were otherwise unobtainable. He proposed that in such cases we should start from "that which is, and is impossible not to be", and he stated clearly that reason cannot usefully be employed if the starting point (premise) is wrong. Following Parmenides, Zeno, also of Elea inadvertently showed that even when the premise seems to be correct the conclusions drawn from what appears to be a rational process can still be wrong because either the premise, the reasoning or both are wrong. Zeno was not attempting to make this point, however. Rather, he was attempting to show by a *reductio ad absurdum* argument that permanence and change cannot co-exist in the universe. In developing his reasoning Zeno generated a number of paradoxes for which he remains famous and from which that of Achilles and the tortoise will suffice as an example. Achilles who can run faster than the tortoise is supposed to give the latter a start before attempting to overtake it. Zeno then argues that when Achilles reaches the point at which the tortoise started to move, the tortoise will have moved to a new position some distance forward; that when Achilles reaches that position the tortoise will have moved on again; and that when Achilles reaches . . . ; and so on…. *ad infinitum*: and he concluded that Achilles can never catch the tortoise let alone pass it, from which he invites us to conclude that change and permanence cannot co-exist. It can and does, and the assumption (premise) from which he started is erroneous (c. f. Sections 4.4 and 10.2).

In the 225 years or so from Thales to circa 400 BC, the intellectual activity previously referred to as natural philosophy (c.f. Chapter 10) began to split into the separate disciplines of mathematics, astronomy, geography and medicine, with all texts relating to reasoned enquiry being written in prose and referred to as logos (pl. *logoi*), while those relating to the gods and their doings, usually in verse, were referred to as myths, *muthos* (pl. *muthoi*). Gradually *logos* took on a spectrum of related meanings, including that of rational thought itself. Later still it was used by Philo (born c. 20 AD) to denote the interlocution of God with the world (c.f. Section 4. 1). The Greeks also differentiated between the content (meaning) of the spoken word (*logos*) and the style of its delivery, it being clear to them that the Assembly could be swayed differently by different deliveries of the same content. Parmenides had noted that illogical argument (c.f. Section 10.1) can deviously mislead listeners and Aristophanes in his *Clouds*, showed that Unjust Speech overcomes True Speech by unscrupulous verbal trickery. Thus, while some deplored the use of such rhetorical skills, others (usually teachers of the subject) applauded their use, arguing that such past-masters as

Solon, Thermistocles, and Pericles himself had done the state great service by such means. However, even supporters of rhetoric had to admit that while such paragons had not sought wrongfully to mislead, others might. Thus, Isocrates (436-338) advised that training in moral responsibility had to be integral with training in rhetoric. In defence of rhetoric, however, he argued that the stronger a speaker's desire to persuade, the more he would strive to be honourable and careful of his good reputation.

This argument requiring considerable rhetorical skill to present convincingly, Socrates (470-399 BC) insisted that the pursuit of Truth required us to identify and question all assumptions and to pay strict attention to the meaning of the words used. His pedagogic approach was to pursue the meaning of a word by a series of questions in order to show that successive answers were incompatible or otherwise defective, and that consequently his responder did not know the meaning of words he habitually used. This approach, however, fails to recognise that meaning arises from the experience of hearing a word used in an otherwise intelligible context; that on being asked the meaning of one word, a responder offering another is inescapably conveying a difference in meaning, otherwise the two words would not have separate existence; that a number of such variants may exist; and that the weightings given to them would vary with the respective life experiences of individual responders. Thus, when asked the meaning of 'courage' a responder offers 'endurance' as did General Laches in one of the Socratic Dialogues, it should not be difficult to see that such weightings might differ as between a military man and a philosopher. Thus, it would appear that Socrates is trapped in a misunderstanding as to how words acquire meaning. On the other hand, we have already seen from the Xenophon quotation that Socrates was unsympathetic to empty speculation irrespective of its mode of expression. Indeed, according to Xenophon, Socrates evaluated the pursuit of astronomy as desirable only insofar as it contributed to calendar knowledge and that he evaluated attempts to know the *causes* of the movements of the heavenly bodies as a waste of time. Though, with reference to Xenophon, it is often suggested that Socrates was anti-science, I say that he was opposing empty speculation which is not science anyway, and that he was right to be concerned about the status of truth (knowledge) in rational-belief philosophy, though he didn't fully understand his reason for concern (c.f. Section 10.8).

Nonetheless, Socrates convinced himself that Truth and the Good exist and are inseparable whereas I say that knowledge and reality-evaluation are inseparable. Thus, in his own approach to ethics Socrates sought to expose, account for and resolve the inaccuracies and discrepancies of thinking and speech by establishing what must be True (c.f. Parmenides above), and thus securing the path to the Good. Such an approach is consistent with mathematics where the axioms (truths) are restated in the form of deductions from them, while it fails to recognise that truth (knowledge) is only attainable through reality-evaluation of hypothesis (c.f. Section 10.1). Thus, while reality-validations of belief were unconsciously producing proto-knowledge of human nature and of the Good and while such was already being expressed through mythology and metaphorical drama, the Socratic approach was to define the meaning of words to secure an axiomatic starting point of equal status to the axioms of geometry so that ethical Truth could be produced by rational thought alone, while this in turn failed to recognise that the axioms of geometry had been reality-validated by the craft of surveying. Thus, Socrates remained unaware that Truth (knowledge) cannot be produced by rationality alone.

However, noting that Socrates did not answer his own questions and that Heracleitus believed all things perceived by the senses (reality-evaluation) to be ever in a state of flux, Plato (427-347 BC) concluded that Truth could not be derived from definitions because there could be no True definition of things perceived by the senses. As to Isocrates, Plato concluded that rhetoricians could not be trained to comprehend moral concepts such as good and evil, justice and injustice if

50

the meanings of these concepts could not be ascertained. Thus, for Plato things of the mind (not defined) became more secure than our perceptions of physical reality. Accordingly, he was much attracted to mathematics which does convey a certitude and exactness not available elsewhere and which appears in its abstraction to be more Ideal than are items and objects in the physical world. Thus Plato is Pythagorean in his attitude to mathematics in believing that abstraction under-pins the natural world and somehow 'exists' beyond it. He went on to suggest that all objects and entities in the real world were similarly under-pinned by their Ideal Forms in the Beyond. The Forms, according to Plato, are hierarchically ordered downwards from the superior Form of Goodness, with the Forms of Justice and Beauty, being parts of the Good and necessarily subordinate to it, and so on down to the Forms of everything else in the here-and-now. The Forms were to be comprehended by the soul which Plato believed to consist of three parts: the reasoning (mind), the sensual (hunger, thirst, sex), and the emotional (anger, desire for reputation *etc.*). Thus, Plato believed maturity to be attained when the reasoning part achieved control of the sensual and emotional parts, and when the reasoning part itself grasped the nature of the Forms which he believed it had known all along, but had forgotten at birth. Here we see the Beyond as the realm of the Forms which would later be the point of contact between the Good of Neo-Platonism and the God of Christianity (c.f. Chapter 4).

Plato argues in the *Meno*, that the comprehension of a mathematical proof by an uneducated slave boy is an example of such a recollection of the world of Forms. However, we should note that the existence of such a world beyond sense-experience from which we can derive knowledge is a matter of pure belief, irrespective of the slave's supposed role, this too being another aspect of the same belief. Nonetheless, we should not disbelieve Plato because we happen to believe some alternative. Instead, we should note that his belief is beyond reality-evaluation and recall that we know more of the nature of mathematics in terms of its axioms and internalised-consistency than he did (c.f. Section 5.4.1). On the basis of his belief, however, Plato avers that while the comprehension of mathematical truths is accessible to all 'minds' capable of grasping logic (c.f. Section 10.1), the eternal truths (Forms) of Good, Justice and Beauty require levels of intellect and reasoning possessed by only a very few. Thus, he proposed that promising children (both girls and boys) be trained in the use of reason in the hope that they would develop an understanding of the Forms which would entitle them to join the Guardians, a governing elite with power to act for the good of the governed, to exile those who resist (in the *Phaedo*) and even to execute them (in the *Laws*). In the *Republic*, he states that knowledge of the Forms transcends all knowledge of the world of the senses and, for example, that "we shall approach astronomy as we approach geometry, by way of problems, and ignore what is in the sky." Thus, we see that Plato did not know that the certainty of mathematics was due to its internal consistency in restating its axioms in more useful forms; and that in ignoring the senses (reality-evaluation) he was ruling out the possibility of acquiring any knowledge at all.

Nonetheless, Plato seems to have permitted others to seek reasons for discrepancies between observed (sensory) and calculated (rational) motions of the planets where these offended his sense of perfection. Thus, his pupil Eudoxus of Cnidus (409-356 BC) determined the length of the solar year at 365 days and 6 hours, and accounted for irregularities in planetary movements by invoking secondary and where necessary, tertiary spheres of movement to harmonise mathematical reasoning with sensory observation. Again, Callipus, (a pupil of Eudoxus) having made more precise observations, added more spheres. However, of more relevance to later understanding of celestial motions, Menaechmus, another pupil of Eudoxus, initiated study of conic sections. Thus, when a plane cuts a cone at right angles to its central axis we have a circle; when it cuts the axis obliquely above the base, an ellipse; when it cuts obliquely through cone and base, a parabola; and when it cuts parallel to the axis through cone and base, a hyperbola; these names being introduced later by Apollonius (c.f. Section 3.1.4) who carried out further work on these curves. Other direct followers of Plato contributed to mathematics and some to physiology, but the greatest of them all is Aristotle.

Aristotle (384-322) whose father was physician to Philip of Macedon, became a pupil of Plato in Athens at the age of seventeen. On Plato's death in 347 BC, he moved to Lesbos off the coast of Asia Minor, became tutor to Philip's son Alexander in 342 BC and returned to Athens as a public teacher in 336 BC when Alexander set out on his conquests. Aristotle distinguished living things from the non-living universe referring to the latter study as physics, his distinguishing principle being *psyche* which translates as spirit or soul. However, he believed psyche to be the essence of animate matter without having separate existence. Accordingly, he saw inanimate matter as being *apsychic* (without soul), plants as being *empsychic* (with soul) but less so than animals while within both plants and animals he identified further gradations to distinguish between lower and higher plants and between zoophytes, molluscs, insects, jointed shellfish, octopuses and squids, reptiles and fish, mammals and man. Elsewhere Aristotle appears to distinguish three forms of soul: the vegetative (nutritive and reproductive), the animal (to which is added motile and sensitive), and the rational (to which is added consciousness and intellect). Aristotle also makes clear that he believes life to have a purpose in tending to an objective and being itself evidence of design. In these respects he has been called a teleologist or vitalist, as distinct from a mechanist or materialist such as Democritus. Either way, these are belief options rather than expressions of knowledge.

It can also be noted that the concept of the *psyche* adds nothing to Aristotle's classification of plants and animals. This classification, or *Ladder of Life* as he called it could have been arrived at on the basis of physical morphology, which must have been the basis he actually used. Thus, the adjectives used (bracketed) above to justify the three levels of soul which classify vegetables, animals and man reveal the *Principle of psyche* to be redundant there being no evidence that Aristotle used it in arriving at his classification. Here is an example of a previously held belief-system being imposed on otherwise admirably objective observation. However, apart from his activities in classification, Aristotle diligently observed and reported the lives and breeding habits of animals and discussed some 540 species with special attention to the embryology of the developing chick, the habits and development of squid and octopus, anatomical descriptions of the four-chambered stomach of ruminants and of the mammalian generative and excretory systems, in the course of which he recognised the mammalian nature of porpoise and dolphin, and the modes of development of fish wherein he noted the similarity of the dogfish to mammals. He also recognised the heart and vascular system as central to life and made great use of diagrams to record complex anatomical relationships and as an aid to teaching.

As to his beliefs on physics, Aristotle like Plato was a Pythagorean in his emphasis on the perfection of the circle. He believed that matter was continuous whereas Democritus believed it to be atomic; and that it consisted of the four elements, air, water, earth and fire as modified by the four qualities, cold, wet, dry and hot of Empedocles. In addition, he accepted the belief, further emphasised by the Pythagoreans, that terrestrial and celestial natures were fundamentally different. Thus, he believed much that could not be reality-validated, and in believing that objects fall faster the heavier they are, he believed what he could have refuted by reality-evaluation (c.f. Section 6.1). On such beliefs he constructed his model of the Universe as a central Earth surrounded by the sphere of the atmosphere around which in decreasing density with distance he located the spheres of the fundamental elements, earth (more properly of earthy exhalation), water, air and fire, all of which were believed to be as inaccessible to humans as the celestial realm itself. Beyond the

52

sphere of elemental fire he placed another which he called the ether (Gk. shining) and beyond that the seven crystalline spheres each of which carries a planet and beyond that again the eighth crystalline sphere which carries the fixed stars. Finally there was the furthest sphere, that of divine harmony which caused the revolving movement of the whole celestial system. The Earth at the centre was believed to be stationary because he could find no independent evidence that it revolved and some such as the absence of a unidirectional air-flow to suggest it did not.

Aristotle also contributed to the systemisation of logic to avoid error in rational thought. Thus, he defined the Syllogism as an argument in which certain things being assumed (the premises) something different (the conclusion) follows from necessity. Generalised by use of alphabetical letters, this argument reads: if all As are B, and C is A, then C is B. He also explored the reasons why the conclusion could be invalid in what may appear to be a similar argument. Thus, all As are B, and C is B, but C is not A. An example of such a valid argument is, all men (A) are mortal (B) and Socrates (C) is a man (A), therefore Socrates (C) is mortal (B), while it is invalid to argue all fish (A) swim (B) and all whales (C) swim (B), therefore whales (C) are fish (A). But C is not A. C is B: whales are not fish, though they swim as fish do. This analysis shows that care is needed to avoid accepting an invalid conclusion from what may appear to be an identical argument to one which previously produced a valid conclusion. We see from the two examples given that the first conclusion is valid because Socrates (C) is one of all men (A), while whales (C) are not a sub-set of all fish (A) but of all 'swimmers' (B). We know of course that whales are not fish for reasons unconnected with the ability to swim *i.e.* they are mammals and fish are not. The general point, however, is that even if we didn't know that, or if we were faced with something new to our experience, a formal analysis of the terms of the second argument in comparison with the terms of the first would reveal that the C term in the second does not relate to the A term as it should, but to the B term, thus rejecting the second conclusion. Logic is reviewed in relation to philosophy, belief and knowledge in Section 10. 1.

As to knowledge in general, Aristotle believed it to be liable to subsequent up-grading. Thus, in his classification of living organisms he recognised contemporary difficulties in distinguishing between plants and animals in marginal cases, and he postulated spontaneous generation only when he sought in vain for evidence of the spawning of eels, now known to occur well beyond his reach in the Bermudas. Again, as Aristotle might have expected, his successor Theophrastus of Eresus (372-287 BC) resolved many such postulated cases in plants by identifying their seeds, suggesting that those remaining would be similarly resolvable. In addition and in contrast to Plato, Aristotle sought to create an ethical system based on the realities of everyday life. Thus, in his *Nichomachean Ethics* he remarks on the feelings of recognition and affiliation that link all human beings, stating that virtue is not to be sought outside the world of experience; that it is the state of eudemonia in the here-and-now, defined as living life in a way which realises its highest potential; that this state can only be achieved by the flexible application of reason (to reality); and that while there are no absolutes, human beings cannot escape their duty to accept responsibility for their own actions whatever the circumstances. Furthermore, eudemonia can only be maintained by early parental training of children in acting properly followed by the continuous practical experience of so doing which fixes virtue in the character of the doer. Aristotle also states that altruism defines the truly virtuous; and that the way to virtue is to use reason to bring out tendencies which though innate will not be realised without effort. Thus, his ethics and biology are based on observation as is craft-knowledge, while his cosmology and all of Plato's Idealism are pure belief.

In his *Poetics*, Aristotle analyses tragedy as consisting of six basic elements which he calls Plot, Character, Diction, Thought, Spectacle and Song. He introduces the notion of *mimesis* by which a work of art must 'imitate' or 'represent' universals as distinct from the specifics of history compared to which it must be more 'serious and philosophical'. He also introduced the more concrete idea that drama must provide *catharsis* for the emotions and enhanced knowledge of what it means to be human. He argues that the tragic hero should have a flaw which leads him to tragedy; that this should have particular qualities for the audience to consider its consequences tragic in the sense of invoking pity and possibly fear through the exercise of its moral sense; and that the tragic hero is "a man who is highly renowned and prosperous, but not pre-eminently virtuous and just, whose misfortune is brought upon him not by vice or depravity, but by some error of judgement or of frailty". In his treatment of tragedy Aristotle assumes that we all pass through periods of happiness and misery, fortune and misfortune; that on the one hand there is a moral order in the universe, and on the other an element of chance or luck and possibly of fate or destiny; and that human beings have to contend with all such, whether successfully or unsuccessfully.

Clearly, Aristotle's range was wide and penetrating and though he made some avoidable mistakes he recognised the uncertainty of much which passed for knowledge in his day. Again, while he attributed to the universe the moral sense which I attribute to our innate group-species inheritance, his knowledge of it was reality-validated, and while he was wrongly accepted as an unquestionable authority in Medieval Europe for a time, this misjudgement cannot be attributed to him or to his immediate followers.

Aristotle chose to avoid re-establishing contact with his former pupil (now known as Alexander the Great) because of his then unpopularity within Greece. Nor did he avail himself of the living organisms collected at Alexander's behest by the special force which surveyed, built and maintained roads in his extending territories. Thus, it was Aristotle's follower Theophrastus of Eresus who wrote a number of treatises on such collections and on those assembled at the initiatives of some of Alexander's commanders, most notably his admirals Nearchus and Androsthenes. In these treatises Theophrastus parallels Aristotle's work on animals by making many acute and accurate observations on plants, distinguishing between monocotyledons and dicotyledons, and contributing many plant names which survive today in modern botany. Another contemporary was Autolycus of Pitane (c. 360-300 BC) who worked on the geometry of the sphere for astronomical and geographical purposes. Yet another was Dicaearchus (c. 355-285 BC) whose interest was physical geography and who also drew on information from Alexander's officers, as did Strato of Thrace (c. 300 BC) who believed that the formation of the world was due to natural forces and that nothing should be recognised beyond natural necessity. He also believed that the functions attributed to the soul could be explained as modes of motion, though he disbelieved atomism. After the first generation of pupils, however, the Peripatetic School (so-called from Aristotle's teaching habit of walking around) ceased to produce original work and devoted itself to preservation and commentary on the work of its founder. Thus, the torch passed to Alexandria from about 300 BC onwards (c.f. below).

However, contemporary with the Peripatetic School was that of the Stoics, named after the stoa (corridor) of the Athens marketplace where it met under Zeno (died c. 261BC), not of the paradoxes. Stoics stressed the importance of natural forces as did Strato, but they went on to claim that all of existence is capable of acting or of being acted upon. Thus, they concluded, that force (the active principle) and matter (the passive principle) pervade each other to the extent that there is no real difference between matter and its cause, and that therefore the concept of Deity blends with that of reason or law. This seems akin to Democritus and his belief in atoms (matter) and motion (force) though the Stoics accepted the non-atomic Aristotelian model of the Universe, albeit with some elaborations. Thus, they believed that the four elements in the order fire, air, water, earth,

54

had separated from the pneuma (c.f. Anaximines) now believed by them to be the essence of being with the residual pneuma being the ether of Aristotle. They also believed that the world having been created, we who are part of it must obey its inevitable laws; that individual souls are only temporarily separated from the pneuma; and that all things will again decay into the elements and thence into the pneuma. In addition, they believed that in the embryo the soul is in the vegetative state; that it becomes successively animal and rational; and that it returns to the pneuma in the end. In contrast, Epicurus of Samos (342-270 BC) founded the Epicureans in 307 BC based on the atomism of Democritus and to a lesser extent on the beliefs of Anaxagoras. However, though they expressed interest in physics, logic and ethics, they had little interest in the world's phenomena and with Epicurus deprecating such enquiry, their physics was largely discussion of the Atomic Conjecture (belief).

At this point, it should be noted that the developing knowledge of human nature which is reflected in Greek myth was seamlessly incorporated and further developed by the Greek dramatists to disseminate a deeper knowledge of human behaviour for public benefit; that knowledge was distinguished from myth, though still undifferentiated from belief; that content was distinguished from style of presentation (rhetoric) in argumentation and persuasion; and that logic was developed to avoid fallacious conclusions. As to ethics, it should be noted that attempts to identify ethical axioms from which to reason in the manner of geometry were unsuccessful; that this failure led Plato to believe that knowledge of the certainty of mathematics could be attained in ethics only by accessing the Ideal Form of Good through appropriate training in rationality, while Aristotle showed a preference for accumulating sense-experience from everyday life to achieve (reality-validated) ethical knowledge and for applying it to empirical criticism of contemporary drama to show how knowledge of the good life was conveyed through traditional myth to the general public. As to living organisms in general, Aristotle accumulated much descriptive knowledge through the (reality-validated) observation on which craftsmanship and ethics were based.

It should also be noted that rational thought was advancing the utility of mathematics through the determination of curve-bounded areas and the properties of conic sections; that increased accuracy was being achieved in determining the length of the solar year and in reconciling predicted planetary motions with observation, while more extensive maps of the earth's surface were being produced; that such progress had led to speculations as to the nature of the celestial bodies; and that the reality-evaluation of craftsmanship was also being applied to medical treatments and to the acquisition of anatomical knowledge. On the other hand, it should be noted that belief still reigned supreme in maintaining that the celestial bodies were fundamentally different from the earth; that the earth and the life upon it were mixtures of the celestial non-material essences and spirits (pneuma); that the nature of things partook of the Ideal Forms in the Beyond from which we derived mathematics and from which we could derive ethical knowledge of equal certainty only by the rational thought of suitably trained 'minds', and that such knowledge was more reliable than that derived from sense-experience, though Aristotle showed a preference for the latter in his *Nichomachean Ethics* and in his biology.

3. 1. 3 Alexandrian Thinking: 300 BC-200 BC

After his death, Alexander's Empire broke into sections under each of four of his generals, Macedonia and Greece (Cassander), Thrace and Northern Asia Minor (Lysimachus), Southern Asia Minor, Mesopotamia and Persia eastwards to the Oxus and Indus (Seleucus), and Egypt and the Mediterranean coastal strip including Jerusalem, Tyre and Sidon (Ptolemy). As to the dynasty of Ptolemy which lasted three hundred years to the death of Cleopatra, the first incumbent brought an interest in study and learning and the second founded the Academy through which the city of Alexandria was to achieve world renown.

Euclid (c. 330-260) was among the first called to the Academy from the founding of which mathematics had a prominent and independent position. He had been a pupil in Athens, probably of Plato, and would have been well-grounded in Pythagorean mathematics, in the geometry of Hippocrates of Chios and of Menaechus. To all earlier mathematics Euclid now added logical sequence, clarity of exposition and completeness. In compiling his treatise on the *Elements of Geometry* in thirteen books, he expands beyond geometry to include number theory (three books), proportion (one book), and the nature of irrational numbers (one book). This work, particularly the first six books, was the basis of geometry teaching until relatively recent times. In addition, he produced works on astronomy, optics and music.

Aristarchus of Samos (c. 310-230 BC) agreed with Plato's pupil Heracleides of Pontus (c.388-315 BC) that the Earth rotates on its axis once every twenty-four hours and that Mercury and Venus revolve in circles round the stationary Sun, and he went on to claim that all the other planets, including the Earth, did so too. This brought accusations of impiety such as had troubled Anaxagoras some two centuries earlier. Nonetheless, Aristarchus was undeterred, going on to determine the relative sizes of the Sun and Moon, and their relative distances from the Earth, his reasoning being as follows. At half-moon the line of sight of an observer on Earth makes a right angle with the direction of the light falling on the Moon from the Sun. Under these conditions the observer is looking at half of the fully illuminated hemisphere of the Moon which is facing the Sun and at half of the un-illuminated hemisphere facing away from the Sun, the former being visible, and the latter invisible. Incidentally, the fact that a half-hemisphere facing an observer cannot be seen proves that the Moon emits no light of its own, the visible half-hemisphere being seen only by light reflected from the Sun. If the observer now measures the angle α which the directions to the Sun and Moon make at his eye, the relative distance to Sun and Moon is cos (90 - α), (c.f. Section 4.4) and hence, the relative sizes of the Sun and Moon can be determined by measuring their diameters as viewed from Earth In practice, Aristarchus measured α to be 87°, whereas it is 89° 52', and so he found the Sun to be 18 times more distant than the Moon and 7000 times larger, the modern values being 346 times and 400 times respectively. It is not, however, the accuracy, but the approach and the consequences to which I wish to draw attention. Thus, recognition that the Moon was smaller than the Earth and that the Sun was much larger encouraged astronomers to define the positions of the larger stars in relation to the Zodiac so that future observations might detect relative movements in a realm till then considered fixed and immutable (c.f. Section 3.1.4).

Herophilus of Chalcedon (active c. 300 BC) a contemporary of Euclid, dissected the human body for instructional purposes at the Academy, compared the anatomy of man and animals, recognised the brain as the seat of intelligence and centre of the nervous system, and distinguished arteries from veins, though he failed to attribute his observed pulsation of the former to heart action. Again, Erasistratus of Chios (c. 280 BC) addressed the functions of the organs, and taught that every organ consists of veins, arteries and nerves ever spreading by branching to smaller sizes beyond visibility; that the brain consisted of the cerebrum (main) and the cerebellum (lesser); and that the convolutions were related to intelligence, being more developed in man than in animals. As to animals, he identified the posterior nerve-roots of the spinal cord which transmit body-surface sensations and the anterior which transmit the motor impulses. He also observed the lymphatic vessels which convey food derivatives from the intestine to the liver: and he suggested that air taken in by the lungs is changed into vital spirit (*pneuma*) when passed to the heart; that it is thence distributed throughout the body by the arteries; that it is further changed into animal spirit on reaching the brain; and that it is thence distributed throughout the body by the nerves which for this purpose he assumed to be hollow. He also considered the breathable *pneuma* to be that of the universe, in compliance with the connection between man and Universe, as believed by the Stoics.

Archimedes of Syracuse (287-212 BC), the greatest pure and applied mathematician of antiquity, was not a member of the Academy though he had visited and remained in touch from Sicily by correspondence. On the basis of the determination of areas bounded by curves by Hippocrates of Chios and the idea of 'limits' introduced by Eudoxus for estimating the volumes of certain solids and used by Euclid to prove a proposition in his twelfth book, Archimedes took the idea of 'limits' to a most significant breakthrough. His extended idea is best conveyed by noting that the total length of the sides of a square is less than the length of the circumference of its circumscribing circle and the area of the square is less than the area of its circumscribing circle; that the original inscribed square can be successively replaced by a series of regular polygons of 8, 16, 32, 64, 128, 256 . . . .sides, by successively doubling the four sides of the original square; and that as this process continues the area of the polygon may be thought to become the area of the circle, as the total length of its ever-increasing number of sides approaches the 'limit' at which it equals the length of the circumference of the circumscribing circle. Archimedes's breakthrough was to realise that while this 'limit' can never be reached by drawing, it can be approached as closely as we wish in theory to achieve practical results of ever increasing accuracy.

Thus, having proved that the area of a circle is equal to that of a triangle of base equal in length to the circumference of the circle and of altitude equal to its radius, Archimedes saw that to calculate the area of this triangle and thus of the circle, it would be necessary to know the ratio of the circumference to the diameter of the circle (π); that he could calculate this ratio by seeking the 'limit' which lay between that approached by the side-lengths of the regular polygons inscribed within a circle and that approached by the side-lengths of the regular polygons circumscribed on the same circle; and that by this approach he could determine the value of π. Indeed, by this approach, he found that the ratio, π, lay between 3 and 10/71 and 3 and 10/70, *i.e.* between 3.1408 and 3.1428 (c.f. Section 4.4). He went on to apply this approach to determining the areas within segments of parabolas. Thus, by cutting this conic section by a series of parallel lines the area of interest can be represented as the sum of the areas of the near-rectangles which result. These are near-rectangles rather than true-rectangles, because their short sides are not parallel, but the discrepancy decreases as their individual width decreases as their number increases.

In the modern parlance of Newton's Calculus, we say that the area to be determined tends to equal the sum of the rectangles, becoming equal to it in the limit when their width tends to zero or their number tends to infinity. Similarly the sum of the areas of the identical triangles with apexes at the centre of the circle subtended by the sides of the inscribed and circumscribed polygons of the circle, become equal to the area of the circle in the limit when their bases tend to zero and their number tends to infinity. Newton was able to create an algebraic procedure for handling such limits without drawing diagrams, but Archimedes had made very substantial progress towards Newton's Calculus (c.f. Section 6.3.7). In addition, Archimedes introduced the power system of notation to facilitate the expression of very large numbers, fancying that it was capable of expressing even the number of grains of sand needed to fill the entire universe, and calling it his Sand Reckoner. As we shall see, this development brought him close to the development of logarithms, (c.f. Section 6.2.3).

Archimedes is more widely know, however, for his alleged cry of "Eureka" when he displaced water from his bath and instantly realised how to determine whether a crown supplied to the King of Syracuse contained less gold than it should have, the goldsmith having surreptitiously replaced some of it with an equal weight of less valuable silver. His solution to this problem was to measure the water displaced by total immersion of the crown and to compare it with the amount displaced by equal weights of pure gold and pure silver. The gold displaced least water, being the most dense (weight per unit volume) of the three, the silver most water, being the least dense and the crown displaced an intermediate amount. This result demonstrated not only that the crown had been adulterated with silver but also by how much. From there, he went on to propound the *Principle of Archimedes*, which states that when a body is wholly or partly immersed in a liquid, it receives an upward thrust from the liquid equal to the weight of liquid displaced, and the special case known as the *Law of Flotation* which states that a floating body receives an up-thrust equal to its own weight from displacement of the liquid in which it floats.

Archimedes also explained the principle of mechanical advantage underlying the operation of levers, wedges, inclined planes, pulleys, and screw jacks, presses and pumps, as discussed above (c.f. Section 2.3.5). In addition, he showed that if three forces acting on a body in equilibrium are represented in magnitude and direction by three lines drawn to scale in directional sequence, they always form a closed triangle (the triangle of forces) which enables unknown forces to be calculated from known ones by applying the known geometric properties of triangles. He also showed that equal weights at equal distances from a fulcrum are in equilibrium; that equal weights at unequal distances depress the end at the greater distance, and that the turning effect, (moment or torque), about the fulcrum is expressed as the product of the force times its perpendicular distance from the fulcrum. This last, is the principle which underlies weighing by means of the steelyard and which enables the centre of gravity of any irregular plane body to be determined. Archimedes's craftsmanship was also of a high order. There is evidence that he constructed a heliocentric planetarium showing the relative movements of the Earth, Moon and planets in explication of the occurrence of eclipses, and that he devised and constructed a number of novel engines of war for the defense of Syracuse against the Romans.

Apollonius (active c. 220 BC) who had studied at Pergamum and at Alexandria continued the work on conic sections which had been started by Menaechus. Thus, in considering the relationship between circle and ellipse he showed that plane sections through a cylinder parallel to the base produced circles while oblique ones produced ellipses, the cylinder being a special case of the cone; that if a plane cuts a cylinder horizontally and tangentially between two inscribed spheres, the point of contact of both spheres coincides with the centre of the resulting cross-sectional circle; that if the section is now supposed to assume greater degrees of obliqueness, the circle becomes an ellipse of increasing eccentricity while the spheres move apart as their points of contact with the plane move apart as the foci of the increasingly eccentric ellipse. Given his understanding of the ellipse, it is to be regretted that Appollonius did not suggest elliptic orbits for the heliocentric system proposed by Aristarchus.

Eratosthenes (276-c.194 BC), librarian at the Academy, is best known for measuring the size of the Earth by applying simple geometry to measurements which could be made on the Earth. Thus, he observed that at noon on mid-summer day an upright rod at Syene, (now Aswan) casts no shadow because the Sun is vertically overhead, while at the same local time at Alexandria, 5,000 *stadia* due north of Syene, such a pole casts a shadow because the Sun is not vertically overhead. Thus, he applied Thales' theorems, that the corresponding sides of similar triangles are in constant proportion and that alternate angles are equal, *i.e.* those formed Z-wise when a straight line crosses two parallel lines either obliquely or at right-angles. Thus, Eratosthenes measured the angle at the top vertex of the triangle formed by the pole (altitude) and shadow (base) at Alexandria at 7.5° which is equal to the angle at the centre of the earth opposite the 5000 *stadia* and is thus proportion to 360° as 5,000 is to the circumference of the Earth in *stadia*. As for Aristarchus, I draw attention to the approach rather than to the accuracy obtained, though in this case the result of 250,000 stadia (25,000miles) is quite good. Eratosthenes then turned his attention to measuring distances and to locating known places on common east-west and north-south parallels for the known world, noting that, were it not for the vast extent of the Atlantic Ocean, one might sail from Spain to India along the same parallel. In addition, Euclid having shown by a *reductio ad absurdum* argument that there could be no greatest prime number, Eratosthenes showed that primes could be identified by writing the integers in their natural order and striking out all those divisible by the sequence of primes of lower value to identify the otherwise unknown primes of higher value in the integer listing: an approach now known as applying the *Sieve of Eratosthenes*.

Astronomy continued to be a consuming interest and to facilitate its study and the reporting of results, a number of concepts and terms were now standardised with respect to any observer of the celestial region who, of course, could only see half of it, the other half being obscured by the Earth on which he stood. Thus, his limiting circle of observation became known as the horizon (Gk. "bound" or "limit") and the points around which the celestial sphere appeared to revolve became the celestial poles. However, the observer's horizon was not co-linear with the celestial equator because the north celestial pole, though very close to the pole star, was not coincident with it. In any case, the lines which crossed the celestial equator at right angles and passed through the celestial poles became known as meridians while the point directly overhead for the observer became known as the zenith, these astronomical concepts and definitions being immediately useful in mapping the Earth.

Thus, if the angle between the zenith and the pole star (known as the zenith distance, Z.D.) is measured at a point A on the Earth's surface, then the angle between the horizon and the pole star at A, is 90 - Z.D. Now if the centre of the Earth is O, the point on the equator due south of A is E, and the perpendicular from A meets OE at D, then in the right-angled triangle AOD the angle at A is equal to the Z.D., because they are opposite angles at the intersection of two straight-lines (Thales). Thus, the angle AOE, is also 90 - Z.D. (Thales) and, therefore, the latitude of A is 90 - Z.D, the angle AOE being defined as the latitude of A. In practice, the zenith distance was measured by sighting the pole star and measuring the angle between the line-of-sight and a plumb-line, and this angle subtracted from 90 degrees gave the latitude of the point, A, at which the observation was made. An alternative was to note that at the equinoxes the sun being vertically above the equator, the angle between the line-of-sight of the Sun and the zenith (plumb line) *i.e.* the Z.D of the Sun, is equal to the angle AOE which is the latitude of A.

As to longitude, it had long been the practice to measure time by the shadow clock and later by the Babylonian sandglass. It was also known that times recorded for eclipses and the passage of a planet behind the Moon (occultation) differed for locations east or west of each other. Thus, by determining the time interval between noon (when the shadow of a pole is shortest) and the beginning or end of an eclipse or occultation by means of sandglasses at two separate locations, it was possible to determine their relative longitude. For example, if the same event was observed at one location 10 hours after local noon, and at another 11 hours after local noon, then noon at the second occurred 1 hour earlier than at the first, and therefore it was 360 / 24 degrees, that is 15° east of the first and *pro rata*.

At this point it should be noted that geometry has been more or less completed; that the concept of irrational numbers, of limits and of the circular-orbiting heliocentric solar system have been mooted; that π has been evaluated to two places of decimals, 3.14; that the length of the solar year has been determined to the nearest hour; that eclipses are understood; that more has been learned of conic sections; that the size of the Earth has been measured; and that latitude and longitude (on land) can be determined. As to medicine it should be noted that observational progress akin to craftsmanship has been made in anatomy, comparative anatomy and physiology, though belief in pneuma (essence/spirit) still persists while quantitative knowledge of static equilibrium, hydrostatics and mechanical advantage is now available.

3. 1. 4 Alexandrian Thinking (200 BC -200 AD)

Hipparchus of Nicaea (c. 190-120 BC), on noticing a new star in the constellation of Scorpio in 134 BC, began to prepare a catalogue of star positions against which future generations could assess time-related changes in the celestial region and to this end he determined the celestial latitude and longitude for about a thousand identified stars. To facilitate the detection of such movement over time he particularly noted those groups of three or more stars which lay in a straight line as he observed them. In addition, he reviewed past records over about 150 years to see if he could detect such relative movements, and found that he could, and that he could explain it by supposing a wobble-rotation in the axis of rotation of the Earth in the direction of the apparent motion of the fixed stars, which in turn causes a precession of the equinoxes (they fall a little earlier each year and then a little later) over a cycle of some 26,000 years.

Hipparchus also addressed the long-standing problem of reconciling calculated movements of planets, Earth and Moon with their observed movements, a problem which arose from the persistent belief in circular motions, despite the work on conic sections by Menaechmus and Apollonius which had provided familiarity with the ellipse. Indeed there were by now two circle-based approaches. The one suggested by Apollonius himself, was based on epicycles, in which each planet moves on a circle, the centre of which moves on another circle centred on the centre of the Earth, while the other was based on eccentric motion in which the planet moves round the Earth in a circle whose centre is not at the centre of the Earth, but elsewhere, and which again moves on another circle. However, by placing the Sun on a fixed excentric and the Moon on a moving one, Hipparchus achieved closer agreement between calculated and observed movements than had previously been achieved, enabling eclipses of the Moon to be predictable to within an hour or two, though those of the Sun remained less predictable than this.

At this point, having noted that geometry and celestial observation had determined the size of the Earth and the latitude of any location on its surface and having noted that geometry, celestial observation and the sandglass had been used to determine the longitude of any location on its land surface, we should note that the scaled latitude-longitude reference grid which had been introduced for the sphere of the earth to enable any such location to be plotted thereon, had also been adopted for the celestial sphere to enable star positions to be plotted thereon for ease of reference and for detection of possible movement over long time-scales. As to the reconciliation of observed and calculated movements of the Moon and planets, with respect to the celestial sphere, however, we should note that astronomers continued to wrestle with the earth-centred system of epicycles and eccentrics with a preference for the former, no-one yet having substituted ellipses for circles in the proposed heliocentric system, despite knowledge of conic sections: nor had anyone speculated as to the cause of such complex motions within motions.

Progress now declined to the writing of compendia of existing knowledge and after Alexandria had become part of the Roman Empire in 50 BC these tended to respond to specific needs of the Empire. Thus, Apollonius of Citium (c. 100 BC) provided useful illustrations of medical operations and bandaging techniques and by 50 BC, Crateuas (c. 80 BC) was describing medicinal plants by accurate drawings to overcome the inadequacy of verbal descriptions, there being no adequate botanical nomenclature. Thereafter, Hero of Alexandria (c. 100 AD) was a significant compiler of knowledge in accessible form, and being a skilled craftsman was also developing useful equipment and techniques, though some had novelty value only. Thus, for example, his *Pneumatica* describes a jug which would pour or not as a hole in the handle was uncovered or covered by the thumb of the pourer. Though of little practical value, this appears to recognise atmospheric pressure. Most well-known, is his steam-fed sphere which rotated on its axle by the continuous release of steam from two tangential tubes at right-angles to the axle, showing a similar recognition of force and reaction. Of more practical value, his *Mechanica,* describes the operation of levers, multiple pulley-systems, worm-drives, cog-wheels and cranks. In addition, he had an interest in optics, first treated mathematically by Euclid, and showed that the angles of incidence and reflection of light from a reflecting surface are equal, and his Dioptra, a fore-runner of the modern theodolite exemplifies his craftsmanship in that the sighting unit could be rotated vertically and horizontally by two crank-operated screw-threads, each engaging their respective cog-wheels.

Cleomedes (first century AD) was also interested in optics, noting that objects such as oars appear to bend at the water-air interface (by refraction) and applying the same principle to explain how an object lying in an opaque basin and just obscured by the rim, could be made visible by pouring water into the basin. He further applied this principle to the atmosphere in suggesting that the Sun might already be below the horizon when still visible just prior to setting. It is odd, therefore, that he disbelieved earlier reports that in particular lunar eclipses, the Sun appears to be still above the western horizon while the eclipsed Moon appears to rise in the east. Again, Rufus of Ephesus (c. 100 AD), a medical writer, indicates some progress in understanding the eye as an optical instrument in describing its lentil-shaped lens.

Ptolemy of Alexandria (active c. 170 AD) having measured angles of refraction, generalised Cleomedes to state that the light from any star on entering the Earth's atmosphere and penetrating to ever lower and denser layers, must at each stage be increasingly refracted, so as to appear closer to the zenith of an observer than it actually is. Ptolemy's own compilation and synthesis, being the last overview from the classical world was known to the Greeks as *Megale Syntaxis* (the Great Composition). Later translators, changed *megale* to the superlative form *megiste* which in Arabic became *Almagisti,* in Latin, *Almagestum,* and finally and colloquially, *The Almagest.* It reviewed mathematics, provided the basis for development of plane and spherical trigonometry and described the astrolabe for measuring the angle of elevation of celestial bodies and its role in astronomy and navigation, (c.f. Section 3.1.3).

In addition, Ptolemy used the astrolabe to measure the distance of the Moon by parallax. Thus, if at one location L, the Moon is at zenith *i.e.* vertically overhead, then a straight line passing through the Moon M and the location L also passes through C, the centre of the Earth. Again, if at another location O at the same time an observer takes the elevation of the Moon above the horizon, then because the horizon is tangential to the sphere of the Earth, the angle between the horizon and the radius from the centre of the Earth C which passes through location O is a right angle (Thales). Thus, in triangle OMC, we know that the angle at O is one right-angle plus the angle of elevation of the Moon at O, and we can calculate the size of angle at C from the known (measurable) distance from O to L and, therefore the size of the angle at M, because the sum of the angles of a triangle is two right angles (Thales). We therefore know the relative lengths of the sides of triangle OMC and can thus determine the ratio of CM to CO.

Thus, Ptolemy estimated the distance to the Moon as being 59 times the radius of the Earth. This is quite close to the currently accepted ratio. In Ptolomy's day he had the Earth's radius as determined by Eratosthenes with $\pi = 3.14$) and so could calculate the distance to the Moon from his distance ratio, as being 234,879 miles. He had no means of applying this method to the planets, however, because they are too far away to make the angle at O measurably different from a right angle. However he did add to the traditional assumptions regarding relative positions of the Earth, Moon and Sun, the further assumption that the further away a moving object is the slower it appears to move, and thus concluded that the order of occurrence of the orbits outwards from the Earth at the centre, was that of the Moon, Mercury, Venus, the Sun, Mars, Jupiter, Saturn, the crystalline celestial sphere, and finally the *Primum Mobile*. Ptolemy's other work was his *Geograhical Outline* in which he represents the curved surface of the Earth on a plane surface for mapping purposes. Thus, he represents the parallels of latitude by arcs of circles centred on the North Pole, one of which is the equator, one passes through Thule, one through Rhodes, and another through Meroe; and the meridians of longitude by straight lines which converge on the Pole. In this way, Ptolemy mapped out the known world between latitudes 63 north and 16 south.

Before leaving the Alexandrians, however, mention must be made of Diophantus (active c. 180 AD) who took the first significant steps in algebra, which at that time lagged seriously behind geometry. He introduced the use of a symbol for the unknown-quantity, formulated equations involving the unknown and developed solutions (the means by which the unknown was to be determined) for equations of the first, second, and in one case, the third degree. He also introduced symbols in a systematic manner, as he required them, such as those to denote equality, powers, and the negative. Not only does he appear to be the initiator of algebra, he also marks the end of western mathematical development prior to introduction of the Hindu number notation with its symbol for zero. (c.f. Section 5.2.2), though Theon (c. 350 AD) was able to determine accurate square roots based on the equation $(a + b)^2 = a^2 + b^2 + 2ab$ (c.f. Section 4.4).

Mention must also be made of the last and most significant compilation and synthesis on biology and medicine of the classical world which was produced by Galen of Pergamum (131-201 AD). Human dissection having been largely discontinued by his time, Galen reported anatomical observations made on a number of animal species including the Barbary ape on which his physiological system was based. In this, he followed Erasistratus (c.f. Section 3.1.3) in believing that the *pneuma* (world spirit) was breathed into the lung and passed via the "vein-like" artery (now called the pulmonary artery) to the left ventricle of the heart, while the *chyle* (nutrient) flowed from the intestine to the liver. Counter to Erasistratus, however, Galen believed that the liver transformed the *chyle* into venous blood, imbuing it with a second *pneuma* (vital spirit) which he believed to characterise all living substance; that the blood thus vitalised was distributed through the venous system and back to the right ventricle of the heart; and that from there it passed via the "artery-like" vein to the lungs for exhalation of its accumulated impurities before returning thus refreshed to the venous system. In addition, he believed that a small proportion of this blood passed drop-wise into the left ventricle through a septum to acquire more of the world spirit through inhalation; and that it then passed to all parts of the body as red arterial blood through the arterial system. Thus, Galen, having failed to recognise the heart-driven circulation of the blood, believed it to oscillate between the heart ventricles, apart from a slight drop-wise internal transference between them. He believed also, that blood containing world and vital spirit was brought by arteries to the base of the brain from whence it was minutely divided, charged with a third *pneuma* (animal spirit) and distributed throughout the body by the nerves which, in agreement with Erasistratus, he believed to be hollow.

At this point we should note that apart from a late increase in knowledge of optics, Greek innovative enterprise was drawing to a close; that progress in what would later be algebra was seriously impeded by the number notation; that intellectual effort was turning to the compilation, synthesis and use of existing knowledge for the practical purposes of the now Roman Empire; that philosophical belief was useless as evidenced by belief in the circular movement of the planets

62

while computing their actual movements on epicycles and eccentrics; and that belief in the gods was useful only as metaphor for human behaviour.

3.2 THE ROMANS

The gods of Roman mythology had their counterparts in Greek mythology while Athens had its Assembly and Rome its Senate. On the other hand, each Greek city state was self-governing while Rome became the central seat of government for an Empire, making for less responsive democracy than on the Greek model, though the latter ranged from Athenian democracy to Spartan autocracy, Cleisthenes having extended suffrage in Athens only as an expedient to out-manoeuvre his patrician opponents, an expedient familiar to the politicians of Rome and to all their successors. Again, though the Roman army owed much to early Greek influence, its numbers soon expanded far beyond the needs of an independent city-state and though Rome continued to admire Greek culture, the interests, needs and satisfactions of the two peoples were different. Thus, votes had to be cast in Rome, making travel a major disincentive to the wider citizenry while career-minded Romans were not interested in pure mathematics, astronomy or the number-based speculations of the Pythagoreans, though they would not have found their own number notation any more conducive to progress than the Greeks found theirs. As to public duty, however, Romans saw Greek stoicism, rhetoric and compilations on geography, medicine and engineering as relevant to lawyer, administrator, politician and soldier, and were content to deal with practical matters concerning the world and its peoples as found, commissioning further knowledge compilations as reviewed below.

3. 2. 1 Geography
Polybius of Arcadia (204-122 BC) though an historian, had been involved in determining position and distance during a sojourn in Alexandria and having served with the army at Carthage in 146 BC, was employed by Scipio the Younger (185-129 BC) to explore the coast of Africa. Later, his map-making extended to Gaul, the Tagus, the Alps and Italy itself. Again, Eudoxus of Cyzicus explored the Red Sea and made at least two voyages southwards along the east African coast while Strabo of Amasia (born c. 63 BC) travelled from the Black Sea to the borders of Ethiopia while his knowledge of Europe may have assisted Eratosthenes during a long stay in Alexandria. As to the world at large, Strabo discounted Thule to the north and terminated his southern coverage at 3,000 *stadia* beyond Meroe. Thus, his north-south dimension was 30,000 *stadia* compared to the 38,000 of Eratosthenes. As to the territories of the Empire itself, Julius Caesar (102-44 BC) had conceived a complete survey, though responsibility for its realisation passed to his successor and the work supervised by Vipsanius Agrippa, was not completed until 20 BC when it was exhibited in a building erected for this purpose in Rome. This survey having been carried out by surveyors trained for the routing and construction of roads for trade and military purposes, produced a road-map rather than a geographical description of a region of the Earth's surface. Indeed, much remained to be done in mapping even the major features of physical geography as is clear from the geographer Pomponius Mela (c. 40 AD) and from the encyclopaedists Pliny the Elder (23-79 AD) and Tacitus (55-120 AD). Thus, even Agrippa's road map was a significant achievement and by Hadrian's time (117-38 AD) there were some 500,000 *stadia* (50,000 miles) of road from his Wall in the north to the Euphrates in the east and to the Sahara in the south.

Vitruvius (c. 10 AD) describes how surveying instruments were used to determine from known distances, others which could not be measured directly, this being the basic task in all map-making as exemplified in determining the width of a river from a known distance along one bank. The method involves measuring this distance as a base-line by counting the number of revolutions of a wheel of known circumference in the hodometer as it is rolled from one end of the base-line to the other, and by measuring the bearings of a selected point on the opposite bank from each end of the base-line by means of the dioptra (c.f. Section 3.1.4). This information was then used to inscribe on a conveniently flat ground surface, a triangle with base equal to the base-line and base-angles equal to the bearing-angles. The width of the river was then determined by measuring the altitude of this triangle *i.e.* the perpendicular distance from base to opposite vertex by means of the hodometer. Alternately, if space were limited, a smaller similar triangle (angles equal to those measured from the base-line with the dioptra) could be scribed from which the width of the river equals the base-line multiplied by the ratio of altitude : base of the smaller of the similar triangles. This triangulation method is still used in cartography except that we now apply trigonometry (c.f. Section 4. 4) to the bearing angles to calculate the perpendicular distance from the known base-line length.

3. 2. 2 Medicine

The Hippocratic Oath sworn by medical practitioners to this day, appears to be of Roman origin though it honours and perpetuates the memory of the earlier eponymous Greek. Nonetheless, Asclepiades of Bithynia (died c. 40 BC) was the first significant teacher of medicine in Rome, though he believed Hippocrates' "healing power of nature" to be merely a "meditation on death" and expressed a preference for active intervention in all cases. Asclepiades founded a school which later met to discuss matters of common interest with other such schools, teaching colleges being built later. However, the earliest Latin text on medicine appears to be a compilation from Greek sources, by Celsus, which dates from about 30 AD and is couched in ethical terms advocating humane treatments, while Pliny (23-79 AD) later wrote sceptically on contemporary treatments and on the lucrative nature of medical practice among the wealthy. Nonetheless, it is reported that treatment of the wounded by the army was effective at the level of bone-setting, stitching and amputation, the latter including the tieing of arteries and the drawing of skin over the stump to facilitate healing.

The Romans again show practicality in their organisation of medical services and provisions for public health while sanitation was a central feature of Roman life, subterranean sewers (cloacae) having been provided from the sixth century BC and burial within the city having been banned from 450 BC. Again, fresh water was provided to public cisterns and to private households through cement-jointed earthenware pipes or soldered lead ones, and Frontius, formerly a military governor of Britain and latterly director of the Rome water supply, reports in his *De Aquis Urbis Romae* of 79 AD that 200 million gallons of fresh water per day were being supplied to users who paid water rates proportionate to 24 different sizes of supply spout. In addition, a public medical service was established and a statute of Antonius of about 160 AD regulates the appointment of physicians to attend to the needs of the poor. Later, the *Code of Justinian* of 533 AD encouraged these physicians to give their services cheerfully and to prefer them to the more subservient attendance on the wealthy. Although their public salaries were fixed, physicians were encouraged to undertake the private training of pupils for payment. There was also a public hospital system and with extension of the Empire's frontiers military hospitals were founded at important strategic locations with similar institutions being later constructed for imperial officials and their families in provincial towns followed by public hospitals in various centres of population.

3. 2. 3 The Encyclopaedists

Varro (116-27 BC), who had been influenced by Platonism on a visit to Athens and who subsequently tended to Stoicism wrote an encyclopaedia which distinguished the nine disciplines of grammar, dialectic, rhetoric, geometry, arithmetic, astronomy, music, medicine and architecture which became the model for numerous Medieval Treatises on the Seven Liberal Arts, the last two having been deleted by later Latin writers. He was also employed by Julius Caesar to arrange the existing store of Greek and Latin literature for the latter's intended Library. Again, in his eightieth year, he wrote a review on farming, *Res Rusticae*, which recorded his own experience while drawing heavily on the writings of others as a recorder of knowledge rather than an innovator.

Again, Lucretius (c. 95-55 BC) in his very substantial book *De Re Naturae*, provided an overview of natural phenomena and Epicureanism which concluded that the origin and maintenance of the world and all mental phenomena are solely due to atomic interactions devoid of any creative intelligence; that there is "nothing save atoms and the void", everything springing from determinate units (semina certa); and that the cycle of all things is a generation from precursors and subsequent return to them. Thus, he believed that the Earth first produced grass followed by plants and animals of increasingly higher type by spontaneous generation, assuring his readers that many plants and animals continue to spring forth from the earth, formed by rains and the heat of the sun. As support for such claims, he cited other dramatic phenomena for attention, such as thunder, lightening, volcanoes, water-spouts, vapours and pestilences.

On the other hand, Seneca (3 BC-65 AD) moved at an early age from Spain to Rome where coming under Stoic influence he made his reputation as an advocate and public administrator. His book, *Natural Questions* is a general account of natural phenomena covering astronomy, meteorology and physical geography, but for him the study of nature led to a knowledge of man's destiny and thus to consideration of his duty. Indeed, Seneca repeatedly sets out the moral to be derived from the phenomena instanced. He did, however, believe that our understanding would progress with time; that man had only been entrusted with God's mighty work; that God is mightier than His works; and that He can only be reached by the Spirit. Seneca, in noting that we enter a temple with reverence, asks how much more reverent we should be before the celestial bodies and the very nature of God, and concludes that all generations will find subjects for investigation and that we cannot know what and how many discoveries are reserved for the ages to come.

Pliny the Elder (23-79 AD) had a literary education in Rome where he took an interest in plants, but coming under the influence of Seneca he turned to philosophy and rhetoric and to practicing as an advocate. After military service in Germany and having visited Gaul and Spain, he returned to Rome where he completed his *Natural History* dedicated to the Emperor Titus. When stationed at Naples as Prefect of the Fleet he lost his life by investigating too closely the eruption which overwhelmed Pompei and Herculameum in 79 AD. Despite a very busy life, his *Natural History* draws on some 2000 works by 146 Roman and 326 Greek writers in describing animals, plants and their medical uses, the sources of minerals and the metals produced from them as a recorder rather than an innovator. Nonetheless, Pliny believed that all plants had specific medical uses; that nature was designed to satisfy the needs and purposes of man.; that 'deity' means 'nature'; and that if there were a God he would be outside the world and could not be expected to care for it. In reviewing the belief that the movements of celestial bodies influence human affairs, he concluded that consistency requires those who believe in God to recognise that having set the universe in motion He never again intervenes. As to belief in immortality, Pliny concluded that it is nothing more than an expression of the fear of death.

3.3 CONCLUSIONS

It may be concluded that the Greeks came to recognise the mythical and metaphorical nature of their deities as their self-knowledge increased through unconscious reality-evaluation; that this self-reliance led to corresponding developments in self-government; that their philosophical speculation, nonetheless, led to a rejection of sense-experience (reality-evaluation) as a means to knowledge, given what to them was the bewildering uncertainty of the natural world; and that they were beguiled by the certainty of abstract mathematics into believing that ethics and good government could be made equally certain by rational access to the Ideal (imaginary) world of the Forms already believed to be the source of mathematics.

However, it may be concluded that arithmetic and geometry had been derived earlier to satisfy the reality-validated needs of financial accounting and of surveying before the Greeks abstracted them to axioms and general propositions; and that mathematics was extended with the reality-validated needs of craftsmanship geography, astronomy, optics and mechanics to produce quantitative knowledge (reality-validated) through sense-perception (observation), while craft-like observation produced qualitative knowledge of plants, animals and man, all without regard to Idealism. Thus, we may conclude that mathematics is independent of belief in a world beyond the senses; that the proofs of mathematics are rational restatements of their reality-validated axioms in more specifically useful form; that logic is verbal mathematics; that beliefs (hypotheses) capable of reality-evaluation are the precursors of knowledge in all subjects including ethics; and that knowledge cannot be acquired when belief cannot be reality-evaluated.

Thus, it may be concluded that suspension of belief need persist only so long as reality-evaluation remains impossible; that rejection of reality-evaluation for continuity of belief is perverse; and that continuity of belief despite reality-refutation is madness. Nonetheless, the unlimited scope for variation in belief and for consequent intellectual disputation make the religious Ur-belief and the Ur-belief in rationality increasingly attractive when their increasing socio-political influence is making belief more of a presence than knowledge. Such were the conditions at the end of the classical Alexandrian period when Euclidian geometry was already complete, the number systems made algebraic development impossible and Idealistic essences and spirits of the Beyond made fruitful hypotheses generation impossible. Indeed, as time passed, the consequent conflict among irresolvable beliefs in the Beyond became significant enough to destroy the Roman Empire, as now reviewed in Chapter 4.

CHAPTER 4: BELIEF AND ITS CONSEQUENCES

Though effective seekers of knowledge are few enough at the best of times, the above difficulties discouraged even those. Thus, while (reality-validated) behaviour codes and craftsmanship continued to sustain family and cohesive social life irrespective of differing religious beliefs, the intellectually active turned to comparative analysis of religious belief, those of Greek, Roman, Egyptian, Persian, Indian, Judean and Christian origin providing plenty of choice. Accordingly, within the first two centuries AD, rational attempts were made to reconcile and unify aspects of these various beliefs to produce what is now called Middle-Platonism. For Platonists the task was to rationalise the means of communication between the Deity in the Ideal Beyond and humankind in the Real world, though Plato himself had believed such communication to be possible only through specially trained 'minds'. However, even when deliberate rationalisation had amalgamated Christianity with Neo-Platonism and absorbed *Old Testament* Judaism, the resulting synthesis failed to reconcile differences between orthodoxy and its many heresies. This period, therefore, provides an opportunity to examine the impossibility of reaching conclusions by rationality alone in the absence of reality-evaluation, the readiness of disputing believers to resort to violence, and their persistence in it, even to the Fall of Rome.

4. 1 SYNCRETISM, PLATONISM, JUDAISM AND CHRISTIANITY

Syncretism sought to reconcile the God of the *Old Testament* with Plato's Form of the Good. Thus, Philo (born c. 20 BC), believed that such as Abraham and Moses had intimations of the Good prior to Plato; that having existed since the creation from chaos, the Good must be the God of Judaism; and that the essence of God was distinct from his power, the Forms of the Ideal having been transmitted by God to man through rationality while being manifest in the real world as the *Logos* which, for example, spoke to Moses from the Burning Bush. Again, Philo believed that just as real tables are approximations to the Ideal Form of Table, so men such as Moses, Abraham *et al*, were closer than are lesser men to the Ideal Form of Man in their greater proximity to the Form of Good.

These beliefs of Philo were developed over the next two centuries by the various syncretistic writers of Middle-Platonism in which the general belief was that God or the Good was an intelligence which acted in the world through the Forms and which could be reached only by rationality and asceticism after emotion and sensuality had been brought under control; and that the human soul was the highest part of the material world which lay below the Forms. From this point, however, differences arose. Some believed that evil was created by free-acting humans, the Good being incapable of becoming evil. Others believed that the human soul could become so corrupted or imprisoned by the material world as to be incapable of perceiving the Good. Yet others believed that the creator of the world was Evil and that the human soul had to acquire enlightenment (gnosis) in order to achieve ultimate union with the Good on release from the material body. Such Gnostics also believed that enlightenment could be enhanced by the more enlightened through teaching. Thus, in general, there is support for every rational belief option and no way of deciding between them or of ranking their significance in the absence of their reality-evaluation against human nature or the universe itself.

Nonetheless, after sojourning in Egypt, Persia and India, Plotinus (204-270 AD) developed Neo-Platonism in Rome. Though Plato had believed the universe to be eternal, he had not specified the point in eternity at which the Good had imposed order on chaos. Plotinus corrected this oversight by averring that the One (the Good) being self-caused and beyond material existence, must have existed throughout all eternity continuously generating Mind (*Nous*) which is now manifest in the Forms and projected as a composite World Soul onto all animate beings and as the individual souls of humanity. Again, though the soul also exists in the inanimate material world at its greatest separation from the One, it is unthinking at the point where Goodness vanishes away. Furthermore, the One, the *Nous* and the World Soul are of the same 'substance' (*ousia*), each maintaining its individuality (*hypostasis*) and its relative position in the scheme of things. Thus the individual soul is attracted upwards to the *Nous* and the *Nous* to the One, but the individual soul can choose to turn downwards to the material world and thus to evil. For Plotinus, however, the supreme desire of the soul is reunion with the One, a consummation not to be exchanged for anything less. As to personal conduct, Neo-Platonism adopted Stoic ethics with its determinism moderated to free the soul to choose evil *i.e.* to permit free-will. As to the physical world, Plotinus believed that the Good would not interrupt its orderly operation *i.e.* would not perform miracles. Thus, Plotinus agreed with Hippocrates that illness had natural causes and was not 'sent by the gods'.

In contrast to the One of Neo-Platonism, however, the God of Judaism was traditionally believed to intervene in human affairs, to take sides in conflicts and to set aside natural law for the benefit of His Chosen People. Thus, Jews believed that they had a Covenant with their God and that their Laws were God-given. This is rather more than believing in the Neo-Platonic One and relying on a semi-empirical stoicism. Nonetheless the Neo-Platonism of Plotinus feels closer to Judaism in being more of a religious belief than does Platonism itself. Thus, Plato's Form is an abstraction in the mathematical sense, rather than a tenet of religious belief. Readers will recall, that number had been abstracted from specific items and that craftsmen knew from experience that triangles of side lengths 3, 4, 5 and 5, 12, 13 contained right angles, whereas Pythagoras proved that these were only examples of a general principle concerning all right-angled triangles. Plato, however, would have said that they were real examples of the Ideal Form of right-angled triangle when he need only have said that they were specific examples of the abstract (generalised) right-angled triangle, just as he need only have said that real tables were examples of the abstract (generalised) table. Thus, we see that Form is a synonym for Abstract or General); that whatever Plato believed, the Forms have no meaning other than as abstractions; and that whatever Plotinus believed, the One of Plato has no existence other than as an abstraction. On the other hand, the Jews believed in the existence of God as an active agent irrespective of the beliefs of Plato or anyone else.

Nonetheless, there is some common ground between Greek myths and Judaic Scriptures. After explaining creation as in the myths, the Scriptures show a similar evolution in the concept of man's duties and responsibilities to that evidenced by Greek law-givers, ethicists, and dramatists. Thus, Judaism reveals a transition from human to animal sacrifice, from 'an eye for an eye and a tooth for a tooth' to personal atonement and the forgiveness of injury, such being a reflection of growing (reality-validated) understanding of human nature as codified in the *Ten Commandments* while the Greek transition from blood-feud vengeance to an orderly response to murders, injuries and slights through justice and law reflects a similar increase in (reality-validated) knowledge. Again, though Neo-Platonism speaks of the individual soul in life and of its release from the body to join the world soul at death, it has little to say about a personal after-life, concerning which Greek mythology offers few details and to which the Judaic Scriptures make virtually no reference

68

despite the sojourn in Egypt where belief in individual resurrection gave rise to mummification. Thus, while the Sadducee majority continued to leave the hereafter to God, the relatively new Pharisees (orig. second century BC) believed in bodily resurrection and the ascetic Essenes (also second century BC) believed in an after-life for the soul only.

Thus while Neo-Platonists might rejoice in unifying their One with the God of Judaism, some Jews at least would have been less than satisfied. Nonetheless, there is not much to argue about regarding creation myths, their similarities having a common source in our inability to account otherwise for our world and for ourselves. Again, the codifications of belief regarding Deity's requirements of humanity are similar in their common reflection of humanity's (reality-validated) knowledge of itself. As to Christianity, it might never have arisen. Jesus of Nazareth might have been accepted as another Prophet in the continuing evolution of Judaism, as indeed he is by Islam. Thus, the statement that he had come to fulfil (update) the Law and not to replace it, the Sermon on the Mount, the Parables, the exhortations to forgive slights and injuries and to turn the other cheek, the references to the coming of God's Kingdom on earth, and even the miracles, might have been seen in this light. On the other hand, His speaking for and on behalf of God if not actually as God, his miracles as distinct from his being an agent of God in their performance, and his offer of salvation and everlasting life through belief in him, suggest claims beyond those of any previous Prophet of Judaism, fulfilment of the Law now being more like replacement.

Whatever Jesus meant, however, some early Christians believed the coming of God's Kingdom to mean termination of earthly life and its replacement by celestial life for those who could achieve salvation in the limited time now available to them. Accordingly, they focussed on what they must do to be saved, though the requirements were a matter of hearsay in the absence of any authenticated contemporary records of the actions and sayings of Jesus, while the later-written accounts, (perhaps as many as twenty) did little to clarify matters, there being considerable variation among them as to both message and interpretation. Nonetheless, one element at least was clear. Having been crucified, Jesus had risen from the dead; had reappeared on earth in recognisable form; and had ascended to heaven. Of course, for those who believed in the ascent of the soul or spirit to heaven, the ascent of the soul of Jesus would have been no more than expected had no claim been made for his bodily resurrection.

This claim however, transforms the religious Ur-belief to a specific belief that Jesus had been resurrected from the dead in the here-and-now, prior to his ascent to heaven, and in so doing transforms a belief which is not open to reality-validation to one which could have been by virtue of its reference to an event in sense-experience. Furthermore, it was witnessed by those who are claimed to have met and spoken to Jesus after he had been laid dead in his sepulchre. Thus, the question is no longer one of belief in God. It has become a question of belief in human witness, reliance on which raises the familiar problem that our need for emotionally satisfying explanations can override our desire for Truth (knowledge). Thus, when a crime is committed our need to identify the culprit is strong enough to require rules of evidence to reduce the likelihood of error. Similarly, our need to explain the creation and the nature of our place within it has been satisfied by imagining and believing in a creator and maintainer in a world beyond the senses, and we have just heard of the sense-experienced evidence of witnesses attesting to his actual existence. Thus, what we are disposed to believe, we are unlikely to dispute with witnesses however unreliable. In any case, our need for explanations has always been satisfied with belief when knowledge is unavailable as it always is with respect to the Beyond and even to knowable Reality (c.f. Chapter 1).

4. 2 THE EARLY CHRISTIAN CHURCH

At this point, readers will recall my differentiation between the security of knowledge and the insecurity of belief, further to which I now review the development of Christianity to show what can happen when belief is all we have, knowledge being absent or unavailable in principle. Thus, starting with a reality-evaluation of the documentation promoted by Christians in support of their claims for the incarnation of God and the Resurrection, I review the rationality by which religious Ur-belief derivatives were given their Christian character and role in the development of western culture, leaving aside for now the knowledge of human nature which it holds in common with other religions and philosophical systems.

4. 2. 1 Documentation

The earliest available writings are the *Epistles of Paul* (written c. 50 AD) in which he attributes his own conversion to a miraculous intervention concerning which he had no need of what we would describe as evidence. Indeed, he doesn't use the actions and sayings of Jesus to secure belief in others. Instead, he attempts to ensure that already believing communities will be right-thinking and right-acting until saved on the Day of Judgement. To this end, and often in inconsistent ways, Paul adjusted the meaning of his message according to his perception of the needs of the believers to whom it was addressed. This is not conversion so much as preaching to the converted, though with reference to the unconverted in *Romans*, Paul cites humanity's common virtue, in the manner of Aristotle. On the other hand, the actions and sayings of Jesus are the focus of the four *Gospels* written in Greek by named individuals, Mark (at about 70 AD), Luke (later than 70), Matthew (between 80 and 90) and John (at about 100). Nevertheless, while these are evidently based on earlier sources they handle witness-evidence badly and are substantially inconsistent. When written, however, the point at which evidence could have altered belief was well passed and it was the second century AD before a selection of the then existing documentation was accepted as authoritative (canonical) by the Church. However, among Jews who did not accept bodily resurrection and Pagans who rejected miracles and were content with myths, metaphors and abstractions, the central belief of Christianity had little attraction regardless of any haggling over adduced evidence. From the start, therefore it was purely a matter of Faith: take it or leave it.

Nonetheless, to show the unlimited possibilities for belief diversification, I now take a closer look at the *Gospels*. That of Mark (supposedly written for early Christians in Rome) is considered to have run from the baptism of Jesus by John the Baptist to the empty tomb, with the miraculous accounts of birth and resurrection having been added later (c.f. below) while those of Luke (target audience unknown) and Matthew (supposedly written for a Jewish community in Antioch) seem to draw on Mark and a common source now unavailable. All of these refer to Jesus as a man, whereas John's Gospel, the most recent of the four and probably directed at Neo-Platonists, describes him as divine. As sources of evidence they are clearly deficient, the textual development, geographical locations, and selection and placement of the sayings and actions of Jesus, varying substantially from one *Gospel* to another in inconsistent and inexplicable ways, particularly with regard to the resurrection. Thus, in the supposed second century addition to Mark, Jesus appears first to Mary Magdalene, then to two of the disciples and finally to the remaining eleven at table. In Matthew there is an appearance near the tomb and then a pre-arranged meeting with the eleven on a mountain in Galilee. In Luke the meetings are in or near Jerusalem, but in these Jesus is asked who he is by the disciples, suggesting surprise or a change in appearance since last seen. In John, the first meeting is with Mary Magdalene in agreement with the later Mark, but the second and third are with the assembled disciples and are located in Jerusalem and by the Sea of Galilee respectively. However, apart from the lack of consistency, the select nature of these post-resurrection appearances contrast starkly with the public nature of the events prior to the crucifixion (c.f. below).

Meanwhile, other differences are that Matthew, unlike the others, is anxious to link the birth and other events in the life of Jesus to predictions in the *Old Testament*. Matthew also emphasises that Jesus had not come to abolish the Law but to fulfil it; that his criticism of Jews is directed at the Pharisees; that the Kingdom would be taken from those who reject him and given to those who would produce its fruit; and that Peter was the rock on which he would build his church. Such treatment suggests that Matthew was written for Jewish Christians facing opposition from Judaism in Antioch. On the other hand John is the only one to refer to the *logos* in a manner appealing to gentile Neo-Platonists. Thus, as with the *Epistles* the drafting appears to be directed to the requirements of specific audiences without care for consistency or clarity of content. For example, it is not clear from the Gospels what Jesus meant by the Coming of God's Kingdom. In Luke, this could be taken as having arrived with the coming of Jesus, as a last judgement, or as a consequence of some cataclysmic event scheduled for the near future. In Mark it appears to be associated with the overthrow of worldly values and the triumph of Christian belief. Though early Christians appear to have opted for imminent judgemental cataclysm, the passage of time modified this expectation to judgement in heaven and to eternal life therein for righteous believers. This reinterpretation, however, still appears to retain the belief that mortal life is little more than a basis for this final judgement, with intellectual study of this world being a waste of time at best, and at worst a sinful distraction from the eternal. On the other hand, the behavioural attitudes of the Sermon on the Mount appear to apply to continuing life on earth, while the exhortation to "love thy neighbour as thyself" would have been recognised from *Leviticus* as being directed to life in the here-and-now.

Again, it is unclear from Luke whether or not Jesus accepted Messiah status, or whether such claims were added by later writers for whom the meaning may differ from the Judaic. Thus, to the Jews, Messiah (Gk. Christos) denoted anyone anointed by God for some special purpose, having been conferred, for example, on Cyrus of Persia for liberating Israel from Babylonian subjugation, though it was from King David's Line that a future Messiah (of unspecified mission) was expected to come. Thus, Messiah status for Jesus would imply a public mission concerning which he did behave in ways which lent themselves to interpretation as fulfilments of Messianic scriptural prophesies. Thus, he entered Jerusalem on a donkey in apparent fulfilment of a prophesy of Zechariah, and was welcomed in the name of the coming Kingdom of David, being acclaimed Son of David. However, it seems likely that the crowds and acclamations which attended his arrival in Jerusalem would have attracted the attention of Procurator Pilate, responsible to Quintillius, Governor of Syria, and of Caiaphas the high priest, responsible to Pilate for civil order in Jerusalem especially when manifestations of insurrection earlier that year had resulted in Barabbas, the Zealot (independence fighter) being in custody pending execution. Having entered Jerusalem under such circumstances according to all the Gospels except John, Jesus now entered the Temple, overturned the tables of the money lenders, decried the priesthood for this abuse of the temple precincts, and placed Caiaphas in the position of having to support his priests publicly. Thus, Jesus now had the undivided attention of the Judaic and Roman authorities in full public view and his later substitution for Barabbas was clearly a public event designed to subdue the excited crowd by giving them what they wanted. That Jesus died is not the point however. The point is the resurrection. Yet, though wide public and official involvement attended the pre-crucifixion events, the resurrection is reported as a closed and private affair.

As to *The Epistles* and *The Acts of the Apostles* about half of which are devoted to the activities of Paul himself, it appears that he was initially a Pharisee from the Cilician city of Tarsus, a citizen of the Empire and an anti-Christian. In *Acts* we read of his miraculous conversion on the road to Damascus, now dated at about 33 AD. Not having met Jesus, he was introduced by Barnabas to the disciples (Apostles) in Jerusalem and after troubles with the Sadducees and the Greek speaking Jewish community of Jerusalem he returned to Tarsus. Some years later, having been brought by Barnabas to Antioch where the first community calling itself Christian was based, and having become involved with Gentiles sympathetic to Judaism, Paul obtained the agreement of the Apostles led by James, a brother of Jesus, to minister exclusively to Gentiles. Perhaps because he had not met Jesus in person, Paul emphasised his conversion vision and his consequent faith in the Ressurection. Perhaps also he chose to minister to Gentiles because his beliefs with respect to Jesus, the Law, and sacrifice were unwelcome to Judaism. Thus, he believed that Jesus had replaced the Law; and that faith in Him as the risen Son of God ensured salvation and removed need for re-affirmation by sacrifice. Nonetheless, though removal of this need might have been welcomed by Pagans, Paul's beliefs made him impatient with those who sought knowledge and truth in this life through philosophical speculation, and did little to persuade them that he was right.

Thus, Paul faced opposition on matters of faith in his missionary work in both the Judaic and Pagan worlds, while even among converted Christians all was not well. As shown by his correspondence, he was constantly instructing on matters of faith and conduct when in the absence of the second coming the faithful were tending to live outside the Law which he had declared to be superseded. Here, and not for the last time, we have evidence of a belief-driven revolutionary finding it difficult to control his belief-based creation. Nonetheless, on the basis of his efforts to do so, he has a strong claim to be the founder of Christianity as we know it. In addition to defining it, he introduced its rituals of commitment such as baptism, and of continuity such as the communal meal of bread and wine. He also based its administrative structure on elders similar to that of the synagogue though headed by a leader, in the manner of the Essenes, who would later be known as a bishop. There was certainly a need for such a foundation, if Christianity was to survive. Apart from asserting the Resurrection, there is little in the *Gospels* which is not covered by Judaic Scripture, or by Stoic writings in respect of recommended behaviour.

The influence of Paul must have been high, in that Marcion was content with ten of Paul's *Epistles* and a version of Luke's *Gospel* when sifting the available material for inclusion in the first canonical *New Testament.* However, though the son of a bishop, Marcion not only believed with Paul that Christians were right to reject Judaic Law, he also believed Jesus to have demonstrated the existence of a new God superior to the changeable, irascible and warlike God of Israel. Though he was excommunicated in 144, Marcionite communities continued to exist into the third century AD by which time the then Orthodox Church had reasserted itself. That, however, was not the only deviancy raised by this new beginning. It was replete with opportunities for disagreement and being belief-driven, was devoid of any reference in reality by which disputes could be resolved. It could not even draw on such authority and tradition as backed the older belief-systems with which it was now in contention. Thus, in doing his best to interpret and innovate on the basis of flimsy source belief, Paul was also raising further dispute and he had to recognise that the Jews had rejected Jesus as being insufficiently convincing in his claims, while the Gentile world was unimpressed by claims which it had ceased to believe of its own gods. As Paul said to the Corinthians, "while the Jews demand miracles and the Greeks look for wisdom, here we are preaching a crucified Christ: to the Jews an obstacle which they cannot get over, to the Pagans a madness."

4. 2. 2 Doctrine and Politics

We may suppose that the early Christians faced a number of difficulties in that Jesus, whether human or devine, had his origins in Judaism while his claims and teachings had been rejected by its authorities as disturbing innovations, and that in seeking to establish the authenticity of Jesus as the anointed of God and to acquire the respectability of an established tradition they had to invoke Judaic prophesy. Again, while it was clear that wider acceptance in the time available before the second coming would have to be sought in the Gentile world, rejection was again likely because Pagans believed the Christian concept of divinity to be retrograde, particularly regarding the miraculous. However, it appears that the chosen response was to raise Jesus from the anointed to the Divine thus making His rejection by Judaism all the more culpable; to reject Judaism on the basis of this culpability; to appropriate the Judaic Scriptures as being Christian in their foretelling of the coming of Jesus thus conferring authenticity and tradition on novelty; and to develop new Gospel accounts accordingly, incorporating Pagan concepts of the divine to enhance acceptability in the Gentile world.

The Gospel attributed to John (c.100 AD) appears to put the above into effect. It starts by asserting that "the Word (*Logos*) was made flesh and dwelt among us". Though this incarnation, mentioned nowhere else in the New Testament, is expressed in Pagan terms, Platonists did not believe that a Form could enter the physical world. Nonetheless, while the *Synoptic Gospels* place Jesus' entry into Jerusalem and his actions in the Temple as being prior to his arrest, trial and execution, John directly associates the *logos* with these actions now interpreted as fulfilment of much earlier prophesies, themselves now re-interpreted to denote the coming of a Messiah now presented as *Logos*. Thus, John seeks to establish Judaic rejection of its prophesised Jesus and to show willingness to accept Neo-Platonism by offering an innovation potentially acceptable to it. Thus, incarnation of the *logos* responds to Pagan reluctance to accept the resurrection by suggesting that acceptance of a Form (Logos) entering the world (incarnation) permits acceptance of its subsequent departure (resurrection). Again, to reduce the sense of loss at this departure, John invents the Holy Spirit through which the message (*logos*) lives on in the world. As to this message, John asserts that the *Logos* as Son of God intercedes with God the Father on behalf of those who believe in Him as Son to achieve the individual salvation and eternal life of believers *i.e.* re-union with the Form of Good, the One, while guiding and nourishing those who accept Him in this life as the Bread of Life. In this way John moves decisively away from the the irascible God of Judaism and from the descriptions of the day of judgement ascribed to Jesus by the *Synoptic Gospels* and developed by Paul in his *Epistles*. This was indeed the *Good News* intended to create a mass following.

All that remained to be done on the above work plan was to reject Judaism and appropriate its Scriptures, a task undertaken by those who sought prophesies of the coming of Jesus within these Scriptures to show that they properly belonged to Christians, the Jews having rejected the said prophesies. Among these activists were such as Justin Martyr (c. 100-c. 160), Tertullian, a North African Bishop (c.160-c.240) who was the first to write in Latin, Cyprian, Bishop of Carthage *et al*. In any case, the Greek version of the *Old Testament*, the *Septuagint*, was incorporated giving Christianity an ancient history and an authority hitherto lacking, and providing its bishops with canonical texts and absolute right of interpretation. The development of an authoritative hierarchy could now proceed. However, while the interpretation *exegesis* (Gk to explain) of Truth-containing texts such the *Books of the Law* was the Judaic tradition, and while Christian exegetes could now concentrate on the *Prophets*, the Greco-Roman tradition was very different. Thus, apart from such as the *Book of Prophesy of the Sybil*, the majority of texts were either metaphorical and classed as *muthoi* or 'rational' and classed as *logoi* (c.f. Section 3.1.2) any suggestion that the former could be analysed to produce the latter being seen as a misunderstanding of their respective natures. Thus, the appropriation of Judaic texts did little to make Christianity more attractive to Pagans.

However, while early Christians appear to have favoured oral accounts of the life of Jesus, the move to Christian texts facilitated the imposition of central authority over individual Christian communities and the appropriation of the Jewish Scriptures suggested growing Christian confidence with respect to Judaism. In addition the winning of further converts and the avoidance of schisms among existing believers necessitated development of an institutional authority and its central control of scriptural interpretation. Indeed, schism was an ever present danger during the establishment of canonical texts which consequently took longer than had appropriation and incorporation of the Judaic texts, further reinforcing the perceived need for central authoritative control. The task was to consider the large number of competing texts, including, by now, some twenty versions of the Gospel; and to select those most consistent with the current beliefs on doctrine of the Church Fathers, their attitudes to current problems facing the Church, and those likely to be faced in future. In any case, the variations and inconsistencies of the four Gospels which we have briefly reviewed, the *Epistles of Paul*, the *Acts of the Apostles* and the *Book of Revelation* must have presented an extremely daunting task, as may be confirmed by the inconsistencies and contradictions which still remain.

To make matters worse, revelation was itself a problem as exemplified by the Montanists of Phrygia whose individual members claimed individual revelation direct from the Holy Spirit. Now, Christianity was essentially a revealed religion, Jesus himself having claimed to have received revelations as had Paul. Indeed, the *Book of Revelation* (claiming to report those vouchsafed to John the Apostle) was itself a candidate for inclusion in the canon. Clearly, this background would make the elimination of individual revelation difficult. In the end, *Revelations* was included, but with John being identified as the last of the Apostles to be in direct communication with the Holy Spirit, and with the Montanists being formally condemned by synods of Asian bishops prior to 200 AD. However, even with the canon established with the basic doctrine of God the Father and Creator, Jesus the Son whose death and ressurection made salvation possible for all, and the Holy Spirit as the Divine presence in the world, there was still a mass of conflicting interpretation regarding the relationship and purposes of these three entities, on the means to salvation, and on what it meant to be saved. There could be no doubt that Christianity would diversify and fragment as it spread, unless its central authority could be strengthened by establishment of an institutional hierarchy equal to the task.

An early attempt to solve this seemingly intractable problem was made by Irenaeus, Bishop of Lyons (178-200 AD). In his *Adversus Omnes Haereses* he opposed those who claimed individual interpretation to be the only solution to the extensive diversity of the scriptures by asserting that the Apostles were all of one mind in knowing the True Interpretation, and that they passed it down in direct succession according to the pleasure of the Father and that all others should be regarded with suspicion as being either heretics or evil-minded. Since those in direct succession were the bishops of whom he was one, this was clearly a most satisfactory conclusion, though no doubt he had reservations about his fellow bishops. Indeed, recognising the need to reduce the scope for disputes among bishops, he proposed that the See of Rome, where Peter the foundation of the Church had been martyred (allegedly), should be that with which all others must be in agreement. It was soon clear, however, that nothing could easily be resolved and in any case not for long. Soon an argument arose over the suggestion by Cyprian, Bishop of Carthage, that those who had sacrificed to pagan gods to avoid martyrdom, could only be re-admitted on being re-baptised by a bishop not himself lapsed in this way. In response, Stephen, the Bishop of Rome

74

stated that all bishops were equally acceptable, only to receive a letter from Firmilian, Bishop of Cappadocia stating that in cutting himself off from Cyprian and his supporters, Stephen had effected his own excommunication.

The attempt to limit the disruptive influence of individual revelation was compounded by the *Acts of the Apostles* which are replete with miracles and portents, all of which are attributed to the Holy Spirit and are reported as having resulted in mass conversions by demonstrating the superiority of Christianity over its competitors, while the exorcism of demons was also a source of converts to early Christianity. The bishops might want to control all such manifestations of the Holy Spirit as being counter to their desire for central control but they also needed converts. However, those won by such means were not thinking Pagans, these being repelled by the concept of miracles, and even more by a religion in which they formed an integral part of the belief-system. Clearly, the bishops had some problems, but just as they had sought to overcome Christianity's lack of background by appropriating the Judaic Scriptures, they were now seeking to widen their appeal to the thinking elements in society by appropriating Platonism to this end. However, Paul had condemned the 'philosophers' and advocated faith rather than reason, while Celsus (late second century) the first outsider to conduct a survey of Christian belief and practice, had observed that Christianity could only convince the foolish, ignorant and uneducated classes and was otherwise only attractive to slaves, women and children, not recognising that those with least comfort and hope in this life will believe most strongly in the next whatever the specifics of doctrine. Again, Galen, the physician, had summed up Christianity as a rejection of reason in favour of 'undemonstrated laws', not recognising that reason (rationality) is nothing without reality-evaluation. In any case, even if the bishops did not recognise that the argument was about belief only, they recognised that something had to be done.

Justin Martyr made a start by claiming that whatever good the philosophers taught belonged to Christians. Clement of Alexandria (c.150-215) claimed that God had given philosophy to the Greeks as a preparation which paved the way towards perfection in Christ. Such headline claims might be thought somewhat arrogant and unlikely to make friends, but the fine-print was more accommodating. Clement noted of Middle Platonism and Christianity that the Form of Good, or the One, (absolute and perfect) was synomonous with the Christian God; that the concept of the human soul being distinct from the body and having a relationship with the absolute and perfect was common to both; and that the *logos* in reaching from the Forms to the human soul was similar to the then Christian concept of the "thoughts of God". It could be noted also that Middle Platonism remained in good standing in the Pagan world and thus could serve as a bridge. Again Plato's concept that only the capable and trained few could comprehend the nature of the Forms and interpret for the rest was just what the bishops needed for central control of doctrine and to keep the masses in line. Thus, Faith would be preserved not through individual revelation, but through the authoritative decrees of the Church Hierarchy. A marriage made in Heaven: or is it Hell?

Origen (185-254), born to Christians in Alexandria and perhaps the most prolific Christian writer of his time, developed this relationship between Christianity and Platonism while introducing ideas of his own. In his *De Principiis,* he writes that in the beginning all human souls were equal and with God, but all save one (Christ) fell away to varying degrees becoming angels, human souls or demons; and that evil does not have independent existence, but is the degree to which individual souls have fallen from God. According to Origen, human souls retain a memory of their initial state, retain some of the *logos* (rational thought), and may seek to return to God with the help of the *logos* which remains fully with Christ. The first step in this return is to desire to be transformed through contemplation and study with the assistance of Christ, those who choose this way being likened to Plato's Guardians to distinguish them from the less commited. Origen also believed that all would eventually be saved because no other final state was conceivable under the truly good and all powerful God, though bodily resurrection would not be necessary. However, in spite of his contribution to the synthesis desired by the Church, Origen was condemned after the Nicene Creed was formulated in 325 because of his unspecified subordination of Christ to God, rather than believing Him to be an eternal part of the Godhead, and because of his belief that all would be saved, the Church having decided that fear of hell was to be integral with its control mechanisms for the future.

The Church might now be well on the way to appropriating Platonism, but there was still a difficulty in appropriating Platonists who continued to believe that the gods were mythical or allegorical, continued to support traditional rituals and to show tolerance to the beliefs of others while failing to find this tolerance reciprocated by Christians who condemned Pagan practices and rituals and who refused even at pain of death to comply with Pagan requirements even when compliance was made as easy as possible for them. This principled rejection of, and self-imposed isolation from, the politico-religious structure of Roman society was, however, more likely to prevent rather than to facilitate conversions among those responsible for the welfare and good conduct of that society. Thus, the Romans tolerated Judaism as they did the religions of all the conquered peoples, provided their followers "rendered unto Caesar the things that were Caesar's" and they would have shown similar tolerance to break-away Christianity provided this condition were met. Nonetheless, they did tend to deride Christianity as a religion without tradition and therefore more deserving of dismissal than acceptance. They had, however, been initially alerted to it by its claim that Jesus was King of the Jews when, as far as they were concerned, this role had been played by Herod Antipas with whom they had had a working relationship. On the other hand, when Nero tried to blame them for burning Rome to cover his possible complicity, many Pagans sympathised with the Christians.

In fact, the Roman attitude to the relatively few early Christians was mixed, which probably accounts for its official responses to self-proclaimed non-integration being spasmodic and variable. Many parts of the Empire knew little or nothing of Christianity which remained largely an urban phenomenon in the Greek-speaking east. In about 110 AD, Pliny (Governor of Bithynia) found it necessary to ask Trajan for advice on how to deal with troublesome Christians and was told that accusers must bring their case in person and be liable to counter-charges of malicious persecution if their accusations proved unfounded; that the accused should be acquitted, if no longer a member of a Christian community; and that prosecution could be avoided by participation in a Pagan sacrifice witnessed by two officials who would issue a certificate. Many Christians complied and in due course re-applied for church membership. Others refused and thus volunteered for martyrdom in one form or another. Such official responses to non-integrated Christians had depended on the discretion of provincial governors until 250-251 AD, when the first Empire-wide action was taken under Decius to reinforce traditional cults and rituals in response to the military crises of the third century. Even so, it was still possible for Christians to hold senior military and administrative positions and to retain them even under the edict of Decius by offering only a token sacrifice to the state.

Nonetheless, by the fourth century Diocletian felt compelled to reinforce state-cohesion through unified allegiance though he consulted widely, even sending to the oracle at Didyma for advice before taking action. His first edict, in 303 AD, was directed at the confiscation of Christian property, but his health was failing and his power slipping towards Galerius, his Augustus in the east, who favoured a tougher policy. Thus, Diocletian felt obliged to issue a further edict in 303 to the effect that Christian clergy be imprisoned until they were prepared to sacrifice to the gods of

76

the state, and another in 304 which required all Christians to sacrifice or face the penalty of death. However, Diocletian abdicated in 305 and Constantius in the west limited his action under the edicts to the confiscation of property, while Galerius attempted to apply the full rigour of the law in the east. Even so, some provincial governors simply claimed that all Christians had sacrificed, while others merely asked for affirmation of an unspecified Supreme Deity. Thus, enthusiasm for the edict of 304 faltered, faded by 310 and in 311 Galerius died.

It is difficult to estimate the numbers of Christians in the Empire or the percentages martyred during this period, though there can be no doubt that ways to avoid martyrdom were on offer. Nonetheless, Tertullian saw martyrdom as a promoter of growth and the publicity given to it suggests conscious efforts to this end. The fact that all the early bishops of Rome were claimed as martyrs whether true or not, suggests that martyrdom was made integral with Christianity regardless of any true accounting of the phenomenon. Again, the early histories of Christianity attempt to hide the disputations and violence between its own groupings of differing belief, though it was the general civil disorder thus created which caused Constantine to attempt integration within the Empire as the only pacification means not yet tried.

The incorporation of the Hebrew Scriptures into Christianity had presented few problems because the Christians were not seeking an on-going relationship with Judaism. On the contrary, they had decided to reject and ignore it. The subsequent attempt to appropriate Platonism had also been easy compared to the difficulty of incorporating Pagans. Nonetheless, though Constantine was now attempting co-existence if not full integration, he must have recognised these and other difficulties. Thus, while the Judaic God was sufficiently warlike for the purposes of a Roman Emperor, the Jesus of *The Gospel* was clearly not. Again, the Pagan and warlike citizens of Rome on whom the Emperor depended, adhered strongly to Pagan cults which the Christians abhorred. In addition, he must have known that the sources of civil unrest arising from the disputes and rivalries of Christian communities (particularly in the east) might not be rendered quiescent by any initiative of his, even one with this precise intention, and that if he were not successful he could face Pagan as well as Christian unrest. Yet, having formed an alliance with Licinius, the successor to Galerius in the east, he issued in 313 a joint declaration, the Edict of Milan, to the effect that "no one should be denied freedom to devote himself to the cult of the Christians, or to such religion as he deems best suited for himself, so that the highest divinity, to whose worship we pay allegiance with free minds, may grant us in all things his wonted favour and benevolence." Could it really be that simple?

Constantine was the son of Constantius who had died at York in 306, and whose military prowess as Caesar in the west had forced Galerius to make him Augustus. Three years later, Constantine claimed independent legitimacy as the son of his father who because he had died in office was believed by some to be a god. Constantine reinforced this belief by claiming descent from Claudius Gothicus whose major victory over the Goths in 269 had notably subdued them for what would be more than a century. He then asserted his right to rule the western Empire, claiming that Apollo had appeared to him in a vision and promised that he would rule for thirty years. He associated himself with the cult of Sol Invictus and issued coins with the Sun (always associated with Apollo and with Plato's Supreme Good) radiating from his head. In 312, he challenged Maxentius, the son of Diocletian's co-Augustus, Maximinian and defeated him three times, before achieving final victory at the battle of Milvian Bridge where Maxentius drowned. This left all of Italy and the provinces of North Africa to Constantine who announced that he owed his victory to the intervention of the Supreme Deity.

His Edict of Milan having been issued within a few months of this victory, Constantine began a substantial programme of church building within a year. He must have judged that his

Pagan credentials were sufficiently established by his god-like status, his personal and public conduct as a follower of Sol Invictus, his claimed vision of Apollo and his military and political successes, to enable him to consolidate his intended new relationship with the Christians by offering them freedom of worship and his church-building programme without undue offence to his fellow Pagans. He no doubt also judged that his neutral reference to the Supreme Deity would be accepted as a diplomatic gesture by both Christians and Pagans, and that it would confer the added benefit of taking a first step towards converting the pacific Christian God to the more war-like nature of a Roman one. Within three years his triumphal-arch in the centre of Rome would be in traditional style, showing no trace of Christian influence and making use of bas-reliefs removed from monuments of the earlier Emperors, Trajan, Hadrian and Marcus Aurelius. Indeed the other reliefs were of the gods of war, Mars, Jupiter and Hercules while the victory at Milvian Bridge was associated with the Sun and the goddess Victory with all being captioned 'Instigation of the Divinity'. In addition, Constantine was shown as making a speech in the Forum and as distributing poor-relief in the traditional manner of a Roman Emperor. For Christians, (Sun)day was the day of the resurrection while the main festival of Sol Invictus was December 25, later chosen for Christmas. His triumphal-arch is a pagan monument, nonetheless, and while its association of the Pagan-Christian Divinity with military victory was perhaps too one-sided to be fully diplomatic, a sufficient amount of compensating church-building may well have been realised and planned by 315.

The support which Constantine offered to Christians beyond freedom of worship and the building of churches, included clergy-exemption from the duty to hold public office and from the obligation to pay taxes. As might have been expected, though it appears to have surprised Constantine, these additional decisions immediately revealed such numbers and diversities of communities calling themselves Christian, that he was forced to consider how he might limit their calls on his generosity. On the other hand, the bishop of Carthage, Caecilian, was judged by his fellow bishops to be ineligible for the Emperor's patronage, because he had surrendered Church scriptures (property as defined in Diocletian's Edict) to be burned by the civil authorities. Thus, citing concurrence with the earlier Bishop Cyprian, they elected Majorinus to replace Caecilian amid such disturbance that Constantine wondered if his own position with the Divinity might be compromised by his negotiations with Christians. However, having referred the matter to two successive councils of bishops in Rome and in Gaul, Constantine withdrew his patronage from the objectors in 316, whereupon they became known as Donatists after their next bishop, Donatus, though they were finally subdued by Augustine in 405 (c.f. Section 4.2.5).

Clearly Constantine's attempts to do business with Christians was going to be difficult. He was not, however, distracted by these disputes from normal business. Thus, between 313 and 315 he had further successes on the northern borders, in 316 he forced Licinius to cede his eastern provinces, in 324 he forced him to abdicate prior to his execution in 325, while his son, Licinius II, who had been appointed Caesar in the east in 317, was killed in 326. Thus, Constantine, now unchallengeable as Emperor, found the more Christianised east even more disputatious than the west, its bishops and sees being virtually at war with one another. In particular, he was immediately involved in a doctrinal dispute between Arius, a presbyter who upheld the belief that Jesus was subordinate to God and Alexander, Bishop of Alexandria who believed them to be one and the same. Most of the bishops agreed with Arius and if the Scriptures are anything to go by, so had Jesus, there being nothing in the Gospels to suggest that Jesus and God are one and the same. A couple of quotations should suffice as a reminder, such as "Father forgive them for they know not what they do" and "Father, why hast thou forsaken me." Again, in recognition of the need to accommodate Platonic thinking, one might recall that the Logos is subordinate to the Form of the Good.

Nonetheless, bishops were lining up on both sides and Constantine's response was to call a council to assemble at the Imperial Palace at Nicaea in Asia Minor, with himself presiding as patron and determined to resolve the dispute through his state and personal authority. By creating this precedent, he must also have intended to increase his future control over the now state-funded church. To this end, we may suppose that any compromise would have satisfied Constantine. His opening speech stressed the need for harmony and the supporting document drawn up by Eusebius, Bishop of Caesarea, was conciliatory in its attempt to produce a summarised doctrine agreeable to all. Thus, he avoided direct reference to the issues raised by Arius, describing Jesus as begotten of God to avoid use of the terms subordination or equality and to allow both sides their own interpretations. Needless to say, it being too late for such a compromise, Constantine had to force an agreement. In such circumstances, he would be likely to enforce his own view and as Emperor this would have favoured central authority over individual revelation and bishops over presbyters which in the long run would be favoured by bishops irrespective of Scripture. Thus, in supporting Alexander against Arius, Constantine would be advancing his own agenda and he does appear to have pushed the assembled bishops in this direction.

Thus, having little time for "gentle Jesus, meek and mild," and preferring unification of the Godhead as a means of bringing Christianity closer to the needs of Empire, there can be no doubt that dissenting bishops were forced to concur. Indeed, Eusebius had to excuse himself on returning home, by telling his flock that although the term *homoousis* (of identical substance) had been introduced to describe the nature of both Father and Son, the Faith prevailed in unanimous form. Clearly he was uneasy about the new Creed, while readers will recall that the terms *ousis* and *hypostasis* of Middle Platonism (c.f. Section 4.1) were more consistent with what was to become known as Arianism. Indeed, Constantine came to realise that his new Creed did little to win the allegiance of the eastern Christian communities who continued their Arian ways: further evidence of the pressure needed at Nicaea. What the Emperor did achieve through the Council, however, was a formal subservience of Church to State, doctrine formulation having been shown subservient to state patronage. For their part, the bishops had seen Imperial Power at first hand with some realising the benefits of cooperation. The Emperor was hugely successful politically and militarily, arguably one of the most successful ever, and the temptation to cast him as the first Christian Emperor must have been strong. Thus, in his *Life of Constantine*, Eusebius presents the Emperor as the first Christian Hero, the equal of Moses, receiver of visions and of divine support for military victories; and the Battle of Milvian Bridge as a triumph of the Christian God: all with Constantine's approval.

No doubt to keep the balance between Christian and Pagan, Constantine authorised the town of Hispellum to build a temple to the cult of his family. Again, in laying out the plans for Constantinople, his new capital, he reserved space for the building of three churches, though their names Hagia Sophia (Holy Wisdom), Hagia Eirene (Holy Peace) and Hagia Dynamis (Holy Power) suggest studied neutrality. Again, while Eusebius tells us that statues of the Good Shepherd were erected in fountains in the city, this was a symbol of significance to Pagans as to Christians as was the Sun. Yet again, there is no record of his ever having attended a church service and his baptism took place only when he realised he was dying. On his death his three surviving sons (he had killed one son and a wife) issued a coin to commemorate their own succession, one side of which depicted the veiled head of Constantine inscribed "The Deified Constantine, Father of the Augusti", while the obverse showed him ascending to heaven in a chariot with God's hand extended in welcome, in the manner of his Pagan predecessors.

Thus, Constantine maintained his sense of balance between Pagan and Christian to the end, having achieved his objectives of severing the Church from its roots in the Jesus of the Gospels and of binding it to government by state patronage of state approved beliefs. The Council at Nicaea had failed to settle an internal doctrinal dispute of the Church, but this would not matter so long as such disputes did not result in civil strife, and the state now appeared well placed to insure that it never would. On the other hand, the Church now had to grapple with a range of questions arising from its new relationship with the State it had previously refused to recognise. These included how best to use its new state-sourced wealth and the status of its internal belief-based authority, given that it had failed to agree on its own beliefs to the extent of having them decided for it as being no longer a purely internal matter. Thus, the internal dispute which the Council of Nicaea had been convened to resolve was whether or not the Son was subordinate to the Father and it had been decided, despite Christian Scripture, that they were one and the same. The source of uneasiness for such as Eusebius was that the Emperor had won the argument he had presided over.

Yet, in permitting Son and Father to be of the same substance (*ousis*) with different personality or grade (*hypostasis*) Middle Platonism could have reconciled Pagan and Christian beliefs at the Council, the new term *homoousis*, (of the same substance) adding nothing to what was already understood by *ousis* applied to both. Introduction of the new term, however, emphasised the identity of Father with Son, thus meeting my supposition that the Emperor had intended to conflate the one with the other. On the other hand, a significant step towards a merger of monotheistic Paganism and Christianity had been taken without ruling out a reinstatement of *hypostasis* at some future date. At this point, however, we should note that harmonisation might have been advanced by formal recognition of the similarities between Judeo-Christian and Pagan ethics, as exemplified by "do unto others as you would have them do to you" (Leviticus/Jesus) and "the fault is mine if I do not give, it is another's if he be not grateful" (Socrates). Again, Aristotle had recognised virtue as being common to humanity, though in need of continuous nurture (c.f. Section 3.1.2). Nonetheless, there was more belief-based conflict to come and readers may already see parallels with the state-funding, cultural/religious and socio-political conflicts. of today.

4. 2. 3 The Internal Politics of the Post-Constantine Church

In reviewing events following the above, my purpose is to emphasise the futility of attempting to reach conclusive belief-based agreement whatever the subject, and to show that such attempts simply prolong disputation and conflict detrimental to social cohesion either directly or through belief-based mediators; that such conflict would not arise or could be resolved were belief open to acceptance, rejection, suspension or submission to reality-evaluation; and that belief-based socio-political disputation and conflict provides more continuity of employment than would knowledge-based resolution.

Thus, the Creed produced by the Council of Nicaea was insecure because Arianism and non-Arianism were but differing interpretations of the religious Ur-belief and as such were inaccessible to resolution by reality-evaluation. Again, as to socio-politics, some appreciated the benefits of central control and recognised that Arianism would be as unacceptable to Constantine's successors as it had been to him, while others adhered to the now canonical Scriptures in believing them more important than state-funding. Thus, a highly disputatious search continued for a form of words which would harmonise majority belief in Son and Father being different, with Imperial and minority inclination to believe them to be one and the same. Clearly the dispute was damaging to civil peace while recognition that it was about beliefs unverifiable either way would surely have dispelled it.

However, Constantine's son, Constantius II futilely continued as mediator to seek a secure belief-based resolution by conceding a degree of subordination of Son to Father with the result that discussions among small groups of eastern bishops produced the four so-called Sirmium Creeds, all

80

of which were based on replacement of the term *homoousis* (of the same substance) by *homoios* (of like substance). However, this change was immediately opposed by those who believed it too general to convey sufficient meaning, though dilution of meaning was surely the intention; by those who suggested *homoousios*, (of similar substance) as an alternative; and by the followers of Arius who believed unlikeness to be the distinction between Father and Son. To simplify matters, Constantius chose the fourth Sirmium Creed, the so-called Dated Creed of 359 as the basis for discussion at two councils to be held in the spring of 360 at Arimium (Rimini) and in the autumn at Seleucia. In the event, the western bishops preferred the earlier Nicaea Creed even though western presence at that Council had been minimal. However, having been unable to put this view to the Emperor because of his absence on campaign, they accepted the Dated Creed and thus informed at Seleucia, the eastern bishops agreed. On this basis, the Council at Constantinople called by Constantius in 360 endorsed the Dated Creed, proscribed the term *hypostasis*, (*homoousis* having now been rejected) and declared all earlier creeds heretical, this then being promulgated by Imperial Edict.

Shortly afterwards, Constantius died unexpectedly in 361 and was replaced by his half-cousin, Julian, most of whose family members had been eliminated by Constantine's three sons in their struggles of succession. Julian had been brought up a Christian, but whether for intellectual reasons or family experience he had become a Pagan who was reported as saying that "no wild beasts are as dangerous to man as Christians are to one another", and that "left to themselves Christians would simply tear one another apart." Thus, he withdrew all the clergy-exemptions enjoyed by Christians and ordered the bishops to allow every man to practice his religion boldly and without hindrance. In 362, the clergy was barred from teaching rhetoric and grammar on the grounds that those who scorned Pagan religion should not teach Pagan culture, but should confine themselves to teaching the *Gospels* in their own Churches. In the period 362-3 AD Julian wrote his *Contra Galilaeos* in which he uses his detailed knowledge of the scriptures (he had been a lector) to point up the inconsistencies and contradictions of the Gospels, the deliberate mis-interpretations of prophesy regarding the coming of Christ, the outdated concepts of God and the sacrilegious claims of His sole commitment to the Jews as in the appropriated *Jewish Scriptures*, and the inferiority of that whole tradition in contrast to the achievements of the Greeks in mathematics, astronomy, medicine, law, philosophy and theology. Julian also argued that belief in a Supreme Deity was in itself no reason for His not presiding over lesser deities, and he referred to a longstanding Pagan belief that the Deity may be more thoroughly reverenced by a multiplicity of belief than by a single belief. He noted too that theological debate was a more civilised affair in the Pagan world than it was in the Christian, and he added for good measure, that if Christians had found the Truth, they had much difficulty in agreeing what it was. Again, to emphasise his Pagan tolerance and perhaps to confound Christian belief that it would never happen, Julian encouraged the rebuilding of the Temple at Jerusalem.

However, after Julian had been killed while campaigning in Sassinid Persia in 363, Christians and Pagans alike were about to face other troubles associated with Roman decline. Thus, having been proclaimed successor by the army, Jovian ceded large areas of the Eastern Empire to the Sassinids before dying eight months later to be succeeded by Valentinian (364-375) the last Emperor to defend the northern frontier successfully. When he in turn died, his brother Valens and Gratian (son of Valens) became co-emperors while the army proclaimed Valentinian II (son of Valentinian) as Augustus. Meanwhile, the northern border was broken through when the Huns from further east drove the Goths across the Danube, and Valens who had hoped to recruit them as auxiliaries, had to face them at Adrianople where he was killed with 10,000 of his men. At this point, the eleven year old Gratian appointed Theodosius as his co-

Augustus while having no option but to allow the Goths to settle in the Empire without having allegiance to it. However in 383, the then sixteen year old Gratian was murdered by some of his men, leaving twelve year-old Valentinian II to emerge as Emperor in the west where being concerned mainly for internal order he resumed Constantine's tolerance of belief for both Pagans and Christians.

Thus, after the Julian interregnum, the Christians were able to resume where they had left-off with the western bishops favouring the conclusion reached at Nicaea, (now referred to as the Nicene Creed), but willing to acquiesce to the Dated Creed. In the east, however, support for Arianism fuelled resentment to the later compromise of Constantius now referred to as the Homoean Creed. To complicate matters further, there was some support even in the west for the version of Arianism adopted by the Roman cleric Sabellius which believed that Jesus on earth was only a temporary manifestation of the Godhead. Nonetheless, things had changed from Arius being traditional and Alexander being deviant, to Arianism being deviant and Alexandrianism being the new orthodoxy, in some form or other. Again, Athanasius, supporter of Alexander at Nicaea and his successor as bishop, having refused Constantine's order to reinstate the excommunicated Arius, had been exiled to Gaul for this defiance among others, had now (c. 356) resumed use of the proscribed term homoousios and had begun to consider how Jesus as *Logos* could suffer as a human being, while the *Logos* being divine could not. Previously, in 350, he had written the first full treatise on the nature of the Holy Spirit which raised much the same difficulties as had the relationship of Jesus to God. Again Athanasius, in emphasising the inherent sinfulness of man, argued that the incarnation of the *logos* as Christ had been to curtail sin's increase since the expulsion from Eden and to provide for its redemption, though he was not as optimistic as Origen that all would be saved. Indeed he was difficult, having spent fifteen years of his forty-five year tenure (328-373) in five periods of exile, and Christianity was anything but unified.

However, a pro-Nicene alliance supported by the bishops of Rome and Ambrose of Milan caused the decline of Sabellianism and with Ambrose's *De Fide* being written in the period 379-381 attention turned to the Holy Spirit, first identified as a distinct entity by Athanasius and later discussed by Hilary of Poitiers (another of the alliance) in his *De Trinitate*. Meanwhile, in the east, the Cappadocian Fathers, Basil of Caesarea (died, 379), his brother Gregory of Nyssa (died, c. 395) and Gregory of Nanzianzus (died 390), expressed the belief that the Godhead is of one substance (ousia) with three personalities (hypostasis) through which it can be represented as Father, Son and Holy Spirit. Now, as we have seen (c.f. Section 4.1), Plotinus, the Neo-Platonist, had believed in three entities, the One (the Godhead), the *Nous* (mind) which presents the Platonic Forms to the material world, and the World-Soul, all of which were of the same substance (ousia) but of different personality (hypostasis). When we also recall that the *Logos* intercedes between the Forms and the material world, we might suppose *Nous* to be a synonym for *Logos*, which in turn is a synonym for Jesus, according to Philo. Thus, it seems that the World-Soul has become the Holy Spirit, permitting God to remain active in the world, Jesus having left it.

However, the Cappadocians still had to deal with the beliefs that God always was; that the Son had been begotten of the Father; and that the Holy Spirit had now proceeded from the Father in some way. Those who were willing to accept the original Nicene formulation would have denied that God could have created a Son, both being one and the same, while the Homoeans would have found a begotten Son difficult to square with an eternal one co-existent with God. Then again the Sabellians would have been content with Philo's belief that the *Logos* had spoken through the Burning Bush only for the time taken to communicate with Moses, and might
82

similarly have been content that it spoke through Jesus only during his time on earth as a temporary manifestation of the Godhead. As to further problems in reconciling the One (the Godhead) with the Trinity, the Cappadocian Fathers were operating in a Homoean rather than a Nicaean context. Rationalism clearly multiplies problems without being able to resolve any of them.

Meanwhile, Valens (364-378) in continuing to support the position reached by Constantius in 360, had been promoting Homoean bishops and had insisted the Goths convert to Homoean Christianity on entering the Empire. However, his successor Theodosius was pro-Nicene and in 380 at his campaign base in Thessalonika he announced that the Nicene Creed as supported by the bishops of Rome and Alexandria, would be the new orthodoxy and that all others would be treated as heresies with loss of tax exemptions and other perks. He then travelled to Constantinople to issue, in January 381, the Imperial Edict expelling Homoeans and Arians from their Churches and installing the formerly Homoean Gregory of Nanzianzus in place of the Homoean Demophilus as Bishop of Constantinople. This Edict also stated that all now classed as heretics would face both the vengeance of God and "such punishment as the state, in accordance with the will of heaven, shall decide to inflict." No record of the preceeding Council survives, the first reference to the Creed from it being its two-fold reading at the Council of Chalcedon in 451, by which time it had been expanded to include the Holy Spirit and the doctrine of the Trinity covered by the earlier Edict of Theodosius.

It is clear that the original Nicene Creed and its subsequent amendment at Constantinople by Theodosius with respect to inclusion of the Trinity were forced through their respective Councils against substantial opposition. There was really no consensus in the Church and to review the respective concepts, the questions raised and the answers attempted is to see that there never could be so long as there were people willing to take part in such debates. There was no truth that could be deduced by such means, the premises on all sides being forever beyond reality-validation. The best that could be hoped for was that outright opponents would tire of the argument, thus permitting a temporary majority decision to be reached among other less divided believers or the Emperor could decide though only temporarily. As to the Emperor's decision, it could decide the distribution of patronage, but it could not decide belief, and therefore could not of itself secure civil harmony. The arguments would continue. Already the expulsions of Homoean bishops had led to riots in many locations and Homoean communities expelled from their Churches were holding their services in the open air. Christianity had been made a state religion to suppress such argument, now the state had become a party to the argument and not always on the same side. However, Theodosius now sought to make acceptance of the Nicene Creed a test of loyalty to the state. Yet, his argument that the defeat of Valens was a judgement of God effected through those (meaning the Goths) whom Valens had perfidiously initiated into Homoean Christianity was more likely to provoke argument than to quieten it. Again, while Theodosius argued thus in the east, Valentinian II Emperor in the west (375-92) remained Homoean and in contention with the Nicene, Ambrose of Milan.

Ambrose, as Province Governor, had been summoned to Milan to keep order on the death of the Homoean bishop Auxentius and though not even a baptised Christian at the time, he was acclaimed by the crowd and accepted as the new bishop by Valentinian, whereupon his mother, Justina, persuaded her son to proclaim freedom of worship for Homoeans and tried to reclaim the Basilica for their use. In the meantime Magnus Maximus had been proclaimed Augustus by his troops and had invaded Italy in 387 hoping to bring the young Valentinian under his influence. This caused Valentinian and Justina to flee to Thessalonika to appeal for the assistance of Theodosius who duly marched into Italy in 388, forced Maximus to surrender, executed him and re-instated Valentinian as Augustus in the west. By then, Theodosius was the fifth Emperor to be served by Ambrose and the first to be wholly in support of the Nicenes. Thus, in making the whole Empire Nicene by repeal of the Homoean proclamation of Valentinian, Theodosius might have expected a quiet relationship with Ambrose the Nicene.

Ambrose appears to have had other plans, however. Thus, when Theodosius included himself with the presbyters on attending mass in the Basilica Ambrosiana, (now Milan Cathedral) Ambrose requested him to join the ordinary faithful. We do not know whether careless preparation had put Ambrose in an embarrassing position with little time to think or whether he had intended to slight the Emperor. However, in 388, a bishop-led Christian mob having destroyed a synagogue in Callinicum on the Euphrates, and Theodosius having ordered the Province Governor to punish the perpetrators and to compensate the victims, Ambrose objected that "a Christian could not re-create a house where Christ is denied" and went so far as to say that he would be happy to accept responsibility for having ordered the destruction. According to Ambrose, the Emperor then cancelled his orders to the Governor. On the other hand, there is evidence that the Emperor had banned Ambrose from the Imperial court. Whatever the outcome, it appears that Ambrose was testing his strength with the Emperor and another opportunity to do so arose in 390. Thus, while in Milan, Theodosius had ordered reprisals for rioting in Thessalonika, in which the garrison commander had been killed. In his rage he may have given the order or the impression that no quarter was to be given or the local troops may have exceeded their orders. Either way, thousands were allegedly killed in a serious over-reaction to which Ambrose reacted by depriving Theodosius of communion and the Emperor responded by asking for penance in the Basilica Ambrosiana. One might say that the Emperor was using the Church as an available instrument in a public relations exercise or that he was being compelled by the Church to seek absolution in its own public interest. Either way Ambrose and the Church were the winners.

Thus, within weeks of his public penance, Theodosius had banned all cult worship at Pagan shrines and Christians thus encouraged began to destroy such shrines. As a further consequence, even the Olympic Games were held for the last time in 395 after a run of nearly twelve hundred years. In the meantime, Valentinian had died in Gaul in 392, and Theodosius had defeated his self-proclaimed successor in 394 just before his own death in Milan in 395. Thus, Ambrose, having first secured the place of Theodosius and the Nicene Creed in the future life of the Church went on through his two sons, Honorius (western provinces) and Arcadius (eastern provinces), to secure the future life of the Church within the State.

It is clear that the problem addressed at Nicaea was that the Arians had faith in the Christian *Gospels,* on any objective reading of which Jesus was subordinate to God. However, harmonisation of Christianity with Platonism was essential to increase its attractiveness to monotheistic Pagans who having rejected lesser gods were uncomfortable with direct communication between man and the Good, and thus with man-gods. Constantine had his own reasons for being uncomfortable with the particular man-god, Jesus, some of which related to the potential for civil unrest through uncontrollable divine revelation among the masses, and so he sought to subsume Jesus with the Supreme Deity who would be more controllable politically. Some Church leaders were also uncomfortable with uncontrolled revelation and so for their own reasons could be expected to go along with Constantine. This shared interest enabled him to produce his Nicaean Edict, though many believed the Scriptures were being ignored and the Son/Father debate was being conducted on Platonist rather than Christian lines.

Thus, with his father having failed to eliminate dissent, Constantius sought compromise through the Homoean Dated Creed, only to find some Church leaders more attracted to central control of doctrine than to compromise. Again, some of these men saw no problem with continuous revelation provided it could occur only through the Holy Spirit which the Church could control (once it had sorted out its differences) without reference to Scripture which being canonical was less easy to change for control purposes. The new concept of the Trinity therefore had the advantage (recognised by Constantine) of subsuming the man-god Jesus into the Godhead. It also had the advantage (recognised by the pro-Nicene faction) of putting Jesus and Scripture in the past, while the new Holy Spirit would be the bishops' source of revelation for any necessary future change, this new merger of interests enabling Theodosius to issue his Edict of Constantinople.

However, differences were not immediately resolved even then. Palladius, bishop of Ratiaria, advised Ambrose of Milan (after *De Fide*) "to search the Scriptures, which he had neglected, so that under their divine guidance he might avoid the Hell to which he was heading on his own." Forty years later, Maximinus, a bishop of the Goths told Augustine in public debate in Hippo "that the Divine Scripture did not fare so badly in Homoean teaching that it had to be improved." However, the Nicenes were about to deploy yet another argument, that of the Cappadocian Fathers, who when cornered, were wont to protest that "all might go mad through prying too deeply into God's secrets." This response, of course, invited the hearer to accept that the Cappadocian explanation was as far as mere humans could go; that it was correct as far as it went; and that faith in the authority of the Gospels must give way to faith in the authority of the Cappadocian Fathers. Following this, we find Augustine transferring this authority to the Church in his reply to critics of the Nicene Creed when he said that "he would not believe the Gospel unless the authority of the Church so moved him." Thus,, orthodox doctrine is whatever Church authority, supported by Imperial Edict, has declared it to be, with Scripture being re-interpreted as the Church deems necessary for its temporal defence. In his *De Doctrina Christiana*, Augustine goes on to state that anything in the divine discourse (the Scriptures) which cannot be related to good morals or the true faith, should be taken as allegorical. For Origen and the more traditional Pagans, allegory was a bridge from belief to reality and *vice versa*. For Augustine, this reality was whatever the Church decreed it to be.

At this point, it should be noted that the difficulty in settling belief, whether by Church authority or Imperial Decree, arises from the circularity of the arguments necessarily deployed. Thus, while a Deity defined as Beyond material existence could be imagined to 'explain' all material existence, all argument for the Deity's existence had to attribute 'non-material' existence to it, hence the focus on (non-material) substance and states of such (non-material) substance, such being akin to the Ideal essences, spirits and Forms earlier believed to embody the materials of the real world (c.f. Section 3.1.1). Again, while belief in non-material substance does not break the circularity, it raises further argument as to how non-material substance can exist in the world of substance and how we who exist in the world of substance can have contact with the Beyond. Thus, having "explained" our own existence by imagining a creator God in the Beyond, believers had to face the problem of explaining how the Beyond could exist and communicate with substantive existence, and how God could wholly or subordinately exist within it. It is no wonder that the Church found Imperial Decree necessary to terminate such otherwise endless argument. Indeed, the only way out of the circularity is to suspend belief in an imagined creator who can do whatever he likes without need for understanding on our part. However, a rational conclusion being desired, the circularity was recycled again and again in different derivative forms. As to such irresolvable derivatives of belief, I now provide examples from specific activities of the Eastern and Western Church.

4. 2. 4 The Eastern Church: Politics and Belief

John Chrysostom from Antioch who had spent some years as an ascetic, claimed in his treatise, *Virginity*, that God's intention had been for Adam and Eve to be asexual, and that Eve had caused sex and its dangers to enter the world. Though John's western contemporary Augustine was one of Paul's followers in having much to say about the difficulty of controlling the sexual urge, the wish to abolish it altogether must surely be an extreme rejection of reality. John was also extreme in his rejection of Jews and Judaism, as evidenced by his sermons which survive in *Against the Jews*. Though recognised as a potential disturber of the peace, he seems nonetheless to have had sufficient popularity to become bishop of Constantinople in 398. However, his attitude to women coupled with his lack of judgement created difficulties with the Empress Eudoxia which enabled the bishop of Alexandria to get the better of him and have him expelled. He died in exile in 404. Clearly John Chrysostom of Constantinople had not used his proximity to an Emperor as successfully as had Ambrose of Milan, though he had shown how belief leads to belief in endless succession so long as reality is absent or rejected.

Such argument between the Sees of Constantinople and Alexandria was maintained for the next half-century by differences in belief as to the true nature of Jesus while on earth. Thus, if it were true under the Nicene Creed, that Jesus was always part of the Godhead, how could He experience suffering as a human being while on earth, as related in the Gospels? In spite of the attempts already made to resolve such questions at Nicaea, Thessalonika and Constantinople, three distinct beliefs were still being identified. These were that Jesus was fully human but adopted by God (Adoptionism); that he was fully divine with only the appearance of being human, (Docetism, from dokeo, I seem); and that he had a human body and divine soul and mind (Apollinarianism, after the bishop of Laodicea). Yet again, Theodore, Bishop of Mopsuestia, believed that Jesus had been conceived twice, once in devine form, and once in human form. Additional considerations were also debated such as whether Jesus was fully man when he suffered, but divine when he performed miracles, or whether he was human then also. Again, when human was he man before the fall, man now or man redeemed? If he were perfect, how could Luke describe him as progressively increasing in wisdom, stature and favour with God and man?

These concerns in turn raised the question of whether the Virgin Mary had been the bearer of a God or a man (Theotokos or Anthropotokos). As to this, Nestorius, now Bishop of Constantinople preferred Christotokos, to avoid re-opening discussions on the nature of Jesus. Seeing this, Cyril, Bishop of Alexandria went for the Theotokos option as an opportunity to undermine Nestorius, having first obtained the support of among others Pulcheria, the elder sister and regent of the young Theodosius II who had succeded Arcadius in 408. There then followed a provocative series of letters from Cyril to Nestorius which sought to illicit and then to exaggerate and distort the latter's beliefs, tactics which culminated in twelve anathemas denouncing Nestorianism. By such means, Cyril caused Theodosius to call the Council of Ephesus in 431 to settle the argument. Cyril by then had long been a source of trouble. When he became bishop in 412 he had recruited strong-arm supporters, the parabalani, who caused such terror that the Emperor had asked their number to be limited to five hundred. However, the City Prefect, Orestes was injured in the exercise of his duties by a mob of monks, synagogues were seized and Hypathia the mathematician was torn to pieces in the street by a Christian mob. Thus, it was not too surprising that Cyril arrived early for the Council of Ephesus with strong-arm supporters, intimidated the presiding Imperial Commissioner, completed the business to his own satisfaction before Nestorius arrived, and subsequently used bribery to keep Theodosius and the Court on his side. Theodosius was thus reduced to negotiating the withdrawal of the anathemas in exchange for his condemnation of Nestorius whose works were burned by imperial decree in 435. When Cyril died in 444, it was said that "a great stone should be placed on his grave to prevent his soul returning to the world when found too evil even for hell."

The arguments raged on, and a second Council was called at Ephesus in 449 to resolve them. This time the proceedings were dominated by Cyril's successor, Dioscorus, who used armed guards to gain control and to push through condemnations which included charges of usury, sorcery, blasphemy, and sodomy against any bishops who could be associated with Nestorianism. Dioscorus even managed to excommunicate Leo, Bishop of Rome whose tome suggesting a resolution of the two natures of Jesus in one person was condemned, and Flavian of Constantinople died of injuries received at or shortly after the Council. In an attempt to restore order, Marcian, Emperor in the east (450-457), an elderly soldier who had married Pulcheria after her brother's death in 450, called a Council to meet at Nicaea. This Council was subsequently relocated in 451 to Chalcedon (closer to Constantinople) to facilitate Imperial control and to allow the attendance of Marcian and Pulcheria at one session. For this Council, the local governor was ordered to secure the surrounding area by expelling 'riotous clergy' and Imperial Administrators conducted the proceedings, insisting on issues being presented in writing and debated as dispositions. In spite of this care and attention many of the sessions were reported as having been chaotic. Nonetheless, the Council of Chalcedon made some changes. The prestige of the see of Constantinople was enhanced by giving it greater authority over its surrounding territories, by taking monks out of secular life in order to regularise their conduct, and by accepting Leo's tome through a compromise interpretation of Cyril's writings which declared that after the Incarnation, Christ was at all times fully God and fully human, with two natures without confusion, without change, without division and without separation. An Imperial Edict followed to the effect that disagreeing with the Council's conclusions was punishable.

Even so Marcian's hopes for uniformity and peace were not realised. The Nestorians who came to adopt belief close to that of Theodore of Mopsuestia, sustained themselves in the eastern regions and in Persia. Those who held the view that Christ had a single nature with divine and human elements (the Monophysites) set up what was to become the Coptic Church in Egypt and the Jacobite (James) Church in Syria. Many felt that the compromise doctrine of 451 violated the doctrine of the Trinity and as late as the 490s there were riots at the news that a phrase suggesting Monophysitism had been added to the liturgy at Hagia Sophia in Constantinople. In 492 the Emperor Zeno felt the need to declare that the Trinity remains the Trinity even when one of the Trinity, God the *Logos*, becomes flesh; and that Christ was *homoousios* with the Father according to his divinity and *homoousios* with us according to his humanity while remaining one Son.

The Emperor Justinian (527-65) set about the final eradication of Paganism in the 530s by withdrawing the religious toleration enacted by Constantine in 313, and by introducing the death penalty for the practice of Pagan cults. In addition Pagan teachers, including philosophers, had their licences (*parrhesia*) withdrawn though these had guaranteed freedom of speech throughout the previous thousand years. This was not a general ban which might be avoided at local discretion, but one directed at specific centres. In this way the last temple dedicated to Isis was closed in 526 and Plato's Academy in Athens was closed in 529 after nine hundred years with its incumbents seeking refuge in Persia. Paganism was still a long way from dying, however, and even within Christianity uniformity continued to be illusive, Justinian finding it necessary to condemn Nestorianism yet again at the Council of Constantinople in 553.

4. 2. 5 The Western Church: Belief and Earthly Power

Though the origins of Christianity were eastern, the western Church looked to Rome on the belief that Peter was the first bishop in the city. Nonetheless, the power was elsewhere as the conflict between Cyprian of Carthage and Stephen of Rome made clear in the third century, and Constantine who was claimed as the first Christian Emperor had motivations other than consolidating Rome's traditional Christian claims when establishing his new capital at Byzantium. We have also noted the response to Leo's tome at the Council of Chalcedon, which even now is generally taken to be the first significant input from Rome to the deliberations of the Councils of the wider Church. Again, even when Theodosius was being encouraged to remove Pagan symbols, it was Ambrose of Milan, rather than Damasus of Rome who achieved the removal of the Altar of Victory from the Senate House.

The problem for the western Church was that Christianity had its sources in the east and was Greek speaking; and the problem for the See of Rome in particular, was that the city remained the centre of the Pagan senatorial aristocracy till the end of the fourth century. Indeed, Tertullian of Carthage was the first bishop to write in Latin rather than Greek, though he could do both. It should be noted, however, that Tertullian, though just as mysogynist and as anti-Jew as John Chrysostom in the east, shared with Paul the robust understanding that the beliefs of Christianity could not be justified by rational debate. Though no belief can be justified by rationality alone, Tertullian made his specific position clear in his statement that "the Son of God died, it must needs be believed because it is absurd. He was buried and rose again; it is certain because it is impossible". This attitude helped the western church to keep its distance from the search for illumination in Platonism, and thus from the interminable arguments of the eastern Church. On the other hand such a man was likely to be 'certain' about individual revelation as a source of truth and he confirmed this in his later years by joining the Montanists.

Another significant figure in the western church was Jerome (c.345-420) who having been educated and baptised in Rome was ordained in Antioch where he learned Greek and Hebrew before his obsession with the dangers of sex and the benefits of asceticism caused him to retreat to the Syrian desert for a number of years. After returning to Rome and becoming secretary to Damasus the bishop, he began at the latter's behest to produce a definitive Latin version of the Bible from earlier second century Latin sources. However, on the death of Damasus about three years later, he was driven from the city by the Roman clergy for criticising their hypocrisy and the lifestyles of prosperous women and for his association with a group of ascetic women, this being construed as scandalous. Thus, Jerome went to Bethlehem with the ascetic Paula whose wealth he used to found two monasteries and having completed his Latin version of the *Gospels* he became occupied on his Latin translation of the *Hebrew Scriptures* for the next twenty years. However, trouble arose from canonical status of the Greek *Septuagint*.

Indeed, Augustine warned of severance from the east were the west to translate it, with the result that Jerome's Latin version was not adopted until Charlemagne's *Bible* of the ninth century. In the meantime, another source of trouble was that in the course of his work, Jerome had referred to the earlier commentaries on the Hebrew and Greek versions of the *Scriptures* by Origen whose unorthodox beliefs had already been criticised. Accordingly, Epiphanius, bishop of Salamis, who believed Origen to be a heretic and an inspiration for Arianism, sent a group of monks to Jerome to persuade him to mend his ways. Consequently, when Rufinus, an old school friend now working on a translation of Origen's *De Principiis* claimed that Jerome shared his view that Origen had been unfairly criticised, the now-corrected Jerome immediately denounced his friend in circumstances which led to Rufinus being branded a heretic. Friendship counted for little when charges of heresy were threatened.

Though Augustine (354-430), had been born in Thagaste, North Africa of a Christian mother, he was initially more drawn to Pagan philosophy having read Cicero while being educated in law and rhetoric. Instead of taking up his intended career in the Imperial Civil Service, however,

88

he became a teacher of literature in Carthage until 383 by which time he had been a Manichean for nine years. The Manicheans, who derived their beliefs from Mani a Persian of the previous century, saw themselves as teachers of a truer Christianity than that of the Church. They drew attention to the contradictions in the Gospels and to the immorality of the lives recorded in the *Hebrew Scriptures*. They practiced asceticism and sought to remove themselves from matter which they considered evil. They permitted sexual relationships but saw the creation of children as the production of yet more evil matter. However, Augustine couldn't accept that all was evil, being in search of a "Good" which could counter it. Thus, in 383 he left for Rome, partly it seems to escape the domination of his mother. Once there, the Prefect, Symmachus who had heard Augustine speak, recommended him for the post of imperial orator for Milan where Ambrose was bishop. Though now attracted to Platonism with its belief in the Good, he suffered an emotional crisis associated with asthmatic attacks which necessitated the cessation of his duties as orator. However, having heard the sermons of Ambrose he came to believe Christianity to be what he had been seeking all along, was reconciled with his mother, and took up celibacy as he recounted in his *Confessions*.

Augustine returned to north Africa in 388, became a priest in 391 and was Bishop of Hippo from 395-430. In his early years as bishop he wrote his *Confessions* which reveal his sense of sinfulness, his concept of original sin, and his belief in a punitive God. In his *Trinitate* he supports the Nicene Creed and interprets Scripture to denounce the Arian and Homoean alternatives, describes the soul as possessing self-awareness, understanding and will, and states the soul to be naturally Christian, rejection of Christianity being a rejection of one's humanity. His *On Order,* seems to accept the Platonist belief in rationality, though it asserts the root of sin to be pride in one's own intelligence and concludes that humility in the acceptance of authority should be modelled on Christ's humility in becoming human, and that certitude is only to be found in acceptance of doctrine as established by the Church. By 390, his *True Religion* shows that his certitude extended to believing in miracles which he asserts to be everyday occurrences among the faithful. In the early stages of *On Freewill* he appears to accept the concept as implying responsibility for the evil one chooses to commit, though later in the same work he says that humans are so controlled by original sin as to have their freewill so limited as to be unable to save themselves without God's Grace, this being achievable only through the sacraments of the Church though there is no guarantee.

From 390 onwards, Augustine studied and wrote commentaries on the Scriptures in an effort to relate them to all the practices and activities of life, but he had no Hebrew and little Greek while the Latin versions which he had to hand were often so poor as to be incomprehensible. Augustine's response was to work on the principle that the test of an interpretation was whether it was consistent with his orthodoxy. Thus, for example, his belief in original sin and all his interpretations of its consequences were based on his belief that we all sin through Adam, whereas the Greek text expresses the belief that the sin which entered the world through Adam's temptation by Eve was an *external* entity with which humanity would henceforth have to contend. It was not passed down individually through the generations as required by his doctrine of original sin. No matter, so long as Augustine's belief gelled with his 'understanding' of what would be acceptable as Church dogma, his belief was 'valid'. Towards the end of his life, his *De Doctrina Christiana* concluded that secular knowledge as provided by philosophers or mathematicians would be valid only in so far as it was consistent with Church doctrine.

When Augustine returned home in 388, the largest Christian community in North Africa was that of the Donatists from whom Constantine had withdrawn patronage following the dispute over re-baptism of those who had earlier surrendered their Scriptures to state authorities. Now,

Augustine's orthodox Church being much smaller, the Donatists insisted on re-baptism of orthodox Christians who wished to become Donatists and saw themselves as having a strong case for recognition as the representative Christian Church in North Africa. Once again the Emperor had to resolve this inter-Christian dispute and in 405 Honorius issued an edict ordering unification of the disputing Churches by declaring the Donatists to be heretics subject to confiscation of property, banning of services and exile of clergy on which basis Augustine drove the Donatists from Hippo and took over their churches. Later, when it appeared that wider implementation of this imperial policy had become relaxed, he petitioned the Emperor to summon a Conference as a result of which Donatism became a criminal offence and Donatists (some 300 bishops and their flocks) were forced to join the orthodox Church. This success through compulsion seems to have led Augustine to look at force in a new light. God having thrown Paul to the ground to effect his conversion, Augustine now concluded that the Church, being divinely inspired, would have the support of God for actions which it might take "in love"; that his success over the Donatists showed that Church procedures over-rode questions of personal merit in priest or hierarchy; and that sacramental validity was the channel for God's Grace without guaranteeing it.

However, apart from questions of force and power, Augustine had difficulties with other Christians over doctrine. A notable opponent was Pelagius, who though from Britain had lived in Jerusalem and Rome, knew and was sympathetic to the beliefs of Jovinian who questioned the virginity of Mary and to those of Rufinus who sought to re-instate Origen. Pelagius believed that salvation could be secured through free will and rationality and that those seeking God would be helped by God to find Him. These beliefs were condemned by one synod in Jerusalem and though supported by another, two further councils in North Africa condemned Pelagianism in 416. Again, while supported by Innocent, Bishop of Rome and initially by his successor Zosimus, rioting in Rome between supporters of Pelagius and Augustine caused Honorius to issue an Edict in 418 condemning Pelagians and ordering them to leave Rome. Julian of Eclanum, forced into exile over this issue, wrote to Augustine to decry the very idea that babies of necessity entirely innocent in themselves would be consigned to Hell because (according to Augustine) they were imbued with original sin, and to point out that such belief was tantamount to attributing to God an action which would be judged criminal among barbarians. Augustine remained unmoved.

In his last work, *The City of God*, Augustine contrasts the worldly city with the heavenly one, pointing out that the Pagan Gods had failed to support Rome; that a worldly city, however Christian in appearance will always be a mixture of good and bad; and that the true City of God can only be attained in heaven after death. He rejects the Pagan idea that the city is the source and cradle of progressive civilisation. Indeed, he rejects the whole idea of earthly progress. Yet, though he accepts war as part of life here below, he recognises the benefits of peace, security and good order for the preservation of the orthodox Church and enjoins Christians to obey those in orthodox authority in Church, state and family. Nonetheless, we may conclude that his need to insist on authoritative orthodoxy establishes the futility of seeking universal acceptance of any derivative of the religious Ur-belief which by definition is beyond reality-evaluation, and that this is confirmed by his own identification of over eighty contending heresies.

In this connection it is worth recalling that the Goths who first sacked Rome in 410 were Homoean Christians, for which action others offered a range of explanations. Some Christians, possibly even the Gothic variety, saw the fall of Rome as the advent of the *Last Times* prophesised in the *Book of Revelation* while some Pagans saw it as a consequence of the abolition of Pagan practices following official acceptance of Christianity. In any case, the Vandals (a Gothic tribe) in over-running North Africa in 430 and laying siege to Hippo permitted Augustine who died on 28 August 430 just before the city fell, to witness heretical Homoeean Christians overcoming

90

orthodox Christians and ex-heretical Donatists. Nonetheless, the See of Rome continued to secure its socio-political position in the western Church despite the military situation. As the leading families of Rome gradually converted to Christianity and new basilicas were built, the power and influence of the Bishop of Rome grew and was consolidated in Leo the Great (440-461) who gradually took command of the western Church through the bishops in Italy, Africa, Spain and Gaul by asserting his position in unbroken succession from Peter. He dealt firmly with heretics, but was careful to act on civil affairs through Valentinian III, Emperor in the west (425-455). His tome on the nature of Jesus had influenced the Council of Chalcedon in 451 and it was he who led the delegation which achieved the withdrawal of Attila the Hun in 452, and again it was he who negotiated leniency when Gaiseric the Vandal entered Rome unopposed in 455.

A century later, with the eastern Church still disputing the nature of Jesus, the Emperor Justinian attempted resolution by re-declaring Nestorianism heretical with the support of Vigilius, Bishop of Rome (537-555), though the latter so prevaricated as to lose both the favour of Justinian and the respect of western bishops to the extent of being refused burial in St Peter's. The next significant Bishop of Rome was Gregory the Great (590-604) considered the founder of the Medieval Papacy. Gregory was the son of a senator, had been Prefect of Rome, a monk, an emissary to Constantinople from the Bishop of Rome, an abbot and finally Pope. He dismissed secular learning, advising the wise to cease from knowledge and recommending his flock to be wise in ignorance and wisely untaught. He believed in miracles, but was more moderate than Augustine in believing in a more merciful God to whom good works and pious practices were of value and in believing the existence of evil in the God-created world to be an unfathomable mystery best left alone. He was also content for clergy to marry and his mission to Britain for the conversion of the Angles was more sensitive than it would have been in other hands. He encouraged the use of music in worship, the Gregorian chant being attributed to him as is the concept of purgatory as a means of increasing the chances of ultimate salvation. Clearly interpretation of Scripture has much to do with the personality and life experience of the interpreter.

4. 2. 6 The Celtic Church: Importance of the Individual

The earliest dates for Christian activities in Britain are difficult to establish, though three bishops, a priest and a deacon attended the Council of Arles in 314 suggesting representation of the four new capital cities of the fourth century Roman provinces in their early stages of Church organisation after its legality had been declared by Constantine in 313. British bishops also attended the Council of Rimini called by Constantius II in 359, though they were so lacking in funds as to be offered free transport *via* the Imperial Post, again suggesting rather less than full Church participation in the socio-political life of Britain. However, some time after the death of Martin of Tours in 397, his acolyte Ninian, the first Christian to attain historical significance on the British scene, arrived in Galloway and built a church at Whithorn.

From this religious community, Ninian conducted missionary work in Scotland, Ireland, northern England and Wales until his death in 432, this accounting for the Church's early presence in Celtic west Britain. We may also discern something of the beliefs of this early Church from the dispute which Ninian's contemporary, Pelagius the Scot, had with Augustine of Hippo and something of its wider influence from the decision of Pope Celestinus to send Germanus of Auxerre to Britain in an attempt to secure orthodoxy by engaging in public debate with Pelagians at Verulamium (St Albans) in 429, to which task he had to return in 435 with still mixed success. Thus, while Dupricius, otherwise known as Dyfrig (425-505) adhered to the orthodoxy of Germanus, his successor, Illtud preferred monasticism to episcopacy in any case, and founded the major monastery of sixth century Britain at Llanilltud Fawr near Cardiff, a preference which the Celtic Church developed and practiced in the isolation of inaccessible coasts and islands of the Atlantic seaboard. Thus, Samson, a pupil of Illtud, went to Caldey Island in the Bristol Channel and hence *via* Cornwall to Brittany where as St. Samson of Dol he is now Patron Saint, while Dewi (530-589) another Celtic monastic similarly took himself off to the western extremity of the Pembroke peninsula and later became Patron Saint of Wales. Perhaps the most extreme example of the desire for contemplative isolation, however, is that of the monks of Skellig Michael who in the sixth century built six beehive-shaped stone shelters and a small church 550 feet up on a pinnacle eight miles off the coast of south-west Ireland. It seems plausible that Celtic Church devotees of those days continued to believe with Pelagius that man could achieve salvation by his own efforts and to reject the doctrine of original sin as he had done.

That this was indeed the case is evidenced further by the despatch of Palladius to the Irish in 431 by Celestinus, the Pope who sent Germanus twice to mainland Britain to correct this heresy. In the meantime, a sixteen year old by the name of Sucat was captured by a raiding party on the Cumbrian shore and sold into slavery in Ireland from whence he escaped on a ship bound for Gaul where taking the name Patrick he was received into the faith by that anti-Pelagian Germanus, though he later studied at the pro-Pelagian monastery of St. Honorat on Isle de Lerins on the Mediterranean coast. Thus equipped, he returned to Ireland where without having been commissioned by Rome, he established and dedicated himself in Armagh to preaching and converting to an extent perhaps unique among contemplative Celtic Christians, later becoming Patron Saint of Ireland.

At about that time, the Scots were leaving Ireland for Ear-Gaidheal (Argyle), later called Dal Riadha, after their source kingdom in Antrim and in due course King Conall of Dalriada gave Calum Cille (Dove of the Church) or Columba as he is now known, the small island of Iona. He had established two monasteries in Ireland, (hence his name) but needed a refuge on being exiled for involvement in armed conflict over monastic possessions. Later, when Aidan Mac Gabrain, himself exiled from Dalriada to the east of Scotland, returned in force to seize the crown, he had Columba legitimise his coronation in 574 in exchange for his public recognition of the new religion. Thus, Iona became a major centre of Christianity under Columba and his successors, though the Picts of the north-west appear to have remained Pagan until the eighth century and beyond. From Iona, however, another Aidan established a monastery on Lindisfarne and converted the Northumbrians whose kings in the seventh century were powerful enough to claim the title of Bretwalda (Britain Ruler). One of these, Oswy (612-670) called the Synod of Whitby in 664 to decide *inter alia* the date of Easter. He, who followed the Celtic Church, had married Princess Eanfled of Kent who had Roman ways, Pope Gregory having sent Augustine in 596 to convert the Angles from his base at Canterbury, the result according to the Venerable Bede being that when the King had ended Lent and was keeping Easter, the Queen and her attendants were fasting and keeping Palm Sunday.

After argument, based as usual on selective quotation from Scripture to which were now added slighting references to offshore islanders by the champions of the 'wider European interest', the Irish bishop Colman conceded that the Celtic Church had no authority to compare with that of the Church of Rome. Nonetheless, he returned to western Ireland *via* Iona with thirty monks intent on avoiding acceptance of the Whitby decision and as late as 687 Aidan's successor, Cuthbert, was still exhorting the Celts to comply. Thus, with some difficulty, was the Church in England unified under the Archbishopric of Canterbury, only Theodore of Tarsus being willing to fill this position. Later the Reformation in Scotland would again expose beliefs which had sustained Pelagianism and the Celtic Church (c.f. Section 6.4).

Meanwhile, however, the Roman Empire was faring badly. The North African provinces having been recaptured for orthodox Christianity by Justinian in the 530s, were lost to Islam in the seventh century, by which time Rome itself was seriously damaged with aqueducts out of action, large areas deserted and with northern Italy having fallen to the Lombards. Thus the social and cultural unity of the Empire was breaking down with Greek becoming unfamiliar in the west and Latin in the east, with classical culture being lost, and with nothing new or creative being done. Meanwhile brains which might have taken an interest in the nature of the world, were now devoted to interpretation and commentary on Christian texts, to Church politics, and to the creation of a Theocratic society. As we shall see however, craftsmanship continued to develop its knowledge despite religious belief and social disorder (c.f. Section 5.7).

4. 3 CONCLUSIONS: THE IRRESOLVABLE NATURE OF BELIEF

Having confirmed in Chapters 2 and 3 that imaginative beliefs are transformed by reality-evaluation to the knowledge which is craftsmanship and empirical ethics we have now confirmed that religious Ur-belief derivatives are limited only by the imagination, being irresolvable to knowledge when beyond reality-evaluation; that consensus can only be temporary, those frustrated by it being a continual source of dispute and violence; and that such beliefs are best left to personal acceptance, rejection or suspension in a manner akin to 'self-revelation'. Thus, it may be concluded that attempts to create a stable orthodoxy through Imperial Edict created the instability which destroyed the power to issue them, that time thus spent is time wasted or devoted to self-destruction, and that persistence in the face of actual destruction is suicidal madness. Nonetheless, Augustine's eighty heresies and the diversity of disputed detail before and after each proclamation of a new orthodoxy exemplify the variability of belief, and explain the recurrence of belief-driven revolutions and wars from the Fall of Rome to the present day whether these are religious, secular/religious or secular, violence being seen as the only option by those who would die rather than agree to suspend belief or to resolve it by reality-evaluation wherever possible (c.f. Chapters 10-12).

On the other hand, it should be recognised that the religious Ur-belief and its derivatives are expressions of human nature in their provision of guidance, comfort and hope; that recourse to such is strongest where the need is greatest; that *Homo sapiens* has always had such recourse even if only as metaphor; and that such is available without conflict when acceptance, rejection or suspension of belief is left to individual decision. Again, it should be recognised that Christianity incorporated empirical (reality-validated) knowledge of human nature from time immemorial as transmitted through the Judaic *Old Testament,* the metaphorical myths, literature and drama of classical Greece, the Ethics of Aristotle, the Stoicism of Greco-Roman culture (c.f. Section 2.5.4) and the *New Testament* teachings of Jesus; that Christianity has created its own cultural tradition on this knowledge (though presenting it as belief) through the ensuing millennia; and that none of this knowledge should be rejected or replaced without reality-evaluation of the benefits of doing so against the constancy of humanity's need for survival through social cohesion.

However, it may also be concluded that this knowledge, having always been treated as religious belief, is as readily replaced by secular belief as is one heresy by another; that this secular replacement has been on-going since the so-called Enlightenment and has been rendered orthodox by cumulative governmental Edicts over the last fifty years or so; and that the resulting mismatch between reality (knowledge) and the beliefs of liberal democracy is more fundamental than the mismatch of orthodox and heretical belief which destroyed the Roman Empire (c.f. Sections 6.4, 6.5 and Chapters 10-12).

4. 4. NUMBER AND MATHEMATICS: REALITY AND ABSTRACTION

Further to belief, it is clear that the Pythagoreans believed number and mathematics to be abstracted from an Ideal Realm which though beyond the senses was accessible to rationality; that for Plato, the Beyond was the source of the socio-political knowledge which he sought to implement in the real world; and that while the early Christians were most concerned to ensure their entry to the Beyond, Neo-Platonic Christianity was concerned to define the nature of God on Earth and in Heaven through application of the rationality which had produced mathematics. As to mathematics, I now turn to the use of abstract number to produce trigonometry from geometry and to facilitate arithmetical computation despite number system difficulties through early steps in algebra, all of which supposed metaphysical success encouraged the Neo-Platonists to seek such certainty elsewhere. I also touch on the computation of probability by the Chinese whose mysticism paralleled that of the Pythagoreans.

As to the application of number to geometry, Thales had shown that triangles with corresponding angles equal (defined as similar triangles) have their corresponding sides (those opposite the corresponding angles) in constant arithmetic ratio to one another, however long or short these corresponding sides may be. Aristarchus had used this knowledge to determine the relative distances from Earth of the Sun and Moon and the relative sizes of both, and Erathosthenes had used this constancy of ratio to determine the size of the Earth. However, when this property of similar triangles was applied to those containing a right-angle, it was observed that the ratios of any two pairs of corresponding sides would always be in constant ratio to one another, the other two corresponding angles remaining constant in size. In particular, it was observed that the ratios of perpendicular and hypotenuse, base and hypotenuse and perpendicular and base of such triangles would remain constant and thus could be used as a measure of the other two angles of the triangle defined in these terms. Thus, if the angle opposite the perpendicular and contained by the base and the hypotenuse is designated angle A, then the above ratios are known as sine A, cosine A and tangent A respectively (sin A, cos A and tan A for short) and their values can be measured or otherwise determined for any angle A. Conversely, the ratios thus evaluated for any angle A can be used to calculate the lengths of any two sides of any right-angled triangle, provided the length of one side and the size of one angle are known or easily measurable, even if one of the lengths to be calculated is the distance of the Moon from the Earth, or whatever. This general observation was the birth of trigonometry.

As to determining the numerical values of these ratios for the range of possible values of angle A, application of the theorem of Pythagoras would suffice in some specific cases. Thus, in a right-angled isosceles triangle, the other two angles are both 45° (Thales) and if its equal sides are one unit in length, we see that the length of the hypotenuse will be of length $\sqrt{2}$ (Pythagoras) from which it follows from the perpendicular, hypotenuse and base ratios defined above, that sin 45, cos 45 and tan 45 are $1/\sqrt{2}$, $1/\sqrt{2}$ and 1, respectively. Similarly we may visualise an equilateral triangle with all of its sides equal to two units and knowing that all of its angles are 60° (Thales), we immediately see, and it can be formally proved, that a perpendicular from one vertex to the opposite side will bisect one of the 60° angles and the opposite side to produce two right-angled triangles which are equal in all respects (defined as congruent triangles) and with the corresponding non-right-angles being 30° and 60° respectively.

If we now focus on one or other of these right-angled triangles we see that it has a hypotenuse of 2 units in length and a base of 1 unit, and that its altitude is $\sqrt{3}$ (Pythagoras). Applying the values thus determined for the lengths of the sides of this triangle we see that sin 60 is

√3/2, cos 60 is 1/2 and tan 60 is √3; and that for the 30° angle of this same triangle the hypotenuse is 2, the altitude is 1 and the base is √3 and that, therefore, sin 30 is 1/2, cos 30 is √3/2 and tan 30 is 1/√3. If we now visualise our 30° angle decreasing in size towards zero, we see that our perpendicular decreases in size and approaches zero in the 'limit' as our hypotenuse tends to become equal to our base, and that therefore sin 0 is 0, cos 0 is 1 and tan 0 is 0. Similarly if the angle of interest increases towards 90°, our altitude and hypotenuse tend to coincide and our base tends to zero in the 'limit', with the result that sin 90 is 1, cos 90 is 0 and tan 90 is infinity.

At this point we recall that neither 2 nor 3 is a perfect square. In other words, there is no whole number which when multiplied by itself gives 2 or 3 as the product. The square of 1 is 1 (1x1=1),and the square of 2 is 4 (2x2=4). The square roots of 2 and 3 must therefore lie somewhere between 1 and 2. In fact √2=1.414 and √3=1.732 correct to three decimal places, this being accurate enough for measurements made by instruments giving consistency up to but not beyond one-in-a-thousand. We could determine such square roots by trial and error. Thus we might guess that √2 would be somewhere around 1.5 but we would find that 1.5x1.5 is > 2 and that 1.4x1.4 is < 2, but that 1.41x1.41 is closer to 2, and so on. However, while this is easy enough with our number notation, scale diagrams were preferred by early mathematicians and accurate enough for their practical purposes. Thus a scale diagram of a right-angled isosceles triangle with the equal sides one unit in length would have a hypotenuse of √2 or 1.4. . . units in length, which could be directly measured with the practical precision of the time. If one of the equal sides was now extended from 1 to 1.4 . . . units in length, the new hypotenuse is √3 or 1.7.. . units (Pythagoras) and if this process is repeated the successive hypotenuses of √4, √5, √6 etc can be measured.

The next step, with respect to easing the computational task, was to combine the triangle with the circle and to demonstrate that if we know the sine and cosine of angle A, we can calculate sin ½A and cos ½A and because sin A/cos A=tan A, we then compute tan ½A also. Thus, if POT is a diameter of a circle with centre O and radius 1 unit, and Q is a point on the circumference, then the angle QOT at the centre of the circle is twice the angle QPT at the circumference subtended on the same arc QT (Euclid). If we now draw a perpendicular from Q to the diameter POT at the point R and another perpendicular from the centre O to the chord PQ at the point S, we see that triangles OSP and QRP are similar and right-angled at S and R. If we now denote by x, the unknown length PS (the base of triangle OSP) and the unknown length OR by y, then the base of triangle QRP has length 1+ y (OP and OQ being the radii of the circle with centre O), SQ also being x and PQ being 2x (PQ being the bisected base of triangle QRP)

If we now refer to the angle QOT at the centre of the circle as angle A and angle QPT at the circumference as angle ½ A (Thales):

we see that	cos A = y/OQ =y, from triangle QOR and from OQ =1, radius of the circle.
and we see that	cos ½A = PR/PQ = (1+y) /2x, from triangle QRP
and	cos ½A= x/OP=x, from triangle OSP, and from OP = 1, radius of the circle
substituting	cos A for y and cos ½A for x, eliminates the unknown quantities,
and we have,	cos ½A= (1+cos A)/2cos ½A
therefore	$2(\cos \tfrac{1}{2} A)^2 = 1+\cos A$
therefore	$(\cos \tfrac{1}{2} A)^2 = \tfrac{1}{2} (1 + \cos A)$
or	cos ½A= √ {½ (1+cos A)}

If we now recall that cos 30 is √3/2 (or 0.866) then cos ½ (30), that is cos 15 can be computed from the above to be 0.966. Clearly the process can be repeated to calculate cos ½ (15), that is cos 7½ which is 0.991, and so on. The sine rule for ½ angles is derived in the same way to give the result that:

$$\sin \tfrac{1}{2}A = \sin A / 2\cos \tfrac{1}{2}A,$$

giving sin 15 as 0.259 and sin 7½ as 0.131. The corresponding tangents (sin A / cos A) are 0.27 and 0.13 respectively. It should also be noted that $(\sin A)^2$ $(\cos A)^2$ and $(\tan A)^2$ and written $\sin^2 A$ and so on.

Other relationships are readily deduced. In a right-angled triangle, the other two angles always sum to 90 (because all three sum to two right-angles, Thales). It follows that, if one of them is angle A then the other is 90-A and it is easy to show from the side-ratios of the triangle, that cos A=sin (90-A) and because cos 15 = 0.966 = sin (90-15), sin 75 =0.966. Similarly sin A= cos (90-A). Again, if we construct two angles with a common line between them, such that angle POS is A and angle SOT is B, then POT is (A+B). Now, if we drop from P a perpendicular PS on to the common line OS and a perpendicular PR on to OT; and from S a perpendicular SQ on PR and a perpendicular ST on OT; and if the line OP has unit length: then we see by inspection that:

$$\sin (A+B) = PR = PQ + QR = PQ + ST = PS \cos B + OS \sin B$$

and that $\qquad\qquad \sin (A+B) = \sin A \cos B + \cos A \sin B$

Again, we see that $\qquad \cos (A+B) = OR = OT- RT = OT- QS = OS \cos B - PS \sin B$

and that $\qquad\qquad \cos (A + B) = \cos A \cos B - \sin A \sin B$

Yet again if the angle A is contained in a right-angled triangle of base b, altitude a, and hypotenuse h = 1, then by the theorem of Pythagoras, $a^2 + b^2 = 1^2$ and therefore, $\sin^2 A + \cos^2 A = 1$. Thus we see that from the evaluation of sines, cosines and tangents of a few angles such as 30, 45 and 60 and by using relations such as those involving half angles, the addition of angles, those such as cos A= sin (90-A) and the relationship, $\sin^2 A + \cos^2 A = 1$, Hipparchus could construct the first trigonometric table of sines, cosines and tangents, circa 150 BC. We must remember, however, that mathematicians such as Archimedes had access to such data before Hipparchus. We must also remember that we have the advantage of having more accurate square roots and a much more convenient number system, including a decimal system of fractions, to make such computation easier for us.

Another approach to square roots was based on the demonstration that an angle at the circumference of a circle, subtended by a diameter of the circle, is a right-angle (Thales). Thus if √2 is required, a circle of radius 1.5 units (the arithmetic mean of the numbers 2 and 1, the factors of 2) may be drawn, a diameter of which may be divided into two lengths x and y of 2 and 1 units respectively and a perpendicular, p, may be drawn from the point of division to the circumference. We now have two smaller and similar right-angled triangles. Thus, their corresponding angles being equal, the ratios of their corresponding sides (those opposite the corresponding angles) are in a constant ratio and thus: x/p = p/y, or $p^2 = xy$, or p = √xy. Thus, the length of this perpendicular may be measured to give the value of √2 because in this case x = 2 and y = 1. Though the level of accuracy is again dependent on that of the scale drawing, the procedure can be extended to produce other roots. To take another example, if x = 3 and y = 2, the radius of the circle is 2½ and the length of the perpendicular is √6. Incidentally, the square root of the product of two numbers, x and y, is referred to as their geometric mean, to distinguish it from the arithmetic mean which is their sum divided by two.

Now, we recall that Archimedes had shown that for all circles the ratio of circumference to diameter was a constant which we designate π, and as we have noted, he showed that the length of the circumference lay between the lengths of circumscribed and inscribed polygons of the same number of sides. I will now describe how he used sines and tangents to calculate π. If the polygons have n sides, the ends of which are connected to the centre of the circle by straight-lines, n triangles will result in each case. If now these triangles are individually bisected by another set of n straight-lines drawn from the centre of the circle to bisect each of the n sides of the polygons into two elements each of length p, there will now be 2n right-angled triangles. If the angle at the centre of the circle in each of these right-angled triangles is the angle A, then for the circumscribed polygon the bisecting straight-lines are radii of the circle and are bases of the small right-angled triangles with respect to the angle A within these triangles. For the inscribed polygon, however, these radii of the circle are the hypotenuses of the right-angled triangles with respect to angle A. Thus, the elements, p, of the boundary of the circumscribing polygon are longer than the corresponding elements of the circumference of the circle and those of the inscribed polygon are shorter, but in both cases they are the altitudes of the right-angled triangles with respect to the angle A.

Thus, if the radius of our circle is chosen to be ½ , then for the circumscribing polygon the boundary element p is given by: $\quad$ $p = ½ \tan (360/2n)$
the total circumscribed boundary, $\quad$ $P_c = n \tan (360/2n)$
and similarly that inscribed, $\quad$ $P_i = n \sin (360/2n)$

We can now see that π can be calculated to whatever level of precision is required by increasing the value of n, referring to the tangents and sines of the correspondingly smaller angles A at the centre of the circle, and averaging the values obtained for P_c and P_i. The following Table shows how the error, calculated with respect to the modern value of π, (3.14) diminishes as n is increased.

Number of Sides	P_i	P_c	Mean π	% Error
4	2.828	4.000	3.41	8.5
6	3.000	3.464	3.23	2.8
12	3.106	3.215	3.16	0.6

We have seen earlier, that Archimedes ended up with a value between 3 and 10/70 and 3 and 10/71 *i.e* between 3.143 and 3.141, which is better than might have been expected. The Egyptians settled for $\sqrt{10}$ or 3.16, but by about 480 AD a Chinese irrigation engineer called Tsu Chung Chih arrived at a value lying between 3.1415926 and 3.1415927. It is not known how he obtained this result but it is supposed that he may have summed a large number of rectangles in the manner adopted by Archimedes for the areas enclosed by conic sections. It should be noted, however, that the approach based on sines becomes inadequate for angles less than about 5 degrees because the number of significant figures in the sine of the angle is insufficient to give more than three significant figures in the result. More modern values are based on series which I discuss later (c.f. Section 6.2.3) though for now it can be seen that Archimedes was more than adequately accurate for the needs of his time.

Archimedes meanwhile was interested in other number progressions or series, some of which had earlier attracted the attention of the Pythagoreans. The simplest progression or series is that of the natural numbers arranged in order, 1, 2, 3, 4, 5, 6, 7, 8, ... The next two to be considered were 2, 4, 6, 8, 10 . . . and 3, 5, 7, 9, 11. . .. Such series, in which successive terms are related by a common difference, d, are said to be arithmetic series. If the first term be a, then the sum to n terms, S_n can be written,

$\quad$ $S_n = a + (a + d) + (a + 2d) \ldots$ on to the nth term, $\{a + (n - 1)d\}$.
and in reverse $\quad$ $S_n = \{a + (n - 1)d\} + \{a + (n - 2)d\} \ldots$ back to, $(a + d) + a$
Therefore adding gives $\quad$ $2S_n = n (2a + (n - 1)d)$, all other terms being seen to be mutually cancelling,
or $\quad$ $S_n = ½ n \{2a + (n - 1)d\}$

Again, geometric progressions or series, in which the terms are related by a common factor, were also recognised. Examples are 2, 4, 8, 16, 32. . . and 10, 100, 1000. . . where the common factors are 2 and 10 respectively. In general, the sum to n terms, S_n can be written,

$$S_n = a + ar + ar^2 + ar^3 \ldots \text{on to } ar^{n-1}$$

and multiplied by r $\quad\quad$ $r\, S_n = ar + ar^2 + ar^3 + ar^4 \ldots \text{on to } ar^{n-1} + ar^n$

Subtracting gives $\quad\quad$ $rS_n - S_n = ar^n - a$, because all the other terms cancel out

Therefore giving $\quad\quad$ $S_n (r - 1) = ar^n - a$

or $\quad\quad\quad\quad\quad$ $S_n = a (r^n -1)/ (r -1)$

All of the above varieties of arithmetic and geometric series can be summed to any desired number of terms by substituting the relevant values for n, a, d and r in the above formulae, and in all cases it can be seen that the larger the number of terms summed, the greater the sum to n terms will be. Clearly the sum to n terms can increase without limit as n is increased without limit. Archimedes, however, appears to have been the first mathematician to realise that this is not the case for geometric series with common factors, $r < 1$. When r is < 1, rS_n is $< S_n$ and so it is appropriate to carry out the above subtraction to give:

$$S_n - rS_n = a - ar^n$$

or $\quad\quad\quad\quad\quad$ $S_n = a (1 - r^n)/ (1 - r)$

When this formula is applied to sum the following series $\frac{1}{2} + \frac{1}{4} + 1/8 + 1/16 + 1/32 \ldots$ where $r = \frac{1}{2}$, it is found that as n is increased, S_n approaches the upper limit value of 1, because $r < 1$ makes smaller and smaller contributions to the total sum of the members as n increases. In other words, r^n tends to zero as n tends to infinity and so S_n tends to the value $\frac{1}{2} (1)/ \frac{1}{2} = 1$. At first sight it is surprising to realise that the infinite addition of a series of members does not yield an infinite sum, even if the individual members are becoming progressively smaller and smaller. But the above analysis shows that this is indeed the case for geometric series with common factors less than 1, and we can see how this mathematical analysis resolves Zeno's paradox of Achilles and the tortoise (c.f. Sections 3.1.2 and 10.2). It is also instructive to note that if a quantity to be determined can be expressed as a limiting series, then the accuracy of the determination can be controlled by choosing the number of terms to be summed. If we add the first five terms of the series $\frac{1}{2} + \frac{1}{4} + $ *etc.*, the sum is 0.96875 which is close to 1 to within about 3%. If we sum the first ten terms we obtain the result 0.9990234375 which is only out by about 0.1% (c.f. Section 5.4.1).

We saw earlier that the Greeks had enough alphabetic letters to write numbers up to 800 in our notation beyond which they had to apply ticks to these letters to denote higher decimal orders. However, in his *Sand Reckoner* Archimedes proposed that high numbers could be represented by multiples of powers of ten, and that if the natural number series were coupled with any simple geometric series, thus:

$$1 \quad 2 \quad 3 \quad 4 \quad 5 \quad 6 \quad 7 \quad 8 \quad 9 \quad 10$$

and $\quad\quad\quad\quad$ $2 \quad 4 \quad 8 \quad 16 \quad 32 \quad 64 \quad 128 \quad 256 \quad 512 \quad 1024$

then multiplication of any two numbers on the bottom series is achieved simply by adding the corresponding numbers on the upper series and reading off the number on the bottom series which corresponds to that sum on the top series. Thus to multiply 16 by 32, add $4 + 5 = 9$ and then read off the answer, 512 opposite the 9 on the upper series. This is multiplication by adding powers because 16 is 2 to the power 4 and 32 is 2 to the power 5. In modern algebraic notation we write $a^m \times a^n = a^{m+n}$. This is the basis of logarithms, but Archimedes did not go on to create tables of logarithms (c.f. Section 6.2.3). The difficulties of handling the number notation were so great, however, that any means of breaking the problem down to simpler steps was helpful. Thus, for the extraction of roots, large numbers were factorised to provide smaller numbers, the roots of which were more readily accessible. It was noted that √ab = √a x √b and so √64 is √4 x √16 = 2 x 4 = 8, and √6 = √2 x √3. In fact, when we know the value of √2 and √3 we can compute, by factorisation, the root of any number divisible by 2 or 3. Similarly, if we also know √5 we can get the square roots of all numbers formed by multiplying fives with twos and threes. A similar approach may be taken to fractions where √a/b = √a/√b.

It has already been mentioned that the Pythagoreans were aware that the square of the sum of two numbers is equal to the sum of their individual squares plus twice their product. This can be demonstrated by dissecting a square into two smaller squares at a pair of diagonally opposed corners and of side lengths a and b, such that the side-length of the original square is (a + b), and observing that the remaining area of the original square has thus been divided equally into two rectangles of side lengths a and b. In this way, it can be seen that $(a + b)^2$ is the area of the original square, as is $a^2 + 2ab + b^2$ and therefore:
$$(a + b)^2 = a^2 + 2ab + b^2$$

This relationship establishes that the general procedure for multiplying factors of the form (a + b)(a + b) is to multiply the terms in the second bracket by the first term of the first to get $a^2 + ab$, followed by the second term of the first bracket to get $ab + b^2$ and then to add. It also enables large numbers to be broken down to ease computation. By way of example, 7 can be broken down to 3 + 4, so that 7^2 can be written as $(3 + 4)^2$, and thus computed as $3^2 + 2(3 \times 4) + 4^2$.

The square can be treated in more ways than this, however. If the above dissection is repeated and one of the squares (now of side y) is subtracted from the whole square of side length x, then the difference equates to the second square plus one of the rectangles of area x (x - y) and the second rectangle of area y (x - y). In this way it can be seen that:
$$x^2 - y^2 = x (x - y) + y (x - y)$$
$$= (x + y) (x - y)$$
This relationship also facilitates computation.

Thus for example, $7^2 - 4^2 = (7 + 4)(7 - 4) = 11 \times 3 = 33$. Again to multiply 37 x 25 we find the arithmetic mean, 31 and then write $(31 + 6)(31 - 6) = 31^2 - 6^2 = 925$. Thus to multiply, all that is necessary is to look up the squares of 31 and of 6 in the tables of squares which were prepared by means of the counting frame and abacus to facilitate such computation, one such table having been found at Nippur (c. 2,000 BC).

These relationships show also that the multiplication of two positive quantities gives a positive result, while multiplication of a positive and a negative gives a negative result. However, Diophantus took matters further by dissecting a rectangle into four rectangles by dividing side a into lengths b and (a - b) and side c into lengths d and (c - d). By joining these points of division by lines drawn parallel to the sides of the rectangle he produced four rectangles of areas b(c-d), (a - b)(c-d), bd, and d(a - b). Since these four rectangles added together are equal in area to the original rectangle of area ac, it follows that:

(a - b)(c - d) + b(c - d) + bd + d(a - b) = ac

therefore (a - b)(c - d) + bc - bd + bd + ad - db = ac

therefore (a - b)(c - d) = bc + ad - bd = ac

subtracting bc and ad from, and adding bd to, both sides of the equation gives

(a - b)(c - d) = ac - ad - bc + bd

This expression now shows that multiplication of two negative quantities gives a positive result and we can now express the rule of signs in the form that multiplication of like signs gives a positive result and that of unlike signs gives a negative result. This new expression provides another simplification the computational task. If it is required to multiply 19 by 28 we can write these numbers in the form (20 - 1) and (30 - 2) and multiply by writing 20 x 30 - 20 x 2 - 30 x 1 + 2 x 1 which is 600 - 40 - 30 + 2 or 532.

Theon (c. 350 AD) prepared multiplication tables to facilitate computation, and he used the relationship

$$(a + b)^2 = a^2 + 2ab + b^2$$

to determine square roots by letting the side of one of the pair of diagonally opposed squares resulting from the dissection of the original square, increase to a value, x, close to that of the original square while that of the other, dx, becomes correspondingly very small. We may then write the above equation as :

$$(x + dx)^2 = x^2 + 2x(dx) + (dx)^2$$

or $\qquad (x + dx)^2 - x^2 = 2x(dx)$ because $(dx)^2$ is very small compared to $2x(dx)$

or $\qquad dx = ((x + dx)^2 - x^2) / 2x$

We now estimate that $\sqrt{2}$ will be a little more than 1.4. Therefore we can say that:

$$(1.4 + dx)^2 = 2$$

and that: $\qquad dx = ((1.4 + dx)^2 - (1.4)^2) / 2(1.4) = (2 - 1.96)/ 2.8 = 0.014$

and thus that $\qquad (1.4 + 0.014)^2 = 2$

or that $\qquad 1.414 = \sqrt{2}$ (approximately)

We can of course re-iterate the process with $(1.414 + dx)^2 = 2$ which gives the more accurate result that $\sqrt{2} = 1.4142$. Theon's method for the accurate determination of square roots and that of Archimedes for the determination of π, are precursors of Newton's calculus (c.f. Section 6.3.7); but with Diaphantus and Theon classical mathematics had reached its limit given the difficulties of its numerical notation.

However, before moving on to the successor Hindu mathematicians (c.f. Section 5.2.2) I will say a word or two more about the Pythagoreans, and about early Chinese mathematicians. Though these groups made very significant contributions to the development of mathematics, the former as already noted were much given to speculation on the significance of numbers beyond their quantification role. For example they noted that the numbers 3, 5, 7, 9. . . were odd and distinguishable from the even numbers 2, 4, 6, 8 . . ., which were divisible by 2, but they went on to say that odd numbers were female, that the even were male, and that the non-prime odd numbers were effeminate. This adds nothing to their mathematical meaning, but it does open the door to all sorts of empty speculation. Thus for example, the prime number 3, together with the even number 2, made the number 5 stand for marriage or fertile union in Pythagorean mysticism. Though such attributions are meaningless, they are all too easily believed to reveal deep meanings from the Beyond, not otherwise accessible to the human brain.

Again, with respect to their triangular numbers, so-called because they could be represented as triangles by arranging the corresponding number as rows of beads each having one more bead than the preceding row, such being the numbers 1, 3, 6, 10, 15, 21, 28 36 . . . , they further noted that adding any two successive numbers in the triangular number series gives a square number consisting of an equal number of beads in rows and columns, the square numbers being 1, 4, 9, 16, 25, 36, 49 . . . , and they proceeded to note that these arrangements of beads would give five-sided figures if square and triangular numbers were combined. Thus they identified 1, 5, 12, 22, 35 . . . as pentagonal numbers, being successively 1, (4 + 1), (9 +3), (16 +6), (25 +10) . . . Then came the hexagonal numbers 1, 7, 19, 37 . . , for which the beads can be arranged in rows as follows (2,3,2), (3,4,5,4,3), (4,5,6,7,6,5,4) . . ; and stellate numbers 1, 8, 21, 40 . . for which the beads are arranged in successive squares, to the four sides of which, the successive triangular numbers are attached thus (4+ 4x1), (9 + 4x3), (16 + 4x6) . . . These activities were not entirely frivolous, however, because series are of significance in mathematics.

In obtaining expressions for the sum to n terms, S_n for the arithmetic and geometric series discussed above, it was necessary to write down an expression for the nth term, T_n in order to proceed. In these cases, this was straight forward because these series were defined by the common difference and common factor respectively. However, with a little more thought it can be seen that any term in the series of triangular numbers is given by noting its numerical position and multiplying it by half the numerical position of the next term. Thus the value of the nth term for the series of triangular numbers is given as: $T_n = n(n + 1)/2$ and for the series of square numbers as $T_n = n^2$. Alternatively, since the square numbers are the combination of the nth term and the $(n - 1)^{th}$ of the triangle number series, it follows that for the square numbers $T_n = n(n + 1)/2 + (n - 1)n/2$, or $T_n = n/2(n + 1 + n - 1)$ or $T_n = n^2$. Similarly the pentagonal series is constructed by combining the $(n - 1)^{th}$ term of the triangular number series with n^{th} term of the square number series, and so $T_n = n/2(n - 1) + n^2$ or $T_n = n/2(n - 1) + n/2(2n)$ or $T_n = n/2(3n - 1)$.

Thus we see that some of the mystically inspired number-related activities of the Pythagoreans, extended knowledge of series and how to handle them to the general benefit of mathematics. On the other hand some of their mystic lore was quite useless. Thus, with the letters of the alphabet being used to represent numbers, those so inclined could attribute value to words by reading their letters as numbers and thus, for example, demonstrate the superiority of Achilles over Hector by noting that the letters which spelled Achilles could be read as 1,276, whereas those of Hector indicated the smaller value of 1,225. We need not delve further than to note that such practices continued into the middle ages in ever extending ways and have their adherents even today; and that even the best brains have the capacity to become misled, when they leave reality for unreality and prefer belief to knowledge.

Now, the Chinese *Book of Permutations* of around 1000 BC shows the same sort of influences in that it classifies the odd and even numbers as male and female respectively, associates them with objects such as sky, earth, fire, water *etc*, and deals with magic squares and puzzles, but among the latter it also considers the number of ways of making choices from a range of options. This is the branch of mathematics which deals with permutations and combinations. The underlying principle can be illustrated by considering how many ways there are of entering a room by one door and leaving by another, if there are three doors available. It can be seen that for each of the three ways of entering there are two ways of leaving, and so there are 3 x 2 ways of entering and leaving. This leads to the general statement that if one operation can be performed in m ways and if in every case a second operation can be performed in n different ways, the two operations can be performed in succession in m x n different ways. If the symbol ^nC_r denotes the number of combinations of n different things r at a time, that is, the number of ways in which r things (r < or = n) may be selected from n different things without regard to arrangement; and if ^nP_r denotes the number of permutations of n different things r at a time, that is, the number of ways in which r things (r < or = n) may be selected from n different things and arranged among themselves, then the principles involved can be further illustrated by consideration of a more specific example. Thus, the combinations of the four letters a, b, c, d, two at a time are:

ab,   ac,   ad,   bc,   bd,   cd so that $^4C_2 = 6$,

and the permutations of the same four letters two at a time are:

ab,   ac,   ad,   bc,   bd,   cd,
ba,   ca,   da,   cb,   db,   dc so that $^4P_2 = 12$

We now have to evaluate ^nP_r in general. To do this we consider the order in which r things are placed to be the order of their selection from n given things. We can see that the first place can be filled in n ways and that once this place has been filled there remain n -1 things and so there are n - 1 different ways of filling the second place. Thus, each way of filling the first place leads to (n

- 1) ways of filling the second. Hence the n ways of filling the first give n (n -1) ways of filling the first two together (c.f. the example of ways of entering and leaving the room). Similarly with each of the ways of filling the first two places there are n - 2 ways of filling the third, so that the first three places may be filled in n (n -1)(n - 2) ways. Proceeding thus and noticing that the number of factors is always the same as the number of places filled, we see that the number of ways in which r places may be filled is n (n - 1)(n - 2) . . . to r factors, and that therefore: $^{n}P_{r} = n(n - 1)(n - 2) . . . (n - r +1)$ so that, for example, $^{10}P_{4} = 10 \times 9 \times 8 \times 7 = 5040$, which means that there are 5040 ordered ways of selecting 4 things from 10 things.

   We now have to evaluate $^{n}C_{r}$ in general. This is done by considering the number of ways in which r things my be selected from n different things, without regard to arrangement. In each of these selections the r things may be arranged among themselves in $^{r}P_{r}$ ways. Therefore the number of ways in which we may select r things from n things and arrange them among themselves is $^{n}C_{r}$ x $^{r}P_{r}$. This is also the number of permutations of n things r at a time.

Therefore: $\qquad\qquad\qquad$ $^{n}C_{r} \times {}^{r}P_{r} = {}^{n}P_{r}$

but $\qquad\qquad\qquad\qquad$ $^{n}P_{r} = n (n - 1)(n - 2) . . . (n - r + 1)$

and therefore $\qquad\qquad$ $^{r}P_{r} = n (n - 1)(n - 2) . . . 3.2.1$

Hence $\qquad\qquad\qquad$ $^{n}C_{r} = \{n (n - 1)(n - 2) . . . (n -r + 1)\} / 1.2.3 . . . r$

so that, for example, $^{10}C_{4} = 10.9.8.7/1.2.3.4 = 210$ which means there are 210 ways in which 4 things may be selected from 10 without regard to arrangement.

   The product of the first n natural numbers, n (n - 1)(n - 2) . . . 3. 2. 1, is called 'factorial n' and is denoted by n! It gives rise to the series 1, 2, 6, 24, 120 . . . , which was known to Euclid who used it in connection with prime numbers, but our interest here is that factorial notation can be used to simplify the above expressions. Thus:

$^{n}P_{r}$ = n (n - 1)(n - 2) . . . (n - r +1)

$\quad$ = {n (n - 1)(n - 2) . . . (n - r +1).(n - r)(n - r - 1) . . . 3.2.1} / {(n - r)(n - r - 1) . . .3.2.1

$\quad$ = n! / (n - r)!

$^{n}C_{r}$ = {n (n - 1)(n - 1). . . (n - r + 1)} {(n - r)(n - r - 1) . . .3.2.1} / {(1.2.3. . . .r)} {(n - r)(n - r - 1) . . .3.2.1}

$\quad$ = n! / {r! (n -r)!}

and we can see, by substituting 2 for r in the above expression, or by inspection as exemplified previously, that the number of ways of selecting a combination of two items from a group of n different items as n increases, $^{n}C_{2}$, is one when n is 2, is three when n is 3, is six when n is 4 and is ten when n is 5. When these results for $^{n}C_{2}$ are tabulated thus:

$^{2}C_{2}$	$^{3}C_{2}$	$^{4}C_{2}$	$^{5}C_{2}$	. . .
1	3	6	10	. . .

we see that 1, 3, 6, 10 . . . is the series of Pythagorean triangular numbers introduced above. When r is 3 the corresponding series is 1, 4, 10, 20 . . . ; when r is 4 the series is 1, 5, 15, 25. . . and when r is 5 the series is 1, 6, 21, 56 . . . ; and so on. These are all triangular number series. Their relationship one to another is revealed by expanding their successive terms to show that each successive series is built on the previous one. The series for r = 3, may be written as 1, (1 +3), (1 + 3 + 6) . . ; for r =4 as 1, (1 + 4), (1 + 4 + 10) . . ; for r = 5 as 1, (1 + 5), (1 +5 + 15) . . . It will be seen that the series in brackets in each case is the preceding series.

   It will be recalled that various plane figures were laid out using beads for the triangular, pentagonal, hexagonal and stellate number series. It may also be noted that solid figures can be visualised by choosing a member of the second triangular series, say 20 and then adding layers of beads in numbers corresponding to successively lower members of the series , 10, 6, 3, 1, to form a three-sided pyramid (tetrahedron). Similarly, with the series of squares starting with any member say, 16 and adding the diminishing series, 9, 4, 1, a pyramid with a square base can be visualised.
102

Regular polyhedra, such as could circumscribe a sphere, or be inscribed by it, can also be visualised by fitting these pyramids together with their faces in contact.

In introducing this review of mathematics to the point now reached, I noted that the Greeks concentrated on geometry because of the inadequacies of their numerical notation; that they nonetheless introduced numbers to geometry to produce quantitative trigonometry; and that they derived the beginnings of algebra from geometry in order to facilitate arithmetical computation. Thus, it may be concluded that all of these mathematical developments were achieved by the application of rational thought to abstractions from reality to the satisfaction of practical need in a manner parallel to that which produced craftsmanship; that some of the motivation for the development of mathematics was the pursuit of "art for art's sake" in appreciation of form, structure and interrelationships of numbers; that this is reminiscent of the craftsman's pursuit of emotional satisfaction in decoration and ornamentation; and that such is taken by some as an intimation of deeper meaning and significance, not otherwise accessible to humanity. Again, while it is possible to be transported to unproductive and sterile by-ways as were the Pythagoreans and some Chinese mathematicians by such emotional considerations, these stimulate the search for further relationships within mathematics itself, which in turn reveal means to satisfy as yet unrecognised mathematical needs in the pursuit of further understanding of reality (c.f. Chapters 6 - 9). However, it has to be concluded that no set of consecutive equations produces any new knowledge. At every stage one thing is said to be another by being equal to it. Thus, in mathematical reasoning, it should be seen that an initial statement (proposition) is progressively rearranged through a series of equivalent statements until that of maximum utility for practical purposes is reached in conclusion; and that in philosophical and religious reasoning no such useful conclusion can be reached when neither the premise nor the conclusion can be reality-evaluated (c.f. Chapters 10 and 11).

Having previously concluded that mathematics could not progress further because of number system difficulties, that the advance of knowledge beyond craftsmanship and direct observation was prevented by belief in essences and spirits, and that religious beliefs intertwined with those of socio-politics had destroyed the Roman Empire (c.f. Sections 3.1.4 and 4.1), I now review the survival of craftsmanship and the development of craft-like knowledge through the Dark Ages to its European Renaissance.

CHAPTER 5: THE MIDDLE AGES (AD 400-1400)

In the west the millennium from 400 and 1400 is referred to as the Dark Ages, though this term is often restricted to the period 400-1100 because classical texts in Latin translations from the Arabic became increasingly available in the period 1100-1300 while the development of western *Humanism* is discernible from about 1250 onwards. These Dark Ages resulted from the social disruption of the western Roman Empire which arose from internal conflict between orthodoxy and heresy and from incursions of heretical Vandals, Goths and Visigoths. As to Britain, the consequent withdrawal of the legions permitted the eastern half of the country from the Channel to the Firth of Forth to be settled by the Angles, Saxons and Jutes during the fifth and sixth centuries. Thus, though the western regions held out for a time without Roman assistance, most of what is now known as England had fallen to the Germanic tribes by the end of the sixth century, with the tribal name Anglii being used by Pope Gregory (d. 604) to denote the newly mixed inhabitants of England irrespective of tribe.

Indeed, the Christian mission sent to England by Gregory in 597 found no indication of demarcation by tribe. Instead it found autonomous kingdoms which by the ninth century would come under the Imperium of King Egbert of the house of Wessex, later to be secured by King Alfred. Subsequently though Cornwall remained independent into the ninth century and Wales more or less held out till 1282, the English came under Norman rule in 1066. Nonetheless, before the end of the seventh century the Church of England had been established and before the end of the tenth, 'King's English' was in standard use for all vernacular writing, no other modern European state having reached full nationhood as early as England. Had this not occurred, the English language might not have survived the subsequent two hundred years of Norman French dominance which otherwise might have reduced England to the condition to which England later reduced Ireland, social cohesion having been the supreme determinant even under a conqueror, as it seems to have been earlier and elsewhere (c.f. Sections 2.5.3 and 2.5.4).

5. 1 EUROPE IN THE DARK AGE

Very little of the intellectual progress reviewed in Chapter 3 and Section 4.4 passed into Christian Europe. Of the works of Plato, only the *Timaeus* in the form of a third century Latin commentary did so to convey the belief that the universe (macrocosm) influences man (microcosm). Of Aristotle, only those on logic were carried forward as translated by Boethius (480-524) whose early death thwarted his expressed intention to translate all of them, though he did translate some Greek sources of elementary mathematics. In addition, Martianus Capella (c. 500) provided an elementary treatment of the seven "liberal arts" in the form of the trivium of grammar, dialectic and rhetoric and of the quadrivium of geometry, arithmetic, astronomy and music, all of which derived from the writings of Varro. Pliny's *Natural History* was also available as were a range of medical texts bearing the names Dioscorides, Hippocrates, Apuleius *et al* which had been translated from Greek to Latin between the fourth and sixth centuries.

In response to the texts then becoming available, Bishop Isidore of Seville (560-636) produced his *Etymology* of the terms used, disparaged 'superstitious' astrology, accepted 'natural' astrology as revealing the influence of the celestial bodies over plant, animal and human life, and advised physicians to study their influence on the humours of man. He, together with Bede (673-735) and Alcuin (735-804) in England and Rabanus Maurus (776-856) in Germany, borrowed each from his predecessor and all from Pliny to pass on what was then Dark Age knowledge and speculation. We may judge how much had been lost by noting that Gerbert (d. 1003) as Pope Sylvester II re-introduced the abacus, the use of which he had learned either in Spain where he had earlier studied or in southern Italy where he later visited the court of Otto II in 970, both these areas having come under eastern influence through Islam. However, he appears to have drawn his arithmetic and numerals directly from Boethius (c.f. Section 5. 5).

Apart from suffering from a paucity of cultural-sources in the three centuries following the removal of the last Roman Emperor in the west in 476, Europe was ravaged by endemic warfare as the descendents of various invaders of the former Empire sought to establish themselves. However, the fact that these contending local rulers were all Christian enabled the Papacy at Rome to achieve increasing influence initially through the early Frankish Merovingian Kings and later through a transfer of allegiance to Charles Martel and his grandson Charlemagne. The latter, crowned Emperor of the Romans by the Pope on Christmas Day 800, established a Frankish empire which stretched from the Ebro to the Elbe, south into Italy and through France to the Pyrenees. This unification was something of a renaissance, but it broke up in the ninth century when the Norsemen began raiding the coasts and penetrating the rivers of Europe through their developments in the shipbuilding craft. In due course these ship-borne raiders established the Duchy of Normandy, the State of Kiev, the colonisation of Greenland and the occupation of most of the British Isles. Again, the emerging German Empire defeated the advancing Magyars at Lechfeld in 955 while Christendom's first external military success with the First Crusade in the 1090's.

At this time the social structure was feudal, based on fealty in exchange for military and labour services and on the Church as a major land-owner having an interest in the development of agriculture and craftsmanship while controlling belief and being active against heretics. From about 1100 the Cistercians made significant contributions through clearing forests, rearing sheep and developing the wool industry, while in Italy increasing inter-town trade was laying the foundations of independent city states. Although the Latin texts referred to above were initially the sole source of ancient culture available in Europe, others gradually became available through contacts with Islamic regions to the south. In the meantime, scholars were beginning to leave the monasteries and cathedral schools for independent centres later to become universities, first at Paris, Bologna and Oxford, and there were about eighty such centres by 1410.

5. 2 CONTEMPORARY DEVELOPMENTS ELSEWHERE

Thus while some retentions of earlier culture are discernible in Dark Age Europe the developments which would significantly affect its future were occurring elsewhere.

5. 2. 1 The Middle East
As we have seen, Plato's Academy had been closed by the Christians in 529 with its incumbents migrating to Persia to pursue their interests. Even so, the Greek speaking world maintained a higher intellectual level than did the Latin though the pursuit of new knowledge was dead in both. However, the Byzantine Christian Empire included many Syriac speakers who by the third century had replaced the use of Greek in western Asia. Again, in the fifth century the heretical Nestorian Church persecuted by the Byzantines, became established in Mesopotamia and later moved to

south-west Persia. There, from the sixth century onwards, Nestorians were extremely active especially in Gondisapur, in producing Syriac translations of the works of Aristotle, Archimedes, Euclid, Hero, Galen, Hippocrates and Ptolemy.

However, in resuming the centuries-long conflict between Persia and Greece and Persia and Rome, the Emperor Chosroes II began a campaign in 607 which in ten years won him Syria and Egypt and though these were recovered by Heraclius the Eastern Roman Emperor in the ensuing six years with Chosroes being deposed and murdered by his own nobles in continuance of the usual cycling of fortunes, all was soon to be changed by developments in Arabia, a mainly desert region with little to attract a conqueror and with no previous ability to trouble Persia, Greece or Rome. Thus, little had been known other than that the spice and incense route from the Indian west coast through Sabaea on the Red Sea crossed Arabia *via* Medina and Petra to Syria and on to Europe; that Diaspora Jews were involved in this trade; that Arab religion was idol-worship with elements of Persian fire-worship, Judaism and Christianity; and that it was centred on Mecca where the Kaaba, had reputedly been a gift from God to Abraham of the *Old Testament*.

Be that as it may, in about 570, Mohammed had been born into the Koreishite clan, traditional guardians of the Kaaba, causing major changes to be set in train when he claimed that Judaism's Angel Gabriel had ordered him to preach a New Faith, Islam, the principal tenet of which is "there is one God, Allah, and Mohammed is His Prophet." Such a claim rendered him a heretic to the Koreishites and having attracted few followers he fled to Medina in 622 where his teaching and raiding of caravans empowered his return to Mecca as a conqueror in 630 with followers inspired to spread his message through the world by the sword. Though he was dead by 632, his followers proceeded to do just that. The Christian provinces of Syria quickly fell to Islam and in 642, the Caliph Omar entered Alexandria to complete the conquest of Egypt till then a province of the Christian Roman Empire centred on Constantinople. Again, the Persian Empire fell by the end of the decade and from Persia the Armies of Islam carried the New Faith to Central Asia. From Egypt they advanced along the Christianised coast of North Africa taking Carthage in 698, and crossing the Straits of Gibraltar in 711 they took Toledo the Visigoth Christian capital in 712 and the whole Iberian peninsula except for a northern coastal strip in less than 20 years. From there, they crossed the Pyrenees into the land of the Christian Franks where in 732, a century after the death of Mohammed, they were stopped by Charles Martel. They had also reached the Bosporus by 688, though Emperor Leo III was able to hold Constantinople. However, expansion continued to some extent, Sicily becoming a province of Islam in the late ninth century and remaining so for the next 200 years.

Within the conquered area Arabic became the official language, tribute being paid by those rejecting Islam the lives of whom were very much on sufferance, while Islamic practice was compulsory in Arabia. Nonetheless, Jewish and Christian communities continued to play leading roles in what became Muslim centres of learning. When the Caliph Omar entered Alexandria in 642, he reported the presence of 40,000 tax-paying Jews, 4000 villas, 400 pleasure parks and 4000 baths, the value of which encouraged adoption of an assimilative attitude and practice by the conquerors. When in 750, the Abbasid Dynasty established its 500 year rule in Baghdad, the most significant transmitters of Greek learning through Syriac into Arabic were the Bukht-Yishu (Jesus hath delivered) a family of Nestorian scholars whose activities continued through seven generations into the second half of the eleventh century. From about 750 to 850 translation was mainly from Greek to Syriac, while between 850 and 950 it was predominately from this to Arabic. Yuhanna ibn Masawiah (d. 857), a member of the Bukht-Yishu family and medical adviser to Harun al-Rashid the fifth Caliph, was an active translator into Arabic, later to be known in Latin translation as John Mesue. The seventh Caliph Al-Mamun (813-33) established a translation centre

106

and library of which Honain Ibn Ishaq another Nestorian was the leading figure, spending his life in Baghdad serving nine Caliphs. During this time, he translated into Arabic almost the complete corpus of Galenic writings, a number of astronomical and mathematical works and some Hippocratic writings, while making a start on Ptolemy's Almagest and on some works of Aristotle.

Baghdad replaced Gondisapur as the Caliphs and their nobles provided the means for Christian (Nestorian) scholars to travel in search of Greek manuscripts for translation. In this way, most of the Aristotelian writings were rendered into Arabic, including those on botany, mineralogy and mechanics. Many Greek alchemical works were also included, though it appears that many alchemical methods were of Persian origin. There was also contact with India from whence came the system of numeration later to be known as Arabic. In fact, when the Afghan ruler Mohammed of Gor established the Sultanate of Dehli towards the end of the 12th century, all Indian mathematics, craftsmanship and related knowledge came within the sphere of Islam. The geographer Ibn Batuta (c. 1305-) from the region which is now Morocco, spent eight years at the court in Dehli, travelled on an embassy to the Yuan Dynasty in China, to the Muslim trading posts in Ceylon and to the Sultanate of Achin in Sumatra. Closer to home, the Islamic Empire stretched from the Atlantic to India, incorporating that of Alexander and exceeding that of Rome.

5. 2. 2 India

The practice of using only ten symbols (one of which was *sunya*, meaning empty) to designate all numbers, was introduced by Hindu mathematicians sometime between 100 and 150 AD, but it is only with the *Lilavati* of Aryabhata around 470 AD that our knowledge of Hindu mathematics really begins. Therein, he presented the topics of calculation, series and equations; discussed the rules of arithmetic and used the rule of signs which we also have from Diophantus; and gave a table of sines at intervals of 3¾ degrees and π at 3.1416. Aryabhata was succeeded in the sixth century by Bramahgupta who again followed the themes of calculation, series and equations, progress now being greatly facilitated by the number notation which removed the difficulties inherent in those of Greece and Rome. By now, *sunya* had gone beyond designating an empty abacus wire to confer positional values on the other nine symbols by becoming the cipher which also designates zero, while the cipher laws on which arithmetic depends had been stated as

$$x \; 0 = 0, \; a + 0 = a, \text{ and } a - 0 = a.$$

For multiplication, reference was again made to the areas of rectangles in the manner of Diophantus. Thus, we see that the area of a rectangle of side-lengths a and b + c + d, is equal to the sum of its constituent rectangles of width a and lengths b, c and d respectively, and that therefore:

$$a \, (b + c + d) = ab + ac + ad$$

If we now recall that the Hindu order in which we write the modern version of the Hindu/Arabic numerals coincides with the columns of the abacus in which the right hand number-column represents units, the next to the left, tens, and so on for hundreds, thousands. . . millions, we see that we can dispense with the abacus and thus unconstrained by its physical dimensions, we can continue to write numerals further and further to the left to express numbers as large as we wish. Using these understandings we can, for example, multiply 321 by 4, by noting that this means 4 (300 + 20 +1) which by reference to the Diophantus equation above, is equal to 4 x 300 + 4 x 20 + 4 x 1 which can be written as:

$$321$$
$$\underline{4}$$
$$1200$$
$$80$$
$$\underline{4}$$
$$1284$$

Once this was known, it followed that numbers of any size could be multiplied using the 'carrying over' rule from one column to the next on the left, as for the abacus, thus:

$$456$$
$$\underline{321}$$

136800	*i.e.* 300 x 456
9120	*i.e.* 20 x 456
456	*i.e.* 1 x 456
146376	

It is of course, possible to arrive at the result of multiplying 321 x 4 by adding 321 + 321 + 321 + 321. However, for multiplication of two large numbers the operation of multiplication, once known and applied by learning the tables up to 10 x 10, or up to 12 x 12, is clearly very much quicker and much less demanding than learning the multiplication tables on the Greek system (c.f. 2.3.3 and 4.4)

Division, being the reverse of multiplication, is the determination of the number of times one number can be subtracted from another and this is equivalent to the number of times it is contained in the other. This can be determined by the example of dividing 321 into 146376, set out in the form first used by Calandri in 1491 and now familiar in modern times, thus:

```
321 )146376( 456
      1284   taking away 4 times 321
      1797
      1605   taking away 5 times 321
      1926
      1926   taking away 6 times 321
```

In this case there is no remainder, R. Had there been, it would have been the fraction $R / 321$ or later the decimal by continuing the above process by bringing down any numerals or zeros to the right of the decimal point until there is no remainder or until terminated when the desired number of significant decimal figures has been generated.. Early Hindu mathematicians were writing and using fractions as we do, except for the division-bar which was introduced later. We have already seen that to multiply fractions the numerators and denominators are separately multiplied together. Around 850 AD, Mahavira propounded the rule that for division of one fraction by another, the divisor is inverted and multiplied.

The main point to note here is that once the Hindus had adopted their numeral notation from 1 to 9 and their position-value system by their recognition and notation of 0, arithmetical computation for commercial purposes became relatively simple and rapid while the relationship of one number to another became more readily graspable. This in turn enabled such numerical relationships as those which we have already met in surveying and astronomy to be expressed as equations, the solution of which enabled unknown values to be deduced from known ones far more readily than ever before. It also encouraged the development of mathematics for its own sake *i.e.* before the need to solve future practical problems had become apparent. As far as equations are concerned, the Hindus went further than Diophantus in showing how to transpose verbal statements into expressed relationships between known and unknown quantities, and in identifying rules
108

whereby these equations may be operated upon to express the unknown in terms of the known and thus to determine the value of the unknown which otherwise would not be accessible.

Thus, for example, if one number is stated to be four times another and the two add up to 35 we can write the equations of these relationships in terms of what is known and what is unknown as $a = 4b$ and $a + b = 35$, from which we can operate to substitute $4b$ from the first equation for a in the second to re-write it as $4b + b = 35$, from which it follows that $5b = 35$, $b = 7$, and $a = 28$. In general, the equation may be thought of as a balance and the operating rules as requiring whatever is done to one side of the equation to be done to the other to maintain this balance while operating to isolate on the left hand side of the equals sign, the symbol representing the unknown and to isolate what is known on the right and thus to evaluate the unknown. Thus, if we add, subtract, multiply or divide on one side we must do the same on the other as we move towards determining the unknown, which is to say, solving the equation (c.f. Section 5.4.1).

5. 2. 3 China

Although their writing was enormously complicated in requiring some 10,000 characters, the Chinese had adopted (early centuries AD) a relatively simple hieroglyph (matchstick) notation for their number system, and we have already discussed some of their mathematical achievements. Nonetheless, in keeping with all save the Hindus, they failed to introduce a position-value system based on a notation for zero. Nonetheless, the T'ang Dynasty (618-960) after a period of turmoil, re-established central control in China and began to develop internal trade through a civil service the members of which were selected by competitive examination, and through an immense canal-building programme (c.f. 2.3.5). Though their western expansion was halted by Islamic forces in central Asia at the Battle of the Talas River, they extended their influence to the south in trade with India.

Under the T'ang, and its successor Sung Dynasty (960-1279) tea and cotton cultivation had become major industries, mechanical clocks appeared around 700, paddle-boats by 800, wood-block printing around 800, movable clay-type around 1000 and movable wooden-type by 1300, while a paper factory based on Chinese methods was established at Muslim Samarkand in 751. In addition, Sung ships were using the magnetic compass by 1100, Sung armies were equipped with gun-powder explosives before 1200 and with canon by 1300. Again, when the Mongol successors of Genghis Khan, having previously pacified the peoples of the Asiatic Steppe, displaced the Sung and established the Yuan Dynasty at Cambuluc (Beijing) they enabled European travellers such as Marco Polo and Islamic travellers such as Ibn Batuta, to visit China. Thus, though trade with India was well established and contact had been made from further west, China was found to be developing craftsmanship and engaging in large-scale organisation rather than attempting to achieve deeper understanding, and when the native Chinese Ming Dynasty took over in the 1360s it turned in on itself. By then however, all of the above developments in craftsmanship had become known to the west as reviewed in Section 5.7.

5. 3 THE BRIDGE THAT WAS ISLAM

It is clear that an Islam sympathetic to the knowledge available within its conquest-expanded borders was well placed to collect and assimilate it, to contribute to its development and extend its areas of application, and to act as a bridge for its dissemination to regions which had lost contact with it for any reason or had never been aware of it. As we have seen, the very substantial advances made by the Greeks were actively collected and assimilated through translation in

Gondisapur and later in Damascus and Baghdad, while by the ninth century there is no doubt that Hindu mathematics and craftsmanship were available in Arabic through substantial commercial contacts with India and while similar contacts with China afforded yet further opportunities to collect and assimilate yet more mathematics and craft related knowledge.

That Muslims recognised the dearth of Arabian achievement and the plenitude of achievement elsewhere, is illustrated by the ninth century scholar, Abu al-Hasan Tabith who wrote: "who made the world to be inhabited and flooded it with cities . . . who has constructed harbours and conserved rivers . . . made manifest the hidden knowledge . . . made to arise the medicine for bodies . . . filled the world with the correctness of modes of life and with the wisdom which is the head of excellence . . . except the good men and kings of heathenism. Without these products of heathenism the world would be an empty and a needy place and it would have been enveloped in sheer want and misery." In the following sections we will look in more detail at the subsequent contributions made to mathematics, astronomy, physics, alchemy, and medicine within the Islamic world up to and through its Golden Age in the tenth and eleventh centuries. In doing so, we will also see that "the inheritors of the heathenism which is honoured gloriously in this world" (Abu Al-Hasan Tabith) were not content simply to accept earlier knowledge but were willing and able to build on it through reality-evaluation of their own hypotheses, irrespective of which religion they professed. This further advance should not surprise us, however, these peoples having previously made progress under all manner of socio-political control (c.f. Section 2.5.3 and 2.5.4) and having been stopped only by the inadequacies of their earlier number notation. Thus we may conclude that the prospect of new knowledge inspires its pursuit so long as religious/secular believers do not actively oppose it.

Thus, Ibn al-Nafis noted that the blood passed through the lungs and not between the chambers of the heart as Galen had believed. Again, Rhazes and Avicenna also improved on Galen while Rhazes exposed Aristotle to critical comment and improved on his own immediate predecessor Geber. In addition, just as Neo-Platonism had been incorporated within Christianity, so also had Plato's Good, Aristotle's Unmoved Mover, and Plotinus's One been incorporated in attempts to define the nature of Allah. But, alas, strains developed within Islam and heresies began to be detected as had been the case within Christianity. Thus, several sects adhering to Epicureanism and to the atomic conjecture of Democritus, both abhorrent to Aristotelian and Muslim orthodoxy, were established in Mesopotamia though as within Christianity the unorthodox were vanquished by the orthodox in the ensuing struggle for socio-political supremacy. One of these sects, the Brethern of Purity (founded c. 980) produced an encyclopaedia consisting of fifty-two treatises, seventeen of which dealt with the elemental essences, minerals, earthquakes, tides and movement of the celestial bodies. Though this was burned as heretical by the orthodox authorities in Baghdad, it nonetheless reached Spain from whence with other Arab-source material it reached Europe.

Before this stage was reached, however, the knowledge newly accumulated in eastern Islam had been transferred to the west under the Caliphs Ibn ar Rahman III and Al-Hakam II of Cordova where a library and academy were established in 970 to be followed by similar establishments at Toledo and elsewhere. It was, thus through Spain that such western Christians as Gerbert, later Pope Sylvester II, (died 1003) made contact with this eastern knowledge, direct contact with the then debased culture of Christian Byzantium being very limited. However, the west also accessed classical Greek sources from Islamic North Africa through Saracen conquest of Sicily and southern Italy in the eighth century until its Norman displacement in the eleventh. Thus, Salerno on the Gulf of Naples was a notable contact point through its Greek speaking and Jewish communities, the latter having their own direct contacts with the east. Full western benefit from such contacts, however, required translation from Greek or Arabic to Latin and this presented difficulties. The Byzantine Greek to Latin route was difficult because the classical Greek of Aristotle was incomprehensible even to the monastic guardians of his manuscripts and their interests were theological and antagonistic to Greek philosophy as directed to the natural world. Again, while educated Arab speakers of the eleventh century could speak and write classical Arabic, there was little incentive for Muslims to translate Arab texts in either language into Latin, and Arabic was very difficult for Europeans to learn for their own use. The idiom was very different, grammars and dictionaries were unavailable and teachers were hard to find. The only real option was to spend a number of years in an Arab speaking country to learn the language, the technical vocabulary and sufficient knowledge of the subject matter to permit translation of Arab texts with any degree of success. However, it appears that the necessary knowledge was not acquired by western Christians before the late twelvth century at the earliest.

Nonetheless, the northern strip of the Iberian Peninsula, comprising the small kingdoms of Leon, Navarre and Aragon, had remained part of the Latin world and it was southwards from this northern border that Islamic dominance relaxed soonest. Thus, by the early eleventh century the people of Toledo in central Spain, though speaking Arabic, were mainly Christian with a strong Jewish element, and when Alphonso VI of Leon supported by El Cid captured Toledo in 1088, a large Arab speaking population chose to remain in place and Toledo became a major centre for the translation of Arab texts into Latin. Christian intellectual activity being still at a low ebb, however, these translations were undertaken by Jews who had the added advantage of a natural familiarity with Arabic. Among such, the most distinguished were Solomon ibn Gabirol (1021-58?) of Saragosa and Moses ben Maimon (1135-1204) better known as Mamonides of Cordova, the latter city being retaken for Christendom in 1236.

Yet, there were some non-native speakers of Arabic among its translators into Latin. Such were Adelard of Bath (c. 1090-1150) who had spent time in Spain and the Sicilies, Robert of Chester (c. 1110-c. 1160) who lived in northern Spain between 1141-7 and was the first to translate the *Koran*, John of Seville (active 1139-1155) a converted Jew whose translations greatly influenced Roger Bacon, and Gerald of Cremona (1114-1187) who spent many years in Toledo where he was taught Arabic by a native Christian and went on to translate into Latin ninety-two Arabic texts many of great length and significance. Another translator was Michael the Scot (c. 1175-1235) who having visited Toledo, stayed also at Padua, Bologna (1220) and Rome (1224-7) before dieing in the sevice of Frederik II. Translators from Arabic to Latin on the Sicilian route though fewer, include Constantine, the African (1017-87) who took up residence in Salerno around 1070, the Sicilian Admiral Eugenius of Palermo who also translated from Greek and Moses Farachi (d. 1285).

5. 4 DEVELOPMENT OF KNOWLEDGE WITHIN ISLAM

Having introduced the Islamic Bridge prior to reviewing its transmission of knowledge in Section 5.5, I now review the development of classical knowledge and speculation under Islam, treating eastern and western Islam separately and in the order of mathematics, astronomy, physics, alchemy and medicine.

5. 4. 1 Mathematics
It is difficult to date the introduction of the Hindu numerical notation and position-value system based on the use of zero. Nonetheless, we find it in the *Arithmetic* of the Persian Al-Kwarismi (c.

830), from whence it is now referred to as the 'Arabic' system. In addition, Al-Kwarismi's *Algebra* is the first work in which the word 'algebra' meaning 'restoration' is used to denote the transposition of a term from one side of an equation to the other with a change of sign from positive to negative or *vice versa* to maintain (restore) the equality, this being equivalent to the same amount being added to or subtracted from both sides of the equation. He also introduced al muqabalah, to denote the collection of like terms as for example when we have: $a + 2a = x + 4x - 3x$, we may collect terms to give: $3a = 2x$.

In what follows, readers should recall that mathematics is a method of reasoning (of logic) in which no new knowledge is produced. Each equation in the sequence of equations is a statement that the left and right hand sides are equal *i.e.* the one is the other and that the changes wrought to reach the useful conclusion which is the object of the process, are restatements of the initial statement. Thus, Al-Kwarismi showed how to determine the value of an unknown when it appears as a square in an equation, an example of which he gives as $x^2 + 10x = 39$. To start he adopted the geometric approach of drawing a square of side-length x units, and attaching to each of two of the sides a rectangle of width x units and of length 5 units to form an L-shaped figure, the total area of which is:

$$x^2 + 5x + 5x, \text{ or, by collection of like terms, } x^2 + 10x$$

He now completed the large square, of side-length $(x + 5)$ units, by inserting a smaller square of side-length 5 units, within the L-shaped figure, and we see that:

$$x^2 + 10x + 25 = (x + 5)^2$$

We know also, because the initial equation tells us so, that

$$x^2 + 10x = 39$$

Thus adding the 25 to both sides gives $x + 10x + 25 = 39 + 25 = 64$

which can be re-written $(x + 5)^2 = 8^2$

and we see that $x + 5 = 8$

and so, transposing and changing sign gives $x = 8 - 5$ *i.e.* removing 5 from both sides

from which we see that $x = 3$

As we have seen, the *Lilavati* of Aryabhata owes much to Diophantus and we now see that al-Kwarismi relies ultimately on him also. Al-Kwarismi notes, however, that the 25 which is added to both sides of the initial equation is the square of half of the 10 (the coefficient) by which x is multiplied in this initial equation, and he goes on to generalise his method for finding the value of x in such quadratic equations in stating that one adds the square of half the coefficient of x to both sides of the initial equation and then proceeds to solve for x by taking square roots. According to the rule of signs of Diophantus, however, the square root of 64 is not just +8, but also -8, because like-signs multiplied together always give a positive result. Thus, there are two solutions to the above equation, namely $x = 3$ and $x = -13$, because the equation $x + 5 = 8$, may also be written $x + 5 = -8$ which on transposing, gives $x = -8 - 5 = -13$.

Al-Kwarismi's Rule for solution of equations of the general form:

$$x^2 + bx = c$$

may be derived by adding the square of half the coefficient of x to both sides of the equation to complete the square thus: $x^2 + bx + b^2/4 = c + b^2/4$

which may then be written: $(x + b/2)^2 = c + b^2/4$

giving: $x + b/2 = + \text{ or } -\sqrt{\{c + b^2/4\}}$

from which, transposing and changing sign, gives the solution:

$$x = + \text{ or } -\sqrt{\{c + b^2/4\}} - b/2$$

Thus we can now solve all equations of the form: $x^2 + bx = c$, by substituting the specific values of

112

c and b in the above equation. Al-Karismi's rule may also be applied when the coefficient of x^2 is other than unity, in which case the general expression for the quadratic equation may be written:

$$ax^2 + bx + c = 0$$

Now, if we divide both sides by a, we have the above in its initial form:

$$x^2 + bx/a = - c/a$$

and we may now make the appropriate substitutions in the above equation for the determination of x, when the coefficient of x^2 is *one;* or we may go through the exercise of completing the square, taking square roots on both sides and transposing, to arrive at the general solution of the quadratic equation when the coefficient of x^2 has the value a, rather than *one*, namely:

$$x = \{-b \pm \sqrt{(b^2 - 4ac)}\} / 2a$$

However, Al-Kwarismi and his contemporaries were puzzled to find that with equations for which $4ac > b^2$ they were faced with the square roots of negative numbers, knowing that there is no number either negative or positive which multiplied by itself gives a negative result, like signs always giving a positive result according to the rule of Diophantus. Consequently, the square roots of negative numbers came to be referred to as imaginary numbers (c.f. Section 6.2.3)

The ease with which the Hindu number system could reveal number relationships, caused both the Hindus and their Muslim followers to re-visit ancient Chinese number lore of the type which so much caught the fancy of the Pythagoreans. Thus, Aryabhata gave rules for finding the sums of various number series such as the sums of the natural numbers and of their squares and cubes *etc*, and thus made further discoveries in the triangular number systems. Again, as we have already seen with Pythagoras $(x + a)^2$ multiplies out to $x^2 + 2xa + a^2$ and on multiplying again by $(x + a)$ we have the expanded form of $(x + a)^3$. Now, Omar Khayyam, a Persian Zoroastrian who resided in Samarkand for a time, went on to consider the result of multiplying out the general expression $(x + a)^n$, and found that for n = 3, 4, 5. . . the results were:

$$x^3 + 3ax^2 + 3a^2x + a^3$$
$$x^4 + 4ax^3 + 6a^2x^2 + 4a^3x + a^4$$
$$x^5 + 5ax^4 + 10a^2x^3 + 10a^3x^2 + 5a^4x + a^5$$

Now, comparison of the notation ^nC_r, (c.f. Section 4. 4) with the coefficients of all of the above terms will show that the *Binomial Theorem* of Omar Khayyam can be expressed in the general form;

$$(x + a)^n = x^n + {}^nC_1ax^{n-1} + {}^nC_2a^2x^{n-2} + \ldots + {}^nC_ra^rx^{n-r} + \ldots + {}^nC_{n-1}a^{n-1}x + {}^nC_na^n$$

which relates to the triangular numbers (c.f. Sections 3.1.1 and 4. 4) in a quite unexpected manner revealed by setting out the above coefficients of the binomial expansion as they were presented in the *Precious Mirror of the Four Elements* by Chu Chi Kei in 1300 when the Mogul Empire was in contact with the Europe. This arrangement of numbers, now known as Pascal's Triangle, takes the form:

```
              1
            1   1
          1   2   1
        1   3   3   1
      1   4   6   4   1
    1   5  10  10   5   1
  1   6  15  20  15   6   1
1   7  21  35  35  21   7   1
```

This triangle can be expanded as far as we wish by evaluating ^nC_r in Omar Khayyam's expansion of the binomial beyond n = 7 which corresponds to the bottom row of the above arrangement, but already we see by comparison with the results given above for n = 2, 3, 4 . . . , that the successive rows correspond to the coefficients of the binomial expansion, that the oblique rows parallel to the right-hand side of the triangle and reading diagonally downwards from left to right are respectively the series of natural numbers, followed by the first and successively higher series of triangular numbers of the Pythagoreans who together with Chinese number mystics, would have been additionally pleased to note that two sides of the above triangle consist of continuous rows of 'unity, the source of all'.

We have also discussed series where the successive terms are ever-decreasing, and we have noted that when a quantity can be expressed as the sum of a series of such terms, its value can be determined to any desired precision by deciding how many terms to sum, (c.f. Section 4.4). A use of the Binomial Theorem to calculate the value of such as $(1.01)^{10}$ can also demonstrate this benefit of diminishing series. Thus to evaluate $(1.01)^{10}$ it is not necessary to multiply it out. One can instead, express it in the binomial form of $(a + b)^n$ where a =1, b = 0.01, and n =10 such that:

$$(1 + .01)^{10} = 1 + 10(0.1) + 10x9 / 2x1(0.0001) + 10x9x8/3x2x1(0.000001) . . . \text{and so on;}$$

though already, the sum to three terms gives the value sought to seven decimal places as 1.1046221

The binomial series expansion can also be used to determine square roots, which as we have seen are needed for the construction of trigonometric tables. The procedure is to express the square root to be determined in binomial form by following the rule of Archimedes that powers are added in multiplication. Thus, it is shown that $a^{1/2}$ is the square root of a by noting that $a^{1/2} \times a^{1/2} = a^1$, which is a itself. Thus, for example, $\sqrt{2} = 2^{1/2}$ and since negative powers express division, we may write $(\frac{1}{2})^{-1/2} = \sqrt{2}$ which in binomial form we may write as:

$$(1 - \frac{1}{2})^{-1/2} = \sqrt{2}; \text{ and expand as the binomial}$$
$$(1 + b)^n \text{ with } b = -\frac{1}{2} \text{ and } n = -\frac{1}{2} \text{ which gives the series:}$$
$$(1 + b)^n = 1 + (-0.5)(-\frac{1}{2}) + (0.375)(-\frac{1}{2})^2 + (-0.3125)(-\frac{1}{2})^3 . . .$$

However, this series does not converge as rapidly as that of the previous paragraph, because 0.5 to successively increasing powers diminishes more slowly than does the smaller 0.01 successively raised to the same powers. Nonetheless, as the above terms are successively added the resulting sums are 1, 1.250, 1.344, . . . with the addition of nine terms giving the now familiar 1.414. It can also be shown that the sum never gets to 1.4143 no matter how many terms we add.

At this point, we should note that identification of all the innovators in mathematics is difficult. All we know is from the records as we have them. The problem is similar to that which be-devils attempts to identify the locations of mankind's origin and earliest developments when all we know is where the fossils and archaeological remains have been found. It seems likely, however, that the Greeks had absorbed concepts from as far east as China in becoming themselves pre-imminent in geometry. Again, though they appear to have initiated trigonometry and algebra, it was development of the Hindu number system which enabled the then Muslim world to develop arithmetic and mathematics and to apply them to astronomy and physics while pursuing alchemy and medicine.

5. 4. 2 Astronomy and Physics

As to astronomy and its association with astrology, the Jewish writer, Messahala (770-820) produced compendia on these, and Al-Fargani of Transoxiana (d. c. 850) wrote on astronomy and served the Caliph Al Manum who built the observatory at Baghdad in 829. However, the greatest astronomer of the period, was Al-Battani (d. 929) later known as Albategnius who worked mainly at his home Raqqa (Aracte) in Asia Minor. In re-working the observations of Ptolemy, Al-Battani obtained a more accurate measure of the obliquity of the elliptic and of the precession of the equinoxes while discovering through his improved tables for Sun and Moon movement that the Sun's supposed eccentric was changing with respect to the records of Ptolemy. In modern terms, he had discovered that the earth's orbit varies with time (c.f. Section 3.1.4). Again, Arzachel (to the Latins) produced highly accurate astronomical tables (1080) later known as the Toledan Tables while the (1180) attempt by Al-Bitrugi (Alpetragius to the Latins) to replace the Ptolemaic system with concentric planetary orbits would influence Copernicus (1473-1443).

The earliest Arabic writer in what we now call physics was Al-Kindi (813-80) of Basrah and Baghdad to whom no less than 265 works have been ascribed of which fifteen are on meteorology, several on specific weight and some on tides, though his best work deals with the reflection of light. Again, Al-Farabi (d. 951) of Asia Minor produced a work on sound and the theory of music and a classification of knowledge which later became influential. Yet again, Al-Biruni (973-1048) of Persia used the displacement method of Archimedes to produce very accurate determinations of specific weight for eighteen metals and precious stones while being interested in mathematics, astronomy and geography and writing his *Chronology of Ancient Nations* which became an important historical document.

However, Al-Hazen (965-1038) of Basrah produced his main work, *The Treasury of Optics*, while in the service of the Fatimid Caliph Al-Hakim (996-1020) in Cairo. This discusses reflection, refraction, colour propagation, the rainbow, halos and optical illusions while describing methods for measuring angles of reflection and refraction and experiments with transparent spherical segments which come close to an understanding of magnifying-lenses, centuries in advance of his successors (c.f. Section 6.1). He also studied reflection from spherical and parabolic mirrors which he constructed of metal on the basis of calculation, and in his *On The Burning Sphere* he refers to focussing, image-inversion, magnification, and the coloured rings produced by refraction, while making the first recorded reference to what we now call the *camera obscura* by which he observed the Sun during an eclipse as it appeared on a wall opposite a small hole in window-shutters. Again, his name is still associated with the problem of finding the point in a convex mirror (spherical, conical or cylindrical) at which a ray coming from a given position will be reflected to another given position, a problem which gives rise to a fourth degree equation solved by Al-Hazen by recourse to the properties of the hyperbola. As to speculation, he believed light to be "a kind-of-fire" reflected at the spherical limit of the atmosphere which he estimated to be at an altitude of about ten miles. However, he was more correct in rejecting the then currently accepted belief of Euclid and Ptolemy that the eye sends out visual rays to the object seen and in believing that the form of the perceived object passes into the eye to be transmuted by its "transparent body" *i.e.* the lens.

5. 4. 3 Alchemy and Medicine

Although there was brief mention of alchemical practice among the Alexandrians, it is really Geber (c. 850) a Syrian Pagan who was the father of the subject as far as we know. The beliefs on which alchemy was based were that all matter consists of various proportions of the Ideal elements of earth, water, air and fire; that gold is the most unchangeable and therefore the "purest" and "noblest" of all metals, followed by silver, copper and so on in proportion to their relative changeability; that transmutation of 'baser' metals into 'nobler' should be possible by adjusting the proportions of the constituent 'elements'; and that an agent or quintessence might be found which could effect the necessary adjustments. However, such beliefs do not amount to hypotheses because these so-called elements had not been reality-validated as constituents of metals in the first place. Thus, they are only speculation and it is not surprising that alchemy later became associated with superstition and fraud. Nonetheless, motivated by these beliefs, Geber developed craft-knowledge of distillation, evaporation, crystallisation, filtration, sublimation and melting for the preparation of a range of then new substances now familiar to chemists, among which were sal ammoniac (ammonium chloride), cinnabar (mercury sulphide), sulphuric and nitric acids, alkalis and acetates. He also knew that mixed sulphuric and nitric acids, later known as *aqua regia*, dissolve gold.

The first writer on medicine of the Arab-speaking world was the Persian Rhazes (865-925) who had studied Greek, Persian and Indian medicine in Baghdad under a successor of the Nestorian, Honain Ibn Ishaq. Although Rhazes also wrote on alchemy, mathematics, astronomy, theology, and philosophy, his life experience in medicine together with earlier medical knowledge from Greek, Syriac and Arabic sources is compiled in his *Comprehensive Book* while of his total output of some two hundred works, half were medical. He was the first to describe small-pox and measles adequately and when he finally devoted himself exclusively to medicine his reputation attracted pupils and patients from all parts of the Middle East. His *Book of the Art* which deals with his earlier interest in alchemy derives partly from Geber, though it goes further in its descriptions of processes and apparatus and in its classification of substances. Again, while Geber divided them into bodies (such as gold, silver), souls (sulphur, arsenic) and spirits (mercury, sal ammoniac), Rhazes classified them as animal, vegetable and mineral.

However, Rhazes had a prominent contemporary whose works were among the first to be translated from Arabic to Latin when he became known as Isaac Judaeus (c. 900). He was an Egyptian Jew who became physician to the Fatimid rulers of Kairouan in Tunisia from whence his reputation quickly spread to southern Europe and from whence his work *On Fevers* became one of the best known medical texts of the European Middle Ages. Later, Avicenna (980-1037) of Bokhara wrote his *Canon of Medicine* which represents the culmination of all previous medical work and which became perhaps the single most studied medical text ever written, though the classification adopted was unnecessarily complex. Avicenna also wrote on alchemy and it is not surprising to find this continuing association between medicine and alchemy or indeed to find both associated with astrology. After all, most people hope for health, wealth and avoidance of misfortune. Anyway, medical interests appear to have been a vehicle for the east to west transmission of learning within the Islamic world. Thus, a manuscript of Dioscorides sent as a diplomatic present to the Caliphate at Cordova by Constantine VI of Byzantium was translated with the help of a Byzantine monk by Hasdai ben Shaprut (d. c. 990) minister and physician to the Caliphate, while its Muslim physician was known to the Latins as Abulcasis (d. c. 1013) for a medical text in thirty sections the last dealing with surgery previously neglected by Islamic authors.

However, the strains between one belief and another which had first appeared in eastern Islam now began to affect the west. Thus, under the influence of the religious teacher Al-Ghazzali (d. 1111), tolerance gave way to persecution of speculators likely to weaken religious belief in the Creator. As a consequence, independent works of significance became rare, except those by Jews of whom the most eminent contributor was the court physician, philosopher and religious teacher (rabbi), Mamonides (1135-1204) whom I have already mentioned as a translator. Though born in Spain, he spent most of his active life in the service of Saladin in Cairo where some of his medical writings for the Sultan offered criticisms of Galen. He is best known, however, for his advocacy of integrity in commercial and personal dealings and for his beliefs on the Cosmos and on the nature of God some of which later influenced Thomas Aquinas and through him Catholic Europe while his *Guide to the Perplexed,* is considered the most readable medieval text on general philosophy.

Nonetheless orthodoxy's opposition to speculation on the natural world finally caught up with Averroes of Cordova (1126-98) who though a judge and third in his family-line of legal professionals, had studied and practiced medicine while producing extensive writings on

116

philosophy. However, in these last he had expressed the belief that while universe and *Prime Mover* were eternal, everything within the former was continuously being created and changed by the latter, and that the human soul was part of the eternal Divine world soul, by which rejection of belief in a single creation out of nothing, he was decrying both Islamic and Christian orthodoxy, for which he was judged by some Muslim theologians to have become a Jew. In the end, his writings were burned by Decree of the Sultan and he spent the latter part of his life in disgrace. Yet another example of one belief falling foul of another.

5. 5 TRANSMISSION OF KNOWLEDGE AND SPECULATION TO CHRISTIAN EUROPE

Earlier in this chapter, I indicated the paucity of classical documents salvaged from the Fall of Rome and available in Latin to Dark Age Europe. I now review the mainly Greek texts previously lost to Europe and the new texts in Arabic which described the advances made in the meantime in China, India and the Islamic world as reviewed above.

As to the Sicilian route, Arabic texts of many North African Jewish writers such as Isaac Judeus were translated to Latin by the Carthaginian, Constantine the African (1017-87) who arrived in Salerno about 1070 and became secretary to its Norman conqueror, and whose translations remained influential even when better versions later became available. Again, this route supplied early medical texts translated from Greek to Latin by Alphanus (d. 1085) Archbishop of Salerno, while from the Greek also, Ptolomy's *Optics* and *Almagest*, were translated by Eugenius of Palermo while Rhazes's *Comprehensive Book (Liber Continens)* was thence translated by Moses Farachi (d. 1285) at the behest of Philip of Anjou (1220-85), King of the Sicilies. Again, Adelard of Bath (c.1090-1150) who sojourned in both Spain and the Sicilies, translated the *Arithmetic* of Al-Kwarismi and the *Elements of* Euclid into Latin and wrote a compendium of Arabic knowledge in the form of a dialogue entitled *Natural Questions*.

As to the Spanish route, the *Algebra* of Al-Kwarismi was rendered into Latin by Robert of Chester in 1144 who later moved from Spain to London where he produced astronomical tables for the latitude and longitude of the city, based on Al-Kwarismi, Adelard and Albategnius respectively. He also rendered into Latin, an alchemical work derived from an earlier Arab source by Morienus Romanus, a contemporary Arab Christian of Jerusalem. Meanwhile, the *Physics* of Aristotle was translated in Toledo from Arabic to Latin by the Christian Domenigo Gonzales (fl. 1140) while John of Seville (fl. 1139-55) a convert to Judaism, translated the astronomical and astrological works of Al-Battani, Al-Farabi, Al-Fargani, Al-Kwarismi, Al-Kindi, and Messahala together with the Aristotelian treatise which was to influence Roger Bacon. However, the most prolific of all was Gerard of Cremona (1114-87) whose most important translations from the Arabic were the *Almagest* of Ptolomy some twelve years after that from the Greek by Eugenius of Palermo; the *Canon* of Avicenna; *On the Quadrature of the Circle* by Archimedes; a work on optics by Apollonius; many works by Aristotle and derived from him; Euclid's *Elements*; many medical works by Galen, Hippocrates, Isaac Judeus, Rhazes and Al-Bucasis; alchemical works by Geber; mathematical and astronomical works by Al-Kindi, Al-Fargani, Al-Hazen, Al-Farabi and Messahala; and some significant Neo-Platonic works. In addition, Michael the Scot (c.1175-c.1235) translated from Arabic to Latin, the astronomy of Alpetragius, a number of Averroean commentaries and the biological works of Aristotle. He also produced an Aristotelian compendium *Secrets of Nature* from a number of Greek, Arabic and Hebrew sources; a treatise on astrology which brought Alpetragius's non-traditional views on planetary motion to the West; and

Aristotle's treatise on astrology, the first major contribution on this subject available in Latin. Michael appears to have had Jewish and Muslim help which together with his association with Frederick II, arch-enemy of the Papacy, may have contributed to his reputation for sorcery to which reference is made in Scott's *Lay of the Last Minstrel*.

5. 6 RECEPTION OF KNOWLEDGE AND SPECULATION BY EUROPE

I now consider the readiness of Christian Europe to receive this input of material and the means whereby it would be absorbed, modified or rejected. After all, its earlier rejection had been a contributory cause of the Dark Age, the only retained 'illumination' having been the Timaeus in the form of a third century Latin commentary acceptable to Neo-Platonic Christianity, the logic of Aristotle in a Latin translation by Boetius and an elementary treatment of the seven liberal arts derived from Varro, while Nestorian heretics were translating classical Greek texts into Syriac, prior to the birth of Mohammed.

5. 6. 1 Scholasticism

Christian Europe had gradually become aware of developments in the Arabic speaking world with the re-introduction by Gerbert (Pope Sylvester II) of the abacus in the late 900s and its linkage with the Greek-sourced arithmetic of Boetius. In addition, Gerbert had initiated a translation to Latin of an Arab text on the astrolabe. Again, Herman the Cripple (1013-54) who spent his life at the Benedictine Abbey of Reichenau wrote mathematical and astrological works which betray Arab influence possibly conveyed by travellers. Others who were aware of activities in the world of Islam were such as Hugh of St Victor (1095-1141) and Bernard Sylvester of Chartres (c. 1150) who also drew on Herman the Cripple while St Hildegard of Bingen (1099-1180) drew on Bernard Sylvester. To these extents at least, Christian Europe was not wholly surprised when Latin translations became increasingly available from around 1100. In addition, potential centres for scholarship began to appear with the founding of the Cistercian Order around 1100, followed by the Franciscans (or Grey friars) of the gentle St Francis of Assisi in 1209 and the Dominicans (or Black friars) of the austere and orthodox Dominic in 1215. Again, the potential of the new material was recognised in that the Franciscans and Dominicans were providing most of the significant teachers for the universities springing up throughout Europe during the thirteenth century. Thus Alexander of Hales (d.1245), Robert Grosseteste (d.1253) and Roger Bacon (d.1270) were Franciscans while Albertus Magnus (c. 1200-80) and St Thomas Aquinas (1227-74) were Dominicans.

Clearly, Christian Europe had centres of scholarship and individuals capable of absorbing the new material this time round, if they decided to do so, this decision depending on the compatibility of Aristotle's beliefs with the Christian orthodoxy of the time, his range being the most comprehensive of the ancients. Thus, all would be well to the extent that Aristotle appeared consistent with the Timaeus, with Neo-Platonism and with Church belief in the macrocosm/microcosm relationship. More specifically, it would depend on Aristotle's belief in the purity and nobility of the stellar sphere and the successive baseness of the lower spheres being parallel with Church belief in the perfection of the stellar heavens in contrast to the imperfections of the planetary motions through the zodiac and in further contrast to the even greater vagaries of life on earth. Thus Aristotle's beliefs had to be compatible with the Church belief that the stellar sphere of the universe was fixed, perfect and certain as death and resurrection, in contrast to life's vagaries which could nonetheless be predicted, avoided or mitigated by astrological observation of the planetary motions in their respective spheres.

This much appeared possible. On the other hand, there was much more to Aristotle. Thus, he had advocated observation of nature in writings which provide copious evidence of this practice while Augustine had made clear in his *De Fide* that we should be ignorant of the mysteries of the celestial and earthly regions and that he cared not to know the courses of the stars, and in his *Confessions* he had stated his hatred of all sacrilegious mysteries. In short, he considered interest in nature to be sacrilegious in itself. Consequently, even as late as the thirteenth century, there was very little evidence of direct observation of nature even in the encyclopaedias (summae) of such scholastics as the Dominican Vincent de Beauvais (1190-1264) or of the Franciscan (Bartholomew the Englishman (c. 1274). In addition, Augustine's fear of heresy was very much alive as the tens of thousands slaughtered in extirpating the Albigensian heresy and the activities of the Dominican-led Inquisition remind us.

However, perhaps the first scholastic to be acquainted with the full range of Aristotle in Latin was Alexander of Hales and the first to present it systematically with continual reference to Arab-source commentaries was Albertus Magnus. As these Arab sources of Aristotle in Latin became more widely available, however, scholastics turned to translations direct from the Greek, with the Dominican William of Moerbeke (d. 1286) being an important translator in this respect. However, increased availability of the complete Aristotle increasingly exposed his interest in the direct observation of nature while the availability of translations from the Arabic of Al-Hazen further showed what could be achieved by this approach, both catching the imaginations of the Franciscans, Robert Grosseteste (c. 1175-1253), John of Peckham (c. 1220-92) and Roger Bacon (1214-94). Thus, Robert Grosseteste, an enthusiast for Greek and Hebrew who later became Bishop of Lincoln was inspired to repeat for himself the work on mirrors and lenses recounted in Latin translations of Al-Hazen, while John of Peckham again following Al-Hazen, wrote on optics and mathematics before becoming Archbishop of Canterbury and while Roger Bacon who taught at Paris and Oxford drew his interest in optics from the Polish mathematician Witelo (fl. 1270),who had written a commentary on Al-Hazen while working in north Italy. Though Bacon was more encyclopaedist than mathematician or experimentalist, it was he who most enthusiastically advocated experimentation for the acquisition of new knowledge for general benefit, he who castigated the Church for its failure to use long-available knowledge to compute the true dates of its festivals, and he who was embarrassed enough to petition the Pope to reform the calendar accordingly.

Nonetheless, the status of knowledge in respect of the preservation of faith, remained unresolved. Thus, while Hugh of the monastery of Saint Victor in Paris was stating (c. 1215) that knowledge of the natural world did not necessarily threaten belief in God or the authority of the Church, the Faculty of Arts of the University of Paris was forbidding the works of Aristotle even as a basis for discussion. To Albertus Magnus, however, investigation of the natural world was of value for its own sake and could never conflict with faith or its consequences. Similar disputes had arisen in Islam despite earlier acceptance that faith and knowledge of the world would eventually be harmonised in the knowledge of God, Averroes having been rejected by the orthodox though for speculative belief rather than knowledge. Help was at hand within Christianity, however. Thomas Aquinas (c. 1225-74) would incorporate Aristotle into the Christian tradition while transforming the latter into what was to become Roman Catholicism. Born near Naples as a seventh son and thus destined for the Church, he was sent aged five to join the Benedictines at Monte Casino and was later transferred to the more intellectual Dominicans before being sent from their teaching house in Paris to study under Albertus Magnus at Cologne in 1248. This was followed by seven years at the University of Paris and ten in Dominican teaching houses in Italy including a period at the papal court at Orvieto where he again met Albertus. Here also he was introduced to William of

Moerbeke who translated Aristotle direct from the Greek so that Thomas might recover what could have been lost in successive translations from Greek to Syriac, to Arabic and hence to Latin.

During these years Aquinas had completed his *Summa Contra Gentiles,* a defense of Christianity against unbelievers such as Muslims and Pagans in which he argued that in seeking to persuade those having no prior knowledge of Christianity it was best to appeal to that natural reason "to which all men are forced to assent" rather than to argue from the *Scriptures* themselves. In this work he identified only the doctrines of the Trinity, the Incarnation, and the Creation *ex nihilo* as matters of faith alone and he accepted as non-disprovable the non-orthodox belief of Plato, Aristotle and Averroes that matter had always co-existed with God. Sometime prior to 1269, he began his *Summa Theologicae* which he progressed over his three years as professor of theology in Paris and continued as head of a Dominican teaching house in Naples until his death in 1274. In this latter work he accepts the *Nicomachaean Ethics* of Aristotle; derives thence, the importance of reason as a moral arbiter; and accepts his arguments for the need to control the emotions while accepting their beneficial importance. He also recognises with Aristotle, the virtues of temperance, prudence, fortitude, justice and the requirement that they be deliberately cultivated.

In all of his works, Thomas Aquinas recognised that argument cannot be pursued without rationality which he believed to be a gift from God and indispensable to acquisition of the world knowledge necessary for appreciation of God as Creator. Thus, in consequence of believing reason to be our greatest attribute, he believed it wrong to despise the senses through which we observe the world, and wrong to deny the perfection of the creation and its Creator by believing humanity to be inherently corrupted by sin. In addition, he argued that reason implies judgement which implies free-will. Thus, in contrast to Platonic, Pauline and Augustinian belief that the body pulls the separate soul away from God, he argues that the 'en-souled' body is a single entity with the soul (mind) learning from the senses; that the perfection of the creation is impugned if the body's senses are denigrated; and that free-will and cultivation of the virtues allows for increased perfection through a preference for good behaviour over bad in human affairs. Thus, according to Aquinas, God wants us to reach towards Him by exercising our free-will and by applying our reason to seek understanding of his creation while accepting as articles of faith His revelation of matters beyond our finite reasoning.

This was undoubtedly a substantial and illuminating attempt to reconcile those who sought knowledge of the natural world with those who believed such knowledge to be a threat to Christian faith. However, being belief-based, it was necessarily incomplete and Aquinas suffered a breakdown in December 1273 which has been ascribed to exhaustion, a mystical experience or regret for his weakening of orthodoxy. Whatever the true cause, it is likely to have been influenced by self-recognition that he had failed to reconcile the search for knowledge through the senses to all who sought to sustain the faith by traditional means, though he had made the progressive position more defendable and traditional objections more difficult to sustain. However,, in the year of his breakdown, he was strongly criticised in Paris for his perceived denial of God's power to over-rule the natural order by miraculous intervention, and he was summoned by the Pope to a Council at Lyons, no doubt to answer these and other criticisms, but took ill and died on the way. Three years later, several of his theses were formally condemned in Paris and Oxford, the former revoked fifty years later, the latter apparently forgotten. Nonetheless, his canonisation began in 1316, before revocation of the Paris condemnation, and was completed by Pope John XXII in 1323 despite an unsurprising lack of convincing miracles, he himself having denied their possibility.

However, while Aquinas rightly agreed with Aristotle that our innate attraction to the Good coupled with our innate rationality enables us to understand moral precepts, his belief in God caused him to argue a circularity as believers always do, whereas I contend that this Rationality is
120

that of our innate Duality and Trinity; that the Duality produces our belief in God while our attraction to the Good is the innateness without which we simply couldn't survive as the species we are; and that the sense of morality attributed to God by believers is reality-validated knowledge of our group-species innateness as produced by the Trinity. Thus, while Aquinas maintained his belief-based argument he could not explain how the senses responsive to real-world stimuli could be responsive to God from whom we receive no sense-stimuli. Here he relied on the Platonic belief that our rationality accesses the Beyond to let us 'know' what God's precepts are and to let him (Aquinas) know that his own doctrines derive from these precepts. Thus, he was circularly reduced to re-stating his belief that God has revealed His Truths to us; that He would not seek to mislead us; and that Faith compensates for all short-comings in our rational understanding of God.

The difficulties for this position are that our senses and rationality cannot provide direct knowledge of God, though we are aware of the Unknowable; and that our imagination and rationality alone, whether God-created or not, does not lead to knowledge but to endlessly disputable beliefs about God and morality as amply shown by the heresy-plagued history of Christianity. Thus, while my differentiation of knowledge and belief places morality with knowledge, and God with suspended belief, such would have required Aquinas to substitute my 'species innate' for his 'God-given', thus entailing a suspension of belief which in his time and circumstances could well have contributed to his breakdown.

Thus, I recognise belief in God to be beyond reality-evaluation while Thomas Aquinas believed our senses, rationality, and response to the good to be God-given in order to maintain belief in God. Again, I recognise that we give our own species-specific and reality-validated meaning to the Good (or to God) while Aquinas believed there is a God who reveals all such to us. However, instead of arguing about the existence of a God beyond reality-evaluation, I contend that we should reality-evaluate the extent to which derivatives of the religious Ur-belief are beneficial; that this can be done though the Ur-belief itself is beyond reality-evaluation; that all derivative beliefs concerning our nature and behaviour can similarly be reality-evaluated as to what is good or bad for our survival and welfare as a group-species; that socio-political policy makers whether religious or secular should encourage the good and discourage the bad thus defined; and that both should recognise the knowledge-content of 'religious' morality as they do craftsmanship, science and technology, while recognising rejection of the religious Ur-belief to be no more valid or invalid than acceptance, the belief or disbelief being beyond reality-evaluation either way.

In any case, Aquinas's efforts to make Aristotle more acceptable to opponents within the Church, had little effect on the pursuit of knowledge. Prior to any such formal acceptance, Roger of Salerno (c. 1220) and his follower Roland of Parma (1250) were already assimilating at Bologna new Arab sources within a tradition of anatomical investigation which had survived from classical times in southern Italy as being compatible with Church-based care of the sick. This practical approach supported by translations from Avicenna, was maintained (post-Aquinas) by Mondino da Luzzi (1276-1328) whose *Anatomy* became a guide to human dissection as increasingly practiced in fourteenth century European Universities. Again, his contemporary, Peter of Abano (1250-1318) later professor at Paris and later still at Padua, reported that the brain and heart were the sources of the nerves and blood vessels respectively; that air had weight; and that the length of the year was 365 days, 6 hours and 4 minutes. His best-known work, *The Conciliator*, reflects his dual access to Latin translations of Arabic sources and to original Greek sources consequent on his having learned Greek in Constantinople. At this time also, Arnald of Villanova (1240-1311) a Catalan in the medical school at Montpellier was actively describing diseases by the methods of Hippocrates while being heavily involved in alchemy, astrology and a supposed linkage between the 'seven metals' and the 'seven planets'. Though alchemy had come to Europe about one hundred years earlier with Robert of Chester's translation of Morienus Romanus into Latin, Arnald pursued his own programme after his student days at Naples and Salerno by travelling widely in Italy, Sicily, France and Spain, by personal contact with Muslims and Jews, and by his direct access to Arabic and Hebrew. In addition, he provided medical advice to the Papal Curia at Rome and Avignon.

Again, astronomy being closely related to Church-favoured astrology, Alphonso the Wise (1223-84) assembled a group of mainly Jewish scholars who having compiled some genuine astronomical data were commissioned by him to produce the widely used *Alphonsine Tables* which included an accurate calculation of the length of the year. The standard astronomical text of the scholastic period, however, was by John Hollywood (d. 1250) a teacher at the University of Paris who based it on Al-Battini and Al-Fargani. This was later translated into a number of European vernaculars while his *Algorismus* based on the 'Arabic' numeral system, continued in use up to the seventeenth century. However, Leonardo of Pisa (c. 1170-1245) has the prior claim to advocacy of the Hindu numeral and place-value system based on zero, with his *Book of the Abacus* (1202) and the added distinction of having apparently learned of its use in the course of his mercantile travels in Islamic lands rather than from translations of Arab-sources. In addition, the French Jew, Levi ben Gerson produced an astronomical treatise containing a return to the heliocentric system of Hipparchus which inspired Copernicus (1473-1443).

Thus, the conquests and assimilative attitudes of Islam were enabling western Europe to re-connect with its lost classical inheritance in an altogether more fully developed form and with a much more convenient number notation. In addition, though this was more or less seamlessly absorbed in some cases, there was some opposition which Thomas Aquinas set himself to reduce though perhaps opponents were less concerned with knowledge than with the potential affect of Aristotle's beliefs on Church orthodoxy. Nonetheless, there is evidence that with few exceptions, even the most enthusiastic recipients of the new knowledge could do no more than translate, compile, disseminate and comment while the exceptions were limited to making further progress in anatomical dissection in which they were already involved or in the refinement of astronomical measurement in areas of continuous interest. Thus, a further stage would need to transpire before western efforts to advance knowledge of the physical and social world would test the robustness of the Aquinas conciliation. In the meantime, Islamic orthodoxy had become increasingly opposed to counter-speculation though as yet no comparable Islamic conciliator had emerged.

5. 6. 2 The Rise of Humanism

In the meantime, having been re-awakened to classical knowledge and speculation through translations from the Arabic and from access to Greek originals, western Scholastics began to re-discover such literary and artistic works as those of Homer and Hesiod, Aeschylus, Sophocles and Euripedes, Ovid and Virgil, and the styles of classical art and architecture, literature having been as closed and forbidden by Islam as by early Christian Europe. The term Humanism has been applied to this interest and to its development in the Renaissance, though it is my contention that the literary tradition describes humanity with a validity which may be judged by the extent to which readers throughout the ages have recognised themselves within it; and that to this extent it is not in competition with reality-validated knowledge: it is part of it, though as yet undifferentiated from belief. In any case, I now review the collection, assimilation and distribution of humanist material recovered directly from Greco-Roman sources, as I previously reviewed the undifferentiated knowledge and speculation transmitted through Islamic sources.

Thus, once again, recognition of existence led to collection, though this time Italy led the way because its increasing mercantile wealth and its memories of former Roman greatness brought opportunities for cultural expression and an aspiration on which to rebuild. A leading figure in this growing nostalgia, aspiration and expectation was Petrarch (1304-74) with his emphasis on architecture, art and literature, though his tendency to imitate rather than to develop make him a fore-runner of the Renaissance rather than a contributor as were such as the later Leonardo da Vinci, Vesalius and Galileo. Nonetheless, with his friend Giovanni Colonna, he did much through his *Book of Memorable Things* to reconcile Pagan and Christian pasts for his contemporaries and thus to assist in the assimilation of classical culture in all its aspects. The documents now being sought were, however, widely distributed and so expensive that Pope Nicholas V when a monk, had run into debt in the acquisition and copying of documents while Niccolo Niccoli, a friend of the elder Cosimo de Medici, spent his entire fortune on buying documents before being permitted to use the Medici wealth to continue. Many others were similarly active without whom much would have been lost, though translation from the Latin to vernacular Italian was easier than from Greek, Petrarch himself having no Greek though he treasured his copy of Homer.

Compared to the circumstances of the earlier transfer from Arabic, the dissemination of knowledge and belief direct from Latin and Greek was greatly facilitated by the introduction of printing around the middle of the fifteenth century (c.f. Section 5.7.1). However, not surprisingly, the priority of printing was first the Bible, followed by medieval theological, ecclesiastical, legal and medical works in this order, followed by those of classical antiquity among which literary merit preceded technical content, there being fewer scholars equipped to benefit from the latter. An exception was the *Natural History* of Pliny which had continued to be available and thus became the first technical book to be printed (Venice in 1469). Indeed, it was so well known that the name of the editor was omitted by the printer. This was followed by Varro (Rome 1471) a writer also continuously known in the "liberal arts" context; Lucretius (Brescia 1473), not strictly technical; the *Geographica* of Ptolemy (Vincenza 1475); the medical work of Celsus (Florence 1478), the first specifically technical work of the classical period to appear in print; Euclid (Venice 1482); and the works on architecture and construction of Vitruvius, Frontius and Vegetius (Rome, 1486-7). Because Greek type was scarcely used in the early stages of printing, the first Aristotelian material to be printed was the Latin translation by Theodore Gaza (1400-78) of three biological treatises (Venice 1476) though the scholar-printer Aldo Manuzio (1449-1515) later supplied Greek texts of Aristotle and Theophrastus (Venice 1495-98), of Dioscorides (1499), of Pollex (1502) whose anatomical nomenclature was thus established for the Renaissance, and of Strabo (1516). Again, the first Greek printings of Galen (1525) and of Hippocrates (1526) were produced by Aldo's successors in the firm.

The practice of printing was not, of course, restricted to Italy. The first classical technical work to appear elsewhere was that by Manilius (Nuremberg 1472) at the private press of Johannes Muller of Konigsberg (1436-76) otherwise known as Regiomontanus. The *Geographica* of Ptolemy also appeared in Greek as did Euclid (Basel,1533) while the *Almagest* was first published in Latin at Basel (1538) as was a collection of the work of Archimedes (1544). The first English translations from the classical period were those of Euclid (1570) and the *Natural History* of Pliny (1601). However, the most frequently printed works in Greek, Latin and the vernaculars throughout the sixteenth century were those on medical matters by Hippocrates, Dioscorides and Galen, these together with those of Rhazes, Mesue, Avicenna and Albucasis providing the basis of medical practice at that time.

However, we are getting beyond the Dark Ages (400-1400) and entering the Early Renaissance (c.f. Chapter 6) when scholars were finally to move forward on the basis of the knowledge and speculation re-acquired from earlier times. Before considering how and by whom the subsequent progress was made, however, I return to the continuing development of craftsmanship through application of the Rational Trinity regardless of the speculation and religious belief of the Rational Duality.

5. 7 CRAFTSMANSHIP FROM THE DARK AGES TO 1700

Having reviewed craftsmanship to the Iron Age as the product of our innate Rational Trinity and having noted the experimentation of Al-Hazen as a development of craftsmanship not yet properly understood even by those impressed by it (c.f. Section 6.1), I now show that Dark Age craftsmanship continued to develop to 1700 in respect of paper-making and printing, shipbuilding, shipping and navigation, and mechanisation, architecture, building and warfare, without any assistance from science (c.f. Section 8.1).

5. 7. 1 Papermaking and Printing

Paper, as previously noted, dates back to 49 BC in the Shansi province of China where it served for writing and decoration, for making small domestic items and for wrapping and clothing. Initially, it was made from hemp and ramie fibres and later from those of rattan and mulberry, the fibrous material being finely chopped, boiled with wood ash (alkali) and washed to remove extraneous materials before the resulting pulp was spread thinly on porous screens, drained and allowed to dry. Such paper was well established in China by the second century AD and by the fourth it had replaced silk, bamboo and wooden tablets for writing, though bamboo became an additional source of fibres in the sixth century despite its need for repeated boiling with alkali. Subsequently paper-making migrated through Korea to Japan in the seventh century and to Samarkand, Damascus and Baghdad by the eighth from whence it entered Europe.

However, it was the twelfth century before Europe had paper-mills, first in Moorish and Christian Spain, then in France and later in Germany and Italy. In Europe paper was "cloth parchment" being initially made mainly from linen rags, though cotton and even straw were also used. In Spain by 1150 the pulping process was carried out in stamping mills driven by wind or water power, the pulp being lifted from the slurry by rectangular trays with wire-mesh bottoms. After draining the sheet was removed, pressed between cloths to remove excess moisture and hung to dry. Such paper, sized with a mineral powder to improve writing-quality by reducing absorbency, replaced parchment in Europe prior to the inception of book-printing, one sheep having provided no more than 15-17 quarto sheets of parchment.

As to increasing the speed of writing and copying, the Egyptians had simplified their hieroglyphs into a cursive form for the priesthood by about 2800 BC and further simplified this for more general use by 800 BC. Again, Cicero's scribe/secretary, Marcus Tullius Tiro had developed a short-hand by 63 BC. Otherwise, though early Sumerian impression-seals are a form of printing, no further development appears to have occurred until about 400 AD when the Chinese began to ink smooth stone slabs incised with characters to print white (un-inked) characters on a dark (inked) background. From there, relief characters were produced by writing a page of text on thin translucent paper, gluing it face-down to a fine-grained woodblock such as pear, carving away all but the characters, removing the paper from them and inking their surfaces. Printing was then effected by pressing a sheet of paper against the inked relief-characters, repetitive inking and printing being possible until the characters became too worn to be serviceable.

This technique produced an enormous volume of printed matter from the routine to the very ambitious. One example of the latter is the Buddhist *Diamond Sutra*, a 5 metres long scroll containing an intricate picture of Sakyamuni preaching. This is the first printed book to be precisely dated, having been completed on the fifteenth day of the fourth moon of the ninth year of Xiantong (868 AD). Another is an edition of the canon of Buddhism, the *Tripitaka* consisting of 130,000 plates which took 12 years to complete, again before 1000 AD. By the fourteenth century printing had been elaborated through the use of two or more blocks to produce more than one colour per printed sheet, the earliest example printed in black and red being *Notes on the Diamond Sutra*. However, from the late twelfth century, blocks had been prepared for bank-note printing in China by engraving both design and writing on copper plates with a tempered steel chisel (burin), printing being effected by inking the plate, wiping the surface and transferring incision-retained ink to the paper, incision delicacy making counterfeiting difficult. However, the carving of book-pages in this way would have been extremely time-consuming.

Increased production rate by the development of movable-type is attributed to the Chinese block-printer Bi Sheng (c. 1045) whose characters were separately fashioned in clay; hardened by firing; pressed in textual order into a bedding-mixture of wax, resin and ash contained in a warmed iron tray; levelled by a flat board into the warm mixture; and allowed to set solid prior to being inked and printed. Around the beginning of the fourteenth century movable-wooden-type was introduced by Wang Zhen whose rotating storage-frame allowed the printer quickly to extract the desired character with bamboo tweezers and to return it to its indexed storage location within the frame after use. A rhyming mnemonic related characters to indexed locations in the storage-frame each of which contained characters in numbers determined by their average frequency of textual use which together with the large number of individual Chinese characters, necessitated rotating frames of some 2.5 metres in diameter. The selected characters fashioned on the ends of uniform wooden pillars were set up in wooden trays and wedged in place prior to inking. Tin-type had earlier been tried, its malleability and durability being greater than wood, but it would not hold the water-based ink then in use, though this was rectified around 1500 by using copper.

Although the transmission of crafts such as paper-making from east to west is clear enough, it is less clear for printing. Nonetheless, its European development was similar, having started with the block-printing of commercial items such as playing cards in Italy which by then had commercial links with the East. However, by the end of the thirteenth century, the earlier Chinese practice of block-printing books a page at a time is evidenced in Germany and paper money was being printed around 1400 in Italian and Dutch commercial centres using metal plates (intaglio printing). Again, at Mainz Johan Gutenberg who as a goldsmith was accustomed to stamping metal coins in a die, was using movable-type by about 1450. For this, he filed individual letters on the ends of steel punches and stamped them on the ends of mould-cast uniform pillars of tin alloyed with small amounts of lead and antimony, the first extant material from the Mainz press being dated 1454. Again, as in China, the type-setter picked out the desired letters from compartmentalised cases with tweezers (capital letters from the upper case and others from the lower) arranged them in a chase and secured the assembly with wedges.

However, specific European refinements quickly followed with Gutenberg himself introducing oil-based ink which adhered more effectively to the type and reduced smudging. Again, the screw-press, long familiar for the expression of juices and oils, was adapted to supply the necessary printing pressure and to ensure its uniformity. In this refinement the type-chase was laid on a flat bed and the paper to be printed was fixed into a frame with a felt backing (the tympan) which was hinged to the type-chase. When the type was inked the tympan was lowered to contact the paper with type and a flat plate (the platen) was forced down on the paper by the screw, the felt compensating for any irregularities in individual type heights. Further refinements enabled up to sixteen pages to be printed simultaneously and both sides of the paper to be used. Later, the screw (not used in Chinese printing) was further modified to move the platen a large distance for a small movement of the operating handle for greater printing convenience while the reduced pressure associated with this reversal of normal screw design was compensated by reducing the area of the platen to cover only half the paper-sheet which in turn required the chase to be moved on rails between impressions thus permitting type-corrections to be made more efficiently. It is estimated that by 1500 this optimised design had printed some 40,000 separate works which at perhaps 500 copies per edition could have amounted to some twenty million books.

5. 7. 2 Shipbuilding, Shipping and Navigation

My previous review of boat and shipbuilding dealt with the Mediterranean with only passing reference to northern Europe in respect of the lightly framed animal-hide curraghs of the Celtic Atlantic coast. However by the Dark Age, such adventurers as Brendan the Navigator (490-570) had made substantial voyages in such boats possibly even to the New World *via* Shetland, the Faeroes, Iceland and Greenland. However, the next development in shipbuilding occurred in Scandinavia in the form of the Kvalsund boat (sixth century) and the Oseberg and the Gokstad ships of about 800 and 900 respectively.

All of these craft had a true keel attached to stem and stern posts and overlap-fastened planking (known as lap-strake or clinker) as their major structural elements. Light internal-support timbers and rowing thwarts subsequently inserted for completion provided added stiffness to the structure while preserving the lightness appropriate to propulsion by oars or the single square-sail characteristic of the curragh. Again, like the curragh, these ships were 'double-ended'. By this time Mediterranean vessels were edge-to-edge planked (known as carvel) which requires thicker planks to hold the inter-plank caulking not required in over-lapped construction. Carvel planking is therefore heavier and requires attachment to pre-built heavy frames (including integral stem and stern posts) rising from the keel, with additional stiffness being provided by deck-beams and deck-planking. The result is a heavier vessel more suited to cargo-carrying than the lighter lap-strake un-decked (open) vessel. Nonetheless these lighter ships had a carrying-capacity of some 20 tonnes, sufficient for a substantial war-party. The Oseberg ship was 21 meters in length with fifteen rowing positions per side while the Gokstad ship had sixteen, both having the square-sailed mast more or less mid-way between stem and stern. When the ornamental high stems were decorated with a dragon-head these long ships became known as Dragon Ships or Dreki and while this new ship-building practice became widespread in the North, other variations produced the birlinn by which the Norsemen were eventually driven from the west of Scotland, the ships of the Danes and of King Alfred and those by which William the Conqueror invaded England in 1066.

By the thirteenth century, more heavily constructed cogs were being used as cargo carriers by the Baltic Sea countries of the Hanseatic League, by the Netherlands and by England. These still had only one mast, though at some 30 metres in length and 8 metres in beam they encouraged the gradual adoption of superstructures in the form of small forward and larger aft 'castles' from which archers could fire at other ships or at boarding parties from them, these defensive/offensive structures being welcomed by the crews of merchant ships and quickly becoming a necessity for warships. Again, cogs were built for Italian merchants from the early fourteenth century though in keeping with local traditions these were carvel-built and had a smaller mast abaft the mainmast. Later, a still smaller mast was added to the aft-castle (later, the poop), this three-mast rig being mostly associated with Spain and Portugal where such vessels were known as carracks. By 1400 this was the standard ship of the Mediterranean with 250 tonnes being considered large though 1000 tonnes had been achieved by 1500. In that interval, the smaller handier version of the carrack (the caravel) had appeared in Portugal and was used for the voyages instigated by Prince Henry the

126

Navigator in the fifteenth century, while the cob doubled in length and the earlier three-mast option became a middle mainmast with a smaller foremast and mizzen at bow and stern respectively.

However, by far the most significant innovation in ship propulsion was the fore-and-aft sail. The square sail set on a horizontal yard is effective enough when the wind is anywhere abaft the beam, but its effectiveness is much reduced with the wind forward of the beam. Thus, while the Norsemen made headway in the latter conditions by rowing, the triangular fore-and-aft sail was introduced in the East as in the dhow. With this sail, the forward bottom-corner (the tack) was attached to the centre-line of the craft near the stem-head, the leading-edge (the hypotenuse) was set on a spar hoisted aloft from about its mid-point, and the bottom-corner of its trailing-edge (the clew) was attached to an adjustable rope (the sheet) by which the spar and the sail itself could be set at variable angles to the craft's centre-line. With such a sail sheeted close (at a small angle) to the centre-line the craft could point towards 45 degrees of the wind direction and so be obliquely worked upwind by tacking and as the wind came from more astern, the sheet could be increasingly freed to adopt the position of a square sail at its most effective.

Having developed the fore-and-aft triangular sail and having observed that a sailing-craft will only proceed to windward if the sideways thrust of the wind is countered by the lateral resistance provided by the immersed hull, attention turned to the under-water shape (wetted-area) of the hull. Thus, it was found that the lateral resistance of shallow-draught craft such as the Norse long-ship, was inadequate; and that the lateral resistance of deeper draught craft such as the cog was adequate though the high wetted-area of such full-sectioned hulls produced more (drag) resistance to forward motion than did the lower wetted-area of the long-ship. Thus, ogee (wineglass) hull-sections were approached by the finer forward and after sections of the dhow to provide a greater lateral resistance than the long-ship with a lower drag-coefficient than the cog. Again, low lateral resistance being unavoidable in craft operating in the shoal coastal waters of the Netherlands and south-east England this disadvantage was later corrected by introducing the lee-board (and much later still the centre-board) both of which could be lowered as required and otherwise raised. The innovation of fore-and-aft sail was quickly adopted in the Mediterranean as the lateen rig with the draught-related lateral resistance being mainly achieved by load-carrying on the fuller hull sections, such that the Portuguese caravels had sufficient windward capability to ensure the return of explorers such as Fernando Diaz and Vasco da Gama from their voyages east of the Guinea Coast and the Cape of Good Hope respectively.

Other shipbuilding developments of the Dark Age were the replacement of the steering oar of the northern 'double ender' by a rudder hung externally on a straight stern-post, the stern itself being transformed to the flat aftermost section of the ship then known as the transom stern. The first European depiction of such an overhung rudder on a single-mast ship is on a seal of the Hanseatic City of Elbing (c. 1242) whereas such rudder-systems are clearly exhibited by models found in tombs of the Han Dynasty (202BC-220AD). Even more surprisingly, the Chinese had treadmill paddle-propelled ships as early as the end of the fifth century according to Li Kao (c. 782) though rowing would probably have been more efficient. As to Dark Age Europe, carvel construction was adopted in the North as ship-size increased while clinker construction was retained for smaller craft. In any case, heavier construction was strongly indicated by the introduction of canon. Henry VIII's warship, *Henry Grace a Dieu* (*Great Harry*, for short) with her 15cm thick planking in three layers, her forward and aft castles and her unusual four masts required well over 1000 tonnes of timber for her building in 1512. Given that an oak tree might provide 2 tonnes of usable timber and that there might be 100 such trees per hectare of oak forest, the timber production of 5 - 6 hectares and a regeneration time of 100 years would have been required to supply the timber for such a ship for which the average service life was only about 20-

30 years. Thus, by the sixteenth century shipbuilding had become a major undertaking of very great significance.

Now that ships could operate entirely under sail and carry the necessary provisions for long voyages, attention returned to the problems of navigation. Thus, while Eratosthenes (third century BC) had measured the circumference of the earth and while Ptolemy (first century AD) had made maps by measuring latitude and longitude on land, longitude could not be determined at sea there being no identifiable physical features for which local time differences of astronomical events could be used once and for all as on land (c.f. Section 3.1.4). For these reasons, even comparatively late efforts to map the Mediterranean such as the *Carte Pisano* (c.1275) or the fourteenth century *Mappa Mundi* were of limited use to the seafarer out of sight of land, though pilotage maps were beginning to provide localised information on shoals, landmarks, tides and prevailing winds, and sailing directions called rutters from *routier*, were increasingly available from around 1300.

However, though the *Book of the Devil Valley Master* records use of the directional property of lodestone (magnetic iron oxide) by prospecting Chinese jade-miners of the fourth century BC, it was not until the eleventh century that iron magnetised by rubbing with lodestone and free-floated on water was providing a constant direction indicator, and not until 1119 that such a compass was recorded by the Chinese as having been used at sea. Again, though the attracting property of lodestone was known to the Romans, the ability of magnetised iron to orientate itself in a north-south direction was first recorded in Europe by Alexander Neckham around 1190 and it was 1296 before the military engineer Peter Perigrinus described in his *Epistola Magnete* how a piece of lodestone-magnetised iron wire could be mounted on floating wood to indicate the north-south direction. Though more a craftsman than the master of experimentation described by Roger Bacon, Perigrinus went on to produce practical compasses with marked scales and cardinal points, though the needle-point dry-mounting of magnet and compass-card within a gimbals-mounted case was not available until the sixteenth century.

Now that the direction of travel from a known departure point could be determined, measurement of the speed of travel would determine how far one had travelled in any measured time. The method adopted at sea was to throw over the ship's stern a weighted flat board (having minimal movement relative to the seabed) and to count the number of knots on an attached cord passing through the hand at 48 foot intervals as the ship moved forward in a time measured by the Babylonian sand-glass. The first printed account of this log-line and its use was that of William Bourne in 1574. This, in turn, gave rise to "shooting the log", to measuring speed in "knots" and to recording these speed measurements at appropriate intervals in the "log-book" which came to denote the day-to-day account of the voyage. From these measurements of speed, the distance made good in any measured time could be calculated and with the direction of travel being given by the compass, the new position could be marked on the chart, the process being known as dead-reckoning. It was now necessary to consider how best to represent the spherical surface of the globe as a plane surface on which the mariner could represent the compass course to be steered as a straight line on which to mark speed-indicated positions. This problem was solved by Gerhardus Mercator by projecting the meridian circles and the parallels of latitude of the sphere on to the surface of a circumscribing cylinder which on unrolling to a flat rectangle presented circles of longitude and latitudes as parallel north-south and east-west straight lines respectively. This mercator projection of the map of the world was first published at Duisburg in 1569, from whence dead-reckoned positions were plotted on the basis of compass course steered and distance travelled.

Nonetheless, it was clear that errors in direction and speed would become cumulatively significant with time from the last known departure-point, and that while measurement of the

128

zenith distance with respect to the Pole Star (c.f. Section 3.1.3) would determine and thus correct the latitude of the position arrived at by dead-reckoning, only an accurate determination of the time difference between noon at the position now reached, and noon at a known reference position would thus correct the longitude of the position arrived at by dead-reckoning. Alas, the necessary accuracy in time-keeping was not achieved until the latter half of the eighteenth century. On the other hand, the astrolabe of Ptolemy had already been converted to the quadrant and the cross-staff for determination of latitude at sea and these were followed by the back-staff invented by John Davis in 1594 with which the user had his back to the Sun.

5. 7. 3 Mechanisation

Mechanisation from quite early times had provided mechanical advantage to the effort of human and animal muscle (c.f. Section 2. 3. 5) the Romans, for example, having used tread-mills for raising water and water wheels for grinding corn. However, as slaves became less readily available and paid labour scarce after the Black Death in the fourteenth century, the replacement of men by machines became increasingly necessary and it was fortunate that trade-generated wealth made investment capital available for the necessary machines (c.f. Section 10.6).

Thus, though the Roman water-wheel changed little in basic design, it was put to ever increasing uses during the Dark Age as the prime mover for lifting drainage-water and product from shaft-bottoms in mining, crushing ore with trip-hammers, operating bellows, forging metal, sawing wood, making water-pipes by boring logs, and fulling cloth. These varied applications called for both reciprocating and rotary motions which required gearing and power transmissions by connecting rods and cranks, the latter being illustrated in 1430. Apart from riverside installations, floating mills such as those built on the Tiber by Belisarius in 537 continued to be widely used in Europe, usually downstream of bridges. Indeed, the Domesday Book of 1086 records 5,624 watermills south of the Trent alone. Though the estimated 2 horsepower output of such mills was poor, their importance may be judged from the large volume of legislation covering their water-supply. Tide-mills were also constructed at sites where water could usefully be trapped in a reservoir at high tide and allowed to flow through the mill-steam during the ebb, but their contribution was small until the eighteenth century.

Given the early use of wind for boat propulsion, it is surprising that windmills cannot be dated earlier than to seventh century Persia. These earliest versions, having six to eight sails on vertical shafts like Tibetan prayer wheels were located within shuttered walls to direct the wind to one side and to control its force to grind corn without gearing and the grain-scorching otherwise caused by over-heated bearings. This design travelled westward to Spain and eastwards to China where in the thirteenth century six junk-type battened furling sails were mounted on a vertical shaft making the shield-wall redundant. Subsequently in Europe, a change to a horizontal shaft with four sails and appropriate gearing brought increased efficiency because the whole sail area was now in continuous use provided the sails always faced the wind, for which there were two solutions. In the post mill (twelfth century onwards) the whole body of the mill was rotated on a central vertical post by pushing a long tail-pole as wind direction changed. In the tower mill some two centuries later, the body of the mill was fixed and often of masonry construction, while the cap carrying the sails was turned to face the wind. Again, when the early horizontal shaft was found to cause bearing problems immediately behind the sails, an inclined shaft was introduced to transfer some of the weight to a stouter bearing at the inner and lower end of the shaft.

Although these mills were used mainly for grinding corn to about 1430 and thereafter for such other purposes as previously served by water-wheels, they later became notably associated with land-drainage in the Low Countries and the English Fens, estimated outputs by then being about 5 horsepower. Frictional losses were high because bearings, gearings and power transmissions were constructed in wood, occasionally re-inforced with iron, while roller bearings were unused before the early eighteenth century and true ball bearings were unavailable till 1772. However, various mechanical instruments calling for a high degree of precision such as those used in astronomy and navigation at sea were being constructed in metal, many so skilfully decorated as to have become collectors' items principally for this reason. However, the required skill encouraged attempts to produce mechanical clocks of which earlier related examples were the classical clepsydras (water clocks) and planetaria, the second century clepsydra-driven celestial sphere of Zhang Hang, and the eighth century mechanical clock of Yi Xing and Liang Lingzan.

In the first European mechanical clocks (c. 1300) a cord was wound many times round a horizontal shaft which rotated as the weighted free-end of the cord descended, rotation being regulated by a device (escapement) consisting of a pair of rocking arms (foliots) mounted on a vertical spindle (verge) each arm ending in a pawl which sequentially engaged and disengaged with a toothed wheel (crown wheel) mounted on the end of the weight-activated shaft. The contact faces of the pawls and the teeth of the crown wheel were made alternately curved and flat so that rotation of the crown wheel would itself cause engagement and disengagement in a regular oscillatory manner to control the rotation of the shaft and the hand attached to it which showed the passing hours on the clock-face. Early clocks being accurate to about an hour a day, a minute hand was judged unnecessary. Nevertheless this accuracy was sufficiently encouraging for them to appear in public locations and for some quite elaborate mechanisms to be based on them. One of the earliest surviving examples dating from 1386 is that of Salisbury Cathedral, though now without its original escapement, while the astronomical clock of Giovanni de' Dondi of Padua, of which only the description survives was built between 1348 and 1362 to show time in hours and date and the motions of Sun, Moon and five Planets. However, the inaccuracy necessitated frequent time checks against sundials, these becoming more common with the popularity of the clocks.

The next step was the mid fifteenth century substitution of a spring for the weighted cord which permitted the building of table and shelf clocks immediately, and pocket watches by the end of the century. The problem to be overcome with spring-driven clocks was the decreasing driving-force of the uncoiling spring. The first solution was to increase the turning effect (c.f. Section 2.3.5) applied to the shaft in progressive compensation for the decreasing effectiveness of the spring, this being achieved by equipping the shaft with a concentric conical drum (fusee) from the spiral groove of which a fine cord or chain was unwound by the spring so as to increase the radius at which the turning force was applied to the shaft. The fusee made its appearance in the first half of the sixteenth century and further progressive improvements were introduced by Christiaan Huygens (c.f. Section 6.3.5) in the form of a pendulum-driven escapement (1657) for weight-driven clocks and the balance spring (1675) for spring driven ones, at which point it became worthwhile to add minute hands to time-pieces.

5. 7. 4 Architecture and Building

I previously noted that the limited beam-spans of the classical period caused internal spaces in public buildings to be severely constrained by the presence of supporting columns; and that although domed roofs provided more open space, they required circular supporting walls as exemplified by the Pantheon built at Rome in the first century AD. I now show how these limitations were overcome in the Dark Age.

Fifth century attempts to build a dome on a square building were based on the squinch, a corbelled arch-structure built up from the four corners to round them off. Later, the pendent arch

130

was introduced, consisting of portions of vaulting rising from the corner supports of the underlying structure with ribbing on the vault crowns and intersections for additional support. Another problem was that window voids weakened load bearing walls and while the absence of windows might provide welcome coolness in warm countries, the absence of light was unwelcome everywhere. Thus, while the building of Hagia Sophia, completed at Constantinople in 537, used standard Roman technique for the main square building with bricks predominating over masonry, it was surmounted by a dome of 100 foot span supported on pendentives between which windows were inserted to illuminate the opposite lower mosaic-covered walls, an effect which caused Justinian to exclaim, "Solomon, I have outdone thee".

After its re-conquest by Justinian, this new Byzantine approach was introduced to Italy with completion in 547 of the church of San Vitale in Ravenna, the dome of which was constructed of hollow earthenware pots to reduce weight. Byzantine building then spread through Italy, pre-Muslin Spain and thence to the rest of Europe with the counter-earthquake innovations of its homeland being retained, among which were bronze-band column re-enforcement, layers of shock-adsorbent lead beneath columns and lintels, and generous use of wood and iron cross-ties. Europe differed from Byzantium, however, in preferring masonry to brick, though smaller blocks were used for ease of handling and transport on bad roads. Nonetheless, the resulting structures remained heavy as exemplified by the original eleventh century Winchester Cathedral with its rubble-filled cavity-walls of more than 2 metre thickness.

The Romanesque building style was indeed overpoweringly massive with its thick walls, small doors and windows and dark interiors, disadvantages which were addressed around the middle of the twelfth century by introduction of the pointed arch and its combination with the rib vault. The pointed arch first appeared in Mosque building in the late eighth century and entered Europe through Spain. It permits more design flexibility than the semi-circular Roman arch in that the overall height is not controlled by the distance between the supports. Thus, it was used in Europe to produce cross-vaults of equal heights but of differing spans and it was seen to reduce the lateral thrust of pitched roofs on supporting walls which in turn permitted thinner load-bearing walls and more window area in such walls. Again, this led to light-weight vaults and slender piers supported where necessary by external buttresses conjoined or flying, which in turn increased the useable internal space and provided higher levels of natural illumination, these innovations being referred to as the Gothic Revolution, the first example of which was the Parisian Abbey of St. Denis when rebuilt around 1140.

Church windows were initially open and later draped with fabric or protected by shutters, until glass began to be used in the seventh century, the Venerable Bede having brought craftsmen from France to glaze the windows of his church at Durham in 675. However, stained glass was not used in Europe until the twelfth century and painted glass not till the fourteenth. Again, iron which had been used since Greek and Roman times to tie stonework was now used in Gothic building to reinforce mullions in windows and the ribbing of vaults. Wood secured by wooden pins or sometimes with iron was used in substantial quantities for roofing and in locations where it was judged more suitable than masonry. Thus eight oak beams each 16m by 0.80m by 0.50m and weighing 6 tonnes approximately were used in the construction of the lantern of Ely Cathedral in 1322. The Gothic style also embodied copious quantities of ornamental stone-work.

Roofs were erected over vaulting, the pitch depending on anticipated loading which often included that of roofing-lead in ¼ inch thick sheets together with that of snowfall where this was significant. It was also known that the lower the pitch the greater the tendency for the rafter-legs to spread, a problem solved by placing the rafter-feet behind a masonry parapet on the outer supporting wall when the roof was to be close to the arch of the vault. Alternatively the rafter-feet could be tied together with a cross-beam if the outer wall could be raised to allow the cross-beam to clear the arch. A more likely compromise was to tie the rafters together at a height between their feet and the roof-ridge. This last option called for a truss on each side between a rebate in the outer supporting wall and a point on the rafter just below the cross-beam. If more room could be had between arch and roof-ridge, a pair of diagonal braces could be inserted from the foot of one rafter to a point below the ridge on the other, this usually calling for an additional horizontal tie below the intersection of the diagonal braces.

In some buildings where vaulting was omitted and the rafters exposed, the impression of height and space was greatest with the diagonal option. In England, however, the hammer beam truss was a national peculiar which maximised this desirable impression. It consisted of a short horisontal truss projecting inwards from the wall, its outer-end rebated into the wall and locked in position by the downwards thrust of a rafter-foot, while a vertical pillar rose from its inner-end to support this rafter while a curved bracket (similar in function to a hanging-knee in shipbuilding) transferred support from the lower wall surface to the inner-end of the short horizontal truss and thence to the rafter *via* the support pillar. This basic unit could be repeated as many times as necessary until the middle of the span was reached where it met its partner from the other side, at which point the short trusses from both sides became a tie-beam between the rafter pair. In progressing to this point, the successive curved brackets transferred support from the inner end of one short truss to the outer end of the one above. Westminster Hall provides a wide-span example of concept, execution, repetition and ornamentation of the hammer beam truss.

In Medieval Europe timber-framed houses and halls were customary, the spaces between the framework being filled with masonry, brick or wattle-and-daub, the roofs being supported by simpler or more complicated options within the techniques described above as specifically required. Thus, the mansard roof was preferred from the sixteenth century onwards where attic rooms were required. In this, the rafter comprised two lenths of timber of which the lower was more steeply pitched than the upper, the feet of the lower rafter lengths being tied together with a beam doubling as a joist for the attic flooring while the upper-ends of the lower rafter lengths were supported by a vertical pillar rising from this beam/joist. Again, the upper-end of the lower rafter provided support for the lower end of the upper and the two uppers were cross-tied by a short beam near their upper ends. By thus 'flexing' the normal rafter outwards, greater headroom was provided over more of the floor space, the short pillars providing inside wall supports and the upper cross-ties providing attachment for a ceiling. Yet again, the beam/joist prevented rafter-spread while this system could be terminated behind a parapet or extended to form eaves.

5. 7. 5 Warfare

I have already discussed military building and weaponry up to and through the classical period. However, with the coming of the Dark Age the strategy of building for city and frontier defence was abandoned in favour of castle building for tactical local purposes, the design of which can be traced back to that at Sinjerli in seventh century BC Syria.

The Franks began to build such castles about the middle of the ninth century as a defense against Norse invaders and when the Norman descendants of the latter invaded England in 1066 they recognised the need for rapid construction of strong-points from which to secure recently conquered territory. They satisfied this need with the motte and bailey which consisted of a wooden palisade on a mound (motte) of earth raised by excavation of a ditch around the area (bailey) surrounding the mound. Around this a second ditch was dug, the excavated material being used to form a rampart which was completed with a palisade. This complex may be seen as a more permanent version of the fortified camps erected in hostile territory by the Roman Army on the march. The Normans built a hundred motte and bailey "castles" before 1100 for gradual replacement with stone structures for which mottes had to be built up in rammed-hard layers and waterproofed with clay before they were strong enough for masonry work to begin. In these replacements the central strong-point (keep or donjon) became a square or rectangular masonry structure, the palisade being replaced by a stone curtain-wall. The White Tower of London (started 1078) exemplifies such Norman building being 36 x 33 metres and having walls 4.5 metres thick at the base.

After the capture of Jerusalem in 1099 as a result of the first crusade of 1095, Norman motte-and-bailey type 'castles' were rapidly built, but as opposition strengthened and European manpower became less available, the crusaders built more permanent strongholds of which Krak des Chevaliers (started, 1110) is the most impressive with its subterranean water cisterns of 9 million litre capacity. Nonetheless, much was learned on both sides by the early capture and subsequent loss of Saracen strongholds culminating in the fall of Acre after a six week siege in 1291, contact in the meantime having been made with much of Byzantine origin such as portcullises, murder-holes and machicolations. Thus, the Knights Templar who had strengthened the castle at Ponferrada on the pilgrim route to Santiago de Compostela in 1178, brought back to Europe much that was innovative as exemplified by the similarity of the Bab al-Futuh gateway of the Saracen defences at Cairo (started 1087) with its flanking round towers and archery embrasures, to the gate-flanking towers of Harlech Castle (1285) the latter being only one of the many built by the Norman English to subdue Wales, by the Celts in recovering the Western Isles and Highlands from the Norsemen and by the Scots for subsequent defence of the rest of Scotland against the Norman English.

Given that wood was the building material for ships, doors in defensive walls, wall-scaling platforms *etc*, it is not surprising that incendiary devices were used as depicted in Assyrian bas-reliefs of the ninth century BC; that ignited mixtures of bitumen, resin and sulphur were delivered by arrows, projected fire-pots and as fire-ships at the siege of Tyre in 332BC; that fire-bombs containing quicklime (obtained from roasting chalk) which self-ignites on contact with water are described by Pliny; that a flame-throwing device which force-pumped a burning liquid through a bronze tube was used in the defence of Constantinople in 671; that a tenth century Byzantine manuscript shows a boat's crew directing a flame jet at another; and that this so-called *Greek Fire* suggests an origin earlier than the Byzantines who referred to themselves as Roman. Later, the Saracen *naphatun,* (naphtha troops) deployed Greek Fire against the crusaders and as *wild fire* it was apparently used by Edward I at Stirling in 1304. However, its use was curtailed by the advent of gunpowder.

As to this, the Chinese had been using mixtures of sulphur, saltpetre and charcoal as offensive incendiary devices from perhaps as early as the seventh century, their building material being almost exclusively wood. More surely, however, the *Collection of the Most Important Military Techniques* of 1044 gives six parts saltpetre, three parts sulphur and one part charcoal for what we now refer to as gunpowder. Initially, such mixtures were added to flammable materials such as hemp and tar to create a more effective form of Greek Fire, though by 1132 the mixture was being packed into bamboo tubes to produce flame-throwing lances to which round shot was later added. However, the *Tearful Records of the Battle of Qizhou* (1221) refers only to arrows loaded with the mixture and to mixture-filled containers both barbed and un-barbed, there being no reference to projectile delivery by explosion of the mixture.

We now know that explosion is brought about by instantaneous conversion of small-volume solid sulphur, charcoal (carbon) and saltpetre (sodium nitrate) to very much larger volumes of gaseous sulphur dioxide and carbon dioxide by reaction with oxygen concentrated in the nitrate group of solid saltpetre, rather than from the air which would simply cause sulphur and carbon to burn. However, the Chinese had no understanding of this process in theory, and could not realise the full potential of their mixture in practice, their early bamboo tubes bursting before any usefull projection pressure could be generated within them. It was only when they produced bronze or iron tubes (cannon barrels) that they could realise anything like the full potential of their mixture. This they had done by 1332, the date of a canon in the Museum of Chinese History, Beijing, and they quickly used this mixture as a rocket propellant to deliver 'shrapnel' bombs detonated towards the end of their flight by time-fuses. Thus, following the now familiar trade-route, saltpetre became known in Persian as 'China Salt' and in Arabic as 'Chinese Snow', an Arabic military treatise of about 1290 giving directions for its purification and some versions of the *Liber Ignium* of Marcus Graecus giving recipes for its preparation. There is also some indication that Roger Bacon (died 1294) was aware of gunpowder and in any case cannon were in use at Metz in 1324, at Florence in 1326, in Scotland in 1327, and ubiquitously by the mid fourteenth century.

Early cannon barrels were forged with a brazed or welded seam until the eleventh century when the technique for casting bronze bells up to a tonne in weight was applied to the casting of bronze barrels. As to iron barrels, these were initially formed by welding longitudinal rods around a removable core and binding with iron hoops, the barrels being mounted on heavy wooden carriages, muzzle-loaded with a gunpowder charge and stone or iron round shot and discharged by a red-hot iron or a lit fuse of saltpetre-impregnated rope. Early cannon weighed about 70 kilograms rising to 300kg by the end of the fourteenth century. Occasionally special requirements produced heavier weapons such as the iron cannon made at Caen in 1375 which weighed one tonne, that for the Duke of Burgundy in 1377 which fired 200kg shot and that for the Turks at the siege of Constantinople in 1453 which weighed 19 tonnes. Experience showed that fine grained gunpowder tended to burn rather than to explode as desired, and thus, by 1425 the ingredients were mixed wet (safer anyway) and passed through a sieve to form granules which exploded more reliably and to the effect of doubling the projective efficiency of artillery.

This new and powerful means of warfare was usable in the battlefield and in destroying defensive walls while mortars were quickly developed to lob shot over walls. In addition, the time-honoured practice of mining walls was now made more effective by filling the excavated space beneath the wall with explosive and detonating it. As to defence, recoil made cannon difficult to use on the relatively constrained space atop defensive parapets and initially defenders could only strengthen walls against cannon attack as need arose, often by banking earth against them on the inside. However, more massive fortifications were devised to prevent shot penetration. These comprised rounded or oblique wall-surfaces to deflect shot on impact, replacement of curtain-wall towers by bastions strong and spacious enough to house several cannon with an open field of fire for the protection of adjacent lengths of curtain wall and with adjacent bastions having overlapping fields of fire over all approaches to the walls. Satisfaction of these requirements was sufficiently demanding to attract the attention of Leonardo da Vinci and Albrecht Durer. Thus, many polygonal (oblique-walled) structures were built by Sebastien Vauban who as Commissary General of Fortifications in France in 1678 also introduced parallel trenches to protect the advance of besieging forces and the socket bayonet first used around 1650 at Bayonne.

The use of gunpowder in hand-held weapons was slow to replace the longbow (retained until the end of the seventeenth century) because their firing rate was comparatively slow and accuracy poor. Thus, having muzzle-loaded the earliest musket with charge, ball and wadding, discharge was effected by applying a glowing match to some powder in a priming-pan before the charge could be ignited by pulling the trigger. Thus, while it could compete with the cross-bow in firing rate, its inaccuracy made it unsuitable for other than for close-quarter use. However, in the
134

succeeding matchlock the glowing match was applied to the primer by pulling the trigger, enabling the musketeer to use both hands to aim and steady the weapon for greater accuracy. Again by the early sixteenth century a spark was applied to the primer by rubbing a spring-loaded wheel against a piece of pyrites (iron sulphide) while in the flintlock of 1630 a flint could be cocked and released by the trigger to produce a more reliable and timely spark. The flintlock was adopted by the French Army around 1660 and shortly afterwards it became the firing mechanism of the Brown Bess of the British Army. Though it had been recognised as early as the sixteenth century that barrel rifling would cause the bullet to spin in flight and greatly improve accuracy, the required close-fit could only be achieved initially by tapping a suitably soft bullet into the barrel, a slower procedure than for a smooth-bored barrel. Thus, while rifling became popular with sportsmen, it did not enter military use until further development in the seventeenth century.

Though Dark Age knights wore a long hooded tunic in chain-mail weighing up to 40kg augmented by a steel plate helm and by similar plate protection in locations which tolerated such inflexibility, a full suit of articulated plate-armour was so heavy as to be reserved largely for jousting tournaments. Thus, the introduction of gunpowder made full body protection impossibly heavy by the fifteenth century, though various degrees of light plate-armour were still in favour for close-quarter fighting with traditional hand weapons. However, by the mid-seventeenth century this protection had been reduced to little more than breast and back plates and later to nothing at all, though the steel helmet was later re-introduced.

Meanwhile, the techniques of naval warfare had progressed from early ramming as practiced by the Greeks, through the boarding practices of the Romans and the amphibious raiding of the Norsemen, to archery from fore and aft castles for ship to ship fighting and repulse of boarding-parties and on to the advent of cannon and musketry. These latter, could now be used as the bow and arrow had been to keep the enemy at a distance, to discourage his attempts to board and to reduce his defensive strength to permit boarding him. However, cannon also offered the possibility of sinking the enemy and of attacking shore defences in support of amphibious landings. Thus, up to the sixteenth century emphasis was on reducing the enemy by cannon and musket fire prior to boarding while in the two succeeding centuries sinking and shore attack became more realistic options as ships were equipped with ever-increasing numbers of increasingly heavy cannon deployed on up to three gun-decks on the largest 'men o' war'.

5. 8 CONCLUSIONS: FROM TIME IMMEMORIAL TO 1700

Chapter 2 concluded that our innate Rational Trinity as evolved from our ape-like and hominid precursors had produced the craftsmanship and social arrangements which had taken us through our hunter-gatherer stages to the city-states and Empires of the Iron Age. Similarly, Chapter 3 concluded that the same Rational Trinity had increased our knowledge of human nature as reflected in the development of myths, literature, drama, behaviour codes and law, while producing descriptive world knowledge akin to that of craftsmanship in biology, optics and geography while applying craft-derived mathematics to observation of the celestial regions and to the further development of craftsmanship; and that all else was Rational Duality belief and speculation. As to religious belief, Chapter 4 concluded that while the Church acted rationally in appropriating Judaism and in accommodating Paganism to establish Christianity within the Roman Empire, it acted irrationally in destroying the Empire in its struggle to establish an orthodoxy from its violently opposed heresies and in rejecting 'worldly knowledge' while accepting craftsmanship.

As to this Chapter, it may be concluded that such knowledge as was lost in the West with the

Fall of Rome was conserved and enhanced in the East by Pagans, Jews, Zoroastrians and heretical Christians as assisted by the Hindu number system and as permitted by conquering Islam; that it returned to Christian Europe through those conquests and their repulse, around the time of its growing rejection by some interpretations of Islam; and that it could have been opposed again by orthodox Christianity through failure to differentiate religious belief from the speculations of natural philosophy. However, it may be concluded that many Churchmen now saw benefit in this recovered inheritance of undifferentiated knowledge and speculation; that Thomas Aquinas assisted in its acceptance; and that while few if any were immediately able to assimilate and develop its knowledge-content, the West had not totally lost its medical, architectural and 'liberal arts' heritage, much of which was already acceptable to the pre-Aquinas Church and readily assimilated by existing practitioners of anatomy, scholarship and craftsmanship.

However, it may further be concluded that advances in mathematics, observational astronomy and year-length determination, mechanics, medicine, anatomy, plant classification, alchemical technique and craft-like optical experimentation (c.f. Al-Hazen, Section 5.2.1) had all been as neutral to interpretations of Islamic belief as they had been to those of Pagan, Judaic or heretical Christian belief; that western Dark Age advance in the crafts of paper-making and movable-type printing, shipbuilding and navigation, mechanisation (including clock-making), architecture, building and warfare were neutral to contemporary changes in western Christian belief (c.f. Section 6.4); and that our Rational Trinity self-knowledge had maintained the socially cohesive systems which from time immemorial to 1700 had enabled continuous benefit to accrue from craft-use of knife, needle, drill, hammer, axe, saw, chisel and lathe to work animal derivatives and vegetable-fibre, wood and stone, minerals and metals, despite all the confusions and conflicts generated by our Rational Duality beliefs, though we would have been better off without them.

CHAPTER 6: THE RENAISSANCE

The interest in classical literature, art and architecture being greater than that in classical natural philosophy, the concept of distinct cultures of art and science arose despite the true dichotomy being belief and knowledge. However, failure to differentiate these two was paralleled by failure to differentiate cause and effect. Nonetheless, its unconscious presence in craftsmanship was extended to what is now called experimentation and though this was only slowly and fitfully understood, it made the Renaissance not a rebirth but something else entirely.

6. 1 THE DEVELOPMENT OF EXPERIMENTATION FROM CRAFTSMANSHIP

Chapters 2, 3 and 5 have shown that reality-evaluation of belief by direct observation produced behaviour codes, craftsmanship, art and descriptive knowledge of the world as it is, while all was speculation as to its underlying nature. However, as to cause and effect, we should note that craftsmen and artists achieve *predictable* results through control of the tools, materials and procedures of their respective crafts (arts) through direct observation of *cause and effect*, the causes being the tool-use of the craftsman (or artist) who simultaneously observes effects until the final effect completes the work. Similarly, an experimenter seeking to understand a natural phenomenon, imagines a *hypothetical cause and effect mechanism*, creates a system to replicate it, and reality-evaluates his hypothesis by *quantitatively* varying and recording his cause while observing and recording the *quantified* effect in isolation from extraneous causes and their effects, this being the experimentation which produces *scientific* knowledge. A mistaken hypothesis is highly unlikely to re-produce the phenomenon under investigation and confidence is increased when mathematical expression of the cause and effect relationship *predicts* effects from causes, even outside the range of experimentation, from a *quantified initial condition*. Again, assumptions as to the existence of cause and effect from correlations between selected parameters are hypothetical at best and must be considered coincidental until established by designed experimentation. Thus, craftsmen (direct observation) and scientists (designed experimentation) can predict effects from causes on the basis of reality-validated knowledge of mechanism whereas nothing can be predicted on belief alone.

Further to the evolution of experimentalist from craftsman, it may be seen that the craftsman applies his existing knowledge and tools to cause effects on his work-material to create his artefact as product, while the experimentalist applies his existing knowledge and his tools (his experimentation system) to cause effects on his work-material (the phenomenon under investigation) in order to create knowledge of its cause and effect mechanism as product. Again, the craftsman learns by reality-evaluation the cause which will achieve the desired effect in his work-piece, while the experimentalist learns by reality-evaluation how to predict the effect of cause, from knowledge of the cause and effect mechanisms underlying the phenomena of the natural world, the knowledge thus acquired being deeper than that of craftsmen.

Thus, while reality-evaluation was the basis of craftsmanship from time immemorial, its derivative experimentation was not practiced until much later, being first distinguishable from craftsmanship in the optical investigations of Al-Hazen (c.f. Section 5.2.1) though not recognised as such until Roger Bacon (c.f. Section 5.6.1) applied the term experimentalist to such craftsmen as Peregrinus (c.f. Section 5.7.2). Thus, I have eschewed the mistaken practice of others who describe classical speculation (belief) as early science (knowledge), by defining as craftsmen even those who classified, measured and calculated on the basis of direct observation of the world as it is, these activities being well short of experimentation. Thus, I define a scientist as one who determines underlying cause and effect by the reality-evaluation of hypotheses by experimentation and who relies on knowledge thus acquired to produce further hypotheses for further reality-evaluation. Readers may find it helpful to recall this definition of scientist and hence of scientific knowledge in deciding whether named individuals are scientists or believers as we proceed from here through Chapter 10, it being my intention thus to differentiate knowledge from belief and science from pseudo-science before exemplifying in Chapters 11 and 12, the consequences of failure to do so.

As to such differentiation, it should be remembered that chance observation of a correlation between two parameters does not mean that one is the cause of the other, such mistaken attribution now being a major source of the confusion produced by those who do not understand scientific method. Thus, for example, a correlation between decreasing plankton numbers and an increase in the presence of a particular chemical in seawater or an increase in the issuance of TV licences or . . . whatever, would automatically identify the chemical as the cause of the observed effect for belief-driven pseudo-scientists (c.f. Section 11.2.3-11.2.5) despite the absence of a reality-validated cause and effect mechanism making it equally logical to blame television. Thus, correlation without reality-validation of mechanism, defines the nonsense which is pseudo-science. Indeed, definitions of science which are based on its supposed 'refutability' or 'acceptance of one belief until a better one comes along', are definitions of pseudo-science and not of science (c.f. Sections 6.2.4, 6.3.2, 6.3.4, 6.4, 8.3.4, 11.2.1 and 12.1).

6. 2 THE PERIOD 1400 - Circa 1600

While the Renaissance shows some sporadic and incomplete recognition of the experimentation which defines scientific method, most enquiry continued at the earlier craft-like descriptive level in a period more transitional than progressive. Thus, Roger Bacon (1214-94) exemplified experimentation by reference to the benefits conferred by the craftsmanship of such as Peregrinus (Section 5.7.2) while Robert Grosseteste (1175-1253) familiarised himself with the optics of Al-Hazen (c.f. Section 5.4.2). Again, while Nicolas de Cusa (1401-64) sought to eliminate all other causes in his investigation of air as the sole cause of weight-increase in growing plants and wrote a book on use of the balance in what can be described as investigation of cause and effect by experimentation, he was ignored until taken up by Jan Baptist van Helmont (1577-1644). Yet again, though Nicolas de Cusa became a cardinal he was no more successful than Roger Bacon had been in persuading his Pope to reform the calendar. Against this background, I review the Renaissance as a period of transition to something else entirely.

6. 2. 1 Continuation of Pre-Dark Age Methods
With respect to the re-instatement of pre-Dark Age lines of enquiry, Georg Purbach (1423-61) started to prepare a digest of Ptolemy's *Almagest* available to him in Latin translation from the Arabic, but his early death prevented its completion though not before he had calculated and prepared a table of sines for every ten minutes of arc. Later, from Greek originals accessible to him, Johannes Muller also known as Regiomontanus (1436-76) completed Purbach's digest of the

Almagest, produced a table of sines for every minute of arc, tangents for every degree of arc, and the first systematic treatise on trigonometry though this was not published till 1533. Meanwhile, towards the end of his life, Regiomontanus was summoned to Rome to assist in correction of the calendar though this was again deferred.

Again, pre-Dark Age descriptive work on human, animal and plant anatomy was continued by those pursuing greater verisimilitude in their painting. Thus, Antonio Pallaiuolo (1428-98) and Andrea del Verrocchio (1435-99) made careful studies of surface anatomy for this purpose as did Sandro Botticelli for plants while Leonardo da Vinci (1452-1519) investigated musculature and skeletal anatomy through the practice of dissection to improve his representational painting technique as indicated in his working notes. Again, Albrecht Durer (1471-1528) studied the details of human anatomy in respect of changes in structural proportion with growth and age within the sexes, and similarly the structural details, habits and growth of animals and plants for artistic reasons. Thus, all such were engaged in knowledge-acquisition by observation and pictorial description in the manner of earlier workers.

Again, both Leonardo da Vinci and Albrecht Durer developed the theory and practice of pictorial perspective, while the former ranged from mathematics to physiology, embryology, comparative vertebrate anatomy, animal motion, bird flight and the provision of drawings for mechanical devices such as gliders, weaponry and defensive structures, and the latter took an interest in optics and the properties of sound. Nonetheless, while they appreciated the wonder of nature and the benefits of direct observation, they are remembered for their pictorial work and nor for experimentation. However, as to knowledge-acquisition by earlier means we must remember that early Renaissance scholars stood in awe of the ancients and were largely content to produce commentaries on their achievements or to proceed along their established lines, having neither the desire nor the ability to change them.

6. 2. 2 Increasing Scepticism towards the Classical Inheritance

Unlike his contemporaries, Aureolus Philippus Theophrastus Bombastus von Hohenheim (1493-1541) also known as Paracelsus, was not inhibited by respect or modesty in emphasising that it was better to see the world in the "light of nature" than to seek it in ancient texts. Thus, he symbolically burned the works of Galen and Avicenna as an introduction to his lecture course at Basel, though his own writings are obscure and replete with mystical overtones. Thus, for Paracelsus, nature included the influence of celestial bodies on human lives through the microcosm/macrocosm relationship of classical antiquity, though he founded a new school (c. 1525) in medico-chemical treatments, now called Iatro-chemistry. In this connection, Geber (c. 850) had believed that base metals could be treated with a fifth element or quintessence to transmute them to gold and with translations from the Arabic becoming available the 'profession' of alchemy (c.f. Section 5.4.3) rose to a position of considerable importance in post-Dark Age Europe. Thus, it was believed that gold and silver contained or consisted of a pure mercury and a pure sulphur while other metals contained or consisted of varying proportions of 'unclean' sulphur; that transmutation of base to noble metals thus required the sulphur to be 'cleansed' and the proportions of mercury and sulphur to be altered by treatment with the fifth element or quintessence now referred to as the *Philosopher's Stone*; that sulphur and fire were the principles of combustibility and transformation respectively, while 'salt' was the 'fixed part' which remained after metals were roasted in air. Thus, Paraselsus came to believe in the transmutation of illness to health by treatment with an *Elixir of Life* whence it was but a small step to believe *Stone* and *Elixir* to be one and the same.

Thus, while Paracelsus had one foot in the old, his Iatro-chemistry was a step towards the chemistry of life, even if inspired by his belief in the Stone/Elixir. Again, his liberating belief that not everything in the ancient texts was definitive and his uncompromisingly arrogant style of belief presentation in general, must have encouraged his more cautious listeners to pursue evidence (reality-evaluation) for or against questionable beliefs. One of his less flamboyant contemporaries was the mining engineer Georg Agricola (1490-1555) often referred to as 'the father of mineralogy' whose book *De Re Metallica* (1546) summarised the mining and metallurgical knowledge of his day and now reminds us of the extensive craft-knowledge which co-existed with the beliefs of alchemy and much else. Agricola is also credited with founding physical geography as a subject of enquiry and with concluding that fossils were the remains of extinct organisms (c.f. Section 8.3.3) though he contributed nothing to scientific method (c.f. 8.3.4).

Meanwhile, the sixteenth century voyages of exploration collected many new life forms which combined with Iatro-chemical interest in vegetable-based drugs, artistic interest in plant and animal depiction and the timely perfection of woodcut and copperplate engraving, gave rise to extremely high quality prints of plants in particular. Thus, Otto Brunfels (1489-1534) of Mainz was the first to produce an illustrated work on plants based wholly on observation (Strasbourg, 1530) which compares well with the best modern illustrative productions though he misguidedly tried to relate his Rhineland plants to the Mediterranean plants of Dioscorides. In contrast, Jerome Block (1498-1554) of Heiderbach did not attempt to relate to other locations his careful descriptions of plants as found (Strasbourg 1539) and though it was some time before such attempted comparisons were wholly abandoned, Leonard Fuchs (1501-66) produced a guide to the collector of medicinal plants (Basel, 1542) based on his extremely high-quality woodcuts with a glossary of botanical terms without any classification and with little on geography of occurrence or on the nature of plants as a distinct life form.

The same illustrative and printing interests were combined with detailed observation of human anatomy in the work of Andreas Vesalius (1514-64) who studied at Louvain and later familiarised himself at Paris with the work of Galen before becoming professor at Padua in 1537. By this time the successors of Mondino had replaced his practice of direct dissection with lecturing direct from the texts of Galen while a demonstrator indicated the dissected parts to the students. Vesalius, however, "put his own hand to the business" and in five years had completed and printed his great work *On the Fabric of the Human Body* (Basel, 1543). In this book the treatment of the bones and joints follows Galen but the muscles are depicted in the normal degree of contraction in life rather than as dead structures. It is what he has to say about the heart, however, which we should note as evidence of a change in attitude. Readers will recall (c.f. 3.1.4) that Galen believed the blood to pass from one ventricle to the other through a septum by a process of drip-feed. In contrast, Vesalius reports on the evidence of his own dissections to the effect that ". . . not long ago I would not have dared to turn aside a hair's breadth from Galen. But the septum of the heart is as thick, dense, and compact as the rest of the heart. I do not see, therefore, how even the smallest particle can pass from the right to the left ventricle through the septum." Here we see the former reverence for the classical texts, which Paracelsus had decried in his rough and indiscriminate way, now succumbing to the careful observations of such as Vesalius which refute and reject earlier observations or confirm and retain them for further development as appropriate to their own observational experience.

Again, access to Ptolemy's *Almagest* in Latin through the translation of Regiomontanus encouraged more astronomical observation which led to further knowledge and to more accurate calculation. Thus, for example, Leonardo da Vinci explained the phenomenon of the "new Moon in the arms of the old" *i.e.* the dimly visible surface of the Moon when the Sun illuminates only the new crescent as being due to sunlight reflected from the illuminated hemisphere of the Earth which

140

could thus be called "Earthshine". Again, Jerome Fracastor of Verona (1483-1543) observed that the tails of comets always lie in a direction away from the Sun while Jean Fernel (1497-1558) a French physician re-calculated the size of the Earth in 1528 to within 1% of the true value. In addition, the Pole, Nicholas Copernicus (1473-1543) though more of a scholar than an observer in having attended university courses in mathematics, astronomy, law, medicine and theology until he was over thirty years old, eventually became interested "to try whether, on the assumption of some motion of the Earth, better explanations of the revolutions of the heavenly spheres might be found." As a result his book *De Revolutionibus* presents a helio-centric system of circular planetary orbits in distance order from the Sun as Mercury, Venus, Earth circled by its Moon, Mars, Jupiter, Saturn and the Sphere of the Fixed Stars. While this placed the Sun at the centre of a system with a moving Earth and required fewer Ptolemaic epicycles and eccentrics, it still required thirty-four.

On the other hand, the meticulous Danish observer, Tycho Brahe (1546-1601) collected data on planetary and other celestial motions over a period of twenty-two years from which he concluded in 1588 that the Earth was at the centre of the orbits of the Moon and Sun and central to the sphere of the fixed stars; that the Sun revolved round the Earth once in 24 hours carrying the orbits of Mercury, Venus, Mars, Jupiter and Saturn with it; that Mercury and Venus had orbits smaller than the Sun's orbit round the Earth; that the three outer planets orbited outside the Earth and its encircling Moon; and that this system explained the observed planetary movements in a manner identical to that of Copernicus. Brahe also showed by parallax that a comet was more distant than the Moon and thus was in the realm of the Changeless Spheres in contradiction of Aristotle; and that its motion might be "not exactly circular but somewhat oblong" in contradiction of belief in the perfect circularity of celestial motions. Here again, as with Vesalius we see a willingness to prefer the results of observation to the unsupported assertions of the ancients, though again we see that planetary motion could be 'explained' in a number of ways consistent with observation, the actual *mechanism* not as yet having been hypothecated, let alone reality-validated.

In the meantime the Italian Giordano Bruno (1547-1601) having taught at the universities of Lyons, Toulouse, Montpellier and Paris, came to London in 1583 where in 1588 he published three short pieces in Italian, *The Ash-Wednesday Supper*, *On Cause, Principle and Unity*, and *On the Infinite Universe and Its Worlds*. These drew on Nicolas de Cusa (1401-1464) who *inter alia* had suggested a moving Earth and an infinite universe, and on Copernicus whose Earth moved in a heliocentric planetary system. However, Bruno went further to claim that while the Earth moves round the Sun, the Sun itself moves; that the stars are at vast and variable distances from the solar system and are themselves centres of 'solar' systems; that the universe, being infinite in time and space, has no identifiable fixity, no point of absolute rest and no beginning nor end; that it is permeated by a common soul and is subject to uniform natural laws; and that in no sense is the Earth at the centre of the universe. Though this can now be seen as a set of hypotheses for future reality-evaluation, it was then no more than belief counter to that of a sufficiency of Churchmen for Giordano Bruno to be burnt at the stake after an Inquisitorial seven year imprisonment.

However, prior to Bruno's death William Gilbert (1546-1603) personal physician to Queen Elizabeth I published in 1600, *On the Magnet and On Magnetic Bodies and Concerning that Great Magnet, the Earth, a New Physiology*. In addition to its main section which describes with diagrams his experiments on the lodestone and magnet and on orientation, variation and declination with respect to the magnetic poles of the Earth, it contains an account of the universe which is that of Bruno whom he must have met in London though he does not mention him by name. Yet again, after Gilbert's natural death a surviving brother saw through the press in 1651 the second of his works entitled *On Our Sublunary World, A New Philosophy* which quoting Bruno gives a detailed account of the latter's belief that the stars, being at different and individual distances from us, cannot be on the 'celestial sphere of the fixed stars' and are themselves the centres of other planetary systems. Thus, Bruno's beliefs were apparently more acceptable in Protestant England than in Catholic Italy, being thus differently interpreted with respect to the Faith.

6. 2. 3. Development of Mathematics for New Applications

Innovations in mathematical expression and operative symbolism were now added to the recently acquired Hindu number system for even greater facility of use. Thus, though the only Hindu operative symbol transmitted to Europe by the Muslims was the square root sign, the + (plus) and - (minus) chalk-marks used to indicate whether containers were above or below nominal weight, were adopted to denote addition and subtraction in Widman's *Commercial Arithmetic* (Leipzig 1489). Later, Francois Viete (1540-1603) was among the first in Europe to use alphabet letters to represent numbers, a step which paved the way for Descartes' development of analytical geometry (c.f. Section 6.3.5). Again, an English commercial arithmetic by Record published a century after Widman, introduced the sign x for multiplication and the sign = for equals. Yet again, the Flemish Simon Stevin (1548-1620) was among the first, in 1585, to use these innovations in writing and solving equations before introducing his decimal notation for the representation of fractions in 1586. In addition Stevin used experimentation to investigate the free-fall of bodies of different weight on which he reported in 1586 prior to Galileo's investigation of this topic. Again, his investigation of pressure variation with depth in liquids re-launched the subject of hydrostatics in quantitative terms of depth and density. Yet again, he showed that any quantity having magnitude and direction *i.e.* a vector, can be resolved into components acting at right angles to each other such that a force F resolves into components F cos A and F cos (90-A) which is F sin A, a procedure which facilitates the mathematical analysis of the effects on bodies of vectors of force, velocity and acceleration.

Again, though the new Hindu number system facilitated arithmetical computation, the multiplication and division of multi-digit numbers involves more operations than does addition and subtraction while the time required as the numbers increase in size can become extremely burdensome. Again, the calculation of value after periods of applied compound interest involves geometric series. Thus if r is the rate of compound interest per pound invested, it will grow to £(1 + r) in one year and if no interest is paid out, to £$(1 + r)^2$ by the end of the second year and thus by the end of the nth year to £$(1 + r)^n$. Thus, it is clear that fractional compound interest rates and investment periods of many years will increase the labour of multiplying out the expression $(1 + r)^n$, while computing increase in value for fractions of a year involves the additional complication of dealing with fractional powers. Readers will recall, however, that Archimedes had noted that when each of two numbers are expressed by another number raised to a power, then the two numbers can be multiplied by adding the corresponding powers according to the relationship: a^m x $a^n = a^{m+n}$ (c.f. Section 4.4). Again, having seen that $\sqrt{a} = \sqrt{a^1} = \sqrt{a^{½+½}} = a^½$ (c.f. Section 5.4.1) we see that in general, the qth root of *a* is *a* to the power 1/q; and more generally that *a* to the power p/q may be expessed as the qth root of *a* to the power p.

Thus, John Napier, Laird of Merchiston (1550-1617) having began his systematization of algebra in 1573, concluded in 1574 that the lengthy process of multiplication could be replaced by addition, that division could be replaced by subtraction and that roots could be extracted by division of powers which could be looked up in tables compiled "for ever" as he put it, provided the appropriate powers could be calculated and conveniently tabulated. He called these powers "logarithms" and spent the next twenty years developing the theory, conducting the necessary calculations and publishing the results in Latin in his *Description of The Marvellous Canon of*

Logarithms (Edinburgh, 1614). In the meantime he introduced the current notation for representing fractions and subsequently produced his *Rabdologia* in 1617 which contains devices, Napier's Bones, for the simplification of multiplication and division, the 'Bones' being used for more than a century before the logarithms were universally adopted .

The following brief considerations may provide a flavour of the work involved in producing tables of logarithms and antilogarithms to the base ten. The logarithm N to the base ten is written $\log_{10}$ N and because any number to the power zero is equal to unity we have $\log_{10} 1 = 0$. In what follows we will compute the logarithms for the numbers 2 to 9 inclusive. Thus, we see that $2^{10} = 1024$ by repeated multiplication, this being accurate to within 2.5% of 1000. Therefore we may write $2^{10} = 10^3$ approximately and to this extent the subsequent procedure will be approximate but adequate for present purposes. If $2^{10} = 10^3$, then $2 = {}^{10}\sqrt{10^3} = 10^{3/10} = 10^{0..3}$ and therefore log 2 = 0.3. Similarly $3^9 = 19,683$ by repeated multiplication which equals 2 x 10,000 approximately; and, therefore, again we may say that $3^9 = 10^{0..3} \times 10^4 = 10^{4.3}$ and that $3 = {}^9\sqrt{10^{4..3}} = 10^{4.\,3/9} = 10^{0.\,48}$ and that, therefore, log 3 = 0.48. Again, because $4 = 2^2$ we may say that $2^2 = 10^{0.\,3} \times 10^{0.\,3} = 10^{0.\,6}$ and hence, $\log_{10} 4 = 0.6$. We now note that 2 x 5 = 10 and hence $\log_{10} 5 = \log_{10} 10 - \log_{10} 2 = 1 - 0.3$ and that, therefore, $\log_{10} 5 = 0.7$; that since $6 = 2 \times 3 = 10^{0.\,3} \times 10^{0.\,48}$ we see that $6 = 10^{7.\,8}$ and hence log 6 = 0.78; and that since $7^2 = 49 = 5 \times 10$ approximately, we have log (7 x 7) = log 5 + log10 approximately or 2 log 7 = 1.7 and hence log 7 = 0.85 approximately. Now, having come this far and given that $8 = 2^3 = (10^{0.\,3})^3$ and $9 = 3^2 = (10^{0.\,48})^2$ it can readily be seen that $\log_{10} 8 = 0.9$ and $\log_{10} 9 = 0.96$.

We should also note that since $10^0 = 1$ and $10^1 = 10$, the number to the left of the decimal point in the logarithm is zero for all numbers between 1 and 10 and because $10^2 = 100$ this number is 1 for all numbers between 10 and 100 and so on. Similarly, when the number which appears in front of the fractional part of the number whose antilogarithm we are looking up is 1, it means multiply the antilogarithm of the fractional part by 10; while 2 in front, means multiply by 100; 3 by 1000; and so on. In addition, it is usual to omit the subscript 10 when the base 10 is understood. Thus, we can now tabulate the approximate results obtained above and provide examples of its use.

Log N	N	log N	N
0.00	1	1.00	10
0.30	2	1.30	20
0.48	3	1.48	30
0.60	4	1.60	40
0.70	5	1.70	50
0.78	6	1.78	60
0.85	7	1.85	70
0.90	8	1.90	80
0.96	9	1.96	90
1.00	10	2.00	100
antilog n	n	antilog n	n

We can now demonstrate the principle by noting that if we multiply 4 x 5 by adding the corresponding logarithms 0.60 and 0.70 from the second column, we get 1.30 the antilog of which is 20 from the third column. Similarly if we multiply 6 x 8 by adding the corresponding logarithms 0.78 and 0.90 we get 1.68, the antilog of which lies between 40 and 50 and we can interpolate. Thus, the number 1.68 corresponds to four-fifths of the interval between the logs of 40 and 50 and hence the antilog sought is 48 which is 6 x 8 and so our table 'works'. Readers will have appreciated that the preparation of accurate logarithmic tables involved the evaluation by direct multiplication of the base number raised to high powers, that the reverse involves the repetitive extraction of roots of the base number, and that the labour involved would be considerable were logarithms to be calculated to four decimal places.

However, the computation of growth with compound interest by the binomial expression $(1 + r)^n$ where n is the number of years over which the interest rate r applies, suggested that the binomial series expansion (c.f. Section 5.4.1) could also be used for both purposes, providing the benefit of rapid convergence when the numerators of the terms of the expansion are small as for the examples provided earlier (c.f. Section 5. 4. 1). It was for these reasons that Jobst Burgi of Prague, who worked independently of Napier, used 1.0001 as the base of his tables. Indeed, having already seen how quickly $(1 + 0.1)^{10}$ converges (c.f. Section 5.4.1) it can be seen that the expansion of $(1 + 0.0001)^5$ converges even more quickly in that the sums of the first two, three and four terms are respectively 1.0005, 1.0005001, and 1.00050010001, successive terms in this series being always less than a thousandth of the preceding term.

These desirable properties of the binomial expansion led to consideration of what is called the exponential series which leads to 'e', the ideal base for the calculation of logarithms. The exponential series is:

$$e^x = 1 + x + \frac{x^2}{2!} + \frac{x^3}{3!} + \frac{x^4}{4!} + \frac{x^5}{5!} \ldots$$

and when x = 1, we have the series which defines e, thus:

$$e = 1 + 1 + \frac{1}{2!} + \frac{1}{3!} + \frac{1}{4!} + \frac{1}{5!} \ldots$$

from which it can be shown that however many terms are summed, the value of e does not get bigger than 2.7182818285 correct to ten decimal places; and that, for example, the fifth root of e or $e^{1/5}$ is obtained to six decimal places by summing to six terms, the series:

$$1 + \frac{1}{5} + \frac{1}{25} . \frac{1}{2!} + \frac{1}{125} . \frac{1}{3!} + \frac{1}{625} . \frac{1}{4!} \ldots$$

This is a very powerful technique. By the earlier methods one has to go on extracting square roots and cube roots repeatedly and there are no algorithms for odd roots other than the cube. However, we can get any root of e by substituting the appropriate fraction for x in the exponential series. The first logarithms to the base e were published by Seidel in 1619. Logarithms to the base ten are obtainable from those calculated on the base e, by applying the relationship:

$$\log_{10} N = \frac{\log_e N}{\log_e 10}$$

Though de Moivre's theorem is of the seventeenth century it is convenient to refer to it here to show how further consideration of imaginary numbers (c.f. Section 5.4.1) led to a new method of calculating the value of sines and cosines through the exponential series. However, before proceeding we should note that according to the sign rule (c.f. Section 4.4), the square root of -1 (designated i) is the only imaginary number because the square root of any other negative number, -n, may be written as $i\sqrt{n}$; and that in equations such as cos a + i sin a = x + iy we can equate the real parts as cos a = x and imaginary parts as sin a = y, i being thus eliminated. Now, de Moivre's theorem which states that

$$(\cos a + i \sin a)^n = \cos na + i \sin na$$

can be demonstrated by multiplying out for different values of n (c.f. Section 6.2.3). Thus, multiplication for n = 2, gives : $(\cos a + i \sin a)^2 = \cos^2 a + 2 i \cos a \sin a + i^2 \sin^2 a$

144

and by using the expanded expressions for sin (A + B) and cos (A + B) where A and B both equal a (c.f. Section 4.4) we have: $\sin 2a = \sin(a + a) = \sin a \cos a + \cos a \sin a = 2 \cos a \sin a$; and $i^2 = -1$ and we may re-write the product as: $\cos^2 a + i \sin 2a - \sin^2 a$

Again, we have: $\cos 2a = \cos(a + a) = \cos a \cos a - \sin a \sin a = \cos^2 a - \sin^2 a$,

and may re-write the product as: $\cos 2a + i \sin 2a$ *quid est demonstrandum* (QED)

Now de Moivre's theorem may be related to the exponential series by setting $x^a = \cos a + i \sin a$, so that we have $x^{-a} = \cos a - i \sin a$, and by subtraction we have $x^a - x^{-a} = 2i \sin a$. Again, we can represent x as some power of e such as e^y or $y = \log_e x$.

Thus, we can write the exponential series: $x^a = e^{ay} = 1 + ay + \dfrac{a^2 y^2}{2!} + \dfrac{a^3 y^3}{3!} + \dfrac{a^4 y^4}{4!} \ldots$

and

$$x^{-a} = e^{-ay} = 1 - ay + \dfrac{a^2 y^2}{2!} - \dfrac{a^3 y^3}{3!} + \dfrac{a^4 y^4}{4!} \ldots$$

Subtracting, we have

$$x^a - x^{-a} = 2i \sin a = 2ay + \dfrac{2a^3 y^3}{3!} + \dfrac{2a^5 y^5}{5!} \ldots$$

and we can write:

$$\dfrac{i \sin a}{a} = y + \dfrac{a^2 y^3}{3!} + \dfrac{a^4 y^5}{5!}$$

Now when a is expressed in radians $\sin a / a$ tends to 1 and a^n tends to zero when a becomes small. Thus the above becomes $i = y$, and since $y = \log_e x$, $x = e^i$ and $x^a = e^{ia}$, we can now write $\cos a + i \sin a = e^{ia}$ and because $i^2 = -1$, $i^3 = -i$, and $i^4 = +1$ *etc*: $\cos a + i \sin a = 1 + ia - \dfrac{a^2}{2!} - \dfrac{ia^3}{3!} + \dfrac{a^4}{4!} + \dfrac{ia^5}{5!} - \dfrac{a^6}{6!} \ldots$

Thus re-grouping : $\cos a + i \sin a = 1 - \dfrac{a^2}{2!} + \dfrac{a^4}{4!} + \dfrac{a^6}{6!} \ldots + i \left[a - \dfrac{a^3}{3!} + \dfrac{a^5}{5!} \ldots\right]$

and by equating the real and the imaginary parts of this equation we have a means of calculating the sine and cosine of angles expressed in radians (π radians = 180 degrees) which may be compared with the earlier square root approach (c.f. Section 4.4). Thus, with the angular measure being < 1 the above series converges in a very few terms. For example, if we take $\pi = 3.1416$, 15 degrees = 0.2618 radians and the above series gives cos 15 = 0.966 and sin 15 = 0.259 after evaluating only three terms. Thus we see that the square root of -1 is manageable after all, and that it can lead to useful results. Indeed, mathematical treatment of alternating electric current later required the equation $e^{ia} = \cos a + i \sin a$.

6. 2. 4 Failure to Understand Experimentation

While craft-like observation was replacing reliance on ancient texts and mathematics was responding to widening practical needs as the sixteenth century drew to a close, understanding of experimentation remained incomplete and belief in astrology and alchemy remained widespread as the seventeenth opened. This failure to understand experimentation is well illustrated in the case of Francis Bacon, Lord Verulam, (1561-1626) who wrote a good deal on what he mistakenly believed scientific method to be. Thus while his *Proficiencie and Advancement of Learning* (1605) and his *Instauratio Magnum* otherwise known as *Novum Organum,* (1620) have led some to regard him as an initiator of scientific method, he really had no notion of how to proceed or even of how others, such as Nicolas de Cusa, had actually proceeded over a century earlier. Thus, in 1605 Bacon expressed the belief that all the facts having been collected by the investigator, the sieving of these facts by rational thought would cause the resulting knowledge to emerge inevitably. In advocating this approach he at least recognised the need to limit the surrounding facts to those relevant to the matter in hand, and in 1620 he warned against human tendencies which might interfere with the optimal selection of facts by referring to the "Idols of the Cave, Market Place and Theatre" by which he meant our tendency to be influenced by our innate dispositions and prejudices, by the views of our fellows, and by mere words and modes of presentation.

Nonetheless, his approach is the complete antithesis of the experimentation which reality-evaluates a specific hypothesis in isolation from all influences which would otherwise introduce error. Thus, while experimentation should avoid all human influences of the investigator, Bacon's warnings will not avoid such influence if the experimentation is not designed to reveal the cause/effect relationships which Bacon believes will spontaneously emerge as knowledge from the subjective collection of optimal (partially selected) facts. In addition, his method is wide-open to coincidental correlations where no cause/effect relationship exists (c.f. Section 6.1, 6.3.2 and 6.3.3). Thus, though Bacon advocated data collection to avoid the dangers of scholastic reliance on book-sourced 'ancient knowledge', he did not know how to collect it. Nonetheless, his influential position as Lord Chancellor was helpful to those seeking to found the Royal Society for the mutual-support of more effective pursuers of knowledge than himself. It is unfortunate however, that Bacon's approach has current adherents who believe that correlated data and/or partially selected facts are enough to establish cause/effect relationships and to pass off beliefs as knowledge, though such practices produce only pseudo-science (c.f. Chapter 11).

6. 3 THE PERIOD 1600 - 1700

Although Francis Bacon, Johannes Kepler and Galileo Galilei were more or less contemporary and active at the turn of the sixteenth/seventeenth centuries, I closed my account of the sixteenth with Bacon as typifying more closely the scholastic attitudes to knowledge of that century, and I start my review of the seventeenth with Kepler because his case illustrates how difficult it was even for the most capable individuals to overcome old habits and new confusions such as those of Bacon, and thus to take the transitional steps from scholasticism to experimentation as practiced by Galileo whose grasp of scientific method made the seventeenth century more scientifically productive than any previous period .

6. 3. 1 Transition from Old to New
The German, Johannes Kepler (1571-1630) professed astrology as his occupation, sought verification of its general claims in the details of his own life and was strongly motivated by his Platonic Idealism and by his Pythagorean belief in the abstract significance of number and mathematics. Nonetheless, though the models of planetary motion of Ptolemy, Copernicus and Brahe were more or less equivalent in their compliance with observation and though Kepler later worked with Brahe, he always favoured the earlier helio-centric Copernican model, perhaps because it was more 'Ideal' to him. Be that as it may, Kepler's first attempt to apply mathematics to the planetary system was in relation to the number, size and relationship of the circular orbits of the Copernican system. After trying various relatively simple numerical relationships which sometimes called for the introduction of additional planets, he opted to attempt the immensely more complicated insertion of the five regular polyhedra of the Pythagoreans into the the five gaps between the orbits of the six planets then known. Thus, he showed by calculation that each of these polyhedral figures could be inscribed in one planetary orbital sphere while circumscribing the next in order from outside to inside as follows: sphere of Saturn, Cube; sphere of Jupiter, Tetrahedron; sphere of Mars, Dodecahedron; sphere of Earth, Icosahedron; sphere of Venus, Octahedron; sphere of Mercury. This work was published with illustration in Kepler's *Mysterium*

Cosmographicum (Tubingen, 1596) with a second edition appearing in 1621: an achievement motivated by his mystical scholasticism.

Subsequently, Kepler turned his attention to the periods of orbital revolution and the distances of the individual planets from the Sun and found that those furthest away moved too slowly for these parameters to be proportional. Thus, he concluded in the concepts and phraseology of his time that "one moving intelligence in the Sun forces all around, but most the nearest - languishing and weakening in the more distant by attenuation of its virtue by remoteness". Later, on joining Tycho Brahe at the turn of the century, he became involved with Brahe's papers as legatee on his death in 1601 while otherwise engaged on optics and a commentary (1604) on the work of the Polish mathematician Witelo (fl. 1270). In the latter, he discusses conic sections with particular reference to their foci, this being a central influence on his greatest work, *New Astronomy with Commentaries on the Motions of Mars*, published in 1609. In this last, Kepler sets out his first two laws of planetary motion in stating that the planets move round the Sun in ellipses (at last, not circles) with the Sun at one of the foci, and that the movement varies such that a line drawn from the Sun to the planet sweeps out equal areas of the ellipse in equal times. These laws were followed by the third which appeared in his *Epitome Astrolonomiae* (1618) in stating that the squares of the periods of revolution of the planets round the Sun are proportional to the cubes of their distances.

Thus, Kepler now knew that his success in fitting the five polyhedra to spherical planetary orbits had been erroneously fortuitous; that while Copernicus and Brahe had reduced the number of epicycles and eccentrics needed to comply with observed planetary movements in models up to and inclusive of Ptolemy's, his own elliptical orbits had entirely removed the need for them; and that he had now done what could have been done any time in the 2000 years since Menaechmus had first considered the properties of the ellipse as a conic section. Be that as it may, there was nothing in any of these models whether circular or elliptical which would enable a decision to be made as to how the planets were constrained so to move, all calculation methods being silent as to the mechanism which would later be provided by Newton on the basis of the scientific method of experimentation applied by Galileo to moving bodies on Earth (c.f. Sections 6.3.2, 6.3.6 and 6.3.7)

As to Ptolemy's observations on the bending of oars at the air/water interface which Al-Hazen and Witelo had later sought to explain, Kepler reported his measurement of incident and refracted ray directions in his commentary on Witelo (c.f. above) though he still failed to express them in a usable form. However, Willibrod Snell showed in 1621 that the relationship between the angle of incidence i, and the angle of refraction r when a light ray passes from one medium to another is $\sin i / \sin r = \mu$ where the angles are measured with respect to the normal to the interface and μ is defined as the refractive index for the media involved, these being water and air in the case of oars and differing density-layers in the case of light sources viewed through the atmosphere (c.f. Section 3.1.4 and 5.4.2).

6. 3. 2 The New Experimentation

In 1585, Galileo Galilei (1564-1642 began to question Aristotle's belief in the speeds of free-falling bodies being weight dependent, and in 1591 he demonstrated that all fall at the same rate independent of weight though not at constant speed. Thus, he treated the belief which Aristotle asserted as knowledge as being a hypothesis to be tested by experimentation designed to reveal whether it was true or false (reality-evaluation). These experiments amounted to showing that bodies of differing weights simultaneously released from the same height reach the ground simultaneously (air resistance being ignorable) though when he investigated this matter in quantitative detail by experimentation on bodies moving on inclined planes, he discovered an acceleration common to all of them, this being the prime example of the scientific method of reality-evaluation of hypothesis by experimentation (c.f. below and Section 6.2.4).

Meanwhile, it should be noted that Galileo also made deductions from what could be directly observed without conducting experiments as such. Thus, he deduced that a new celestial body which appeared in the constellation of Serpentarius in 1604 must be at a greater distance from us than the Moon and planets because unlike them it showed no parallax from whatever point it was viewed, this being a refutation of another Aristotelian belief that the fixed stars were located in a changeless realm and that new/changing bodies such as meteors and comets must belong to the lower and less perfect regions closer to Earth. Again, in 1609 he deduced that the lunar mountains revealed by his telescope were up to four to five miles high. He also reported in his *Messenger of the Heavens* in 1610 that he had observed moons orbiting the planet Jupiter, stars at least ten times more numerous than previously catalogued, star clusters invisible to the unaided eye and regions within the Milky Way, Orion, the Pleiades and elsewhere which were irresolvable to stars even by telescope. Yet again, in 1612, he observed that dark spots on the Sun narrowed towards its edge suggesting a fore-shortening of surface features on a rotating sphere. In a more generally descriptive way, his *Il Saggiatore* (*The Assayer*) of 1624 distinguished between qualities capable of exact numerical evaluation (primary qualities) and those which are not (secondary qualities), in stating that " . . . tastes, colours, odours and the like exist only in the being which feels, which being removed, these qualities themselves do vanish . . . that (only) size, shape, quantity and motion remain." These categories are now respectively referred to as quantitative and qualitative. However, the reader should note, *pace* Galileo, that while taste, colour and odour are undoubtedly subjective, the properties of materials which invoke these sensations in us do not vanish when we cease to experience them, and that all properties *per se* are ultimately quantifiable (c.f. Chapters 7, 8 and 9).

More controversially, in 1630, Galileo completed his *Dialogue on the Two Chief Systems of the World* in which a debate is conducted between an advocate of the Copernican system and a follower of Aristotle and Ptolemy in the presence of an impartial participator who is supposedly open to persuasion. Prior permission had been obtained from the ecclesiastical authorities on condition that the subject be treated hypothetically and not on a factual basis, but he ignored this condition. Thus, the Copernican supporter adopts the mixture of knowledge and belief of Nicolas de Cusa as developed by Giordano Bruno and totally rejects the belief that the stars are fixed on a crystal sphere. Instead they are said to be at vast and differing distances in an infinitely extended universe with the lack of observable parallax cited in support, while the Earth moves with all the other planets round the Sun. The reader is left in no doubt concerning Galileo's own mixture of knowledge and belief on these matters, and in the course of the dialogue he sets out his *Doctrine of Uniformity*, meaning that corresponding causes produce corresponding effects everywhere in the universe. The Copernican advocate has the best of the argument, of course, and the follower of Aristotle and Ptolemy is presented as obstinate and stupid. Nonetheless, nobody yet knew the mechanism by which the planets moved round the Sun. In 1632, the book was prohibited and submitted to a special examining commission. Though the verdict went against Galileo forcing him to recant, he was free to set out his results on "coherence and resistance to fracture" and on "uniform, accelerated and violent or projectile motions" in his *Discourses Concerning Two New Sciences* of 1638.

In the first, he distinguished between the cohesive strength of fibrous ropes and that of metals and stones which do not exhibit a fibrous structure and he concluded that coherence must be due to the tendency in all materials for the minute particles of which they are composed to adhere to one another. This led him to conclude that columns of materials suspended vertically from their upper ends would break under their own weight if they exceeded a limiting length. This, in turn, led him to reason that structures and machines would become progressively weaker if scaled-up, because the weights of their corresponding constuction members and the forces required to move them increase as the cube of their linear dimensions while the strength conferred by cross-sectional area increases only as the square of their linear dimensions, and thus to conclude that weight would eventually overcome strength.

In the second, he defined accelerated motion as equal increments in velocity in equal intervals of time, and by careful experimentation and measurement of bodies descending inclined planes (under the action of gravity), he showed that the velocity attained depended on vertical height dropped regardless of the angle of inclination of the plane. From this, he argued that the motion of a projectile (neglecting air resistance) is compounded of a constant horizontal component of projected velocity and a vertically upwards component of this velocity which is decelerated to zero and accelerated downward (by gravity) during the time for which it remains in the air, component velocities being independently treated (c.f. Section 6.2.3). Thus, he showed that a projectile launched at any angle to the horizontal will follow a parabolic trajectory; and that projectiles launched horizontally at a point above the ground will also follow parabolic paths because in equal intervals of time they all move equal distances horizontally forward while they fall distances which increase as the square of the elapsed time until they reach the ground. He went on to describe a family of parabolas for different angular velocities of projection and showed that the range of a projectile over a horizontal plane is maximised when the projection-angle is 45 degrees. Thus, readers should note that Galileo reported his most fundamental work after his earlier and specific recantation of his preference for the beliefs of Copernicus over those of Aristotle and Ptolemy (c.f. Section 6.3.1).

As to significance, Newton's more celebrated work on lunar motion (c.f. Section 6.3.6) was dependent on Galileo's elucidation of the motion of projectiles from his experimentation with bodies on inclined planes, the elucidation being that bodies move at constant speed unless accelerated by an imposed force, which in the case of falling bodies is the attractive force of the Earth. Thus, Galileo reality-refuted Aristotle's intuitive beliefs that "terrestrial bodies tend (of their own nature) to rest at a level which is natural for them and that all motion sooner or later ceases when its cause is removed". Thus, while refutation appears counter-intuitive at first sight, it recognises that the force which gives the projectile a flying start ceases to act on it thereafter, that it is the momentum (mass x velocity) initially imparted to it which continues, and that its downwards acceleration is caused by a previously unsuspected force of attraction to the Earth. This elucidation predates what are now known as Newton's first, second and third laws of motion *viz.* that a body remains in a state of rest or uniform motion in a straight line unless acted on by a force, that a force F causes an acceleration α in a mass M such that $F = M\alpha$, and that every action has an equal and opposite reaction (c.f. Section 6.3.7) though this last was set out more clearly in a short work on static mechanics written early in Galileo's career, though not published until after his death. Thus, while Newton developed Galileo's dynamics in applying it to the Moon, mechanics remains essentially as Galileo left it. Again, Galileo's concept of acceleration by gravity had been initiated when aged eighteen he had confirmed by counting his pulse-beats that the period of swing of a chandelier (pendulum) remained constant while its arc of swing decreased.

In addition, Galileo's rapid improvements to the telescope made him its effective inventor while he was the actual inventor of the compound microscope by which an entirely unsuspected microscopic world could now be studied and shown to comply with his macroscopic universal

Doctrine of Uniformity. In passing, it may also be noted that in the commissioning of telescopes, microscopes and other specialist apparatus, Galileo initiated the craft of scientific-instrument maker. Furthermore, he applied his knowledge of the mechanics of structures and machines 'bigger means weaker' to the animal kingdom to explain the size-limits of species, the largest being marine because their body weight need not be borne by their skeletons, being supported by buoyancy forces equal to the weight of water displaced (Archimedes). Nonetheless, he never worked directly on biological systems, his primary and secondary properties recognising them less accessible to experimentation and mathematical analysis than physical systems.

The first to be inspired to apply Galileo's quantitative approach to biology was his fellow professor at Padua, Santorio Santorio (1561-1636) whose investigations involved the measurement of weight and temperature, the latter by means of Galileo's thermometer (c.f. Section 6.3.4). Thus, in his *De Medicina Statica* of 1614 Santorio *inter alia* attributes weight loss of the human body on exposure to "insensible perspiration". Again, William Harvey (1578-1657) after studying at Padua (1598-1601) went on to demonstrate the circulation of the blood through weight considerations. Having shown that blood leaves the heart in one direction only and noting that it beats 72 times a minute, he measured heart-capacity to be about 2 ounces of blood and reasoned that the heart in beating 72 times per minute must deliver 2 x 72 x 60 ounces of blood per hour (540 pounds per hour) and that since this is equivalent to about three times the weight of the body the blood must circulate. In addition, Giovanni Alphonso Borelli (1608-79) in his *On The Motion of Animals* (1680) applied the mechanical principles of the lever and turning-effect of a force about a fulcrum (moment or torque) to the actions of bone, joint and muscle.

Thus, by 1650 or so, it should have been clear that Galileo's methods of direct observation, experimentation and mathematical analysis were applicable to physical systems both terrestrial and celestial, and to human, animal and plant biology down to the microscopic level; that knowledge thus acquired was superior to belief-based speculation; and that while speculation could fall foul of religious beliefs, knowledge whether acquired by craftsmanship or scientific method was immune to belief whether religious or non-religious. At this point, readers should note that scientific method involves reality-evaluation by knowledge-based observation of reality as it presents itself or by submission of hypotheses on its underlying nature to designed experimentation. The nature of scientific method will be further clarified by noting its presence or absence in this Chapter, by its sustained application as in Chapters 7, 8 and 9, and by its absence in pseudo-science as in Sections 8.3.4 and 11.2).

6. 3. 3. Continuance of Confusion and Obscurantism

In 1633, Descartes (1596-1650) had been about to publish his cosmological beliefs in *The World*. However, the Church's response to Galileo in 1632 caused him to publish his resolutions for the conduct of science in his *Discourse on Method* of 1637. Thus he resolved "never to accept anything for true which he did not clearly know to be such, avoiding precipitancy and prejudice, and comprising nothing more in his mind than was absolutely clear and distinct in his mind; always to divide problems under examination into as many parts as possible; and always to proceed in his thoughts from the simplest and easiest to the more complex, assigning in thought a certain order even to those objects which in their own nature do not stand in a relation of antecedence and sequence - *i.e.* to seek relation everywhere; to make enumerations so complete and reviews so general as to be assured that nothing was omitted."

As to these resolutions, the first appears to be circular and not a basis for progress. Again, though it is reminiscent of the Parmenides exhortation to accept for true only premises of which it can be said, "it is and it is impossible not to be", it relies heavily on the "idols" of Francis Bacon regarding what should be avoided. His fourth resolution is again reminiscent of Bacon's call to collect all relevant data while the other two seem to be futile steps towards doing so. This is not just disappointing: it is astonishing in purporting to describe a successful scientific method without making any reference to direct observation or designed experimentation *i.e.* no reference to the very methods which Galileo had actually used and concerning which Descartes ought to have made himself aware. Reference to his own practice is no more helpful. Thus, the phrase "I think, therefore I am" is intended to certify his existence by his awareness of his thinking. Yet, his existence does not guarantee that everything he thinks is true simply because he thinks (believes) it, his own "resolutions" being less than reassuring on this point. In any case, even if he believes his own thoughts, he surely would not believe those of others with similar indulgence. Indeed, he asserts "the separation of soul from body to be clear and obvious and therefore true" while asserting the belief of others in revealed religion to be "superfluous". Thus, we are back to belief versus belief with no reference to reality-evaluation by experimentation, after which he belittles Galileo as a mere mechanic who unlike Descartes "conducted no analysis of the basic concepts of force, motion, matter, space, time, number, extension and so on". Thus, while Galileo could be said to have neglected metaphysics (c.f. Section 10.2) he could not be said to have neglected physics. Surely, it is game set and match to Galileo.

As to Descartes' own analysis of these "basic concepts", we find little but empty speculation, assertion and circular argument of which a few examples will suffice to show how easily even the gifted can be diverted to futility. Thus, of his cosmology he states that the form of the world is inevitable, his reasoning being that "had God created more worlds, provided only that He had established certain laws of nature and had lent them His concurrence to act as is their wont, the physical features of these worlds would inevitably form as they have done in ours." He states as a probability "that matter was created as a momentary act and that this act is that by which the creation is now sustained; that the universe is infinite and devoid of any empty space; that the movement of any part of matter results in movement of all matter; and that the movement takes the form of vortices the contacts of which grind matter down to finer and finer particles. Furthermore the matter itself has the primary quality of extension and secondary qualities of divisibility and motion, is undifferentiated and basic though divided and configured in endless variety. The finest particles are of 'first matter' which forms the Sun and Stars, these particles acquiring a centrifugal action which forms enveloping atmospheres of 'second matter', the centrifugal tendency of which produces rays of light in the form of waves which reach our eyes, while certain other particles in the process of vortex formation are detained on their way to the solar or stellar centres to form 'third matter' which can be recognised as sun-spots and certain other celestial phenomena. In addition, major vortices are responsible for planetary movements, minor ones for terrestrial phenomena and gravity is created by the centripetal action of vortices". This is certainly imaginative and Descartes may have believed it all, but there is no hypothesis for submission to reality-evaluation by experimentation in any of it.

To complete his world picture Descartes felt obliged to consider living organisms. Here he favours us with the belief that he "remains satisfied that God first formed the body of man wholly like to ours . . . out of the same matter; that at first he placed in it no rational soul, nor any other principle, beyond kindling in the heart a flameless fire similar, as I think, to the heat generated in damp hay or to that which causes fermentation in must". By way of justification he goes on to say "for, when I examined the kind of functions which might, as consequences of this supposition, exist in the body, I found precisely all those which may exist within us independently of all power of thinking, and consequently without being in any measure owing to a soul; . . . functions in which the animals void of all reason may be said wholly to resemble us; but among which I could not

151

discover any of those that, as dependent on thought alone, belong to us as man, while on the other hand, I did afterwards discover these as soon as I supposed God to have created a rational soul, and to have annexed it to this body." Thus, we learn that Descartes believed man to differ from animals in possessing a soul and rationality, though we can only be astounded that he believed the argument presented above to be other than circular and devoid of any logical justification let alone reality-validation. But there was more: he located the soul by simple assertion in the pineal gland of man, whether animals had pineal glands or not. So much for his cosmology and scientific method, though his mathematics is another matter entirely, (c.f. Section 6.3.5). Nonetheless, the above musings again show how difficult it was to reject scholasticism and to grasp the significance of scientific method in its early days, though the desire to do so has not been ubiquitous, then or since (c.f. Section 10.8 *et seq.*).

6. 3. 4. Further Use of Experimentation

The overthrow of Aristotelian belief in the seventeenth century is usually attributed to the increased knowledge of force and motion which explained the mechanism underlying the lunar and planetary orbits of which more later (c.f. Section 6.3.6). However, increasing knowledge of matter and of biological systems through the scientific method of experimentation was no less significant in contributing to this overthrow. In this respect we should recognise the contribution of Jan Baptist van Helmont (1577-1644) who in devoting himself to investigation as advocated by Paracelsus, repeated the experiments of Nicolas de Cusa and recognised that vapours may differ in properties though they be similar in appearance. Nonetheless, though his work was published by his son as *The Fount of Medicine* in 1648, it was obscurely written and had little influence until the 1670s when it was clarified for a wider readership. In it he had coined the word "gas" to describe that physical state of matter, possibly derived from 'geist' the German for 'spirit' which was how undifferentiated vapours had previously been designated, or alternatively from 'chaos' phonetically transmuted by his Flemish speech. Either way, the gaseous state was now formally recognised as taking its place with the liquid and solid states earlier differentiated.

More indirectly, air was confirmed to have weight through the following considerations. Galileo had erroneously believed that the failure to raise water more than 34 feet by pumping as in mine drainage *etc* was due to cohesion-failure in water columns at this limiting height. More profitably, his pupil and secretary Evangelista Torricelli (1608-1647) hypothesised that such columns of water were held up by atmospheric pressure acting on the water-surface external to the delivery pipe when the pump had removed the air which at atmospheric pressure had equalised the water surface levels within and without the delivery-pipe. Thus, Torricelli reasoned that the pump 'sucked' air, not water as previously believed; that since mercury is about 14.5 times denser than water, the atmosphere would support a mercury column of about 30 inches in height; and that this hypothesis (belief) could be tested by experimentation.

Thus, a 4 foot long heavy gauge glass tube closed at one end was filled with mercury, displacing all air from the tube. The open end was then sealed by a finger and the tube inverted to place this end beneath the surface of mercury in a basin. When the finger was removed the internal mercury level dropped sharply as mercury transferred to the basin until the mercury surface in the tube stood 30 inches above its surface in the basin. This left a void (absence of air) 18 inches in height at the top of the closed tube (later called the Torricellian vacuum) which exerted no downward pressure on the mercury surface within the tube, thus allowing the external atmospheric pressure on the surface of the mercury in the basin to hold the column within the tube at the observed height just as it supported a 34 foot water column in a pipe from which air had been removed by pumping, as hypothesised. This experiment not only confirmed that the hypothesis
152

was correct but also that air has weight, is material and not spirit or *pneuma*; and that the weight of the atmosphere exerts a pressure equal to that of a column of water 34 feet high or of mercury 30 inches high in inverse proportion to their respective densities.

This implied that at high altitude the column-height would be less because there would be less atmosphere to support it and this was confirmed (reality-validated) when Pascal (1623-1662) took the apparatus to the summit of the Puy de Dome and after further work by Huygens, Halley and Leibnitz, the principle of the mercury barometer was established with the pressure of one standard atmosphere being defined as that in equilibrium with a column of mercury 30 inches high which is 15 pounds per square inch, the pressure at any point in a liquid being equal to its depth multiplied by the density of the liquid. Thus, P (pressure) = d (depth) x ρ (density) where d and ρ are expressed in corresponding units such as feet and pounds per cubic foot to give P in units of pounds per square foot or in cm and g/cm^3 to give P in $g/cm.^2$ (c.f. Section 6.2.3). That the atmosphere has weight and thus exerts force per unit area was dramatically demonstrated by Otto von Guericke (1602-86) who built a pump specifically to extract air from his Magdeburg Hemispheres after placing their flanges in contact and proceeded to show that sixteen horses in two teams could not pull them apart. Later, von Guericke's air pump was improved by Robert Hooke (1635-1703).

Apart from pressure, temperature is an important parameter in the study of the gaseous state and reference has already been made to Galileo's thermometer. This consisted of a glass bulb blown at one end of a glass tube, the other (open) end of which dipped into water in a basin to contain and isolate the air within the bulb and tube. This trapped air could be observed to expand or contract in accordance with changes in temperature because the water level in the tube fell or rose accordingly as water was pushed into the basin or pushed from it. Though this system was very sensitive to temperature change, it was also sensitive to atmospheric pressure changes which induced water level changes within the tube similar to those of mercury level in Torricelli's barometer: a reminder of the importance of avoiding extraneous effects which mask the effect sought (c.f. Section 6.1). Accordingly by 1612 Galileo moved on to thermometers in which a liquid was sealed in a glass tube and bulb to eliminate atmospheric pressure effects. This dependence on expansion and contraction of liquids with change in temperature is now current practice, though construction difficulties were not wholly overcome until the eighteenth century.

The separate effects of temperature and pressure on the volume of a fixed mass of gas were thoroughly investigated later (c.f. below) and would eventually lend support to the atomic theory of Democritus, interest in which was revived by the French philosopher Pierre Gassendi (1592-1655) in his review of Epicureanism in 1649. Galileo himself, had earlier invoked the attraction between particles (atoms) to explain the cohesion of materials and Robert Boyle (1627-91) would later use Gassendi's nomenclature when he began to develop his chemistry (c.f. below). In addition the German teacher Joachim Jung (1587-1657) had enunciated his concept of the chemical elements in 1634, published them at Hamburg in 1642 and communicated them to Boyle by letter in 1654. However, Robert Boyle is remembered in the eponymous Law which states that the volume of a fixed mass of gas at constant temperature is inversely proportional to its pressure and the means by which he determined this relationship is usefully illustrative of the scientific method of experimentation (c.f. Sections 6.1 and 6.3.2).

Thus, Boyle made a glass U-tube with a long and a short limb (more correctly perhaps, a J-tube) and closed the end of the short limb. He then introduced just enough mercury into the open limb to isolate some air in the closed limb after shaking to allow sufficient air to escape to permit the mercury now located in the bend to reach the same level in both limbs. At this stage the air isolated in the short limb was at atmospheric pressure (as was that in the open limb) and its volume was directly proportional to the height of its column above the mercury level common to both limbs, the cross-section area of the tube being constant over its entire length. Boyle now measured the height of the enclosed air column, poured more mercury into the open limb and measured the resulting height of the isolated-air column in the closed limb to obtain its new volume (constant cross-section) and the difference in the mercury levels in the open and closed limbs, let us say h_1 (inches or cm) to give the new pressure of the isolated air as atmospheric + h_1, the atmospheric pressure being measured by means of a Torricelli barometer at the time of the experiment. Thus, by adding successive amounts of mercury to the open limb, he could progressively measure the difference in the mercury level each time as h_2, h_3 . . . and by adding the atmospheric pressure each time he could determine the pressures of the enclosed air, while the heights of the isolated-air column gave its corresponding volumes whereby he showed that when such paired pressures and volumes were multiplied together they gave a constant result.

Thus, when the head of mercury in the open tube was say 30 inches, the pressure of the isolated-air was two atmospheres, and its volume was half that at one atmosphere, and so on. Boyle also observed that the air expanded according to the same relationship when the pressure was reduced *i.e.* the process was reversible. Such a relationship can be expressed as P x V = K (a constant) or as $P_1 V_1 = P_2 V_2$ enabling either volume or pressure to be predicted if the other is specified and any previous pressure and corresponding volume for that mass of gas (the quantified initial condition) have been previously measured (c.f. Section 6.1). Once again, as in the Torricelli example, we see the power of the new scientific experimentation method for reality-validation of hypotheses, and for posing further questions. What, for example is the nature of air if it can expand and contract in this way? We shall see that such behaviour provides evidence for the existence of atoms and molecules (c.f. Section 7.1.3).

In the meantime, Boyle and Hooke (of the air-pump) showed by experimentation that air was necessary for respiration and combustion, that only part of the air was consumed in these processes, and that therefore, air must be a mixture of at least two different gases. Again, in 1661 Boyle's *Sceptical Chymist* presented his belief that the elements were "certain primitive and simple bodies; which not being made of any other bodies, or of one another, are the Ingredients of which all those call'd perfectly mixt Bodies are immediately compounded and into which they are ultimately resolved." Boyle himself, isolated elemental phosphorus, and in his *Origin of Forms and Qualities* of 1661 he postulated a universal matter, the *prima naturalia* to consist of solid particles each with its own determinate shape, these associating to form secondary corpuscles of individual shape which do not, or at least very rarely, dissociate into their constituent particles. In these postulates we can discern our atoms and molecules, but much more detailed experimentation would be needed before any degree of certainty could be reached. Boyle's postulates were simply intended to point the way to hypotheses capable of reality-evaluation by experimentation.

Boyle also introduced the use of 'indicators' which change colour when solutions change from acidic to alkaline thus indicating the neutral point when one was progressively added to the other. Again, Franciscus Sylvius (1614-72) professor of medicine at Leyden now began to investigate biological systems in terms of their chemical processes. Thus, he studied the functions of saliva and the secretions of the stomach and pancreas in trying to understand digestion in terms of acid and alkali interaction and of fermentation in the course of which he recognised salt formation as an expression of the affinity of acids and alkalis for each other. In contrast, Georg Stahl (1660-1734) propounded his *laws of the sensitive soul* of which chemical processes were *the slaves*. Though this was a throw-back to Aristotle, Stahl nonetheless progressed chemistry. Thus, by noting that Geber (c.776) had identified sulphur with *the principle of flammability* (c.f. Section 6.2.2) and that Becher (1667) had attempted to account for the many combustibles containing no sulphur by postulating his more inclusive *principle of terra pinguis*, Stahl postulated *phlogiston* (Gk. I set on fire) as the substance released when a metal was converted to its *calx* by heating. We now retain the term *calcination* for the process of heating a metal in air to form its oxide by uptake of atmospheric oxygen. However, for Stahl this reaction was written as: Metal - phlogiston = calx.

However, as to reality-evaluation of this *Phlogiston Theory*, it had long been known that heating a so-called metal calx with carbonaceous material produced the metal (c.f. Section 2.4.4); that this suggested carbon to be rich in phlogiston which it gave to the calx to produce the metal, that this richness was consistent with carbon's own combustibility which produced solid residues negligible enough to be dismissible as impurities; and that a good deal of what was then known about other chemical reactions could be explained by similar reasoning. On the other hand, the theory was known to have at least one serious defect in that it failed to account for Boyle's observation that a component of air was necessary for combustion. Thus, to harmonise the Theory (belief) with this knowledge, supporters of phlogiston had to argue that something in the air took up the released phlogiston. To this the supporters of Boyle responded that the air component involved in combustion was itself consumed. More significantly, however, Rey had already shown by experimentation in 1630 that the calx was heavier than the metal which gave rise to it, to which the phlogistonists could only respond that phlogiston had negative weight. As we shall see later (c.f. Section 7.1.1), its final overthrow was achieved by Lavoisier (1743-94) who showed by experimentation that the active component of the air was oxygen and that all outstanding conflict could be resolved by substituting *uptake of oxygen* for *loss of phlogiston*.

This example provides further evidence of the power of the experimental method. A postulate may be questionable: yet, it may provoke recognition of the relevance of earlier knowledge to the development of *reductio ad absurdum* arguments or to full elucidation by designed experimentation which would not otherwise have been initiated. Thus, in noting that the scientific method can turn even a doubtful postulate to new knowledge by reference to existing knowledge and reality-evaluating experimentation, we see that a hypothesis should be based on existing knowledge and be designed so that its reality-evaluation will answer a specific question; that it should thus act as a bridge from existing to new knowledge; and that, in these respects, Stahl's Phlogiston Theory was inadvertently a bridge from belief in the 'spirits' of classical Idealism to knowledge of the 'substance' of chemistry (c.f. Section 11.2.1)

In the meantime, the Rev. Stephen Hales (1677-1761) made an important contribution to the future characterisation of gases by devising a simple method for their collection, referred to as the pneumatic trough. This comprised a glass delivery tube from the glass reaction vessel in which the gas was produced to a cylindrical glass vessel (gas jar) filled with water and inverted on a second open-bottomed cylinder (bee-hive shelf) provided with a hole in the side for entry of the gas delivery tube and a hole in the top through which the delivered gas could enter the gas jar with downward displacement of water to a basin (pneumatic trough) containing sufficient water to immerse the inverted lip of gas jar and thus keep it full of water prior to gas delivery. When full of gas, a flat glass disc (cover-slip) was slipped under the flanged lip of the gas jar to retain the collected gas when jar and cover-slip were removed from the trough. By this means Hales measured volumes of gas produced from weighed quantities of various solids on heating, though at the time he believed he was collecting "air" in all cases, this having been supposed to act as a binder for the constituent particles of his solids prior to heating. It was left to his successors, through use of his pneumatic trough, to distinguish one gas from another by specific reactivity tests.

Again before the end of the seventeenth century, Galileo's compound microscope enabled

Marcello Malpighi (1628-94) at Bologna, Robert Hooke (1635-1703) and Nehemiah Grew (1641-1712) in London, Jan Swammerdam (1637-80) in Amsterdam and Antony van Leeuwenhoek (1632-1723) in Delft to investigate the mechanical organism to a much finer level of detail than ever before. Thus Malpighi and Leeuwenhoek discovered the corpuscles of the blood, the "capillary vessels" of the circulatory system, the secretory functions of glands and the fibrillary character of muscles. They also revealed similarities in the fine structure of animals and plants, identified spermatozoa and recognised the similarities between the sexual reproductive processes in plants and animals, though they were much given to speculation on what they saw and to imaginings beyond that, both of which were valueless in being beyond reality-evaluation.

However, microscopy did help to resolve the question of spontaneous generation of life. Readers will recall that Aristotle allowed only the possibility of such, though this was enough to give authoritative credence to the common belief that corpses 'bred' worms; rotting meat, maggots; dirt, vermin . . . and so on. Counter to these beliefs Malpighi showed that plant galls believed to be spontaneously generated, were in fact caused by insect larvae and Antonio Vallisnieri (1661-1730) showed that the larvae derived from eggs deposited in the plants by parent insects. Leeuwenhoek, however, saw microscopic creatures appear in clear infusions of hay which became cloudy with their presence within a few days or even in some cases a few hours. These seemed to be generated spontaneously or to have grown from something beyond the power of the microscope to see. On the other hand, Francesco Redi (1621-97) reported in 1668 that: "I. . .began to believe that all worms found in meat were derived from flies, not from putrifaction. I was confirmed by observing that before the meat became wormy, there hovered over it flies of that very kind which later bred in it. Belief unconfirmed by experiment is vain. Therefore, I put a (dead) snake, some fish, and a slice of veal in four large, wide-mouthed flasks. These I closed and sealed. Then I filled the same number of flasks in the same way leaving them open. Flies were seen constantly entering and leaving the open flasks. The meat and fish in them became wormy. In the closed flasks were no worms, though the contents were now putrid and stinking. Thus the flesh of dead animals cannot engender worms unless the eggs of the living be deposited therein." He goes on, "Since air had been excluded from the closed flasks I made a new experiment to remove all doubt. I put meat and fish in a vase covered with gauze. For further protection from flies, I placed it in a gauze-covered frame. I never saw any worms in the meat, though there were some on the frame, and flies, ever and anon, lit on the outer gauze and deposited their eggs there."

Here we have another example of experimentation through the use of a carefully designed system and procedure to confirm as far as possible the validity of an initial belief. This example serves to show that observation of what nature offers us may not be sufficient and that for confirmation we must test its sufficiency by a suitable and carefully designed experiment or series of experiments. Redi would not allow himself to be convinced by his initial belief. His experimentation was designed to confirm the validity of the conclusion he tentatively drew from it.. Indeed, despite these results he rightly reserved judgement on the general question of spontaneous generation on the grounds that after all, he had only shown that worms were generated from flies eggs. Other aspects remained to be settled by other experiments such as those arising from Leeuwenhoek's work on hay infusions. Nor was he convinced that Malpighi and Vallisnieri had settled the question of gall generation (c.f. Sections 8.2.5 and 8.2.6).

6. 3. 5. Further Developments in Mathematics and Measurement
To see how mathematics developed in the seventeenth century we must return to Descartes (1596-1642), whose contribution was to realise that equations in the form y equals an expression in x, (more properly a function of x, written f (x)) represent positions or loci of points whose co-

ordinates (x, y) are the paired values of y and x as the value of y changes in equality with the value of f (x), as the value of x is changed. This becomes clearer when it is referred to graph paper with an origin at O in the centre of the sheet and orthogonal axes X'OX (the x-axis) and Y'OY (the y-axis) with respect to which positive x-values are plotted to the right of the origin O and negative to the left; and positive y-values are plotted above the origin O and negative downwards for all paired values x and y. It will become clearer still when we take an equation as an example and substitute a series of values for x to evaluate the corresponding values of y; when we plot these paired-values of x and y (loci) with respect to the above axes on the graph paper; and when we draw a line through all the plotted points. It will become even clearer when we think of the continuous line as joining not only all the plotted locus points, but also all intervening locus points which we did not actually plot, though in principle (though not in practice) we could have. Thus the drawn line is the locus of points all of which satisfy the equation. It is in fact, a picture of the function f (x).

For example, let us take the equation $y = 2x + 3$ and substitute the series of values 1, 2, 3 . . . for x to give the corresponding values of 5, 7, 9 . . . for y, and plot the points with paired x and y co-ordinates (1, 5), (2, 7), (3, 9) . . . and draw a line joining them. We see that the result is a straight line. We also see that it crosses the y-axis at $y = 3$ and that the tangent of the angle which it makes with the x-axis is 2, this being the gradient of the line with respect to the x-axis. Again, because the axes are orthogonal the tangent of the angle of gradient (A) of the straight line is always given by the difference between the y co-ordinates of any two points on the line divided by the difference in their corresponding x co-ordinates i.e.:

$$(y_2 - y_1) / (x_2 - x_1) = \tan A$$

In general, equations of straight lines are in the form $y = mx + c$ where m is tan A and c is the intercept on the y-axis. By the same process of generating paired co-ordinates it can be shown that equations of the form $x^2 + y^2 = r^2$ are circles, those of form $y = ax^2$ are parabolas, those of form $x^2/a^2 + y^2/b^2 = 1$ are ellipses and those of form $x^2/a^2 - y^2/b^2 = 1$ are hyperbolas where m, c, r, a and b are constants.

Readers will recall the general formula for determining the two values of x for quadratic equations of the form $ax^2 + bx + c = 0$. These values of x are those at which the curved-line of the function crosses the x-axis i.e. at those points were $y = 0$. It is, of course, now possible to determine these values i.e. to solve the equation by the above line-drawing process and reading off the values of x where it cuts the x-axis. We have already seen that such quadratic equations can be solved by the process of completing the square (c.f. Section (5.4.1). There is, however, no general formula or procedure for solving cubic or higher order equations. Consequently, the only way to solve them is by generating paired co-ordinates, drawing the curve and reading off the values of x at which the plotted curve crosses the x-axis. Similarly, we can draw the curve of the function $ax^2 + bx + c$, which as we have seen represents all the values that that function of x can have, and from which we can find the value of x which satisfies and equation $ax^2 + bx + c = d$, by drawing the horizontal straight line $y = d$ on the same x - y diagram. If it intersects the curve we read off the values of x at the points of intersection which are the solutions of the equation. If the straight line does not intersect the curve, there are no solutions to the equation. Thus, it can be seen that Descartes' co-ordinate or analytical (often called Cartesian) geometry represents a substantial advance. The Calculus of Newton and Leibnitz would not have been possible without it (c. f. Section 6.3.7).

At this time also: Blaise Pascal (1623-62) contributed advances in probability theory and invented the first computing machines; John Wallis (1616-1703) professor at Oxford whose *Arithmetica Infinitorum* of 1655 was read by Newton, had applied mathematics to the tides, suggested that the mass of a body might be assumed to be at its centre for the purposes of calculation, considered possible interpretations for imaginary numbers and introduced the symbol for infinity; and before the age of twenty, Christian Huygens (1629-95) had done significant work on the quadrature of the circle and on conic sections which led Descartes to predict a glowing future for him. In due course, Huygens improved the telescope to the point of showing (1653-6) that the "the horns" of Saturn seen but unresolved by Galileo, were in fact a disc orbiting the planet at an angle of inclination to the elliptic of 28°. Other improvements by Huygens were to increase the focal length of his lenses in order to reduce chromatic aberration *i.e.* interference from the rainbow colours of diffracted light; to introduce the 'Huygenian' eyepiece; and to apply the micrometer to telescopes for measurement of small angular distances (c. 1640) following its invention by the Englishman William Gascoinge (1612-44).

More importantly, however, Huygens devised the pendulum clock escapement to hugely improve the accuracy of time measurement and elucidated the principles of dynamic oscillatory motion to the extent that his *Horologium* of 1658 is the foundation of the clock making craft while his *Horologium Oscillatorium* of 1673 goes beyond Galileo in its significance and genius, Newton's *Principia* being largely based upon it. Thus, Huygens had invoked the force of gravity to account for the accelerations determined experimentally by Galileo and himself, and prior to Newton he had written with more assurance than Galileo that "If gravity did not exist nor the atmosphere obstruct the motions of bodies, a body would maintain for ever, with equable velocity in a straight line, the motion once impressed upon it." Although this statement is now referred to as Newton's first law of motion, it was first enunciated in this form by Huygens. He also used a 'seconds pendulum' in which the distance between suspension point and centre of gravity was adjustable and accurately measurable to establish a period of one second per swing at any geographical location and thus to determine the acceleration due to gravity as 32.16 feet per second per second. Assuredly Newton "stood on the shoulders of giants" as he said himself. There were no giants comparable to Galileo and Huygens.

6. 3. 6 Union of Experimentation with Celestial Observation

It was Newton (1642-1727) however, who saw that the force of gravity which induced the acceleration which caused the curvilinear motion of projectiles and the constant period of pendulum-swing, was that which caused the Moon to orbit the Earth and the Planets to orbit the Sun in conformity with the Principle of Uniformity postulated by Galileo. Nonetheless, it was the experimentation on curvilinear and oscillatory motion by Galileo and later by Huygens which provided the crucial concept that speed in a straight line is a scalar quantity *i.e.* it has magnitude only, while velocity is a vector quantity *i.e.* it has both magnitude and direction (c.f. Section 6.2.3) and therefore a force is required to change the direction of a moving body even if its speed remains uniform. Thus the suspended pendulum arm provides the (centrifugal) force which counters the gravitational force to maintain its oscillatory motion (its swing) in the arc of a circle. Similarly, the tension force in the rope connecting the bolas to the hand of the thrower maintains its circular motion until on release it moves off tangentially in a straight-line prior to having curvilinear motion again impressed upon it by the force of gravity.

Newton, therefore, reasoned that unless the force of gravity acted between the Moon and the Earth, the Moon would move off in a straight line tangential to its orbit; that he knew to some degree of accuracy the distance of the Moon from the Earth and the period of the Moon's revolution round the Earth; and that he could, therefore, calculate the instantaneous speed of the Moon at any point in its orbit and hence the tangential distance which it would travel in one second, if the force of gravity were absent. Thus, from the point which the Moon was thus calculated to have reached in one second in the absence of gravity, Newton considered the secant drawn through the centre of the Earth. Now the secant and tangent theorem of Euclid states that the square on the tangent from a circle to an external point is equal to the product (multiplication) of the whole secant times its part external to the circle. Thus, by choosing the secant which passes through the centre of the earth, the diameter of the earth being known, Newton calculated the length of the external part which is the distance which the Moon had 'fallen' towards the Earth in orbiting for that one second. He then reasoned, having regard to the relationship between base-area and height of the cone, that the Earth's gravitational force of attraction for any other body would decrease as the square of the distance of separation between the Earth and the body. Thus, if he now compared the distance which the Moon had 'fallen' in one second with the distance fallen by a stone in one second when released close to the Earth under the gravitational acceleration of 32.16 feet per second per second, as measured by Huygens, he could then write:

$$\frac{\text{Distance fallen by Moon}}{\text{Distance fallen by Stone}} = \frac{(\text{Distance of Stone from Earth's Centre})^2}{(\text{Distance of Moon from Earth's Centre})^2}$$

Thus, the reality-validation of Newton's reasoning on the basis of the results of earlier experimentation depended on whether substitution of the relevant values in the above expression would demonstrate its equality. In 1666 he found that all was not as he had hoped, the distance fallen by the Moon being only seven eighths of that required for this equality. Indeed, it would be some years before all the relevant quantifications were precise enough to satisfy Newton as to this equality (c.f. Section 8.2.2).

6. 3. 7 Yet Further Development in Mathematics

In the meantime, Newton turned to what is now called the Calculus. Readers will recall that a straight line in Cartesian geometry has a constant gradient, the tangent of which is the ratio $(y_2 - y_1) / (x_2 - x_1)$ *i.e.* the ratio of the difference between a pair of y co-ordinates divided by the difference between the pair of corresponding x co-ordinates. Thus for gradient angle A we may write $\tan A =$ (diff. y) / (diff. x), or $\tan A = \Delta y / \Delta x$. Now, though a curved line has an ever changing gradient, we can in principle draw a tangent to any point on any curve drawn with respect to the Cartesian axes. Thus, we can visualise the gradient of this tangent as the gradient of the curve at the point of contact as the difference between the y co-ordinates of points on the curve which bracket this point of contact, and the difference between their corresponding x co-ordinates as these differences become ever smaller as the two points on the curve come closer and closer *i.e.* as they tend to merge with the point of contact between tangent and curve. Of course, tangents can be drawn by eye and their gradients computed from the ratio of differences in appropriate y and x co-ordinates. However, Isaac Barrow, another of Newton's teachers, appears to have realised from the above visualisation that careful draughtsmanship was unnecessary. He saw that the gradient of the tangent to the curve measures the rate of change of the quantity represented along the y-axis for unit change in the quantity represented along the x-axis. Thus, finding the gradient of any curve whose equation is known or as we say differentiating y with respect to x, amounts to deriving an expression for $\Delta y / \Delta x$ (or as we now write dy/dx) from the equation of the curve.

Now, we know that the particular curve which is the straight line has the equation $y = mx + c$, and that $dy/dx = m$, because $m = \tan A$. If we now consider the equation of the parabola $y = ax^2$, having regard to our two points P_p and Q_q either side of the point of contact between tangent and curve we may write:

$$\frac{dy}{dx} = \frac{ax_q^2 - ax_p^2}{dx}$$

$$= \frac{a.\,(x_p + dx)^2 - ax_p^2\,)}{dx} \text{ points p and q being very close}$$

$$= \frac{a.\,(x^2 + 2x\,dx + (dx)^2\,) - ax^2}{dx}$$

$$= 2ax + a.dx$$

$$= 2ax \text{ because dx is close to zero}$$

This process can be repeated for $y = ax^n$, when series expansion of the resulting binomial to the power n, will show that for $y = ax^n$, $dy/dx = nax^{n-1}$ which embodies the rule for differentiation which removes the need to draw the tangents. Again, as to the straight line equation $y = mx + c$, we see that since this can be written $y = mx^1 + cx^0$, it follows that $dy/dx = m$ (which we deduced earlier) is compliant with the rule. When the process is repeated, the second differential is written d^2y/dx^2.

The invention of the differential calculus is attributed to Newton who made much use of it in relation to velocity and acceleration (c.f. next paragraph but one). However, many others were involved in one way or another and if one were to be singled out for having the primary idea it would be Newton's teacher, Barrow. Similarly, recognition that the determination of areas, amounts to solving a differential equation is mainly due to Leibnitz who also introduced the dx/dy symbol which continues to be used to this day. But, even here, others were involved, such as Wallis (c.f. 6.3.5). In fact Leibnitz who had studied mathematics in relation to astronomy under Huygens, developed his differential calculus for this purpose independently of Newton and had published in 1684 while Newton's *Principia* did not appear until 1687, long after Newton had completed the work reported therein, Halley having spent many years trying to overcome Newton's reluctance to publish for the reasons given in Section 6.3.6.

As to the determination of areas, let us suppose that a curve is drawn entirely above the x-axis for values of x between a and b and that the verticals (ordinates) to the curve from $x = a$ and $x = b$ are labelled AF and BG respectively, then the area in question is that of the figure AFGB. Following Archimedes (c.f. Section 4.5) the procedure is to represent this area by two series of vertical rectangles, one series being inscribed within the curve while the other circumscribes it in such a way that the area Δ of the figure AFGB lies between the sum of the smaller inscribed rectangles and the sum of the larger circumscribed rectangles, both of which approach the value Δ as the width of the rectangles becomes smaller and the number of rectangles correspondingly increases. This summation is called the integral, and we now have to consider how to evaluate it in terms of the equation of the curve. Without going into its derivation, integration is the reverse of differentiation *i.e.*, if $dy/dx = ax^n$, then $y = \{a/(n+1)\}x^{n+1}$. Again, just as the integral gives the area between the curve of f (x) and the x-axis between the limits $x = a$ and $x = b$, it turns out that the volume obtained by revolving the curve about the x-axis between the planes perpendicular to that axis at $x = a$ and $x = b$ is π times the integral of f (x). Thus, the area and the volume in question are evaluated by evaluating the integral for the ordinate $x = b$ and subtracting from it the value of the integral for ordinate $x = a$.

Now, returning to Newton's use of the calculus, we can see that because velocity is the rate of change of displacement x with time t, we can write $dx/dt = V$ (velocity) and acceleration being the rate of change of velocity V with time, we can write for falling bodies which accelerate downwards at g feet per second per second that

$$\frac{d^2x}{dt^2} = g$$

which on integration gives

$$\frac{dx}{dt} = V = gt + C$$

C is the constant of integration which must always be allowed for, because on differentiation as we have seen, constants vanish, being effectively coefficients of x^0. Inspection of the situation, however, reveals that at t = 0 there might have been a velocity which we will call u, the initial velocity.

Thus $\quad\quad\quad\quad\quad\quad\quad\quad\quad\quad\quad\quad V = gt + u$

Integrating again gives displacement $\quad\quad x = \frac{1}{2}gt^2 + ut + C$

But inspection of the initial situation reveals $\quad x = 0$ when t = 0, if the origin for x is taken as the point of projection, and so C = 0. Hence $\quad\quad x = \frac{1}{2}gt^2 + ut$

The above are the equations of motion, enabling displacement (distance covered) and velocity attained after any time interval to be calculated, if acceleration and initial velocity are known. Although the acceleration caused by gravity, g, has the measured value of 32.16 feet per second per second in the above, these equations have general application to all moving bodies whatever their accelerations, be they projectiles, aircraft, automobiles, trains, planets, stars, interstellar gas, dust clouds, or whatever. It can again be seen that differentiation is the reverse of integration, by applying it in reverse order to the above equations. Again, we may check that integrals relate to areas by remembering that if a graph of distance against time is plotted, the resulting straight line or curve will show the rate of change of distance with time for which the integral (area under the curve) is velocity and similarly, a plot of velocity against time is the rate of change of velocity with time for which integration gives the area under the velocity curve which is acceleration.

Though Newton had completed his calculus by 1671, it was not until 1687 that his *Philosophiae Naturalis Principia Mathematica* finally appeared *The Principia*, as it is usually called, had established the force of gravity and its induced accelerations as the mechanism which could explain Kepler's elliptical orbits of the planets with the Sun at their common focus and that of the Moon around the Earth. It had also established Newton's *Laws of Motion* to the effect that bodies remain in a state of rest or of uniform motion in a straight line unless acted on by a force; that force equals mass times acceleration; that to every action there is an equal reaction; and that the gravitational force between two bodies is proportional to the product of their masses and inversely proportional to the square of the distance between them, the last being known as the *Law of Inverse Squares*. Without going into details, it also followed that the potential energy released by a falling body from height h is hg, that the kinetic energy of motion is $\frac{1}{2}mv^2$, and that momentum is mv. In addition, it had established the universality of all scientific laws and principles by showing that both earthly and celestial bodies move according to a single relationship between force, mass and acceleration. Thus, such universality as believed in by Bruno and Galileo, had been demonstrated by Newton on the experimentation by which Galileo had refuted Aristotle's beliefs regarding motion.

6. 4 BELIEF AND KNOWLEDGE TO 1800

My reviews to 1700 having shown that the religious opposed only beliefs and speculation counter to their own, while accepting useful and demonstrable knowledge, and having shown that socio-political leaders continued to rely on the rationality which had failed to avert the Peloponnesian

War or the Fall of Rome, it might have been expected that Enlightenment philosophers would have renounced reliance on rationality alone, given the success of the scientific method of experimentation prior to 1800. Alas, they chose to ignore experimentation, in their conflation of rationality with science, and their depiction of religion as irrational in order to propound secular belief in their own self-interest.

In contrast, while the Church had burned Bruno as a heretic in 1601 for believing the universe to have had neither beginning nor creator, it had recognised by 1631 that house-arrest was sufficient punishment for scornful treatment of the Pope in publicising what could be verified by anyone with a telescope. Again, with all early supporters of the new knowledge having been churchmen and with Thomas Aquinas having argued the neutrality of knowledge/speculation to Church Doctrine, a little more diplomacy on Galileo's part might have saved him inconvenience. In any case, Galileo published his seminal scientific work after his house arrest while his successors retained their religious beliefs with few or none having any motivation to be publicly anti-religious or anti-church. Indeed, by agreeing with Aquinas and Newton that the new approach used God-given faculties to explain His creation, the Church had no reason to oppose the new knowledge however it defined it, and had it chosen to recognise its moral code as a knowledge-based (reality-validated) product of our nature as created by God rather than as God-given through our God-created rationality, and had it permitted beliefs beyond the possibility of knowledge to be accepted, rejected or suspended as belief or metaphor, it would have substantially negated the efforts of secularists to achieve popular rejection of both Faith and code (c.f. Sections 5.6.1 and 12.1).

However, the hypocritical life-styles of many Renaissance Popes and their subordinates at all levels together with the Church's collusion with socially defective feudal governments, caused many believers to agree with Martin Luther's Confession of Augsburg (1530); to support the Reformation's emphasis on personal responsibility and self-improvement as earlier advocated by Pelagius (c.f. Section 4.2.5 and 4.2.6); and thus to support a return to some form of classical democracy despite its belief-based defects having been discerned by Thucydides, Isocrates, Socrates and others (c.f. Section 3.1.2)). Thus, these changes within religious belief and towards secularism, produced religious wars across Europe, the revolts which preceded the British Civil War (1642-1651) and execution of Charles I in 1649, the dissatisfactions which produced the US War of Independence of 1766, the French Revolution of 1789, the Terror and the subsequent Napoleonic Wars to 1815, all of which could have been avoided or mitigated by more knowledge and less belief, even Bruno's execution of 1601 having been due to differences in the latter as were all other stake-burnings of their time. Nonetheless, Britain avoided the belief-driven madness of the French Revolution, the Commonwealth of 1649 being terminated by the peaceful Restoration of Charles II in 1660 and followed by socio-political changes more empirically consistent with social cohesion through the Glorious Revolution and beyond, though knowledge remained undifferentiated from belief throughout the so-called Enlightenment to the present (c.f. Sections 10.5, 10.6 and 11.2.2).

Thus, we should note the extent to which secularism took over from religion as the cause of socio-political mayhem, though it self-presents as an improvement on religion by conflating rationality with science, by misrepresenting traditional behaviour codes as irrational religion, and by ignoring their knowledge-content to promote its own beliefs as 'knowledge'. Thus, while secularism hails the 'Enlightenment' as the triumph of 'rationality' over 'irrationality', it is the triumph of non-religious belief over religious belief to the detriment of scientific method and of empiricism in ethics and political philosophy (c.f. Sections 10.4 - 10.6) while doing nothing to prevent conflicts of belief whether religious or secular (c.f. Chapter 11).

162

Again, by ignoring the inaccessibility to reality-evaluation of the Ur-belief in religion, the secular claim Newton's deterministic universe to have destroyed the rationale for religious belief without explaining how it justifies their disbelief, and without mentioning its dependence on the experimentation which they ignore in conflating knowledge with rationality and in protecting their own beliefs from reality-evaluation. Thus, given the ease with which Newton's achievement can be detached from its underpinning experimentation and presented as 'rational knowledge', there are many who follow Voltaire (1694-1778) in thus promoting a future devoid of religious belief or of any social cohesion based upon its empiricism. In addition, this denial of experimentation encourages those engaged in social-science to conflate ethical empiricism with religious 'irrationality' and thus to replace it with alternate beliefs without reality-evaluation, even to the extent of ignoring failure on implementation. Again, it encourages those engaged in physicochemical science to ignore their professional reliance on experimentation when advancing or endorsing socio-political belief-based aspirations on rationality alone.

6.5 CONCLUSIONS

It may be concluded from this Chapter, that renaissance of the classical inheritance was slow; that the centre of scholastic learning was the Church from the monastic-orders of which relatively independent universities were being established; that scepticism developed towards classical anatomical sources as direct observation resumed; that designed experimentation was slow to develop and slower to be understood by those writing about it even after Galileo and his immediate followers had demonstrated its unique ability to produce new and deeper knowledge; that advances in mathematical analysis intended to assist commercial development were also assisting this new scientific method of reality-evaluation by experimentation; that astronomical observation and calculation were still steeped in classical Idealism which though capable of replicating observed movement by various arrangements of epicycles and eccentrics was bereft of mechanism until Newton supplied it by applying the force of gravity to Kepler's elliptical orbits; that while this force could not be removed in experimentation (c.f. Sections 8.3.4 and 11.1), the effect of its hypothetical removal was consistent with direct observation; and that while this new physical knowledge arose from experimental refutation of classical belief regarding motion, chemical knowledge was also accruing from refutation of classical belief in essences and spirits by this same scientific method of experimentation.

At this point, it may also be concluded that the beliefs of humanism and secularism had begun to influence education, politics and law-making, in a process previously controlled by the Church; and that this transfer of control culminated in the Enlightenment's conflation of knowledge with rationality *via* spurious interpretation of Newton's achievement; that this conflation was obscured by avoiding any submission of secular beliefs to the reality-evaluation without which there is no knowledge; that this in turn reinforced the general tendency to philosophise (c.f. Chapter 10) and encouraged the so-called social-sciences towards pseudo-science (c.f. Chapter 11) and all scientists to socio-political speculation. Again, it may be concluded that while descriptive knowledge can be acquired by direct observation as in astronomy and biology, knowledge of the mechanism of phenomena inaccessible to direct experimentation can only be obtained by demonstrating compliance with the results of accessible experimentation, Newton's Theory being thus compliant; and that while knowledge can be acquired by calculation from direct observation as in Galileo's determination of lunar mountain heights from shadow-lengths, knowledge cannot otherwise advance beyond the collecting and describing of specimens which physicists liken to stamp collecting.

Thus, it may be concluded that religious-belief and Church-authority were attacked by secular pseudo-science rather than by knowledge; that religious belief is beyond reality-evaluation though it reflects our self-knowledge; that its associated behaviour codes are always accessible to reality-evaluation against our group-species survival requirements; that to the extent of their current knowledge-content they have been thus validated; that recognised knowledge replaces belief and has no need to debate its superiority; that knowledge can only be replaced by belief when it is misrepresented as alternate belief; and that while the debating of beliefs does not lead to knowledge, scientists are not above engaging in such debate or even in pseudo-science when seeking socio-political influence and/or funding.

Further to these conclusions, Chapter 7 now shows how the scientific method advanced our knowledge of the physicochemical world in the period 1700-1900 while Chapter 8 shows how this knowledge transformed craftsmanship to technology and provided astronomy, geology and biology with the knowledge of underlying mechanism available only from physicochemical experimentation. Again, Chapter 9 shows how continuing experimentation produced twentieth century physicochemical knowledge and how it was applied to astronomy, cosmology, earth-sciences and technology. However, in contrast, Section 8.3.3 shows that eighteenth century speculations on the mechanism of biological evolution are unsupported by reality-evaluation; that the observed fossil record is circularly misused by Darwinists to support their conjectured mechanism of 'survival of the fittest' to discredit religious belief, as others misuse Newton, the joint purpose being to replace empirical ethics with alternates now derived one way or another from this conjectured mechanism of evolution regardless of our need for social cohesion.

Thus, having concluded that the Renaissance was much more than a rebirth in that the scientific method of experimentation is something else entirely, I now proceed to exemplify in Chapters 7, 8 and 9 how experimentation has produced today's physicochemical knowledge, how this knowledge differs from theories of biological evolution which lack reality-evaluation by experimentation (c.f. Sections 8.3.3 and 8.3.4) and how experimentation-based physicochemical knowledge reality-validates hypotheses in fields otherwise inaccessible to experimentation (c.f. Sections 8.2, 9.3 and 9.4), all of which differentiates science from pseudo-science as my critique of philosophy in Chapter 10 differentiates knowledge from belief and sets the scene for reality-refuting socio-political beliefs as exemplified in Chapter 11 and demonstrating how knowledge can replace belief and why it must as exemplified in Chapter 12.

CHAPTER 7: THE NATURE OF THE PHYSIOCHEMICAL WORLD 1700-1900

We saw in Chapters 3 and 4 that real world substance was believed to be the embodiment of essences, spirits, qualities and forms from the Beyond; that these essences of earth, water, air and fire were the constituent elements of the physical world; that the forms encountered in the real world were embodiments of the Ideal Forms of the Beyond; that the air, spirit and soul of animation were continuous with the universal soul or God; that the entities of the Holy Trinity were differing substances or different qualities of the same substance in the Beyond and in the Real; and that the abstraction of number from the Beyond conferred a higher status on rationality of the 'mind' than on bodily sense-perception of the real.

Clearly, such belief in the existence of the real world being contingent on existence of the Beyond was inaccessible to reality-evaluation. Nonetheless, we saw in Chapters 2 and 5 that craftsmanship and social arrangements continued to develop through reality-evaluation, while in Chapter 6 we saw how craft methods evolved to scientific method after Europe had reconnected with the undifferentiated knowledge and speculation of the classical world and had access to the Hindu number system for the first time. Against this background I now review the progress made in explaining the nature of 'material and non-material substance' in the eighteenth and nineteenth centuries, in further explication of the *Scientific Method of Reality-Evaluation by Experimentation*.

7. 1 UNDERSTANDING THE NATURE OF MATTER

Sixteenth century attempts to understand the nature of material substance through experimentation can be discerned in its alchemy and iatro-chemistry (c.f. Section 6.2.2) though their hypotheses were not based on knowledge. Again, though Francis Bacon (1561-1626) in his *Cogitationes De Natura Rerum*, published posthumously in 1653, had stated that "it is sufficiently clear that all things are changed and nothing really perishes and that the sum of matter remains absolutely the same", it was well into the seventeenth century before air was recognised as having weight and as being a mixture of gases with different properties (qualities) as evidenced by reaction or non-reaction with other material substances and in respiration, such recognition being sufficient to re-activate interest in the theory that substance ultimately consists of atoms distinguishable by their respective properties, as presented by Boyle in his *Sceptical Chymist* of 1661 which again supported belief in the constancy of substance (c.f. Section 6.3.4).

However, those who take contemporary science for granted cannot appreciate the difficulties faced by those seeking to replace belief in the essences of earth, water, air and fire with knowledge of the natural world when apart from craft knowledge they knew next to nothing. Nonetheless, some appreciation of these difficulties can be had from considering how they were overcome. To this end, and further to explicate Scientific Method, I now review the clarity of thought and the suspensions of belief needed to formulate the parallel and sequenced hypotheses which had to be reality-validated by experimentation before individual conclusions and their syntheses could progress the tentative initiative of the sixteenth century to its fulfilment in the knowledge of the nineteenth and twentieth.

As an example of the clarity of thought initially required, Newton had distinguished between mass and weight. According to his second law, the mass of a body is proportional to the force which produces a given acceleration in the body. For a falling body, the force involved is the weight of the body which gives its mass an acceleration of 32 feet per second per second. Thus, the weight is the force which exists between the body and the earth. However, while this force varies as the inverse square of the distance between the two, the matter of which the body consists is invariant (*Law of Conservation of Matter*) and so at any given location, such as at the surface of the Earth, the weight of a sample of matter must be constant. Thus, it follows that any observed change in the weight of a sample of matter indicates a transformation (chemical reaction) in which matter has been added from elsewhere or subtracted to elsewhere to the extent of the weight difference, and that belief in weightless essences of earth, water, air and fire can be accepted as irrelevant.

7. 1. 1 Constancy of Combining Weights of Elements in Compounds

Before the nature of matter could be investigated through its chemical reactions by weighing, however, some postulates (not yet hypotheses) were needed as to what constituted a chemical reaction. In reviewing the chemical knowledge then existing, the Dutch physician, Hermann Boerhaave, (1668-1738) clearly postulated in his *Elements of Chemistry* of 1732 that all chemical events (reactions) would ultimately be reducible to a few simple categories and that all vital processes would ultimately be expressible in chemical terms. These postulates had the very necessary effect of encouraging the practice of experimental chemistry at a time when the task of developing an understanding of inanimate, let alone animate matter, must have looked daunting to say the least. The next essential postulate was that of chemical affinity by which is meant the selective tendency of one substance to react chemically with some but not all other substances. The French physician Etienne Francois Geoffroy (1672-1731) who was influenced by Boerhaave compiled tables in which acids were arranged in order of their affinities for certain bases (alkalis) and metals for sulphur. Relative affinity was based on observation of the tendency of one reagent to replace another of similar type in a compound containing the latter, *i.e.* one acid replacing another or one metal replacing another. Readers will recall that Roman metal workers knew that one metal would plate out on another, but not in reverse.

Joseph Black (1728-99), of the University of Glasgow (founded, 1451), was the first to investigate a series of related reactions by measuring weight differences. Being interested in the mechanism of kidney-stone formation he observed that chalk when heated gives off a gas which Stephen Hales had called 'air' and which he had suggested was the cement which bound the particles of chalk together in the solid. Although Black observed that the heated solid chalk was indeed transformed to a fine powder, he also observed that the resulting powder had different properties from the original unheated chalk. Thus, it did not effervesce in acids as chalk did and it took up water with the emission of heat, while chalk did not. In addition, Black noted that the powder having taken up water, would subsequently react with a mild alkali to produce a strong alkali plus re-constituted chalk. Further, he observed that a weighed amount of chalk whether subsequently heated to the powder or not, neutralised equal volumes of the same strength acid. Again, he observed that this neutralisation took place with effervescence and loss of weight if the chalk had not been previously heated, and without effervescence and loss of weight if it had been previously heated to the powdered state. Black also observed that chalk was re-constituted when the powder resulting from heating chalk was exposed to the atmosphere.

166

Thus, in the course of the above, Black had discovered a gas which was different from air (because unlike air it did not support combustion) which was capable of existing in both the free and combined states and which was capable of transferring from combination with one substance to combination with another in a Geoffroy-style replacement. He called it "fixed air" to distinguish it from atmospheric air and he recognised it to be a constituent of the atmosphere. We call it carbon dioxide and write it CO_2. It would, of course, have been easy to set out all of the above reactions in the modern way using the symbols which have come into use to denote the elements both free and in combination in order to clarify the transformations which Black was investigating. My purpose at this point, however, is to show how the state of knowledge at the time made it difficult for the early workers to understand their observations fully, even when those observations arose from experiments which they had deliberately set up to elucidate the phenomena under investigation. Thus, my description of results as they were reported at the time is intended to give readers an understanding of the difficulties faced by those seeking knowledge of matter by experimentation which, as often as not, revealed entirely new and as yet inexplicable phenomena.

Further to this, Henry Cavendish (1731-1810) in his paper *On Fractious Airs* (those prepared in the laboratory and distinct from "natural" air) reported in 1766 that the action of acids on metals produced a gas which he called "inflammable air". We call it hydrogen and write it H_2. Cavendish determined that one part by weight of inflammable air was released in the presence of acids by 24 parts of iron, 28 of zinc or 50 of tin. He considered these amounts to be 'equivalents' and he used this term in 1766 to describe the different weights of different alkalis which neutralised a fixed amount of a given acid. He was also the first to determine the weights of equal volumes of different gases. Again, in his *Experiments on Air* of 1784 he reported that the only product of the reaction of 'inflammable air' and 'dephlogisticated air' was water. We call the latter, oxygen and write it O_2 and we write water H_2O.

The term 'dephlogisticated air' had been coined by the Unitarian Divine, Joseph Priestly (1733-1804) who had prepared oxygen (1774-5) by heating certain oxides (calxs), but had interpreted this result according to Stahl's phlogiston theory of 1702 (c.f. Section 6.3.4). In the course of his work Priestley improved the means of gas handling and had prepared and investigated the properties of what we now call ammonia, hydrogen chloride, sulphur dioxide, nitric and nitrous oxides, nitrogen peroxide, nitrogen and silicon tetra-fluoride besides his misinterpreted oxygen (c.f. below). Again, Carl Wilhelm Scheele (1742-86), a Swedish apothecary who carried out most of his investigations prior to 1773, seems to have isolated oxygen before Priestley, having reported in his *Treatise on Air and Fire* of 1777 that air consisted of two distinct gases which we now call oxygen (O_2) and nitrogen (N_2). In addition, he prepared a wide range of compounds which, if we make further use of modern nomenclature, included chlorine, silicon tetra-fluoride, hydrofluoric acid, hydrogen arsenide, manganese, baryta, various inorganic acids, an extensive range of organic acids, glycerol, copper arsenide (Scheele's green) and many more, these being deduced from his preparative descriptions.

In spite of the success being achieved through quantitative experimentation under the guidance of the new postulates, the old elemental essences of earth, water, air and fire had not been wholly superseded at this time. Thus, it was still widely believed that prolonged boiling converted water into earth because the residue remaining after evaporation seemed consistent with ancient belief regarding the formation of sedimentary deltas in river mouths. Nonetheless, in 1770 Antoine Laurent Lavoisier (1743-94), the first to concentrate on chemistry as a distinct subject, showed that when a weighed sample of water is totally evaporated to steam, condensed and weighed again, the weight difference corresponds to the weight of the solid residue. Though not conclusive, this result suggested to Lavoisier that the solid had simply been dissolved in the water and was not transformed from it. This experiment did, however, prove that no weight had been gained by the process of boiling the water whereas the original four element theory implied that changes in weight were expected when air became water (rain) and when water became solid (earth) through some transformation of immaterial essences into material substances and *vice versa*.

Lavoisier next dealt with the phlogiston theory by showing (1774-78) that the increase in weight which occurs when a metal forms a calx was caused by "something" taken up from the atmosphere, that this "something" was also consumed in respiration and combustion, and that the products of respiration were Black's "fixed air" (CO_2) and water (H_2O). During the period 1772-83, he coined the name oxygen (acid maker) for this constituent of the atmosphere because he also recognised that when non-metals such as sulphur reacted with it, the products dissolved in water to form acids. He repeated Cavendish's experiments on 'inflammable air' (hydrogen) and concluded that his 'dephlogisticated air' was oxygen, and in 1784 he further concluded that water was a compound of these two gases. Thus, while Priestley had previously isolated the constituent of the atmosphere which Lavoisier later called oxygen, he was now seen to have misinterpreted his result when he called it 'deplogisticated air' in his then continuing acceptance of the phlogiston theory. Lavoisier was therefore credited with the discovery of oxygen because he had understood its nature in terms of its reaction products, had closed off the phlogiston theory, and had opened up a major avenue of further experimentation and productive interpretation.

Lavoisier went on to clarify the concept of chemical elements as used to-day, though he called them "simple radicals". Following Boyle, he defined them as substances which cannot be further sub-divided into simpler substances and he divided them into four groups: the "imponderables", light and caloric (heat); the gases, oxygen, nitrogen (air minus oxygen), and hydrogen (the water former); non-metals such as sulphur, phosphorus and carbon which react with oxygen to form oxides which yield acids when dissolved in water; metals (he distinguished seventeen) which react with oxygen to form oxides which yield bases (alkalis) when dissolved in water. He also recognised the "earths" which included lime, magnesia, baryta, alumina, silica, together with the alkalis potash and soda, none of which had yet been resolved into their constituent elements, though he correctly believed them to consist of oxygen and other elements. Thus, Lavoisier recognised twenty-three elements correctly in the modern sense, though his list was considerably longer. Again, in *A New Chemical Nomenclature* written jointly with de Morveau and Bertholet in 1787, Lavoisier began to name substances according to their chemical composition, thus replacing random alchemical names with many still in use today. Yet again, in 1789 he published his *Elementary Treatise on Chemistry* which first established it as a systematic experiment-based discipline. In this, he makes clear that the same weight of constituents can be extracted from compound bodies as have been put into them, and that compound bodies have the combined weight of the simpler bodies and ultimately of the elements of which they are composed. It seems poor recompense that Lavoisier was guillotined in a secular revolution supposedly intended to benefit humanity.

Having now clarified the nature of the elements and their tendency to react to form compounds, the next step was to hypothesise that the elements which formed a given compound would always be found in constant proportions in that compound, in response to which, Joseph Louis Proust (1755-1826) demonstrated that in all his examples of quantified preparation and analyses of pure substances, a definite compound always contained the same elements in the same proportions by weight, whether formed in nature or in the laboratory. This hypothesis was found to be so inviolate that it is now known as the *Law of Constant Composition.* Working on Proust's conclusions, E.G. Fischer (1754-1831) prepared a table of equivalent weights for a range of elements based on data collected by J. B. Richter (1762-1822), these being the experimentally determined weights in which elements would be expected to react to form compounds in those instances where their affinities caused them so to do.

7. 1. 2 Existence of More than One Compound of the Same Elements

This initially confusing possibility came to light when Tobern Olaf Bergman (1735-84) reported that there might be two equivalent weights for each element depending on whether reaction took place in aqueous solution or in the dry state, and that in some cases the reaction could not be carried to completion unless one of the reagents was present in excess of its equivalent weight. In addition, Geoffroy's affinity table had been criticised by Claude Louis Berthollet (1748-1822) in his *Essay on Chemical Statics* of 1803, and the latter now agreed with Bergman on the need for excess reagent in some cases. In addition, Berthollet reported that when two substances competed to react with a third, the outcome depended not only on chemical affinities but also on the quantities present, and he erroneously concluded that the constituents of the compounds formed were not in constant proportion, but in proportions which depended on the conditions of their formation. Now, these results were valid as observed, but rather than being necessarily evidence that Proust was wrong, they were evidence of the need to consider wider issues, such as the influence of the concentrations of reagents and product on reaction *rate* as distinct from the constancy of proportion on reaction *completion*. Indeed, these rate-related aspects of chemical reactivity later became the subject of a new field of investigation which today is referred to as reaction kinetics. In any event, regardless of reaction conditions, rate, and the degree of completion, the composition of the compound formed is always one of constant composition as claimed by Proust, any excess in the reagents being simply left un-reacted and thus not forming product.

Nevertheless, it is not always the case that there is only one product. There are two oxides of lead. In the red oxide (red lead) the relative portion of oxygen to lead is in the ratio of 64 : 621, while in the yellow-white oxide (litharge) it is 64 : 828. In addition, there are two oxides of carbon in which the ratio of oxygen to carbon is 8 : 3 and 8 : 6, and five oxides of nitrogen in which the amount of oxygen associated with 14 parts of nitrogen are 8, 16, 24, 32, 40 respectively. Such observations led John Dalton (1746-1844), a Quaker teacher of Manchester, to the generalisation that where two elements combine to form more than one compound the different weights of one which combine with the same weight of the other are in simple proportion. This is now called the *Law of Multiple Proportions*. In addition, Jons Jacob Berzelius (1779-1848) published in the interval (1810-1812) the results of a careful series of experiments on the weights of combining elements which showed that 100 parts of iron, 230 parts of copper and 381 parts of lead are equivalent because they combine with 29.6 parts of oxygen to form oxides and with 58.7 parts of sulphur to form sulphides; and that hence, if sulphur and oxygen form a compound, 58.7 parts of sulphur should combine with 29.6 parts of oxygen or taking the *Law of Multiple Proportions* into account, with some simple multiple or sub-multiple of 29.6 parts of oxygen. As to this possibility Berzelius then showed that in sulphur dioxide 58.73 parts sulphur are combined with 57.45 parts of oxygen, where he should have found 2 x 29.6 = 59.2 parts of oxygen. Though the disagreement between 59.2 and 57.45 is rather large even for the analytical precision of the time, modern repetition has given agreement close to 1 in 50,000. Now, with J. B. Richter having reported similar relationships for reactions of acids and bases (alkalis), it was concluded that the weights (multiple or sub-multiple) of the various elements which react with a fixed weight of any element taken as a standard, also react with one another in simple proportions, this being the *Law of Reciprocal Proportions*.

Thus, while differing compositions of the type which caused Berthollet to disagree with

Proust do exist, they are in compliance with Proust's Law in that they represent separate compounds each with its own constant composition. Thus, it was now possible to state that the combining weight (or chemical equivalent) of an element is the number of parts by weight of it which combine with or replace 8 parts by weight of oxygen (taken as standard) or the combining weight (chemical equivalent) of any other element. The resolution of this earlier-seeming inconsistency is an example of yet another aspect of the scientific method. It is always found that when inconsistent results arise from two or more different but equally valid experimentation procedures, an opportunity immediately arises to achieve a deeper or wider understanding of the phenomenon which gave rise to the inconsistency. In such cases, deeper knowledge will eventually be provided by experiment-based investigation of the inconsistency. This is a consequence of the fact that properly verified scientific results cannot be wrong. When the apparent inconsistency is resolved, the sets of 'conflicting' data remain valid in their respective contexts as sub-sets within the even wider data set which now constitutes fuller knowledge of the wider issue as now resolved.

7. 1. 3 Growing support for the Atomic Theory of Matter

Another aspect of scientific method is that the drawing together of knowledge from a variety of sources can often provide vindication of an earlier conjecture not previously believed related to any of the individual sources. Thus, as we shall see, all of the progress reviewed in this Section 7.1 may be taken *inter alia*, as vindicating the Atomic Conjecture of Democritus (c.f. Section 3.1.2).

This vindication had started in 1790 when Joseph Priestley concluded "from a very coarse experiment" that "fixed and common air expanded alike from the same degree of heat". Subsequently, John Dalton stated in 1801 that all gases expand equally with equal increments in temperature. Shortly afterwards, Joseph Louis Gay-Lussac (1778-1844) quoted some experiments in support of the more general statement that "the same rise of temperature produces in equal volumes of all gases the same increase in volume, provided the pressure be kept constant". This is now referred to as *Charles's Law* in memory of J. A. C. Charles who according to Gay-Lussac had made some crude experiments on the subject some fifteen years before his own publication of 1802, though some still refer to the relationship as *Gay-Lussac's Law*. This relationship was combined with Boyle's Law (c.f. Section 6.3.4) to give the general gas equation in the form: $(P_1.V_1) / T_1 = (P_2 .V_2) / T_2$. Clearly gas volumes as measured must be converted *via* the gas equation to standardised conditions of temperature and pressure if quantified use is to be made of them. The standard adopted is 0° Centigrade and 1 atmosphere pressure (760mm of mercury, referred to as normal (normalised) or standard temperature and pressure, NTP or STP. In respect of Charles's Law, it should be noted that when the volumes of a fixed mass of gas are plotted against corresponding centigrade temperatures, the line drawn through the plotted points extrapolates to cut the temperature axis at zero volume at a temperature of -273° C, this consequently being absolutely the lowest temperature attainable in nature, while 0° C is equivalent to 273° Absolute, the temperatures used in the above gas equation being thus on the Absolute (or Kelvin) temperature scale (c.f. Section 7.2.8)

Now, Dalton's approach to gases was *via* meteorology in which he kept long term records of temperature, pressure and relative humidity in an effort to relate such variable parameters to weather forecasting. However, his chemical analyses of the atmosphere showed that while the oxygen and nitrogen were present in constant proportions, there were relatively small and variable quantities of carbon dioxide and water vapour; and that despite their differing densities the atmosphere was uniformly mixed. In addition he observed by experimentation that when non-reacting gases are brought together they form a homogeneous mixture despite their density differences; and that each exerts the same pressure as it would if it alone occupied the containment space. Thus *Dalton's Law of Partial Pressures* is $P = p_1 + p_2$ where P is the total pressure of a non-reacting gas mixture and p_1 and p_2 are the partial pressures which each gas would exert if it occupied the whole space on its own. This Law extends to mixtures of any number of gases. It follows, of course, that when a prepared gas is collected over water in the pneumatic trough, the presure P in the gas jar is equal to the partial pressure (p_1) of the collected gas plus the partial pressure of water vapour (p_2). The latter being considerable at ambient temperatures, the measurement of the quantity of gas collected over water requires subtraction of the partial pressure of water vapour from the total pressure in the gas jar (P) which is equal to the atmospheric pressure at the time of collection. In addition, for comparison of one volume of collected gas with another, their partial pressures must be converted to NTP through application of the gas equation as discussed above. To allow for the partial pressure of the water vapour, however, its value needs to have been measured previously.

This is done by inserting with a small pipette, a few drops of water into the foot of a dry mercury column in a Torricellian barometer (c.f. Section 6.3.4). When these drops rise up to the vacuum space they evaporate and exert a pressure equal to the resulting drop in the level of mercury in the barometric column. If this process is continued until liquid water appears at the top of the mercury column *i.e.* the space above it is saturated with water vapour and no more can evaporate, the lowering of the mercury column is the maximum vapour pressure of water, in mm of mercury, at the temperature and atmospheric pressure at the time of the experiment. If the barometer tube is surrounded with a jacket through which warm water can be passed, the maximum pressure of water (or other) vapour can be measured at a range of temperatures, and results have been tabulated for routine use. In this way, the true quantity of gas collected over water can be calculated by application of Dalton's Law of Partial Pressures and as we shall see later, accurate determination of gas quantity is fundamental to subsequent progress in chemical understanding, while the physical mixing of gases begins to make atoms more than conjecture.

Again, as we have seen, Gassendi had re-introduced the Atomic Conjecture in 1649 and Boyle had returned to it at intervals (between 1661 and his death in 1691) with regard to his ideas on the nature of the elements. Again, Newton had had to assume space to be a vacuum in his consideration of lunar motion. The realisation now dawned, however, that a vacuum had been accessible here on Earth at the top of every Torricellian barometer tube since the middle of the seventeenth century. Now, when Democritus conjectured that matter is discontinuous and consists of discrete and indivisible atoms, it might have been supposed that otherwise continuous matter could be cut or otherwise divided into smaller and smaller pieces until further subdivision would produce two pieces neither of which would be the original material. This *reductio ad absurdum* reasoning leads to matter having a limit to its subdivision which is the atom, defined by Democritus as that which cannot be further subdivided. According to this reasoning, matter is discontinuous only because its subdivision terminates at the atom, while continuous matter would presumably be capable of infinite subdivision.

There is more to it than this however. According to Democritus, the atoms exist regardless of our supposed process of sub-division, and Lucretius (c.f. Section 3.2.3) forces us to consider where they exist when he says that "nothing exists save atoms and the void." Thus, what we intuitively think of as matter is not matter alone: it is also the void which contains the atoms of matter. This is altogether different in that it disallows continuous matter, whether limited in its subdivision or not On this basis, reality is the counter-intuitive and ubiquitous void within which atoms of gases and of vapours can exert pressure on the atoms of liquids and solids (liquid surfaces or the walls of containers) which themselves consist of atoms in the void, while the emptiness of the void is the space in which all atoms whether of gases, vapours, liquids or solids have their being, and which is co-extensive with the universal void. Thus, the Torricellian vacuum is not just an absence of atoms: it is a sample of the void.

However, with regard to the immediate concerns of chemistry, Dalton now turned to Proust's recently formulated Law of Constant Proportions, assumed that chemical combination would occur in the simplest possible way, and concluded as a working hypothesis (*Dalton's Hypothesis*) that one atom of one element would combine with one atom of another and where two elements could form more than one compound, simple whole number ratios would still apply. Thus he supposed that water would be composed of one atom of hydrogen and one of oxygen, that ammonia would consist of one nitrogen and one hydrogen atom, and that since carbon and oxygen combined to form two compounds one would consist of atoms in the ratio of 1 : 1, and the other in the ratio of 1 : 2. Dalton also concluded that though atoms must be far too small to be weighed, it should be possible to determine their relative weights by determining the relative weights and the relative numbers in which they combined to form a given weight of compound. He could not as yet, however, determine these relative numbers, but he was getting close to demonstrating the existence of atoms. Indeed, the compressibility, expandability and miscibility of gases, strongly suggested void volumes containing individual moving atoms or their small number combinations.

7. 1. 4 The Number of Atoms in the Molecule of a Compound

The next step in determining the number of atoms in molecules and thus in vindicating the Atomic Conjecture was taken in 1808 by Gay-Lussac in reporting that the volumes of reacting gases were in very simple numerical ratios to the volumes of their gaseous products. Thus, for example, one volume of oxygen combined with two volumes of hydrogen to form two volumes of water vapour, and one volume of nitrogen combined with three volumes of hydrogen to form two volumes of ammonia gas. From these simple relationships, Amadeo Avogadro (1776-1856) reasoned in 1811 that the atoms must exist in groupings (not as single atoms) within the volumes of combining and combined gases. Thus, he explained Gay-Lussac's results by assuming that the atoms must exist as pairs in the isolated gases, that these were separable in their reactions, and that they re-grouped in forming the reaction products. Furthermore, he called these divisible and re-formed groups molecules (Latin, little masses), hypothesised that "equal volumes of all gases under the same conditions of temperature and pressure contain the same number of molecules" (*Avogadro's Hypothesis*) and on this basis explained Gay-Lussac's observation as one volume of oxygen consisting of diatomic molecules (O_2) combining with two volumes of hydrogen consisting of diatomic molecules (H_2) to form two volumes of water vapour consisting of tri-atomic molecules (H_2O), now written as $O_2 + 2H_2 = 2H_2O$. Similarly the reaction between nitrogen and hydrogen could now be written $N_2 + 3H_2 = 2NH_3$ and we see that both sides of these equations have the same number of atoms in compliance with the requirement that matter be conserved.

Though Avogadro's Hypothesis is one of the most productive in the history of chemistry, he had not yet solved the problem of determining the number of atoms in compounds. The remaining difficulty is that while Dalton's Hypothesis defines an atom as the smallest particle of an element which can enter into or be expelled from chemical combinations, only the weight ratios of the elements in a compound can be determined by chemical analysis. Thus, while chemical analysis shows that the weight ratio of oxygen : carbon = 8 : 6 in carbon monoxide, the carbon monoxide molecule may consist of one oxygen atom with two carbon atoms each with a combining weight of 3; or of one oxygen atom and one carbon atom with a combining weight of 6. Thus, we do not *know* how many atoms are present in Avogadro's gaseous molecules, and similar difficulties arise with all

172

combinations of elemental atoms, including Gay-Lussac's reacting gases, though Avogadro's assumption of two atoms per molecule is very plausible on the basis of the reactant and product volume ratios. Thus, the concept of the atom was now indistinct in being useless for deriving atomic weights from analytically determined combining weights. Nonetheless, here we can identify yet another aspect of the scientific method in that hypotheses are retained (suspended) so long as they are potentially useful which is until their refutation or validation by reality.

In the present case, the potential usefulness of Avogadro's Hypothesis was pursued by measuring vapour densities. The absolute density of a gas is defined as the weight of a litre of the gas as measured under standard conditions while its relative density is defined as the number of times it is heavier than an equal volume of hydrogen at the same temperature and pressure, hydrogen being the least dense of all the gases. Now, because Avogadro's Hypothesis states that equal volumes of all gases contain the same number of molecules, it follows that the relative density of a gas is proportional to its molecular weight. Thus, if we can establish the number of hydrogen atoms in the hydrogen molecule we can determine molecular weights for all other gases and vapours from their measured densities, and since the molecular weight of a substance is equal to the sum of the atomic weights of all the atoms in the molecule, it follows that we can determine the values of atomic weights of the elements from the numbers of atoms present in combination, though this is impossible from Dalton's and Avogadro's Hypotheses either separately or together.

Now, elucidation of the number of hydrogen atoms in the hydrogen molecule being crucial to progress, the relevant considerations were as follows. Gay-Lussac, had observed that one volume of hydrogen combines with one volume of chlorine to form two volumes of hydrogen chloride. However, were we to write the reaction 'equation' as $H + Cl = 2HCl$ we would see that the product on the right hand side has two hydrogen atoms and so the hydrogen molecule must contain *at least* two atoms of hydrogen and similarly the chlorine molecule must contain *at least* two atoms of chlorine, and so our molecular equation could be written $H_2 + Cl_2 = 2HCl$, in order to at least balance it as required by matter conservation. However, as exemplified above for carbon monoxide, the problem is that such balance can also be achieved if hydrogen and chlorine molecules contain equal multiples of 2 atoms and the HCl molecule contains half this number of hydrogen and chlorine atoms, *i.e.* it could not be said that these reacting molecules have only two atoms each and the product molecules only one of each. It was known, however, that HCl is an acid in aqueous solution and in common with all other acids contains hydrogen replaceable by metals; and that acids differ from each other in the number of stages in which their hydrogen can be replaced to form an equal number of distinct salts. Thus, the hydrogen can be displaced in three stages to form three salts with orthophosporic acid; in two stages to form two salts with sulphuric acid; and in only one stage to form only one salt with many other acids. Consequently, if hydrochloric acid had the formula H_nCl_n we should expect to find the hydrogen being replaced in n stages to form n identifiable salts. In fact it can only be displaced in one stage, only the chloride salt, being observed. It can thus be inferred that the molecule of hydrogen chloride may be written HCl and that therefore the molecules of hydrogen and of chlorine may be written H_2 and Cl_2 respectively as in the above equation. Thus, we infer that there are two hydrogen atoms in the hydrogen molecule and the way is open to determine molecular weights from vapour pressure measurements on this basis.

Evidence of an entirely different kind supports this conclusion. Joseph Black, in addition to his work on chalk also investigated Lavoisier's "imponderable" caloric (c.f. 7.2.1) as a consequence of which his instrument maker James Watt introduced his separate condenser to improve the efficiency of steam engines (c.f. Section 8.1.1). In order to pursue his work Black had defined heat capacity (or specific heat) as the amount of heat required to raise one gram of a substance (liquid or solid) by 1° Centigrade. However, because a gas is heated by compression and cooled by expansion, it is necessary to define two specific heats, that at constant pressure c_p and that at constant volume c_v. Without going into details, it can be shown that the ratio c_p / c_v (γ) for a monatomic gas should be 1.667 on theoretical grounds. Experimental determination of this ratio for a range of gases now showed that there was a group in the range 1.4 to 1.3 inclusive and another below 1.3 which were clearly poly-atomic gases such as methane, ethane, benzene *etc.* For hydrogen and nitrogen the value is 1.41; for oxygen and carbon monoxide, 1.40; for hydrogen chloride, 1.39; for chlorine, 1.32; while for methane it is 1.27 and for benzene it is 1.09. It seemed reasonable, therefore, to take these results as supporting evidence that hydrogen, nitrogen, oxygen, and carbon monoxide were all diatomic, this being further confirmed when the value of γ for the rare gases was later observed to be 1.66 showing them to be monatomic as would be expected from their lack of reactivity (c.f. Section 7.1.7).

Now if we define gram-molecular volume at standard temperature and pressure (STP) (c.f. Section 7.1.3) as the volume occupied by the number of grams of gas numerically equal to its molecular weight, Avogadro's Hypothesis tells us that it will be the same for all gases and that if we can calculate it for one gas we will have it for all. Thus, the atomic weight of the hydrogen atom was set at unity and the atomic weights of all other elements relative to it. Now, having measured the density of hydrogen gas to be 0.09 grams per litre at STP, the volume of 1 gram-molecular (2 atoms) weight of hydrogen (weight / density), was calculated to be 22.4 litres on which basis the molecular weight of all gases should be twice the measured vapour density according to Avogadro. Accordingly, attention now turned to the measurement of vapour density as a route to molecular weight and hence to atomic weights from knowing the number of atoms in their molecules and their elemental composition. Nonetheless, though the number of molecules in the gram-molecular weight of any gas at STP was now denoted by N, and referred to as Avogadro's Number, its value was not determined till much later. The most direct method is that of Rutherford (c.f. Section 9.1.3) who counted the number of α-particles emitted by a quantity of radium and calculated N, knowing that each α-particle is an ionised helium atom. Again, N was deduced from determining the electron mass to be $1/1836^{th}$ of the mass of the hydrogen atom (c.f. Section 9.1.3) and later from Einstein's deduced relationship of N to Brownian Movement from which Perrin determined N by experimentation. The current value of N is 6.025 x 10^{23}.

In the meantime, in order to make use of the still provisional relationship that molecular weight = 2 x vapour density, vapour densities had to be measured. This was done for permanent gases either as absolute density by determining the weigh in grams of 1 litre of gas at 0° C and 760mm pressure, the weights being corrected to sea level at latitude 45° or as relative density which is the weight of a given volume of the gas divided by that of an equal volume of hydrogen measured and weighed under identical conditions. In the Globe (or Regnault's Method) an evacuated globe was weighed, filled with the gas at a known pressure and temperature, and reweighed. The volume of the globe was then determined by weighing it full of water of which the temperature and density were known. To obtain results of the highest possible accuracy, however, the globe must be absolutely dry and the gas as nearly as possible at 0° C and 760mm pressure. To allow for changes in relative humidity, temperature and pressure, the air in the balance room was monitored, the globe was counterbalanced against an exactly similar globe and both were always treated in exactly the same manner. To calculate shrinkage of the globe on evacuation it was placed inside a closed vessel with its orifice tube passing through one of two holes in the vessel top, the other having been fitted with a calibrated vertical capillary tube; the vessel was otherwise filled with water and immersed in a constant temperature bath; and the fall in water level in the capillary was measured on evacuating the globe. Finally, the density as determined above was further corrected by dividing by the factor (1- 0.0026 cos 2λ - 0. 000000196h) where λ and h are latitude and altitude of the place of observation. Because this technique would be subject to un-quantifiable adsorption of gas on the internal surface of the globe, it is limited to non-absorbing gases such as the rare gases and nitrogen (Rayleigh, 1892) and the permanent gases hydrogen and oxygen (Morley 1895).

In addition, mention should be made of the Volumetric Method of Guye and Pintza which is based on measuring the volume of gas such as hydrogen driven off from previous solution in palladium by heating, or by absorbing gas such as nitrogen in charcoal contained in a globe immersed in liquid air, and on measuring the associated weight-change. Again, the Buoyancy (or Microbalance) Method depends on equating the buoyancy experienced by an evacuated quartz bulb surrounded by the gas of unknown density ρ' at measured pressure p' with that of a gas of known density ρ at measured pressure p, the relationship being $\rho'/\rho = p/p'$. Furthermore, the unknown density of a gas ρ' can be determined by comparing its diffusion rate r' through a porous membrane with the measured diffusion rate r of a gas of known density ρ, the relationship being : $r'/r = (\rho/\rho')^{1/2}$, *Graham's Law of Diffusion*, (c.f. Section 7.2.2).

In the case of substances which are solid or liquid at ordinary temperatures, density measurement must be made above the volatilisation temperature. In Dumas's Method some 6 to 10 grams of the compound in question are placed in a glass retort (long-necked flask) of 100 to 200 ml capacity immersed in a suitable bath at some 20 - 30 degrees above the boiling point of the compound, until vapour ceases to issue from the neck of the retort, whereupon it is sealed and the bath temperature and barometric pressure are read. The flask is then cooled and weighed, its sealed tip broken under water or mercury, weighed full of liquid and again empty. In Hoffman's Method, a modification of an earlier (1811) method of Gay-Lussac, a small stoppered glass bulb containing a weighed amount of the chosen compound is introduced to a Torricellian barometer tube in which it ascends through the mercury to vaporise in the void space, the barometer tube being surrounded by a jacket through which passes the vapour of a liquid of boiling point some 20 degrees above that of the compound in question. When all is in equilibrium, the vapour volume, the mercury column height, barometric pressure and temperature of the apparatus are read. In Victor Meyer's Method of 1877 the volume of air displaced by a known weight of vapour is determined. This involves having a tall tubular vessel with a side-tube leading from its top end to a pneumatic trough (c.f. Section 6.3.4) enclosed within an outer vented jacket containing a small amount of liquid of boiling point some 20-30 degrees above that of the compound in question. With this liquid boiling in the jacket a calibrated water-filled gas jar is placed over the delivery tube to the pneumatic trough, a small (stoppered) bottle containing a weighed amount of the compound is vaporised by causing it to drop into the jacketed length of the tall tubular vessel. Thus, air/vapour is displaced into the graduated gas jar where its volume is measured by downward displacement of water of which the temperature is measured, together with barometric pressure. Vapour density is calculated from the measurements made in each case.

7. 1. 5 Equivalent Weights, Atomic Weight, Molecular Weight and Valence

To take the search for a once and for all means of determining atomic and molecular weights a stage further, it is necessary to return to the equivalent weights for reacting elements. It may be recalled that the concept of equivalence in relation to compounds had arisen earlier when Cavendish in 1766 referred to a given weight of potash as the equivalent of another (different) weight of lime when both exactly neutralised the same weight of an acid, and when Richter in 1792 published a table of equivalent weights of acids and bases. Volumetric analysis is based on this concept whereby a normal (N) solution is defined as one which contains the gram-equivalent weight of a substance in one litre of solution, the gram-equivalent weight being the number of grams of the substance numerically equal to the equivalent weight. Solutions of known concentration are made up at any convenient strength, usually 0.1N by accurate weighing of the appropriate reagent. A known volume, usually 25ml, is then reacted with solutions of unknown concentration to determine the volume needed for the reaction to be complete, thus determining the number of equivalents in the unknown solution and hence the weight present in grams. The process of determining the completion point is called titration and the 'end point' is determined by a colour change in an indicator a few drops of which are added at the beginning of the titration (c.f. Section 6.3.4). Again, equivalent weights of compounds can be related to the equivalent weights of elements. Thus, the equivalent weight of an acid is that which contains one equivalent weight of replaceable hydrogen; and the equivalent weight of an oxidising agent is that which contains one equivalent weight (8 parts by weight) of available oxygen. Since the molecule of hydrogen consists of two atoms, its equivalent weight will be half its molecular weight, and hence the gram-equivalent weight of hydrogen will occupy 11.2 litres at STP. The determination of equivalent weights of the elements is not only fundamental to all quantitative work including quantitative analysis, but also to the determination of Atomic Weights.

It may be recalled that all of the above progress was made despite continuing uncertainty as to how many atoms were actually present in the molecules of their respective compounds; that Dalton had made the purely arbitrary assumption that when only one compound of two elements was known, its molecule would contain only one atom of each, elements existing as separate atoms; and that Berthollet *et al* took the view that molecular composition was variable and dependent on the conditions of formation. As a result of this lack of certainty and associated confusion, it was difficult to maintain early enthusiasm for the search for a means of determining the relative weights of atoms, *i.e.* their atomic weights. Again it will be recalled that Gay-Lussac's work on combining volumes of gases was very suggestive as to the relative numbers of atoms in molecules before and after reaction, but it was still not definitive; that Avogadro indicated a way forward which was consistent with the results of Gay-Lussac, though on its own it was not the answer; and that nonetheless it did encourage measurement of vapour density, there being some independent evidence from replaceable hydrogen in acids for the hydrogen molecule containing two atoms and thus for molecular weights being twice the measured vapour densities. Again, the Laws of Constant Composition, Multiple Proportions and Reciprocal Proportions having been propounded, work continued on the determination of equivalent weights for the quantification of reactions. Thus, we see how scientific method proceeds on a number of fronts though their interconnection remains unclear, in this case there being no definitive route to the number of atoms in the molecules of elements and compounds though equivalent weights were being determined and consistently used.

However, the remaining uncertainties were addressed in 1858 by Stanislao Cannizzaro (1826-1910) through his comprehensive consideration of a range of volatile compounds of carbon, namely carbon monoxide, carbon dioxide, methane, ethylene, propylene, and carbon disulphide.

176

These were analysed to determine their percentage composition by weight and molecular weights were assigned from vapour density measurement as discussed above. In addition, Cannizzaro calculated the amount of carbon per molecule in relation to the hydrogen, oxygen, or sulphur as appropriate in each case. The result was that the smallest weight of carbon in a gram-molecular weight (as determined by vapour pressure) of any of these compounds was 12, from which he assumed 12 to be the atomic weight of carbon, that of hydrogen being unity. Indeed, from that time to this no compound of carbon has given other than 12 for the atomic weight of carbon. Thus, Cannizzaro's method for finding atomic weights involved selecting a set of purified compounds containing the element of interest and which were volatile without decomposition; determining their molecular weights as twice their measured vapour pressures to determine the lowest amount of the element in the set of molecules by chemical analysis; and assuming that the lowest value was the atomic weight of the element. Of course, there was the possibility that the chosen set would not reveal the true minimum, and that the value thus found would later have to be replaced by a sub-multiple. However, this possibility was minimised by including the simplest known compound of the element of interest in the first set chosen, which in the case carbon is carbon monoxide.

In the meantime, in measuring the specific heats of solid elements, P. L. Dulong and A. T. Petit in 1819 had found that the atomic weight A and specific heat (heat capacity) C (c.f. Section 7.2.1) are related such that $A \times C = 6.4$ though the constancy is not exact because of variations in crystalline form and in the proximity of the fusion temperature to that of specific heat determination for each element. Nonetheless, *Dulong and Petit's Law*, with some important exceptions such as carbon, silicon, boron and beryllium, computes the approximate atomic weight for any solid element whose specific heat can be determined and complements vapour density measurements for molecular weight determination of volatile compounds.

However, it was found that the approximate atomic weights provided by Dulong and Petit could be transformed to the accuracy of equivalent weight and percentage composition determinations. The reasoning was that the ratio of specific heats at constant volume and pressure and the staged replacement of hydrogen by metals as earlier discussed, made it highly probable that hydrogen rarely if ever combines with more than one atom of any other kind; that, therefore, an element which combines with hydrogen has an equivalent weight e and an atomic weight a such that $e = a$ for such an element. Similarly, if a compound contains an atom of the element combined with two atoms of hydrogen, then $e = a/2$ for that element. In general, if the atom of the element is combined with V atoms of hydrogen, then $e = a/V$. Now since V is the number of hydrogen atoms combined with the element, V must be a whole number since atoms are indivisible, and it must be small. We can now rearrange our equation and write, atomic weight = equivalent weight x a small whole number.

This small whole number V, the number of hydrogen atoms with which an atom of another element can combine, was now called the valence of the element, and we know from the Laws of Multiple and Reciprocal Proportions that some elements combine together in more than one proportion to form different compounds; and that a given element may have more than one equivalent weight though it has only one atomic weight. Now, it follows from our equation $e = a/V$ that an element with more than one equivalent must correspondingly exhibit more than one whole number valences; that an accurately determined equivalent e can be divided into an approximately determined atomic weight a^* to give a valence V^* ($a^*/e = V^*$) which approximates to the whole number V; that this can be rounded off to the whole number V because it *has to be* a whole number; that this whole number when multiplied by the accurate equivalent (Ve) gives the atomic weight a to the accuracy of the equivalent; and that atomic weights to this accuracy can thus be derived from those approximately determined by *Dulong and Petit's Law*, while valence V and its variability (multi-valence) provides a new measure of the chemical affinity of one element for another.

Having seen how the task of determining atomic weights had inspired careful measurement of gas and vapour density, it will not surprise readers that it now inspired careful measurement of combining equivalent weights. The methods pursued may be classified as hydrogen displacement, oxidation/reduction, chloride formation, metal replacement, electrolysis and conversion of one compound to another. Hydrogen displacement involves determination of the equivalents of metals by measuring the volumes of hydrogen displaced by known weights of metal and calculating the amount needed to release 11.2 litres of hydrogen at STP. Oxide methods involve weight determinations of the amounts of elements which combine with the gram equivalent of oxygen either by direct oxidation (synthesis), indirect oxidation (indirect synthesis through an intermediate nitrate for example) or reduction of the oxide to constant weight of element. Chloride formation involves precipitation of the chloride of the element by addition of silver nitrate, the equivalents of silver and chlorine being attainable with great accuracy. Replacement methods involve the plating out of one metal from a solution of its salt by another element going into solution. The electrochemical method (c.f. Section 7.2.5) involves passing the same amount of current through the solutions of the salts of two metals in series, the weights of the metals released being proportional to their equivalents. Examples of the conversion method are the conversion of an oxide to a chloride, a chloride to a sulphate or a chlorate to a chloride. In all of these methods the known equivalent of one element is used to determine the equivalent of another.

The determination of atomic weights from equivalent weights requires individual experimental ability and dedication exceptional in any generation. Among such are J. S. Stas (1813-91) whose skill and patience excelled all his predecessors. After very careful search for an optimal method Stas focussed on converting the element to its chloride or bromide, treating it with silver nitrate to precipitate silver chloride or bromide and relating the quantitative results so obtained to the equivalent weight of oxygen. This he did by heating potassium chlorate to determine the loss in weight associated with the release of six oxygen equivalents); by treating the resulting potassium chloride with silver nitrate to precipitate potassium chloride, the equivalent weight for silver having been determined by reacting pure silver in a current of chlorine. In this way Stas devoted his life to determining the equivalent weights of a limited number of elements. Nonetheless, his successor T. W. Richards (1868-1928) on proceeding to use his predecessor's values for silver and chlorine in his own work, found discrepancies which led him to identify systematic errors. Thus, Richards found that the most carefully prepared potassium chlorate always contains some chloride; that silver chloride when precipitating always carries down traces of the potassium chloride which cannot be removed by washing the filtrate; that the silver chloride solution used by Stas had sometimes contained solid chloride; that the quantities used by Stas rendered precipitate washing difficult; that Stas had not allowed for the slight solubility of silver halides and the effect of excess of one or other of the reagents on them which rendered their precipitation ever so slightly incomplete; and that the silver used by Stas had contained oxide

As a consequence of the above, Richards and his co-workers (at Harvard) determined the weight of silver in a given weight of silver chloride; the weight of silver chloride obtained from a given weight of ammonium chloride; and the weight of silver nitrate formed from a given weight of silver. From these results the atomic weights of silver, nitrogen and chlorine were calculated independently of each other and of any other on the bases of the atomic weight of oxygen being 16 and that of hydrogen being 1.0076. Without going into the details of how all of Richards's reagents were prepared and purified, how he investigated the completeness of his chosen reactions and the extent and ingenuity of his experimental techniques and specific equipment developments,

178

readers may obtain some impression of the care taken to build on Stas's achievements and inadvertent oversights by reference to some of Richards' results, such as 1.00000 gm of silver gave 1.57497 gm of silver nitrate and 1.00000 gm of silver chloride was precipitated by 0.373217 gm of ammonium chloride, from which by calculation, the atomic weights of silver, chlorine and nitrogen were given as 107.8810, 35.4574, and 14.0085 respectively.

Stas had made oxygen at atomic weight 16 the standard (1860-65) for all other atomic weights, rather than hydrogen at atomic weight 1 because determination of combining weights of hydrogen with oxygen was insufficiently certain, and Richards had concurred in using the oxygen : hydrogen ratio of 16: 1.0076, this being the ratio determined by Morley (1895). In 1842, Dumas had synthesised water by passing purified hydrogen over red hot copper oxide and collecting the water formed. Thus, he avoided the difficulties of weighing volumes of gas by weighing the copper oxide before and after to obtain the weight of oxygen in his collected water and to obtain the weight of hydrogen in this water by difference. In contrast Morley weighed both the hydrogen and the oxygen used and the water formed, whereas his immediate forerunners had determined one of these quantities by difference. Morley was therefore able to assess the accuracy of his work by the concurrence which he obtained for these three quantities. Again without going into the details of gas preparation, purification, use of adsorption and de-sorption in palladium, apparatus and technique, the degree of care and attention may be judged from his result that the hydrogen used was 3.7198 gm, the oxygen used was 29.5335 gm and the water formed was 33.2530 gm which on the basis of the atomic weight of oxygen being set at 16 means that 16 parts by weight of oxygen combine with 2.0152 parts by weight of hydrogen to form 18.0152 parts by weight of water and that on this basis the atomic weight of hydrogen is 1.0076.

Although we are now straying beyond 1900, Burt and Edgar in 1915 reported as the result of fifty-nine determinations that the combining volumes of oxygen and hydrogen in water were in the ratio of 1: 2.00288, from which the combining weight ratio can be deduced by applying the respective gas densities. Now Morley, in addition to determining this weight ratio directly as described above, had also determined the absolute densities of hydrogen by the Globe Method (c.f. Section 7.1.4) his results being that one litre of hydrogen and of oxygen at STP weigh 0.089873 gm and 1.42900 gm respectively. When these densities are applied to the volume ratio of Burt and Edgar we find the weight ratio to be 16 : 1.0077 which is in satisfactory agreement with Morley's direct weight determination of 16 : 1.0076.

Thus, by 1900 chemistry could be said to have emerged successfully from an extremely difficult period, in which there had been no conceptual framework which could integrate the apparently disparate progress being made on separate frontal sectors and thus facilitate progress across the whole front. In the end Cannizzaro connected various sectors of the front for molecular weight determination for volatile compounds, Dulong and Petit added their specific heat approach for determination of the atomic weight of elements and the remaining frontal sector of equivalent determinations enabled a self-consistent approach to atomic and molecular weights to be attained, together with provision of a new concept of chemical affinity in terms of multiple valence, this latter providing an explanation for the Laws of Multiple and Reciprocal Proportions. Thus, as in section 7.1.2 we have another example of how the scientific method brings the results of disparate investigations together, over extended periods of time when necessary (in this case from 1790 to 1858) to reach a composite advance and completion of details by 1900. It does not jump to premature conclusions nor does it take a vote after belief-driven debate, references to 'scientific consensus' being oxymoronic.

7. 1. 6 Chemical Symbols, Nomenclature, Formulae and Equations

Although much of the chemical activity of the first half of the nineteenth century was devoted to resolving the confusion of conflicting results through clarification of the issues surrounding molecular and atomic weight determinations, progress was nonetheless being made in yet other areas. Thus, Jon Jacob Berzelius (1779-1848) in addition to his work on the combining weights of the elements in relation to atomic weight determination, also founded the entirely new field of electrochemistry (c.f. Section 7.2.5) in the pursuit of which he developed the concept and coined the name radical for groups of atoms which remain unchanged in chemical reactions as though they were elements. Again, he established chemical symbols and nomenclature as we now have them by using the capital initial letter of the name of the element from the Latin where necessary; supported by a lower case letter where further distinction was needed, and by subscript numerals to indicate the numbers of the atoms present in a molecule or radical. Thus, to give a few examples, we have C for carbon, Cl for chlorine, S for sulphur, Sn for tin (Latin, stannus) and H_2O for water with the subscript 2 indicating two atoms of H (for hydrogen) and one atom of O (for oxygen) in these molecules. Such combinations of symbols and subscript numbers became the formulae for expressing the chemical composition of substances whether they existed as molecules or not. Thus, the molecular HCl gas dissolves in water to produce hydrochloric acid, the hydrogen of which may be replaced by the metal sodium to produce the salt sodium chloride (common salt) but when the salt is obtained in the solid state by evaporation of the water it is not molecular. Instead it consists of sodium and chloride ions (c.f. Section 7.2.5) arranged in a three-dimensional matrix, though its chemical composition is still represented by the formula NaCl,

Again, as we have seen, it was now possible to write chemical reactions in the form of equations, the equality being that the same number of atoms are present on both sides according to the Law of Conservation of Matter. Furthermore, now that we have atomic weights we can replace symbols with numbers. Thus, we can write the reaction of atmospheric carbon dioxide with rain water to produce carbonic acid thus: $CO_2 + H_2O = H_2CO_3$ and we can substitute the appropriate atomic weights thus: $(12 + 2 \times 16) + (2 \times 1 + 16) = 2 \times 1 + 12 + 3 \times 16$ i.e. $44 + 18 = 2 + 12 + 48$, or $62 = 62$. Again, this equation enables us to see that 44 parts of carbon dioxide produce 62 parts of carbonic acid and thus we can calculate how much carbonic acid will be produced from any given weight of carbon dioxide. For if 44 parts produce 62 parts then say, 5 tonnes will produce by simple proportion $62 \times 5 / 44$, or 7.045 tonnes and *pro rata* for any weight units chosen.

In this period also, more elements were identified. Thus, Humphrey Davy (1778-1829) used electric current (1807-8) to resolve Lavoisier's alkalis, potash and soda, and his alkaline earths, baryta, strontia, lime and magnesia into their elements which turned out to be oxygen in all cases together and a series of individual metals which he appropriately called potassium K, sodium Na, barium, Ba strontium Sr, calcium Ca and magnesium Mg. Again, in 1810 he showed that the gas chlorine Cl_2, prepared by Scheele in 1774 and thought to contain oxygen, was really an element. In addition, he reviewed and organised for the first time, the chemical knowledge then relevant to agriculture in his *Elements of Agricultural Chemistry* of 1813 which contained the first use in English of the word element defined by the statement: "all the varieties of material substances may be resolved into a comparatively small number of bodies, which, as they are not capable of being decomposed, are considered in the present state of chemical knowledge as elements." By 1813, forty-seven elements had been recognised and in 1815 the physician William Prout (1785-1850) in drawing attention to the closeness of atomic weights to whole numbers, proposed that hydrogen was the primordial substance, the *materia prima* from which all else was derived by processes unknown. Though this was too approximate to be well received, its significance was later explained (c.f. Section 9.1.3).

180

We are now in a position to clarify Black's earlier work on chalk (c.f. Section 7.1.1). Thus, Black's carbonate grouping, CO_3, is an example of what Berzelius refers to as a radical. It arises from the solution of carbon dioxide in water as discussed above. It exists in chalk, $CaCO_3$ in association with the metal calcium, Ca, and it transfers from association with the metal sodium Na back to calcium in converting the mild alkali sodium carbonate, Na_2CO_3 to the strong alkali sodium hydroxide NaOH. Again the OH is another example of a radical, transferring from the calcium to the sodium. This exchange of element and radical is common in chemistry and has become known as double decomposition. Now, in Black's first reaction, chalk was heated to produce quicklime with the release of the gas carbon dioxide, which may now be written $CaCO_3 = CaO + CO_2$. The quicklime, CaO, was then slaked with water to give calcium hydroxide thus, $CaO + H_2O = Ca(OH)_2$. The alkalis inter-converted thus, $Ca(OH)_2 + Na_2CO_3 = CaCO_3 + 2NaOH$. The unheated chalk when treated with hydrochloric acid HCl gave calcium chloride, water and carbon dioxide gas, thus, $CaCO_3 + 2HCl = CaCl_2 + H_2O + CO_2$ while the heated chalk, $i.e.$ CaO when treated with the same acid, gave calcium chloride and water, thus, $CaO + 2HCl = CaCl_2 + H_2O$. Finally quicklime when exposed to atmospheric carbon dioxide gave chalk, thus, $CaO + CO_2 = CaCO_3$.

Readers may confirm that the same number of atoms appear on both sides of all chemical equations in accordance with the Law of Conservation of Matter; that the sodium, hydrogen, and chorine atoms are univalent as is the hydroxyl radical; that the atoms of calcium and oxygen and the carbonate radical are divalent; and that the carbon within the carbonate radical appears to be quadrivalent (c.f. Section 9.1.7) Indeed, by this time, the chemistry of carbon was becoming a major focus of investigation because of the exceptionally wide range of carbon compounds which appeared to exist, the chemistry of life being essentially that of carbon, a fact which would lead carbon chemistry to be known as organic chemistry. An early and major figure in this field was Justus von Liebig (1803-73) who as professor of chemistry first at Giessen and later at Munich had inscribed over his laboratory the text: "God has ordained all things by measure, number and weight." Though, organic chemistry would not really take-off until the twentieth century, its involvement in nineteenth century physiology is reviewed in Section. 8.2.5, and its twentieth century systemisation is reviewed in Section 9.2.

7. 1. 7 Classification of the Elements

With some forty-seven elements having been recognised, attention turned to their possible classification. We have already seen that Lavoisier had classified them as metals and non-metals, but this was too broad to be of much use because the dozen or so distinguishing properties available varied gradually from one element to another, a difficulty which was scarcely lessened by introducing the metalloid class for those lying between the clearly metallic and the clearly non-metallic. Another problem was that these distinguishing properties were physical rather than chemical. Thus, while metals form basic (alkaline) oxides which dissolve in mineral acids with release of hydrogen to form salts (metal + acid radical) and while non-metals form acidic oxides which do not usually dissolve easily in mineral acids, almost all other distinguishing features relate to physical parameters such as phase state (solid, liquid or gas), volatility, density, light reflectivity, electric conductivity, malleability and ductility, apart perhaps for atomicity in the vaprous state and the degree of hydroysis (dissociation in water) of chlorides. Clearly more was needed for a useful chemical classification of the elements.

However, some regularities in the atomic weights of chemically similar elements were observed between 1816 and 1829 by J. W. Dobereiner. Thus, such similar elements had almost the same atomic weight as in the case of iron, cobalt and nickel, or else they exhibited an almost constant difference in atomic weight again in groups of three as for calcium, strontium, and barium; chlorine, bromine, iodine; and sulphur, selenium, tellurium. These groupings were referred to as

Dobereiner's Triads though it was subsequently observed that they might be manifestations of a more general relationship. Thus, when between 1863 and 1866, J. A. R. Newlands arranged the elements in ascending order of their atomic weights he noticed that every succeeding eighth element was "a kind of repetition of the first." in the sense that elements in the vertical groups so formed had similar chemical properties. Referred to by Newlands as his *Law of Octaves*, this periodicity with increasing atomic weight from left to right produced three rows repeating on the eighth as follows:

H (Hydrogen) Li (Lithium) Be (Berillium) B (Boron)   C (Carbon) N (Nitrogen)   O(Oxygen)
F (Fluorine) Na (Sodium) Mg (Magnesium) Al (Aluminium) Si (Silicon) P (Phosphorus) S(Sulphur)
Cl (Chlorine) K (Potassium) Ca (Calcium)   Cr (Chromium) Ti (Titanium) Mn (Manganese) Fe (Iron)

Perhaps because Newlands rather overdid his supposed analogy with the musical scale, his idea was not immediately accepted. Indeed, it seems to have been ignored despite having been independently proposed by A. E. B de Chancoutois in 1862. Nonetheless, Lothar Meyer (1830-95) and Dmitri I. Mendeleeff (1834-1907 had better luck when quite independently and apparently in ignorance of the earlier efforts of Newlands and de Chancourtois, they extended the comprehensiveness of the idea. Somewhere about 1869, Mendeleeff and Meyer noticed a general periodicity, and as Mendeleeff said " . . .if the elements be arranged in order of increasing atomic weights, their properties vary from member to member in a definite way, but return more or less nearly to the same value at fixed points in the series." Thus we have Mendeleeff's conclusion that the properties of the elements are a periodic function of their atomic weights, not only as regards graded similarities in chemical properties in the vertical Groups which had commended themselves to Dobereiner and more extensively to Newlands, but also with respect to the gradual and continuous trend in chemical properties in each of the horizontal rows or Periods in what he called his *Periodic Table of the Elements.*

Lothar Meyer calculated atomic volumes by dividing the atomic weight of the elements by their specific gravities (numerically equal to density in gm/ml) in the solid state and found that they plotted against atomic weight to give a clearly defined periodic curve which showed decrease in atomic volume from lithium to boron, followed by increase through carbon, oxygen and fluorine to sodium, whereupon it decreased again through magnesium down to aluminium, and increased again through silicon, phosphorus, sulphur and chlorine to potassium. Thus, the alkali metals, lithium, sodium, potassium . . , occupy distinct peaks on the curve while elements such as boron, aluminium, cobalt, and nickel . . . *etc* occupy the intervening troughs. This suggested that the octaves of Newlands, (as shown above), should be re-arranged to place fluorine to the right of oxygen, and chlorine to the right of sulphur. This left hydrogen on its own though being univalent as are the alkali metals (lithium, sodium . . .) and the non-metallic halogens (fluorine, chlorine . . .) it might be allocated to either group. D. I. Mendeleeff favoured the former allocation and O. Masson the latter whereas the *Electronic Theory of Atomic Structure* would latter support Mendeleeff (c.f. Section 9.1.6)

This periodic system was undoubtedly superior to all earlier classifications of the elements because of its comprehensiveness, its compatibility with Cannizzaro's reasoning and its encouragement of atomic weight determinations. In addition, as Mendeleeff pointed out, his Table not only classified the elements chemically it also provided a means of estimating the approximate atomic weights in cases where they had not yet been determined, of indicating the accuracy of atomic weights already determined, and of predicting the properties of unknown elements, not all of them being known at that time. In fact gaps had to be left in the tables of both Meyer and

Mendeleeff, for elements presumed unknown in order to arrange the known ones in the correct groups and periods on the basis of their atomic weights and chemical properties. As an example of how the Table assisted in the allocation of atomic weights we have the element indium which according to Winkler had an equivalent weight of 37.8 on the basis of which a valence of 2 and a corresponding atomic weight of 75.6 would allocate it to a position in the Table for which it is chemically unsuited, whereas attribution of tri-valence by Mendeleef gave an atomic weight of 37.8 x 3 =113.4 and allocation to a position which suited its chemistry very well and in advance of confirmation by determination of its specific heat at 0.0577. The accepted atomic weight now is 114.76.

Thus the location of gaps in the atomic weight sequence suggested not only the approximate atomic weights of unknown elements but also their likely chemical properties as guides to the search for them. To avoid giving names to unknown elements, however, Mendeleeff designated them as analogues of known elements, pre-fixed as necessary with the Sanscrit numerals for one, two and three. In this way he predicted the existence of eka-aluminium, eka-silicon, (later to be named gallium and germanium when found), eka- and dwi-caesium and tri-manganese for example. The existence of the inert rare gases could not at that time be predicted none of them being known. However, after the discovery of argon and helium their atomic weight order placed them between the acidic halogen group and the alkali metals in the Table suggesting the probable existence of others, and krypton, neon and xenon were duly discovered. Being un-reactive, however, their atomic weights could not be determined from chemical equivalents. Instead they were determined by Raleigh, Ramsay, Whytlaw Gray *et al* by the method of vapour density determination by weighing and by determination of γ at 1.66 giving an atomicity of unity confirming their lack of reactivity (c.f. Section 7.1.4). In cases where determination of atomic weight by vapour density or equivalent weight faced practical difficulties as was the case with indium, beryllium, uranium and a number of rare earth elements, Mendeleeff's adjustments to fit his Table were helpful guides to the more accurate determinations which confirmed the allocated positions in due course.

When the known elements had been arranged in order of increasing atomic weight, initially with gaps for unknown elements which were later filled, it was found that the horizontal Periods had 2, 8, 8, 18, 18 and 32 elements allocated to them. Period 1, the first short period, has hydrogen in Group I and the inert gas helium in Group VIII. Period 2, the second short period, has lithium in Group I followed by beryllium, boron, carbon, nitrogen, oxygen, and fluorine in Groups II to VII respectively, and is completed with the inert gas neon in Group VIII. Period 3, the third short period, has sodium, magnesium, aluminium, silicon, phosphorus, sulphur, chlorine and argon in Groups I to VIII respectively. In periods 4 and 5, (the first two long periods), however, it was necessary to insert not eight elements but eighteen before one of similar properties to the first was reached. Thus in Period 4, potassium in Group I is an alkali metal closely related in properties to sodium (Period 3, Group I) and to lithium (Period 2, Group I), while calcium in Group II of Period 4 relates to magnesium (Period 3, Group II) and to beryllium (Period 2, Group II). Before reaching rubidium, however, the next alkali metal in Period 5, Group I, an extra ten elements have to be accommodated, which *do not* Group-relate to the members of the preceding Periods. Consequently, these elements are referred to as the first transition series which consists of scandium, titanium, vanadium, chromium, manganese, iron, cobalt, nickel, copper and zinc. These are inserted in that order into Period 4 after calcium, and the period then continues as per Periods 3 and 2 with gallium, germanium arsenic, selenium, bromine and krypton in Groups III to VIII respectively, the vertical Group-relationship having been re-established.

Similarly in the second long period, Period 5, after rubidium in Group 1 and strontium in Group II, a second transition series of ten elements is inserted. These are, yttrium, zirconium, niobium, molybdenum, technetium, ruthenium, rhodium, palladium, silver and cadmium, after which Groups III to VIII resume with indium, tin, antimony, tellurium, iodine and xenon. The third long period, Period 6, starts with the alkali metal caesium in Group I, barium in Group II, and lanthanum in Group III, after which a fourteen member series, the rare earths, has to be accommodated before the ten member series which would in any case have been expected in this third long period. This time the ten member transition series starts with lanthanum, and is continued, after insertion of the fourteen member series, with hafnium, tantalum tungsten, rhenium, osmium, iridium, platinum, gold, mercury. This period then continues to fill Groups III to VIII with thallium, lead, bismuth, polonium, astatine and radon, while the fourteen-member rare earth transition series, inserted after lanthanum, consists of cerium, praseodymium, neodymium, promethium, samarium, europium, gadolinium, terbium, dysprosium, holmium, erbium, thulium, ytterbium and lutetium. Period 7 starts with the alkali metal francium in Group I and radium in Group II, followed by the actinide transition series, consisting of actinium, thorium, protactinium and uranium.

This Tabulation of the Elements in order of their Atomic Weights was not completed in Mendeleeff's lifetime, but with its completion the efforts of many chemists over many years reached a consummation in which all material substance was explicable in terms of ninety-two elements and their chemical interactions. This is an achievement which deserves wide recognition, though it is absent from histories of science which select aspects more favourable to the Enlightenment practice of conflating science with rationality. In contrast, creation of the Periodic Table illustrates how the experimentation of scientific method converts belief to knowledge *via* hypothesis, as I hope I have shown. However, my account of the twentieth century shows that the atomic weights and chemical properties which underpin Mendeleeff's *Periodic Table of the Elements* have deeper explanations than those which sustained his predecessors and himself in their labours (c.f. Sections 9.1.5 - 9.1.7). In the meantime, I show how the elucidation of non-matter by the experimentation of scientific method lent further support to the Atomic Theory.

7. 2 UNDERSTANDING THE NATURE OF NON-MATTER (ENERGY)

Readers will recall that substance was intuitively believed to be synonymous with existence in reality, while soul and spirit were believed to have non-material existence both in the Beyond and in reality. Thus, in equating matter with existence in reality, Lavoisier believed heat to be a form of matter though being weightless he called it "imponderable" caloric. On this basis, the warming of metals by hammering was the pressurised release of heat as a fluid substance from pores in the metal while friction-generated fire was a similar release of this fluid substance. Again, imponderable static electricity was believed to be a fluid substance produced by rubbing certain substances together as was the magnetism transferred to iron from certain minerals by rubbing. In addition, the light and sound released with heat from an ever-widening variety of chemical reactions were yet further manifestations of imponderable substance. However, prior to Lavoisier, Boyle in 1664, Hooke in 1665 and Huygens in 1690 had suggested that heat, light, sound, chemical reaction, magnetism and electricity would all be explained as forms of force-related movement of the particles of matter, not as forms of matter in themselves.

7. 2. 1 Temperature and Heat

As already noted, Galileo's open-ended air thermometer of about 1592 had made temperature measurable for the first time, this being followed by Rey's open-ended water version in 1632 and by a sealed alcohol instrument, probably due to Ferdinand II, grand Duke of Tuscany, which appeared in 1641. However, all such instruments had arbitrary scales until 1701 when Newton suggested standardisation on a scale which took the freezing point of water as zero degrees and the temperature of the healthy human body as 12 degrees. To extend this rather small temperature range, Newton used his thermometer to measure successive temperatures of a cooling body, plotted them as a function of time, extrapolated his plot back to earlier times and read-off earlier temperatures above his measurement range, *Newton's Law of Cooling* being that the rate is proportional to the difference in temperature between the body and its surroundings when such differences are small. However, by 1715 the mercury thermometer of D. G. Fahrenheit (1686-1736) with its scale between the freezing and boiling points of water had enabled quite significant temperatures to be measured and compared at different places and times.

Now, with such a thermometer Joseph Black (1728-99) was able to measure heat for the first time. Black reasoned on the basis of observation that when a body adsorbed heat its temperature rose and when it lost heat (cooled) its temperature dropped. He then hypothesised that different materials might have different capacities for heat; that were this to be so, there would be a relationship between the amount of heat adsorbed or released by a body, its heat capacity, and the rise or fall in temperature which it exhibited; and that he could measure heat capacities. To this end, he defined the calorie as the unit of heat which would raise the temperature of one gram of water by one degree or be released when it cooled by one degree. He then reasoned that if two masses of water of known weight m_1 and m_2 and temperatures T_1 and T_2 were mixed and the temperature of the mixture was assumed to be t, then the amount of heat given out by the hotter water in falling from T_1 to the temperature of the mixture t would equal the amount of heat taken in by the colder water in rising from T_2 to the temperature of the mixture t. Thus, weight times temperature-range times specific heat for the cooling water = weight times temperature-range times specific heat for the heating water, and since the specific heat of water has been deliberately set at unity in the definition of the calorie we can write $m_1 (T_1 - t) = m_2 (t - T_2)$, this equation being solvable for t, all other quantities being known from measurement, thus allowing the calculated and measured temperatures of the mixture to be compared and found to agree, provided no significant heat losses to the surroundings had occurred in the meantime. In such work heat losses to the surroundings are minimised by mixing in a calorimeter, a device in which the mixing container is isolated from its surroundings by slender suspension within suitable shielding.

With this approach Black could proceed to measure the heat capacities of other substances in comparison with that of water, these being referred to as specific heats and later used *inter alia* in the determination of atomic weights by Dulong and Petit (c.f. Section 7.1.5). Meanwhile, Black's approach to the determination of specific heats was to heat a weighed amount of the metal m_1 to the standard temperature of boiling water, to transfer it to a known weight of water m_2 in a calorimeter at a measured temperature T_1 and to measure the temperature of the 'mixture' t which in this case is the temperature of the water after it reaches equilibrium with the transferred metal. In this case, the heat given out by the metal equals the heat taken in by the water. Thus we write $m_1 (100 - t)$ x specific heat of the metal = $m_2 (t - T_1)$ x specific heat of water. Since the specific heat of water is unity, the only unknown is the specific heat of the metal which can be determined by solving the equation. Black chose a metal of low specific heat (copper, specific heat 0.1) for the construction of his calorimeters and thus allowance could be made for the heat taken up by calorimeters of known weight in all subsequent thermal measurements.

185

Black was also able to measure temperatures beyond the range of available thermometers much more effectively than Newton had estimated them from his *Law of Cooling*. Thus, Black determined the specific heat of iron as above, heated a weighed m_1 piece of iron to 'red heat' (unknown temperature, T_1), transferred it to a known amount of water m_2 in his calorimeter at temperature T_2 and measured the 'mixture' temperature t. Once again, the heat given out by the iron equals the heat taken in by the water plus the heat taken in by the calorimeter of weight m_3 which, if made of copper, has a specific heat 0.1. Thus: $m_1 (T_1 - t)$ x specific heat of iron = $m_2 (t - T_2) + m_3 (t - T_2)/10$, by which equation the temperature T_1 corresponding to 'red heat' is determined. Black also showed that his *Method of Mixtures* could measure the amounts of heat absorbed in melting and evaporation and released in freezing and condensation. Thus, he passed a convenient amount of steam (100° C) into a known weight of water at a measured temperature T in his calorimeter, determined by re-weighing, the weight of steam condensed to water and measured the resulting 'mixture' temperature t, of the water and calorimeter. He then reasoned that the heat given out by the steam at 100° condensing to water at 100°, plus the heat given out by the condensed water at 100° in cooling to the temperature of the "mixture" must be equal to the heat taken in by the original water and calorimeter in rising to the temperature of the 'mixture'. The only unknown in this equation is the heat released in condensation and so it can be determined by solving the equation. It is expressed as amount of heat released per unit weight of steam. Similarly, by putting into a known weight of warm water at measured temperature T, a convenient amount of ice and by subsequently measuring the temperature of the "mixture" and re-weighing the water to determine the weight of ice melted, he could determine the heat absorbed in melting per unit weight of ice. Black called these quantities the latent heat of steam and the latent heat of ice respectively.

7. 2. 2 Heat as Motion of Atoms and Molecules

Though the above progress had been made irrespective of whether heat was a material substance or not, the American Benjamin Thompson (1753-1814) addressed this question by considering the nature of heat. Otherwise known as Count Rumford of the Holy Roman Empire, Thompson had come from Austria to England where he became engaged in the boring of canon at the Woolwich Arsenal. By recording the temperature rise in a mass of water surrounding the boring point, he reported in his *Inquiry Concerning the Source of the Heat which is Excited by Friction* of 1798 that such heat appeared to be inexhaustible; that "any thing, which any insulated (isolated) body or system of bodies can continue to furnish without limitation, cannot possibly be a material substance"; and that heat must, therefore, be "a kind of motion." He subsequently, used a balance sensitive to one part in a million to show (1799) that there was no change in weight in a mass of water on its conversion into ice or on its re-conversion into water despite a latent-heat change sufficient to raise 9.75 ounces of gold from freezing point to red-heat. This also, strongly suggested to him that heat was not "a substance distinct from, and accumulated in, the heated body." Rather, it was "an intestine vibratory motion of the constituent parts of heated bodies." He also compared the heat generated steadily and inexhaustibly by the paired-horses employed in the boring of canon with the heat produced by combustion of the same amount of food as eaten by the horses. Nonetheless, though Black and Watt (c.f. Section 8.1.1) had also come close to recognising the inter-convertibility of heat and work, this would not be fully achieved until the middle of the nineteenth century (c.f. Section 7.2.8).

Before that happened, however, further progress was made towards demonstrating that heat was indeed the motion of the atoms and molecules of matter. We have already noted that gases compress and expand with change in pressure and temperature according to the Laws of Boyle and

Charles and that liquids introduced to the Torricelli vacuum vaporise to fill the available void volume. We have also noted Dalton's Law of Partial Pressures of 1802 which states that in a mixture of non-reactive gases, each exerts the same pressure as if it alone occupied the containing volume, the total pressure being the sum of the pressures due to each gas separately. It is impossible to understand such behaviour if matter is continuous and not discrete atoms or molecules moving in otherwise empty space. One is thus forced to conclude that matter must be discrete atoms and molecules consistent with the Periodic Table; that these are distributed in a void of total volume much greater than that of the atoms or molecules within it; and that when evaporated into the Torricelli void they cannot come to rest in fixed positions.

Indeed, rapid motion is further suggested by the immediate production of a homogeneous mixture when the cover slips are removed from a jar of low density gas such as hydrogen inverted over another containing a much denser gas such as air despite the expectation that the density difference would maintain their relative positions for an observable time at least. However, Dobereiner, in 1823 observed that hydrogen collected over water in a cracked flask escaped at a greater rate than air entered through the crack, the water of the pneumatic trough rising up in the flask neck to compensate for the net loss of flask content, a phenomenon investigated in turn by measuring the pressure differences associated with such differential rates of diffusion through the walls of porous pots, concerning which Thomas Graham was able to state in 1832 that under constant conditions, the relative rates of diffusion are inversely proportional to the square roots of gas densities. This is now known as Graham's Law of Diffusion (c.f. Section 7.1.4).

We are now in a position to understand yet another feature of the scientific method. In this example we assume that gases consist of discrete atoms or molecules which are in constant motion, that as such they will obey Newton's Laws of Motion, and that mathematical analysis should thus be able to account for the Laws of Boyle, Charles and Graham, and for the Hypothesis of Avogadro, all of which apply to the gaseous state. Thus, according to Newton, the moving particles will continue to move in straight lines unless acted on by a force and we can assume that they will thus change direction only on inter-particle collision and on collision with the container walls Again, we can assume that the particles are of negligible size compared to the space which they occupy; that they do not exert any attraction on each other; and that their collisions being perfectly elastic, their momentum and kinetic energy will be conserved. These assumptions are perfectly reasonable because, if atoms and molecules exist at all, they must be extremely small (c.f. Section 9.1.5) and because we are dealing with non-reactive gases, there is no inter-particle action. Again, if the collisions were inelastic, gases would spontaneously condense to liquid over time, because energy would be lost on each collision.

Suppose now, that we have confined in a cube of side-length l cm, n molecules of gas each of mass m and that the average speed of these molecules is V, where V is the root mean square velocity *i.e.* the square root of the sum of the squares of all the speeds of the individual molecules. The zig-zag motion of the colliding molecules can be resolved into three mutually perpendicular velocities parallel to the edges of the cube, (c.f. Section 6.1.3) and because there is no tendency for the molecules to accumulate in any particular region of the cube, we can assume that $1/3(n)$ molecules are travelling with velocity V parallel to any particular edge and therefore perpendicular to the two corresponding mutually opposed sides of the cube. One such molecule will take l/V units of time to pass from side to side and will thus collide with a side $\frac{1}{2}V/l$ times per unit time. At each collision with the side of the cube there is a change of momentum from $+mV$ to $-mV$, i.e. $2m$V. The total change in momentum for $1/3(n)$ molecules colliding with a side $\frac{1}{2}$ V/l times will, therefore, be the product of these factors *i.e.* $1/3(nmV^2/l)$. This is the total force exerted on one side of the cube of area l^2 and so the total pressure p exerted is $p = 1/3(nmV^2/l^3)$.

Now l^3 is the cube volume v and of the gas contained within it. We may, therefore, write $pv = 1/3(nmV^2)$. If we now note that the right hand side of this equation can be written 2/3 x ½ nmV^2; that ½ nmV^2 is the total kinetic energy of the n molecules each of mass m; and that this must remain constant provided the temperature does not change; we see that 2/3 of a constant being a constant, we may write pv = a constant, which is Boyle's Law. Again, the product of pressure and volume (pv) of a gas being equal to two-thirds of the total kinetic energy of that gas, it follows that if the temperature be altered while the pressure remains constant, the kinetic energy will alter in proportion, as will the volume. This may be expressed as volume, V = a constant x temperature T, which is Charles's Law. In addition, since the same volumes of two gases at the same pressure and temperature have the same value of the product pv, it follows that $n_1 m_1 V_1^2 = n_2 m_2 V_2^2$ and that since James Clerke-Maxwell showed that the average kinetic energy per molecule in such systems is the same, it follows that ½ $m_1 V_1^2$ = ½ $m_2 V_2^2$ and that therefore $n_1 = n_2$, which is Avogadro's Hypothesis. Finally, since $pv = 1/3(nmV^2)$, and density $d = m/v$ it follows that the mean velocity V $= (3 \, pv/nm)^{1/2} = (3 \, p/d)^{1/2}$. Thus, the mean velocity of a gas molecule is inversely proportional to the square root of the gas density which is Graham's Law of Diffusion.

Thus, this *Kinetic Theory of Gases* not only supports these previously discovered laws of gas behaviour of Boyle, Charles and Graham together with the Hypothesis of Avogadro, it also enables the mean velocity of gas molecules for any gas at pre-determined temperatures and pressures to be calculated. Thus, by making the appropriate substitutions in the equation V $= (3 \, p/d)^{1/2}$, it can be calculated that the mean velocity of the hydrogen molecule at 1 atmosphere pressure and 0° C is approximately 60 miles per minute. Though this indicates velocities greatly in excess of the rates of diffusion of the gas as a whole, the explanation is that the molecules can never move far in one direction without colliding with each other, the frequency of collision being calculated to be of the order of 10^{28} per ml per second at STP, and that consequently the gas as a whole only diffuses at a relatively slow rate.

In contrast to gases, it is clear that the particles (molecules) of liquids definitely attract each other. This is the reason why liquids exhibit the phenomenon of surface tension and why liquid drops are spherical in shape. Now, in relation to Charles's Law (c.f. Section 7.1.3) reference was made to minimum gas volume at Absolute zero (-273° C) which, according to the above Kinetic Theory is the temperature at which all motion ceases. Thus, application of the Kinetic Theory to liquids at temperatures above 0° A (or K) indicates that molecular motion still occurs despite the molecular interactions which characterise liquids. Now, the kinetic energies of individual molecules will vary considerably with some reaching the liquid surface with sufficient energy to overcome inter-molecular attraction and escape to the atmosphere with consequent reduction in the mean kinetic energy of the liquid and thus in its temperature. This is the phenomenon of evaporation which is always associated with cooling. Again, if the temperature is to remain constant during evaporation, heat must be supplied from the surroundings, this being the latent heat of evaporation measured earlier by Joseph Black. Now, the molecules which escape from a liquid in this way constitute its vapour, while if its temperature is far removed from its temperature of liquefaction, it is referred to as a gas. For example, oxygen and nitrogen at normal temperatures are gases while water and alcohol would give rise to vapours. However, the kinetic energy of vapour molecules will vary with some being recaptured by the liquid phase with an increase in the mean kinetic energy of the liquid and thus in its temperature. Again, if the temperature is to remain constant during this condensation, heat will be given up to the surroundings, this being Black's latent heat of condensation.

Now, if we suppose a liquid to be evaporating into a Torricellian vacuum space the fleetest molecules will accumulate in the vapour phase and depress the mercury column by the amount equal to the vapour pressure. This will continue until the same number of molecules are escaping from the liquid surface as are being re-captured by it. At that point the vapour is said to be saturated at the maximum vapour pressure for the temperature of observation and the liquid and vapour phases are said to be in equilibrium. However, such dynamic equilibrium can be disturbed by changes in external conditions. Thus, an air current passing through the liquid or a rise in temperature will increase the rate of evaporation, though temperature may be raised so high as to exceed the rate at which high kinetic energy molecules can escape through the surface area of the liquid at which point vapour bubbles will form within its volume in what we refer to as boiling. Again, when the vapour pressure equals the external pressure to which the liquid is subjected, further increase in heat supply does not raise the temperature, it increases the rate of vapour bubble formation as long as any liquid remains. Conversely, if the external pressure is reduced, boiling occurs at lower temperatures. Thus, water at a pressure of 4.6 mm of mercury boils at $0°$ C and liquids which decompose at their atmospheric pressure boiling points can be distilled at lower temperatures without decomposition by reducing the pressure in what is called vacuum distillation.

Just as liquids generate vapours by evaporation, gases may condense to liquids. In 1869, T. Andrews found that carbon dioxide decreases in volume more quickly as a function of applied pressure than would be predicted by Boyle's Law and begins to liquefy; that from this point decrease in gas volume occurs without further pressure increase as the liquid volume increases; and that further increase in pressure confirms the general incompressibility of liquids. Thus, at $0°$ C carbon dioxide begins to liquefy at a pressure of 35.4 atmospheres, at $13.1°$ C liquefaction starts at 48.9 atmospheres and at $31°$ C, 70 atmospheres are needed. On the other hand, at temperatures above $31°C$ no pressure, however great, will liquefy carbon dioxide. It turns out that for each gas there is a temperature beyond which it cannot be liquefied by pressure alone. Andrews called these the critical temperature and critical pressure.

Thus, as the applied pressure reduces the volume of a gas its molecules come closer together and eventually experience inter-molecular attraction sufficient to reduce their kinetic energy to the point of liquefaction, provided the thermal energy is not greater than that at the critical temperature of the gas. Now, the gas equation $PV = RT$ was derived from the Kinetic Theory of Gases on the assumption that the molecules were of negligible volume compared to the total volume in which they move, and that there was no inter-molecular attraction. However, in 1888 Van der Waals took account of Andrews's observations by replacing the pressure factor P and the volume factor V in the gas equation by $(P + a/V^2)$ and $(V- b)$ respectively. His reasoning was as follows. As the pressure increases and the volume decreases, the inter-molecular distance becomes closer to that in a liquid and so inter-molecular attraction forces cause the applied pressure to have a greater compression effect than it would in the absence of such attraction. If it is assumed that these attractive forces are inversely proportional to volume and therefore equal to a constant times $1/V^2$, they should increase the effective pressure P by the term a/V^2. Again, as the volume decreases with increasing pressure the time will come when the volume of the molecules will cease to be insignificant compared to the total volume in which they are moving and so the effective gas volume will be smaller than the measured volume and so should be reduced by the term b as liquefaction approaches.

Experimentation shows that for all gases other than hydrogen and helium, the product PV deviates slightly from the constancy expected from Boyle's Law in first decreasing and then increasing with increase in pressure; and that the corrections introduced by Van der Waals correct both these deviations from constancy. At the lower pressures the correction for molecular attraction predominates over that for molecular volume, while the correction for the latter predominates over the former when the gas volumes are very small at the higher pressure range. Using experimentally determined values for a and b of 0.00874 and 0.0023 respectively, E. H. Amagat in 1893 obtained constancy of the product 'PV' over a total pressure range of from 1 to 500 atmospheres with discrepancies only showing in the third decimal place between observed and calculated (Van der Waals) values.

Again, while Andrews had identified the critical temperature for the gaseous state, Caignard de la Tour had previously noticed that when liquid is heated in a sealed tube the surface of separation between liquid and vapour (gas) disappears and the whole content of the tube becomes homogeneous at a definite temperature, thus demonstrating the critical temperature for the liquid state. In fact, the transition from the one state to the other proceeds in a continuous manner. Thus, physical properties such as density, surface tension, viscosity, refractive power, heat of vaporisation, compressibility *etc* gradually lose their distinctive character and merge at the critical temperature.

Now, the fact that steam (vapour) condenses to water when cooled suggested that other gases might be liquefied by cooling even though they could not be liquefied by pressure alone, Natterer having failed to liquefy nitrogen, oxygen and hydrogen even at pressures up to 2790 atmospheres and Andrews having discovered that some gases exhibited a critical temperature in this respect. Thus attention now turned to the possibility that the so-called 'permanent' gases might be liquefied if sufficient cooling could be applied to them. W. Cullen seems to have been the first to notice in 1755 that the temperature of a sample of air is decreased by rarefaction and increased by compression and Dalton attempted to quantify these effects. Thus, a gas expanding against atmospheric pressure does work equivalent to the product of the atmospheric pressure and the change in volume and therefore the gas cools while the work done to compress a gas is equivalent to the product of the pressure and the decrease in volume and therefore the gas heats as everyone now knows who has inflated a bicycle-tyre with a hand pump. However, we are concerned here with the cooling effect which Cailletet used to achieve sufficient cooling to liquefy small quantities of permanent gases by sudden expansion of highly compressed samples.

However, expansion of a gas into a vacuum should not produce any such cooling because there is no external pressure against which it is doing work. Indeed, when J. L. Gay-Lussac, in 1807 and J. P. Joule in 1845 carried out such experiments they duly reported the absence of cooling. However, following the work of Van der Waals, it was known that such an expanding gas must still be doing work against the internal attractions of its constituent molecules and it was concluded that the effect must have been too small to be detected by the experimental arrangements of Gay-Lussac and of Joule. Thus, when between 1852 and 1862, Joule and W. Thomson (Lord Kelvin) carried out more precise experiments, the cooling effect due to inter-molecular attraction was observed. These workers found by forcing a steady stream of gas through a porous plug of cotton or silk contained in a box-wood tube, that the gas was cooler after transiting the plug than before reaching it and that the work done against inter-molecular attraction caused a fall in temperature $F = 75.35 \, (p_2 - p_1)/ \, T$ where pressures, p_1 and p_2 are in atmospheres and temperature T is in degrees Absolute (K). For example, for a pressure drop from 4 to 1 in atmospheres at a temperature of $0°$ C, the fall in temperature is (75.35 x 3)/273 or $0.828°$ C.

Although at first sight this seems insignificantly small, this *Joule-Thomson Effect* was applied to the large-scale industrial liquefaction of air in 1894-5 by Linde in Germany and by Hampson in England, and by the end of the nineteenth century all gases except helium had been liquefied by this effect, many such as hydrogen and fluorine being liquefied by James Dewar who to solve the problem of storing such liquefied gases devised the Dewar or vacuum flask. This now common device was initially a double or triple walled vessel of glass with the space between the walls evacuated and the walls silvered, glass being a poor conductor of heat, vacuum being a non-conductor and the silver-coating being an effective reflector of radiant heat. Still-air being itself a very poor conductor of heat, such open-necked vessels plugged lightly with cotton wool could store and transport liquid air with acceptably little evaporative loss. Liquid oxygen (boiling point -183° C) and liquid nitrogen (boiling point -195.8° C) are separated from liquid air by fractional distillation. Although we are moving into the twentieth century, we should note here that helium having a critical temperature of only -267.9 ° C, was liquefied by Kammerlingh Onnes in 1907 and solidified by Keesom in 1926 at a temperature of 0.89° A (K).

In further vindication of the Atomic Theory, I now turn to homogeneous solids which in the great majority of cases consist of aggregates of crystals even if these are very small. A crystal is thus a solid with a definite geometrical shape characterised by plane faces bounded by distinct linear edges whereas a solid which has no definite shape and cannot be obtained in crystalline form is said to be amorphous. Examples of amorphous solids are sulphur, glass and flint though many solids once thought to be amorphous have turned out to consist of exceedingly small crystals. Now, every crystalline substance of definite chemical composition has a characteristic crystalline form even though the faces of its crystals may vary in size and shape, the defining characteristic of individual crystalline forms being the constancy of their interfacial angles as first announced by D. Guglielmimi in 1688. This constancy, in turn, ensures constancy of the face relationships of the crystalline forms of each substance, though truncated edges result in smaller facial areas, more vertices and hence additional facets. Another characteristic of crystals is their tendency to split along definite planes of cleavage, sometimes parallel to the faces of the original crystal and sometimes not, this being the basis of gem-stone cutting though the shapes of gems, cut and polished to accentuate ornamental value should not be confused with crystal structure: nor is cut glass properly described as crystal, glass being a non-crystalline super-cooled liquid.

Now, it has long been realised that the structure of crystals can be understood on the basis of an aggregate of particles arranged in space in an orderly manner. Hauy showed in 1788 that simple geometric shapes such as spheres or cubes could be arranged in regular arrays to produce 3-dimensional shapes analogous to those of actual crystals and in 1848 Bravais modified and extended this idea by replacing Hauy's solid unit shapes with small particles placed at their centres to produce an open arrangement referred to as the space lattice. Such an arrangement can also be visualised as rows of points in three-dimensions which in turn may be visualised as a series of cells all of which are parallelepipeds. Bravais and others went on to show that 230 space lattices were theoretically possible and that these could account for the thirty-two types, the seven systems, and the symmetry characteristics of these systems into which the great variety of crystals formed by different substances had already been classified.

The seven crystal systems are the triclinic, monoclinic, rhombic, tetragonal, trigonal, hexagonal and cubic. The symmetries which relate to these systems are two-fold. Firstly, a plane of symmetry divides the crystal into two mirror-image halves. Secondly, a crystal may be rotated about a definite axis through an angle such that the faces, edges and vertices (corners) are brought to a new position for which the aspect is identical to that prior to rotation, and we speak of dyad, triad, tetrad and hexad axes of symmetry according as there 2, 3, 4 or 6 identical aspects in one complete rotation of 360 degrees. On this basis, the triclinic system has no planes or axes of symmetry, examples being copper sulphate, boric acid, copper selenate *etc*; the monoclinic has one plane of symmetry, or one dyad axis of symmetry, or both a plane and a dyad axis, examples being borax, sodium carbonate, and cane sugar; the rhombic may have three planes of symmetry and three dyad axis of symmetry, examples being zinc sulphate, sulphur deposited from solution, iodine *etc*; the tetragonal may have five planes of symmetry, one tetrad, and maybe four dyad axes of symmetry, examples being mercurous chloride, tin, strychnine sulphate *etc*; the trigonal may have three planes of symmetry, one triad, and three dyad axes of symmetry, examples being antimony, bismuth, graphite *etc*; the hexagonal may have seven planes of symmetry one hexad, and six dyad axes of symmetry, examples being cadmium sulphide, zinc, calcium *etc*; and the cubic may have nine planes of symmetry, six dyad, three tetrad, and four triad axes of symmetry, examples being diamond, sodium chloride (common salt), iron *etc*. The classification of crystals is thus determined by their symmetry and not by the external form of a given crystal.

We have now seen that the low levels of inter-molecular attraction of the permanent gases are too low to prevent their expansion to fill the space available; that the inter-molecular attraction in liquids is sufficient to prevent such expansion except when in the vapour phase, and only sufficient to maintain their cohesion as flowing liquids at temperatures below their boiling points and above their freezing points; and that solids maintain not only their cohesion but also their shape because their internal attraction forces are sufficient to locate their constituent particles within a 3-dimensional lattice, though even here there is temperature-related internal vibratory motion at these locations. We also now see that the solid, liquid and gaseous states of matter consist of atoms or radical or molecular groups of atoms, whether they be elements or compounds, and if the latter, whether they be inorganic or organic in origin. We further see that the internal vibratory motion of solids can be increased to the freer movement of the melted (liquid) state and hence to the gaseous state by the progressive overpowering of internal attractive forces through the application of appropriate quantities of heat.

7. 2. 3 Heat Associated with the Bonding of Atoms in Molecules

All of the above phenomena and their explanations in terms of the thermal energies associated with the internal motions of gases, liquids and solids adds credence not only to the Atomic Theory of matter but also to the concept of heat as a form of kinetic energy. In addition to being associated with the movement of molecules, however, energy is also associated with the bonds between the atoms within the molecules and radicals which constitute chemical compounds. This bond-related energy reveals itself by the evolution or absorption of the heat which accompanies the re-arrangement of inter-atomic bonds which constitutes chemical reaction, the study of such heat changes being referred to as thermo-chemistry. Thus, any chemical system, whether comprising a single substance or group of substances, contains a definite amount of intrinsic energy depending on the mass, chemical nature and physical condition of the system. This remains constant so long as the system remains unaltered, but when a chemical reaction takes place the reaction products constitute a new chemical system of different intrinsic energy. We can readily determine the change in total intrinsic energy between reagents and products while ignoring the absolute initial and final intrinsic energies. Thus, provided no external work is done during the reaction, the decrease or increase in intrinsic energy will be the measurable heat evolved or adsorbed in the reaction

Experimentation shows that the heat evolved or absorbed in any chemical change is constant for a given quantity of the reactants. The standard *Heat of Reaction*, however, is defined as the quantity of heat associated with the gram-formula quantities of the reacting substances as indicated by the equation of the reaction. This quantity of heat is usually expressed in kilogram-calories (Cals.), one Cal being the quantity of heat required to raise the temperature of one kilogram of water by 1° Centigrade. For example, the equation $C + O_2 = CO_2 + 94.3$ Cals. indicates that 12 (atomic weight) grams of carbon combine with 32 (molecular weight) grams of oxygen to form 44 (molecular weight) grams of carbon dioxide with the liberation of 94.3 Cals of heat. When a gas is generated at atmospheric pressure, the external work done is given by the gas equation $PV = RT$ where R has the value of 1.988 gram-calories and T refers to the Absolute temperature scale. For example, if the gram-formula weight of zinc is dissolved in sulphuric acid to liberate the gram-formula weight of hydrogen the *measured* quantity of heat evolved is 34.2 Cals. at 16° C. For this temperature, RT has the value 575 gram-calories, or 0.575 Cal., so that the heat of reaction is 34.2 + 0.575 = 34.775 Cals to take account of the work done in gas expansion against atmospheric pressure. Conversely, if gas is absorbed, a quantity 1.988T must be subtracted from the *measured* value to account for the atmospheric work done in contracting the gas.

The quantity of heat liberated or absorbed when the gram-formula weight of a compound is formed from its elements is called the *Heat of Formation* of the compound and the heat liberated when one gram-formula weight of an element or compound is completely oxidised is called the *Heat of Combustion*. Compounds which are formed or reactions which take place with the liberation of heat are said to be exothermic and those associated with the absorption of heat are classified as endothermic. Heats of Reaction are measured by observing changes in temperature in suitably designed calorimeters developed from those used earlier by Joseph Black. In 1840, G. M. Hess measured the heat associated with the formation of a compound made in several different ways and concluded that the quantity of heat evolved during the formation of a given compound is the same whether the compound is formed directly and all at once or in a series of progressive intermediate stages. This is now known as *Hess's Law* which is associated with the corollary that the thermal value of a reaction is the sum of the heats of formation of the final products less the heats of formation of the reacting substances. This allows the heat of formation of a compound from its elements to be computed when a direct determination is either impractical or very difficult. Similarly, it enables the thermal value of a reaction to be deduced when the heats of formation of the different substances which take part in the reaction are known or can readily be measured.

Count Rumford had suggested around 1800, that motion was associated with heat, and had compared the heat generated in the boring of cannon with that to be derived from combustion of the food eaten by the horses employed to turn the drill-bit. Now, the Kinetic Theory of Heat at the atomic and molecular levels and the new subject of thermo-chemistry had led to the conclusion that animals and humans were basically heat engines energised by the heat of combustion (respiration) of ingested food, just as steam engines were energised by the heat of combustion of coal.

7. 2. 4 The Void

At this point, we have concluded that heat, though other than matter, is a manifestation of the movement of the atoms and molecules of matter in an otherwise all pervasive void. Further evidence for the existence of this void and for atoms and molecules within it, will now be considered. Thus, not only were gases found to diffuse (dissolve) in gases as discussed above, but gases were also found to dissolve in liquids and solids. Likewise, gases, liquids and solids were found to transform smoothly from one phase to another. Such inter-mixing and transformation phenomena strongly suggest the presence of an all pervasive void in which fundamental particles (atoms radicals and molecules) of one substance exist and can penetrate the void between those of another regardless of their normal respective states.

Thus, when a small quantity of a solid, such as sodium chloride (common salt) is added to water it seems to disappear. A similar result can be achieved with the coloured salt, potassium dichromate, except that its colour allows the diffusion to be followed visually. Nonetheless, the solubility of a solid (solute) in a given quantity of a liquid (solvent) is limited and constant for any given solute-solvent pair at any given temperature, this limit occurring when the solution is said to be saturated. Solubility is generally expressed as the number of grams of solute which can be dissolved per 100 grams of solvent. However, when this is measured for different solutes in the same solvent for a range of temperatures, the resulting plots (solubility curves) show that solubility generally increases with increasing temperature; that the rate varies from one solute to another; and that, just occasionally, as with sodium sulphate in water, the curve reaches a maximum solubility before decreasing again for further temperature increase.

The abnormal solubility curve exemplified by sodium sulphate in water is characterised by a change in gradient at 32.4° C. The explanation is that sodium sulphate can be associated with ten molecules of water of crystallisation with a formula of $Na_2SO_4.10\ H_2O$ when its crystals are monoclinic and it is known as the decahydrate, or it can exist in the anhydrous form simply as Na_2SO_4 when its crystals are rhombic. The solubility curve below 32.4° is that of the decahydrate, the solubility of which rises relatively rapidly with temperature because the greater association with water molecules is stable at the lower temperatures, and the solubility curve above 32.4° degrees is that of the anhydrous form, the decahedrate being unstable at the higher temperatures and the solubility correspondingly lower. At 32.4°, the transition temperature, both forms are in equilibrium. Abnormal solubility curves can also arise when two salts are dissolved together in water and crystallise to form double salts. In this way, potassium sulphate K_2SO_4 and $Al_2(SO_4)_3$ crystallise in the cubic system with 24 molecules of water of crystallisation to form alum with the formula $K_2SO_4.\ Al_2(SO_4)_3.\ 24H_2O$.

Dissolved solids cannot be recovered by filtration because solutions consist of separate molecules such as those of sugar or, in the case of salts, of dissociated ions (c.f. Section 7.2.5) which are homogeneously distributed among the molecules of the solvent. However, when a hot saturated solution is cooled, the quantity of solute in excess of the saturation limit at the lower temperature will re-crystallise out of solution. Thus, we see that the solid is transformed into its individual molecules (or dissociated ions) when it dissolves and it is re-constituted in its initial form when it re-crystallises from the dissolved state. Thus, the solubility of solids provides a convenient means of purification by separating soluble substances from insoluble ones by dissolving in an appropriate hot solvent, filtering the impurities and allowing to cool. Again, the considerable differences in the solubility of solids at different temperatures provides a means for their separation one from another by arranging to re-crystallise one while leaving the other in solution. Dissolved solids can also be recovered by evaporation to dryness and pure solvent can be recovered by distillation or by freezing. It was recorded as early as the time of Aristotle that drinkable water could be obtained by melting sea-ice, any traces of salt in such ice having been added mechanically to its surfaces by sea movement. Similarly, the continual removal of ice from the surface of cider stored in North American barns was practised in former times as an alternative to distillation in the home production of strong (high alcohol content) liquors. However, in all cases the presence of the dissolved substance (solute) depresses the freezing point of the solution in proportion to the amount of solute present, as expressed in *Blagden's Law* of 1788, and as utilised in the salting of roads in winter.

If we examine the freezing of solutions in more detail taking that of potassium chloride (KCl) in water as our example and considering a plot of temperature on the vertical axis against % KCl on the horizontal axis, it is found that the temperature at which ice begins to separate from the KCl solution, thus increasing the concentration of KCl in the remaining liquid is gradually reduced to -10.64° C, at which point the liquid solution contains 19.5% of KCl when the whole of the remaining liquid freezes *en bloc*. The solution at 19.5% KCl is called the eutectic mixture, and -10.64° C, the eutectic temperature. It was suggested by T. Guthrie that the eutectic mixture was a definite compound; and that by analogy with the water of crystallisation of hydrated salts, eutectics could be called cryohydrates. However, they are now known to be mechanical mixtures of ice and salt *i.e.* to consist of two distinct phases rather than one as for a compound or a solution, on the evidence that cryohydrates are opaque and ill-defined, are heterogeneous under the microscope, give rise to open networks of salt when the ice is removed by dissolving in alcohol, and have variable salt to water ratios. This concept of phase thus required clear definition being rather more complicated than simply a matter of either solid, liquid and gas, with ice, water and water vapour (steam) all being able to co-exist in dynamic equilibrium as homogeneous entities separated by surfaces in a heterogeneous system of three phases.

In the period 1876 to 1888, J. Willard Gibbs produced a generalised treatment of such heterogeneous systems now known as the *Gibbs Phase Rule* for which he defined a phase as a homogeneous portion, the components as the least number of independently variable elements or compounds present, and the variance or the degrees of freedom of the system as the number of independent variables which must be fixed for the state of the system to be defined without ambiguity. Thus, in the heterogeneous system of water and its vapour there is only one component, namely H_2O, whereas in the two systems discussed immediately above, the components were water (H_2O) and sodium sulphate (Na_2SO_4), and water (H_2O) and potassium chloride (KCl) respectively. As to degrees of freedom, it will be recalled that the equilibrium condition of a gas with respect to temperature, pressure and volume is defined by the equation $PV = RT$, where R is a constant. In such an equation of three variables, two must be fixed so that the third can be calculated to define the state of the system without ambiguity. The two fixed variables are said to be arbitrary or independent variables, while the third to be calculated from the equation is said to be the dependent variable. Thus, we see that the gas system has two degrees of freedom. On the basis of such considerations and definitions the *Gibbs Phase Rule* states that a system will be in equilibrium when its variance (number of degrees of freedom) F is equal to the number of components C less the number of phases P, increased by two. Thus, $F = C - P + 2$.

Thus, the system of liquid water and water vapour has two phases, one component (H_2O) and two variables (vapour pressure and temperature) of which the one is dependent and the other independent. It is therefore univariant as confirmed by substituting the appropriate values in the equation, $F = C - P + 2$, thus $F = 1 - 2 + 2 = 1$. The system liquid water, water vapour and ice involves three phases and interfaces namely solid-vapour, vapour-liquid, and liquid-solid. The three inter-phase curves on the vapour versus temperature plot for this system meet at a point called the triple point the co-ordinates of which for the water system are pressure, 4.57 mm of mercury and temperature, 0.0076° C. At the triple point, the system is invariant because C is 1 (H_2O) as before but now there are three phases, solid, liquid and vapour, giving $F = 1 - 3 + 2 = 0$. Thus, if the pressure or temperature at the triple point is varied to any extent at all, one of the phases will disappear and a two phase system will exist in which the state of the system will be represented by a point on one of the three inter-phase curves, for then $P = 2$, $C = 1$ as before and hence $F = 1$, the system being univariant with one variable having to be known before the state of the system can be determined. To take another example, the system comprising a saturated solution in contact with an excess of solute is also univariant, but it is bivariant if unsaturated. In the former case there are two components (solvent and solute) and three phases (solid, solution and vapour) for which $F = 2 - 3 + 2 = 1$ (univariant); while in the latter, there are two components (solvent and solute) and two phases (solution and vapour) for which F = 2 -2 +2 = 2 (bivariant), with two variables having to be known before the state of the system can be determined. Thus, systems having the same variance behave analogously with change in temperature, pressure, and volume or concentration: and the Phase Rule groups systems into classes on the basis of variance and indicates the conditions for phase equilibrium in heterogeneous systems.

When a coloured solute such as copper sulphate is placed at the bottom of a tall jar and allowed to dissolve into the water then added to fill the jar, it will be seen that the interface between solute and water slowly loses its clarity and becomes obliterated over time as the solute gradually diffuses into the solvent eventually producing a uniform concentration of solute throughout the jar. Such diffusion of a solid into a liquid was recognised to be analogous to the diffusion of one gas into another as discussed above. We have also noted that if the diffusion of one gas into another is arranged to occur through a permeable partition (membrane) a pressure difference between the two sides of the membrane will be measurable. It will therefore not surprise readers to learn that the diffusion of the particles (molecules or ions) of a dissolved substance will exert a similar pressure when a membrane is placed between a solvent and a solution of solute in that solvent, provided the chosen membrane offers no resistance to the transfer of solvent molecules through it, but resists those of the dissolved solute. Such a membrane permeable to solvent but not to solute is said to be semi-permeable and the passage of water through a membrane in this manner into a solution of solute in water is called osmosis (Gk. osmos, to push). The pressure exerted between water and a solution of sugar in water was called the osmotic pressure of the sugar solution by W Pfeffer in 1877. More generally, osmosis is the passage of solvent from a dilute solution to a more concentrated one through a semi-permeable membrane.

On this basis, J. H van't Hoff showed in 1885 that the osmotic pressures of different solutions of the same solute are proportional to their concentrations at constant temperature; that the osmotic pressure of a solution at constant concentration is proportional to the absolute temperature; and that these relationships could be expressed in the form: $P/C = KT$, where P is osmotic pressure, C is solution concentration, T is absolute temperature and K is a constant. In addition, since concentration is inversely proportional to the solution volume, this equation may be written as $PV = KT$, where V is the volume of the solution in which a given amount of solute is dissolved. This is reminiscent of the Gas Equation and we can go a stage further. If we substitute for P and V, values obtained by experiment at a given temperature (V being expressed as the volume of solution containing one gram-molecular weight of solute), we can find the value of K. By this means Berkley and Hartley obtained a value within 1% of the value of the gas constant R, calculated from the gas equation and thus justified writing the equation for the osmotic pressure of dilute solutions in the form of the gas equation for n gram molecular weights of solute as $PV = nRT$. Now, Van't Hoff further developed the parallel of mixed gases and solutes in solvents through theoretical considerations of thermodynamics and the nature of the semi-permeable membrane to conclude that the osmotic pressure of a solution is equal to the pressure which the dissolved substance would exert in the gaseous state if it occupied a volume equal to that of the solution. In addition, by re-writing the osmotic equation as $P = nRT/V$, we see that the osmotic pressure is proportional to the number of gram-molecular weights of solute in a given volume of solution; or that equimolecular solutions of molecular substances (c.f. electrolytes Section 7.2.5) have the same osmotic pressure; and that, therefore, osmotic pressure measurement provides a means to determine the molecular weights of solutes.

However, just as the equation $PV = RT$ applies to a *perfect* gas to which actual gases conform to varying degrees of proximity as discussed above, so also does the osmotic pressure equation $P = nRT/V$ apply only to an *ideal* solution to which actual solutions conform to varying degrees. The deviations

196

which occur with actual solutions are thus accounted for by considerations similar to those applied to real gases by Van der Waals, namely those relating to the attractions between molecules of solute and between molecules of solute and solvent, and the volume corrections needed to account for the volumes of the molecules themselves in relation to the overall liquid volume. However, in both cases we have a vindication of the atomic/molecular theory of matter with gas pressure being the result of the continuous bombardment of gas molecules with the walls of the container, and with osmotic pressure being due to the differential bombardment of the semi-permeable membrane by molecules of solvent and solute respectively. Examples of such membranes are those produced by the deposition of copper ferrocyanide in the walls of a porous pot by procedures which need not be described here, or those consisting of the thinnest grades of commercial cellophane. It was assumed by the early workers that such membranes acted as a sieve which permitted passage of individual solvent molecules but not the larger solute molecules. It is now recognised that the actual pore-diameter of copper ferrocyanide membranes is too large to prevent the passage of molecules even as large as those of sugar, thus requiring modifications to the basic theory of permeability, one being that the effective pore-diameter is reduced by the presence of adsorbed layers of water molecules on the pore-walls which stops the passage of solute molecules while allowing water molecules to make their way through.

Having discussed the nature of heat in terms of the movement of the atoms and molecules hypothesised to explain the chemical reactions which led to the Periodic Table, and having now further validated the atomic/molecular structure of matter by reviewing the physical nature of gases, liquids, solids and their solutions one with another with respect to the void, we now turn to "imponderable", electricity.

7. 2. 5 Electricity

Until the end of the eighteenth century, only static electricity had been recognised with C. F du Fay (1698-1739) having introduced in 1730 a theory of two fluids which were supposed to be separated by friction and neutralised by contact, with conduction and insulation having been demonstrated in 1731, and with the accumulation of charge on a system of two conductors separated by a non-conductor having been demonstrated with the Leyden Jar invented by two Dutch workers in 1746. Thereafter, Benjamin Franklin (1706-90) observed that charge could be drawn off easily by metal points and proposed, in his one fluid theory of 1747, that "electric fire was a common element in all bodies"; that a surplus should be designated 'plus' and a deficiency 'minus'; that lightening was electrical; and that benefits could be derived from the lightening conductor which he described in 1749 and tested in a practical way in 1752.

Again, though Priestley had suggested in his *History and Present State of Electricity* of 1767 that the force of electrical attraction would obey Newton's inverse square law, and though in 1786 an attempt was made to verify this by relating charge magnitude to the angle of leaf separation in a gold-leaf electroscope, verification was first achieved in 1785 by the French engineer Charles Augustus Coulomb (1736-1806) who measured the force required to bring two equally charged (repulsive) pith-balls ever-closer together by means of a torsion balance constructed for the purpose. Yet again, John Hunter in 1773-5, Ingenhousz in 1773 and Cavendish in 1776 attributed the shocks delivered by the skate-like torpedo fish and the eel Gymnotus to electricity. This in turn, led Luigi Galvani (1737-98) of Bologna to demonstrate in 1791 with the legs and spinal column of a frog that electricity produced by dissimilar metal contact, could produce muscular contraction. This, again led Alessandro Volta (1745-1827) to find that when the free ends of a pair of different metals joined in a V-shape were placed one in the mouth and one in contact with the eye, the sensation of light was immediately experienced; that a silver and gold coin held against the tongue produced a salty taste when connected by a wire; that electric current was produced for the first time by a series of paired discs of silver and zinc separated by cards soaked in brine; and that later his *couronne des tasses* of 1800 in which two different metals dipping into salt water or dilute acid contained in each cup and connected with wire similarly produced current electricity.

Again, it was noted that the passage of such current through water and though aqueous solutions produced chemical decomposition. Thus, Humphrey Davy observed that water was decomposed in this way with release of hydrogen at one electrode and oxygen at the other, the volume of hydrogen given off being twice that of the oxygen, thus confirming the composition of water. Again, as we have seen, he used such electric current to isolate a range of previously unknown elements from Laviosier's "earths" and alkalis for the first time (c.f. 7.1.6). To explain these decompositions, Grotthus hypothesised in 1805, that passage of the current caused successive decomposition and recombination of water or solute until these were separately and continuously liberated at their respective terminal electrodes.

However, Ohm showed the relationship between the current I flowing in a metal conductor of resistance R under a potential difference V to be I = V/R where current is in amperes (amps for short), resistance in ohms and potential difference in volts, these units being named after Ampere, Volta and Ohm himself, and when this relationship now known as *Ohm's Law* was shown to apply to solutions of decomposable solutes in water (electroytes) it became clear that the energy of the current overcomes the resistance of the solution, and that none of it is used to decompose the solute (c.f. below). In addition, Michael Faraday (1791-1867) gave this process of electrolysis quantitative expression in 1834 when he showed that the mass of product liberated is proportional to the quantity of electricity passed; and that the same quantity of electricity passed through solutions of different substances liberates products in proportion to their chemical equivalents, the unit quantity of electricity (amps x seconds) being the coulomb, after August Coulomb. Thus, *Faraday's Laws of Electrolysis* can be summed up in the statement that one gram-equivalent of any substance is liberated by the passage of 96,494 coulombs of electricity, which quantity is now known as the Faraday (c.f. Section 7.1.5).

Ohm's Law having thus refuted the hypothesis that solutes were decomposed by the current, Clausius hypothesised in 1857 that electrolytes in solution are already dissociated into charged particles, irrespective of the presence or absence of an applied voltage; that these particles exist at low concentrations in equilibrium with un-dissociated electrolyte molecules; that the former migrate to the electrodes when a potential difference is applied, there to be discharged and liberated as the observed products of electrolysis; and that further dissociation occurs to maintain equilibrium between the particles and un-dissociated molecules as the electrolysis proceeds. These hypotheses, in turn, were taken forward by Arrhenius in 1887 with his *Theory of Electrolytic Dissociation*. According to Arrhenius, dissociated charged particles consist of atoms or groups of atoms carrying charges equal to the valence (c.f. Section 7.1.5) of the atom or radical resulting from the dissociation. The total charge carried by these dissociated particles was thus algebraically zero, the process of their dissociation being considered partial, reversible and almost complete in very dilute solutions.

The presence of such charged particles in solution, irrespective of the presence or absence of electrodes or current, accounts for Ohm's Law applying when current is actually flowing because the current flow is their movement towards the electrodes and the resistance is that of the solvent to their movement. It also accounts for the fact that the products of electrolysis appear only at the widely separated electrodes where the charges on the individual particles are neutralised and the corresponding substances liberated, the metals at the cathode (negative electrode) and the radical at the anode (positive electrode). If we assume that all univalent particles each carry a charge of magnitude e, the quantity of electricity which passes through the solution will be proportional to

198

the number of such particles discharged and hence to the quantity of substance liberated. This explains Faraday's *First Law of Electrolysis*. If the charged particle is bivalent and thus carrying a charge of 2e, the quantity of substance liberated by the passage of current corresponding to e units will be equal to the weight of the particle divided by its valency, or in other words to its equivalent. This is Faraday's *Second Law of Electrolysis*. Thus we see that the Theory of Electrolytic Dissociation is consistent with the observed facts of electrolysis and provides further support to the atomic/molecular theory of matter.

Now, in developing his theory of solutions, Van't Hoff had noted that solutions of acids, alkalis and salts show osmotic pressures greater than would be expected from their molecular weights. To normalise this situation he introduced the factor i into his osmotic pressure equation which he now wrote as $P = iRT/V$ for one gram-molecule of solvent, finding for sodium chloride and similar univalent salts that in moderate strength solutions i has a value of about 1.8 and tends to a value of 2.0 at high dilution, and that for sodium sulphate i varies similarly from 2.2 to about 3.0. On this basis, Arrhenius hypothesised that the need for Van't Hoff's factor arose from the dissociation of the molecules of electrolytes into charged particles which resulted in the presence of more particles than would otherwise exist in the solution and that these extra particles gave rise to the anomalous osmotic pressures observed for electrolytes.

Thus, Arrhenius reasoned that if one gram-molecule of an electrolyte dissociates into n particles in dissociating to the fractional extent α, there will be $1 - \alpha$ gram molecules of un-dissociated electrolyte and $n\alpha$ gram-molecules of particles; that therefore there will be a total of $(1 - \alpha) + n\alpha = 1 + (n - 1)\alpha$ gram-molecules of solute particles altogether; and that, therefore, the ratio of the number of total solute particles to the number which would be there if no dissociation occurred is $\{1 + (n - 1)\alpha\} : 1$, which is Van't Hoff's factor i. Consequently Arrhenius could write $i = 1 + (n - 1)\alpha$, and hence $\alpha = (i - 1) / (n - 1)$. Thus, applying this reasoning to a sodium chloride solution for which $i = 1.85$, Arrhenius showed that the degree of dissociation is 85%, and that in general, electrical conductivity and osmotic pressure measurements are related to particle dissociation in this way. However, in developing this Electrolytic Dissociation theory Debye, Huckel and Onsager replace the 'charged particle' of Arrhenius with the modern term 'ion' in their *Ionic Theory*, and while this term was introduced after discovery of the electron (c.f. Section 7.3.1), I make the replacement now.

Before proceeding, however, it should be noted that while the specific resistance (in ohms) of a metal is that of a 1 centimetre cube and the specific conductance is its reciprocal (in mhos), the specific conductivity of a solution is not that of a one cm cube of solution located between two electrodes each one square cm in area and 1cm apart, because the conductivity depends only on the ions present and not on the totality of the material between the electrodes. Thus, for comparison of the conductivities of solutions of different solutes they must contain equivalent amounts of solute, equivalent conductivity being defined as the conductivity of one gram-equivalent of the substance dissolved in solvent in a conductivity cell whose opposite walls 1cm apart form the electrodes. Again in contrast to metals, the potential-difference driving the *direct* current for electrolysis induces a counter potential-difference such that the measured resistance is not of the solution alone while to avoid the extraneous conductivities of impurities, the aqueous solvent needs to be extremely pure. In responding to the former in 1869 Kohlrausch measured *alternating* current resistance with the Wheatstone Bridge while the impurities in ordinary distilled water were found to preclude accurate measurement of electrolyte conductivities, such impurities including carbonic acid from atmospheric carbon dioxide.

To give readers some appreciation of the water purities progressively achieved, the conductivity of ordinary distilled water is between 3 and 6 x 10^{-6} mho at 18° C while that used for general conductivity measurements has a conductivity of 0.9 x 10^{-6} mho and for the most accurate work the conductivity is reduced to about 0.043 x 10^{-6} mho, this being referred to as equilibrium water its conductivity arising from its own very slight dissociation into the ions H^+ and OH^-. These various degrees of purity are achieved by re-distillations of ordinary distilled water over acidified potassium permanganate followed by barium hydroxide and finally into a block-tin condenser in a stream of carbon dioxide free air. Further refinements involve condensing only part of the vapour while allowing gaseous impurities to escape with the other part. Of course, such ultra-pure water requires exclusion of atmospheric air from all subsequent operations and measurements. Thus, Kohlrausch found that the equivalent conductivity of all electrolyte solutions increases with dilution and tends to a maximum referred to as the equivalent conductivity at infinite dilution. He also stated what is now *Kohlrausch's Law* that the equivalent conductivity at infinite dilution is the sum of the mobilities of the positively and negatively charged ions, now known respectively as cations and anions, this relationship being written $\lambda_{inf} = \lambda_c + \lambda_a$.

Now, according to Arrhenius the increase in conductivity with dilution is due to the increase in dissociation of the solute into its constituent ions, the limit being reached at infinite dilution when complete dissociation has occurred. This being so, the degree of dissociation (ionisation), denoted by α at any given dilution will be given by the ratio of the equivalent conductivity at that degree of dilution (λ_v) to the equivalent conductivity of the same solute at infinite dilution (λ_{inf}), or $\alpha = \lambda_v / \lambda_{inf}$ usually expressed as a percentage. For substances which exhibit high equivalent conductivity at moderate dilutions (the so-called strong electrolytes) the value of the equivalent conductivity at infinite dilution can be obtained easily by extrapolation. For the weaker electrolytes Kohlrausch's Law is used to determine the equivalent conductivity at infinite dilution from the contributions made to this conductivity by each ion, these having been determined from the equivalent conductivities of strong electrolytes containing these ions. Thus the conductivity at infinite dilution of the weak electrolyte acetic acid may be calculated from the experimentally determined values of the conductivities at infinite dilution of the strong electrolytes sodium acetate, hydrochloric acid and sodium chloride, thus:

λ_{inf} (for sodium acetate) = 78.5 (by experiment and extrapolation) = $\lambda_{Na} + \lambda_{Ac}$ . . . (1)

λ_{inf} (for hydrochloric acid) = 380.4 (by experiment and extrapolation) = $\lambda_H + \lambda_{Cl}$ . . . (2)

and λ_{inf} (for sodium chloride) = 109.0 (by experiment and extrapolation) = $\lambda_{Na} + \lambda_{Cl}$ . . . (3)

Therefore λ_{inf} (for acetic acid) = $\lambda_H + \lambda_{Ac}$ {by adding equations (1) & (2) and subtracting (3)} = 349.9

Thus we have another example of the way in which scientific method pursues separate lines of enquiry to reach confirmation through consistency, the values obtained by Arrhenius for α {the degree of dissociation (ionisation)} of various electrolytes at different dilutions λ_v, and those based on conductivity measurements of λ_{inf} as illustrated above, being both found to agree with the values inferred from the Van't Hoff factor *i*, obtained from osmotic pressure measurements.

Thus, having seen that the properties of gases, liquids and solids and of their solutions one with another, require matter to be atomic and molecular; and "imponderable" heat to be a manifestation of atomic and molecular motion, we now see that the "imponderable" electricity is also closely associated with the atomic and molecular nature of matter with the dissociation of electrolytes (acids, alkalis and salts) in solution being manifest in the electrical conductivity of such solutions; that normal osmotic pressures are analogous to gas pressure and can be used as can vapour pressure to determine molecular weights; that the anomalous osmotic pressures observed with electrolytes are explained by molecular dissociation; and that measurement of anomalous pressures and conductivities permit the degree of dissociation to be determined, even though the relationship between these phenomena was not anticipated at the outset.

Thus, we see that the scientific method can produce knowledge unforeseen when particular experiments were designed for the reality-evaluation of initially unrelated hypotheses; and that this unforeseen knowledge causes other experiments to be designed to pursue other hypotheses to further knowledge and so on. Thus, at the outset, heat was believed to be a material fluid, but it was revealed to be a form of energy manifest by the movement of the constituent atoms and molecules of matter. At the outset, electricity was also believed to be a material fluid associated with certain forms of matter, but it was shown to be carried under certain circumstances by matter itself, thus leading to the further hypothesis that the equilibrium dissociation and re-association of electrolytic solutes might somehow be electrical in nature; and that, consequently the bonding of atoms in general might be electrical. As we shall see in Chapter 9, these hypotheses were also transformed to knowledge in due course.

7. 2. 6 Magnetism

Though Michael Faraday had elucidated the relationship between matter and electricity with his Laws of Electrolysis (c.f. Section 7.2.5) he also elucidated the relationship between electricity and "imponderable" magnetism, though others had earlier investigated this relationship using current electricity from voltaic cells, there being no dynamos prior to Faraday's elucidation of these earlier observations.

Thus, Hans Christian Oersted (1777-1851) demonstrated the relationship between the new electricity and the more familiar magnetism, by showing that when a wire in an electric circuit is positioned parallel to a magnetic needle and the current is switched on, the needle is deflected, and that it is un-deflected when the wire is initially positioned at right angles to it. He also showed that the direction of deflection depends on whether the wire is located above or below the needle and on the direction of the current. In addition, Francois Arago (1786-1853) showed in 1820 that a spiral of copper wire attracted iron filings when an electric current was flowing along the wire, and that the filings dropped off when the current was switched off. He also showed in 1824 that a copper disc rotating in a horizontal plane caused a magnetic needle suspended above it to rotate. In the meantime, Andre Marie Ampere (1775-1836) showed that two parallel current-carrying wires attract each other when their currents flow in the same direction and repel each other when their currents are opposed, and he hypothesised that magnetism could be an effect of electric currents at the molecular level. In addition, such work and especially that of Ampere gave rise to new instruments for detection and measurement of electric currents, initially on arbitrary scales. These galvanometers consisted of a magnetic needle suspended at the centre of a multi-turn coil of wire, the deflection of the former being a measure of the current flowing through the latter.

From his own investigations based on the foregoing, Michael Faraday recognised that an electric current creates what he called a magnetic "field of force"around the wire in which it flows, and he graphically represented cross-sections of this "force field" by a series of circles concentric with the wire. He then hypothesised that this force field could cause a magnet to move round a current carrying wire and such a wire to move round a magnet. Now, these lines of magnetic force had been around as a hypothesis since Gilbert's time (1546-1603) and they could be demonstrated by alignment of iron filings by a magnet. In addition, Arago had shown that a current-carrying wire acted as a magnet and Oersted had shown the movement of a compass needle above and below such a wire to be consistent with such force lines.

Therefore, to validate his hypothesis Faraday constructed the following circuit. A wire was fixed at the end of a horizontal suspension arm from which it dipped into the centre of the surface of mercury contained in a tall cylindrical glass container and a second wire was flexibly suspended from the other end of the arm to dip into the mercury surface in a second tall container in such a way as to freely describe the surface of a cone were it to rotate. Now, the first glass container was fitted with a bar magnet, one end of which was flexibly mounted in a central position to its base, the other end projecting above the mercury surface and free to describe an 'inverted' cone were it to rotate, while the second container was fitted with a similar bar magnet in a fixed central vertical position to its base and projecting above its mercury surface. Now, the lower ends of the two magnets were electrically connected through the bases of the containers and the two suspended wires were connected through the suspension arm to a source of electricity, and when this circuit was completed through a switch, the magnet in the first container and the wire in the second immediately rotated as permitted by their flexible mountings and continued to do so until the current was switched off. Thus, he reality-evaluated his hypothesis of complementary rotation.

Faraday then hypothesised that because a wire behaves like a magnet when it carries current, a magnet should be able to produce current in a wire. To reality-evaluate this hypothesis he wound two separate wires around two arcs of an iron ring, one of which was connected to a galvanometer and the other to a source of electric current. On making and breaking the voltaic circuit the galvanometer showed that a current also flowed for an instant in its circuit, and that these 'making and breaking currents' were in opposite directions. Next, he wound a wire round an iron rod which he placed between the north pole on one bar magnet and the south pole of another, the other two ends being in direct contact. He then connected the ends of the coiled wire to a galvanometer and again demonstrated that when contact between these ends was made and broken the galvanometer registered momentary current flow. Faraday next wound a wire round a wooden bobbin and connected its ends to a voltaic cell, and round this 'primary' coil, a 'secondary' and much longer coil was wound the ends of which were connected to a galvanometer. Again, as with the metal ring experiment, making and breaking the electrical circuit produced momentary currents in the separate coil as indicated by the galvanometer.

Faraday realised that all of the above magneto-electric effects, including the induction of current in a secondary circuit by current flow in the primary, must be due to the growth and decay of fields of force associated with movement of magnet or coil, or with making or breaking a circuit or contact; and that these movements affected the force-line distribution, the magnet or coil being correspondingly urged away from the strong region of the field to the weak. On this basis, Faraday placed Arago's copper disc between the poles of a horse-shoe magnet, connected the axis and edge of the disc to a galvanometer and showed the presence of an induced current when the disc was rotated. He was also able to explain Ampere's observation of current-carrying coils attracting or repelling each other with same and opposite direction currents respectively, by showing in the former case that lines of force are drawn together when being driven from strong to weak regions of the field while in the latter they are driven apart. The next step was recognition that an electric current would be induced in a conductor wire which was moved so as to continuously cut the force-lines of a magnetic field, thus generating continuous current electricity.

Thus, the dynamo is a conductor built up of many coils of wire continuously rotated in a magnetic field to produce current electricity. However, because the current direction changes during each revolution, alternating current is produced, though direct current can be supplied by "rectifying" the output by reversing the reverse current each time the rotating coils pass between a pair of suitably arranged off-take contacts (c.f. section 8.1.3). The electric motor is a similar device in which instead of rotation producing electricity, electricity produces rotation. In 1851, the Parisian instrument maker, H. D. Ruhmkorff (1803-1877) produced the type of coil which bears his name and thus made the electric motor a practical reality.

7. 2. 7 Light

In spite of the antiquity of optics, there was no agreement on the nature of light itself, the corpuscular theory and the wave theory still being in contention at the end of the eighteenth century. Newton had favoured the former in believing that a luminous body emitted streams of corpuscles in straight lines (rays) which on impact with the eye produced vision. On this model, refraction was believed due to the bending of the rays towards the denser medium on close approach. Newton dismissed the alternative belief that light was a form of motion by saying that "a bell may be heard behind a hill . . . but light is never known to bend into the shadow". In other words light travels in straight lines only, this being consistent with the expected behaviour of a stream of corpuscles. Here again we see an initial preference for "imponderable" substance, this time in the form of 'corpuscles'.

However, the wave theory was taken forward in 1678 by Huygens and presented more fully in his *Treatise on Light* of 1690. This theory supposed the universe to be pervaded by an elastic medium, the ether, through which the waves are propagated spherically from a light-source in analogy with the propagation of sound waves through matter. However, though substance as corpuscles is now replaced by substance as all-pervasive ether, the significance of this change lay in its preference for a wave theory. Thus, any point on the surface of the spherical wave may be regarded as a light source emitting its own spherical wave all of which at any distance from the original source may be regarded as combining to form a wave-front. Again for sufficiently distant light sources any small part of the wave-front may be regarded as flat or in section linear, while the lines, rays, radiating to it from the source may be regarded as parallel. On this basis, Huygens explained refraction more satisfactorily than on the basis of corpuscles. Thus, when the plane wave-front at right-angles to its direction of advance arrives obliquely at the surface of the denser medium, points on the wave-front progressively reach the surface and thus some will find themselves moving in the denser medium before others have reached it, and so in equal intervals of time they will travel less far, in the denser medium than those still travelling in the less dense medium. Thus, the wave-front plane makes a smaller angle with the surface of the dense medium which it has entered than it did prior to entry and so its direction of advance will be bent towards the normal to the interface in compliance with Snell's Law (c.f. Section 6.3.1).

Again, when Thomas Young (1773-1829) admitted sun-light through a pin-hole to form a cone of light in a dark chamber and interposed a card to produce a shadow on the opposite wall, he observed faint fringes of colour on either side of the shadow, and in the shadow itself a series of faint dark and light vertical bands with a faint light band in the middle, and he reasoned that the light which passed each side of the card must spread behind it as Huygens might have expected, though the dark and light bands were unexpected. Again, on finding that the banding disappeared when he prevented the light from passing one edge of the card, he reasoned that light spreads out equally behind the card when allowed to pass only one side of it, and that when it passes both sides, the two sources of spreading light interfere to produce the observed bands. Thus, in two papers in 1801 Young explained the above as follows: "suppose a number of equal waves of water to move upon the surface of a lake with a certain constant velocity and to enter a narrow channel leading out of the lake; suppose then, another similar cause to have excited another equal series of waves, which arrive at the same channel with the same velocity and at the same time as the first. One series of waves will not destroy the other, but their effects will be combined. . . . in such a manner that if the elevations of the one series coincide with those of the other, they must together produce a series of greater joint elevations; but if the elevations of one series are so situated as to correspond to the depressions of the other, they must exactly fill up those depressions, and the surface of the water must remain smooth - at least, I can discover no alternative, either in theory or experiment.

Now, I maintain that similar effects take place whenever two portions of light are thus mixed, and this I call *the general law of the interference of light*." Thus Young argued by analogy that light must be a wave-form, though his analogy with water still implied a medium (substance) of propagation. Young also showed by allowing a beam of light to pass through a slot in a screen, that it does indeed bend into the shadow behind the screen on either side of the slot and that this can only be explained on the basis of Huygen's wave theory which allows the wave-front to spread in all directions in the required manner.

Now, it was known that light did not travel equally in all directions through all transparent media. Thus, when it passes successively through two crystals of the mineral Iceland Spar it usually produces two beams of unequal brightness with one disappearing entirely depending on the relative orientation of the crystals. Again, Etienne Louis Malus (1775-1812) had found that he could obtain comparable effects with light reflected from transparent surfaces and misunderstanding the underlying mechanism he called the phenomenon polarisation. In any case, it was not explicable on wave theory until August Jean Fresnel (1782-1827) developed it in correspondence with Young, the explanation being based on a comparison between the vibration modes of sound and water waves together with an extension of the latter. In sound-waves the transmitting particles vibrate in a direction parallel to the wave propagation in a mode referred to as longitudinal vibration while in water-waves the transmitting particles move up and down at right angles to the forward direction of the wave in what is called transverse vibration. Fresnel now supposed ether particles to vibrate transversely in all directions at right angles to the direction of the ray, so that they could be represented in a cross-section of the circular ray as diameters of length signifying the extremes between which the ether particles vibrate. He then supposed the particles of crystalline Iceland Spar to be arranged similarly to a set of railings which would allow passage of the advancing planes of vibration of a light ray only in alignment with the gaps between the rails such vibrations being said to be polarised, all the others being stopped.

Fresnel went on to estimate the wavelength of light in 1821. To do this he admitted light to a dark chamber through a pin-hole in one side and reflected it from an angled mirror on to an end-wall. Thus, looking into the mirror an observer would see a 'virtual image' of the pin-hole as far behind the mirror as the end-wall is in front of it. If now the mirror is replaced by two mirrors side by side, so that they may be rotated very slightly out of the plane of the original single mirror, the observer will now see two virtual images of the pin-hole, A and B. If the mirrors are now adjusted to be in the same plane, these two images will coincide and appear on the end-wall at C midway between A and B. Now, by imagining any point P on the end-wall in an area which receives light from both virtual images A and B, it will be seen that if P is on the B-side of C then PA will be longer than PB, but the difference becomes less the nearer P is to C. Again, this difference PA minus PB can be calculated from the known dimensions of the experimental arrangement and it can be observed that P sometimes shows a dark and sometimes a light band because the variable limits of P receive light from two sources, namely the virtual images A and B which may be in phase or out of phase on arrival at the end-wall and so may reinforce or cancel. Thus, it follows that the difference PA-PB is a measure of the half wavelength of the light. As to the velocity of light, this was determined in 1849 by Jean Leon Foucault (1819-68) working with Hippolyte Louis Fizeau (1819-96) to be about 3×10^5 kilometres per second.

7. 2. 8 Mechanical Equivalence of Heat and Unity of Electricity, Magnetism and Light
We have seen that by the end of the seventeenth century knowledge of the effects of static and dynamic force had been completed and that the latter had been applied to celestial bodies by Newton through the concept of the gravitational field. We have also seen that by the end of the

nineteenth century a unified and coherent body of knowledge on the constitution of matter and its transformations had been achieved in terms of the chemical properties and reactions of ninety-two identified elements on the basis of *Matter Conservation*, and that imponderable non-matter had given way to coherent bodies of knowledge on heat, electricity, magnetism and light, with matter being unified with heat and electricity through motion, with electricity being unified with magnetism and with light being shown to be wave-like rather than corpuscular. We are now about to see how knowledge of heat as motion led to the unification of heat and work by Carnot, Joule, Helmholtz and Thomson, how knowledge of electromagnetism was unified with light in the electromagnetic spectrum of Maxwell, and how these imponderable unifications led to the overall unification of energy as the capacity to do work and to the equivalence factors for conversion of one energy form to another on the basis of *Energy Conservation*.

Thus, Sadi Carnot (1796-1831), in his *Reflexions on the Motive Power of Fire* of 1824 defined work as "weight lifted through a certain height", showed that heat and work are equivalent and interchangeable and that the efficiency of a heat engine depends on the temperatures between which it works. In *Carnot's Cycle* (of operations) all the heat taken in by the engine enters at constant temperature T_1 from a hot body maintained at constant temperature T_1 and all the heat discharged is given out at constant temperature T_2 to a cold body maintained at a constant temperature T_2, these isothermal (no change in temperature) and adiabatic (no heat loss) operating conditions implying an ideal engine. In the first operation the working substance is compressed adiabatically until its temperature is T_1. In the second operation the working substance is allowed to expand isothermally, heat being taken in from the external source at constant temperature T_1 to the extent of Q_1 units. The third operation is to allow the working substance to expand adiabatically until the temperature has fallen to T_2. The fourth is isothermal compression of the working substance at constant temperature T_2 during which Q_2 units of heat are discharged to the external cold body until the initial conditions of pressure and volume are attained. This completes the cycle in which external work ($Q_1 - Q_2$) is done by the working substance if not dissipated as heat within the engine. If a Carnot engine is operated in reverse, the cold body loses heat equal to the quantity which it gained in the forward mode, the hot body receives a quantity of heat equal to that which it supplied in the forward mode, and the quantity of heat ($Q_1 - Q_2$) is equivalent to the external work which must be done on the working substance to drive it in reverse, in which mode the engine may be described as a heat pump.

These insights were taken forward by J. P. Joule (1818-89) who had been a pupil of John Dalton. He began by emphasising the need to establish units of measurement for the transformation of chemical activity into electricity, for the electrical generation of heat and for the transformation of heat into mechanical work. He showed that when a given amount of zinc is dissolved in acid a certain measurable amount of heat is given off. If, however, the zinc dissolves in a battery in the course of producing electricity the amount of heat available to drive an electric motor is the heat available from simple solution less the amount used up in heating the electrical circuitry and the amount of heat left to drive the motor is equivalent to the work done by the motor. His paper *On the Calorific Effects of Magneto-Electricity and on the Mechanical Value of Heat* of 1843 presents what is now called *Joule's Equivalent*, this being the amount of heat required to perform a unit of work. Thus, what is now known as the *First Law of Thermodynamics* states that heat and mechanical work are mutually convertible and that in any operation involving such conversion 4.18×10^7 units of energy or of mechanical work (ergs) are available for each unit of heat (calorie) expended. Thus, Joule's paper, *Matter, Living Force and Heat* of 1847 announced the indestructibility of his *Living Force* or Energy as we now call it, and Hermann Helmholtz (1821-94) published *Erhaltung der Kraft* (Conservation of Energy) in the same year.

Following the work of Carnot, Joule and Helmholtz, William Thomson (1824-1907) recognised that the quantity of work performed by a heat engine operating between two temperatures will be greatest when the lower of these temperatures is the lowest temperature attainable. In his paper on the *Dissipation of Energy* (1852) he considered that a series of heat engines operating in sequence over the successive temperature differences of one degree Centigrade from the boiling of water T_1 on down, would perform equal quantities of external work while successively discharging heat to the next engine in the sequence until the last engine performing that quantity of external work would be unable to discharge any heat to a further engine, having reached T_2, the lowest attainable temperature. Thus, he showed that the maximum external work (100% conversion of total input heat to available work) would be obtained at - 273° C which he called Absolute Zero, on which basis the freezing and boiling points of water become 273° A and 373° A respectively, this Absolute Zero coinciding with the zero of the gas (air) thermometer scale discussed earlier (c.f. Section 7.1.3). Such temperatures are now quoted as degrees Kelvin in memory of Thomson, later Lord Kelvin, after the river at the University of Glasgow. Thus the Carnot Cycle gave rise to the *Second Law of Thermodynamics* which states that it is impossible to transfer heat from a cold body to one at higher temperature without doing work, and that useful work cannot thus be made available.

Now, to return to Lavoisier's "imponderable" light, we start by noting that the force between two electric charges or two magnetic poles is the product of their respective magnitudes divided by the square of the distance between them; that this was initially seen to be analogous to the force of gravity between two masses at a distance; and that the electric or magnetic fields surrounding such charges or poles were initially seen as being analogous to the gravitational field envisaged by Newton. Faraday, however, believed that such a model was over-simple, not least because he had shown that moving current-bearing coils and moving magnets induced complimentary magnetic and electric fields respectively; that such varying fields might have the physical ability to push each other through otherwise empty space in some kind of wave, and that light itself might be just such a wave or *vice versa*. Though Faraday lacked the mathematical ability to proceed from there, James Clerke Maxwell (1831-1879) did not.

Though Carl Friedlich Gauss (1777-1855) and others had already proposed equations for moving-charges which seemed to comply with the earlier Newtonian-based approach, Maxwell introduced changes to these equations largely for mathematical reasons not suggested by the experimental results but consistent with them, and found that they now implied an oscillating magnetic field which induced an oscillating electric field which in turn induced an oscillating magnetic field and so on in a manner consistent with Faraday's experimental results and his own mathematical innovation. Thus, one of Maxwell's equations describes how the electric field changes with time in response to the magnetic field and electric current at any instant, while a second describes how the magnetic field is changing with time in response to the electric field at any instant, while the third describes how the electric field is related to the distribution of charges, and the fourth analogously describes the magnetic field. Now, when Maxwell used this approach to calculate the speed with which these effects would propagate through space, he found that it was the speed of light as measured experimentally by Foucault and Fizeau in 1849.

Meanwhile, it had been shown that electric charge can be built up and stored between two conductors separated by a non-conductor as in the Leyden jar (c.f. 7.2.5) and it was well known that such a 'condenser' could subsequently be discharged by contact with a conductor. However, Lord Kelvin had more recently shown by calculation that when the two parallel-plate conductors of a condenser were connected by a conductor of sufficiently low resistance, the charge did not simply disappear: it oscillated between the plates. Now, according to Maxwell's electromagnetic theory any sudden change in the electric field anywhere causes a disturbance to travel through space at the speed of light, from which it followed that the oscillatory field due to the discharge of a condenser must propagate outwards as electromagnetic oscillations. Similarly, electric currents in wires must produce such effects at wave lengths other than those of visible light, this being confirmed in 1888 when Heinrich Hertz demonstrated the existence of such (radio) waves.

Later we shall see that various individual frequency bands of James Clerke Maxwell's electromagnetic spectrum were successively established by experiment (c.f. Section 7.3.1 and 7.3.2). For now, however, we should note that while Newtonians spoke of the gravitational field, the equations of dynamics concerned bodies the existence of which was independent of the field; and that in contrast, Maxwell's equations were true field equations out of which the waves arose in association with definite amounts of energy for the calculation of which Maxwell provided an explicit mathematical expression and for the existence of which Hertz provided proof by experimentation. At this point also we should note that Maxwell demonstrates yet another aspect of the scientific method. Thus, while Newton used equations based on experimentation to provide a dynamical knowledge of planetary motion which though consistent with observation, could not be directly experimented upon, Maxwell went further with a mathematical innovation which not only provided deeper knowledge of electromagnetism than that achieved by Faraday's observations but also predicted the existence of phenomena not previously observed at all, suggested how and where such might be observed, and lo, confirmatory observations (reality-validations) were duly made which would lead to much new knowledge and practical applications (c.f. below).

7. 3 FURTHER ELUCIDATION OF MATTER AND NON-MATTER (ENERGY)

The next step is to review how the new knowledge of electricity and magnetism led to further knowledge on the nature of matter and non-matter. Readers may recall that for Berzelius, Davy and Faraday, electric currents had readily passed though water and aqueous solutions of various substances; and that the quantities released in electrolytic decomposition were related to their chemical equivalent weights and to the amounts of electricity involved. In contrast, however, it was found that gases were such poor conductors of electricity as to be classed as insulators, air, for example, requiring a potential difference of 30,000 volts for conduction to take place at atmospheric pressure. Nonetheless, this conductivity was eventually investigated by reducing gas pressure (by means of an air-pump) in glass-tubes through the ends of which electrodes were sealed and connected to an induction coil (c.f. Section 7.2.6). In such an arrangement conduction typically occurs at a pressure of around 0.03 mm of mercury with a blue glow proceeding from the cathode (negative electrode) to produce a green fluorescence on striking the tube wall, this conductivity and its associated phenomena eventually ceasing on further evacuation of the tube.

7. 3. 1 Cathode Rays: the Electron and X-rays
In 1858 Plucker showed that the direction of the above cathode emanation (named cathode rays by Goldstein in 1876) could be altered by a magnetic field and in 1869 Hittorf showed that a solid object (a Maltese cross) placed between cathode and anode or between cathode and tube-wall would cast a true shadow on the glass. Crookes in 1879 found that cathode rays impinging on the vanes of a axially suspended wheel caused rotation and similarly caused specific mineral samples to glow. Furthernore, when cathode rays were focussed on to a metal sample by means of a concave cathode, the metal could be brought to incandescence or even melted. Again in 1895

Perrin showed that cathode rays consisted of negatively charged particles by passing them into a small metal cylinder and showing that an electroscope externally connected to it accumulated negative charge or was discharged if initially positive, this being in agreement with the magnet-induced deflections observed by Plucker. In the meantime, Lenard had shown in 1894 that whatever they were, cathode rays could pass through thin sheets of metal.

Finally, in 1897 J. J. Thomson hypothesised that these negatively charged particles, named "radiant matter" by Crookes, arose from "disintegration" of the gas atoms within the conduction tube; and that these particles, being identical regardless of source-gas, must be constituents of the atoms of all the gases thus far observed. Thomson then determined the ratio of charge to mass (e : m) of these particles as being 1.2×10^7 electromagnetic units per gram by measuring deflections in their direction of travel induced by applied electric and magnetic fields. Later, more accurate determination gave 1.758×10^7 e.m.u per gram which by reference to Faraday's Laws of Electrolysis was 1,836 times the e : m for the hydrogen ion (charged hydrogen atom) suggesting that either the mass of the hydrogen ion was 1,836 times greater than the electron, the charges being numerically equal, or that the masses were equal and the charge on the electron was 1,836 times that on the hydrogen ion. As we shall see later, the negative particle is now called the electron and the positive hydrogen ion when combined with it constitutes a neutral hydrogen atom. Thus, towards the end of the nineteenth century, it was concluded that all atoms must have internal structure in that they must contain electrons, the first sub-atomic particle to be discovered.

However, before the end of the century further study of the electrical conductivity of gases was to reveal more surprises. Thus, Rontgen observed in 1895 that the glass opposite the cathode becomes brilliantly fluorescent and rays proceed outside the tube when the latter is evacuated close to the limit of its conductivity range. These rays, now called X-rays, were immediately seen to be different from cathode rays (electrons) because they passed through the glass wall of the vacuum tube (and much else besides) whereas cathode rays do not. Indeed, this penetration power increases with tube evacuation which in turn requires higher potential differences thus providing the initiating electrons with correspondingly higher energies while less highly evacuated tubes produce X-rays of lower penetrating power, the former being referred to as hard X-rays and the latter as soft. Further differences between X-rays and cathode rays are that the direction of the former are unaffected by magnetic or electric fields and that they constitute yet another band of Maxwell's electro-magnetic spectrum though their wavelengths were not immediately determined. Nonetheless, they were quickly found to differ from the visible band of this spectrum (light) in conferring electrical conductivity on gases through which they pass, in fogging photographic plates even when wrapped in black paper, and in passing through soft-tissue more readily than through bone.

7. 3. 2 Radioactivity and the Electromagnetic Spectrum

In 1896 Becquerel having placed several samples of phosphorescent salts of uranium on photographic plates double-wrapped in black paper in a drawer in the absence of light for about 24 hours, found on development that silhouettes of the samples appeared on the plates. Although Niepce had observed the same phenomenon some thirty years earlier and G. le Bon in 1896 had called the responsible radiations "lumière noire", they came to be known as Becquerel rays and the emitting substances as radioactive. In 1898 Madame Curie and G.C. Schmidt independently found that thorium was similarly radioactive and on subsequently finding that a number of uranium minerals were more radioactive than could be explained by their uranium-contents, Madame Curie isolated a new radio-element to which the name radium was given. Though we shall see in Section 9.1 how these new radiations provided deeper knowledge of the Periodic Table and the electromagnetic spectrum, I now review the latter as it was known by the end of the century.

208

Readers will know that Newton had passed a beam of light through a glass prism to reveal its constituent colours by refraction. Though a single prism produces a relatively compressed spectrum, this can be expanded into a long ribbon of colour by successive passage through a train of prisms or by passage through a prism-shaped bottle containing the highly refractive carbon disulphide. When this is done it can clearly be seen that the colours change from a dull red at one end to a brighter red followed by orange, yellow, green, green-blue, blue and violet towards the other, the intensity falling gradually from its greatest level in the yellow band. In addition, while the heating effects of the different coloured bands can be distinguished by measuring temperature along the spectrum, the greatest heating effect is detected in the dark space just beyond the red end, known as the infrared. If, on the other hand, the spectrum is allowed to fall on a sensitive photographic plate, subsequent development shows the greatest image intensity to be beyond the violet end, known as the ultra-violet. Thus, Maxwell's electromagnetic spectrum was shown to extend beyond the region to which the human eye is sensitive.

Now, while bodies at ordinary temperatures do not emit radiations which affect the eye, temperature-rise can cause a solid body to emit a dull red colour at about 700° C as its radiation reaches the red end of the visible spectrum, when it is said to be red-hot. If its temperature continues to rise its radiation extends progressively through the successive bands of the visible spectrum until it emits all of them, when it is said to be white-hot and to present a continuous spectrum. In contrast, the spectra of gases and vapours when hot enough to be visibly luminous, consist of lines or short bands, and it is additionally found that any vapour absorbs at any temperature that part of the visible spectrum which it emits when at higher temperatures. Thus a continuous spectrum passed through a vapour exhibits dark (absorption) lines characteristic of the elemental constituents of the vapour, and these correspond to the bright line spectra of these elements when emitting at higher temperatures, phenomena which provide powerful means for identification of individual chemical elements as was recognised in 1859 by G. R. Kirchhoff (1824-1887) and R. W. Bunsen (1811-99)

The story had begun in 1802 when W. H. Wollaston (1766-1828) observed dark lines across the coloured band of the solar spectrum by coupling a prism with a telescope, continued in 1814 when Joseph Fraunhoffer (1787-1826) showed that dark (Fraunhoffer) lines always appeared in the same positions and led Kirchhoff and Bunsen to discover two new elements, caesium and rubidium in the laboratory and Kirchhoff to identify a large number of elements in the Sun. These solar observations arise from the white light emitted by the extremely hot outer shell of the Sun (the photosphere) being absorbed at wavelengths (dark lines) characteristic of the elements present in its cooler and surrounding chromo-sphere through which the light passes on its way to observers on earth. During the eclipse of 1869 such analysis revealed the presence of an element not detected on Earth until 1896 and named helium.

Thus, having elucidated matter, non-matter and their inter-relationships by reality-evaluations of a series of hypotheses from around 1700, the scientific method closed the nineteenth century by revealing new relationships between atoms and radiation and by extending our physicochemical knowledge beyond our Earthly confines.

7. 4 CONCLUSIONS

Following the achievements of Galileo, Huygens and Newton in elucidating the nature of force, mass and acceleration, attention turned to the elucidation of substance (matter) by means of measuring weight changes associated with the reaction of one substance with another in what became known as chemistry. Thus, it was shown that all natural substance could be understood in terms of ninety-two basic elements each of which consisted only of atoms of the element; that these atoms combined together in simple ratios into molecular compounds; that these in turn could exist as either gases, liquids or solids depending on the strength of their inter-molecular attractions as a function of temperature; that the concept of atoms was further supported by measurements of equivalent weight, atomic weight, molecular weight and valence of the respective elements, all of which were consistently summarised in the Periodic Table of the Elements on the basis of their atomic weights and interactive properties.   In addition, the postulated existence of atoms in otherwise empty space was shown to be consistent with the expandability and compressibility of gases, with gases, liquids and solids being inter-dissolvable without volume-increase, and with gas partial pressures and solvent/solute osmotic pressures being due to the movement of molecules and ions.

As to the non-material and weightless, it was found that heat and heat capacities could be measured by the method of mixtures having defined the calorie as the amount which would raise the temperature of one gram of water by $1°$ C, having defined temperature in terms of expansion and contraction in gases or liquids, having calibrated temperature scales between ice/water and water/steam transitions and having defined the heat capacity of water as unity. It was also found that heat is the motion of atoms and molecules; and that heat thus being kinetic energy is capable of doing useful work for which the conversion factor for the mechanical equivalence of heat was quantified. Again, it was shown that electricity was produced by chemical reactions and could cause chemical reactions when flowing through aqueous solutions wherein it was carried by dissociated and moving charged particles (ions); that electricity was also produced by the movement of metallic conductors in magnetic fields; that light consisted of electromagnetic waves rather than particles; that it extended beyond the visible to the infrared and ultraviolet and was extendable by induced vibration of electric charge to produce the radio waveband; and that all of the 'imponderables' were interchangeable forms of energy. Yet again, it was shown that spectroscopic analysis of electromagnetic radiation could identify emitting/absorbing elements even in the Sun without recourse to their chemical properties; that electrical conductivity in gases revealed the sub-atomic electron 1,836 times smaller than the hydrogen atom; that these electrons explained electrical conductivity in metallic conductors and electrolyte solutions; that when impinging on metal targets they produced electromagnetic X-rays; that these could pass through matter opaque to visible light; and that other penetrating rays were emitted by radioactive minerals.

Thus, given our progress in craftsmanship from time immemorial and in science from 1600-1900 (c.f. Chapters 2 -7) there can be no gainsaying the success of our Rational Trinity especially when compared with the failure of our Rational Duality to produce anything other than disruption, revolution and war (c.f. Chapter 4 and Section 6. 4) and more especially when we recognise that the Rational Trinity is also the source of the social cohesion required for such success even in periods otherwise dominated by Rational Duality mayhem, a feature of our history to which I return in chapters 10, 11 and 12. Meanwhile, I review how physicochemical science (c.f. Chapters 5, 6 and 7) transformed craftsmanship to technology while providing deeper insights to otherwise descriptive science.

CHAPTER 8: CRAFTSMANSHIP, TECHNOLOGY AND OTHER SCIENCES, 1700-1900

Having shown that craftsmanship gained little or nothing from non-craft knowledge prior to about 1700 (c.f. Section 5.7), I now show how physicochemical knowledge transformed craftsmanship to technology and provided a physicochemical basis for otherwise descriptive sciences while continuing to be ignored by philosophers still in thrall to the Ur-belief in rationality undeterred by on-going socio-political confusion and violence, though for a brief period they appeared to accept the impossibility of acquiring knowledge by rationality alone before abandoning knowledge for postmodernism (c.f. section 10.8).

However, in anticipation of wider benefits from early knowledge and speculation, facilitating societies had arisen prior to 1700. Indeed, successors of the *Brethren of Sincerity* founded in Islamic Sicily around 983 were the *Accademia Secretorium Naturae* (Naples 1560), the *Accademia Lincei* in 1603 and the *Accademia del Chimento* in 1657, this last attracting Medici support as the centre of knowledge moved to the north where such as Galileo, Torricelli and Borelli were active. As to northern Europe, *The Royal Society* was founded in 1660 under the patronage of Charles II followed by the *Paris Academy of Sciences* in 1666 and the German *Societas Regias Scientiarum* in 1770 while the Courts of Sweden, Denmark and Hungary were similarly encouraging. In contrast, there were no comparable developments in Spain where the focus was on importing wealth from the Americas and in exporting the Faith. However, academic recognition of science generally remained weak with Oxford and Cambridge virtually ignoring other than mathematics, with many Royal Society Fellows being self-improved craftsmen, and with Harvard having been founded solely as a liberal arts centre as late as 1636.

However, despite the desire of some scientists for socio-political recognition, knowledge is generally unwelcome in belief-based socio-politics, opportunities for its insertion being fewer than naivety expects. Against this background, I now review how physicochemical science transformed craftsmanship to technology, created new technologies, provided deeper insights to descriptive sciences and created new sciences while the political establishment was limited to a facilitating role prior to its now active collusion in the corruption of scientific knowledge and method in defence of the beliefs of so-called liberal democracy (c.f. Chapters 10, 11 and 12).

8. 1 CRAFTSMANSHIP AND TECHNOLOGY

Having previously shown that craftsmanship arose from the conversion of belief to knowledge through reality-validation in respect of tool making and artefact production, and that experimentation evolved from it to produce knowledge of the physical world at a deeper level than was available to craftsmen, I now review the extent to which such deeper knowledge helped craftsmen in ways not otherwise open to them, and the extent to which they achieved their objectives through their own efforts in any case. To these ends I consider steam-power and internal combustion; electricity generation and storage; marine technology; road, rail and air transport; agriculture and food preservation; textiles, porcelain and mass production; mining, tunnelling and canal excavation; mineral processing, metal extraction, iron, steel and machine tools; new metals, alloys and coatings; coal, gas, oil and chemicals; electricity transmission, water and sewage treatment; printing, telecommunications, entertainment and recreation. In all of the above fields, readers should note how opportunity led to fulfilment through the Rational Trinity, the degree to which the progress we now take for granted derived from private enterprise rather than from government involvement, and the extent to which it was completed prior to 1900.

8. 1. 1 Steam Power

Torricelli having demonstrated that the atmosphere exerts pressure consequent on air having weight, the attention of craftsmen turned to harnessing this pressure to perform useful work by alternating it with a vacuum (or partial vacuum) to move a piston in a cylinder, the mechanistic means of transmitting this motion to the work-point having long been known (c. f. Sections 2.3.5 and 5.7.3). Thus, while Huygens suggested in 1680 that the detonation of gunpowder beneath a piston would drive it upwards for atmosphere pressure to drive it down again as the gaseous products cooled and contracted in volume, his assistant Denis Papin proposed the sequential evaporation and condensation of water to produce volume and pressure changes of 13,000 : 1, and in 1690 he sought to apply external heat to evaporate sufficient water to push a piston to the top of its cylinder against the atmospheric pressure which on external cooling would return it to the cylinder bottom . . . and so on. Alas, having been defeated by the difficulty of fitting piston to cylinder closely enough, he turned to the simpler task of developing his digester (pressure-cooker with no moving parts) knowing (Torricelli again) that boiling point increases and decreases with pressure. Thus, by containing the steam to attain water temperatures above 100° C he decreased cooking times in a device later used as a sterilizer (c.f. Section 8.2.6).

This left Thomas Savery to take out a patent in 1698 for the first practical steam-driven device for draining mines, supplying water to towns and powering mills. In this device, steam pressure pushed water up a pipe to be retained above a valve when closed, the steam in the lower pipe being condensed to create a vacuum so that atmospheric pressure could push water into the foot of the pipe to be lifted in turn by a new charge of steam when the valve was re-opened, and so on. Thus, by means of appropriate valve-control a single boiler could operate two vertical pipes, one discharing water upwards while the other filled from below. Such a system overcame the 34 foot lift-limit provided the steam pressure was greater than atmospheric. At risk of boiler explosions, Savery achieved pressures of 3 atmospheres and thus with his 'piston-less' pump situated about 30 feet above the surface of the water to be pumped he could deliver a total lift of about 120 feet and though horsepower rating would only later be introduced by Watt (c.f. below) we know that Savery achieved about 1horsepower.

Subsequently, Thomas Newcommen succeeded with the Papin-type cylinder and piston, the latter linked to a centrally-pivoted beam in order to transmit the motion to other machinery such as a pump. Steam was admitted with the piston at its lowest point to force it and its associated beam-end to rise and the other end to descend. A spray of cold water then condensed the steam in the cylinder causing the piston and associated beam-end to fall under atmospheric pressure, the far end to rise, and so on. However, because of patent difficulties with Savery, it was 1712 before Newcommen's first beam engine was built, installed and operated at 12 strokes per minute to deliver just over 5 horsepower for mine drainage at Dudley Castle, Worcestershire. Though his cylinders were cast, the precision-boring limit being 7 inch diameter for cannon barrels, he solved Papin's problem by sealing the top of his pistons with a leather disc covered with a layer of water. Thus equipped for steam retention, Newcommen's engines were widely used in the tin mines of Cornwall and in coal mines elsewhere in Britain, and by his death in 1729 they were in use in

France, Belgium, Hungary and elsewhere in Europe. By 1730 cast-cylinders of 29 x 108 inches were in demand and by 1765 this had risen to 74 x 126 inches. At such sizes a steam-tight fit between cylinder and piston could not be achieved and even in the nineteenth century tolerances of 'a bare sixteenth' of an inch or 'a full thirty-second' were the best achievable.

Thus, apart from the initial scientific work of Torricelli, practical steam engines were entirely due to craftsmen. It was not until 1763 that science once again lent a hand when Joseph Black explained his work on latent heat to James Watt, his instrument maker. This led the latter to avoid cooling the cylinder and piston at each stroke by introducing his small separate condenser thus increasing the thermal efficiency of the Newcommen engine by a factor of three. Watt then entered into partnership with the craftsman Matthew Boulton at his works near Birmingham and the firm Boulton & Watt thereafter produced some 500 engines while enjoying a 25-year extension of Watt's original patent of 1769. The next improvement was again craft-based when in 1770 John Smeaton, who had ten years earlier built the Eddystone lighthouse, developed a new boring machine which improved the fit between cylinder and piston and almost doubled the performance of beam engines. One of Smeaton's engines with a two meter cylinder was installed for pumping water from the dry-docks at Kronstadt, while Watt's engine was again craft-improved by making both the downward and upward strokes deliver power (double-acting); by admitting steam early in the piston's motion for its expansive force to complete the stroke; by converting the reciprocal beam motion into rotary motion for which Watt crafted his sun-and-planet gearing, the more obvious crank-shaft solution being closed to him by patent; and by introducing in 1787 his centrifugal governor for maintenance of constant speed under varying load.

Despite Savery's boiler explosions, high pressure steam was attractive for its higher power : weight ratio and lower fuel consumption, benefits first realised in practice by Richard Trevithic who used steam at ten atmospheres pressure at Coalbrookdale in 1802 with a boiler-casing 1.5 inches thick, a cylinder of only 7 inch diameter and a piston-stroke of only 3 feet. Such were the benefits of this advance, that Trevithic built fifty high pressure engines within two years while from 1803 onwards Arthur Woolf increased the efficiency of the Watt engine by 'compounding' it with high-pressure and low-pressure cylinders and in 1845 John McNaught introduced a short stroke with his high-pressure cylinder. In the meantime, the use of vertical pistons to ensure even wear was seen to be unnecessary and horizontal pistons became increasingly common from 1825 onwards.

The first Newcommen engine having been imported to North America in 1753 to drain a copper mine at Newark, New Jersey, the total number in America was still only about half a dozen when at the end of the century a major step-change was brought about by the craftsman Oliver Evans who between 1804 and his death in 1819 built some 50 engines based on a double-acting cylinder of 6 inch diameter and 8 inch stroke operating at about 8 atmospheres pressure and running at 30 r.p.m. Evans also reduced the size of the beam by placing his cylinder and crank-shaft under the same end of his beam, with a new straight-line linkage for the upper end of the piston, rather than having effort and load at opposite ends as was customary. Evans was a contemporary of Trevithic and by then there was almost a century of British experience in steam engine design, building and operation. Nonetheless, it was Evans's work which Olinthus Gregory, mathematics teacher at Woolwich, chose to describe in his *Treatise on Mechanics* of 1807. Evans's achievement is an example of 'technological catch-up' and provides an early illustration of the difficulty of maintaining a lead in technological fields.

As we have seen, the next scientific input occurred in 1824 with the publication by Sadi Carnot of his theoretical work on heat engines though this had to await the fuller exposition by William Thomson (Lord Kelvin) in 1849 before its value was recognised. In the meantime, the craftsman and his products carried on with beam engines working at about 3 atmospheres pressure continuing to be built up to the end of the nineteenth century and with some continuing in use well into the twentieth. In the meantime, however, machine tools were developing to make machine parts with ever increasing precision at acceptable price and with a tolerance of one thousanth of an inch being attained by the end of the nineteenth century. Thus, by the latter half of the century British engines were developing up to 180 horsepower at rather less than 100 rpm while American engines ran at higher speeds particularly when applied to the task of driving dynamos (c.f. Section 8.1.3). Again, from 1863 engines of 168 horsepower and 350 rpm were being built in Philadelphia and later in England under licence and by the end of the century engines of nearly 3,000 horsepower were available. Thus by a combination of craftsmanship and some scientific input over a period of some two hundred years the early engine had progressively increased in power output, its thermal efficiency having improved from 0.5% to over 20% for the big triple-expansion marine engines which were about as far as the steam engine as such could be developed.

Though the steam turbine had first been demonstrated by Hero of Alexandria in the first century AD with his rotating sphere driven by the reaction of steam escaping through equatorially tangential jets, it was not until 1629 that Giovanni Branca conversely rotated a wheel by causing steam-jets to impinge on vanes attached to its circumference. Again, Trevithic reverted more closely to Hero in causing steam at 7 atmospheres pressure to escape from the ends of a 15-foot tube pivoted at its mid-point to produce his 'whirling engine'. However, it was only when the demands of the electricity generating industry could no longer be satisfied even by the 1,000 rpm reciprocating engines (produced by Peter Brotherhood from about 1870) that serious attention was given to the need for higher rpm. To satisfy this requirement, Charles Parson's first steam turbine of 1884 achieved 18,000 rpm. This unit consisted of a stationary outer casing fitted with internal vanes and an inner co-axial rotor carrying vanes alternate with those on the stator so that vane interaction with axially admitted high pressure steam would cause rapid rotation of the rotor. Though between 1889 and 1893 he had to adopt the alternative approach of radial steam flow because of patent difficulties, he subsequently reverted to axial flow in 1897 for his turbine powered launch Turbinia which achieved the then astonishing speed of 34.5 knots at the Spithead Naval Review while his two 1500 kilowatt turbo-generators for Elberfeld where the biggest in the world in 1901.

8. 1. 2 Internal Combustion Engines

In spite of such successes there were those who remembered the pre-steam efforts of Huygens and sought alternatives to gunpowder. Thus, in 1794 Robert Street lodged a patent for a piston engine to be fuelled by gas derived from oil-tar or turpentine with flame ignition internal to the cylinder, while Phillipe Lebon pioneer of the coal-gas industry (c.f. Section 8.1.11) filed a patent for a double acting coal-gas engine with cylinder ignition by means of Volta's battery of the previous year. Again, coal-gas having meanwhile become cheaply and widely available, Etienne Lenoir implemented its use in 1859 though with a poor power : weight ratio. However, this was significantly improved by 1862 when Alphonse Beau de Rochas compressed the gas/air mixture before ignition, an innovation taken up by Nikolaus August Otto and Eugen Langen who went on to win the gold medal for their gas engine at the Paris Exhibition in 1867. Though such progress was encouraging, these internal combustion engines were all Newcommen-type atmospheric engines in which the explosion of the gas/air mixture drove the piston upwards to be pushed down again by atmospheric pressure when the explosion-products decreased in volume on cooling.

The big break-through came when Otto announced his four-stroke cycle in 1876. The first piston stroke drew the explosive-mixture into the cylinder, the second compressed it and just at the
214

start of the third the mixture was ignited, the explosion driving the piston to complete the third (power) stroke, and the fourth (exhaust) stroke expelled the combustion products from the cylinder. Once the cycle of strokes was established by spinning the associated fly-wheel to achieve the initial power stroke, it was maintained by successive power strokes with the spinning fly-wheel also smoothing the delivery of power there being only one power stroke in four, compared with every stroke being a power-stroke in the double-acting Watt engine. It is now accepted that Otto had conceived this cycle independently, but his patent of 1876 was invalidated in 1886 on the grounds that Beau de Rochas had described it earlier. The original Otto-Langen atmospheric gas engine was manufactured under licence (1869) by Crossley Brothers of Manchester who between 1869 and 1900 had sold some 40,000 and by 1900 there were some 200,000 gas engines in use, the majority being in Germany, Britain and America.

The next step was to make Otto's four stroke gas engine independent of its fixed fuel source and thus provide a freely mobile power source and, indeed, one which might be self-propelled. In 1869 Otto took charge of the business side of gas engine production and exploitation leaving Langen to concentrate on the development and engineering side with Gottlieb Daimler and Wilhem Maybach as assistants. Initially they considered the use of bottled gas and a working system was introduced in 1871 to supply electric lighting on German railway carriages, but the weight of the equipment and the difficulties of supply and transportation precluded the wider use of this approach. Attention turned to alcohol, ether, and finally to petrol (gasoline) which at that time was an unwanted (and therefore cheap and readily available) product of the growing petroleum industry (c.f. Section 8.1.11). It should be noted that all of these gas and petrol based developments are examples of waste recycling.

Maybach had already run a stationary gas engine on petrol vapour before 1882 when Daimler left Otto and Langen taking Maybach with him to set up on their own. Though initially the petrol vapour/air mixture was supplied by drawing air over liquid petrol, a float-feed carburettor which injected a fine spray of petrol into the air-stream had been devised by Maybach by 1893. This brought mobile power sources a bit closer to realisation though problems arose with ignition at the 600-900 rpm engine-speeds envisaged for road-vehicle applications. In response, Daimler and Maybach inserted into the cylinder a tube kept permanently hot by an external petrol-fuelled flame while Karl Benz re-visited the work of Lenoir and in 1885 introduced electric-spark ignition based on a chargeable accumulator (c.f. Section 8.1.3) for his slower running engine. Again, though Benz also used a surface-evaporation carburettor, his engine's slower running speed made it inferior to that of Daimler and Maybach. In any case, neither the latter's V-type two-cylinder petrol engine car nor one by Benz caused much excitement when exhibited at the Paris Exhibition of 1889. Meanwhile, Britain made no notable contribution to automotive engineering until the carburettor of Frederick W. Lanchester drew air over wicks fed from a petrol reservoir in 1897.

The above account shows that the development of heat-engines owed more to craftsmen than to scientists and illustrates the craftsman's imaginative power to recognise requirement and opportunity and to produce hypotheses for reality-evaluation to these ends from time immemorial without any external assistance. Viewed from this angle, it is unsurprising that scientific knowledge of the nature of the world would be slow to assist the craftsman's use of the world given the recent derivation of scientific method from the craftsman's long-established method in any case. In thus establishing the predominance of craftsmanship over science it should for example be noted that Thomas Newcommen and Oliver Evans had been ironmonger and wainwright apprentices respectively; that James Watt (though advised by Joseph Black) was an instrument maker and the son of a carpenter; and that his partner Matthew Boulton was a buckle-maker. As to the role of formal education, we should note that foreign efforts to 'catch-up' with Britain included establishment of the Ecole Central in Paris; Polytechnic Schools in Germany, Holland and Switzerland, and the founding of land-grant colleges in the USA from 1862 onwards and of the Massachusetts Institute of Technology (MIT) in 1865 some 200 years after Harvard University of the Liberal Arts. However, while Daimler and Benz had certainly attended the Technische Hochschule in Stuttgart and Karlsruhe respectively and while it is customary to argue that Britain's failure to maintain its early lead was due to not having established its own technical college programme until 1889, reasons for our subsequent decline other than a shortage of technical college places or of university places for that matter should be sought, given that it is impossible to stay ahead just by being ahead when at any time others can emulate and surpass as Oliver Evans had done without formal education or even prior training beyond the building of horse-drawn carts (c.f. Sections 11.2.3) .

Thus, it is with Rudolph Diesel (1858-1913) who attended the Hochschule in Munich that we first see a relationship between formal education and industrial innovation in the one individual. In Munich, Diesel studied thermodynamics under Carl von Linde now known for his work on the liquifaction of air; went on to Paris in 1880 when the significance of Carnot's cycle for the efficiency of heat-engines was at last being recognised; and published *The Theory and Design of a Rational Heat Engine* in 1893, though note his misuse of 'rational'. This described the three innovations on which his new engine was based and patented prior to his building it. His first innovation was to compress air alone (not the air/fuel mixture) so highly in the compression stroke that its temperature rose sufficiently for spontaneous ignition of the fuel when it was injected into the cylinder, thus dispensing with the need for a separate ignition system. The second innovation was that combustion took place at constant pressure as the piston moved down in the power stroke, this being more efficient thermodynamically than in the Otto cycle where it takes place at constant volume at the beginning of the power stoke. The third innovation was that a less volatile and therefore safer fuel was used. The new engine attracted considerable attention when exhibited at the Munich Exhibition of 1898, though at that stage it had the disadvantage of running less smoothly than its petrol alternate and being necessarily of heavier construction was more suited to stationary than to vehicular installation.

8. 1. 3 Electricity Storage and Generation

Readers will recall that Alessandro Volta had shown in 1800 that discs of dissimilar metals such as zinc, silver or copper separated by brine-soaked felt produced an electric current and that this system became known as a voltaic pile. Later, in 1886 George Leclanche produced electric current when zinc and carbon rods were placed in a solution of ammonium chloride which in the twentieth century gave rise to the dry-cell battery of everyday use. Such systems produce direct current spontaneously as a consequence of internal chemical reaction but become exhausted when the chemical reaction is completed in use. They are known as primary batteries. However, as early as 1803 secondary batteries were devised in which completed electricity-producing chemical reactions could be reversed by subsequently passing direct current through the battery to re-charge it. Because such devices stored electricity supplied from elsewhere they became known as accumulators and in 1860 Gaston Plante devised the lead-acid accumulator which is still in use, single cells of which give about 2 volts with higher voltages being available from series connection.

However, the non-chemical generation of electricity by Michael Faraday in 1831 almost immediately led to the building of electricity generators on the principle of a coil of wire rotating between the poles of a permanent magnet (c.f. Section 7.2.6) one such being demonstrated to the *Academie des Sciences* in Paris by Hyppolyte Pixii as early as 1832. Improvements were then

216

made by replacing the permanent magnets by electromagnets activated by batteries, and by 1886 Cromwell F.Varley had patented self-excitation by which the electricity for the magnets was provided by the generator itself. By then multiple coils had replaced the single coil in what became known as an armature so that a fairly steady voltage was delivered. Electricity could now be produced at will by coupling the dynamo to a suitable engine to spin the armature in the field provided by the electromagnets, this having produced the need for high speed prime-movers which encouraged the development of steam turbines as noted above.

Although waterwheels are of great antiquity, Claude Burdin (1790-1873) was still giving a course on them as professor at the St Etienne School of Mines when he coined the word turbine to decribe a system in which rotation was produced by a radial outward flow of water from a vertical-axis rotor. One of his students, Benoit Fourneyron sequentially constructed a 6-horsepower and a 50-horsepower turbine on this principle to work on a water pressure of 100 metres at rates upwards of 2000 rpm. Such turbines being suitable for dynamo-generated electricity were installed in the Niagara Falls hydroelectric plant by the end of the century. However, for the slow-flowing rivers of Europe the axial flow turbine, in which the waterflow and rotor were horizontal, was more suitable and such a device was introduced by N. J. Jonval in 1841 while from 1850 such were also used in America. A third type in which the water flowed radially inwards was described in 1826 by Jean Victor Poncelet. Though never built in France, a few were built in New England by Samuel Howd from 1838 onwards, while in Massachusetts James Francis combined both radial and axial flow in what became known as the mixed-flow turbine.

Again, as already noted, the late arriving wind-mill was progressively developed from manual to automatic orientation of sails to wind-direction by around 1850, with iron being substituted for wood particularly for gear wheels, and with diversification of use beyond flour-mills and water-pumps to wood-saws, trip-hammers and manufacturing machinery of various kinds. Nevertheless, the unreliability of wind as a power source was recognised as a serious disadvantage except where storage of product could off-set intermittent operation. Since electricity cannot be adequately stored because of the limited cost-effectiveness of accumulators, no attempt was made to drive dynamos with wind driven turbines their intermittency disadvantage already having been overcome by steam and water turbines. It was concluded therefore that power extraction from wind had been terminated by its intermittency at the applications previously described (c.f. Section 5.7.3) though this conclusion is now being ignored (c.f. Section 9.5.1).

8. 1. 4 Marine Technology and Canal Building

The determination of longitude at sea was still a pressing problem in 1675 when the Royal Observatory was established at Greenwich and the first Astronomer Royal John Flamstead proposed the preparation of lunar position tables which would solve the problem by observation of the Moon's position with respect to a fixed star as an alternative to comparing local time with reference meridian time now taken as that of Greenwich. As to the latter alternative, the sailor could determine local noon *i.e.* the time of highest Sun altitude as observed locally with the type of instrument already in use for determination of latitude (c.f. Section 5.7.2) but to determine the time difference between this and noon at Greenwich he would need a clock which would continue to keep Greenwich time throughout his voyage. Thus, with such a clock at the unknown position showing Greenwich time, the sailor could read the time at which he observed the Sun to be at its highest altitude knowing that every hour of difference before or after that local noon-time equates to 15° east or west of Greenwich respectively and *pro rata* for fractions of an hour. The problem with this second approach was building a clock of sufficient accuracy, the earliest clocks having had insufficient accuracy to require a minute hand and though Huygens had improved the accuracy of pendulum clocks such would be useless at sea. This problem was considered so intractable, both mathematically and mechanically that the *Board of Longitude* established in 1714 was authorised to award a prize of £20,000 for a proven practical solution.

Though the lunar approach had proved even more complex and difficult than initially expected, the lunar distance tables of the German mathematician, astronomer and map maker Tobias Mayer were evaluated by observations conducted at Greenwich by the third Astronomer Royal, James Bradley and were used by the Reverend Neville Maskelyne later to become the fifth Astronomer Royal to determine longitude during a voyage to St. Helena in 1761. In the end, however, craftsmanship triumphed over the mathematical approach when in 1760 John Harrison won the prize after submission of a series of developments based on the spring and balance wheel approach. These were his H-1 to H-4 of 1737, 1741, 1759 and 1760 respectively though it required the intervention of George III to overcome the personal interests of his mathematical and more influential competitors before Harrison actually received the prize.

Though ships had been propelled by sail and built of wood, attention now turned to steam propulsion and other construction materials. The former was first demonstrated on the River Saone in 1789 with the 185 tonne *Pyroscaphe* and four years later the 50 foot stern-wheeler *John Fitch* (named after its originator) steamed on the Delaware at Philadelphia powered by an engine by Henry Voight a local clock-maker. Meanwhile in Scotland in 1788, Patrick Miller had increased the speed of his manually driven paddle-wheeled experimental catamaran to 4 knots by a Watt type steam engine installed by William Symington. Impressed by this success, the Secretary of State (and governor of the Forth and Clyde Canal) Lord Dundas commissioned Symington to build a steam tugboat for use on the canal. This wooden *Charlotte Dundas* of 1802 was a 58 foot stern-wheeler powered by a 12 horsepower single cylinder engine. She is generally considered the first successful steamboat though withdrawn after a month of regular use because her wash was damaging the canal banks. In turn, the American Robert Fulton was sufficiently impressed by the *Charlotte Dundas* to install in 1807 a Boulton and Watt engine on the 100 tonne side-paddle *Clermont* with which he achieved immediate commercial success on the Hudson River. After two seasons Fulton ordered a sister ship *Phoenix* to be built in Hoboken, the 100 mile delivery of which to the mouth of the Delaware made her the first steam ship to make an open sea passage though in the next few years regular short-haul steamship services were established on numerous routes such as Glasgow-Fort William, Brighton-Le Havre and London-Leith. In 1819 the American full-rigged ship *Savannah* which could lift her side-paddles clear of the sea when not in use, crossed the Atlantic in 27 days 11 hours though her paddles were used for only 85 hours in total, while in 1825 the British ship *Enterprise* reached Calcutta in 103 days of which her engine had been used on more than half.

Although these were sailing ships with auxiliary engines, the 1,300 tonne *Great Western* was a steamship with auxiliary sails when she inaugurated in 1833 the Great Western Railway Company's regular Bristol-New York service, to which the British and American Steam Navigation Company responded with the even larger *British Queen*. However, delivery having been delayed, they chartered the *Sirius* which thus became the first ship to cross the Atlantic under steam alone arriving in New York from Cork with almost empty bunkers while the *Great Western* later arrived from Bristol with more than 200 tonnes to spare. Side-paddle effectiveness being reduced by variation in immersion-depth in the presence of waves, the centre-line screw was introduced as far below the ship's waterline as possible though a practical demonstration of the benefits of the latter was not achieved until 1838 when the Swede John Ericsson was so successful with his installation on the *Archimedes* as to cause Isambard Kingdom Brunel to change his 4,000 tonne *Great Britain* from paddle to screw during its construction. In 1845 the overall superiority of the screw was convincingly demonstrated when the screw frigate *Rattle* towed the otherwise identical paddle frigate *Alecto* backwards at a speed of nearly 3 knots. Nonetheless, Brunel's 19,000 tonne *Great Eastern* of 1854, five times bigger than any other ship afloat, was equipped for both screw and paddle propulsion to carry 4,000 passengers on the Australia *via* India run. However her fuel-consumption having been seriously under-estimated, she was relegated to the Atlantic service and was further demoted to telegraph-cable laying, transatlantic in 1865 and Aden to Bombay later. However, this lack of commercial success prompted development of the triple-expansion steam engine, the Parsons steam turbine and the diesel propulsion units which entered marine service before 1900.

As to alternatives to wood for construction, John Wikinson had launched a 70 foot iron barge on the Severn in 1787 while the first iron steamship crossed the English Channel in 1825 and the 60 foot *Codorus* was the first iron vessel launched in the USA. The size of wooden ships having been constrained by the natural dimensions of trees, iron was initially used in similarly short lengths in compliance with traditional construction methods, its greater resistance to hull-hogging and sagging not being fully utilised until the middle of the nineteenth century when main frame members were available in single rolled or cast pieces and standard-size skin-plating was being fastened by red-hot riveting. In addition, from the 1850s steel was available on request and by 1890 its replacement of iron was almost complete and hand-hammer riveting had become pneumatic by the end of the century.

Canals having been used to move heavy goods from earliest times, a 4,000 mile network of canals had been constructed in Britain by 1831 following the opening of the Sankey-Warrington canal in 1757. Meanwhile the Erie Canal Project to link Albany on the Hudson with Buffalo and Lake Erie was completed in 1825. Earlier in France the Canal du Midi between La Manche and the Mediterranean had been completed in 1681 followed by the canal linkages of the Somme, Oise and Seine to the Marne, Rhone and Rhine, all of which were in place by 1881 while within Germany the Dortmund-Ems canal was completed in 1899. In addition, to satisfy world-trade requirements for the passage of heavy freight and passengers, the Suez Canal had been opened in 1869 and the Panama Canal project was started in 1881 though not completed until 1914.

8. 1. 5 Road, Rail and Air Transport

Because of the low power : weight ratio of steam engines it was 1769 before the first steam traction unit appeared on the road, this being an innovation of the French military engineer Nicolas Cugnot at the behest of Jean-Baptiste Gribeauval, a general of artillery. In this unit the power of a two-cylinder high-pressure steam engine was transmitted to a single front wheel by a crank mechanism to tow a 3-tonne canon at walking speed. However, having started in 1785 it was 1802 before Isaac de Rivaz had a steam carriage on the road in Switzerland though Oliver Evans had driven on the streets of Philadelphia in 1800. Again, William Murdoch designed a steam carriage which James Watt patented in 1784 though Murdoch made only a working model in 1786, Boulton & Watt being focussed on stationary engines while Richard Trevithic achieved 8 mph in 1801. However, there was a regular London-Birmingham service by 1833 and by 1838 Sir Goldsworthy Gurney's service between Gloucester and Cheltenham was covering the 9 miles in 45 minutes. Also in 1838, a London omnibus service which lasted for 5 years was inaugurated by Thomas Hancock pioneer of the rubber industry. However, further UK development was discouraged by the Red Flag Act of 1865 which restricted the speed of mechanical road vehicles to 4 mph. (3 mph. in towns) and demanded an additional crew member to proceed the vehicle with the said flag. In France, *au contraire*, development continued with Leon Serpollet introducing his red-hot steel piped flash boiler to raise steam more quickly, driving a steam tricycle so-equipped from Paris to Lyons in 1887 and achieving a speed of 80 mph on pneumatic tyres by 1903. Again at the century's turn, the Stanley brothers of Newton, Mass., introduced their 'Stanley Steamer' though by then the future was internal combustion.

However, this growing interest in road vehicles drew attention to the poor state of the roads concerning which a notable pioneer was Thomas Telford, road, bridge and canal builder, whose stone bed and cambered surface directing rainwater to a system of lateral ditches and cross drains was widely adopted after it greatly improved the Glasgow-Carlisle road for which Parliament had voted £50,000 in 1814. Again, though wooden railways had smoothed the way from earliest times, their lack of durability finally caused their replacement by iron rails at Whitehaven Colliery in 1738, a replacement which spread quickly when Abraham Darby began casting iron rails at Coalbrookdale. One such 10-mile installation linked the Pen-y-Daran ironworks with the Glamorgan Canal and Trevithic who had installed a stationary steam engine to drive the rolling-mill there in 1803 now used it as a locomotive to pull five wagons of 10 tonne capacity on these rails at 5 mph in 1804. Cast-iron rails having proved inadequate for this task, however, the engine reverted to stationary use, while a second locomotive was built for a colliery near Newcastle in 1805 and Trevithic ran a demonstration locomotive and passenger carriage round a circular track in Euston Square in 1808. Nonetheless, there was widespread doubt that the frictional grip of traction wheels would be sufficient to pull laden wagons on gradients manageable by horses, doubt which caused John Blenkinsop to devise a cogged traction wheel to engage a toothed rail in 1811. However there being a growing number of private industrial railways, an Act of Parliament of 1801 sanctioned a horse-drawn public railway from Wandsworth to Croydon and by 1820 George Stephenson had begun to manufacture steam locomotives at Killingworth.

In 1821 another Act approved a horse-drawn wooden railway from Stockton to Darlington for the transport of passengers and freight and Stephenson who was appointed engineer in 1823 had the experience and enthusiasm to succeed in converting it to an iron railway with provision for some steam traction. When it was opened in 1825 Stephenson's *Locomotion* pulled 12 wagon loads of freight, 21 wagon loads of ordinary passengers and a coach load of directors. This demonstration of the superiority of steam traction over draught horses led to the Liverpool and Manchester Railway, the first to rely wholly on steam. When opened by the Duke of Wellington, then Prime Minister, the first train was drawn by Stephenson's *Rocket* chosen on the results of the competitive Rainhill Trials of 1829. It had separate cylinders on each side driving the wheels through short connecting-rods in what was to become the standard arrangement and a multi-tubular boiler for efficient heat transfer designed by Marc Seguin of the St Etienne-Lyons railway, the first in France. These early successes led to the widespread construction of railways, there being 250,000 navvies working on construction projects with paid-up capital in excess of £250 million by mid-century and in excess of £1000 million by 1900 in the UK alone.

This provided previously undreamed of travel opportunities for the general public with Thomas Cook introducing his package holidays in 1841 and the railways bringing six million visitors to the Great Exhibition of 1851 to see the wonders of Victorian technology. Thus, by 1860 the general desire to travel in the UK had produced a railway network of 10,000 miles and by 1885 this had doubled. Railway developments on this scale had a major impact on canal operators who had long enjoyed a virtual monopoly on the movement of heavy freight. So severe was this impact that the Manchester Ship Canal, completed in 1894 was the only major canal project in the UK after 1831. In America, long distance transport had remained rudimentary though in 1817 the Erie Canal Project came to be seen as a threat to the trade of Philadelphia and a deputation came to England to assess the likely benefits of a railway. The upshot was the Philadelphia-Columbia railway opened in 1831 for public use with horse-drawn wagons though it had acquired locomotives and rolling stock by 1834. Although these early locomotives were imported, such as the *Stourbridge Lion* for the Delaware and Hudson Railway in 1829, home production soon got under way and by 1838 some 350 locomotives of which no more than a quarter had been imported were running on 1500 miles of rail-track. Although this was a similar mileage to that of the UK at the time, the latter reached its peak around 1900 with some 22,000 miles of track while the USA reached 30,000 miles by 1860 and exceeded 200,000 miles by 1900. The American Civil War of 1861-5 was the first conflict in which railways made a significant contribution and because of their relative distribution at the time, they conferred yet another physical advantage on the Union.

As the railways expanded so did the desire for speed. By 1847 the Great Western Railway was running some scheduled services at a mile a minute and in 1904 its *City of Truro* achieved 100mph. Greater rail adhesion was achieved from 1859 by coupling the driving wheels while greater boiler length was supported by pushed and trailed bogies. The Belgian engineer Egide Walschaerts introduced improved valve gear in 1844, the Swiss Anatole Mallet compounded a small high pressure and large low pressure cylinder in France in 1878 while the German Wilhelm Schmidt introduced super-heated steam to reduce condensation losses in 1898.

The next step was based on the realisation that just as a dynamo supplies electricity when rotated by an engine, so a dynamo supplied with electricity will rotate as an engine. Such a 3 horse-power locomotive unit drawing low voltage electricity from a central rail and pulling up to 30 passengers round a narrow gauge circular track at 4 mph was displayed at the Berlin Exhibition of 1879 by Werner von Siemens. Again, by 1883 Magnus Volk had opened a narrow-gauge railway along the seafront at Brighton and in 1884 the Siemens & Halske Company had established an electric tramway between Frankfurt-am-Main and Offenbach which drew current from an overhead cable. Also in 1884 Frank Julian Sprague electrified the bogies of the New York Elevated Railway and in 1897 he devised the means by which all the motorised cars could be controlled from the leading car to produce the first multi-unit train. Meanwhile, the Metropolitan Railway built in 1863 to link some of London's principal mainline railway stations through covered cuttings demonstrated the need for electric power to replace its smoke emitting steam locomotives, and when the City and South London Line was to be constructed between 1887 and 1890, electric traction was chosen from the start.

Improvements to early railway technology were quick and numerous. Thus, the brittle cast-iron rails were first replaced by the more flexible wrought-iron and then by steel from about 1860 onwards. Fish-plates were applied at rail-joints to supplement the chair which alone had initially aligned them. Counter-balancing weights were added to the driving-wheels of locomotives to reduce their pounding action and the various gauges were unified. The recognised need for signalling was satisfied by Claude Chappe's military semaphore system of 1793 and its progressive developments, and subsequently by the electric telegraph, first in America and later in Britain from 1839. Improved signal transmission led to the block system in which track sections were barred to train entry until the previous train had proceeded from them, and pressure operated braking-systems were superseded by the vacuum-operated system of George Westinghouse. Passenger comfort also received attention with progressive introduction of lavatory, sleeping and dining facilities, culminating in the carriage conversions of George Pullman from 1864 onwards. In addition, gradient tolerance increased from Stephenson's favoured 1 in 330 to the stiffer 1 in 40 on which locomotives were required to maintain 12 mph with 80 tonne loads for service on the Semmerling Pass by 1848. Even so, improvements in mining practice were adapted for the tunnelling which remained essential to railway construction. Thus, when tunnelling beneath the Thames (1825-43) Marc Isambard Brunel developed and used a shield which provided temporary circumferential tunnel support while the work-face was being excavated prior to installation of permanent support-lining, a technique improved by James Henry Greathead whose steel shield was advanced by hydraulic rams while compressed air prevented water ingress. In addition, excavation rates were increased three-fold when Germain Sommellier developed the pneumatic drill for the 8-mile long Mont Cenis tunnel project of 1870.

With such developments in the means of travel by sea and land being achieved in the period between 1600 and 1900, attention turned to air-travel. Though in the west Archytas of Tarentum is considered to have invented the kite in the fourth century BC, there are references to man-carrying kites being used for observation during a seige in China at that time. In any event, by the time Leonardo da Vinci was drawing his flying machines, the 'lift' experienced when kites are appropriately deployed to wind direction must have been long known, this experience being immediately available to any kite-flyer. From there it is a small step to imagine that 'lift' would be experienced by any object gliding through still air. Nonetheless, Leonardo did not get his bird-wing designs to glide though it has recently been shown that some balancing tail-plane modifications might have given him a degree of success. Perhaps because of this failure of the gifted, attention turned to the principle of a genius and thence to balloons.

Thus, from the *Principle of Archimedes* and its corollary *Law of Flotation* it follows that a balloon inflated with a gas of lower density than air and receiving an up-thrust greater than the weight of its envelop and contents will rise (float), and that it will lift any attached load provided the overall weight remains less than the weight of the air displaced. Hot air being less dense than an equal volume of cold air has the potential to provide load-carrying lift and is readily provided by heating air as it enters through a small hole on the under-side of the balloon envelop to replace cooling air which is escaping through another small hole at its top, an arrangement which also confers a lift-control mechanism through varying the intermittency of heat application to the entering air. The first to achieve lift-off with such a hot-air balloon were the Montgolphier brothers in 1782 and in 1783 two passengers in the gondola (basket) remained airborne for half an hour, reached a height of 330 feet, and travelled 5.5 miles. By 1785 the English Channel had been crossed and by the end of the century the armies of Britain, France and the USA were using balloons for observation. The next steps were to fill a sealed envelop with a lighter than air gas such as hydrogen at a pressure just above atmospheric and to equip the gondola with an engine and propellor. The steam engine being too heavy, a battery powered electric motor was used in 1884 for the 5-mile flight of the cigar-shaped airship *La France*. Later, rigid airships in which the gas-envelop had a slender metal frame were developed by Graff Ferdinand von Zeppelin who flew his first in 1900. However, as early as 1799 Sir George Cayley knew that lift was generated when a wing was presented to an airflow at an appropriate angle and had shown diagrammatically that he understood the concepts fundamental to gliding and to powered fight with fixed wing aircraft.

8. 1. 6 Agriculture and Related Activities
The first thousand years after the fall of Rome saw no significant change in the craft of agriculture except that experience had taught the benefits of crop rotation with a fallow season and use of animal manure. This had led to the three-strip system in which each was cropped in turn with winter wheat, spring wheat or left fallow; the un-enclosed land being worked in long strips in multiples of three with animals for meat and milk allowed to graze the surrounding land or the strips themselves immediately after harvesting. However, the seventeenth century saw a greater use of traditional forage crops such as clover and alfalfa, and the introduction of new ones such as turnips as a winter supplement to hay. This was accompanied by an increased interest in livestock improvement through out-breeding to develop desired characteristics and in-breeding to stabilise

them. These motivations to improve productivity and profitability led to the British Enclosure Acts between 1727 and 1845 which brought more than 8 million acres of agricultural land under more unified management and led in turn to the need and opportunity for mechanisation especially with the Industrial Revolution drawing labour from countryside to town

The situation was initially rather different in the new territories in which European settler populations were small in relation to the available land. In America this land was suitable for cattle and grain, and further south for tobacco, cotton and sugar cane; in Australia and New Zealand for sheep, cattle, wheat, apples, and grapes for a wine industry; in South Africa for sheep and wheat; and in Argentina for cattle. Nonetheless, when the Declaration of Independence was signed in 1776, the settler population in North America was no more than 2.5 million and by 1843 that of Australia was still only 200,000. Thomas Jefferson had said in 1800 that the object in Europe was to make the most of the land, labour being abundant, while in the USA it was to make the most of labour, land being abundant. However, while the British population had risen from about 9 million in 1760 and to above 24 million by 1830, the ever-increasing industrial demand for manpower was reducing the availability of agricultural labour and decreasing the ratio of food producers to consumers in this increasing population. It was thus becoming obvious even in Britain that to get more out of the land, increased levels of mechanisation would be as necessary as in America and the other new territories where efforts were being made to produce exportable surpluses for the ever-increasing industrial populations of Europe. Thus, there was widespread need and opportunity to turn industrialisation to the mechanisation of agriculture.

Thus, the medieval supply of farm implements in wood and wrought-iron by individual carpenters and blacksmiths to satisfy local need was gradually replaced by batch production by small manufacturers to satisfy regional and even national markets as the implements themselves were progressively improved. Thus, the all-iron plough having appeared in Europe in the latter half of the eighteenth century, Robert Ransome in 1789 patented a self-sharpening ploughshare by cooling one side of it more quickly than the other, opened a factory at Ipswich to produce ploughs constructed from interchangeable parts which simplified repair, and offered a choice of shares to satisfy the range of soil conditions encountered across the country. Again, James Oliver of Indiana produced a light plough which sold well in North America, Britain and other Northern European countries. Again, from 1850 onwards steam engines were replacing draught animals for ploughing, these being self-propelled to locate themselves to operate in stationary mode by drawing the plough across the field by cable, the plough being reversible to make each traverse productive . Thus, while draught animals might pull a two-shared plough in light soil, the steam plough could haul multi-shared ploughs on the heaviest soils at up to 12 acres per working-day. Again, the mallets used to break-up clods left after ploughing successively gave way in the first half of the nineteenth century to smooth rollers in wood or stone, serrated rollers, the zig-zag iron harrow and the disc harrow.

Soil drilling for the sowing of seed having begun in Italy in the sixteenth century, Jethro Tull introduced his seed drill in 1701 and advocated its use to facilitate subsequent weeding by horse-drawn hoe in his *Horse-Hoeing Husbandry* of 1731. By 1786 Andrew Meikle had replaced manual threshing and winnowing with his combined machine in which the harvested crop was fed into the space between a rotating drum and its surrounding casing, the released grain being shaken through a riddle into sacks and the chaff blown away by a rotating fan while by the middle of the nineteenth century both these operations were being carried out by steam-driven machinery. By 1800, the rotating-tine hay tedder was speeding its drying, by the 1830s the mowing-machine was in use while horse-operated reaping machines were introduced by Patrick Bell in Scotland and by Cyrus McCormick in the USA though neither attracted much attention until the Great Exhibition of 1851. Again, in 1860 the American L. O. Colvin developed an electric milking machine based on continuous suction and in 1895 Alexander Shields of Glasgow introduced his pulsating system which being more akin to hand-milking avoided the inflammation and bleeding associated with continuous suction.

Although the application of animal-manure supplemented by bone, hoof, seaweed and fish-wastes had long been recognised as conducive to soil fertility, it was often difficult to maintain the appropriate balance between stock-rearing and crop-growing. In any case, prior to fodder cropping it had been impossible to keep more than a small fraction of stock through the winter. However, in the nineteenth century it became possible to identify the fertilising elements, to quantify application rates in relation to need, and to augment natural supplies artificially to meet this need. For the study of such matters, a carefully managed estate was established at Celle in Saxony by Daniel Thaer in 1802 with similar initiatives elsewhere in Germany and France. In Britain, Humphrey Davy was lecturing on soil fertility at the *Royal Institution*, his *Elements of Agricultural Chemistry* appearing in 1813 and John Bennet Lawes established the *Rothamsted Agricultural Research Station* in Hertfordshire in 1834. In addition, Justus von Liebig's *Chemistry in its Application to Agriculture and Physiology* appeared in 1840. Thus, it was found that phosphorus, nitrogen and potassium were essential elements for soil fertility and that phosphorus could be solubilised from bone by sulphuric acid treatment.

As a consequence the physician James Murray began to process his super-phosphate in Ireland in 1817, discovering that phosphate rock could be used in his process instead of bones. By 1843 Lawes (of Rothamsted) had established a super-phosphate factory which thirty years later had an annual output of 40,000 tonnes. In addition, substantial quantities of bird droppings (guano) and sodium nitrate mined as cliché were imported from Chile as sources of fertiliser nitrogen from 1839 onwards, and wood-ash, a forestry by-product was imported from Canada as a source of potassium, while from 1860 onwards the potassium mineral *carnalite* was imported from Germany as an alternative to the wood-ash. Again, in Europe by 1900 the demand for sodium nitrate as a source of nitrogen fertiliser to supplement that from animal wastes was running at around a million tonnes annually while in the USA where the separate concentrations of arable farming and stock raising were non-conducive to delivery of animal manure from the latter to the former, reliance on the artificial fertiliser industry was almost total. Thus, mixed fertiliser production began in Baltimore in 1849 and by the end of the century some two million tonnes were being produced annually, rock phosphate being mined in South Carolina from 1868 onwards.

With increased food production and increased distances between producer and consumer in some cases, attention turned to improvements in the traditional means of food preservation. With Napoleon having offered a prize for improvements suitable for use by the French Army, Francois Appert investigated the efficacy of heating food in glass jars surrounded by boiling water followed by hermetic sealing. His approach was belief-based, however, the role of micro-organisms in food spoilage being then unknown, and he did not perfect his process and open his first processing factory at Massy until 1810. That year also, Peter Durant in England patented the use of tin-plate canisters as a cheaper alternative to glass and by 1812 Brian Donkin was supplying the Royal Navy from a cannery in Bermondsey in which the cans were made individually by hand. However, by 1847 can manufacture had been mechanised and by the end of the century the use of rubber seals had automated the process of filling and sealing. This latter process when adopted in the USA in 1817 resulted in the huge meat canning operations of the Chicago area which from 1880 onwards were synonymous with the name P. D. Armour. By then a wide range of canned fruits and vegetables were also cheap and readily available throughout the world.

In addition, canned milk previously condensed by evaporation, was now available, quickly to be followed by dried milk (1855) and malted milk (1883). Again, Laval's turbine-based cream separator of 1878 increased the efficiency of the traditional transformation of perishable milk into longer-lasting butter and cheese, these having become factory procedures in Australia, Canada and America before 1900. Margarine first made by Hippolyte Mege-Mouries in 1869 as an emulsion of beef suet, skimmed milk, cow udder and pig stomach and initially sold in bulk, was later improved in taste and texture by addition of vegetable oils to the point of being packaged as for butter in the USA from the 1890s, with 50,000 tonnes being imported annually by Britain by 1900, by which time refrigeration was enabling European importation of meat from New Zealand, Australia and Argentina.

8. 1. 7 Textiles and Related Activities

The textile industry was transformed over half a century by a series of craft-based inventions. Formerly a single weaver had thrown the shuttle through the shed of threads with one hand and caught it with the other while broadcloth required an operator on each side of the loom to throw the shuttle to and fro. Thus, the first invention was the flying shuttle of the Lancastrian John Kay in 1733 which enabled broadcloth to be made more quickly by a single weaver than had formerly been possible with two. Of course, more rapid weaving required more rapid spinning and in response to this need James Hargreaves had produced his hand-operated eight-spindle spinning jenny by 1764 though he failed in his patent application of 1770. Meanwhile Richard Arkwright, being successful with his larger horse-driven machine in 1769 had entered into partnership around 1770 with the hosiers Samuel Need and Jedediah Strutt in opening a water-driven mill at Comford for the manufacture of cotton thread, an initiative regarded as the start of the factory system. Thereafter between 1774-9 Samuel Compton combined features of the machines of Hargreaves and Arkwright in his spinning mule and in 1785 a Boulton and Watt steam engine was installed to power a mill at Papplewick.

As spinning capacity now began to outstrip weaving capacity, attention turned to power-weaving though this proved to be more difficult. Although Edmund Cartwright installed his power-loom at his own works at Doncaster in 1787 this could only be considered a prototype in need of improvements and these were slow to appear, there being only about 2000 power looms in Britain by 1800 while by 1825 some 250,000 hand looms were producing the same output as the then 75,000 power-looms. Nevertheless mechanisation even at these rates produced levels of unemployment which caused Ned Ludd to destroy some stocking-frames in Leicestershire in 1782 and seriously destructive rioting by the so-called Luddites occurred in 1811 and 1818. Nevertheless, mechanisation produced a huge expansion in British cotton production which overtook and surpassed the longstanding woollen industry. Thus, while in 1751 the export value of cotton goods had been £46,000, by 1800 it was £5.4 million and in 1861 it was £46.8 million when that of the woollen industry was £11million.

In addition, new processes were changing the basic properties of cotton and wool. Thus, in 1823 Charles Macintosh perfected his rubberised fabric and within ten years the term 'Macintosh' became synonymous with the new waterproof coat while in 1844 John Mercer discovered that cotton could be given a lustrous sheen by treating it with caustic soda. It was also found that chlorine-treated wool could be dyed more easily and could acquire crease-resistance. Again, in 1856 the early industrial organic chemist William Henry Perkin produced his synthetic (artificial) azo-dyes and opened the prospect of more synthetic products in the future. Thus, by 1892 Charles Frederick Cross and Edward J. Bevan had demonstrated the viscous rayon process for the production of 'artificial silk' from cellulose though this had to await the early twentieth century for commercial introduction.

Though natural silk, being a low-volume luxury item presented less incentive to mechanisation than had cotton and wool, Joseph Jacquard in France in 1801 devised a new loom which dispensed with the draw-boy who had performed pattern-producing operations with warp and weft as instructed by the weaver. With the Jacquard loom, the weaver controlled these operations with the aid of a treadle and a punched-card device, the hole-distribution of which controlled the pattern in the woven silk as later it would programme early computers. While such developments raised the prospect of a ready-to-wear clothing industry, the chain-stitch sewing machine introduced by Balthazar Krems in 1810 failed for a number of reasons and it was 1851 before Isaac Singer patented his lock-stitch machine which not only made mass-production clothing a reality but was also popular for home use in the USA and later in Europe as his light-weight 'family' machine of 1858, factory production being further facilitated by G. P. Eastman's reciprocating knife which could cut through 50 layers of fabric in one movement.

8. 1. 8 Porcelain

As we have seen the Chinese were producing high quality porcelain from the eighth century onwards using kaolin (China clay) mixed with the mineral petuntse (weathered granite containing quartz and feldspar) at kiln temperatures of 1300° C. However, when from the fourteenth century such porcelain was reaching Europe *via* the Silk Road attempts were made to imitate or replicate it. Thus, by 1570 Florentine potters were producing soft-paste porcelain by replacing the petuntse with powdered glass which permitted lower firing temperatures and though this technique spread to the leading centres in France at Paris (St Cloud) and Rouen, it was around 1707 before Johan Bottger alchemist to Augustus II (Elector of Saxony and King of Poland) was able to produce porcelain equal to that of China. His approach was to evaluate the ability of various calcareous fluxes for the clays of Saxony and to devise a suitable glazing technique to produce porcelain from these fused clays. In 1710 the Meissen Pottery was founded near Dresden with Bottger as manager and in France the search for a hard-paste pottery process culminated in 1738 with the establishment of a pottery under Royal patronage at Vinciennes which having moved to Sevres in 1756 began in 1770 to produce hard-paste pottery equal to that of Meissen.

The first to succeed in producing true porcelain in Britain was William Cookworthy, a Quaker preacher in business as a chemist in Plymouth who in 1745 began to experiment with local clays and discovered an ideal source of kaolin and petuntse at St Austell. However, his patents after transfer to his partner Richard Champion were challenged by a group of Staffordshire potters, one of whom was Josiah Wedgewood who already famous for his stoneware and tinted and polished stone-like jasper, had been experimenting with additives to local clays to produce hard-paste porcelain at New Hall in 1791. Meanwhile other British potters had been attempting to improve the quality of soft-paste porcelain by use of additives including bone-ash which resulted in the production of bone china at Stratford-le-Bow in London from about 1750, and in the addition of bone-ash to hard-paste porcelain by Josiah Spode around 1800. Again, from about 1751 the Worcester potteries were adding the local soapstone, steatite, to their pastes to produce high-quality low-volume porcelain items which could be hand-painted as desired.

Meanwhile, in the 1740s in response to a long-standing demand for mass-produced products for general use, Ralph Daniel introduced the technique of pouring a very mobile clay suspension (slip) into moulds which after drying sufficiently were fired in the usual way. To speed drying, the original metal-moulds were replaced with porous plaster-moulds and to speed shaping, the plaster-mould was rotated while a shaped-jig was lowered into it. For such mass-production a cheap, plain glaze was sufficient to which from about 1750 patterns could be transferred and enhanced by varying degrees of hand-painting.

8. 1. 9 Mining, Mineral Processing, Metal Extraction, Iron and Steel, and Machine Tools

Industrialisation called for increased scale and efficiency of mining and by the seventeenth century gun-powder was being used below ground to enhance age-long pick and shovel methods and by 1831 William Bickford had introduced his safety-fuse in Cornwall. Again, Christian Schonbeim of Basle discovered in 1845 that a more powerful explosive than gunpowder could be prepared by treating cotton or other forms of cellulose with nitric acid and Ascanio Sobrero in Italy discovered in 1846 that glycerine could be substituted for cellulose though nitro-glycerine was too dangerous for general use. However in 1865, Alfred Nobel stabilised it by mixing to a dough with the clay mineral kieselguhr to produce a safe-working explosive five times more effective than gunpowder which he marketed as Dynamite and for which the demand rose in ten years to 3,000 tonnes per annum for rock blasting alone. Meanwhile, the pneumatic drill of the St Cenis Tunnel project of 1870 either with rotational or hammer action was being used for shot-hole drilling in mining until both were combined in the same tool. Again, the earth-moving techniques of open cast mining benefited from excavation experience in the Panama Canal project.

While the steam engine had been used underground since 1698 for drainage and winch-wire hauling this stationary mode of operation had been compatible with its emissions and waste heat being exhausted up a vertical shaft, though it precluded use at an advancing workface. Thus, the need for general ventilation had caused John Buddle to introduce his wooden air-pump in 1807 and John Nixon his steam-driven pumps by about 1840 which by the end of the century were achieving extraction rates of 6,000 cubic metres per minute though this still failed to prevent explosions from coal-seam release of methane gas (fire-damp) and naked flame illumination. Thus, having invited the submission of safety lamp designs, *The Sunderland Society* endorsed Humphrey Davy's Lamp of 1816 which enclosed the flame in a metal gauze to thermally isolate it from the external atmosphere and thus preclude explosion without reducing illumination. Thus, advances in health and safety assisted in satisfying the growing demand for coal, this having risen from a largely house-hold requirement of about 3 million tonnes annually in 1700 to about 6 million tonnes by 1800, 60 million by 1850 and 225 million by 1900 as industrial demand accelerated.

The demand for metals also accelerated and with the earliest known and richer deposits becoming exhausted, attention turned to poorer and to mechanical means of ore enrichment, the increasing demand having overwhelmed the earlier hand-sorting processes. With heavy ores such as those of lead much of the associated crushed and broken strata (gangue) could be washed away with water in the manner of gold-panning. In some cases, powerful water jets were directly used to wash down and separate exposed ore while in others mechanical dredgers collected it from lagoons created in the washing process. Again, in 1895 A. R. Wilfley introduced his vibrating-table separator which had parallel grooves or riffles across which the ore concentrated for discharge from the lower side of the table while crushed magnetic iron oxide (magnetite) could be separated from the gangue by electro-magnets, such a plant with a capacity of 5,000 tonnes per day having been built by Thomas Edison at Ogden in the Appalachians in the 1890s. However, the most generally applicable ore enrichment process is flotation and this was first used in 1865 to separate low-grade sulphide ores such as copper pyrites from the gangue. The process involves agitating the crushed mixture with oil and water, allowing the oil entrapped ore particles to form a floating layer on the underlying water in which the gangue has sunk. It was later found that oil requirements were reduced by bubbling air through the system to carry the ore to the water surface on oil-coated air-bubbles, a technique first used in 1901 at Broken Hill, Australia, to concentrate zinc blende.

As to extracting metals from their ores the available procedures had remained much as I have already described them, the task now being to satisfy ever increasing demand. In the case of iron smelting we have already noted that the high melting point of iron makes it difficult to remove impurities as slag by the method applied to lower melting point metals, and that this difficulty had necessitated slag removal from iron by beating in the forge (c.f. Section 2.4.4). For the tonnages now demanded, however, this manual-beating stage would be insurmountably difficult. In addition, the supply of charcoal for smelting was becoming unsustainable in the face of ever increasing demand. Thus, attention turned to achieving sufficiently high smelting temperatures to allow slag removal from molten iron as for lower melting point metals and to replacing charcoal with coal. Higher temperatures were initially achieved by blowing air into the mixture of metal oxide and charcoal in what became known as the blast furnace, said to have been devised in Germany about 1350 and in Britain about 1500. However, the use of raw coal is precluded because its sulphur content weakens the iron so produced, necessitating prior oven roasting to produce coke with removal of sulphur as sulphur dioxide as first practiced by Abraham Darby for his blast furnace at Coalbrookdale in 1709, his local low-sulphur coal ensuring few early competitors (c.f. below).

The charge of oxide-ore and coke was fed in at the top of the blast furnace, the molten slag collecting on the molten iron surface at the foot of the furnace tower. However, the operating temperature was still too low to melt *pure* iron and so the melt within the furnace contained dissolved carbon from the coke together with the silicon, sulphur, phosphorus and manganese not completely removed in the tapped slag while the melt separately tapped at intervals, run into moulds (pigs) allowed to cool and known as pig-iron could not be worked by heating and hammering because on heating the brittle solid immediately melts to a liquid instead of softening to a workable state. Thus, further purification had to be effected by re-melting in a separate furnace (cupola) heated by coke after which it is known as cast-iron on being poured into moulds. This cast iron is still relatively brittle though it can be heated and worked into articles not required to sustain undue shock or strain.

However, in 1784 Henry Cort introduced his puddling process in which pig iron (carbon content 1.5 - 4%) was melted on a bed of iron oxide in a reverberatory furnace where the oxide reacted with the carbon in the pig iron to form carbon monoxide which burns as 'puddler's candles' to carbon dioxide at the molten metal surface while the silicon, manganese and other impurities formed a separable slag. As the metal became purer its melting point increased forming pasty balls which were spongy because of their residual slag content. When removed from the furnace these balls were worked under a steam-hammer to remove the remaining slag as far as possible to form what is known as wrought-iron though the Swede Christopher Pohlen was using steam-driven grooved rollers in place of the steam-hammer to finish iron bars at much reduced cost and Cort later introduced this practice to Britain. Thus, while cast-iron melts at about 1200° C, wrought-iron melts at 1,537° and softens at about 1000° at which temperature it can be forged and welded. It is tough, malleable and stress resistant and as such was used for ship and bridge building and similar purposes. However, production declined from 3 million tonnes in 1882 to about 0.8 million tonnes in 1937 as mild steel replaced it.

Steel, as we have seen, has much the same antiquity as iron though the making of any considerable quantity by the ancient methods (c.f. Section 2.4.4) again presented substantial problems. From about 1300 the earlier process of cementation which had 'steeled' small iron articles such as sword blades was scaled up to the point when iron bars were packed with charcoal into firebrick boxes and heated in a furnace for eight to eleven days at red-heat (1000° C). Under these conditions carbon monoxide forms and diffuses into the hot iron where it forms iron carbide (Fe_3C) to an average carbon content of about 1%. The bars were then removed and subjected to an elaborate forging process to distribute the carbon as evenly as possible. However, in 1740, Benjamin Huntsman of Sheffield succeeded in melting such carburised bars in a small crucible and thus achieved uniform carbon content more easily than by forging. Again, high grade crucible steel was produced by melting high quality wrought-iron with a definite proportion of charcoal while a lower grade was obtained by melting a mixture of wrought-iron with the appropriate amount of cast-iron.

Such slow batch processes limited production to the extent that Britain, the largest producer by far, had an annual output of only about 60,000 tonnes of steel as late as the mid-1800s. However, Kelly and Bessemer working independently in the USA and Britain were about to change this very substantially. In 1847 Kelly, a manufacturer of sugar kettles, noticed that a blast of air over the surface of molten iron raised the temperature to white-heat because the carbon in the iron was reacting (burning) with the oxygen of the airblast. On this observation he built seven experimental converters for the conversion of iron to steel between 1851 and 1855 and in 1866, having heard of Bessemer's work he lodged a patent in the USA. Meanwhile, Bessemer had found with respect to the rifling of field guns during the Crimean War, that he could decarburise fused mixtures of iron and steel by blowing air through them, had patented this process in 1855 and in 1860 its associated tilting converter of iron-plate construction and siliceous brick lining. With the air-blast in operation the temperature of the charge in this converter rises because of the heat liberated in oxidation of the carbon, sulphur, silicon and phosphorus impurities. The carbon initially forms carbon monoxide which later burns to carbon dioxide at the mouth of the converter while the oxides of the other impurities (with the exception of the oxides of phosphorus, as it turned out) form a slag with the siliceous lining. The right moment to stop the air blast can be judged by observing the flame and at this point the correct amount of an alloy of manganese and iron, *spiegeleisen,* (containing < 20% iron) is added to reduce residual iron oxide to iron in the converter, the air blast being briefly resumed to offset the otherwise untoward effects of the other remaining oxides during this brief period.

However, Bessemer having unwittingly used phosphorus-free ores from Sweden, his licensees found their steel from phosphorus-rich British ores to be un-forgeable when hot and brittle when cold because the phosphorus oxides did not slag with the furnace lining. This problem was solved in 1878 when S. G. Thomas and P.G. Gilchrist substituted dolomite for the siliceous lining of the converter, added lime to the pig-iron charge and somewhat prolonged the air-blast causing the oxides of phosphorus, sulphur and silicon to react with the lime to form a basic slag which could be used as a fertiliser by virtue of its phosphorus content. The terms acid and basic are now applied to the process according to whether the siliceous or the dolomite lining is required. When first introduced, the Bessemer process reduced the steel price from £70 to around £15 per ton.

Nonetheless, by the end of the century more steel was produced by the rival Siemans-Martin open-hearth process developed in Germany and favoured by the Scots-American steel magnate Andrew Carnegie. In this process the furnace is charged with a mixture of pig-iron, scrap iron and haematite ore free from carbon and melted in its shallow rectangular trough (or hearth) by the combustion of producer gas (c.f. next paragraph). When a test shows that the product contains the right amount of carbon, ferro-manganese is added as in the Bessemer process. If the furnace-bed is lined with siliceous material we have the acid process in which the proportions of carbon, silicon and manganese are reduced during the treatment though the amounts of sulphur and phosphorus remain fairly constant. In contrast, when the lining is dolomite we have the basic process in which there is a steady decrease in the phosphorus and sulphur content during the treatment as in the basic Bessemer process. The open-hearth process owes its commanding position to the uniformity of the product, the ease with which the composition of the steel can be controlled, the ability to recycle steel scrap, the smaller loss of iron in the process (4% compared with 15% in the Bessemer) and the larger quantities which can be processed per operation. Its principal disadvantages in comparison with the latter are the 10 hours instead of 20 minutes to complete a charge and the need for external heating.

The fuel-gas used in the Siemans-Martin process is produced by passing air through incandescent coke. When the air enters the bottom of a coke-bed in an air-tight cylindrical furnace (the producer) made of sheet iron lined with fire-brick, it oxidises some of the coke to carbon dioxide according to the equation $C + O_2 = CO_2$ and as this gas passes further up the coke-bed it is reduced to carbon monoxide by the excess hot-coke according to the equation $CO_2 + C = 2CO$. The equilibrium between the amounts of carbon dioxide and carbon monoxide moves towards the latter the higher the operating temperature of the producer. Such producers are usually designed to operate at about $1000°$ C when the issuing gas consists essentially of carbon monoxide and the nitrogen of the air used. This gas, known as producer gas, is a cheap source of heat when burned according to the equation $2CO + O_2 = 2CO_2$. Having low calorific value, however, it is always made *in situ* and used as it is made to minimise heat loss. Another fuel-gas conveniently made on industrial premises is known as water gas. When steam is passed up a tower packed with red-hot coke they react according to the equation: $H_2O + C = H_2 + CO$, producing a mixture of hydrogen and carbon monoxide (water gas). Although this endothermic process cools the coke, replacing the steam with an air supply returns it to red-heat according to the exothermic equation: $C + O_2 = CO_2$. Thus, both reactions can be operated alternately in paired-towers to give a constant supply of water gas with replacement of consumed coke as required. The water gas is burned in air exothermically (as is producer gas) as a source of heat according to the equation $H_2 + CO + O_2 = H_2O + CO_2$.

The production of iron and steel in large quantities not only provided for the manufacture of larger numbers of small items but also for much larger items, the manufacture of which required machine tools which for the basic operations of turning, planing and milling could themselves be massive. Recognition of this growing mechanisation of production had inspired Denis Diderot to compile between 1751and 1772 his *Encyclopedie ou Dictionnaire des Science, des Arts et des Metiers* to which Adam Smith referred in his consideration of the *Division of Labour*. Thus Diderot describes the precision gear-cutting machinery and screw-cutting lathes needed by clock and instrument makers at one end of the scale and at the other, the steam-engine manufacturers' need for accurately bored cylinders up to 2 metres in diameter and up to 3 metres in length, together with heavy machinery such as steam-hammers for forging and shaping, mills for rolling red-hot ingots of many tonnes into sheet and plate, and grooved rollers and slitting mills to produce bars and rods from sheet. For example, James Naismyth's steam-hammer of 1839 could forge a steel ingot nearly a metre in diameter into a steam-boat paddle-shaft. In this way 20 tonne ingots were being shaped by mid-century and Alfred Krupp could roll a steel ingot of 130 tonnes into naval armour-plate 30 cm thick and 14 x 3.5 metres in area by 1900.

Machine tools were also required for accurate and fast repetitive work as exemplified by the machinery installed at Plymouth Dockyard by Marc Brunel in the first decade of the nineteenth century for the production of wooden pulley-blocks for the Royal Navy. In this production unit, 43 machines driven by a 30-horsepower steam engine turned wood into three sizes of pulley-block at the rate of 130,000 per annum. Such precision mass production greatly extended the manufacture of interchangeable parts as was increasingly practiced in Europe, though this became known as the American system by virtue of its enthusiastic adoption by Eli Whitney, Simeon Worth and Samuel Colt in the production of muskets and pistols for the US Government. By 1853 Colt had 14,000 machine tools in operation though it was only after this mass-production system was demonstrated at the Great Exhibition that it was first adopted in Britain by the Royal Small Arms Factory at Enfield. Machine tools were also needed to satisfy the growing demand for wire for hawsers, springs and fencing including barbed-wire, for the electricity-supply industry, and for telegraph and telephone communications, all of had specific requirements.

8. 1. 10 Aluminium, Alloys and Coatings, Platinum Metals, and Nickel and Cobalt

Hans Christian Oersted had isolated aluminium in 1824 by treating aluminium chloride with sodium (later with potassium) both of which had previously been obtained by electrolysing their fused salts. Although this new metal had the very attractive characteristics of lightness, strength and corrosion resistance, the costs of production appeared prohibitive until 1879 when Hamilton Young Castner reduced the cost of sodium by heating caustic soda with carbon in the presence of iron as catalyst at 1000° C according to the equation: $6NaOH + 2C = 2Na + 3H_2 + 2Na_2CO_3$ and began manufacturing sodium at the rate of 50 tonnes per annum at Oldbury, England in 1888. Later he reduced costs again by electrolysis of fused caustic soda and again by electrolysing fused sodium chloride. However, with Charles M. Hall in the USA and Paul Louis Tousaint Heroult in France having independently produced aluminium by direct electrolysis of a fused mixture of bauxite (aluminium oxide) and cryolite in 1886 and with increasing availability of cheap electricity from new hydroelectric schemes such as at Niagara, Castner turned to supplying sodium cyanide for a wet-chemical method of extracting gold as the cyanide in America, South Africa and Australia. However, aluminium was the first new metal since classical times, and from an annual production rate of around 10,000 tonnes in 1900 it quickly increased to millions of tonnes per annum.

Though zinc metal had been known in the ancient world and had long been a constituent of brass, it was being used with copper and nickel to make the new alloy German silver by the nineteenth century, and a brass, Muntz metal containing 40% zinc was being used instead of copper to sheath the bottoms of ships. Again, while zinc extraction for the production of brass had been established by William Champion at Bristol about 1740, thin corrugated iron sheets were now being dipped into baths of molten zinc (galvanising) to increase corrosion resistance when such sheets were used as cheap roofing for farm and factory buildings. Yet again, the annual demand for copper (the other constituent of brass) rose dramatically during the nineteenth century from about 10,000 tonnes to 525,000 tonnes, around half of the increase being attributable to the needs of electricity transmission.

Apart from aluminium which went into general use because of its lightness and strength, a number of other metals began to be used for first-time specialist purposes in the nineteenth century, these being the platinum metals, nickel and cobalt. Although there is an uncertain reference to the former in the term 'aluta' in Pliny's *Natural History*, the first authenticated reference is the Spanish use of the term Platino del Pinto in South America. However, the properties of platinum were described in 1750 by Wood, Brownrigg and Watson, its hardness and very high melting point (1773.5° C) making it difficult to work though the natives of Ecuador and Colombia had overcome this difficulty by mixing it with small granules of gold to facilitate melting to intimate contact and diffusion of one metal into the other and by forging to produce an alloy workable into desired artefacts.

Prior to 1823 South America was the main source of platinum though it was found in the Urals in 1819 and began to be exported in 1824. Meanwhile, investigation of native platinum had revealed the presence of associated metals, osmium and iridium being discovered by S. Tennant in

1802-3 and rhodium and palladium by William Hyde Wollaston in 1803-4, while ruthenium was later discovered by K. Claus in 1845. The details of platinum metal processing are something of a trade secret, Wollaston having set up and run his own manufactory in London until his death in 1828 when leadership of the industry passed to Johnson Matthey in the UK and Engelhardt in the USA. Like iron, platinum softens before melting and so can be welded. This fact together with its high fusion temperature and resistance to attack by air or by strong acids enables it to be used in the manufacture of apparatus such as crucibles, stills and dishes for many chemical operations which could not readily be performed in contact with other materials of containment. Indeed, the analysis of many minerals could not be conducted as at present were it not for the unique properties of platinum. In addition, having nearly the same coefficient of thermal expansion as glass, platinum wires can be fused through glass in an air-tight fashion. These properties further commend its use for contacts in electrical apparatus, for surgical instruments, in jewellery and as a catalytic metal in many industrial processes and for the catalytic abatement of pollution from motor vehicle exhaust.

Again, platinum-iridium wire with platinum wire is used in bimetallic thermocouples for the measurement of temperatures up to 1000° C, platinum-rhodium wire with platinum is used in a similar way for temperatures up to 1400° C, and an alloy of 90% platinum and 10% iridium was chosen for the preservation of the International Standards of length and weight. At the Paris Exhibition of 1867 Johnson Matthey showed equipment constructed in platinum to a total weight of 500kg, an impressive sight when the total world production of platinum by 1919 was only 6.5 tonnes. Iridium has the advantage over platinum of not forming a brittle carbide when heated in the presence of carbon and is used for crucibles and other apparatus where such contact cannot be avoided. It is also used to tip gold pen-nibs to increase wear-resistance. Palladium is used for absorption of hydrogen and for the detection of carbon monoxide and its high malleability permits its use analogous to gold as palladium-leaf for corrosion protection. Rhodium is alloyed with platinum for special apparatus and for resistance-wire windings in laboratory electric furnaces. It can also be plated on silver-ware where a layer-thickness of 0.00002 inches is amply sufficient for complete tarnish-protection with the added advantage of its reflectivity being the highest of all metals. Ruthenium is alloyed with platinum or palladium for use in jewellery. Osmium, formerly used for light-bulb filaments has been replaced by tungsten on cost grounds, though Osmium tetroxide is still used in histology to stain and harden organic tissues.

The word 'Kobalt' appears in the writings of Valentine and Paracelsus to denote the goblins who were believed by the old Teutons and Scandinavians to haunt mines and mischievously interfere with miners. The term was later applied to what were called false-ores *i.e.* those which did not yield metals when subjected to the standard methods of metal extraction. Later still it was restricted to those minerals which imparted a blue coloration to glass (cobalt blue). In 1735 Brandt hypothesised that the colour was indicative of a new metal which he called cobalt rex and which he isolated as the new metal cobalt in 1742. Similarly, the term kupfernickel (false-copper) was applied to an ore which had the appearance of being one of copper, though the standard methods of extraction produced no copper. In the interval 1751-4, Cronstedt hypothesised that the brown colour inparted to glass by kupfernickel was due to a new metal while le Sage hypothesised it to be a compound of cobalt, iron, arsenic and copper. Finally, Bergman showed that nickel retains its individual nature when arsenic is absent, that solutions of nickel retain their individuality when no signs of cobalt or copper can be detected, and that he could not make nickel from mixtures of le Sage's supposed constituents. Thus, was nickel established as a new metal.

Electricity having been used to extract metals from their fused compounds, attention turned to the electro-deposition of metals of attractive appearance onto less attractive metallic articles, workers in precious metals always having welcomed opportunities to extend their markets by coating baser materials. One method of great antiquity was to apply gold-leaf, the gold being beaten out as thin as fine paper. Later, Vannoccio Biringuccio (sixteenth century) developed a technique for gilding iron and other metals by means of gold-amalgam and in 1742 Thomas Bolsover produced what became known as Sheffield plate by fusing a thin silver plate to a thick plate of copper and rolling it out while hot for use in his button and belt-buckle trade and later in the production of other articles such as candlesticks. However, though Sheffield plate was widely used for about a century, it was displaced from 1840 onwards when the Elkingtons of Birmingham introduced electroplating first commercially operated by Thomas Prime. Though gold and silver were the first to be plated, nickel became popular because of its silvery appearance and tarnish-resistance while cobalt, chromium and cadmium were similarly used later.

Once these new metals had become commercially available, attention turned to alloying them to produce metals with specific properties as had occurred with the platinum metals. Cobalt and nickel were of special interest because of their magnetism. Thus, Alnico, an alloy of cobalt, nickel, copper and iron was favoured for the production of permanent magnets for magnetos and later loud-speakers while alloying cobalt and nickel with iron in varying proportions and with other metals such as chromium produced steels for high-speed cutting tools and for gears and crankshafts for internal combustion engines. Again, nickel-brass alloying produces a series of tarnish resistant nickel-silvers while Monel metal, an alloy of 70% nickel - 30% copper is very corrosion-resistant and is thus much used in the chemical industry and for domestic purposes. Again, the British 'silver' coinage is now an alloy of 75% copper - 25% nickel.

8.1.11 Coal-Gas, Chemicals and Petroleum

The heat-treatment of coal in the absence of air to produce the coke first used by Abraham Darby for iron smelting in 1709 also produced a gaseous mixture (coal gas) consisting largely of hydrogen, carbon monoxide, methane and other hydrocarbons in varying proportions, these being an unusable waste at the time. Unsuccessful attempts to promote its use for street-lighting cost the ninth Earl of Dundonald (father of Admiral Cochrane) most of his wealth before William Murdoch installed such a gas-plant to light the works of Boulton and Watt in 1798. With this success the company proceeded to supply the necessary equipment to a large Lancashire textile-mill and subsequently on a wider commercial basis to create an entirely new gas-supply industry. By the middle of the century, streets, public buildings and the homes of even the poorest town-dwellers had benefited from gas-lighting and by the end of the century coal-gas was also being used for domestic heating throughout Europe, the consequent changes in the leisure habits of the general population being very considerable. In the USA, however, the introduction of coal-gas was overtaken at an early stage by the use of natural gas and before the end of the century US oilfields were also being exploited (c.f. below).

This distillation of coal also produced liquids in the form of an aqueous layer containing ammonia, ammonium sulphide, phenol (carbolic acid), pyridine and small quantities of other organic compounds; and a 'tar' layer insoluble in water and consisting of a large number of hydrocarbons such as benzene, toluene, naphthalene *etc, etc*, towards which the attention of a significant proportion of early industrial chemists was directed for investigation and production of many new organic compounds of subsequent commercial significance. It was also found that the higher the distillation temperature the greater the proportion of gas to liquid, and that the lower luminosity of the resulting flame could be off-set by the incandescent mantle produced from thorium oxide mixed with an essential 1% cerium oxide. However, the preparation of coal gas for delivery to users required many chemical engineering developments later indispensable to the development of the chemical industry in general. Thus, while the earlier producer gas plant (used as the heat-source for coal distillation) handled gas only (c.f. Section 8.1.9) coal distillation itself had to take account of gas, vapour and liquid products if use was to be made of them. Thus, vapours had to be condensed out of the gas stream while ammonia and sulphur dioxide had to be removed by adsorption in water scrubbers. Again, while some of the hydrogen cyanide, hydrogen sulphide and carbon dioxide are removed with the ammonia in these scrubbers, the remainder of the first two had to be removed in two sequential purifiers one of which absorbed the former in a solution of ferrous sulphide and sodium carbonate while the other removed the latter in packed layers of ferric hydroxide.

When the ferric hydroxide had thus been converted to a mixture of Fe_2S_3, FeS and free elemental sulphur, it was discharged to the air for 24 hours, spread out to a depth of twelve inches and turned over repeatedly to expose fresh surfaces for atmospheric oxidation of the sulphides for re-cycling as ferric hydroxide. However, after about sixteen cycles of re-use, the content of elemental sulphur having progressively risen to about 55%, further recycling was no longer cost-effective. At that point it was saleable as a source of sulphur in sulphuric acid manufacture, and later its iron content after a preliminary treatment was recycled in blast furnace feed-stock. After initial treatment, however, the coal gas could still contain small amounts of carbon disulphide which when burned would give rise to unwelcome sulphur dioxide. To remove this hazard, the South Metropolitan Gas Company introduced the practice of passing the gas over a nickel catalyst at 450° C to convert the carbon disulphide to hydrogen sulphide which could be removed reliably in a second absorber. This brief account of the early gas industry shows that recycling of wastes, environmental protection and concern for health and safety were recognised long before these terms became common currency, the gas industry itself being a recycling of the wastes from coke production for the production of steel, a process which itself recycled scrap steel. Indeed, the steel industry recycled its phosphorous bearing wastes to fertiliser production and sulphur bearing wastes to sulphuric acid production as did the gas industry its sulphur bearing wastes, its iron wastes going to steel production.

In 1775 the French Academy of Sciences offered a prize for a manufacturing process for sodium carbonate (Na_2CO_3) which was won by Nicholas Leblanc though he never received the prize, the Revolution having intervened. At least he was not guillotined as was Lavoisier. Leblanc's process involved three stages. In the first, sodium chloride otherwise known as common salt (NaCl) was reacted with sulphuric acid (H_2SO_4) to produce sodium sulphate (Na_2SO_4) together with hydrogen chloride (HCl), which dissolved in water to yield another valuable product, hydrochloric acid, thus:

$$2NaCl + H_2SO_4 = Na_2SO_4 + 2HCl$$

In the second stage, the sodium sulphate was heated to a high temperature in a revolving furnace with limestone and coke to produce the desired sodium carbonate, together with calcium sulphide and carbon dioxide gas which is vented, thus:

$$Na_2SO_4 + Ca_2CO_3 + C = Na_2CO_3 + CaS + 2CO_2$$

In the third stage, the soluble sodium carbonate was extracted by leaching with water and purified by crystallisation, the insoluble calcium sulphide which remained being utilised as a source of sulphur.

The Leblanc process was gradually supplanted by that devised and patented in Belgium by the Solvay brothers in 1861. Though this Solvay Process took another ten years to become fully operational, it was producing nine-tenths of the annual consumption of two million tonnes of sodium carbonate by 1900. In this process ammonia derived from ammonium chloride is reacted

234

with carbon dioxide obtained by heating limestone (chalk) in kilns and brine (NaCl) usually obtained by pumping *in situ*. In the first stage these reactions produce sodium bicarbonate, thus:

$$2NH_3 + CO_2 + H_2O = (NH_4)_2CO_3$$
$$(NH_4)_2CO_3 + 2NaCl = Na_2CO_3 + 2NH_4Cl$$
$$Na_2CO_3 + CO_2 + H_2O = 2NaHCO_3$$

The sodium bicarbonate, being insoluble, is filtered off and heated to form the normal carbonate, thus: $2NaHCO_3 = Na_2CO_3 + CO_2 + H_2O$ the carbon dioxide released in this reaction being recycled to the continuous process.

Sulphuric acid requirements for such as the Leblanc process were initially met on a manufacturing scale by burning sulphur with nitre in large glass vessels of 40 to 60 gallons capacity (Ward, 1740) though it had been prepared from the late middle ages by distilling ferrous sulphate crystals from which its early name was *oil of vitriol*. The burning was repeated until the acid which collected at the bottom of the vessels was strong enough for subsequent concentration in glass retorts for sale as 'oil of vitriol made by the bell'. However in 1746 Roebuck and Garbett substituted lead chambers for Ward's glass vessels and in 1793 F. Clement and J. B. Desormes showed that the process could be made continuous. The difficulty in the manufacture of sulphuric acid is that the sulphur burns in air to produce sulphur dioxide which when dissolved in water produces sulphurous acid, H_2SO_3, thus:

$$S + O_2 = SO_2 \text{ followed by } SO_2 + H_2O = H_2SO_3$$

whereas what is required is oxidation to SO_3 and solution in water to produce sulphuric acid H_2SO_4, thus $2SO_2 + O_2 = 2SO_3$ followed by $SO_3 + H_2O = H_2SO_4$

The role of the nitre in the Ward and the Lead Chamber processes was to effect this second oxidation of sulphur dioxide to sulphur trioxide with the oxygen of the nitrate radical (NO_3). However, in 1870 the German chemist Rudolf Messel succeeded in producing sulphur trioxide by passing the sulphur dioxide over a platinum catalyst in air, and after the first World War a vanadium pentoxide catalyst was found to be a cheaper alternative.

Organic chemistry, as investigation of carbon compounds came to be called (c.f. Section 9.2), had shown that long chains of linked carbon atoms existed in some natural products such as vegetable and animal fibres; and that long protein chains could readily be broken down into smaller molecular units, such as the amino acids (c.f. Section 9.2.1). Thus, attempts were soon made to modify natural products and to synthesise new polymeric (Gk. many parts) materials from smaller molecules. Thus in 1869 John Wesley Hyatt patented celluloid made by treating the natural polymer cellulose (c.f. Section 9. 2. 1) with nitric acid and blending with camphor, another natural product. This was used as a substitute for ivory in the manufacture of billiard balls, for the production of dental plates and later as a base for photographic film. Again in 1872 Adolf von Baeyer mixed phenol and formaldehyde with a view to a polymer, though he produced only a dark non-crystalline sludge which he rejected as being irrelevant to his interest in molecular structure. However, Baekeland and Swinburne later produced from this sludge, the first industrially important fully synthetic thermosetting plastic, Bakelite. Again in 1897 a semi-synthetic polymer was produced in Germany from milk casein and used for buttons and other small items while in respect of textile developments we have already noted the new artificial fibre of Charles Frederick Cross and Edward J. Bevan, and the new synthetic azo-dyes of Henry Perkin (c.f. Section 8.1.7).

Although petroleum occurs in vast underground deposits, natural surface-releases permitted its use in masonry-jointing, leak-prevention and lubrication from earliest times, and Marco Polo found petroleum-gas being burned at a fire-temple in Baku in 1272. Again, in the 1840s James 'Paraffin' Young was distilling lighting-oil from Scottish shale deposits and George H. Bissel encouraged by oil contamination at shallow depths in water and brine drilling operations, began to drill for oil in Pennsylvania where his contractor, Edwin L. Drake, was successful at 21 metres depth on 29 August 1859. Around this time, oil wells were producing in Romania, the Nobel brothers were active in Baku in developing oil pipelines and having Swedish-built oil tankers delivered *via* inland waterways, while annual Russian and North American production levels were each around 12,000 tonnes by the end of the century. Though early freshwater and brine wells had been sunk by the Chinese method of shattering rock and penetrating soil by manually raising and dropping a heavy steel tool and progressively lining the hole to prevent collapse and to facilitate debris removal by water-flushing, steam power had replaced manpower by the 1850s and by the 1920s depths of 2,500 metres were being achieved. Again, though rotary drills had been used in Europe for accessing underground water, they could not be used for the hard-rock oil-drilling required in America until hard alloy drill-bits and abrasives such as tungsten carbide or industrial diamond had been successively introduced and though the turbo-drill was introduced in the Russia of the 1920s, it was not widely used until after 1945. Nonetheless, by 1894 sub-sea oil deposits were being accessed by drilling from jetties at Santa Barbara and by the 1920s fixed offshore drill-rigs were operating in the Caspian Sea and mobile barge-mounted drill-rigs off the US Gulf Coast and elsewhere.

However, the components and properties of crude oil vary with source and require processing to produce useable products. The most volatile fraction, petrol (gasoline) was considered a dangerous waste until found suitable for fuelling the internal combustion automobile engine while the less volatile paraffin (kerosene), was initially and increasingly required as a lamp-oil. Less volatile again was a viscous fraction which only gradually found use as a fuel oil particularly for ships, and an even less volatile and more viscous black pitch. Clearly, if the demand for lamp and Primus-type stove oil was to be satisfied, markets had to be found for the fractions which were otherwise wastes. While the subsequent growing demand for petrol could initially be met by distillation, attention focussed on the viscous wastes with the intention of 'cracking' their large molecules into the smaller paraffin type for which there was the greater demand. Thus, from the 1860s to about 1900 high temperature 'cracking' produced dozens of process patents and increasing paraffin yields from crude oils while it took until about 1914 for petrol demand to exceed supply by distillation. However, from about 1900 the far sighted could see a coming need to 'crack' down to the petrol fraction. Thus, in 1913 William M. Burton of Standard Oil of Indiana patented a high-temperature and high-pressure process for 'cracking' the heavy fuel oil fraction to petrol and the company had increased its cracking units to 800 by 1923. Meanwhile, in 1915 Jesse Dubbs and his son Carbon Petroleum Dubbs patented an improved process which was licensed to Shell in 1919, the demand for petrol having increased substantially during the 1914-18 War. However, little further progress was made till 1937 when Eugene Houdry's catalytic cracking process substantially reduced costs just before US demand for warplane fuel alone rose from 40,000 barrels per day to 600,000 barrels by 1945. Once again we see wastes being progressively put to use within industry without external agitation from anyone.

8. 1. 12 Electricity Supply, Water Purification and Sewage Treatment

Though early on-site gas plants had served large consumers such as cotton mills, other localised plants could only supply more numerous small users within delivery pressure limits of a few kilometres. Similarly, electricity supply in the 1870s was a small-scale affair with early generators being installed in factories, theatres, railway stations and large retail premises solely for lighting arc-lamps and later incandescent filament lamps. The first district supply was installed at Brighton in 1887, the year the *London Electricity Supply Corporation* was founded by Basil de Ferranti. Nonetheless, before widely dispersed users could be supplied, the energy-loss through heating the transmission lines had to be reduced, this being possible only through the principle of induction whereby current flow is reduced by increasing the generator voltage by a step-up transformer for transmission and by decreasing it again by a step-down transformer for reception by users. Thus, Basil de Ferranti proposed a power station on cheap land with access for fuel delivery at Deptford to supply a large populated area of London some seven miles distant for which he designed a new cable consisting of 6-metre copper conductors separated longitudinally by waxed-paper insulators for his intended 10,000 volt transmission.

In this early period of local electrical power supply, alternating and direct current had their respective supporters because accumulators and electric motors required direct-current while alternating current was essential for transmission transformers. However, Nikola Tesla a Serbian electrical engineer working in Budapest introduced his alternating current motor in 1881 and marketed it in 1889 after emigrating to the USA. Even so, the electrical generating industry remained localised with differences in frequency and voltage, there being 250 separate suppliers in Britain and 3000 in the USA as late as 1900, causing difficulties for electrical appliance manufacturers and users. However, despite the desirability of unifying on alternating current, direct current suppliers were still to be found in London as late as 1950.

The most important public service industry of ancient times had been that of urban water-supply and sanitation, both of which reached a high standard before the fall of Rome (c.f. Section 2.5.4). By the nineteeth century, however, the countryman still depended on local streams, springs and wells with the possibility of collecting rainwater in a cistern against occasional periods of drought. For the townsman the same basic sources were now being exploited much more intensely, not only for the rising domestic requirements of population growth but also for rising industrial requirements particularly for textiles. Response to increasing demand involved the use of steam-engines to raise more water from the larger rivers, the use of cast-iron pipes able to withstand higher pressures than those of earlier wooden pipes, the use of improved drilling techniques for deeper access to underground water especially where artesian pressure would circumvent the atmospheric limitation on pumping, and the construction of reservoirs where the terrain was suitable. Even so, only the better class of dwelling had its own direct supply usually to a single tap in the kitchen, while a stand-pipe in the street more usually served a number of tenements, and while the water-carrier selling by the bucketful was by no means unusual.

Again for the countryman, human excreta could be mixed with farmyard manure and spread on the land or buried, whereas for the townsman, wastes of all kinds were thrown into the street with alternatives being slow to enter general use. Thus while a water closet flushed from an overhead tank had been installed in his Somerset home by Sir John Harrington in 1589, while an automatic flushing system activated by removal of the user's body-weight from the seat had been introduced in 1780, and while the U-bend water-seal appeared in 1882, nothing at all was done to improve final disposal arrangements. The initial water flow simply conveyed the wastes to a cess-pit which had to be emptied periodically or to waste pipes or open sewers leading directly to the nearest water-body. This for preference might be the sea or more likely the nearest river which in all likelihood would be a source of drinking water. Wells too, might be contaminated by damaged under-ground sewage pipes or by ingress of contaminated surface-water through poorly protected well-heads.

Meanwhile, the UK population increased from 9 to 24 million between 1760 and 1830, and to 42 million in 1900 while urban New York grew from less than 1 to 3.5 million between 1860 and 1900. Thus with Parliament unable to sit at Westminster in the summer because of the stench from the Thames and with the London Cholera outbreak of 1854, Parliament voted the money and Bazalgette rebuilt the London drainage system substantially as it remains to this day based on the separation of storm water carried to the river and of sewage to the eastern estuary. Later, pre-discharge treatment arrangements consisting of filter beds and delay-ponds to remove and decompose organic matter enabled innocuous water to be discharged to the estuary while innocuous sludge was dumped at sea from specially designed hopper-barges. Again, in the 1870s, Louis Pasteur established the relationship between disease and micro-organisms thus emphasising the health dangers of over-crowding and associated water contamination (c.f. Section 8.2.6).

8. 1. 13 Printing, Tele-Communication, Entertainment and Recreation

In 1772 the Scottish goldsmith William Ged made a plaster mould of a page of moveable-type and cast the whole page in metal stereotype thus permitting retention for later multiple use in a manner impossibly uneconomic with individual moveable type. In 1800 Lord Stanhope introduced his iron-frame press which being stronger than its wooden precursors permitted a sharper print-impression and a print-rate of 250 sheets per hour while papier-mache had replaced plaster for page-casting by 1829. Meanwhile in 1810 Frederick Koenig had replaced earlier flat presentations with his steam press in which the paper was rolled over the inked type by a revolving cylinder to which a second paper-carrying cylinder was quickly added so that two sheets could be printed on a forward and backward movement at a rate of 1100 sheets per hour. Next, Richard Hoe wedged the type to a cylinder in 1846 New York, this being further improved by cylindrical stereotypes and continuous paper rolls from about 1860.

During this period attention turned to increasing the speeds of both type-casting and type-setting through mechanisation. The first machine for the former task appeared in the USA in 1838 and the first for the latter in 1842 when Henry Bessemer introduced his "piano" key-board for type and space selection from storage magazines. This was superseded in 1886 when Ottmar Mergenthaler combined the casting and setting of type in whole lines (lines o' type) or Linotype in a single machine at a rate of 6000 characters per hour and in 1887 by the Monotype machine which cast, set and justified individual characters making easier the correction of errors for high quality work such as book production. As rates of newspaper production increased it was no longer necessary to break up type after each edition. It was melted and recast. Again for material requiring only a few copies, Christopher L. Sholes designed the typewriter in 1867, later produced by the Remington Company in 1874. This early machine incorporated the strike-bar characters and QWERTY keyboard to minimise the risk of bar clashing, and the inked-ribbon and carbon paper for the associated small copying requirement. This design remained standard until the introduction of interchangeable metal character bands provided a range of type-faces in William A. Burt's VariTyper of 1933, of line-justification in 1937, and of the "golf-ball" head of the IBM Selectric in 1961.

In 1753 a correspondent to the *Scots Magazine* suggested that messages could be sent to a receiving system comprising alphabetically labelled pith balls each paired with a wire to which the ball could be attracted in sequence to spell out words when the wire was activated by static electricity by the sender. In the event, Francisco Salva transmitted such signals over a distance of 1 kilometre in 1804 using the voltaic cell invented less than four years previously, Samuel T. von Somering increased the distance to 3 km in 1812 using electrified wire identification by hydrogen bubble release from weak acid, and Baron Schilling identified the electrified wires by the movement of suspended magnetic needles in 1832. Again, William Cooke and Charles Wheatstone used this type of detector in their patented telegraph of 1837 in which five wires and detectors operating in pairs identified the transmitted letter. Yet again, with the wire-identification requirement reduced to two, the code developed by Samuel Morse in 1835 was being used to send messages as long and short strokes on a paper-strip by 1842. By 1855, David Hughes had devised

238

a printing telegraph in which the message was typed out on a keyboard by the sender and printed out again for the receiver, and by 1870 the multiplex system enabled several messages to be sent simultaneously over the same wire. Meanwhile Britain which already had 6,400 kilometres of message line was connected to France in 1851, to the USA in 1858, to India in 1868, while a submarine cable was laid across the Black Sea to Varna in Bulgaria during the Crimean War. By the end of the century there were 25,000 kilometres of wire in Britain where the public was sending 400 million telegrams per annum, while in Europe and in the USA there were 130,000 and 80,000 kilometres respectively.

The principle underlying the telephone is that the sound waves of the caller's voice vibrate a reed or diaphragm and cause a corresponding fluctuation of electrical signal to pass along a wire connected to another reed or diaphragm which is caused to vibrate to reproduce the sound waves of the caller for the listener's ear. The first to file a patent (14 February, 1876) was the Scotsman Alexander Graham Bell who beat the American inventor Elisha Gray by a few hours. Bell subsequently emigrated to the USA and founded the *Bell Telephone Company*. As with the telegraph the new system developed rapidly, the first exchange with 21 subscribers opening in New Haven Connecticut in January 1878, the first telephone company being founded in Britain the same year, Boston and New York being linked in January 1884 and there being one million telephones in the USA by 1900. Meanwhile in 1889 Almon B. Strowger of Kansas City had devised an automatic system by which connections could be made by push-buttons or later by a numbered dial though this was not adopted by Bell Telephones until after the 1914-18 War when women exchange-operators were readily recruited. Meanwhile in 1882, the Belgian engineer F. van Rysselberghe had introduced anti-interference 'chokes' which permitted telephonic messages to be carried on existing telegraph lines and by 1891 Britain was connected to the 20,000 kilometres of Continental telephone-telegraph lines. However, long distance telephony required signal boosters at intervals and this presented difficulties even for overland links which were not solved until the early twentieth century. Early telephones had only one vibrator (microphone) used alternately for speaking and listening until in 1877 Thomas Edison introduced separate ear and mouthpieces.

We have seen that James Clerk Maxwell's mathematical work on electromagnetic waves followed by Heinrich Hertz's demonstration that such waves could be generated by an electric spark and detected at a range of 20 metres was a major unification of knowledge of the physical world. However, on reading of Hertz's results in 1884 the 20 year old Gugliemo Marconi quickly transmitted such signals over 2 kilometres pulsed as required for Morse code, went to London where he attracted the interest of the Post Office engineer-in-chief, established his own company by 1897, later the *Marconi Wireless Telegraph Company* of 1900, and sent a signal across the English Channel in 1899. The next step was to transmit pictures by wireless telegraphy. Thus, again in 1884, Paul Nipkow had devised a system of scanning pictures by rotating a disc provided with a series of small holes arranged in a helix whereby bright areas of the picture passed light strongly through the holes while darker areas passed dimmer light causing differing intensities to fall onto a photoelectric material *i.e.* an electron emitter in response to incident light (c.f. Section (9.1.1), the electric pulses thus generated being transmitted to a distant receiver where the reverse transformation of electricity to light was effected, passed through a rotating Nipkow disc and allowed to fall on a screen to reproduce the original picture. This approach was followed by John Logie Baird, though as with Gugliemo Marconi these new developments would only be fully realised in the twentieth century (c.f. Section 9.5.6).

Meanwhile Thomas Edison had built his first sound-recording device, the phonograph of 1877 on the principle of allowing the sounds to vibrate a thin metal diaphragm and transferring these vibrations by means of a spring-loaded steel stylus to a sheet of waxed paper wrapped around a rotating cylinder into the wax of which the stylus cut a spiral groove to depths corresponding to the sound vibrations, reversal of the procedure reproducing the original sounds. Later, tinfoil was substituted for waxed paper. Later still, in 1886 Chichester Bell used a hard wax cylinder in his graph phone and in 1888 Emile Berliner introduced the disc-record to be played on his gramophone. At this stage the stylus was caused to vibrate laterally and the original recording was transferred to a copper disc from which large numbers of copies could be made in hard shellac resin.

In the late seventeenth century the *camera obscura* was used by artists to transfer an image to paper and early in the eighteenth Johan Heinrich Schulze had noted that silver salts darkened in colour when exposed to light, though the fixing of such an image was not achieved until 1826 when Joseph Niepse utilised the photochemical hardening of bitumen. This first photograph was achieved by using a lens to focus an image on a light-sensitive bitumen-coated plate contained in a darkened box (camera) for an eight-hour exposure time. Returning to silver salts, Louis-Jacques-Mande Daguerre in 1839 used a coating of silver iodide on a copper plate in exposures of 30 minutes in bright sunlight, followed by development by exposure to mercury vapour to obtain what came to be known as a Daguerreotype. Also in 1839 William Henry Fox Talbot used silver salts on transparent paper to produce a negative from which any number of positive copies could be made. With this approach exposure times were reduced to just over a minute making portraiture just possible. Again, by 1851 Frederick Scott Archer had reduced exposure times to about half-a-second for brilliantly lit subjects with his wet-plate process in which a glass plate was dipped into silver nitrate solution immediately before exposure and developed immediately after to give a sharper image than did paper. To reduce the amount of photographic paraphernalia, the dry plate appeared in 1853 with the additional advantage of not needing immediate development. In 1874 George Eastman moved from dry plates to paper and then to celluloid strips which were tightly rolled on spools while his Kodak camera of 1888 opened photography to the amateur mass market with his slogan "you press the button, we do the rest." Though initially the camera had to be returned for reloading (enough film for 100 prints), only the exposed film was subsequently returned for development and printing and by the end of the century exposure times had dropped to 1/25 of a second. However, colour film for popular use was a twentieth century development

Image persistence on the retina already recorded by Ptolemy, was used in the nineteenth century to convey the illusion of animation by viewing a sequence of progressively intermittent pictures of such as a dancer at the appropriate rate of exposure to the eye. Thus, Edward Muybridge a professional photographer produced his zoopraxiscope with which in 1877-78 he investigated the action of a galloping horse with a system of 24-cameras with exposure times of 1/1000th of a second. This investigation settled a long-standing argument by showing conclusively that at certain points in the action all four feet of a galloping horse are off the ground. This success encouraged the French physiologist Etienne-Jules Marey to develop his 'photographic gun' which permitted a rapid succession of images to be recorded around the circumference of a photographic plate (and later on a roll of film) for subsequent projection on a screen for the investigation of phenomena in natural and slow motion, all of which was achieved by 1890. Also around 1890 Muybridge had the idea of combining his zoopraxiscope with Edison's phonograph, but was rejected, Edison producing his own Kinetoscope in 1891 with which one person at a time could view about fifteen seconds of action in entertainment halls. Though Edison subsequently added music and voice in 1896 he did not patent it abroad, thus allowing the Lumiere Brothers to adapt it for viewing on a screen with the result that the first showing of a 'motion picture' to a paying audience occurred in Le Grand Café, 14 Boulevard des Capucines, Paris, on 28 December 1895.

The bicycle is another familiar item of the modern world, the development of which was substantially complete by 1900. In 1818, Karl von Drais produced his two-wheel Draisine or Dany-horse on which the rider sat astride and pushed against the ground for propulsion. In 1839 the Scottish blacksmith Kirkpatrick Macmillan added pedals which drove the rear wheel through a system of cranks and in 1861 the French coach-builder Pierre Michaux attached the pedals and cranks directly to the front wheel. Such velocipedes were being manufactured in Coventry where in 1870 James Starley increased the diameter of the front wheel to about 2 metres to gear the rider's effort to a comfortable pedalling rate in what became known as the 'penny-farthing'. This gearing requirement was met in the 'safety' bicycle of 1885 by arranging for the rider to transmit his pedal action to the rear wheel by means of a chain passing round a large sprocket-wheel on the pedal shaft and a smaller one on the rear wheel axle while placing the rider closer to the road between two wheels of equal size. The next significant innovations were W. T. Shaw's enclosed gearing of 1885 (fore-runner of the Sturmley-Archer three-speed hub of 1902) and John Dunlop's pneumatic tyre of 1888. By 1887, Thomas Stevens had completed a 19,000 kilometre cycle tour (started in 1884) which took him across the USA, Europe and on to Asia. Again, in the autumn of 1888 the Reverend Hugh Callan cycled from Glasgow to Jerusalem and back and in Paris J. Michael attained a speed of just under 75 kilometres per hour in 1902.

8. 2 THE RELATIONSHIP OF PHYSICS AND CHEMISTRY TO OTHER SCIENCES

Physics is concerned with the nature of matter and energy (atoms and radiation) and chemistry with the energy-dependent reactive properties of atoms, molecules, ions and radicals. Thus, chemistry having established by experimentation the existence of these and the nature of heat, and physics having established by experimentation the nature of electricity, magnetism and light by which chemistry deepened and quantified its understanding of chemical reaction, I now show how physicochemical knowledge deepens and quantifies the knowledge of other sciences beyond their early descriptive stages just as it deepens and widens craftsmanship to technology. Thus, while all knowledge begins with observation such as in craftsmanship and ethics, quantitative experimentation is required to establish cause and effect relationships mathematically, concerning which Lord Kelvin said: "if you can't measure it you don't know anything about it." Consequently, in conditions where direct experimentation is impossible deductions from observation must be treated as hypothetical until shown compatible with earlier or subsequently conductible experimentation. Thus, having shown, in Section 8.1, how earlier physicochemical knowledge took observational craftsmanship to technology between 1700 and 1900, I now show how it took observational astronomy, geology and life sciences to quantitative predictability through knowledge of their cause and effect mechanisms in more or less the same time interval, while deferring consideration of observational but experimentation-lacking whole body biology to Section 8.3.

8. 2. 1 Astronomy
We have already seen that early classification by observation in astronomy was extended by the physics of the telescope while knowledge of mechanism required the experimentation of gravitational dynamics. Again, we saw that knowledge of the constitution of the Sun depended entirely on physicochemical spectroscopy while precise astronomical measurement depended on craftsmanship and mathematics.

As to precision, the first Astronomer Royal John Flamstead determined the positions of some twenty thousand stars in the period 1676-1689 while Edmond Halley (1656-1742) Astronomer

Royal from 1720, sailed for St Helena in 1676 on the hypothesis that discrepancies between the observed and Newtonian predicted paths of Saturn and Jupiter might be explained by celestial measurements possible only from the southern hemisphere. There, over a period of eighteen months, Halley determined the positions of 341 previously uncharted stars, improved the seconds pendulum of Huygens and made meteorological observations published in 1686 which explained the main features of the global wind system. In 1680 he began to measure the movement of comets which Newton had suggested might be in elliptical orbits round the Sun (regular re-appearances) though of such high eccentricity as to be indistinguishable from parabolas (one appearance only) when close enough to the Sun to be observed from Earth. In 1682 Halley determined the elliptical path of such a comet to be in conformity with previous appearances in 1531 and 1607 showing it (now known as Halley's comet) to orbit the Sun according to Newton's Laws as a member of the solar system with a re-appearance interval of 75 years.

Again, James Bradley (1693-1762) who succeeded Halley as Astronomer Royal, measured in 1729 the extent to which star positions were subject to elliptical variation as observed from the orbiting Earth in order that star position measurement could be corrected for this phenomenon in future. Also in pursuit of ever-greater accuracy, he showed that the long-term precession of the equinoxes is not only caused by the circular motion of the Earth's north and south poles as deduced from Newton, but is additionally subject to yet another influence which causes the circumference of these circles to be sinusoidal with a small but detectable amplitude. Since Bradley's time, further influences on the orientation of the Earth's axis have been quantified as to variation in solar radiation intensity at the Earth' surface and hence as to possible variation on global temperatures as distinct from any earth-sourced variation (c.f. Section 9.4.3).

In addition, a combination of great work-capacity and skill in observational instrument-making enabled Frederick William Herschel (1738-1822), a Hanoverian who came to England in 1757, to conduct four complete reviews of the observable universe, to discover the planet Uranus in 1781 by harmonising discrepancies between the observed and predicted orbits of the planets known up till then, and to discover the satellites of Uranus in 1787 and of Saturn in 1789. Again, after further instrumental improvements he showed that our solar system was located somewhat less than halfway to the centre of our Milky Way galaxy; that the galaxy was lens-shaped with a diameter about five times its maximum thickness; and that there were many hundreds of what he called nebulae. Subsequently, by increasing the power of his telescopes in the period to 1791 he resolved some of these nebulae into star clusters which he concluded were island galaxies separate from our own while those which he could not resolve he concluded to be true nebulae of a shining fluid which he suggested in 1814 might be in the process of condensing into stars (c.f. Section 9.3.1). As to the movement of certain stars relative to each other (the so-called proper motions known since Alexandrian times) Herschel concluded in 1805 that the solar system itself was moving towards a point in the constellation of Hercules. Again, Herschel selected certain closely associated pairs or 'double stars' for observation at six monthly intervals *i.e.* from points 180 million miles apart across the Earth's orbit for estimation of the relative distances of the members of each pair from the Earth and showed in 1802 that they moved round each other according to Newton's law of gravity in all of the cases studied to this detail. Herschel's discovery of the planet Uranus and his work on paired stars thus extended and confirmed Newton's work on the Earth and Moon.

Also in pursuit of ever greater accuracy, Leonard Euler of Basel (1707-83) showed that the effects of certain variations in the earth's movement had accumulated since the time of Ptolemy and were explicable by supposing that the axes of the earth's orbit had altered by about 5 degrees in this time interval. Again, while it had been known since Galileo that the non-rotating Moon alternately reveals and conceals lunes (c.f. Section 3.1.2) close to its edge, it was explained in 1764 by J. L. Lagrange (1736-1813) as being due to the Moon and the Earth rocking slightly with respect to each other because neither is truly spherical and so gravity is not acting from truly spherical centres. With respect to other subtle effects, Lagrange showed that the gravitational influence of one member of the solar system on another depends not only on their relative positions and masses but also on the dimensions and relative inclinations of their orbits and that the latter produce small-scale orbital disturbances which exhibit periodic cycles. In addition he showed that these mutual disturbances were cumulative and either self-correcting or non self-correcting over time, and he called the former "periodic" and the latter "secular".

In further consideration of such disturbances, P. S. Laplace (1749-1827) showed in 1787 that the very slow increase in orbital speed of the Moon around the Earth was explicable on the basis of a correspondingly slow decrease in the eccentricity of the Earth's orbit round the Sun; that the latter was due to the gravitational influence of the other planets; and that these changes amounted to a decrease in the length of the month of about $1/30^{th}$ of a second per century. Again, irregularities in the motions of Jupiter and Saturn which had been suspected since about 1650, substantiated by Halley in 1676, and believed to be secular in nature (as Lagrange would say) were shown by Laplace to be periodic and self-correcting over a period of 900 years. Subsequently, Lagrange and Laplace undertook (1773-84) a systematic investigation of the supposed secular disturbances from which they concluded that there is a constant amount of eccentricity within the solar system; that if the orbital eccentricity of one planet be increased, that of another must decrease; and that the *Law of Constant Eccentricity* may be seen as an expression of the stability of the solar system, all disturbances being self-correcting in a periodic manner.

Laplace's *Celestial Mechanics* (1799-1825) showed that all apparent discrepancies between observation and prediction for all members of the solar system were resolvable by careful application of Newton's Law of Gravity to such levels of accuracy as to suggest that any future discrepancies, if found, would be smaller and in any case resolvable by more precise application of the said Law. This represented a successful culmination of the efforts of the followers of Newton to validate his Law of Gravity. For present purposes it illustrates yet another aspect of the scientific method. Here we have a demonstration of the extent to which care and accuracy of measurement coupled with mathematical analysis can provide almost incredible levels of precision in our prediction of future conditions when the underlying mechanism of cause and effect is understood in mathematical terms. Again, in his *Essay of the System of the World* of 1796 Laplace having pointed out that all of the motions of the members of solar system were in the same direction and recalling Herschel's suggestion that nebulae condensed into stars, suggested that the solar system itself, star (Sun) and planets together, had condensed out of such a gaseous nebula. This in turn demonstrates how one thing leads to another in scientific method, for this suggestion in turn implied that all of the elements comprising Earth and Sun, whatever these might be, would be distributed throughout the universe in general, a suggestion which chemical spectroscopy in the hands of Fraunhofer, Kirchhoff and Bunsen was shortly to reality-validate as we have already seen (c.f. Sections 7.3.2 and 9.3)

Again, in purely numerical way J. E. Bode (1747-1826) noted in 1772 that the proportionate distances from the Sun of Mercury, Venus, Earth, Mars, Jupiter and Saturn could be represented by the sequence of numbers 4, 7, 10, 16, 52, 100 which could be generated by adding four to each of the members of the sequence 0, 3, 6, 12, 24, 48, 96 except that the number 28 is absent from the first series, and suggested that the apparently missing planet between Mars and Jupiter might be found. He searched at the indicated distance and duly found a small planet which he named Ceres about a quarter the size of the Moon. This turned out to be the first member of the asteroid belt almost all of which orbit between the orbits of Mars and Jupiter and might be thought to be the remains of a disintegrated planet as meteorites might be, or debris which failed to accrete to a planet (c.f. Section 9.4.5). Again, more conventionally, on the basis of observed discrepancies in the orbit of Uranus, John Crouch Adams (1819-92) and U. J. J. Verrier (1811-77) independently searched for a planetary cause at the indicated location and announced their discovery of the planet now called Neptune. As to the wider universe, measurements on the double-stars first reported by Herschel continued to be refined by F. G. W. Struve (1793-1864) and his successors at St Petersburg, and the proper motions of single stars including a few reported by Herschel continued to be measured by F. W. A. Argelander (1799-1875) who by 1837 had identified about 400.

To extend work on the motion of stars, their distances had to be accurately determined and so attention returned to the parallax method previously applied to double-stars by Herschel. This approach, however, involved ever more accurate measurement of the increasingly small angle subtended for ever more distant stars even when the subtending chord was the 180 million miles across the Earth's orbit. In addition, the distances involved required a more convenient unit of distance than the mile. This latter need was met in 1832 by Thomas Henderson working between 1798-1844 though it remained unpublished till 1893, while H. L. Bessel (1784-1846) had published his results in 1838. This new unit, the parsec, is the distance at which the angle at a star subtended by the earth's distance from the sun is 1 second of arc, this distance equating to 3.086×10^{13} km. This in turn equates to 3.2616 light years, one light year being the distance travelled by light in a year at 186,000 miles per second, this being the unit subsequently introduced for distances beyond measurement by parallax (c.f. Section 9.3.2)

8. 2. 2 Measurement of the Earth

The circumference of the Earth had been measured in classical times and the length on the surface corresponding to a degree of latitude or longitude had been taken to be 60 miles until Jean Picard (1620-82) undertook a re-determination for the *Academie des Science* in the period 1669-1671. Using essentially the same method as Eratosthenes, he arrived at a figure of 69.1 miles. The *Academie* then mounted an astronomical expedition 1671-1674 to Cayenne in French Guiana at latitude 5° north where it was found that a pendulum set for Paris in latitude 49° north had to be shortened, suggesting that the Earth was not spherical. Here again, we see physics and craftsmanship contributing to the accuracy of measurement. Thereafter, a long series of pendulum measurements were undertaken in France between 1684 and 1714 by G. D. Cassini (1625-1712) and his son Jacques (1677-1756) and several expeditions were mounted to make pendulum measurements elsewhere, the most important of which left Paris in 1735 for South America under C. D. de la Condamine (1701-74) to decide whether the earth was a prolate spheroid (rotation of an ellipse about its major axis) or an oblate spheroid (rotation about its minor axis), a question settled in favour of the latter option by P. L. M. Maupertuis (1698-1759) who had been on such an expedition to northern Sweden.

During this period, further improvements were made in the precision of instruments. Thus, George Graham (1673-1751) constructed his mercurial pendulum which compensated for thermal expansion of the rod with expansion of mercury in a container suspended by the rod to maintain a constant centre of mass and thus constant effective length, improved astronomical instruments for Halley and Bradley and improved geodetic instruments for Maupertuis. Again, John Harrison (1692-1776) of longitude fame produced in 1726 his grid iron pendulum in which thermal expansion in opposing directions was mutually compensating and his maintenance mechanism by which clocks kept time while being wound. In addition, Jesse Ramsden (1732-1800) produced his 'equatorial' of 1744 to achieve automatic telescope tracking of any identified point in the heavens, and his redesigned theodolite to achieve more land survey accuracy.

Such instrument improvements encouraged a more precise approach to cartography. Thus, Picard's numerous longitudes were incorporated in a map of France prepared for the *Academie* in 1679 by G. D. Cassini who also produced a much improved map of the world in 1694 while J. B. Bourguignon d' Anville (1697-1783) broke with tradition in omitting fanciful entries and legends from his maps by leaving blank the interior of Africa and omitting the Antarctic continent which some believed to account for half the southern hemisphere. In 1718 he produced a map of China based on surveys by Jesuit missionaries while his *Carte Geometrique de la France* of 1793 based on the surveys carried out in the period 1744-1783 by C. F. Cassini (1714-84) and his son Jacques Dominique (1748-1845) was for many years the best topographical presentation of France. In 1787 General William Roy used a Ramsden theodolite to establish the base line for the triangulation of the British Isles which led to the Ordnance Survey of which the first inch-to-the-mile sheet was issued in 1801. Again, during the three voyages which occupied the last twelve years of his life, Captain James Cooke (1728-79) mapped the Pacific Ocean and two French naval officers, J. F. de Galaup, Compte de la Perouse (1741-89) and J. A. Bruni d'Entrecasteaux (1739-93) began to map Chinese and Japanese waters.

8. 2. 3 Meteorology, Oceanography and Terrestrial Magnetism

In his account of global winds of 1686 Halley had described such features as the temperate variables and the more reliable trade and monsoon winds of the tropics between 30° north and south in terms of the general distribution of solar induced temperatures at the earth's surface. To this early account, George Hadley (1685-1768) added the hypothesis in 1735 that the rotation of the earth deflects the movement of colder denser air moving from the north and south to replace hotter less dense air which is rising in the equatorial region thus providing a fuller explanation of the trade wind system. This hypothesis was supported by the chemist John Dalton (of atomic theory fame) and by the mathematician Jean le Rond d'Alembert (1717-83) in his general work on global winds in 1742, such deflection now being attributed to the Coriolis Force. This was followed by investigations of atmospheric water reported in 1783 by H. B. de Saussure (1740-99), by studies of the composition and properties of the atmosphere at altitude during balloon assents in 1804 by the chemist Gay-Lussac, by introduction of the wind speed scale also in 1804 by Admiral Beaufort (1774-1857) and by dew formation as reported in 1814 by the American Charles Wells (1775-1859). In addition, Friedrich Heinrich Alexander von Humboldt (1769-1859) made the first general study of temperature and pressure over the globe and introduced isotherms and isobars in 1817.

From 1839 onwards, the American naval officer Matthew Fontaine Maury (1806-73) extracted data on winds, currents and related temperatures from ships' logbooks and collated them on charts with the objective of shortening the duration of sea passages. The success of this endeavour was sufficient for an international conference to be called for 1853 to consider the organisation of further observations of this type and Maury's *Physical Geography of the Sea* of 1855 laid the foundations of physical oceanography, encouraged the establishment of several governmental meteorological offices and initiated the international meteorological service, while in 1855 Admiral Fitzroy (1805-65) of the eponymous barometer was appointed first director of the (UK) Meteorological Office. Prediction of tidal heights and times at any required location was still some way off, however, though Kepler and Galileo had discussed the tides and Newton had placed them on a gravitational footing in his *Principia* of 1687.

The extent to which the magnetic compass deviates from true north is known as its declination or variation and Halley had reported compass declinations in his map of global winds of 1700 in the form of isogonic lines of equal declination. Again, Graham showed in 1724 that declination at any given place was subject to diurnal change and between 1756 and 1759 John Canton (1718-72) showed that declinations were erratic when the Aurora Borealis was visible. Soon afterwards it was realised that both these phenomena were related to Sunspot activity. In addition, the strength of the magnetic force was observed (in the period 1798-1803) to vary from place to place in equatorial America and (in 1804) to decrease from pole to equator by Alexander von Humboldt (1769-1859). Again, in 1827, Arago showed that magnetic force also shows diurnal variation and the mathematician Karl Friedrich Gauss (1777-1855) dedicated the first laboratory to the study of terrestrial magnetism at Gottingen in 1834, an initiative followed in 1840 by the establishment of a number of centres throughout the British Empire under the leadership of Edward Sabine (1788-1883) who produced (1823-1871) numerous publications on terrestrial magnetism.

8. 2. 4 Palaeontology and Geology

In 1669 the Dane Niels Steno (1648-86) discussed the formation, displacement and destruction of the stratified rocks of Tuscany and drew attention to the organic origin of fossils (c.f. Sections 6.2.2 and 8.3.3). This produced much subsequent activity in Italy and Britain while in France George Louis Leclerc, Compte de Buffon (1707-88) produced the earliest account of the formation of the Earth and its fossils in his *Epoques de la Nature* of 1778. This did much to set the scene for future work by drawing attention to the heat content of the earth as distinct from that of solar radiation, to the role of the former in altering the rocks and to the presence of a wide variety of fossils in a wide variety of situations. Thus, marine fossils were present in the limestone of mountain tops, those of large terrestrial animals more or less similar to living forms were in near-surface strata, and those of clearly extinct forms were at greater depths. In respect of the heat content of the Earth, Buffon emphasised the formative role of volcanoes and earthquakes while Abraham Gottlob Werner (1750-1817) of the school of mines at Freiburg emphasised the role of water in the formation of rocks. On this issue, the followers of Buffon became known as Vulcanists while those of Werner became Wernerians or Neptunists. Again, Georges Cuvier (1769-1832) adhering to the constancy of species as implied by Linnaeus (1707-78) believed that the succession of populations of fossil species was evidence for successions of catastrophe-related extinctions and creation events. In contrast, Jean Baptiste Pierre Antoine de Monet de Lamarck (1744-1829) believed that the alterability of species more readily accounted for the successions of fossil forms (c.f. Section 8.3.3).

The occurrence of fossils in stratified (sedimentary) rocks had been reported by James Hutton (1726-97) in his *Theory of the Earth* of 1795 as evidence that their layer-structure had been caused by gradual deposition of fine particles on the beds of ancient seas, lakes, marshes *etc*. Again, from his experience in cutting canals William Smith showed in his *Stratigraphical System of Organised Fossils* of 1817 that strata may be characterised by their fossil content though some fossils may occur in more than one adjacent layers, and that the earlier (deeper) the layers, the less the fossils resemble contemporary forms. Furthermore, Charles Lyell (1797-1875) saw that the relative ages of the more recent deposits could be estimated from the proportions they contained of living and extinct mollusc fossils, and he also showed in his *Principles of Geology* of 1830-1833 that rocks are currently being broken down by the processes of erosion and are being deposited in rivers, lakes and seas just as in times past. In addition, G. Poulett Scrope (1787-1876) in his *Considerations on Volcanos* of 1825 recognised the role of heat in the origin of volcanic rock while that of water continued to be recognised in erosion and the formation of sedimentary rocks and clays, thus complementing Vulcanism and Neptunism. Again, Roderick Murchison (1792-1871) in
246

his *Silurian System* of 1839 expounded the chronological correspondence of rocks, introduced much of the nomenclature now in use, and explained the nature and occurrence of many scenic details, while Thomas de la Beche (1796-1855) began the Geological Survey of England and Wales in 1832, this being earlier in inception and execution than any comparable initiative elsewhere. Meanwhile, Jean Louis Agassiz collected evidence in the 1830s for the previously unsuspected sequence of glacial and inter-glacial periods throughout geological time (c.f. Sections 9.4.3).

Thus, by the early decades of the nineteenth century, Earth studies which had started as additional pursuits of chemists and physicists with naturalists taking an interest in fossils, had become the science of geology with its own subdivisions comprising the distribution and arrangement of rocks (stratigraphy), their structure and composition (petrography) and the nature and affinities of their fossils (palaeontology) the word Geology itself being introduced by H. B. de Saussure of Geneva in 1779. In time the study of Earth magnetism and other obviously physical aspects would give rise to the science of geophysics while stratigraphy and petrography would continue to make calls on chemistry, with geochemistry becoming a field in its own right, and with palaeontology continuing to rely largely on whole body biology. Later the sciences of meteorology and oceanography would develop from the early steps reviewed above while continuing to make calls on physics, chemistry and biology as appropriate with the separate speciality of marine biology being recognised later still.

8. 2. 5 Physiology, and Spontaneous Generation of Life

The early chemists had sought knowledge of both chemical and biological processes at the atomic and molecular levels. Thus, Priestley in his *Experiments and Observations on Different Kinds of Air* of 1774 had reported that plants immersed in water give off the gas (now called oxygen) and Lavoisier had demonstrated that the products of its consumption in animal respiration are carbon dioxide and water. Similarly, the Dutch engineer Jan Ingenhousz (1730-99) working in London with the Scottish surgeon John Hunter (1728-93) had published his *Experiments upon Vegetables, discovering their power of purifying the common air in the sunshine and of injuring it in the shade and at night* which reported that plants release oxygen while absorbing atmospheric carbon dioxide in sunlight and re-release a little of the latter in the dark. Hunter always emphasised similarities in living organisms as distinct from the older Linnaeus and the younger Cuvier who as classifiers were always looking for differences. Indeed, Hunter believed that organisms share a common chemical basis regardless of differences in structure and habit.

However, progress towards identifying that common basis only got going when living processes became interpretable in physicochemical terms from the nineteenth century onwards. In 1828, Friedrich Wohler (1800-82) showed that urea, a typical organic chemical excreted by mammals and birds, could be prepared simply by heating to dryness an aqueous solution of ammonium cyanate, a perfectly typical inorganic substance; that nothing is gained or lost in this transformation; and that the constituent atoms of ammonium cyanate simply alter their structural arrangement (isomerise) to that of urea under the action of heat. Thus, Wohler took a step in showing that chemicals are chemicals, and that there is no vital difference between organic and inorganic chemistry. Such was the strength of belief in vitalism, however, that this simple transformation had to be repeated many times before it was accepted. In the meantime, Justus von Liebig (1802-73) professor of Chemistry at Giessen introduced a method for the quantitative analysis of urea in solution (a human adult excretes about 30g of urea every 24 hours) and for many other compounds of significance in the metabolic processes of living organisms. He also classified food intake in terms of carbohydrates, fats and proteins, recognised that plants are the source of all food; that they derive from the carbon dioxide and nitrogen of the atmosphere; and that animal heat derives from the combustion of food, and is not 'innate' as taught by the vitalists (c.f. below).

Meanwhile, Henri Dutrochet (1776-1847) had observed in 1832 what he called stomata, little openings in plant leaves which communicated with the leaf body as the channel of gaseous interchange between the atmosphere and the plant, and in 1837 he had shown that only those plant cells which contain green matter absorbed the carbon dioxide. As to nitrogen, however, Liebig showed in 1840 that this was absorbed through the root system as ammonium salts and nitrates, thus reality-refuting earlier belief in the direct absorption of humus; that the inorganic compounds, carbon dioxide, water, ammonium salts and nitrates provided all the carbon and nitrogen necessary for the production of vegetable matter in all its forms; and that these compounds were also the ultimate products of putrefaction and decay. Thus, Liebig enunciated the cycle of life in which the appropriate assembly of chemical elements is built-up into organic forms by external energy ultimately from the Sun and in accordance with understandable chemical laws, followed by their dissolution according to the same chemical laws when the assembly becomes unsustainable, and so on. Again in the 1850s Jean Baptiste Boussingault (1802- 87) showed that plants can grow in soil devoid of carbon compounds provided only that nitrate is present, thus confirming that all plant carbon must be derived solely from the carbon dioxide of the atmosphere. Yet again, Julius Sachs (1832-97) who had worked on plant nutrition since 1857 showed in 1865 that the chlorophyll is not distributed uniformly throughout the plant; that it is contained in specialist bodies called chloroplasts since 1883; that these absorb carbon dioxide in the presence of light; that the effectiveness of this assimilation depends on the quality of the light; and that it does not occur at all in the total absence of light (c.f. Section 9.2).

Though this new knowledge of the relationship between organisms and their inorganic surroundings re-awakened belief in the spontaneous generation of life-forms, the manner in which this question of cause and effect was finally resolved provides further explication of scientific method. Thus, though Aristotle had been content to leave open the question of spontaneous generation (c.f. Section 3.1.2), and though Francesco Redi had shown maggots arose from flies' eggs rather than spontaneously (c.f. Section 6.3.4), vitalists still believed in the spontaneous generation of Leeuwenhoek's microscopic 'animalcules', and so Louis Joblot (1645-1723) was obliged to return to the fray in 1710. Thus, having boiled such a hay infusion, divided it into two portions, placed one in a baked (sterilised) and closed container and the other in an open container, he showed that the open container teemed with animalcules in a few days while the closed one remained free of them for as long as it remained closed. These results suggested that an infusion once freed of life was incapable of spontaneously generating it; and that life appeared only when it had been transferred from elsewhere as Redi had shown, or where it had not been previously eliminated by heat-treatment as Joblot had now shown. On the other hand, Joseph Needham (1713-1781) carried out similar experiments in 1749 in which life developed in his heated-closed vessels as well as in his open-unheated ones, thus supporting his vitalism, though we now know that his heat-treatment was insufficient to kill heat-resistant spores of which nothing was known in his day.

In any case, Lazzaro Spallanzani (1729-99) proceeded to conduct a series of such experiments with hay infusions, urine, beef-broth and similar organic media in which after sufficiently prolonged heating no animalcules appeared in the closed containers. To this Needham replied that prolonged heating had destroyed the 'vegetative force' of the organic matter on which he believed spontaneous generation of life to depend. Spallanzani responded by showing that he had not destroyed any such capacity by heating the infusions in the closed tubes because animalcules developed in them when they were finally opened to the air and according to the non-

248

vitalists, its dust borne life-forms. To this, the vitalists advanced the counter-argument that air was continuously necessary for spontaneous generation, citing Lavoisier's discovery of oxygen in 1775 and his demonstration that a continuous supply of air was necessary for the life support of all respiring organisms. To address this new vitalist argument, the previously heated infusions of meat or hay were allowed to remain open to the air only after it had passed through sulphuric acid or potassium hydroxide solutions which would eliminate dust borne life-forms (Shultze, 1836) or through very hot glass tubes with the same objective (Schwann, 1836), their belief being that otherwise the air would introduce living forms into the infusions. However, when the infusions exposed to such treated air failed to develop animalcules, the vitalists simply re-ran the Needham-type argument that such treatments destroyed the 'life-giving' properties of the air, thus preventing spontaneous generation.

Finally, in the period 1854 to 1861, Schroder and Von Dusch sought to overcome these arguments by avoiding both chemical and thermal treatment. They simply allowed air to pass through cotton wool and showed that no animalcules appeared in the heated infusions until the containers were opened to air which had not passed through cotton wool. It thus became sufficiently apparent that the method of air treatment had nothing to do with the failure of animalcules to appear; that these did not generate spontaneously; that there were living forms floating on the dust in the air which were killed by heat, acids and alkalis, but which could be caught and held by cotton wool alone; and that such living forms grew and developed in the infusions to which they had entered. Later, Pasteur demonstrated the presence of these life-forms (micro-organisms) on the retaining cotton wool.

8. 2. 6 Microbiology

Louis Pasteur (1822-1895) having been asked to study spoilage in French wine and beer concluded that micro-organisms were the cause; that these were introduced from the air with the ingredients or were present on the internal surfaces of the manufacturing apparatus; and that when beer and wine contain no living organisms they remain unaltered. Pasteur's solution, to what were called the 'diseases' of wine and beer was to hold them at a temperature of between 50-60° C for a few minutes before sealing for storage or transport, and milk was later 'pasteurised' by heating to 62° C to kill undesirable micro-organisms. However, Pasteur also foresaw that the diseases of man and animals might be caused by other specific micro-organisms which could invade from the surroundings and he showed the vitalists that micro-organisms float in the air attached to dust particles; that heat-sterilised infusions and broths can be preserved from the development of animalcules in open flasks, provided only that the necks of these flasks be drawn out and formed into U-bends where dust-borne micro-organism can settle before reaching the flask contents; and that only when a flask is tilted to bring its contents into contact with this dust and allowed to run back into the flask or when the neck is broken off close to the flask-body, does animalcule growth occur in the flask. After Pasteur's work, no serious person felt obliged to refute the beliefs of the remaining vitalists, some of Pasteur's flasks having remained sterile for many decades.

Pasteur also provided an understanding of Jenner's observation that smallpox could be prevented by the prior contraction of the milder cowpox by noting his chance observation that inoculation with attenuated germ-cultures could induce a mild attack of the associated disease and immunity to its recurrence, and his fame was assured when he successfully intervened against rabies by a post-exposure vaccination. For later reference, it should be noted that Pasteur's lifelong interest in chemistry was rewarded during his work on wines by his discovery that the tartrates exhibit a new phenomenon with respect to their transmission of polarised light (c.f.

Section 7.2.7) which he generalised by concluding that some chemically identical organic molecules can alter the plane of light polarisation to the right, (dextro-rotary) or to the left, (laevo-rotary) because they exist in two molecular forms each the mirror-image of the other. This phenomenon is now called stereo-isomerism (c.f. Section 9.2.4).

Pasteur's work on spoilage caused Joseph Lister (1827-1912) to recognise that micro-organisms from the air, the skin of the surgeon or the instruments used might infect wounds during and after surgical operations. Thus, from 1827 onwards he took steps to render all surgical instruments sterile, to operate in a fine mist of carbolic acid solution and to use sterile dressings. Thus, Lister's work led to the current general practice of asepsis which instead of destroying germs after their effects are observed, excludes their presence in the first place by means of sterile clothing and facemasks, sterile instruments and dressings and sterilisation of the patient's skin before any incision is made. Again from 1847 onwards Ignaz Semmelweis had insisted on the need for thorough hand-washing by doctors and mid-wives to reduce the incidence of puerperal sepsis though he died from an infected finger in 1875 before his contribution had been fully appreciated. Meanwhile, Robert Koch (1843-1910) health officer for Wollstein became involved with anthrax and decided to study the causative micro-organism in his spare time. However, at that time micro-organisms had to be observed in the living state, usually in a drop of fluid on a piece of glass and this was difficult because of their transparency, their own motility or the movement induced by the Brownian movement of the suspending fluid. To mitigate these difficulties Koch spread an anthrax-infected droplet as a thin film on a glass microscope-slide and allowed it to dry to render the bacilli motionless without shrivelling or otherwise altering them in any obvious way. Though this succeeded in immobilising his specimens, they were still colourless, substantially transparent and difficult to observe in any detail either directly or photographically.

In the meantime, staining techniques were being used to clarify cell structure at the mcroscopic level in the parallel field of histology and the natural dyes initially used such as carmine were being replaced by some of the new synthetic dyes of Paul Ehrlich, successor to William Perkin of coal-tar dye fame. One of these, methyl-violet, having been found in 1875 by Weigert to reveal the presence of bacteria in histological cell preparations, Koch adopted this staining technique to render his bacteria easy to find and to study, a practice soon widely followed. Again, in 1884 the Danish bacteriologist, Gram, found that bacilli stained with methyl-violet and iodine in sequence could either be decolourised or not by subsequent alcohol treatment, which led to the former being classified as gram-negative and the latter as gram-positive in the Gram test which continues to be the first step in the standard procedure for identifying an unknown bacterium. Meanwhile in 1870 Koch introduced the 'plating-out' technique which involves smearing suspensions of bacteria or liquids suspected of containing them onto solid growth media contained in shallow glass (Petri) dishes, replacing the lid to avoid subsequent airborne contamination and incubating in a suitable oven to promote growth of single organisms to visible colonies for identification and investigation. In the subsequent five years the causative organisms of a range of diseases were identified such as those of diptheria, cholera, erysipelas, lockjaw and pneumonia.

Meanwhile, by 1888 Beijerinck had isolated from the nodules of leguminous plant roots, bacteria of the Genus Rhizobium which symbiotically aid the plants in the direct fixation and utilisation of atmospheric nitrogen, and between 1890 and 1900 Winogradsky, Beijerinck, Omelianski *et al* showed how ammonia formed in the soil by amino acid decomposition is oxidised to nitrite by the genera *Nitrosomonas* and *Nitrosococus* and hence to nitrates by the genera *Nitrobacter* and *Nitrocystis,* nitrate being the form in which nitrogen becomes available to plants other than the leguminous varieties. These workers also clarified the molecular pathways by which micro-organisms chemically make use of sulphur, carbon and other elements in the soil. In addition, von Behring, Kitasato and Fraenkel discovered in 1890 that guinea pigs could be immunised by injections against tetanus and diptheria toxins and that their blood then contained antitoxin which could protect other animals from these diseases. Again, in 1892 Iwanowski discovered a disease-producing agent which was invisible and could not be cultivated on inanimate media, but could pass through filters capable of collecting even the smallest known bacteria. This was the first identified virus, the causative agent of tobaco mosaic disease (c.f. Section 9.2.6).

8. 2. 7 Cellular Structure and Mechanism

In 1805 Lorenz Oken (1779-1851) compared infusoria with the mucous vesicles of which all larger animals are composed and suggested that larger organisms are agglomerations of infusoria. Gradually the term cell came into use, the cell nucleus was recognised, and by 1831 Robert Brown (1773-1859) had recognised that the nucleus was a constant feature of plant cells also. Again, in 1835 Johannes Evangelist Purkinje (1787-1869) drew attention to the similarity of packed cell masses in animals to those in plants while Felix Dujardin (1801-62) recognised unicellular organisms as such, and noted the inseparable association of life with the mucilaginous substance which Purkinje called protoplasm in 1839. Yet again, Karl Ernst von Baer (1792-1876) discovered the microscopic eggs of mammals in 1838 on the bases of which Theodore Schwan (1810-82) produced the first overview of the cell. Thus, he noted that the eggs of hens, frogs and mammals though differing in size, were all essentially cells having a nucleus, protoplasm, membrane *etc*; that development proceeds by cell division; and that subsequent differentiation occurs to produce five cellular types which give rise to the corresponding tissues. These he characterised as having cells which are isolated, separate and independent as in the blood, independent though pressed together as in the skin, coalesced to varying degrees as in cartilage, teeth and bones, elongated into fibres as in tendons and ligaments; and coalesced as in muscles and nerves. Thus, he concluded that the entire animal or plant is composed of cells and the products of cells, that the cells have a life of their own to some extent though subject to the life of the organism as a whole. To this overview, Max Schultz (1825-74) added that cells were nucleated protoplasm (1861) and that protoplasm was the physical basis of life presenting chemical and structural similarities in plants and animals in their higher and lower forms and in all tissues wherever encountered (1863).

The viscous nature of protoplasm attracted the attention of Thomas Graham (1805-69) who had initiated the study of matter in the colloid state in 1850. Colloids are high molecular weight polymeric structures which exhibit high surface tension and are insoluble in water. Graham suggested that the surface energy of colloidal droplets might be the source of vitality at the cellular level. Following this, Emil Fischer (1852-1919) began work on the polymeric class known as proteins in 1882 and showed that they are built up from individual molecules of particular amino-acids of which the amino-group (NH_2) of one links with the acid-group (COOH) of another to form the long chains which are the protein molecules; and that the individual properties of proteins depend on the number and order of the particular amino-acids involved (c.f. Section 9.2.1). Thus, the chemical processes taking place at any moment in a single cell were expected to be many and various and in 1878 Willy Kuhne (1837-1900) introduced the term enzyme to refer to those molecules which act as organic catalysts in facilitating specific chemical reactions within the cellular dimensions of living organisms (c.f. Sections 9.5.2 - 9.5.4)

These developments, in turn, enabled Johannes Muller (1801-58) to review the cellular and comparative anatomical aspects of organisms and to present them as physicochemical mechanisms in his *Handbook of Physiology* covering the period 1834-1840. Nonetheless, he remained a vitalist in believing in something beyond physicochemical mechanism in life processes. His particular contributions were in the mechanism of sense-perception of the external world, his *Principle of Specific Nerve Energies* setting out the specificity whereby sight involves physical stimulation of the optic nerve to produce images in the brain while parallel arrangements exist for all of the other senses. Thus, regardless of the mode of stimulation, the sense impression is always specific to the sensory system stimulated, *i.e.* whether the optic nerve is stimulated by light, heat or electricity the impression is always visual, and similarly for the other senses.

However, for Claude Bernard (1813-78) the organs of the body did not act independently though they had specific functions. Thus, he showed that the liver builds from blood-borne nutrients a store of substances such as glycogen which it subsequently modifies and distributes to other parts of the body as needed. He also showed that digestion did not involve only the stomach, the pancreas providing secretions to the intestine near the exit from the stomach which emulsify and split food proteins and fats into fatty acids and glycerine, which convert insoluble starch into soluble sugars for distribution through the blood, and which hydrolyse and dissolve those proteins not fully hydrolysed in the stomach. (c.f. Section 9.2.1). In addition, Bernard showed that the muscle-fibres in the walls of the smaller arteries (discovered in 1840) were controlled by the nervous system to contract and relax for the regulation of blood supply as required by the body. On the basis of such inter-related organic functions, he defined the basic characteristic of living things as their ability to preserve internal conditions (homeostasis) despite external change, through control of organ function by the nervous system throughout life.

The observable anatomy of this nervous system had been known from the work of Albrecht von Haller (1708-77) and from his *Elementa Physiologiae* of 1759-66 while the electrical nature of its operation in relation to muscle contraction had been revealed by Galvani and Volta. Later, Emil du Bois-Reymond (1818-96) showed that a nervous impulse is always associated with a change in electrical state which passes along the nerve, and he and others went on to show that chemical changes in muscle always accompany contraction switched on by the nervous impulse/change in electrical state. In the meantime Charles Bell (1774-1842) had shown that of the double spinal roots from which most of the body's nerves arise, one conveys only sensory impulses while the other conveys only motor responses, and that it is thus possible to investigate the action of individual nerves. Again, in 1873 Camila Golci (1844-1926) deposited metal salts within cell structures to show that those of the central nervous system are irregular polygons from the vertices of which project axons which terminate in complicated branch structures, dentrites, which in turn form twig-like arborisations round other dentrites linked similarly to other cells and ultimately with terminal cells associated with sense organs, glands and muscles. Comparative studies were also conducted on a range of nervous systems while Cuvier based his classification system in part on a comparison of nervous reactions, having himself worked on the nervous systems of molluscs, starfish and crustaceans. However, It was not until Thomas Henry Huxley (1825-95) produced his *Manual of the Anatomy of the Invertebrated Animals* in 1877 that attention focused on the varying degrees of nervous system complexity across the animal kingdom.

In this connection, Paul Broca (1824-80) had made comparative studies of human and ape brains and began to identify the areas of the brain which could be associated with specific activities prior to 1886 when he was able to demonstrate by post-mortem examination the relationship between loss of speech and injury to a specific area of the cortex, now known as Broca's area (c.f. Section 2.1). In addition, Gustav Fritch (1838-91) and Eduard Hitzig (1838-1907) found while working together in 1870 that stimulation of certain parts of the cortex reliably produced contraction of certain muscles and David Ferrier (1843-1928) went on to show in 1876 that other non-muscle related areas of the cortex were functionally differentiated in other respects. Again, Marshall Hall (1790-1857) had introduced the term 'reflex action' to describe non-conscious

252

response to sensory stimulation such as breathing, digestion *etc* now considered to be innate reflexes, while Ivan Petrovitch Pavlov (1849-1936) demonstrated that the saliva glands of dogs could be activated by the sound of a bell previously associated with the imminent provision of food, such involuntary responses being acquired rather than innate are said to be conditioned reflexes.

As to suppression of the nervous system, early surgeons had recourse to various painkillers such as henbane, hemp, opium and alcohol. Nonetheless, much depended on the speed and dexterity of the surgeon and on the ability of surgical assistants and various kinds of harness to restrain movement of the patient, reliable anaesthesia not being available until the eighteenth century. Although Humphrey Davy had prepared nitrous oxide in 1799 and discovered its anaesthetic properties, its side effect as 'laughing gas' was its most noted feature until 1844 when Horace Wells used it for dentistry in the USA. Two years later, ether was being used by another US dentist, William Morton and the Scot, Robert Liston introduced it to Europe. Meanwhile Sir James Young Simpson had introduced chloroform in Edinburgh and their fellow Scot William MacEwan began to administer it through a trachea-tube by about 1880. In addition, the French physicians Charles Gabriel Pravaz and Pierre Ore respectively invented the hypodermic syringe in 1857 which introduced intravenous anaesthesia using chloral by 1878 and injection between lumbar vertebrae by the turn of the century, though needle-breakage was a serious concern until 1950. Meanwhile, Carl Koller had used cocaine in eye surgery by the end of the century, though this was quickly replaced by the synthetic variant, procaine, and after various barbiturates had been tried, Emil Fischer introduced barbital (veronal) in 1902.

8. 3 WHOLE ORGANISM BIOLOGY

Having reviewed the method by which physicochemical science explained the movement and composition of astronomical bodies, the underlying nature of the phenomena observed in the earth sciences and those in biology at the functional level of micro-organism, cell and organ, I now turn to the external observation of animals and plants which precedes physicochemical experimentation and to theories of biological evolution which have preceded even the establishment of cause and effect.

8. 3. 1 Classification

Although Aristotle had made a start in distinguishing between mammal, reptile, bird, fish and plant, the development of an effective and convenient system of classification between and within these groupings became increasingly urgent as the number of different animals and plants increased with exploration of the Earth. Of the many attempts to satisfy this need, the most successful was that of Karl Linnaeus (1707-78) which appeared in his *Philosophia Botanica* of 1751. In it, he arranged the plants into Classes and these into Orders. Thus the Class Monandria was divided into the Orders Monandria Monogynia (with one style), Monandria Digynia (with two) and so on. The Orders were then divided into Genera and these into individual Species. For the animals, Linnaeus added the Insects and Vermes Classes to those previously distinguished by Aristotle, and whereas all of Aristotle's four classes comprised animals with red blood (as he described them), these are now vertebrates, the Classes introduced by Linnaeus containing Orders with and without vertebra. However, the feature for which Linnaeus is most remembered is his binomial nomenclature, first introduced in his *Systema Naturae* of 1735, modified and amplified over many successive editions and finalised in 1758 with a particular species being first identified by its genus and secondly by its species within this genus. To take an example from microbiology, the first name recalls the morphology, characteristic behaviour or its discoverer, and the second recalls something specific about the species, such as its colony colour, the disease of which it is the causative agent, or its discoverer. Thus, the name *Bacillus anthracis* indicates that the organism is rod-shaped, aerobic and spore-forming (properties of the genus *Bacillus*) and specifically that it is the causative agent of anthrax.

Classification expresses different approaches to the observed differences between animals and between plants. These approaches are taxonomy, the comparison of external characteristics of forms closely related to each other; morphology, the comparison and distinction of form and structure between different organic types; palaeontology, the comparison of fossil forms; and embryology, the study of developmental stages in relation to the structure of adult forms. Augustin Pyramus de Candolle (1778-1841) who introduced the term 'taxonomy' in 1813, was active in the classification of the higher plants. Another significant plant taxonomist was Joseph Dalton Hooker (1817-62) who became Director of the Botanic Gardens at Kew. In morphology, the significant figures are Robert Brown (1773-1858) of Brownian motion, Georges Cuvier (1769-1832) who divided the animal kingdom into vertebrata (with back-bone), molusca (slugs, oysters, snails *etc*), articulata (jointed animals, insects, spiders, lobsters *etc*), and radiata (all remaining animals), Etienne Geofroy St. Hilaire (1772-1844 who had differences with Cuvier), Johannes Muller (1801-58) and Richard Owen (1804-92) who became the first director of the British Museum of Natural History. In palaeontology, the significant figures are Charles Lyell (1797-1875) who introduced the term in 1838, Richard Owen (1804-92) listed above as a morphologist, and the palaeo-botanist William Crawford Williamson (1816-95). In embryology, we have Karl Ernst von Baer (1792-1876) and Louis Agassiz (1807-73) who became aware of earlier Ice Ages (c.f. Section 8.2.4).

8. 3. 2 The Geographical Distribution of Classified Plants and Animals

The exploratory voyages of the eighteenth century collected a wealth of material for classification. One of the earliest and most significant was that of the *Endeavour* to the Pacific Ocean in the period 1768-1776 under Captain James Cook (1728-79) with Joseph Banks (1745-1820) as naturalist and provider of equipment, supported by a pupil of Linnaeus as botanist and several illustrators. This voyage and Cook's subsequent two voyages were very productive, as was that of the *Beagle* (1831-1834), under Captain Robert Fitzroy (1805-65) with Charles Darwin (1809-82) as naturalist, and that of the *Erebus* and *Terror* to Antarctica (1839-1843) under Sir James Ross (1800-62) with Joseph Dalton Hooker as naturalist. However, perhaps the greatest biological exploration of all was that undertaken by the British Admiralty vessel *Challenger* (1872-1876) fully equipped for six naturalists under Charles Wyville Thomson (1830-82) which covered 69,000 nautical miles visiting every ocean and many of the least frequented parts of the globe, the resulting collections of samples and data being evaluated onshore by a veritable army of investigators under John Murray (1841-1914) and the results being issued by the UK Government in fifty large volumes. This was followed by the cruise of the US Government steamer *Tuscarora* which studied the floor of the Pacific Ocean and by other American and Norwegian expeditions in rapid succession, the prominent American oceanographer of this period being Alexander Agassiz (1835-1910) and the most prominent Norwegian being Fridtjof Nansen (1861-1930).

It became clear that life existed in the oceans in a wide range of forms across a wide range of conditions. In the surface waters the striking feature is the microscopic flora and fauna to which the term 'plankton' (Greek, drifting) was given in 1888 by Victor Hensen (1835-1924) of Kiel. In these surface waters, light penetration is sufficient to sustain photosynthesis to biomass productivity levels greater than those achieved on land (~ 80% of the total). Light penetration

254

ceases, however, at depths below 400 metres so that biomass at depths from there on down is ultimately dependent on the photosynthetic processes in the water between there and the surface, though there are chemosynthetic organisms at greater depths.. At the greatest depths, conditions are substantially uniform across the globe in that there is no light, seasons nor currents, little temperature variation and high pressures (about 1 atmosphere at 10 metres and *pro rata*) and while there is life everywhere, no new Classes or Orders have been found.

In contrast, it had long been known that different countries presented different life-forms and the collections made by Charles Darwin on the *Beagle* cruise between 1839-1843 confirmed this association of geographical and meteorological differences with differing distributions of land animals and plants. Thus, Alfred Russel Wallace (1823-1913), in his *Geographical Distribution of Animals* of 1876, divided the land-surface of the globe into six zoogeographical regions. Though such division depends on the particular animal and plant groups chosen, these having different modes of dispersion and geographical/ geological age, the modern division based on mammals and perching birds is similar to that of Wallace. In any case, there are striking faunal differences from region to region, none more so than between the Islands of Bali and Lombok across the 'Wallace Line' which separates the Oriental and Australian zoogeographical regions. However, division of plants into distinct geographical regions is more difficult, temperature and moisture being overwhelmingly significant for them, the flowering plants being geologically younger than the animal groups which define the zoographical regions, the non-flowering plants being geologically older, and the seed-dispersal of the flowering plants being freer than the movement of animal groups. Nonetheless, Alexander von Humbolt was able to demonstrate relationships between the forms and habits of plants and the climatic conditions and soils of their habitats in his *Kosmos,* written between 1845-1847, while certain similarities between the flora of Africa, South America and Australia which had puzzled Humbolt and others were explained by Joseph Dalton Hooker in 1847 in terms of land-bridges in the Jurassic. However, the overwhelming importance of climate caused plants to be classified as being of the North Temperate, Tropical, or South Temperate Zones.

8. 3. 3 Postulated Agencies of Evolutionary Change

The first attempts to relate the area and time distribution of living forms was made by William Crawford Williamson (1816-95) who influenced by William Smith began work on fossil plants in 1858 drawing attention to the similarities of the gigantic fossilised plant-forms in coal to existing flowerless plants such as horse-tails, ferns and club-mosses, and making use of the well-defined cell walls of plants to examine their fossils in minute detail as to their reproductive processes and relationships between forms and groups of forms. However, the similarities and differences between living and fossil forms had already given rise to the belief that organic forms evolve from one to another. Thus, Hook (1635-1703) and Oken (1779-1851) had more or less overtly expressed this belief and its general circulation is evidenced by its denial by Linnaeus (1707-78), Haller (1708-77), Cuvier (1769-1832) *et al* who insisted that species remain fixed as created and do not arise from earlier species. Indeed, even the unlikelihood of Cuvier's explanation of the fossil record as a succession of creations and extinctions, did not make him believe the malleability of one form to another to be more likely, the earliest use of 'evolution' in this specific sense being in Lyell's *Principles of Geology* of 1831in which he discusses Lamarck's belief in such malleability.

However, the first naturalist to discuss changes in existing species in relation to changes in circumstance and habit, was George Louis Leclerc, Compte de Buffon (1707-88), who regarded his forty-four volume *Natural History* as paralleling Newton's *Principia*. Thus, un-attracted by Linnaeus's distinct species, Buffon traced identifiable features through long-term change, noted that animals possess features no longer of use to them and concluded that species alter their activities while retaining vestigial features of earlier usage such as the lateral toes of the pig. These beliefs were well received by Erasmus Darwin (1731-1802) in his search for evidence of external influences on organism development. Thus though not strictly *a propos*, his *Zoonomia* or the *Laws of Organic Life* of 1794-96 cited natural transformations in animals after birth, such as from the crawling caterpillar to the winged butterfly or from the dissolved-oxygen breathing tadpole to the air-breathing frog; the increasing strength and swiftness bred into horses and the strength, swiftness, courage and odour-acuity similarly bred into dogs; changes from hair to sheep-wool and to winter white in hares and ptarmigan; transfer of inherited characteristics and non-transfer of acquisitions such as mutilations; and the structural similarities of all warm blooded animals including man. In any case, Erasmus Darwin believed that a malleable living-filament ran through all, that natural changes to the filament through *reinforcing* transmission to offspring produced different species in the course of geological time; and that acquired characteristics might even be transferred through an act of will.

Again, for Jean Baptist de Monet de Lamarck (1744-1829) whose beliefs on evolution had been discussed by Lyell in 1831, there were no barriers which would render species permanently fixed. From noting that all dogs had been selectively bred by man from natural variations in a common ancestor, he believed that similar variations could account for natural change in the wild, that the agent of change is the external environment in both cases, that species remain constant only so long as their environment does not change them, that the mechanism of natural change could be encapsulated in his *Law of Use and Disuse* (c.f. Buffon, above), and that these organic changes are transmitted to offspring. Thus, he suggested by way of examples, that a grass grazing deer-like creature forced by environmental change to eat the leaves of trees would increase its neck length through the usage of upward straining and become in time the beast recognised as the giraffe while conversely the eyes of animals living in darkness would gradually cease to function and finally disappear through non-usage.

At this point readers should note that while Buffon, Erasmus Darwin and Lamarck believed that species change to other species in response to their environment, none developed specific hypotheses for reality-evaluation as to the mechanism of such change; that they spoke only of change within *existing* species; that analogies between the developmental stages from ova and sperm to adulthood and between controlled and wild breeding within single species were rather poor analogies for diversification of one species to another; that argumentation from analogy proves nothing in any case; and that they said nothing as to the mechanism of evolution of species from the primordial single-cell organism to the multi-cellular diversity exhibited by the fossil record and all living organisms.

However, in 1798, the Rev. Thomas Robert Malthus (1766-1834) produced his then anonymous *Essay on Population* which called attention to the inevitability of starvation as population growth outstrips food supply and which Charles Robert Darwin (1809-82) read with the *Principles* of Lyell in 1831, thus combining survival under stress as derived from Malthus with evolution (Lyle's term) as propounded by Lamarck and others including his grandfather Erasmus Darwin.. Thus, Darwin began to believe that the natural malleability of individual species could be enough to ensure the survival of the variants best fitted for success in the struggle for food, so that only they would procreate while the less fit died of starvation before procreation; that only the survivors would thus pass their survival fitness to their offspring; and that a *new* species would thus come into existence.

Though Darwin now had his *Theory of Evolution*, readers should note that it requires a natural variant to arise within an existing species; that this variant survive long enough to procreate under conditions in which all other variants must die before procreation; and that such 'natural selection' in the wild is as effective in controlling procreation as is the animal breeder in choosing and isolating his mating pairs. However, readers should also note that no evidence has been proffered for a mechanism to generate such variation or for such effectiveness in procreation control in the wild, other than the evolution which it circularly purports to explain; that while there is evidence for the survival of all the natural variants from which the animal breeder makes his selection, there is none for the pre-procreation death of the un-selected; that no new species arises from the survival of the initial species as a variant; and that diversification of one species to another is not explained or even addressed.

Nonetheless, in 1837, Darwin had begun to make this process of natural selection of spontaneous variants by survival of the fittest the basis of what was to become his *Origin of Species* and had taken it through a first draft in 1842 and a second in 1844 prior to receiving a letter from Andrew Russell Wallace seeking advice on the possible validity of this process The outcome was the hurried appearance of the outline of the theory co-authored with Wallace in 1858, followed in 1859 by Darwin's book entitled *The Origin of Species by Means of Natural Selection, or the Preservation of Favoured Races in the Struggle for Life.* However, despite the long-recognised anatomical similarities of man and ape, Darwin expressed no opinion on the possibility of human evolution from earlier ape-like creatures. Nonetheless, Thomas Henry Huxley immediately drew attention to this possibility. Indeed, three years previously in 1856 bones had been discovered in a small ravine in Prussia which Huxley had already classified as those of *Homo neanderthalensis* while Darwin's beliefs on that score only appeared in 1871 with his *Descent of Man*.

Even before any of Darwin's publications, however, evolutionary concepts had been applied to human culture in what came to be known as anthropology. Thus, in 1830 Jacques Boucher de Perthes (1788-1868) discovered in the gravels of the Somme certain flints which appeared to have been crafted and in 1846 he found such flints in association with the remains of elephant, rhinoceros and other tropical or extinct life-forms. Again, in 1863 he found a human jaw in association with crafted flints in a Pleistocene deposit near Abbeville and in his *Antiquites Celtiques Antediluviennes* covering the period 1847-1864 he demonstrated the existence of man-like creatures in the Pleistocene and early Quaternary from their associated artefacts, such demonstrations being cautiously accepted by Lyell in his *Antiquity of Man* in 1863, again without any hypotheses as to how species generate other non-interbreeding species.

8. 3. 4 Belief, Scientific Method and Knowledge

In all of the foregoing, I have been showing that reality-evaluation is the difference between knowledge and belief, that craftsmanship is on-the-job reality-validation of belief and that science is reality-validation of belief by experimentation, while my critique of the above theories of evolutionary mechanism has contrasted what is craft and science with what is neither craft nor science.

As to science, I have shown that it arises from direct observation such as of the fossil record and from designed experimentation as to the reality-evaluation of hypothetical mechanisms of cause and effect; that Newton applied the *Laws of Motion* as experimentally determined to explain the mechanism of lunar motion; that his successors applied these *Laws* to the whole of the observable universe in demonstrating the reliability of the mechanism to ever more extensive and astoundingly precise degrees; and that to this extent the *Laws of Motion* and the *Theory of Gravity* were reality-validated. Similarly, I have shown that chemists reality-validated the *Laws of Chemical Composition* by experimentation whereby they explained the mechanism of chemical reactivity, inter-phase solution, ionic conductivity and heat in terms of atoms, molecules and their movement; and that to these extents *The Atomic* Theory and the *Periodic Table* were reality-validated as indeed was chemistry as a whole. Again, I have shown that physicists resolved all 'non-material substance' into aspects of interchangeable energy by experimentation; and that to these extents the *Laws of Thermodynamics* and the *Equations of the Electromagnetic Spectrum* were reality-validated as indeed was physics as a whole. Yet again, I have shown that this physicochemical knowledge provides other sciences with reality-validation not otherwise available to them while creating technology from craftsmanship.

As to what is not science, it is clear that there were no experimentally determined '*Laws of Biology*' on which to establish a mechanism for evolution or *vice versa*; that the existence of different species and of time-sequenced changes in their characteristics does not explain the mechanism by which these changes came about; that attempts to explain the former by reference to the latter or *vice versa* require reality-validation of at least one or the other; that the need to explain the mechanism of biological evolution from primordial unicellular species through the myriad forms of the fossil record to the present day might have suggested hypotheses formulation at the cellular level of fossilised plants and/or at the living cells of microbiology and physiology; that while 'survival of the fittest' might be operative after changes had occurred within pre-existing species, it could not be the cause of such changes whatever their consequences might be for the species; and that the diversification of pre-existing species to others with which they could not breed was another matter entirely, concerning which stock-breeders unconvinced by belief assertion might have judged Darwin's choice of book title to be over-selling its contents.

Such considerations may explain Darwin's reluctance to publish until Wallace seemed likely to beat him to it, though he too appears to have had doubts. Thus, while observation of differences within species and similarities between species had given rise to a postulate that 'survival of the fittest' might be the mechanism underlying both observations, Darwin and Wallace must have known that eighteenth century theories as to the mechanism of evolution did not arise from knowledge, could not themselves be reality-validated and could not produce hypotheses for reality-evaluation; and that they should have been suspended as beliefs pending the formulation of such hypotheses. However, instead of proceeding thus in a scientific manner, Darwinists have sought socio-political dominance over religion by redundantly attacking a metaphorical creation myth with the fossil record, by presenting nature as 'red in tooth and claw' to destroy belief in a beneficent creator, and by replacing knowledge-based behaviour codes with alternates based on belief in 'the survival of the fittest', to which ends they keep their Theory of Evolution in the public consciousness by continuous reference to its author as *scientist par excellence* (c.f. Sections 11.1 and 12.1), though there are many more deserving candidates for that honour.

Meanwhile, the mechanisms of species-change and species-diversification as distinct from their observed consequences, are likely to be elucidated through molecular genetics. Indeed, the first steps towards identifying a cellular genetic-carrier were taken by Gregor Mendel (1822-84) in his investigation of character transfer in successive generations of the pea-plant (1857-1869). Though this failed to attract attention, it was rediscovered in 1900, given a molecular basis by X-ray crystallography in the 1950s, and now provides opportunities for reality-evaluation of hypothetical mechanisms of biological evolution for the first time (c.f. Section 9.2.5, 9.2.6, 9.4.4, 9.5.3 and 9.5.4). As to the degree to which Darwin's mechanism is without reality-validation, readers should compare it with the reality-validation of physicochemical science (c.f. Chapters 6, 7, 8 and 9) which in turn supports the mechanisms currently advanced for stellar and geological evolution (c.f. Sections 9.3.1, 9.4.2 and 9.4.3).

8.4 CONCLUSIONS

It may be concluded that craftsmen and entrepreneurs operated initially without scientific assistance (c.f. Chapters 2, 3 and Section 5.7); that nuggets of scientific knowledge were subsequently enough for such craftsmen and entrepreneurs to develop technology between 1700 and 1900; that this was achieved despite their education being no more specialised than at any previous time, tools, machines and artefacts having been progressively developed in response to requirements and opportunities by application of the Rational Trinity since time immemorial; and that even scientists and technologists were self-taught to the point of applying the Rational Trinity to specific sectors of the unknown.

Thus, Torricelli having demonstrated the weight of the atmosphere by producing a vacuum, craftsmen knowing that steam condensed to a vacuum, had all they needed to develop the atmospheric engine to the point where knowledge of Black's latent heat enabled efficiency to be enhanced by Watt's separate condenser. Again, the wainwright Oliver Evans assimilated and surpassed the previous hundred years' development with his own high-pressure engine of 1804, while Huygens's suggestion that sequenced explosions would move pistons led craftsmen to develop internal combustion engines to the point where Sadi Carnot's scientific work was incorporated by Rudolf Diesel. Furthermore, while science had been greatly advanced by the former book-binder Michael Faraday and while the more formally educated James Clerke Maxwell had elucidated electromagnetism in a way which had eluded Faraday, electric generators, motors, transformers, radios *etc,* were almost immediately built by craftsmen.

Even where commercial exploitation was more directly in the hands of chemists than in those of physicists, all practical progress depended on craftsmanship. Indeed transfers of innovative knowledge from physics and chemistry to craftsmen produced a corps of engineers and technologists who quickly became capable of improving and diversifying without further transfers, while entrepreneurs such as John Boulton (buckle-maker) Josiah Wedgewood (potter) and Andrew Carnegie (office boy) continued to fund improved and diversified marketable products all of which show that the relationship between formal education and commercial success is less direct than now believed, the ability to read, write and count having been adequately acquired by such twelve year old school leavers as Carnegie and by all such craftsmen and entrepreneurs whether remembered or forgotten.

Transfer of knowledge from a more fundamental to a more descriptive science is a similar process, though mathematics is necessary to replace qualitative description with quantitative knowledge. Thus, astronomy would be purely descriptive without the quantitative understanding of celestial motion and stellar composition provided by Newtonian dynamics and physicochemical spectroscopy. Similarly, knowledge of the Earth was largely descriptive until mathematics, physics and chemistry improved the accuracy of geographical measurement and created the new sciences of meteorology, oceanography, geophysics and geochemistry. Again biology was purely descriptive until attention turned to the chemical basis of life which led to the new sciences of physiology and microbiology with their conceptualisation of the living cell as a physicochemical entity.

Meanwhile the exponents of purely descriptive biology, encouraged by the collection of new species on voyages of discovery and of fossils in time-sequenced strata, began to speculate as to the mechanism of species evolution. However, in contrast to the reality-validation which characterises physics, chemistry and their derivative sciences, these speculators could not refute rational objections to their speculations, let alone produce hypotheses for reality-validation in their support.

Nonetheless, having been adopted as a tenet of secularism, the defects of Darwin's Theory were ignored as Darwinists pursued their belief-driven socio-political objectives through corruption of social-science to pseudo-science (c.f. Chapter 11) while leaving the species diversification mechanism to molecular investigation, Darwinism itself being an investigative dead-end (c.f. Section 12.1).

CHAPTER 9: THE TWENTIETH CENTURY

Chapter 7 showed that the existence of atoms was comprehensively consistent with the reality-validations which culminated in the Periodic Table of the Elements, in heat and temperature being manifestations of the movement of atoms and molecules, in the phase changes from solid through liquid to gas, and in the accommodation (solution) of the atoms and molecules of one phase within the void space of another. Again, Chapter 7 showed that the electromagnetic energy-field was similarly established by the comprehensive consistency of the reality-validations which culminated in the unification of light, electricity, magnetism, radio-waves and radiant heat as forms of energy, and in the transformation of one form to another through appropriate equivalence factors and units. In addition, Chapter 7 showed that atoms were found to contain even smaller particles (electrons); that these electrons under an applied voltage produced electromagnetic X-rays on colliding with atoms; and that some atoms emitted radiation spontaneously by processes unexplained in the nineteenth century.

Thus, just when matter had been explained in terms of atoms and their chemical reactions and the "imponderables" had been explained as specific manifestations of the electromagnetic energy-field, the relationship between matter and energy was raising further and deeper questions. Central to these, was the mechanism of energy distribution between particles and fields, one manifestation of which was the energy absorption lines (frequencies) characteristic of each element in the vapour phase, while others were associated with thermal radiation, the photo-electric effect, X-rays and radio-activity, all of which were equally inexplicable. In this Chapter, therefore, I now review the success of the Rational Trinity in explaining all of those, prior to reviewing their applications in organic chemistry, astronomy, earth sciences, and technology in the twentieth century.

9. 1 PHYSICS AND CHEMISTRY ENTER A NEW ERA

Explanation of the relationship between particles and fields came in the form of the *Quantum and Relativity Theories* which in turn deepened our knowledge of the atom and of the chemical bond in relation to the Periodic Table; of the molecular structure of organic (carbon) compounds and the chemistry of life in ways not otherwise available; of the creation of atoms and the Cosmos itself; and of the Earth and of Life itself; while providing wider opportunities for new technologies all of which render our physicochemical knowledge ever more comprehensively consistent. However, to appreciate these achievements it is necessary to review the individual and collective explanations provided by reality-evaluating experimentation for all of the phenomena listed above.

9. 1. 1 Quantum Theory, Photo-electron Emission, and Wave-Particle Duality
Black-body radiation provides a focus for considering the interaction of particles and fields because here we have constituent particles of the body emitting electromagnetic (thermal) radiation. On the basis of existing knowledge, Rayleigh and Jeans predicted by calculation in 1900 that all the energy would be transferred from the particles to the field at ever-increasing frequencies, particles being defined by six parameters (three for position and three for momentum) while the field appeared to have an infinite number of potential frequencies. Although observation showed that

these predictions were correct for the lower frequencies of field oscillation, the distribution of energy was not as predicted for higher frequencies. In fact, it increased and then fell to zero, maxima occurring at a specific frequency for any given temperature such as those of red, yellow or white heat. Thus, theory and observation were in disagreement until later in 1900 when Max Planck proposed that electromagnetic oscillations only occur at permitted frequencies whose energy E is related to frequency f by the equation: $E = hf$, where h is a new constant (Planck's constant) with a value of 6.6×10^{-34} joule seconds. While this bold initiative enabled Planck to explain the observed results of black-body radiation, it implied that energy exists in discrete amounts (or packets) and is not continuous, just as matter is atomic and not continuous, these packets being the Quanta of the Theory.

On this new basis, Einstein suggested in 1905 that when a particle (atom) emits a quantum of energy it continues to exist and that a beam of light must therefore be a stream of such quanta each of energy hf which in the case of light are referred to as photons. On this model, light intensity diminishes with distance from a point-source because the number of photons per unit area is diminishing as the light spreads with distance from source and not because the energy of individual photons is diminishing. The energy of the photon cannot diminish according to Planck. Thus, with regard to photo-electric emission, Einstein suggested that when a photon collides with an electron its energy cannot be distributed over more than one electron because its energy cannot be sub-divided. Instead, the incident photon must either be reflected with no loss of energy or it must lose all its energy to the electron. Thus the number of electrons emitted by a photo-irradiated surface per unit area per unit time must be proportional to the intensity of the radiation i.e. to the number of photons traversing the unit cross-sectional area of the irradiating beam per unit time, the emission of each electron being instantaneous with the transfer of photon energy to it, the kinetic energy of the emitted electron being what is left after overcoming the forces which bound it to the surface. Thus, Einstein's photo-electric equation as reality-validated is $hf = W + \frac{1}{2} mv^2$ where W is the energy required for electron release and $\frac{1}{2} mv^2$ is the kinetic energy with which it is released.

Thus Plank's explanation of black-body thermal radiation and Einstein's of photo-electron emission implied that the electromagnetic field itself exists only as discrete energy units which in turn implies that light must be 'particulate' as Isaac Newton had believed. On the other hand, surely Thomas Young had established that light consisted of waves! In 1923, Prince Louis de Broglie looked at matters from the converse position and in his doctoral dissertation proposed that material particles would sometimes behave as waves. Thus, de Broglie's wave-frequency f for any particle satisfies the Planck equation while through Einstein's equation (c.f. Section 9.1.2) its mass m is related to frequency f such that $hf = E = mc^2$ and accordingly there is no discontinuity between particles and fields. Particles may be waves and wave-fields may be particulate. Anything which oscillates with a frequency f can exist in discrete particles of mass mc^2/h and anything with a mass m can be an oscillation of frequency of hv/c^2. Thus, we live in a world where particles and field oscillations are the same thing or where ultimate reality cannot be described as one or the other, but rather as something 'in between' which appears to be one or the other depending on the type of observation made. This is now referred to as *Wave-Particle Duality*.

Now, readers will recall Thomas Young's *General Law on Interference of Light* which resulted from his experimentation to establish the wave-form of light. When light is passed through a narrow slit it does indeed demonstrate wave-properties in that the screen beyond the slit shows the characteristic interference pattern of lighter and darker bands. However, if the intensity is reduced far enough the illumination of the screen can be seen to consist of individual spots in agreement with the particulate-form of photons. If now a second parallel slit is opened the screen shows an interference pattern consistent with the wave-form of photons. If, however, the intensity is again reduced to the point when no more than one photon at a time is arriving at the slits, the interference pattern persists suggesting that a single photon can travel through both slits at once and interfere with itself or that the single photon (particle) is itself a wave which enters both slits. This duality is reinforced by observing that when only one slit is open (and it doesn't matter which one) the photon travels this route as a particle, and by observing that when both slits are open the photon doesn't travel either route as a particle, it travels both as a wave. Though this experimentation result is remarkable for its counter-intuitiveness, it is necessary to grasp that at the quantum level there are different alternatives open to a particle and that these can cancel each other when it behaves as a wave on its own. In classical (pre-quantum) physics a particle was determined by its position in space and its future position could be predicted from its known momentum. In quantum physics the position which a particle might have is an 'alternative' available to it.

Meanwhile in 1913, Niels Bohr had used early quantum theory to model the electronic structure of the atom, though his explanation of absorption and emission spectra was rather *ad hoc* (c.f. Section 9.1.5). Consequently, more mathematically satisfactory treatments of quantum theory were separately advanced as matrix quantum mechanics by Werner Heisenberg in 1925 and in 1926 as wave mechanics by Erwin Schroedinger, these being shown to be equivalent when subsumed into a more comprehensive and general scheme by P. A. M. Dirac which took account of special relativity (c.f. Section 9.1.2) and electron spin (c.f. Section 9.1.6), both omitted by Schroedinger. However, in Schroedinger's approach the alternatives available to the particle are combined together by multiplication and addition of probability amplitudes expressed as complex numbers of the form a + ib where a and b are alternatives and i is the square root of -1 (c.f. Section 6.2.3). It turns out that the squared modulus of the quantum complex amplitude gives what would be a probability in classical physics. Thus, the *quantum state* of a particle is the collection of such complex number amplitudes, denoted ψ and called the *wave-function* of the particle, this having a specific value for each position x, denoted $\psi(x)$, this in turn being the amplitude for the particle to be at x while the probability of finding it at x is $|\psi(x)|^2$.

As to momentum, it turns out that the wave function already contains the various amplitudes for the alternative momenta and the application of what is called harmonic analysis to the function is all that is needed to determine what are referred to as the *momentum states*. When ψ-curves are suitably plotted (on what is known as the Argand diagram) they are seen to be helixes, the degree of tightness being proportional to momentum with zero momentum being a straight line. This is consistent with Plank's equation where frequency (tightness) is proportional to energy. Alternatively, a function of momentum p rather than of position x can be constructed $\Psi(p)$ which gives the amplitude for the particle to have momentum p and the probability of finding that it has momentum p is $|\Psi(p)|^2$.

In 1927, Heisenberg addressed the problems which clearly arise when attempts are made to transpose the intuitive (common sense) concepts of classical physics to the atomic and sub-atomic realm in a paper entitled *On The Intuitive Content of the Quantum-Theoretical Kinematics and Mechanics*. The intuitive idea inherent in Newtonian dynamics (kinematics) is that in principle it is possible to know precisely both the position and momentum of a particle at the same time. The mathematical development of Heisenberg's ideas, however, led to the conclusion that this was not so at the quantum level and that the inherent uncertainties in position and momentum are expressed by the relationship, $\Delta x. \Delta p > h/2\pi$, where the Δ (delta) functions x and p denote uncertainties in position and momentum respectively and h is Plank's constant. Since the uncertainties multiplied together are greater than or equal to a constant, it follows that as one increases the other decreases, this relationship now being known as *Heisenberg's Uncertainty Principle*.

We can now apply this principle to Schroedinger's wave mechanics. The ψ-curve is a helix at a constant distance from the x-axis and the amplitudes for different positional values all have equal squared moduli. In other words, if a position measurement is performed the probability of finding the particle at any one point is the same as finding it at any other, which is the same as saying that the position of the particle is completely uncertain. If, however, we know the position state of the particle the ψ-curve is replaced by a delta function at that position, the amplitudes for all other positions being zero. Thus the particle would be precisely located. On the other hand, the Ψ-curve would still be a helix with all momentum amplitudes having equal squared moduli and so the particle's momentum would be completely uncertain. However, if position and momentum are uncertain in the manner of Heisenberg, then the ψ-curve and corresponding Ψ-curve are no longer helixes with constant amplitudes. Instead they have appreciable amplitudes in a short region of the axis beyond which they decrease to zero. Thus the squared moduli are appreciable only in a limited region of position space and of momentum space. Such a quantum state is called a wave-packet and is often taken to be the closest approximation to a particle in quantum theory. Schroedinger's basic objective, however, was to formulate a theory applicable to electrons bound in atoms and he continued to believe that atomic processes could be visualised by classical imagery. Thus, while Schroedinger's wave equation was not so much derived as concocted, it was justified by its prediction of the correct energy levels for the hydrogen atom without the quantum jumps required by Bohr's classical planetary model of the atom (c.f. Section 9.1.5). However, Heisenberg's mathematically more rigorous matrix approach though based on un-visualisable bound particles had by 1925 solved a number of other problems not amenable to either the Schroedinger or the Bohr approach..

Meanwhile, Heisenberg's mentor Max Born was interested in 'free' electrons moving through space, a problem beyond the scope of both quantum mechanics and wave mechanics. In his paper of 1926, however, Born proposed that Schroedinger's wave function did not represent the electron's visualisable charge distribution as a wave surrounding the nucleus (as Schroedinger understood it) nor did it represent a group of charge-waves moving through space. Instead, the wave-function was totally abstract and non-amenable to visualisation. Thus, rather than calculating density of electricity, one calculates a probability density for the electron to be present in some region of space. On this basis, Schroedinger's equation does not tell us the path of a particle in time (as per Newton),but rather how the probability of the particle's detection changes with time. Thus, while Bohr came to believe that quantum mechanics as propounded by Heisenberg should point the way to reality however counter-intuitive it seemed, Schroedinger remained un-reconciled as indeed did Einstein. Nonetheless, Schroedinger's wave-mechanics focussed on matter as waves, offered a visual representation of the bound electron and in addition to accounting for the line spectrum of hydrogen without quantum jumps, it proved to have a wide range of applications in chemistry as we shall see later (c.f. Section 9.1.7). Meanwhile Heisenberg in continuing to develop quantum theory and its applications, accounted for the spectrum of the helium atom in 1926 and in showing that particles can attract one another by changing places rapidly he explained the bonding of the hydrogen molecule (c.f. Section 9.1.7) and was the first to account for the stability of the atomic nucleus.

9. 1. 2 Theories of Special and General Relativity

I now review the implications of the speed of electromagnetic wave propagation for Galilean-Newtonian physics. The principle of Galilean relativity is that physical laws remain unchanged on passing from a stationary to a uniformly moving frame of reference, which means that we cannot ascertain whether we are stationary or moving at uniform speed in a straight line simply by looking at objects moving with us. In addition we intuitively expect that our measurement of the speed of light would vary with our own velocity (speed and direction) relative to the light during the act of measurement, this being our experience with all other examples of relative motion. Yet, James Clerke Maxwell tells us that his electromagnetic waves (light) have a fixed speed, c, however and wherever it is measured. In considering this problem, Einstein and Poincare independently found that Maxwell's equations also remain unchanged on moving from a stationary to a uniformly moving frame of reference, though under conditions incompatible with those of Galilean-Newtonian physics. Thus, one or other set of equations must be modified or the principle of relativity must be abandoned no matter what the conditions.

In attempting to deal with this fundamental impasse Einstein noted that all the phenomena compatible with Galilean-Newtonian physics involved speeds negligible in comparison with that of light; and that the equations which relate to light are those of Maxwell. Accordingly, he concluded that the equations in need of modification were those of Galileo and Newton. Thus, the relativity conditions required by the Maxwell equations were reported by Einstein in 1905 in what is now called his *Special Theory of Relativity* to distinguish it from the *General Theory* which came later. This principle is difficult to grasp because our limited experience of everyday life on Earth renders it counter-intuitive. However, help in understanding the Special Theory was provided by one of Einstein's teachers, Herman Minkowski, who showed that our intuitive conceptualisation of time and three-dimensional space as independent entities has to be replaced by a uniform four-dimensional space-time entity incompatible with Euclidean geometry. Nevertheless, regardless of how counter-intuitive these concepts may be, their consequences are reality-validated by experimentation. For example, the decay-times of unstable sub-atomic particles show protraction in accordance with the predictions of special relativity when travelling at speeds approaching that of light as when approaching the Earth in cosmic rays or as produced in particle accelerators. Again, 'atomic clocks' (in which time is measured by the oscillation frequencies of atoms in crystals) are now able to measure time-slowing effects as predicted by the theory when they are transported by fast aircraft even though such speeds are still well below that of light. Perhaps the best-known example of a consequence of the Special Theory is that expressed by Einstein's equation: $E = mc^2$ where E is the energy generated by the annihilation of mass m with c being the velocity of light, this being reality-validated by the energy release in nuclear fission. Thus, having met energy equivalencies and their associated conversion coefficients we now meet that for energy and matter with its coefficient c^2.

The next step was to reconsider the validity of the Galilean-Newtonian concept of gravity despite all its reality-validated consequences. According to Galileo all objects free-fall to earth under the influence of gravity from equal heights in the same time regardless of their individual masses and according to Newton the Moon free-falling in space under the influence of this same gravity is following its appropriate 'canon-ball' trajectory in orbiting the Earth. Now to a space-walking astronaut his space-station and himself appear to be stationary or in uniform motion while orbiting together, he being unaware of falling or of gravity. Thus, for an observer in the accelerating reference of free-fall the sensation of gravity is eliminated and this equivalence of free-fall with motion in a straight-line was referred to by Einstein as the *Principle of Equivalence*, free-falling bodies being conceptualised as following paths analogous to orbits in space which he called geodetics in space-time. Thus, with space-time possessing a curvature which replaces gravity with free-fall and with space-time being independent of gravity in Minkowski's description of *Special Relativity*, Einstein combined these concepts in his *General Theory of Relativity*.

However, irrespective of these profound changes both Einstein's curved-space-time and

265

Newton's gravity give identical results (reality-validations) provided velocities are small in relation to that of light c and gravitational fields weak enough to keep escape velocities this small also. As speeds increase towards c, however, the results differ, Newton's becoming increasingly divergent from Einstein's which remain in agreement with reality-validation. Thus, clocks run at rates dependent on the strength of gravitational fields, appropriate variations being observable in aircraft flying at different altitudes at constant speed, while light and radio signals approaching Earth are observed to curve (bend) as they pass close to massive bodies such as the Sun and are delayed by the appropriate times. Again, Einstein more closely describes the orbits and trajectories of planets and space-probes than does Newton. Thus, the anomalous motion of the planet mercury, known as the perihelion advance since 1859, was resolved by application of Einstein's General Theory in 1915 and his explanation of binary pulsar observations is consistent with the existence of gravity waves analogous to electromagnetic waves. Nonetheless, though these successes and many more are beyond the scope of Newton's theory the latter remains reality-validated for the relatively low speeds and gravitational environment concerning which it was devised. The way in which the dynamics of Newton and Einstein coincide at low velocities and increasingly diverge as velocities approach that of light can be shown by comparing Newton's equation which expresses momentum p as the product of mass m and velocity v such that $p = mv$ with Einstein's equation in which mass is now expressed by masses m and m_0 to allow for the increase in mass with increase in velocity, while velocity v is now expressed as a fraction of the speed of light v^2 / c^2 as per the General Theory. Thus, $pv = mv = m_0v / /(1 - v^2 / c^2)$ from which we see that as v decreases with respect to c, $(1 - v^2 / c^2)$ tends to 1, m_0 tends to m, mv tends to p, and Einstein tends to Newton as speeds decrease from c to those of daily experience.

9. 1. 3 X-Rays, Radio-activity, Positive-Rays, and Early Model of the Atom
In 1906 C. G. Barkla showed by increasing the energy of bombarding electrons that all elements could be made to emit X-rays; and by measuring X-ray absorption coefficients in a standard substance, such as aluminium, that these emissions were characteristic of the individual elements. In 1912 Laue, and Friedrich and Knipping, showed that X-rays were diffracted when passed through crystals and that this diffraction permitted measurement of their individual wave-lengths according to the following reasoning. If we suppose that the distance between the planes of the ions in a crystal such as rock-salt is d, that the angle which the incident X-rays make with the crystal planes is θ, and that one ray reflects from the surface plane and a parallel one reflects from the one beneath it at distance d, then the two reflected rays will interfere and reinforce when in phase and cancel when not in phase, a condition which may be expressed by the equation $n \lambda = 2d \sin \theta$ where n is a small integer, and λ is the wave-length of the X-rays under study. This being so, d can be calculated from the density and atomic weights of the rock salt crystal which causes the diffraction and by substitution in the equation, λ, the wavelength of the X-rays, is determined. It follows, of course, that when the wave length is known the inter-atomic distance d of an unknown crystal can be calculated from this relationship and as we shall see (c.f. Section 9.2.5), this approach can be extended to determine molecular structures.   Here we note that the logarithms of X-ray wave-lengths characteristic of the elements were shown by H.G. Mosley in 1913 to plot as a straight line against the ordinal numbers of their positions in the Periodic Table, while against their atomic weights the plot was irregular, suggesting that atomic (ordinal) number was the more significant, and that the atom was more complex than had been supposed. On this basis Mosely proposed that the atomic number was numerically equal to the net positive charge on the nucleus and to the number of orbiting electrons in Rutherford's model of the atom of 1903 (c.f. Section 9.1.5).

Following the discovery of radioactivity by its effect on photographic plates, it was quickly found to cause phosphorescence in certain minerals such as zinc blende and to discharge an electroscope by rendering air electrically conducting. Later by subjecting the radiation from Madame Curie's new element radium to magnetic fields and by interposing screens of different materials and thickness in the subsequent paths of the radiation, it was shown to be of three distinct types. Thus, the α-rays are positively charged, have a limited range in air (about 7cm) and can be screened by the thickness of a few sheets of paper or thin metal foil, the β-rays are negatively charged and can be screened by thin sheets of aluminium, and the γ-rays have no charge and can penetrate lead at a thickness of up to about 15 centimetres.

In addition, Rutherford discovered that the element radium emitted a gas which he referred to as an emanation and in 1910 Ramsay and Whytlaw-Gray determined its atomic weight to be 222 and showed chemically that it was a member of the rare gas Group of the Periodic Table, then called niton and now called radon. Similarly, the complexity of the atoms of radio-active elements was indicated in 1908 when Rutherford and Royds collected α-rays in an outer evacuated tube after they had passed through the walls of a very thin inner glass tube which contained their radium source, saw that the collected α-rays emitted the helium spectrum on passing an electric discharge through them and concluded that α-particles were positively charged helium atoms *i.e.* helium ions. Again, β-rays were shown to be indistinguishable from cathode rays *i.e.* they were electrons, though ejected at speeds approaching that of light; that the γ-rays were short wavelength X-rays; and that the relative penetration of aluminium by the three types α, β and γ were in the ratios of 10 : 10^3 : 10^5. There were other surprises. The initial radium emanation, the rare gas radon (niton), was found to be radioactive in transforming spontaneously (decaying) into a radioactive solid and helium gas, the former decaying through a series of radioactive products to non-radioactive lead, each decay being associated with the emission of either α-rays (now referred to as α-particles) or the emission of β-particles together with γ-rays.

Again radio-activity was found to be unaffected by compound formation or by any physical conditions to which it might be exposed. To account for these unique features Rutherford and Soddy proposed the *Theory of Spontaneous Disintegration*, in 1903 according to which the atoms of radio-active elements are complex in structure, potentially unstable and capable of spontaneous disintegration (decay) at a rate which diminishes exponentially over time. This, in turn suggested that some radio-active elements could have existed in earlier times and now be extinct, and that since a radio-active atom is liable at any moment to disintegrate, the fraction of the total number disintegrating at any one time is constant. This statement is equivalent to saying that the rate of disintegration at any time is proportional to the number N present at the time. Thus, by calculus we have the differential equation:

$$dN/dt = -\lambda N$$

This equation can be rearranged to read: $\quad dN/N = -\lambda\, dt$

which on integrating gives: $\quad \log_e N = -\lambda t + c$

Now, if the initial number of nuclei is N , then the above equation gives $N = N_0$ when $t = 0$ and so:

$$\log N_0 = c$$

and, therefore, $\quad \log_e N = -\lambda t + \log N_0$

and $\quad \log_e (N/N_0) = -\lambda t$

or $\quad N/N_0 = e^{-\lambda t}$

or $\quad N = N_0\, e^{\lambda t}$

This equation also permits calculation of the time taken for half the nuclei present to disintegrate

i.e. the half-life of the nuclide. Thus if the half-life is represented by $T_{1/2}$, then when $t = T_{1/2}$ and $N = N_0/2$ $$N_0/2 = N_0 \, e^{-\lambda T_{1/2}}:$$
and thus $$\log_e 2 = \lambda T_{1/2}$$
or $$T_{1/2} = 0.6931/\lambda$$
The half-lives characteristic of the individual nuclides may also be expressed as 0.6931 times the period of average life and so each radio-element may also be characterised by its average life.

Thus, in a series of radio-active transformations the amounts of each element present at any time are proportional to their half-lives and Rutherford estimated that the radium then on earth would be virtually extinct in a about 25,000 years and that therefore it would already be extinct were it not continuously created. In fact it is created in a series of radio-active transformations initiated by the spontaneous disintegration of the heaviest known natural element uranium, the rate of which is so slow as to indicate an average life of 8×10^9 years. In fact there are three series of radio-active transformations in nature, one starting from uranium which passes through radium and goes on to end with lead, another starting with thorium and the third with protactinium, an element separated from pitchblende by Debierne in 1899, both of which also end with lead. By 1913, several investigators had suggested that the emission of an α-particle would move the element two horizontal places in the direction of reduced atomic number within the Periodic Table *i.e.* the atomic number would be reduced by two units, and that conversely the emission of a β-particle would cause the element to increase its atomic number by one unit in moving one place to the right. This *Displacement Rule* causes the chemical nature of the product of such displacement to be identical with that of its new position in the Periodic Table.

Applying this Rule to the thorium series, we see that thorium emits an α-particle to become mesothorium I which emits a β-particle to give mesothorium II which emits a β-particle to give radiothorium which emits an α-particle to give thorium X. Thus, we have two single moves to the right and one double move to the left bringing mesotherium I and thorium X to the same position in the Periodic Table and to chemical identity despite a difference of four units in their atomic weights. Entities with identical chemistries and which therefore cannot be chemically separated were called isotopes by Frederick Soddy who worked on these natural radio-active series. Thus, ionium (one of the members of the uranium series), thorium and radiothorium are isotopes, mesothorium is isotopic with radium and the three types of lead identified as terminating the three radio-active series are isotopic, as Soddy discovered in 1914.

In 1920 Chadwick confirmed Moseley's suggestion of 1913 that the atomic number was the measure of the net positive charge on the nucleus and the number of its orbiting electrons. He did this by observing the scattering of α-particles (positively charged) as they passed through thin sheets of the metals, platinum, silver and copper, from which he was able to calculate the repulsive positive charges on their respective nuclei as being 77.4, 46.3 and 29.3 in good agreement with their atomic number positions in the Periodic Table of 78, 47 and 29. Now, we may recall that the atomic number and atomic weight for hydrogen are both unity and that when the hydrogen atom loses an electron the resulting positive ion H^+ is called the proton. We also recall that the α-particle is actually a helium ion having mass four units on the scale which sets hydrogen at unit mass, a positive charge of 2 units, and an atomic number of 2. Thus, the helium atom has two protons in its nucleus each carrying a positive charge and two orbiting electrons for electrical neutrality and ought to have an atomic weight of two units when in fact it is four, reasoning which concluded that there must be yet another sub-atomic particle with a mass equal to that of the proton but carrying no charge, and hence named the neutron. At this point we should recognise that the β-particle, though an electron, is emitted from the nucleus in radioactive decay and not from the

268

complement of orbiting electrons (c.f. Section 9.1.5); that such emission transforms a neutron into a retained proton; and that this (newly formed) proton in the nucleus accounts for β-particle emission being associated with increase in atomic number by one unit in compliance with the Displacement Rule.

The discovery of isotopes among the radio-elements together with the developments in atomic theory which accounted for them, led to consideration of the possible presence of isotopes among the stable elements. Very careful determination of the atomic weights of stable lead, derived from various sources by Richards in 1914, showed variations, later confirmed by other investigators, which ranged from 205.927 to 207.9 while from lead sulphide (galena) it was 207.21. However, while these results suggested the presence of isotopes, their individual atomic weights and the relative amounts present could not be determined, isotopes being chemically identical and the radioactivity indicative of radioisotopes now being absent. On the other hand, an alterative approach was under development. In 1882 Goldstein had noticed that in a cathode ray tube with a perforated cathode, luminous so-called canal rays passed backwards through the perforations, these later being shown by J. J. Thomson to be positively charged particles of atomic size by means of his deflection method of particle analysis (c.f. Section 7.3.1). Thus, in the course of his work on the positive rays from neon, Thomson had observed an additional mass to charge ratio of 22 which was initially attributed to doubly-charged carbon dioxide (CO_2) from the stop-cock grease of the gas handling system until cooling the system with liquid air removed the singly-charged CO_2 particle at line 44 while leaving the line at 22 unaffected.

However, after the discovery of isotopes among the radio elements and the demonstration that stable lead from different sources had different atomic weights, the suggestion was made that Thomson's results revealed the existence of two stable isotopes of neon with atomic weights of 20 and 22. Thus, if the neon-22 was present to a lesser extent than neon-20 the determined atomic weight of neon of 20.12 could be explained and similar considerations could be applied to other fractional atomic weights determined for other elements. Further investigation of stable isotopes was now undertaken by Aston and by Dempster and Bainbridge who developed Thompson's method into a very sensitive instrument which Aston called the mass spectrograph. This subjected the stream of positively charged particles to the combined action of transverse electric and magnetic fields which caused them to move in mass-dependent parabolic trajectories to impact in different positions on a photographic plate to produce lines from the location of which the mass of the particle could be calculated. Again, with Dempster and Bainbridge also having built highly sensitive instruments though with differing detection and recording systems, the accumulated results showed that with 23 exceptions all the stable elements exist as mixtures of two or more isotopes. Tin has ten and 26 others have from five to nine.

In view of the plethora of stable isotopes it is remarkable that the chemically determined atomic weights of the elements are constant across all sources including that of meteorites, lead being the only exception for the reasons given by Soddy in 1914. Thus, it may be concluded that the isotopes have been thoroughly mixed to constant proportions since their formation or that the formation process itself produced them in fixed proportions. In addition, we now see that the proximity to whole numbers of the atomic weights available to Prout which led to his hypothesis of 1816 that hydrogen was the building unit for all the elements (c. f. Section 7.1.6) was due to mixtures of individual isotopes with whole-number masses, the proton (hydrogen nucleus) and the neutron being of equal whole number mass and 1,836 times heavier than the electron. It now became clear that if the individual isotopic masses and their percentage abundances could be determined for the elements their atomic weights could be computed and compared with those determined by traditional chemical methods (c.f. Section 7.1.5). The refinements introduced to mass spectrometry by Aston, Dempster and others enabled this to be done with an accuracy which caused some chemical determinations to be repeated to improved accuracy. It is a further testimony to the scientific method that two methods so essentially different should give results concordant to this degree.

9. 1. 4 Nuclear Transformation and Energy Release

Since radio-active nuclei had been found to undergo transformations on emission of particles, it was a natural step to investigate whether transformations could be induced in non-radioactive nuclei by bombarding them with such particles. Thus, in 1926, Rutherford bombarded nitrogen with α-particles and found that he had transformed the nitrogen into hydrogen and oxygen by the nuclear reaction:

$$^4_2He + {}^{14}_7N = {}^1_1H + {}^{17}_8O$$

In such nuclear equations, the superscript is the Mass Number and the subscript the Atomic Number of the respective elements. In the reaction we see that the α-particle (helium ion) of 4 units of mass (2 protons and 2 neutrons) coalesced with the nitrogen atom of 14 units of mass to produce an unstable entity of 18 mass units (not shown) which stabilised to an oxygen nucleus of mass 17 with emission of a hydrogen nucleus (a proton) of 1 mass unit, and that the sums of the Mass and Atomic Numbers are conserved in the transformation. Many more such reactions were quickly investigated and in the course of such work Mme Curie-Joliot discovered in 1934 that the new nucleus which she had produced was itself radioactive. Thus, having bombarded aluminium with α-particles she produced a neutron and a radioactive isotope of phosphorus (unknown in nature) which emitted a positron $i.e.$ an electron mass with a positive charge:

$$^{27}_{13}Al + {}^4_2He = {}^1_0n + {}^{30}_{15}P$$
$$^{30}_{15}P = {}^{30}_{14}Si + {}^0_1p$$

In the decay of phosphorus of atomic number 15, one of its protons becomes a neutron by losing its positive charge by emitting a positron to produce a nucleus of atomic number 14 which is that of silicon.

For many years it has been standard practice to produce radioactive isotopes of the naturally occurring stable elements to investigate the reaction-routes of the latter in biochemical and medical research by following the path taken by the former by its radio-emissions both being chemically identical and the former being referred to as a radioactive tracer. Thus, for example, a radioisotope of calcium can be used to follow (trace) the route of metabolic calcium uptake in bone formation in mammals and radiocarbon (carbon-14) produced by neutron bombardment of nitrogen is used to follow the serial reactions of natural carbon compounds in biochemistry. Again, carbon-14 produced in the upper atmosphere (c.f. Section 9.3.2) and subsequently photosynthesised can be used to date the termination of photosynthesis and hence of archaeological artefacts from the extent of its subsequent decay, the rate being known.

Although all known nuclear reactions (transformations) prior to 1932 were associated with spontaneous emissions of particles or were induced by bombardments with such particles, as exemplified above, J. Cockcroft and E. T. S. Walton in that year split the lithium nucleus into two helium nuclei by the latter means. This was followed in 1938 by Liese Leitner and Hans Strassman splitting the uranium nucleus into two nuclei of approximately equal masses; by Leitner and her nephew Otto Frisch recognising in early 1939 that this splitting (fission) released large amounts of energy relative to those of chemical reactions; by Frederic Joliot and his wife Irene Curie-Joliot observing in April 1939 that this fission could take the form of an accelerating chain reaction because more neutrons were produced by the fission than were required to cause it; and by Niels Bohr and J.A. Wheeler reporting on 1 September 1939, the day Germany invaded Poland that of the three uranium isotopes (mass numbers 234, 235 and 238) only that of mass 235 (present to only 0.76%) readily underwent fission on neutron bombardment.

In the meantime (1934) Enrico Fermi had sought to create elements of atomic number higher than the highest naturally occurring uranium. To do this he bombarded uranium with neutrons and reported the production of an isotope of uranium and a new element of atomic number 93. It is more likely, however, that he was dealing with fission products. Nonetheless, the search for trans-uranic elements continued and the new elements neptunium (Np) and plutonium (Pu) were established thus:

$$^{238}_{92}U + {}^{1}_{0}n = {}^{239}_{92}U \text{ (radio-uranium)}$$
$$^{239}_{92}U = {}^{239}_{93}Np + {}^{0}_{1}e$$
$$^{293}_{93}Np = {}^{239}_{94}Pu + {}^{0}_{1}e$$

Here, the initially produced uranium isotope of mass 239 undergoes radio-active decay emitting a β-particle to produce neptunium of atomic number 93. This, in turn, undergoes radio-active decay emitting another β-particle to produce plutonium of atomic number 94. Thus, neptunium and plutonium are true trans-uranic elements of which some nineteen short-lived radio-nuclides have since been created by such means, thus extending the Periodic Table to include the actinide transition series. The plutonium nucleus was also found to undergo fission under neutron bombardment, releasing further neutrons and was thus capable of sustaining a chain reaction as does that of uranium.

It was subsequently found that the fission of one gram of uranium-235 or of plutonium causes an almost instantaneous release of energy equivalent to that produced by the combustion of 18 tons of coal. This energy arises from the conversion of about 1% of the mass into its equivalent in energy according to Einstein's equation: $E = mc^2$. Later similar mass-related energy release was associated with the fusion of the hydrogen isotopes deuterium and tritium to form helium and a neutron, thus:

$$^{2}_{1}H + {}^{3}_{1}H = {}^{4}_{2}He + {}^{1}_{0}n$$

Such fusion reactions are the source of the Sun's energy, the high initiation temperatures required having been produced by heat release from the gravity-induced condensation of the hydrogen cloud which initially formed the Sun (c.f. Section 9.3.1) Though controlled release of fusion energy has not yet been usefully realised (c.f. Section 9.5.1) the excess neutrons from controlled fusion-energy production might one-day transform the radioactive wastes from the fission-energy process to stable products thus offering an alternative to the current storage and decay option.

9.1.5 The Structure of the Atom

Following his discovery of the electron around the turn of the century J. J. Thomson had proposed that the atom consisted of a spherical positive charge in which electrons were somehow imbedded to the extent required for electrical neutrality. To investigate this matter further Geiger and Marsden under the direction of Rutherford arranged in 1909 for α-particles scattered by very thin metal foils to be observed on arrival at a glass screen by the light scintillation of their impact on its zinc sulphide coating. Thus, they found that while the majority were scattered through small deflection angles, about one in eight thousand were deflected by more than 90 degrees, leading Rutherford to propose in 1911 that the infrequent large-angle scattering was due to a single, more or less head-on encounter between an α-particle and an intense positive electric field; that the atom therefore consisted of a positively charged core (the nucleus) containing most of the atomic mass surrounded by orbiting electrons; and that the nucleus accounts for only a small proportion of the total space within the atom which is otherwise void (c.f. Sections 7.1.3 and 7.2.4). On this basis he calculated that the number of α-particles deflected through an angle θ should be proportional to cosec ½ θ, and Geiger and Marsden validated this prediction in 1913, giving a radius of about 10^{-15} m for the nucleus and about 10^{-10} m for the atom as a whole thus validating the Thomson-Rutherford model as far as these experiments went and indicating the extent of the apparent void space within the atom. This is perhaps more easily visualised on a scale on which the nucleus is a centimetre in diameter and the nearest electron is about three kilometres distant.

In fact, atoms could not exist on this basis alone, a constantly orbiting electronic charge being an emitter of electromagnetic energy as evidenced by radio-transmission. Again, the mutual electrostatic attraction between the negative electron and the positive nucleus might be expected to draw the electron out of orbit by causing it to spiral into the positive nucleus as energy was lost by radiation. However, this difficulty was removed by Niels Bohr in 1913 by incorporating Plank's *Quantum Theory* whereby the energy of the electron could not continuously decrease as it would were it to spiral into the nucleus, its permitted energy levels having to be whole number multiples of hf (c.f. Section 9.1.1), on which basis Bohr predicted the wavelengths of the optical line spectrum of atomic hydrogen to a high degree of accuracy. Thus, on the Bohr model the permitted energy levels of the electrons are E_1, E_2 ... E_n, corresponding to particular orbital radii, the electrons being able only to jump from one permitted energy level to another by absorbing or emitting electromagnetic quanta whose frequency f is given by: $E_2 - E_1 = hf$ where h is Plank's constant. Thus, the electron cannot have energy values between those permitted and so cannot continuously radiate as it would otherwise do.

The electron energy levels in an atom are usually represented as horizontal lines one above the other. The single electron of hydrogen normally occupies the lowest level, known as the ground state, with an energy value of -13.6 electron volts, 1 eV being the kinetic energy of an electron in a potential difference of 1 volt, this being equivalent to 1.6×10^{-19} joules. If the atom gains energy by collision or by absorption of electromagnetic radiation the electron may be promoted into one of the higher energy levels, this being equivalent to its having jumped into an orbit further from the nucleus, in which case the atom is said to be in an excited state from which after a short but random time interval it may fall back to the ground state re-emitting the energy initially absorbed. Each energy level is characterised by what is called a quantum number n where n = 1 for the lowest level, n = 2 for the next higher and so on to n equal to infinity at which final point the energy is zero and the electron is no longer bound to the atom which becomes a positive ion and a free electron. The energy levels of the hydrogen atom corresponding to n = 1, 2, 3, 4, 5, and 6 are -13.6, -3.39, -1.51, -0.85, -0.54 and -0.38 eV respectively. Thus the energy required to ionise a hydrogen atom is 13.6 electron volts. We are now in a position to explain the adsorption/emission line spectra of hydrogen (c.f. Sections 7.3.2 and 9.1.1)

Thus, if the electron in a hydrogen atom is excited to the energy level characterised by n = 4 and after a short time interval returns to the ground state for which n = 1 it can take four possible routes. These are: to go from n = 4 step-wise through n = 3, and n = 2, to n = 1; to go in one jump from n = 4 to n = 1; to go from n = 4 to n = 3 and then in one jump to n = 1; or to jump from n = 4 to n = 2 and then to n = 1. In these four routes, six individual transitions can be identified by inspection. Each of these transitions results in an emission of electromagnetic radiation the frequency of which is given by the energy difference between the two levels involved according to the equation $E_2 - E_1 = hf$. In using this equation to obtain frequency in Hertz, electron volts have to be converted to Joules by multiplication by 1.6 x 10^{-19}, Plank's constant being expressed in Joules. Now, on this basis the three most obvious groups of lines in the spectrum of atomic hydrogen, the Lyman Series in the ultraviolet, the Balmer Series in the visible and the Paschen Series in the infrared, are due to transitions from higher levels back to n = 1, to n = 2 and to n =3 respectively and this agreement between calculated and observed line frequencies in this spectrum of atomic hydrogen provides further reality-validation of the Rutherford-Bohr model of the atom.

9. 1. 6 Atomic Structure, Spectra of the Elements and the Periodic Table

The electron orbits in the hydrogen atom were considered to be circular about the nucleus which consists of a single proton. However, consideration of the atoms of elements of higher atomic weight W and atomic number N and with nuclei containing N protons and W - N neutrons, led to the additional concept of elliptical orbits with various degrees of eccentricity and to the concepts of magnetic moment and spin for the electron. These concepts supported by investigation of spectra (as indicated above for the simpler case of hydrogen) and knowledge of chemical properties (as previously summarised in the Periodic Table) enabled the distributions of electrons within the atoms of all of the elements to be determined. It has thus been concluded that the extra-nuclear electrons are located in shells denoted by the letters *K, L, M, N, O, P, Q* (derived from the notation of X-ray spectra) the K shell being nearest to the nucleus. The condition or state of each electron is characterised by four quantum numbers: the first, or principal quantum number *n* defines the shell, with *n* =1 for the *K* shell, *n* =2 for the *L* shell and so on; the second quantum number *l* determines the eccentricity of the orbit; the third *m* is the magnetic quantum number and the fourth *s* is the spin quantum number. The different values of *l* deduced from investigations of spectra are denoted by s, p, d and f corresponding to the sharp, principal, diffuse and fundamental spectral series. Further requirements are that the assignment of electronic configuration to an atom must comply with Pauli's *Exclusion Principle* which states that no two electrons in one atom can have all four quantum numbers identical; and that the assignment of electrons to atoms must be consistent with re-appearance of similar properties after progressing through 2, 8, 8, 18, 18, 32 elements as indicated by the Periodic Table.

It is found that all requirements are met by assigning electrons to shells and orbits according to quantum numbers *n* and *l* by progressively adding one electron to the orbit of next lowest energy level which becomes available in passing from one element to the next across the Periodic Table. Thus for hydrogen the single electron is in the K shell with quantum number n = 1 and quantum number *l* = s, it is a 1s electron. In helium both electrons are in 1s orbits and the K shell is complete as befits the inert chemistry of a rare gas. The next element lithium having two 1s electrons in its K shell, the third goes into the 2s orbit of the L shell (n = 2) which being further from the nucleus is more easily removed making lithium more reactive than helium. With beryllium the 2s orbits are full so the next electron goes into a 2p orbit of boron of which there are three capable of accommodating two electrons each which progressively account for carbon, nitrogen, oxygen, fluorine and the next rare gas neon with six 2p electrons making eight electrons in all for the second period comprising the K and L shells. The third period is a repeat of the second with the eleventh electron of sodium entering the 3s orbit and the thirteenth of aluminium entering the 3p orbit and with the 3p orbit being complete at the rare gas neon to complete the M shell.

In the fourth period the nineteenth and twentieth electrons of potassium and calcium respectively complete the 4s orbits of the N shell, but the twenty-first of scandium does not enter the 4p orbit of the N shell. Instead, it enters a deeper 3d orbit of the M shell, this being of lower energy. The process of filling the 3d orbits continues as we pass along the fourth period until all five 3d orbits are filled with ten electrons, the number of 4s electrons remaining unchanged at two, except for chromium where one of these drops into a 3d orbit until there are eighteen electrons in the 3s, 3p and 3d orbits at copper. The thirtieth electron of zinc then enters the 4s orbit vacated at chromium and the succeeding elements gallium to the rare gas krypton fill the 4p orbits as in periods two and three. The filling of 3d orbits thus accounts for the first transition series scandium to zinc.

The fifth period closely resembles the fourth. It begins with rubidium and strontium filling the 5s orbits after which the five 4d orbits are filled to account for the second transition series yttrium to cadmium and thereafter the three 5p orbits are filled from indium to the rare gas xenon. In this second transition series, however, one of the two 5s electrons falls into the lower 4d orbit from niobium (element 41) to silver (element 47) as occurred for chromium in the fourth period. The sixth period starts as usual with the addition of one and two electrons to the 6s orbits of caesium and barium. The third transition series (the lanthanides) then begins with lanthanum adding an electron to a 5d orbit but sequential filling of the 5d orbits is interrupted, by sequential filling of the seven inner 4f orbits from cerium to lutetium (the rare earths), before 5d filling of the lanthanides is resumed from hafnium to mercury. Thereafter the 6p orbits are successively filled from thallium to the rare gas radon and the 7s and 6d orbits to Uranium (c.f. Section 7.1.7).

9. 1. 7 Electronic Theory of Valence and Wave Mechanics in Chemistry

The above discussion of quantum theory and of atomic structure has provided deeper knowledge of the manner in which the Periodic Table achieved its success in summarising the chemical properties of the elements (c.f. Section 7.1.7). Again, as a consequence of knowing the distribution of electrons within atoms, we can now achieve a deeper knowledge of the laws of chemical combination and of the valence whereby elements combine with one another in small whole number ratios to form compounds of constant composition. We start by recalling that bonding within compounds is likely to be of two distinguishable types from the fact that there are two general classes of compounds, namely electrolytes whose aqueous solutions conduct electricity and non-electrolytes which are non-conducting.

With regard to electrolytes W. Kossel assumed that elements with fewer electrons or more electrons in their outermost shells than the rare gases might accept or donate electrons so that both when combined would have the stable, non-reactive, rare gas complement of electrons. Thus the atom of sodium has two 1s, two 2s and six 2p electrons equivalent to that of the rare gas neon, plus one 3s electron more than the rare gas neon. On the other hand chlorine while having the same number of 1s and 2s electrons as sodium, has only five 2p electrons which is one short of the rare gas neon. If, therefore, the outermost 3s electron of the sodium atom is transferred to the chlorine atom the result will be a sodium ion with one positive charge and a chlorine ion with one negative charge, both ions having the stable electronic structure of neon and both being held together by electrostatic attraction. Again, the magnesium atom has two 3s electons in its outer shell which it can transfer singly to each of two chorine atoms to form one magnesium ion with two positive charges and two chlorine ions each with one negative charge, all three having the electronic structure of the rare gas neon and held together by electrostatic attraction.

In the solid state such bonding is consistent with the arrangement of ions in orderly crystalline structures and with their free movement in water, the high dielectric constant of which reduces the force of electrostatic attraction. It also explains the whole number ratios of combining elements and demonstrates that the valency of ions is numerically equal to the value of their electrical charges. However, as an explanation of bonding such *electrovalence* is restricted to elements which differ by having more or fewer electrons in their valence shells than a

274

corresponding rare gas, the shells of which are considered to be complete and are themselves chemically inert. However, it is immediately obvious that the existence of molecules consisting of atoms of the same element such as oxygen 0_2 and hydrogen H_2 cannot be explained in this way. In general this difficulty applies to all non-ionisable compounds and these are the great majority with those of carbon being more numerous than those of all other elements taken together.

In 1916 G. N. Lewis overcame this difficulty by suggesting that the stable electronic configuration of the rare gases could be achieved by the sharing of a pair of electrons to form what he called the *covalent* bond. Thus for example, two hydrogen atoms each with one 1s electron could by sharing achieve the 2s configuration of helium. Similarly, two oxygen atoms each with two 2s electrons and four 2p electrons in their valency shell could share two pairs of electrons (a double bond) to achieve the eight electron configuration of neon. Again, two hydrogen atoms can share one electron each with one oxygen atom to provide the hydrogens with helium configurations and the oxygen with the neon configuration to form water (H_2O) and three hydrogen atoms can each share an electron with one nitrogen atom (two 2p and three 2p electrons) to provide the hydrogens with the helium configuration and the nitrogen with the neon configuration to form ammonia (NH_3), this sharing being referred to as *covalence*.

For still other compounds, however the bonding could not be explained by electrovalence or covalence. In these, a bond is formed when both of the shared electrons are contributed by one of the atoms involved. This is called the *co-ordinate* bond in which the atom supplying the pair of electrons is the *donor* and the recipient the *acceptor*. As an example the atoms of oxygen and sulphur are both two electrons short of the outer shell configuration of eight (two s electrons and six p electrons) of their respective rare gases neon and argon. Thus, if a sulphur atom which has six valence electrons (two s electrons and four p electrons) shares a pair of electrons with one oxygen atom (which also has six) to form a double covalent bond and donates a pair to another oxygen atom to form a co-ordinate bond, a molecule of sulphur dioxide is formed (SO_2), in which each atom has a completed rare gas octet of electrons. However, at this stage the sulphur still retains a pair of valence electrons which it can donate to another oxygen atom to form a second co-ordinate bond and a molecule of sulphur trioxide (SO_3) is formed. Co-ordinate bonds would be expected to have a polar character and as such have been called co-ionic, dative or semi-polar bonds. The dipole moment of such molecules is small but measurable, being of the order of 10^{-18} electrostatic units and such measurements demonstrate the existence of co-ordinate bonds.

Now, in its initial form Schroedinger's wave theory visualised the electron bound within the atom as a vibrating string with its energy levels depending on the nature of the vibration. In the hydrogen atom the string was visualised as being fixed (bound) at both ends and vibrating with one half wave-length between these ends, constituting the electron's lowest energy level. At the next energy level the string was visualised as vibrating with two half wave lengths between its ends, the third with three half wavelengths and so on. Schroedinger then set down the electron's possible energy levels (eigenvalues) each denoted by E and his wave function ψ which together describe its behaviour in relation to a mathematical operator (the Hamiltonian) H representing the total energy of the atom by means of his wave equation. This in its simplest form may be written: $E\psi = H\psi$ though its use involves partial differentiation in three dimensions and considerable computational labour now greatly reduced by computers. Nonetheless, it was by this means that Schroedinger calculated in 1926 the correct energy levels for the hydrogen atom, without invoking the quantum jumps introduced by Bohr, by visualising the atom-bound electron as a charge distribution in space based on the probabilities inherent in the wave-function, though Max Born interpreted the wave-function as a probability of finding the electron at any point (c.f. Section 9.1.2).

Either way, the charge-density/probability approach has been very fruitful in the development of chemistry. Thus, together with Heisenberg's notion of bonding through rapid interchange of position it enabled Walther Heitler and Fritz London to provide in 1926 a deeper explanation of the bonding of the two atoms of the hydrogen molecule and later it showed that the charge densities of the atomic electrons s, p, d and f had directional properties in space and thus conferred the directional properties of inter-atomic bonding which accounted for the overall shape (stereochemistry) of the resulting molecules. Thus the two electrons of lowest energy and opposite spin in the K shell occupy a spherically symmetrical orbit about the nucleus, the probability of finding an electron occupying this orbital decreasing with distance from the nucleus in any direction. Again, in the L shell two electrons occupy another s-orbital of greater radius than that of the K shell because they are of higher energy, while there now are up to six more electrons to consider in the three p-orbitals each of which are hour-glass shaped and lying mutually perpendicular to each other along the x, y and z axis with origin at the centre of the nucleus.

Now, it turns out with respect to the carbon atom that one of the s-orbital electrons can be excited into a vacant p-orbital, there being only four p-electrons in the carbon atom; that these s and p orbitals can produce four equivalent Indian club-shaped sp^3 hybrid orbitals disposed tetrahedrally from the nucleus; that each of these can form a directional covalent bond by mergence with the spherical orbital of the valence electron of a hydrogen atom or with the Indian-club-shaped orbital of another carbon atom; and that these bonding molecular orbitals, having rotational symmetry about the bond-axis are called σ-bonds. It also turns out that the s-orbital can combine with two of the p-orbitals to form three sp^2 hybrid orbitals of India-club shape disposed in a plane at 120 degrees to each other; that the un-hybridised hour-glass shaped fourth p-orbital is perpendicular to this plane; that each of the three hybridised orbitals contains a valence electron which can pair with valence electrons from other atoms to form three σ-bonds; and that the electron in the remaining p-orbital can pair with another in a neighbouring carbon atom to form the molecular orbital of a π-bond. Two atoms thus double-bonded will resist rotation and so atoms or groups to which they are also bonded will be fixed at the four corners of a rectangle giving rise to the possibility of geometric isomerism. Again, triple-bonding between two carbon atoms can also arise when the s-orbital and one of the p-orbitals of each produce two sp hybrid orbitals which extend outwards on opposite sides of the carbon nucleus and are available to form two σ-bonds while the other two p-orbitals whose axes of symmetry are perpendicular to each other and to the bond-axis merge with those of the other atom to form two π-bonds between them. Thus, in multiple bonding between two carbon atoms there is always one σ-bond, the other two being π-bonds. On this basis I now introduce carbon chemistry.

9. 2 CARBON CHEMISTRY: EIGHTEENTH-TWENTIETH CENTURY

Carbon dioxide naturally present in the atmosphere dissolves in water (rain) to produce the weak (relatively un-dissociated) carbonic acid which gives rise to the carbonate salts such as calcium carbonate (chalk). However, the vast majority of natural carbon compounds have their origin in the photosynthesis of atmospheric carbon dioxide which produces all the constituent compounds of vegetable and hence of animal matter. Thus, the chemistry of carbon is the chemistry of life and is for this reason referred to as organic chemistry. Because of the multiplicity of organic compounds early organic chemists faced an even more daunting task than had inorganic chemists, there being more compounds of carbon than of the other ninety-one elements. Nonetheless, the new task yielded to the same systematic experimentation-based approach as had the previous one. From its

276

position in the Periodic Table carbon is expected to form covalent bonds and to be quadrivalent. However, carbon has the ability to concatenate (self-bond in long molecular chains) and though silicon its Periodic Group analogue exhibits this property to a lesser extent in the silicate minerals, carbon can do so not only through the single bonds of silicon but also through double and triple bonds, these properties of carbon being the source of its unique compound-multiplicity. Truly, life is a property of the carbon atom.

9. 2. 1 Classification of Carbon Compounds

Organic compounds which contain only carbon and hydrogen are called hydrocarbons. The simplest are the shortest chain lengths of the paraffin series: CH_4 (methane), C_2H_6 (ethane), C_3H_8 (propane) and C_4H_{10} (butane), the general formula for which is C_nH_{2n+2}. Re-writing these formulae from ethane respectively as: $H_3C.CH_3$, $H_3C.C(H_2).CH_3$, and $H_3C.C(H_2).C(H_2).CH_3$ we see that the carbon to carbon and the carbon to hydrogen bonds are single; that the terminal carbons are bonded to another carbon and to three hydrogen atoms; and that all non-terminal carbons are bonded to two carbon and two hydrogen atoms.

Where double bonded carbon atoms are present the simplest formulae may be written: $H_2C:CH_2$ (ethylene), $H_3C.C(H):CH_2$ (propene), $H_3C.C(H):C(H).CH_3$ (butene) and $H_3C.C(H):C(H).CH_2.CH_3$ (pentene) with the general formula of this olefin series being C_nH_{2n}. In this series from butene through higher members, the double-bond (:) can be in different positions in the carbon chain. Thus, as written above the double-bond in butene is between carbons 2 and 3, but it could have been written $H_2C:C(H).C(H_2).CH_3$ with the double-bond between carbons 1 and 2. Now, whether this bond is between carbons 1 and 2, or 3 and 4 makes no difference, being at the end of the molecular chain as it is in propylene. However, with the central double bond between atoms 2 and 3, two distinct structural arrangements are possible, the cis-form in which the two single hydrogen atoms associated with these carbons are on the same side of the molecule and the trans-form in which they are on opposite sides, the double-bond unlike the single-bond, being non-rotational (c.f. Section 9.1.7). Again with pentene, the double bond can be between carbon atoms 2 and 3 as written above to give rise to cis- and trans-forms as with butene or between carbons 1 and 2 to give the terminal double bond as in butene and propylene while placing it between carbon atoms 3 and 4 gives the option of cis- and trans-forms again. However, with the six carbon chain of hexane the double bond between carbon atoms 3 and 4 gives additional central cis-and trans-form options. Thus we see that as chain length increases the number of possible positions for the double-bond increases as do the possibilities for different cis- and trans-chain lengths on either side of the double bond. In addition, the possibilities for more than one double bond also increase with chain length.

Where triple bonded carbons are present the simplest formulae may be written $HC*CH$ (acetylene), $HC*C.CH_3$ (propylene) and $HC*C.C(H_2).CH_3$ (butyne) with the general formula for the acetylene series being C_nH_{2n-2}. Again as chain length increases, the number of different locations for the triple-bond (*) increases as does the number of possibilities for their being more than one.

From the above, it can be seen that chain length increases when a hydrogen atom bonded to a terminal carbon is replaced by a $-CH_3$ (methyl) group. When such hydrogen replacement involves a non-terminal carbon, however, a branched chain results. Such branches can be of different lengths as when replacement involves the ethyl group $-CH_3.CH_2$, propyl group, and so on. In addition, such hydrogen replacement may involve atoms of other elements, most commonly those of bi-valent oxygen and tri-valent nitrogen. In the former case one hydrogen is replaced by a single bonded oxygen, the second valence of the oxygen being satisfied by bonding to another hydrogen

277

to form the hydroxyl group, or two hydrogen atoms are replaced by a double bond between the oxygen and the carbon atom. In the latter case one hydrogen is replaced by a single bonded nitrogen of which the second and third valencies are satisfied by hydrogen atoms.

Thus, taking $H_3C.CH_3$ (ethane) as an example, we may have $H_3C.C(H_2).OH$ or $H_3C.C(H).O$ or again, $H_3C.C(H_2).NH_2$. The first of these transformations produces an alcohol (-OH group), the example given being ethyl alcohol, the second an aldehyde (-C(H).O group), the example being acetaldehyde while the third produces an amine (-NH_2 group), in this case ethylamine. In addition, the single hydrogen attached to a carbon in acetaldehyde may be replaced by a hydroxyl group thus, $H_3C.C(OH).O$ to form the carboxylic acid group, more commonly written -COOH as in acetic acid CH_3COOH. The long chain acids of this form are often referred to as the fatty acids and when they contain C.C multiple bonding they are said to be unsaturated fatty acids, being unsaturated (deficient) with respect to hydrogen content.

The single hydrogen attached to the carbon of an aldehyde group may also be replaced by a methyl group to give the ketone group as in $H_3C.C(CH_3).O$ normally written CH_3COCH_3, in this case di-metyl ketone otherwise known as acetone. If replaced by an ethyl group, the result would be methyl ethyl ketone and so on. Again, the hydrogen of the OH group, as for example in ethyl alcohol, can be replaced by a methyl, ethyl or longer chain radical as in $CH_3.CH_2.O.CH_3$ to form ethyl methyl ether, diethyl ether *etc.* Furthermore, if one of the hydrogen atoms bonded to the carbon adjacent to the acid group COOH were replaced by the amine group NH_2, the result would be an α-amino acid whatever the chain length, an example being $R.CH(NH_2).COOH$, where R represents an alkyl chain of unspecified length and α denotes the carbon position adjacent to the acid group to which the NH_2 group is bonded, the β position being the next along the alkyl chain and so on..

Again, one of the hydrogen atoms on each of the carbons in a straight chain may be replaced by a hydroxyl group to form what is referred to as a carbohydrate, the names of which end in -ose. Thus, we could have the compound $CH_2(OH).CH(OH).CH_2(OH)$ which having three carbon atoms in the chain would be triose, longer chains being tetrose, pentose, hexose *etc.* Such compounds may also be referred to as polyhydric alcohols. Thus, the triose is also known as 1,2,3-propane triol otherwise known as glycerol. Such compounds may, however, contain aldehyde or ketone groups in place of a hydroxyl in which case the prefix aldo or keto is used. Thus, we have $CH_2(OH).CH(OH).CHO$, aldotriose, otherwise known as glyceraldehyde, and we may have ketotriose $CH_2(OH)CO.CH_2(OH)$.

Now, acids react with alcohols to form esters. Thus, acetic acid with ethanol forms the ester, ethyl acetate in a manner analogous to hydrochloric acid and sodium hydroxide forming sodium chloride as shown by the following equations:

$$CH_3.COOH + CH_3.CH_2(OH) = CH_3.COOCH_2.CH_3 + H_2O$$
$$HCl \quad + \quad Na\,OH = NaCl \quad + \quad H_2O$$

In this way the naturally occurring fats (solids) and oils (liquids) are found to be esters of the higher fatty (aliphatic) acids and glycerol because of which they are also called glycerides. If unsaturated acids are involved the resulting fats and oils are said to be unsaturated, being convertible to corresponding saturates by addition of hydrogen (hydrogenation). In addition, the amino-acids will also react with alcohols to form esters, but more importantly the acid group of one may react with the amine group of another to form a peptide. Thus, $CH_2(NH_2)COOH$ amino acetic acid or glycine will react with itself to form the di-peptide $(NH_2)CH_2.CONHCH_2COOH$ through the -CONH, (amide linkage) and the process can be repeated at both ends of the di-peptide to form the tri-, tetra-, and higher polypeptides, the number of such linked units ranging from 300 to 1000.

278

Again, the proteins are peptide-linked polypeptides involving a number of different amino acids in specific sequences on which their properties and functions depend, the possibilities being very numerous. With three different amino acids and no repetitions there are 3! (factorial 3) or 6 ways of creating a tri-peptide and this rises to 3,628,800 (10!) ways for a deca-peptide. By breaking the amide linkages (hydrolysis) of proteins around two dozen individual amino acids have been identified some of which can be synthesised in the animal body while others have to be supplied in the diet. Without going into details, the sequences of amino-acids in peptide and protein chains were determined by sequential *End-Group Analysis* introduced by Frederick Sanger in 1945.

The basic carbohydrate unit is the monosaccharide while those linked together may be disaccharides or polysaccharides. The most important of the monosaccharides is glucose while the commonest disaccharide is sucrose (cane sugar) consisting of the monosaccharides glucose and fructose linked through a C-O-C linkage formed with the elimination of water. Polysaccharides contain several such mono-units which may be pentoses as in the xylan of wood, hexoses as in starch or cellulose, or a mixture of pentoses or hexoses as in wood gums. Starch is found in almost all plants and is stored in all grains and tubers as a future food-supply for the germination of seeds. On hydrolysis, starch yields only glucose whereas the inulin of potatoes yields only fructose. Cellulose, the most widely distributed polysaccharide is the chief constituent of plant cell walls and hence is the structural material of the vegetable kingdom comprising about 50% of wood and about 90% of cotton. As with starch, cellulose consists of glucose units linked together at the 1 and 4 carbons whereas in dextran made by fermenting sucrose as a substitute for blood plasma, the glucose units are linked between carbons 1 and 6 (c.f. Section 9.2.3)

It should also be noted that divalent sulphur can occur instead of divalent oxygen to give, for example, the mercaptans and alkyl sulphides. Thus, the mercaptans RSH are analogues of the alcohols ROH while the alkyl sulphides, otherwise known as the thio-ethers, have formulae RSR or RSR' as in dimethyl sulphide or in methyl ethyl sulphide.

9. 2. 2 Consideration of Molecular Structure

As we have seen, carbon chain-length, number of double and triple bonds, chain branching and the presence and arrangement of hetero-atoms such as oxygen, nitrogen and sulphur can vary almost without limit. Thus, instead of the straight chain pentane we might have a branched pentane which would be specified as 2-methyl butane in which the second carbon of the butane chain (carbon 2 as designated in the name) has a methyl group bonded to it in addition to the methyl and ethyl groups which with itself constitute the four-carbon butane straight chain. In addition, straight chain amines RNH_2 can take the form RR'NH and RR'R''N, which are known as the primary, secondary and tertiary amines respectively, nitrogen being trivalent.

A further structural variation arises, however, when the carbon chains form rings in what are known as the alicyclic compounds. Many plants, especially those of the families *Coniferae* and *Myrtaceae* and genus *Citrus* contain volatile oils in their leaves, blossoms and fruits which have been steam distilled for use in perfumery since antiquity. These oils called terpenes are mixtures of unsaturated alicyclic compounds of empirical formula $(C_5H_8)_n$, the C_5H_8 being known as the isoprene unit, the individual terpenes being classifiable as open-chain, monocyclic, bicyclic, sesqui-cyclic or otherwise poly-cyclic and being unsaturated, cis and trans forms are distinguishable. Thus, one pair of such isomers is Nerol (cis) and Geraniol (trans) and the aldehyde Citral corresponding to the alcohol Geraniol is the essence of lemon.

Again because of the tetrahedral bonds, carbon chains are zigzag with the bonds making angles of 109 degrees 28 minutes with each other. Such zigzagging coupled with rotation about single-bond axes enables the two ends to approach each other in the course of thermal agitation so that rings of carbon-carbon single bonds are possible though these are not planar. Thus, if we imagine a six member ring as a hexagon and number the carbon atoms 1 to 6, we see that while carbons 2, 3, 5 and 6 can lie in the same plane, the diametrically opposed carbons, 1 and 4 would be tilted at 109 degrees 28 minutes either above or below the plane. If both are tilted up we have what is called the boat form while one is up and the other down gives the chair form. Such rings in which bond angles are thus maintained are also possible for larger rings. Only one form of cyclo-hexane has been isolated, however, suggesting that in this case there is a rapid thermal inter-conversion between the two forms. These possibilities led Hassel to introduce conformational analysis in 1943.

In fact distortion of the tetrahedral bond angle does not prevent formation of cyclo-pentane, cyclo-butane and even cyclo-propane though these rings are planar with bond angle distortions of 0.44 minutes, 9 degrees 44 minutes and 24 degrees 44 minutes respectively and with relative reactivity to ring opening being proportional to release of the strain caused by these deformation levels. Indeed, the even greater reactivity of the alkene double-bond is consistent with this relationship on the basis of its being a ring of two carbon atoms with a bond deviation angle of 54 degrees 44 minutes. Again, as with the double-bond these rigid planar rings with pairs of hydrogen atoms above and below the ring, are capable of substitution to give cis and trans forms of more complicated stereo-isomerism as ring size increases.

Further to rings, the structure of benzene first isolated from coke oven condensates in 1825 and of benzoic acid, benzyl alcohol and methyl benzene (toluene) later isolated from gum and tolu balsam, were found by Kekule (1829-1896) to be based on a six-carbon unit which survived routine chemical changes and degradations. He also found that though they had a low hydrogen : carbon ratio they did not undergo the addition reactions usually indicative of un-saturation and that the simplest member of this group of substances was benzene of formula C_6H_6 whereas a fully saturated chain paraffin with six carbons would have the formula C_6H_{14}. Again, while bromine Br_2 adds readily to the alkene double-bond to give a dibromide, benzene could only be persuaded with difficulty to substitute one bromine atom for a hydrogen with the formation of C_6H_5Br, bromobenzene and HBr, hydrogen bromide. In addition, Kekule showed that ethane and benzene gave only one mono-substituted product while propane gave two mono and four di-substituted products showing that all the hydrogen atoms in ethane and in benzene were equivalent in contrast to those at two distinct locations in propane, consistent with its formula $CH_3CH_2CH_3$. He also found that only three di-substituted products are available from benzene. Thus he showed that the benzene molecule consisted of a regular hexagonal ring of six carbon atoms bonded to each other by alternating single and double bonds with each carbon atom being single bonded to a hydrogen atom to satisfy the quadri-valence of carbon and with the alternate single and double bonds oscillating between their two possible forms rendering them chemically indistinguishable.

In wave mechanical terms (c.f. 9.1.7) when several sp^2 hybridised carbon atoms are bonded in a chain with the axes of symmetry of their third un-hybridised p-orbitals all parallel and overlapping with those of their neighbours on either hand, the resulting molecular π-orbitals extend over all of them. Such delocalised π-orbitals contain two electrons of opposite spin as do localised π-orbitals, though when written as alternating double and single bonds these are said to be conjugated. This delocalisation (conjugation) confers greater molecular stability and less reactivity than would otherwise be expected from alternate single and double bonds. Thus, the open chain of 1,3-butadiene is conjugated and more stable, un-reactive, to additions than that of 1,4-pentadiene with its two non-conjugated double bonds. As to cyclic benzene, the inter-carbon distance (bond-length) of 1.40 Angstrom units is intermediate between the 1,54 of alkane single bonds and the

1.34 of alkene double bonds in compliance with Kekule's resonance hybrid of two oscillating forms.

The di-substitution of benzene can occur at carbons 1 and 2 to give the ortho, at 1 and 3, to give the meta and at 1 and 4 to give the para forms. As with the open chain molecules, the usual functional groups may be present such as OH to give phenol C_6H_5OH for example, polyhydric phenols and other aromatic alcohols; CHO and CO to give benzaldehyde, aromatic ketones and quinines; COOH to give benzoic and other aromatic acids; and NH_2 to give aromatic amines, diazo compounds and dyes. In addition alkyl side chains arise such as with toluene $C_6H_5CH_3$ to which side chains the functional groups can again be added. In addition, we should note di-phenyl in which two benzene rings are single-bonded between a carbon in one ring to a carbon in another, tri-phenyl methane in which three benzene rings are substituted for three of the hydrogen atoms of methane, and the condensed honey-comb structures of the so-called polynuclear aromatics such as naphthalene (two such rings sharing ortho and meta carbons), anthracene (three in a row with ortho and meta sharing) and phenanthrene (with the third condensed, as it were, between the otherwise non-condensed rings of diphenyl).

The remaining ring compounds are those which contain one atom of an element other than carbon within the ring itself, such being known as heterocyclics. Thus, in five member rings with two pairs of double-bonded carbon atoms and a hetero-oxygen atom we have furan, with a hetero sulphur atom, thiophene and with a hetero nitrogen atom, pyrrole. In a six member ring with three double bonds and a hetero nitrogen atom we have pyridine which may be visualised as benzene with one carbon atom replaced by a nitrogen atom. Once again we can have substitutions for the hydrogen atoms bonded to ring members in all such heterocyclics. Such compounds are ubiquitous in the plant and animal kingdoms and there are complex structures of basic units and side-chains as for example in chlorophyll, the basic structure of which consists of four pyrrole rings with their respective nitrogen-adjacent ring carbon atoms (*i.e.* those at the 2 and 5 positions) linked through a side chain carbon atom, and with their hetero nitrogen atoms (at position 1) bonded to a central magnesium ion. Haemin has a similar structure with a central iron ion. In addition, pyridine can fuse with benzene to share the ortho and meta carbons of the latter to form quinoline or at the meta and para positions to form isoquinoline, the alkaloids being plant-source hetero-cyclic compounds with structures based on pyrrole, pyridine, quinoline and isoquiniline, many being physiologically active with quinine being used to prevent malaria, morphine for pain relief, cocaine as a local anaesthetic, atropine in eye surgery and with nicotine being the chief alkaloid in tobacco leaves.

9. 2. 3 Chemical Determination of Structure

It is clear from the above that the characterisation of organic compounds involves both analysis of elemental composition and deduction of the structural arrangement of those elements within the molecule. Thus, a new substance is first purified prior to determination of its empirical formula which through measurement of molecular weight by vapour or osmotic pressure determines the molecular formula in terms of the number of the various atoms in the molecule by applying a small whole number multiplier to the empirical formula (c.f. Section 7.1.5). Secondly, the nature and numbers of the functional groups are identified through their reactions with group-specific reagents. Thirdly the molecule is taken apart by specific reagents and the positions of its functional groups are determined by their positions in the molecules of the identified break-down products, all derivatives produced by specific reagents and all break-down products being similarly identified. The fourth step is to synthesis the compound in question from known reactions devised for the synthesis of complex molecules from simpler ones of known structure. The fifth step is to show by comparison that the synthetic compound is identical in all respects to the compound in question.

This general approach is modified as required for specific tasks as these are identified, but all such modifications are consistent with it. We have already seen that Kekule showed by reaction with bromine that all the hydrogen atoms (taken as functional groups) in benzene were equivalent and that this provided evidence for a ring structure rather than for an open chain where terminal hydrogen atoms have different bonding-environments from those in the chain. Again, the presence and number of carbon-carbon double bonds is usually determined by quantitative hydrogenation which for benzene reveals four double-bond equivalents, three for the double bonds and one for ring opening. Again the presence of a carbonyl group can be revealed by such means and identified by reactions specific to aldehyde, ketone or carboxylic acid groupings. Yet again, oxidation of carbon-carbon double bonds produces an aldehyde group if the double bond is adjacent to a straight chain and a ketone if adjacent to a branched chain. Thus, in the molecule $CH_3.C.(CH_3):CH.CH_3$, the oxidation products would be acetone and acetaldehyde, and this would be enough to show that this pentane was branched with a methyl group at carbon-2 and that the double bond was located between carbons 2 and 3. That it was a hydrocarbon with one double-bond equivalent would have been revealed by confirming its empirical formula of C_5H_{10} as its molecular formula by quantitative hydrogenation to C_5H_{12} or by vapour pressure determination of molecular weight

At this point the investigative power of this particular aspect of scientific method can be further demonstrated by a return to carbohydrate chemistry. The molecular formula for glucose is $C_6H_{12}O_6$. When glucose reacts with acetic anhydride a penta-acetyl derivative is formed, indicating the presence of five OH groups in the molecule. Reaction with phenyl hydrazine confirms the presence of a carbonyl group. It reduces Tollen's reagent and Fehling's solution while gentle oxidation with bromine water gives a mono-carboxylic acid, indicating that the carbonyl is that of an aldehyde. In addition, this mono-carboxylic acid when strongly oxidised by nitric acid gives a di-carboxylic acid without loss of carbon, indicating that this second carboxylic acid group must have arisen from a CH_2OH group as distinct from a CHOH group. Again, reduction of glucose by phosphorus and hydriodic acid produces normal (straight chain) hexane, indicating that the carbon skeleton is non-branching. In addition, the monovalence of the aldehydic carbonyl CHO and alcoholic CHOH groups, indicate that they occupy the terminal positions in the six-carbon chain. The four hydrogen atoms still not accounted for can then be allocated to the non-terminal carbon atoms according to valence requirements and the structure can be written:

$$CH_2(OH).CH(OH).CH\,(OH).CH(OH).CH\,(OH).CHO$$
$$\quad 1 \qquad\quad 2 \qquad\quad 3 \qquad\quad 4 \qquad\quad 5 \qquad\quad 6$$

9. 2. 4 Further Consideration of Structure

Consideration of the above structure in the light of the tetrahedral orientation of carbon bonding reveals that the four inner carbon atoms each have two possible arrangements for their hydrogen and hydroxyl attachments such that one will be the mirror image of the other. Thus, 3-dimensionally, if we draw a line from carbon-4 in the plane of the page from left to right to carbon-6 through carbon-5, we see that the H and OH bonded to carbon-5 would be in the plane of the page with either one being towards the top and the other towards the foot of the page thus giving two mirror image possibilities. Further consideration shows this asymmetry to apply to carbons 2 to 5 and that consequently the glucose structure allows for 2^4 or 16 distinct isomers. All of these have been synthesised, but only three occur in nature, namely glucose, mannose and galactose.

Similar considerations apply to the hydroxy and to the amino acids. Thus lactic acid $CH_3CH(OH)COOH$ has an asymmetric central carbon atom. This is the phenomenon which gave rise to the optical activity observed by Pasteur in his work on the tartaric acids (c.f. Section 8.2.6) whereby the two isomers rotate the plane of polarisation of light transmitted by Iceland spar to the right, *dextro* (*d*) and left, *laevo* (*l*) respectively. There are two asymmetric carbon atoms in the tartaric acids, however, which permit the existence of a meso form in which the rotations due to the carbons cancel each other within the molecule. These three isomers may be represented as being:

HOOC.HCOH.HCOH.COOH (*dextro*), HOOC.HOCH.HOCH.COOH (*laevo*) and

HOOC.HCOH.HOCH.COOH (*meso*)

This internal (meso) cancellation of rotation is distinct from that due to the presence of equal amounts of *d* and *l* isomers in what is known as a racemic mixture. Naturally occurring amimo acids are all of the *l* form whereas laboratory synthesis always produces the racemic *dl* mixture because natural enzymatic synthesis shows a preference, a handedness, which is not reproduced in (non-enzymatic) laboratory synthesis. It is not possible, however, to separate such mixtures by solubility, boiling point or other physical means nor can it be done by direct chemical means because these optical isomers (enantiomorphism) are in these respects identical. Nonetheless, Pasteur was able to make the first separation (resolution) by hand-selection of crystals because of a rare tendency exhibited by the tartrates to crystallise in separate mirror image forms. A second approach relies on biological preference to enhance the %age of one form by elimination of the other through exposure to micro-organisms.

The best approach, however, involves reacting a racemic mixture with an optically active substance to produce a pair of diasterioisomers which unlike enantiomorphs do differ in physical properties relevant to subsequent separation such as by fractional crystallisation from a suitable solvent. Thus, a *dl* mixture of lactic acid can be neutralised by an optically active base such as *l*-strychnine, *l*-brucine or *l*-quinine to form a *d*-acid *l*-base salt and an *l*-acid *l*-base salt to be separated by fractional crystallisation and separately treated with mineral acid to release the separate optically active acids. Similarly a racemic base can be separated by use of an optically active acid such as the readily available *d*-tartaric acid.

9. 2. 5 Confirmation of Chemically Determined Structures

Having considered the chemical determination of molecular structure in section 9.2.3, I now turn to the chemical synthesis of such pre-determined molecular structures. The former involved detection and identification of functional groups by their specific reactions, ring opening and the break-down of long carbon-chains to shorter chains for chemical identification. Conversely, the latter involves chain lengthening, ring closures and the introduction of functional groups as required to produce the intended molecular structure, using the appropriate reagents from the known range at any time or the invention and reality-validation of new reagents to meet such new requirements, many such innovations being named after the chemists who introduced them. Some such reactions involve the introduction of a hetero atom to the molecules of one compound by one reaction followed by its removal by another to produce molecules double their original length. Thus, for example, alkyl iodides can be prepared from their respective alcohols by reaction with phosphorus tri-iodide, itself prepared by reacting phosphorus with iodine:

$$2P + 3I_2 = 2PI_3$$
$$3ROH + PI_3 = RI + H_3PO_3$$
$$RI + RI + 2\,Na = R\text{-}R \ + 2NaI \ (\text{ Wurtz Synthesis})$$

Again, alcohols can be prepared by substitution of OH for X in the alkyl halides RX where X stands for F, Cl or I by treatment with aqueous sodium hydroxide:

$$RX + NaOH = ROH + NaX$$

while ethers are produced by the removal of water from alcohols through treatment with sulphuric acid at 170° C while alkenes are produced at the lower temperature of 140° C, thus for example, diethyl ether and ethylene from two or from one molecule of ethyl alcohol respectively:

$$2\ H_3C.C(H_2)OH = H_3C.C(H_2)OC(H_2)\ CH_3 + H_2O$$

$$H_3C.C(H_2)OH = H_2C:CH_2 + H_2O$$

and similarly, aldehydes and ketones are produced from primary and secondary alcohols on treatment with dilute potassium dichromate, respectively, thus:

$$RCH_2OH = RCHO + H_2O$$

$$RR'CHOH = RR'CO + H_2O$$

Meanwhile, secondary alcohols are prepared from aldehydes by the Grignard Reagent (alkyl magnesium halide), thus: $RCHO + R'MgX = RR'C(H)OH + Mg (OH)X$

In addition, carboxylic acids can be prepared by the oxidation of aldehydes with potassium permanganate or through conversion of an alkyl halide to a nitrile by reaction with potassium cyanide which increases the alkyl chain by one carbon, followed by oxidation by potassium permanganate to the resulting acid amide and hence to the carboxylic acid one carbon atom longer than the carbon chain of the initial halide, thus: $RX + KCN = RCN + KX$

$$RCN + H_2O = RCONH$$

$$RCONH_2 + H_2O = RCOOH + NH_3$$

Alternatively Grignard Reagents will react with carbon dioxide to produce a carboxylic acid of chain length one carbon atom longer than the initial alkyl chain, thus:

$$RMgCl + CO_2 + H_2O = RCOOH + Mg (OH)Cl$$

There are also the so-called condensation reactions in which two molecules combine to form a larger one with elimination of a simpler substance, usually water. Thus, the dimerisation of acetaldehyde when warmed in the presence of dilute sodium hydroxide to form β-hydroxybuteraldehyde, thus:

$$2CH_3CHO = CHC(OH)HCH_2CHO + H_2O$$

Another is when two acids combine to form their so-called anhydrides, as for example when two acetic acid molecules combine with elimination of water thus:

$$2CH_3 COOH = CH_3 CO.O.COCH_3 + H_2O$$

Again, the Perkin Reaction is a condensation in which benzaldehyde C_6H_5CHO reacts with acetic anhydride $(CH_3CO)_2O$ and sodium acetate to form cinnamic acid $C_6H_5CH:CHCOOH$ in which the side chain of the benzene ring has been extended by two carbon atoms with a double-bond between two of them. This reaction is capable of wide extension to produce many substituted cinnamic acids.

Thus, in principle, any naturally occurring organic molecule can be synthesised by such reactions as exemplified above and others like them too numerous to mention here. The point is that every molecule of the plant kingdom is synthesised from carbon dioxide and by photons of light and every molecule in the animal kingdom is derived either directly or indirectly from those of the plant kingdom. There is no distinction to be drawn between chemicals and natural organic products: everything in the plant and animal kingdoms is an organic compound all individuals of which are identical whether synthesised naturally, in a laboratory or in an industrial process. Indeed, it is standard practice to confirm the analytically deduced molecular structures of naturally occurring substances by synthesising them to show natural and synthetic to be identical in all respects.

Now, as shown in section 9.1.3, the diffraction of X-rays can provide information on crystal structure and the spatial relationship of atoms. As to carbon itself, the X-ray diffraction pattern obtained from diamond confirmed the three dimensional tetrahedral structure predicted from the directional properties of the sp^3 hybridisation of the electron orbitals of the carbon atom, that from graphite confirmed the two-dimensional planar structure predicted from sp^2 hybridisation and those from crystals of organo-metallic complexes such as lead tetraethyl or cobalt hexapropyl confirmed their spatial arrangements as predicted by the directional properties of the dsp^2 and d^2sp^3 hybridisations of their respective metal-atom orbitals. It was a small step from there to confirm the structures of the organic components (ligands) of such complexes by X-ray diffraction and from there to introduce a general technique for confirming the molecular structures of organic molecules deduced by the analytical and synthetic means described in the previous sections, provided they could be made available in pure crystalline form.

Thus, while the information contained in X-ray diffraction patterns is insufficient to enable unknown structures to be deduced from them alone, it became a routine matter to confirm chemically deduced structures from them by computer-based calculations before they were further confirmed by chemical synthesis. Later, it became possible to determine structures by hypothesising their completion from partial chemical analysis and reiterative recourse to the computer to achieve ever-closer agreement between hypothesised and actual diffraction-patterns: and finally to confirm purely hypothetical structures in this way. Thus it was that the structures of progressively more complex natural products were determined, *e.g.* by Dorothy M. C. Hodgkin for penicillin, insulin and vitamin B_{12}, and by James Watson and Francis Crick for their hypothetical double helical structure for molecular DNA in 1953, Erwin Chagraff having established the basic components of DNA and Linus Pauling and R. B. Corey the α-helical structure of proteins in 1950.

9. 2. 6 Precursors to Life

As a prelude to the following reviews of astronomy, earth sciences and biotechnology (c.f. Sections 9.3, 9.4, and 9.5.2-9.5.4) it is appropriate to note that ultraviolet light has been shown to induce water, methane and ammonia to auto-synthesise compounds of up to 20-30 atoms among which amino-acids predominate. Though the energy stored in the chemical bonding of such structures (c.f. Section 7.2.3) would ordinarily be expected to break them down again with spontaneous release of energy, its disposal in small incremental steps as such simple molecules inter-react to produce those of ever-increasing complexity is the journey towards the threshold life at which molecular complexity becomes sufficient to act as a template for its own reproduction from simpler compounds produced as above from the action of sunlight on the even simpler.

However, the virus is a level of complexity which can reproduce only within the already living cells which it invades, though the enabling template for the reproduction of viruses and living cells is the DNA which controls the growth, develop and maintenance of all cells, organs and organisms in all species-specific, individual and personal ways. Again, while life may have begun in shallow coastal waters with molecular adsorption on solid silicate structures overcoming the paucity of inter-molecular contact at high water dilution, it seems likely that water, methane, ammonia and other gases out of which solids were condensing prior to planet accretion, would have been exposed to more ultraviolet radiation than would later reach sea level on Earth; and that the material of planetary accretion could have contributed some complex molecular structures to the primeval oceans of planet Earth (c.f. Section 9.4.4).

9. 3 ASTRONOMY AND COSMOLOGY

Until the end of the nineteenth century astronomy was largely confined to observation, prediction and confirmation of the movements of celestial bodies and to spectral determinations of stellar composition. Thereafter, physics and chemistry provided the opportunity to address star and galaxy formation and the processes by which stars generate energy and synthesise the chemical elements which give rise to the planets and to all life-forms. Thus, just as Newton had been stimulated by the laboratory based physics of Galileo and Huygens to investigate the Earth-Moon system so also was the imagination of later astronomers stimulated to interpret the workings of the universe on the basis of the latest laboratory-based reality-evaluations of physics and chemistry. We must always be aware, however, that while cause and effect within the universe is accessible to such means, the cause of the effect which is the universe is not, and that no other means are available to us.

9. 3. 1 Star Formation and Evolution

The observation that our Sun is 90% hydrogen and that the universe consists of stars and interstellar hydrogen clouds, prompts the hypothesis that stars are formed by the gravitational contraction of hydrogen. On the other hand, it is known from laboratory investigations that gas temperature increases with contraction, that molecular velocities increase with temperature and that molecules might thus escape from the gravitational field of the cloud at some point short of contraction to a star, thus preventing star formation by this hypothetical mechanism. Again while it is possible to postulate an initial mass of gas large enough for gravitational contraction to continue despite the temperatures reached, a mass equal to that of our Sun would be insufficient for its formation in this way. Yet again, a mass sufficiently large could either contract to produce individual stars hugely in excess of the sizes observed, or it could produce stars in the numbers and sizes actually observed in open star clusters such as the Pleiades.

As to the latter, it has been shown that though the first stage of contraction would be slow, hundreds if not thousands of millions of years being required, a cloud of say 10 parsecs diameter would have shrunk to about 0.1 parsec in attaining a temperature of about 3000° C and a density increase from say 10 atoms per ml to about 10 million (10^7) per ml; that at this temperature the hydrogen molecules having dissociated to atoms and its infrared opacity having been removed by vaporisation of its interstellar dust, further contraction could proceed within a number of sub-centres because further temperature rise could now be moderated by radiation from the interior of these sub-clouds as their gravitational fields intensify with their increasing gas densities; that while this first stage of cloud separation would take only a few thousand years, there is still a long way to go to reach the density of stars which for the Sun is around 10^{24} atoms per ml *i.e.* about fifty times the density of water; that nonetheless a second set of sub-centres would develop within each of the first set of sub-clouds and so on; and that for six successive sets of multiple sub-centre contractions, the total time required is only 25% longer than for the first.

Thus, a star is eventually formed when its internal pressure balances the weight of its outer layers and when the energy which it generates within balances the radiation from its surface, the two features most open to observation being the amount of light emitted in a given interval of time *i.e.* the brightness and the distribution of the light with respect to wavelength *i.e.* the colour. From the second feature the surface temperature can be estimated and from surface temperature and brightness the mass of the star can be calculated. Now, when the visible light emission (brightness) of stars compared to that of the sun is plotted against their surface temperature in thousands of degrees C on log-log axes we have the Hertzsprung-Russell Diagram on which the position of a star is found to depend only on its mass and its composition. Now when stars of different mass having the same composition, origin and age as the Sun (consisting of 0.25% metals, 1% carbon, nitrogen, oxygen, neon and other non-metals, 10% helium and the rest hydrogen) are plotted on the H-R diagram, they lie on a line known as the *Main Sequence* which runs from top-left to bottom-right, (the horizontal axis of surface temperature increasing from right to left) it is found, for example, that a Main Sequence star of 1/5 the mass of the Sun has 0.1% of solar brightness, that one twice the Sun's mass is 10 times brighter, that one 10 times the mass is 1000 times brighter, and that their respective surface temperatures are 3000, 10,000 and 20,000° C.

As to the internal source of stellar energy, it is now known that for stars not more than 10 times the brightness of the Sun (up to, say, twice its mass) the nuclear reactions known as the proton-chain are responsible. Thus, thanks to H. A. Bethe and C. L. Critchfield we have:

$$^{1}_{1}H + p = ^{2}_{1}H + ^{0}_{1}p$$
$$^{2}_{1}H + p = ^{3}_{2}He + \gamma$$

and thanks to C. Lauritsen we have: $\quad ^{3}_{2}He + ^{3}_{2}He = ^{4}_{2}He + 2p$

all of which were further investigated by E. Salpeter. Now, whether a positron (positive electron) is emitted as in the first reaction, or an electron as we have previously seen in others it is usually referred to as a β-process, while the emission in the second is a γ-ray *of* wavelength shorter than for X-rays and in the third it is two protons amounting to two mass units. For larger more luminous stars, however, the so-called carbon-nitrogen nuclear cycle (Hans Bethe again, and later W. A. Fowler) is of greater importance than the proton-chain. Thus, we have:

$$^{12}_{6}C + p = ^{13}_{7}N + \gamma$$
$$^{13}_{7}N = ^{13}_{6}C + ^{0}_{1}p$$
$$^{13}_{6}C + p = ^{14}_{7}N + \gamma$$
$$^{14}_{7}N + p = ^{15}_{8}O + \gamma$$
$$^{15}_{8}O = ^{15}_{7}N + ^{0}_{1}p$$
$$^{15}_{7}N + p = ^{12}_{6}C + ^{4}_{2}He$$

from which series of reactions, the overall result is fusion of hydrogen (protons) to helium as in the proton chain though this second fusion is catalysed by the carbon-nitrogen-oxygen-carbon nuclear reaction cycle. In addition, because positron emission is always accompanied by a neutrino, the above equations show that the released energy is in the form of neutrinos, γ-rays, positrons and the kinetic energy of the helium nuclides, all of which (less the neutrinos which escape) is absorbed by the star in maintaining its pressure and energy in balance with gravity and surface radiation.

Now, if the helium mixes as it forms, the surface temperature and luminosity do not increase much with time, the star moving only slowly from bottom right to top left with only slight deviation to the right of the Main Sequence in the H-R diagram. If, on the other hand the helium remains as a growing central core, then the evolution of the star in time is dramatic. If we take the Sun as an example we may expect it to deviate to the right of the Main Sequence line and subsequently move at approximately right angles to it towards the top right of the H-R diagram. The Sun has been slowly moving towards this deviation for the past 4 - 4.5 billion years and may take another 5 billion to get there, but once embarked on the right-angle movement its evolution will speed up as its brightness increases and its surface temperature drops with increase in size. A doubling in brightness will be enough to bring Earth temperatures to the boiling point of water and further increase will be enough to vaporise the Earth while the accompanying increase in the size of the Sun will engulf the existing orbits of Mercury, Venus and possibly the Earth. Thereafter, it is expected to shrink with a reduction in brightness and a rise in surface temperature as it moves to cross the Main Sequence line higher up and further to the left of its earlier deviation point, by which time it will have become a blue star of about its present size but very considerably brighter. Stars of greater mass than the Sun evolve more quickly and those of lesser mass more slowly so that at this point in time the former should be found at different points on the evolution curves of the H-R diagram. As to reality-validation, plots for the stars of the globular cluster M 3 by R.A.

Sandage and of M 92 by H. C. Arp and by Arp, Baum and Sandage are in compliance with the H-R evolution curves predicted for differing mass.

As to the mechanism of this stellar evolution, Gamov and Critchfield hypothesised that hydrogen fusion would be initiated at the star's centre where the temperature and density caused by the gravitational contraction of its formative gas cloud are highest; that this could continue in a thin skin surrounding a growing helium core; and that with no further energy production in the helium core itself, there being no hydrogen, the core might contract further converting gravitational to thermal energy as a contribution to energy generation in the skin surrounding the core which continues to maintain the energy balance by radiation transfer through the surrounding region, by convection outwards of this region, and finally by radiation from the photosphere to space. Such a stellar structure was first proposed by Gamov and Keller in 1945 for stars of medium mass at the point of deviancy from the Main Sequence line of the H-R diagram. Again, calculation shows that though the core contracts, the star as a whole remains constant for a time before expanding very considerably as indicated in the H-R diagram. In considering why the core does not continue to contract S. Chandrasekhar recognised that it no longer consists of molecules as in the early stages of star formation the ambient radiation intensity having now stripped all atoms of their electrons; that the bare *nuclei* now resisted further gravitational contraction by what he called degeneracy pressure; and that contraction would stop with both tendencies in balance provided the core mass did not exceed what is referred to as *Chandrasekhar's Limit* which he calculated to be 1.44 times the mass of our Sun (c.f. Section 9.3.4).

Thus, on cessation of contraction at a temperature of 15-20 million degrees C the core resumes its growth through accumulation of helium, the convection zone continues to deepen almost to the energy generating skin of the core and the star continues to maintain its energy and pressure balances through size increase until the core temperature reaches 100 million degrees C, when a new energy generating fusion process begins. This is the conversion of helium through carbon and oxygen to neon, thus:

$$^4_2He + 2\ ^4_2He = \ ^{12}_6C + \gamma$$
$$^{12}_6C + \ ^4_2He = \ ^{16}_8O + \gamma$$
$$^{16}_8O + \ ^4_2He = \ ^{20}_{10}Ne + \gamma$$

The onset of helium fusion in the core amounts to a nuclear explosion, but the overburden of stellar material is sufficient to limit its consequences to a rapid expansion of the core which is over in a few minutes, this containment of what would otherwise be a destructive explosion being referred to as the 'popping of the core'. It marks the transition from growth to contraction of the star as it moves downwards and to the left on the H-R diagram towards the empty region caused by Sandage having omitted to plot the oscillating stars of the cluster M 3 which amount to about 150, those of the cluster M 92 being 6 only. These are the so-called 'RR Lyrae stars' which for reasons unknown oscillate in size and brightness in two distinct ways, one with periods varying from a day at the right of the H-R gap to 8 hours at the left, the other with periods of close to 10 hours. In addition, it is found that the evolution curve after crossing the Main Sequence line from right to left, extends further to the left before gently curving downwards and to the right in step with helium exhaustion into the realm of the white dwarfs, so-called because of their shrunken size and white hot surfaces, these being typically about the size of the planet Jupiter though 1000 times more massive.

Given that the agreement obtained between the mass-dependent prediction of stellar evolution and its observation in clusters M 3 and M 92 is based on their common origin, composition and age, we might expect less agreement in considering the totality of stars in the

Milky Way which may vary not only in mass, but also in age and composition. Nonetheless, when this totality is classified as dwarfs (plain, white, red, and sub), giants (plain, blue, red, sub and super), and oscillators (regular and irregular) and all are plotted on the H-R diagram each class is found to group in specific regions. Thus, at formation stars lie on or near the Main-Sequence with those of large mass (the blue giants) lying high on the sequence and those of smaller mass, (the red dwarfs) at the lower end below the Sun which itself is a plain dwarf. As to its subsequent evolution, a star such as the Sun at the lower end deviates to the right of the Main Sequence into the region of the sub-giants and from there to the giants after which maximum growth, it contracts through the RR Lyrae region and after crossing the main sequence finally enters the region of the dying white dwarfs. Again, a star more massive than the sun, starting its evolution higher on the main-sequence evolves to the right higher on the H-R diagram through the region of the super-giants, while the smaller red dwarfs evolve lower on the diagram through the region of the red giants. Yet again, stars which start out above the dwarfs on the main-sequence *i.e.* those with a brightness from 10 times that of the Sun to perhaps 400 times, evolve through the region of the regular Cepheid variables which lies above that of the RR Lyrae region transited by lower mass stars, while the irregular variables appear to occur just after the onset of contraction from the giant phase of medium sized stars. As to the evolution of stars of greater mass still and with brightness greater than 400 times that of the Sun, there is little evidence for super-giants in the expected region far to the right of the Main Sequence and high on the H-R diagram, a circumstance now deferred for later discussion (c.f. below).

Now, while some stars in their contraction phase consume their hydrogen entirely as observed by Bidelman and Greenstein, it was suggested by Mestel that were the popping of helium-cores to occur in the near-surface regions of residual hydrogen there would be insufficient overburden to contain the explosion; and that some of the residual surface hydrogen could be explosively ejected with the star exhibiting a luminosity of up to 100,000 times that of the Sun for several weeks if the energy released were thermal rather than kinetic. Such phenomena, called novae, are indeed observed by brightness increase and explosive ejections of stellar material, the former ranging from about 30 times that of the Sun to the levels suggested by Mestel for about two weeks with ejection speeds of up to 2000 km per second. Furthermore, with the amounts ejected being about 1/1000 of that required to rid a star of its residual hydrogen and with the evolution period of such stars and their number within the Milky Way being known, there should be about 20 to 30 novae each year which for the Milky Way agrees with observation.

Having thus considered the evolution of the Sun together with stars of lesser mass and those of up to twice its mass in terms of their nuclear processes, I now turn to stars more significantly above Chandrasekhar's limit, the nuclear processes of which might build all the elements of the Periodic Table and the super novae explosions which might distribute these elements across space (c.f. Section 9.1.3).

With these more massive stars, helium fusion produces an inner core of oxygen and neon while hydrogen fusion continues outside the skin of the concentric layer of helium. This mechanism suggests that hydrogen (protons) and the innermost oxygen-neon core are separated by a layer of helium and do not mix. However, if even a small quantity of protons penetrated to the helium fusion skin, it has been suggested by W. A. Fowler, G. Burbridge and M. Burbridge that a supply of free neutrons could arise according to the following reactions:

$$^{20}_{10}Ne + p = {}^{21}_{11}Na + \gamma$$
$$^{21}_{11}Na = {}^{21}_{10}Ne + \beta$$
$$^{21}_{10}Ne + {}^{4}_{2}He = {}^{24}_{12}Mg + n$$

and that such could produce heavier elements than iron, if such were present in the originating gas cloud (c. f. later). In any case, the oxygen-neon core can itself increase towards Chandrasekhar's limit in these massive stars to undergo its own gravitational shrinkage with temperature increase from 300 million upwards to 600 million degrees over some millions of years to the point when the neon of the core is gradually replaced by magnesium. During this phase the core consists of oxygen and magnesium surrounded in outward sequence by concentric layers in which neon, helium, hydrogen are being respectively fused in what is now a four-zoned star. The next phase, when the star runs out of neon, is that the inner regions shrink again and oxygen fusion starts with the temperature rising to 1,500 million degrees. In this phase, with the reactions being too intricate to describe here, the star now builds aluminium, phosphorus, chlorine, argon, potassium and calcium in increasing atomic weight and in different amounts to produce a six-zoned star consisting of a core of magnesium, aluminium, silicon, phosphorus, sulphur, chlorine, argon, potassium and calcium with oxygen as the energy generator; surrounded in outward sequence by zones of oxygen, sodium and magnesium with neon as energy generator; oxygen and neon with carbon as generator; oxygen, carbon and neon with helium as generator; the outer layer of hydrogen; and with mixing between zones. Eventually when there is no more oxygen, core shrinkage again occurs with further increase in temperatures at which point the γ-ray intensity is sufficient to dissociate the nuclei themselves into their sub-atomic particles.

Calculation shows that in the range 2000 to 5000 million degrees the dissociated particles of the previously produced nuclides of the so-called 'silicon group' rearrange themselves into the 'iron group' comprising scandium, titanium, vanadium, chromium, manganese, iron, cobalt, nickel, copper and zinc in the abundances found in nature *e.g.* on the Earth. At this point the star has an iron group core surrounded by concentric zones in outwards order comprising: the silicon group; magnesium with oxygen as energy-source; neon with oxygen as energy-source; oxygen and neon with carbon as energy-source; helium; and hydrogen. In this phase, the neutrino loss associated with the change of neutrons into protons for increase in atomic numbers from hydrogen to zinc causes an energy loss which cannot be made good by the gravitational shrinkage of the inner regions of the star. When the internal temperature has risen to 3000 million degrees, a shrinkage which would have been appreciable in millions of years is achieved in one year, at 4000 million degrees it is achieved in one month and the rate of shrinkage continues to increase as temperature increases further to 5000 million degrees, at which point the nuclides revert to helium with an absorption of energy equal to that previously generated in the nuclide building process. In addition, the process of inner shrinkage over its previous evolution has increased the density to the extent that one ml would contain 10 to 100 tonnes of central star material. This massive imbalance in energy and pressure causes the collapse of the star in about one second and the in-fall of material from the outer regions releases gravitational energy with associated temperature increase to around 3000 million degrees, sufficient in about one second to release all the available energy from the nuclear reactions of the remaining oxygen and neon zones of the outer regions of the star. The result is an explosion reminiscent of a nova but on a vastly greater scale: a super nova.

For comparison a nova might release a mass of material equal to about one ten thousandth of the mass of the Sun whereas a super nova might release a mass equal to that of the Sun which would equate to the release of as much energy in one second as the nuclear reactions in the Sun would yield in 1000 million years. Again, both novae and super novae impart velocities of 2000 to 3000 km per second to ejected material irrespective of the masses involved, even though the super novae radiates 200 million times more intensely than the rate of the Sun for about two weeks and is 10,000 times brighter than a nova. Such an event occurred in 1054 which though unrecorded in

Dark Age Europe was documented by Chinese astronomers and interpreted 900 years later by Baade with reference to modern knowledge of stellar evolution and direct observation of the Crab Nebula which reveals the outward streaming of gases at 1000km per second and a central white dwarf which could well be the remnant of the star which exploded in 1054. In addition it is observed that Sirius and Procyon are doubled with a white dwarf of mass less than that of the Sun, suggesting previous doubling with a larger partner which underwent a super nova explosion in each case.

Thus, a star proceeds along its evolutionary loop of the H-R diagram only as long as the mass of hydrogen transmuted does not appreciably exceed Chandrasekhar's limit: otherwise it explodes. This explains the apparent dearth of super giants. Again, the extent of evolution along the loop is determined by the fraction of mass which comes to reside in the core of the star, it being calculated that this fraction is 10% at the point of deviance to the right of the main-sequence, that it is 40 % at the point of maximum expansion of the star, and that it approaches 100% as the star contracts back towards the Main Sequence in completing its evolutionary loop. The explosion point, however, is determined by the total mass in the core irrespective of the fraction that it represents. Thus, a star of mass 1.5 times that of the Sun will not explode until almost all of its mass resides in the core in the late stages of the evolutionary loop towards the main-sequence line, whereas a star of mass 15 times greater than the Sun will explode when only about 10% of its hydrogen has been transmuted to core material *i.e.* almost at the beginning of its evolutionary loop. Thus, we see that stars appreciably above the Sun on the main sequence do not evolve along the loop of expansion and contraction because their evolution is quickly terminated by explosive loss of mass which results in the stellar remnant immediately taking its position in the white dwarf region of the H-R diagram; and that the stars of clusters M 3 and M 92 plot over the whole of the evolutionary loop of the H-R diagram with an absence of large stars to the right of the main-sequence: all such having exploded.

In addition, the above implies two types of super nova. Type I comprises those which being just above Chandrasekhar's limit occur late in the evolutionary process and are consequently hydrogen poor, whereas Type II are those which being well in excess of the limit, occur early and are hydrogen-rich. It follows that Type I energy release should arise from nuclear reactions involving oxygen, neon and carbon, whereas that of Type II should be enhanced by the contribution from hydrogen reactions with the expectation that the speed of ejected material and the radiation-energy released would be greater for the Type II than for I, other things being equal. Thus, the relatively low ejection speeds of 1000km per second, observed for the Crab Nebula suggest that it is an example of a Type I super nova. On the other hand, the visual brightness of observed Type II super novae appears less than for Type I in contradiction of the above, unless the apparent deficit is made good by substantial radiation in the ultraviolet. Again, metal production was incompletely understood in the 1950s. Thus, while stellar production of helium and carbon to zinc appeared to be explained by the above together with a mechanism for their distribution in interstellar space, the production of lithium, beryllium and boron which lie between helium and carbon, and of gallium to uranium which are heavier than zinc could only be explained by extension of the neutron and proton additions applicable to the lighter elements. Again, though the metal contents of older stars are lower than for younger suggesting metal accretion from earlier super novae in the interstellar hydrogen clouds from which younger stars form, no older stars were without metal content. Thus, by mid-century, stellar evolution had not explained the existence of all ninety-two elements (c.f. Section 9.3.3).

9. 3. 2 Distance Measurement, Cosmic Rays and Radio-Sources
In the meantime, progress was being made in distance measurement (c.f. Section 8.2.1). Having refined

bearing angle measurement to 1/30 of a second of arc to determine distances out to 10 parsecs reliably and decreasingly reliably out to 100 parsecs, attention turned to determination of even greater distances by comparison of apparent brightness with intrinsic brightness provided the latter could be independently determined. In brief, the H-R diagram for the cluster M 3 allowed the intrinsic brightness of the RR Lyrae stars to be 100 times brighter than the Sun, with the additional advantage that such stars could be identified by their characteristic oscillations wherever located. On these bases, and having shown that the frequency of occurrence of RR Lyrae stars peaks at the centre of our galaxy, Walter Baade showed that the centre is about 8,000 parsecs from us (Baade's value was actually 8,140); that our galaxy and its associated halo of stars was about 60,000 parsecs across with satellite galaxies beyond 30,000 parsecs from its centre, and that the effective limit for this method lies at about 200,000 parsecs distance. Again, the Cepheid variables having been calibrated against the RR Lyrae stars in the Magellanic Cloud and shown to be intrinsically 1000 times brighter, *i.e.* 100,000 times brighter than the Sun, Baade showed that our neighbouring major galaxy, the Andromeda Nebula (M 31) is 450,000 parsecs away with a halo which extends some 50,000 parsecs from its centre and with two satellites both of which are more significant than any of ours; and that beyond M 31 some 1000 other galaxies are visible, one of which lies at a distance of 2,500,000 parsecs. Again, it is possible to compare intrinsic and apparent sizes. Thus, the emissions of material at 1000km per second for 900 years from the super nova of 1054 suggested an emission cloud of about 2 parsecs across by the mid 1950s, and comparison of this intrinsic size with its apparent size suggested a distance of about 1000 parsecs.

Progress was also being made in cosmic rays, magnetic fields and radio astronomy. The arrival of cosmic rays at the Earth's upper atmosphere was first deduced from sea-level detection of mesons otherwise known only as products of particle-collisions in the large accelerators at the Brookhaven and Berkley laboratories. After a number of false starts it became known that these rays consist of a range of highly energetic particles which includes free neutrons and protons (unbound in nuclei) which collide with the nuclei of molecules in the atmosphere in an extremely violent manner. One such reaction with nitrogen nuclei is that which produces the carbon isotope now used in carbon-14 dating, thus:

$$^{14}_{7}N + n = {}^{14}_{6}C + p$$

This radioactive carbon is subsequently absorbed with the carbon dioxide of photosynthesis and its rate of decay enables the date of death of the plant and often of its transformation into an artefact to be determined. Again, in 1948, photographic plates borne aloft by balloons established the presence of heavy nuclides in the cosmic rays which were presumed to be emitted from stars, though the energies appeared to be unexpectedly high. It was recalled, however, that in 1949 Fermi had hypothesised that heavy charged nuclides might pick up energy through interaction with interstellar gas clouds moving in magnetic fields as had the particles in the cyclotron accelerator of E.V. Lawrence. Thus, heavy nuclei would be accelerated more than the more numerous protons and neutrons in agreement with cosmic ray observation. In the meantime, the role of intervening dust-clouds in the polarisation of light from some stars was being investigated by Hall and Hiltner when Davis and Greenstein suggested that the necessary uniformity of dust-particle orientation could be provided by the said magnetic fields.

In turn, this led to a search for radiation at radio frequencies because such would penetrate the Earth's atmosphere the opacity of which to the higher γ - and X-ray frequencies had hitherto limited astronomy to optical frequencies only. Accordingly, radio-frequency emissions were found to emanate from cool hydrogen clouds; the Sun; hot hydrogen within the plane of our Galaxy; sources outside the plane yet still within our Galaxy; discrete sources of exceptional power within our Galaxy; discrete sources from outside our Galaxy; and a location in its centre. It was also found that cool hydrogen emitted at a wave-length of 21 cm, while the other sources emitted across the whole waveband. As to the former, Henyey and Keenan showed that we see hydrogen clouds by means of the light which they emit on recombination of hydrogen ions with electrons previously released from hydrogen atoms by the photo-electric effect of stars in their vicinity; and that we detect them by their radio-frequency emissions when this recombination does not occur. Later, the hot clouds first detected within our Galaxy as an agglomerate by Ryle and Scheuer, were resolved into separate clouds by Haddock, Meyer and Sloanaker by focussing on the 9.4 cm wavelength. Again, the collision of moving gas clouds would be a source of radio-emission as from the Crab Nebula where super nova ejection is colliding with the latter and where the radiation intensity is 100 times larger than expected from free electrons and protons. It is also to be expected that magnetic fields would accelerate electrons by the Fermi mechanism to emit radio waves while all strong radio sources are found to contain gaseous masses with rapid and random internal motions up to 300km per second. Colliding galaxies also involve gas cloud collisions and the constellation Cygnus in which two are colliding is a particularly strong radio-source. With ever-increasing numbers of large discrete radio-sources being found with even distribution in all directions, Gold suggested that they might be galaxies at great distances radiating as do ours and neighbouring Andromeda, rather than being more local stars within our own galaxy and neighbourhood, the balance of evidence having moved towards the former by the 1960s, though since then black holes have been added to our list of radio-sources.

9.3.3 Expansion, Continuous Creation and Big Bang

It was already known that motion of a light source towards or away from an observer causes its spectral lines to move respectively to the blue (short wavelength) or to the red (long wavelength) this phenomenon having been used to study the relative motion of Herschel's binary stars and the edges of the sun to determine its rotation rate *etc*. However, when this relationship was applied to the galaxies by Hubble in 1929 he found that all apart from our local group of galaxies are receding from us at speeds linearly related to their distances from us. Thus, for example, those at a distance of the order of 400 million parsecs are receding at a speed of 40,000mph as a consequence of which the average density of matter continues to diminish with time from what must have been an infinitely dense state when all of creation issued from a singularity. To determine when that singular incident occurred as accurately as possible, one selects a galaxy cluster sufficiently far away to ensure that any random internal movements contribute only negligibly to the red-shift measurement which determines its recession speed and one divides its distance by that speed, the quotient being the so-called Hubble Constant. At such distances, however, the previously described star-based methods of distance estimation cannot be used. To determine the Hubble constant more accurately than Hubble did, it has been necessary to compare the intrinsic brightness of the largest and nearest galaxies such as M 31 and M 81 with that of our own using standard distance measurements; to assume that only such large galaxies will be visible at the furthest distances; and to determine those distances by comparing apparent brightness at those distances with the intrinsic brightness of such as M 31 as measured. Thus, the Hubble constant has been evaluated at 7000 million years, agreeing with the result obtained by comparing the apparent size of these distant galaxies with the intrinsic size of such as M 31 and implying that the *Big Bang* occurred 7000 million years ago.

The counter-intuitiveness of concluding that everything came into being, say 10 billion years ago prompted a search for possible alternatives. Thus, it was suggested by Fred Hoyle that the decrease in density associated with a postulated Big Bang might be incompatible with the density increases needed for star and galaxy formation, and that the combination of overall expansion with local contraction implied gravitational attraction at densities above a certain limit and gravitational repulsion below this limit if the relatively condensed galaxies were subsequently to be driven apart.

Hoyle also suggested that the need to consider an infinitely dense singularity might be avoided altogether if the matter present in the universe before the latter expansion began had been less than the amount now present. Thus, as an alternative to the Big Bang and to gravitational repulsion, Hoyle proposed his *Steady State Hypothesis* in which the continuous creation of hydrogen at the rate of one atom per second per 4.096 million cubic km of space would maintain a steady density of matter in a universe expanding in compliance with Hubble's constant.

Of course, hypotheses are only useful if they can be reality-evaluated. In this case, the derived rate of hydrogen creation is too low to be directly measured as is the density at gravity reversal which has to be lower than that for star and galaxy condensation which was considered to have begun at 10^{-27} times the density of water, while as to the Big Bang alternative, there appeared to be no evidence for its having happened. Again, George Gamov sought to explain the billion year expansion prior to local contractions to stars and galaxies as being the time it took for the Big Bang radiation energy to be embodied as matter (wave/particle duality) and thus to exhibit gravity, while he, Alpher and Herman alternately suggested that all the nuclides of all the elements could have been built up in a succession of neutron captures in the first few minutes of the Big bang, and that their widespread existence is evidence that it did indeed take place. This latter argument is circular however. If the Big Bang is the source of everything, then anything is evidence that it took place. In any case, Hoyle countered that the ratios of the heavy elements to hydrogen are lower in older than in younger stars, that this was evidence for successive star generations each contributing heavy metals to interstellar space, that this succession was incompatible with a one-and-only Big Bang source, and that it was compatible with his Steady State hypothesis. On the other hand, were there no Big Bang origin the universe would be infinite in time, making it impossible to limit the number of previous cycles of element generation from hydrogen even in theory, and thus making it difficult to explain why heavy-element : hydrogen ratios are as low as they are.

In contrast, hypotheses concerning stellar evolution can be reality-evaluated by observing stars at different stages in this evolution with respect to the H-R diagram, and in 1987 further reality-evaluation of such evolution was provided by observation of a super nova explosion of a previously known blue giant of about 20 solar masses as it was actually happening over the weeks of its peak luminosity and the years of its subsequent cooling. However, the creation of all nuclides up to uranium in stellar interiors and the nuclear reactions associated with the Big Bang became more clearly understood as knowledge of the binding forces within the atomic nucleus increased from mid-century onwards. Thus, it is now known from collision experiments with hydrogen and helium nuclei at energy levels simulating those of the Big Bang that about 23% of the hydrogen present would have been converted to helium during expansion and cooling from an initial billion degrees to about 3 million in the first few minutes, and that apart from traces of deuterium and lithium no higher nuclides would have been produced because the cooling rate was too rapid for their formation. As to reality-evaluation, this level of helium production is supported by observing that the helium content of even the oldest stars is never less than 23-24% while that of young stars such as the Sun is 27%, anything over 23% reflecting a finite succession of stellar contractions of inter-stellar gas and internal processing, as does the higher levels of other constituents in younger than in older stars. Indeed, there was even support for the Big Bang itself when in 1965 microwave radiation was found to be coming from all directions in space, and when in the 1990s its spectrum was confirmed as indicative of a black-body source to an accuracy of one part in 10,000 by NASA's Cosmic Background Explorer Satellite (COBE), this was interpreted as evidence that the universe had a temperature of 3000 degrees after helium creation and prior to star and galaxy formation in the course of cooling to its current 2.728 degrees K and average density of 0.2 atoms per cubic metre.

294

Further refinements having suggested that helium formation began at about one second after the Big Bang, attention turned to even earlier events for which experimental support becomes increasingly unobtainable. Thus, while the density at about 10^{-3} seconds would be that of a neutron star, little is known of the physics of such entities. Again, even the Large Hadron Collider at Geneva will not provide energies relevant to all of the particles present within the first 10^{-14} seconds of the Big Bang. Nonetheless, many crucial features of our observable universe would have been manifest at say 10^{-35} seconds or earlier. Nonetheless, we should note that hypotheses relevant to these timescales might be reality-evaluated by observations in the current universe and even be guides to the development of physics instead of being totally dependent on existing physics as has been the case till now. However, as to there being a limit to this subdivision of time, we know that energy is proportional to frequency, from Plank's equation $E = h\gamma$; that frequency is the inverse of wavelength; that ever shorter wavelengths are required to probe ever-finer detail, X-rays being able to locate atoms in crystals while light-rays cannot; and that there is nonetheless a limit to the energy which can be packaged in quanta as wavelength decreases to the so-called Planck length which is 10^{19} times smaller than a proton, a distance traversed by light in the Planck time of 10^{-43} seconds. Thus, it is impossible to measure shorter distances and time intervals than these limiting quanta, which means that we cannot tell which of two events happened first when separated by less than the Planck time. Accordingly, post Big Bang time runs from 10^{-44} seconds though a period of energy-particle interactions (wave/particle duality) to helium production between 1 and 200 seconds, to a gaseous 'fireball' lasting for about 300,000 years, to a dark era which preceded the star and galaxy formation period from about 1 billion years ago till now.

Now, if stars are needed to produce all the nuclides of the Periodic Table we still have to explain star formation from the dark uniformity of hydrogen and helium at a density of less than one atom per cubic metre and at well below their formation temperatures. However, any density differences which did arise in the uniformity of the primordial expansion would be magnified and would lag behind those of average density by differential deceleration due to gravity, until their over-density caused their own expansion to cease as they condensed and grew at the expense of the surrounding gas into stars, galaxies and clusters of galaxies, all bound together by gravity at a tightness expressed as the ratio of the energy required to break them up to their total energy (mc^2). It is found that this ratio, Q, has a value of the order of 10^{-5} for stars, galaxies and clusters which means that gravity is weak enough for Newton's Theory to be applicable to their movements as we know it is. Again, having recognised that a record of the density variations of the embryonic universe might be carried by the background microwave radiation already detected, it was extremely gratifying to find that instrumentation on the COBE satellite detected directional variations in intensity of the magnitude required. Yet again, the input to mathematical computer models of hypothetical initial conditions including density irregularities corresponding to specified values of Q have simulated the generation of galaxies from dark gas through successive stages of pre-galactic gas condensations, temperature increase sufficient for gas condensations equivalent to a million solar masses to emit light, and fragmentation of such masses into proto-stars prior to producing groups of stars, a single super star or a quasar with gas continuing to fall into them. Thus, we see that the earlier difficulty of harmonising local condensations with overall expansion has been resolved, at least to the above extent.

In addition, we see that whether this expansion continues for ever or eventually slows, stops and reverses to a Big Crunch depends on the balance or imbalance of gravitation and expansion energy; and that knowing the speed of the expansion now, this question turns on knowing the total gravitating mass now in motion. As to balance (neither expansion nor contraction), the critical average density of the universe is calculated to be 5 atoms per cubic metre while the observed average density is 0.2 atoms per cubic metre. Now, with Ω defined as the ratio of the actual density to the critical density we would expect an ultimate Big Crunch for values of $\Omega > 1$, whereas Ω has a value of 1/25 (0.04) when density is calculated from the matter observed from its visible, infrared and micro-wave radiations. Thus, with $\Omega < 1$, the universe should be expanding as observed. On the other hand, we know that the unobservable (dark) matter must be ten times more than the observable matter, because the speeds at which stars and gas-clouds are observed to orbit within our galaxy and others, would not otherwise be possible; that these speeds, being still well below that of light, we can rule out relativistic changes in effective mass; and that we must therefore seek to identify this unobserved dark matter by some means or other, possible candidates being interstellar dust, brown dwarfs, neutrinos, other exotic sub-atomic particles and black holes.

As to such candidates, we know that there is some non-radiating dust in our galaxy because it scatters and attenuates starlight, but if it were to account significantly for the missing dark matter we would see nothing of the stars at all. We also know that individual brown dwarfs too small to be luminous by fusion, can reveal themselves in passing across the face of a star by focussing its light to appear magnified, but we have no way of knowing how many there might be. However, photons and neutrinos are expected to have reached equilibrium in the second after the Big Bang and we know that there are 3/11 as many neutrinos as there are photons at equilibrium; and that there are now 412 million photons per cubic metre in the residual Big Bang radiation. In addition, since the 1980s, the neutrino is no longer thought of as a zero-mass entity thanks to the Kamiokande experiment in Japan. Thus, whatever its mass turns out to be, there are hundreds of millions of neutrinos for every atom in the universe. Furthermore, there is a long list of hypothetical particles which might exist and might have survived from the Big Bang in sufficient numbers to make significant contributions to the missing dark matter. Thus, the search for such non-charged particles as the neutrino and even heavier entities which can pass through the entire Earth is being conducted deep underground by several groups of physicists. Further confirmation of this dark matter having ten times more mass than we can directly observe, has recently been provided by the Hubble telescope in observing the light from remote galaxies to be focussed by relativistic-bending by the required amount on passage through less remote star clusters on its way to Earth.

However, the inferred amount of dark matter in galaxies and clusters is still only ten times that which provides the average apparent density of 0.2 atoms per cubic metre *i.e.* even if included, Ω would still be less than unity. Thus, additional dark matter beyond that which influences internal motions of clusters and the light bending due to clusters, would only betray its presence by affecting overall cosmic expansion. To make progress on this line of enquiry we need to determine whether the expansion is slowing down or is constant. Thus, super novae out to the limits of visibility were chosen as standard light sources and the luminosities and red-shifts of about a dozen of the most suitable were measured on ten-metre ground-based telescopes or by the Hubble space telescope by several teams led or encouraged by Saul Perlmutter of the Lawrence Berkley Laboratory, all of whom reported in 1998 that the expansion was accelerating rather than decelerating or constant. Now, when Einstein developed his Theory of General Relativity in 1917 there was nothing to suggest expansion or contraction and with his equations implying one or the other, he introduced his "cosmological constant" λ whereby a cosmic repulsion exactly balanced gravitational attraction and maintained a static universe, prior to Hubble discovering its expansion. However, if expansion is accelerating and thus overwhelming gravity, λ cannot be zero. Indeed, in the late 1990s, the degree of non-uniformity in residual Big Bang radiation enabled calculations based on observed gravitational focussing to suggest that were Ω 0.3, then λ would be 0.7.

9. 3. 4 Atomic Structure, Black Holes and Grand Unified Theory

In the meantime, though radioactivity, nuclear transformations, chemical bonding, and stellar evolution had been explained in terms of the atom as described in Sections 9.1.3 - 9.1.7, the nature of the force which stabilised the nucleus by overcoming the mutually repulsive force of its positively charged protons was not known. Thus, Yukawa suggested that protons and neutrons might be held together by a strong force field, the vibration frequency of which could be associated with a detectable particle (wave/ particle duality) and from what was already known about nuclear forces he predicted the existence of new particles having masses two or three hundred times that of the electron. The first such particle, the μ-meson (or muon) was found in cosmic rays, though it was the later (1947-48) π-meson which had the required mass. Again, Glashov and Weinberg, and t'Hooft, and Abdus Salam, showed that the weak force involved with radioactivity and neutrinos would have come into being with the cooling of the universe and later, Salam and Weinberg identified their predicted particles for this force field in the CERN accelerator at a simulated temperature of 10^{15} degrees, corresponding to that of the universe at about 10^{-12} seconds.

However, by the 1950s and 60s so many particles were being discovered that property-related groupings were discerned in a manner reminiscent of the Periodic Table. Thus, those associated with the strong force are baryons, those with the weak force are mesons, while those which interact only very weakly with nuclei are the electron, the muons (one of which is 206 times heavier than the electron) and the 'zero mass' neutrinos (one of which is associated with the electron). Again, in 1964 Gell-Mann and Zweig introduced *The Quark Model* in which quarks have charges 1/3 or 2/3 that of the proton and for which Freedman, Kendall and Taylor produced support by showing, in the newly commissioned Stanford Linear Accelerator, that electrons were scattered by protons as though each proton consisted of separate charges of 2/3, 2/3 and -1/3 of the total charge. Yet Again, by the 1970s, the so-called *Standard Model* had emerged in which the electromagnetic force and the weak nuclear force had been unified, the strong nuclear force had been interpreted in terms of quarks held together by yet another particle called the gluon, and nine different types of quark had brought order to the otherwise bewildering number of sub-atomic particles. Nonetheless, the gluon does not fully explain the nuclear forces, 0.7% of the mass of the two protons and two neutrons which combine to the helium atom being converted to energy as expressed by $\varepsilon = 0.007$, further transmutations of helium up to iron releasing a further 0.001. For a fuller explanation, the next step is to unify the electromagnetic and weak forces with the strong force into the so-called *Grand Unified Theory* (GUT) though even this will not include gravity which came into being with the cooling of the universe to 10^{28} degrees at an age of 10^{-35} seconds, conditions which could not be simulated by an accelerator without it being much larger than our solar system.

In the meantime, further consideration was given to Chandrsekhar's Limit in respect of masses too large to stabilise by degenerative pressure when contracting under gravity in stars, and which would thus continue to contract without limit. Though such Black Hole singularities were theoretical concepts initially, they have now been shown to explain a number of otherwise inexplicable observations. Thus, though invisible, their presence is inferred from their gravitational effect on masses and light rays which happen to pass close to them, or when paired with an ordinary star in a binary system, on the basis of which there are estimated to be many millions in our galaxy, each of about ten solar masses. Again, the relatively rare "γ-ray bursts" which for a few seconds outshine a million galaxies are attributed to black holes at the point of creation. Yet again, the black hole at the centre of our galaxy (detected by the otherwise abnormal speeds of stars under its influence) is equivalent to 2.5 million solar masses and is 6 million km in radius, while some other central galactic holes are of several billion solar masses and up to diameters as big as that of our solar system. Now, though Einstein's General Theory predates consideration of black holes, it can describe their distortion of space and time and the shape of their boundary surface (membrane) between our space-time and quantum realms across which no signals reach us and nothing which enters escapes.

Again, because Einstein's space-time is a smooth continuum without limitation of scale, there is nothing in the theory to stop black holes being as small as an atom or as large as our observable universe. By definition, however, black holes are objects in which gravity has overwhelmed all other forces, be they electromagnetic or nuclear. Thus, were a black hole to be the size of an atom, 10^{36} atoms would have been squeezed to the dimension of one. For black holes to exist down to the Planck Length, however, the force of gravity would need to be much larger in the (micro) quantum world than we observe it to be in the (macro) world of everyday objects, planets, stars and galaxies. At present neither General Relativity nor Quantum Theory satisfies this need, which is why the search is on for the *Grand Unifying Theory*, the so-called *Theory of Everything,* and why consideration of black holes and the Big Bang (the reverse of a universal black hole) must be the route to it. The most promising consideration thus far assumes that at the creative instant t = 0 all the forces were as one; that they spit into the four which we now identify as strong and weak nuclear, electromagnetic and gravitational by the time the universe had cooled to about 10^{15} degrees at an age of about 10^{-12} seconds; and that the subatomic particles previously considered to be fundamental are themselves different harmonics of different modes of vibration of so-called string loops which vibrate on the scale of the Plank length, not in four dimensional but in ten dimensional space. Again, though all physical theories are expressed in known mathematics, even Einstein's four dimensional space being expressible in the non-Euclidian geometry of Minkowski, *String Theory* poses questions which cannot be answered on the basis of current mathematics.

Nonetheless, since 1995, it has been shown that the extra dimensions of *String Theory* "wrap up" into five distinct classes of six-dimensional space at a still deeper mathematical level; that these may be separate but related structures of eleven dimensional space; that the concept of one dimensional strings may be broadened to two dimensional membranes and, indeed, to higher dimensional surfaces referred to as three-branes and so on; and that gravity turns out to be integral to what is now called *Super String Theory*, the dimensions having been increased from ten to eleven. Again, given that all material becomes standardised on entering a black hole, Bekenstein noted in the early 1970s that this is equivalent to a loss of information and order, which is equivalent to an increase in randomness otherwise known as entropy in thermodynamics; and that black holes should, therefore, have a temperature. This train of thought was supported when Hawking calculated that black holes did actually emit radiation, though at levels too weak to be detected by astronomers. Nonetheless, this could be helpful should mini black holes arise from particle interactions in the Large Hadron Collider, recently commissioned at Geneva.

9. 4 EARTH SCIENCES

As with astronomy and cosmology, developments in physics and chemistry enabled progress to be made in the earth sciences which would not otherwise have been possible. Accordingly, I now resume my review of the earth sciences from the mid 1800s (c.f. Sections 8.2.2 - 8.2.4).

9. 4. 1 Age of the Earth

By the 1860s, William Thomson (Lord Kelvin) was attempting to estimate the post-accretion cooling period of the Earth (c.f. Section 9.4.5). To this end, he assumed that the accretion temperature was that of molten volcanic lava (~ 1100° C); that it had cooled by conduction to its current atmospheric temperature; and that the relevant thermal conductivity was consistent with the temperature-depth gradients observed in mines. On these assumptions he obtained in 1862 a cooling time of between 20 million and 400 million years, and had narrowed this range to between 20 to 40 million by 1897. Again, in 1899, John Joly assumed that rivers were the sole contributors to sea-water salinity, and compared the salt content of rivers with that of the sea to produce an age estimate of 99 million years. By then, however, Rutherford had recognised that radioactivity was a continuing source of heat additional to the initial gravitational heating on planet accretion, and that any estimates based on cooling rates of initially molten rock which omitted radioactive heating would be erroneously brief, a conclusion to the general satisfaction of those who believed very substantial timescales to be necessary to account for observed geological changes.

However, Rutherford showed in 1905 that radioactivity would provide absolute time measures for what had previously been a sequence of geological periods having only relative (sequential) timescales. Thus, he showed that α-particles, being actually helium ions made it possible to age the formation of uranium-containing minerals from their helium contents and went on to show that a mineral sample, found in Connecticut USA, was at least (perhaps some helium had escaped) 500 million years old. Subsequently R. J. Strutt used the same approach to show that a thorium mineral was at least 2,500 million years old. Later, lead being the final product of radioactive uranium decay and much less likely to escape than helium gas, the ages of minerals were determined from their uranium: lead ratios, on the assumption that when a uranium rich mineral such as zircon first crystallizes from cooling molten granite it contains no lead. Thus, from 1911 to 1927, the geologist Arthur Holmes showed that what geologists termed the Phanerozoic (shell) Period was at least 400 million years old; that earlier periods such as the Precambrian are billions of years old; and that the Earth's crust was about 3.6 billion years old. Again in 1971, Stephen Moorbath dated Greenland rock samples at 3.75 billion years old, the earliest yet identified.

9. 4. 2 Ocean Depth, Crust Thickness, Magnetic Anomalies and Plate Tectonics,

Meanwhile, in *Die Entstehung der Kontinente und Ozeane* of 1915, Alfred Wegener presented his evidence for all of the continents having been conjoined in one land mass which he called Pangea before drifting to their present locations separated by the present oceans. His evidence was that the continental outlines could obviously be fitted together; that when this was done the rock formations coincided like the lines of print on previously torn newspaper; that their fossilised flora and fauna had similarities which could not otherwise be explained if the continents had always been in their present positions; and that they must still be moving. In spite of this rather convincing evidence there were problems in understanding what the continents were moving on, the movement of ice-flows on water to which Wegener referred, being an insufficient analogy (c.f. Darwin's use of insufficient analogy) while what had been learned of the inter-continental ocean basins from the *Challenger* voyage of the 1870s appeared to contribute nothing directly in support of Wegener. Thus, it was known from lead-line sounding that the continents were surrounded by shelves out to water-depths of about 200 metres though this technique was seriously inconvenient for the ocean depths beyond. Thus, the continental shelf edges were presumed to slope gently to these greater depths as were those rising to the mid-ocean ridges which were about 1000 km wide and about

2500 m high at most, the horizontal and vertical dimensions of the basins being thus disproportionate and the continents having no definite edge. As to the general nature of the seabed itself, geologists could only assume that the rocks resembled those of the continents and that they were covered by a layer of continental sedimentary detritus, possibly up to a depth of 5 km.

This lack of knowledge was first addressed in the 1950s by the precision graphic recorder (PGR) which provided a continuous record of water depth by measuring the time taken for an acoustic echo to return to the survey vessel after the fashion of submarine detection in the Second World War. When PGR surveys were first made in the Pacific Ocean the seabed was found to be hilly, not smoothed out by a thick layer of continental detritus and therefore not as old as expected. The second technique produced seismic waves by explosive means, these being capable of penetrating beneath the seabed before returning to a series of widely spaced microphones towed behind the survey ship. This seismic technique had already been applied to the continents and had revealed a surface zone in which the vibrations moved slower than in the zone beneath, the first being referred to as the crust of the Earth and the second the mantle. However, in contrast to the continental crust thickness of 35 kilometres, the result first obtained in the Pacific was that seafloor crust was only about 7 kilometres thick. In addition the vibrations were found to move slowest of all in the top kilometre of the seabed which was taken to be the depth of the sediment cover. Another surprise was the PGR discovery by William "Bill" Menard of a step-feature about 2000 m high and extending over 1000km in an east-west direction on the Pacific seabed and of several more by 1953 which he now called fracture zones one of which extended some 5000km in the eastern Pacific. In the meantime, Bruce C. Heezen and Marie Tharp were assembling the PGR data to produce in 1956 the first detailed topographical map of the world's seafloor. This showed that the oceans are generally about 4 km deep; that each has a mid-ocean ridge the summit of which averages about 2500m below sea level with numerous elongated hills parallel to the main ridge; and that only in the abyssal plains below the shelf escarpment is the seafloor smoothed by a thick cover of sediment delivered by river runoff from the continents. By 1958, it was clear that the mid-ocean ridges form a connecting system right round the globe; that for the most part it has a longitudinal central valley reminiscent of the East African Rift Valley; and that the whole system is broken by Bill Menard's fracture zones.

In 1955, it was agreed that a high resolution coastal depth survey planned out to 600km by the US Coast and Geodetic Survey could be accompanied by a proton magnetometer search for anomalies in the earth's magnetic field. The result was that Arthur Raff recorded a sequence of highs and lows of about 10% of field strength which correlated with the same sequence on parallel ship's tracks and by 1958 he had produced a map of these regular magnetic anomalies showing their widths to vary from a few km to a few tens of km, quite unlike the random anomalies on land associated with the presence or absence of localised magnetic rocks. Raff also noted that his stripes were parallel to the mid-ocean ridge, while it was also found that identical stripe sequences could be observed on both sides of Bill Menard's fracture zones, in some cases displaced side-ways by as much 1000km. Now, it was recalled that iron-rich minerals such as haematite and magnetite lose their magnetism when heated above their 'Curie temperature', and are re-magnetised (acquire remanent magnetism) on cooling in a magnetic field; and that in studying certain (cooled) volcanic rocks Motonari Matuyama had discovered in 1920 that his older samples exhibited reverse polarity to that of the Earth's present magnetic field, suggesting a polarity reversal a few million years ago. Again, it was known that naturally occurring radioactive potassium decays to argon; that all such argon would be released from molten lava; that any argon found in lava-source minerals would have accumulated since cooling; and that the time-lapse could be determined from the accumulated quantity of argon and its rate of production from the half-life of potassium decay. This dating
300

technique, developed in the 1960s at the University of California (Berkley) and applied to appropriate lava samples, showed the Earth's magnetic field to reverse every million years or so.

Thus, by the mid-1960s, it was known that ocean basin floors were spreading from the volcanic activity of their mid-ocean ridges towards their continental margins with their record of reversals in magnetic polarity showing that no part of the ocean floors were more than 200 million years old, whereas the continents were on average around 2 billion years old. Again, it was clear that on reaching the continental margins the ocean floor was subducted beneath them towards the Earth's interior, such zones being characterised by an offshore sub-sea trench, a parallel arc of onshore volcanoes, intermittent major earthquakes and continuous small earth tremors, the latter named after Hugo Benioff who discovered them in the early 1950s. On these bases, the *Theory of Global Plate Tectonics* was advanced in 1967, according to which the Earth's crust and underlying lithosphere of about 100 km in total thickness consists of a number of rigid plates some of which are topped by ocean crust only, while others have a topping of adjacent continental and ocean crust, all of which are moving relative to each other, sometimes apart at mid-ocean ridges or rift zones, past each other along transform faults or together. Indeed, on the basis of the time sequence of polarity changes and anomaly separation distances, the rate of ocean floor spreading has been quantified at about 4 cm per annum, a rate supported by the ages of organisms found in sediment-cores at increasing distance from mid-ocean ridges, while the relative rate of tectonic plate movement as measured by satellite global positioning can be 20cm per annum though averaging < 10 cm.

As to the onshore volcano arc, Leonore Hoke has shown that while the material emitted in eruptions is characteristic of the earth's mantle (the layer beneath the lithosphere) it also lends support to subduction by having characteristics of marine sediments. Thus, while the ratio of the ^{4}He : ^{3}He isotopes at the Earth's surface reflects the constant release ^{4}He (α-particles) from the radioactive decay of the uranium and thorium content of the crust, that from Andean fumaroles is 500 times richer in ^{3}He suggesting mantle-source subduction material for which the concentrations of uranium and thorium is much lower while the water and nitrogen concentrations are more representative of a wet marine sediment source rich in nitrogen from marine organism decomposition. In addition, the argon concentration in these emissions is much less than in air, tending to confirm that the nitrogen content is non-atmospheric. Again, the water content causes the emissions which solidify to create new crust with a different composition and density from mantle material. Thus, as molten rock rises and cools, the water keeps it molten longer than would otherwise be the case and enriches it in silica SiO_2 from which the silica enriched components of the crust such as quartz, mica and feldspar are eventually formed. Thus, crust rocks average about 60% silica, being roughly three parts basalt (50% silica) to one part granite (75% silica) while the association of metal ores with volcanic areas is also due to such fractionation by water.

Earthquake (seismic) waves are now interpreted in terms of intermittent tension release when subduction layers or tectonic plates are in relative movement. However, these waves had previously been classified as primary (P) when in the direction of motion and secondary (S) when perpendicular to it, both being analysed with respect to speed/density relationships as a means of investigating the interior of the Earth through which they travel from source to detector. Thus, the speed of a P wave in the crust is typically about 6 kilometres per second while below the Mohorovicic discontinuity discovered in 1909, speed increases in the mantle from about 8 km/s at the top to nearly 14 at the bottom at depths of about 700 kilometres. Inside the mantle, a core was discovered in 1897 because it deflected the P waves and more recently it has been shown that S waves do not travel through the core either, thus confirming it to be liquid, while more detailed analysis of reflected P waves has revealed an inner molten core at about 5000 kilometres depth.

Now, with the oceanic crust being about 7 kilometres deep and those of the continents averaging about 35 kilometres, mantle material brought by volcanoes from depths of several hundred kilometres consists of the minerals olivine, garnet and pyroxene which melted together as volcanic lava produce basalt which contrasts with the silica rich minerals of the crust. In parallel, meteorites are either the more common chondritic which consist largely of iron, oxygen, magnesium and silicon or the metallic which is an alloy of iron and nickel. Now, were the Earth to be an accretion of such meteorites it would have the density it is observed to have from its total mass and volume. Again, the composition of chondritic meteorites less their iron is similar to that of olivine and pyroxene while this iron together with the iron and nickel of the metallic meteorites would account for the Earth having an iron-nickel core. In support, laboratory experiments under pressures corresponding to a depth of 700 kilometres have shown that olivine and pyroxene transform to the more closely packed structure of perovskite which consequently may well be the most abundant mineral in the earth, while under pressures corresponding to the iron-nickel core they have shown that it should melt at about $5000°$ C, such pressures being produced momentarily in the laboratory between two diamond points driven together by hydraulic rams.

Now, this core temperature being inconsistent with extrapolated temperature gradients in mines and the conduction assumed by Lord Kelvin, suggested convection in the mantle. However, convection depends not only on temperature difference, on the distance between top and bottom of the layer and on thermal expansion producing adequate density differential between top and bottom; but also on thermal conductivity which can be an alternative means of heat transfer, and on viscosity which limits the cycling between bottom and top which is the heat transfer mechanism of convection. Thus, Lord Rayleigh having combined these factors in his Rayleigh Number, and having shown that convection ensues when it has a value greater than 1000, it became a matter of applying this approach to mantle materials in the laboratory to decide whether mantle convection could be the mechanism of tectonic plate movement. Now, as to estimation of mantle viscosity for this purpose, it was noted that post-glacial rebound over the last 18,000 years in previously ice-covered regions has amounted to a rise in land surface of about 120 metres with an estimated 200 metres still to come; that this could be explained on a mantle viscosity of 10^{22} poises (water has a viscosity of 10^{-2} poise or 1 centipoise); and that such a mantle viscosity would ensure vigorous mantle convection while ensuring sufficient stiffness to transmit seismic waves. Thus, convective up-welling beneath mid-ocean ridges and down-welling in subduction zones may provide the motive-power for plate tectonics, the plates existing because they are colder and stronger than the underlying mantle though otherwise part of the convection system.

A further example of flow under gravity is provided by the movement of India as discussed by McKenzie and England. Thus, India having closed up the intervening Tethys Ocean in making first contact with the southern margin of Asia some 55 million years ago has advanced a further 2000 kilometres since then, while raising the Himalayas as it slips beneath them. Similarly, the Himalayas having reached their natural height in this process began to flow to the north, to widen the range to the north, and to create the Tibetan Plateau with the whole creating further ranges to the north again. One consequence of this general elevation of the earth's crust was that atmospheric convection above the Tibetan Plateau drew moist air northwards as the Monsoon which on rising to cross the Himalayas caused increased rainfall and subsequent river-borne rock debris to move back to the sea *via* the Indus and Ganges while rendering East Africa drier, transforming rainforest to savannah and causing tree-living apes to become the savannah-living precursors of *Homo Sapiens* (c.f. Section 2.2).

9. 4. 3 Climatic and Biological Consequences of Plate Tectonics

The ice sheets of our current Ice Age began to form in Antarctica and in the Arctic about 34 million and 2.5 million years ago respectively to reach a maxima and to decline thereafter through a series of peaks and troughs in a period of generally increasing global temperature, the last seriously cold period of which occurred about 18000 years ago. However, we only became aware of this Ice Age when Jean Louis Agassiz began to interpret the debris found on mountainsides below existing glaciers as material deposited from their undersides as they melted and withdrew, such material becoming known as glacial drift. The remains of earlier drift deposits in the geological record have since revealed that previous Ice Ages peaked at around 290 million, 450 million, and 600 million years ago; that Ice Ages are relatively short term events being significant for only a few tens of millions of years; and that global temperatures have generally been warmer than those of today as we approach the close of our current Ice Age. However, once again recourse to isotopes provides more detailed information.

Though isotopes of the same element are chemically identical their differing densities cause differing diffusion rates of $^{235}UF_6$ and $^{238}UF_6$ (c.f. Section 9.5.1) and differing reaction rates. Thus, the two most common isotopes of oxygen ^{16}O and ^{18}O reacted at different rates indicative of the ambient temperature at which they were incorporated as carbonate (CO_3) in the shells of marine organisms. Thus, mass spectrographic analysis of separated samples of plankton (top 50 metres of the ocean) from benthos organisms (deeper waters) taken from time-sequenced slices of sediment cores enables top and deeper temperatures to be determined for any geological period. Thus, the record of marine temperature shows that ocean surface temperatures are essentially constant while the deeper temperatures have declined from the highest recorded point of $20°$ C in the Cretaceous Period (140 - 65 million years ago) to today's average of nearly zero, reflecting the transition to our current Ice Age. Again, this record shows a marked cooling of deep water about 35 million years ago, coincident with the appearance of glacial drift in sediment cores from around Antarctica, a further drop at 15 million years ago when the Antarctic ice sheet attained roughly its current size (c.f. below), and another with the appearance of drift in the Arctic about 2.5 million years ago.

Again, the differential rates for temperature-dependent evaporation of water ensure that the lighter of the two isotopes of oxygen present in land ice (re-precipitated water) preserves a record of past temperature in time-sequenced ice-cores submitted to mass spectrographic analysis. However, temporary temperature rise during an ice age, causes the oceanic proportion of the lighter isotope to increase by melt-water return to the ocean which affects subsequent evaporation, and while this latter effect is insignificant in the early stages of an ice age when there is little land ice anyway, it makes ice-core temperature data unreliable from about 15 million years ago, though thereafter it provides estimates of ice volumes instead. Such ice volumes identify periods over the last six million years when the ratio of ice to water was higher and sea levels were lower than today, and *vice versa*, thus confirming the previous evidence from glacial drift and showing that ice volume started to increase about 2.5 million years ago in compliance with the inception of the Arctic ice sheet at that time.

However, it is isotope ratios from the Greenland icecap which provide the most detailed account of temperature change in more recent times. Thus, for the last 10,000 years, the Holocene, temperatures have been constant with only small changes such as those which permitted colonisation of Greenland around 800 and Ice Fairs on the Thames in the eighteenth century. Prior to that, there were rapid temperature swings of up to $10°$ C every few thousand years for a period of about 100,000 years with which *Homo Sapiens* had to cope in his hunter-gatherer stage, and in which the average temperature remained below that of the Holocene. This variable cold period reached its maximum about 18,000 years ago, its last cold interval being the Younger Dryas Event which terminated with a rise in temperature of about 7° C over 50 years around 11,500 years ago. Prior to this variable cold interval, the fossil record confirms the end of hippopotamus and elephant in southern England about 115,000 years ago and though equatorial forests were never annihilated, ice sheet growth and associated sea-level fall continued until 18,000 years ago. Thus, during our current Ice Age there have been warm intervals in the north, while at its maximum severity the forests which had extended to the poles during the Cretaceous merely contacted towards the tropics where conditions were perhaps a little drier and perhaps 2 to 3° C lower than today.

In considering the possible causes of such global temperature changes, Milutin Milankovich calculated in 1920 the variations in solar radiation intensity caused by cyclic variation in the eccentricity of the Earth's orbit, in the obliquity of its spin axis, and in the axis wobble which causes precession of the equinoxes, the cycle periods of which are respectively 100,000, 41,000 and between 19,000 and 23,000 years. When these calculated intensity variations were compared with temperatures derived from oxygen isotope ratios from deep sea sediment cores it was concluded by a UN Committee in 1970 that solar intensity variation could account for at least 60% of the earth's climatic fluctuation while perhaps 40% has been due to variation in atmospheric greenhouse gas concentrations over tens and hundreds of thousands of years. However, while it is known that water vapour, carbon dioxide, methane *etc* retain atmospheric heat as does the glass of a greenhouse by allowing solar ultraviolet radiation to enter while reducing subsequent escape of infrared, the belief which required committee consensus is that anthropogenic emissions of carbon dioxide are currently increasing global temperatures while the contribution from natural sources of this gas are insignificant (c.f. below). Again, while ice-core samples from the Russian Vostok base in Antarctica time-sequenced over the last 150,000 years correlated isotope-determined temperatures with concentrations of carbon dioxide and methane in gas bubbles retained within them, it should be noted that the principle atmospheric greenhouse gas is water vapour which itself is radiation dependent; and that these correlations do not distinguish the effect of one gas or vapour from another (c.f. Section 6.1).

However, any anthropogenic variation in atmospheric carbon dioxide concentrations has to observable against the equilibrium concentration produced by the natural biological and geological recycling mechanisms. Thus, carbon dioxide is removed from the atmosphere by photosynthesis and returned to it by oxidative degradation (rotting) of fallen vegetable and animal matter, a cycle which cannot of itself alter the atmospheric concentration of carbon dioxide and though the burning of fossil fuels adds to the natural release of vegetative carbon at any point in time, it is still only returning that which would already have returned had the vegetative matter rotted in the natural way instead of being buried and fossilised as coal and oil in the first place. Again, deposits on the seabed of photosynthetic carbon from the marine food chain are subducted and returned to the atmosphere in volcanic eruptions while being replaced by further debris from on-going photosynthesis. Yet again atmospheric carbon dioxide dissolved in rain reacts as carbonic acid with silicate rocks to form limestone in the reaction named after Harold Urey with these rocks being eroded and returned to the sea by rivers. As to whether current fossil fuel combustion could affect these cycles we need to consider past inputs, abstractions, effects and timescales.

Thus, calculations by Robert Berner suggest that the Ice Age at the end of the Precambrian (between 700 and 600 million years ago) was caused by global cooling due to abstraction of atmospheric carbon dioxide as photosynthetic single cell organisms began to colonise shallow seas; that subsequent atmospheric carbon dioxide levels peaked at ten times today's levels around 280 million years ago even with extensive ice sheets covering Gondwanaland which then comprised the land masses of today's southern hemisphere; that carbon dioxide levels were five times today's levels about 100 million years ago when forests stretched to the poles and large cold-blooded dinosaurs roamed the land. Since then there has been a steady cooling which Maureen Raymo and William Ruddiman attribute to depletion of atmospheric carbon dioxide levels by the Urey reaction in the Himalayas, Tibet and Central Asia and in the Andes where plate tectonics has been raising and exposing new silica rock to this process before its return to the sea by erosion. Indeed, this Urey reaction coupled to mountain growth is so massive in its effect that it might have stripped the atmosphere of carbon dioxide long ago, were there no return by subduction.

Again, isotope ratios show temperature ranges to be greater towards the poles than the equator, despite heat transfer by ocean currents. Thus, north bound currents such as the Gulf Stream carry heat to northern regions, mirroring this process to the south. However, when tectonic plate movement separated Antarctica from South America 15 million years ago it established the circum-Antarctic current which isolated the new continent from the southern flow of Pacific and Indian Ocean water and caused a marked cooling. Again, the plate-induced closure of the Isthmus of Panama about 2.5 million years ago disconnected the Pacific and Atlantic Oceans and could have caused the Arctic glaciation initiated at that time. As to the Gulf Stream, water density increases with surface freezing and general cooling which causes it to sink and return south at deeper levels thus maintaining heat transfer by circulation. On this basis, Wallace Broekker suggested that had the ice sheets melted fast enough in one of the intermittent swings in temperature referred to above, the density of arriving Gulf Stream water would have been too low for it to sink, thus stopping the thermohaline circulation with onset of the Younger Dryas Event; that the ensuing lower temperatures would have stopped the melt and restarted the circulation; that the restart might account for the temperature rise of 7 degrees in 50 years as revealed by isotope ratios; and that such current induced effects may account for greater temperature ranges in polar than in equatorial regions.

Thus, with our overall record of natural temperature change, doubt as to whether we are currently in cooling phase or are warming towards the end of our current Ice Age, and the constancy of temperature since the Industrial Revolution being within natural oscillation limits, 'consensus predictions' of future temperature increase from fossil fuel combustion need to be treated with caution (c.f. Section 11.2.4).

9. 4. 4 Origin, Evolution and Extinctions of Life on Earth

The earliest evidence for life on Earth depends again on isotope ratios. Thus, because living organisms enrich the proportion of $^{12}C : ^{13}C$ over the inorganic ratio, mass spectrographic analysis of this ratio indicates when chemo-synthetic and photosynthetic life began. Thus, despite there being no fossil organisms in the 3.8 billion year old Banded Iron Formation (BIF) of western Greenland, isotope ratios indicate the start of life within 700 million years of the Earth's formation now dated at 4.55 billion years ago. Thereafter, fossilised single cell organisms dated at 3.5 billion years ago have been found in cherts formed by silica precipitation from hot springs in volcanic regions, such as those living today in the similar conditions of volcanic activity on mid-oceanic ridges where hyper-thermophiles tolerate temperatures up to 100° C, obtain energy from inorganic chemical reactions and grow by chemo-synthesis rather than photosynthesis. Again, while colonies of photosynthetic algae similar to the stromatolites still found in Shark Bay western Australia first appear as fossils in rocks from about 3.5 billion years ago, the oxygen which such photosynthetic organisms release to the atmosphere still appears to have been insufficient to affect the BIF of western Australia or of Michigan which though dating from 2.5 and 2.1 billion years ago show no sign of oxidation during deposition. Thus, apart from photosynthesis being added to the earlier chemo-synthesis the only apparent change in life forms prior to about 600 million years ago was size increase in single cell organisms with perhaps the advent of a cell nucleus and the encoding of DNA information in genes (c.f. sections 8.3.3, 8.3.4 and 9.2.6).

Though these early single cell organisms suffered a mass extinction between 900 and 600 million years ago as the first super-continent Rodinia formed and moved towards the south pole with the oscillating conditions of an Ice Age, multi-cellular organisms definitely appeared in the subsequent warming as evidenced by the jellyfish-like fauna (Ediacara) found in the eponymous mine in the Flinders Range in Australia in 1946. Thereafter, from around 550 million years ago the number of orders of animals doubled every 12 million years or so with almost all of today's phyla of animals starting to appear in the fossil record in this Cambrian 'explosion of life' as worms, crabs, shellfish, sea urchins, sponges, tunicates and centipedes. Contributory factors could have been that volcanic activity at mid-ocean ridges associated with the break-up of Rodinia contributed chemical elements conducive to skeletal formation and carbon for chemo-synthesis; that ocean ridge formation displaced seawater onto low-lying continental margins providing an increased area of photosynthetic waters; that ocean current development recycled nutrients from deeper to surface waters; and that specialist single cells would have associated into multi-cell assemblies and subsequent organisms with a pooling of DNA information, though all essential details remain obscure regardless of Darwin's alleged explanation. Be that as it may, the diversity of life tripled in the Ordovician which ended around 440 million years ago and though the first fish had appeared, the converging landmass of Gondwanaland comprising the present day southern continents was moving towards that pole and initiating the second Ice Age the advances, retreats and associated sea level oscillations of which wiped out nearly three-quarters of all marine species in less than a million years.

For the rest of the Palaeozoic (old life) the northern continents converged on Gondwanaland to form Pangea while some marine animals made the transition across inter-tidal shores to join the first Ordivician plants for life on land. During this period through the Silurian, Devonian and Carboniferous, the first millimetre high plants were succeeded by trees tens of metres high, the latter initiating the deposition of coal. On the other hand, the land animals did not increase in size beyond worms, snails and myriapods (ancestors of centipedes and millipedes) from which insects subsequently evolved. Otherwise, such size increase awaited the development of an internal mineralised skeleton in marine creatures, without which larger animals could not move around out of water. Thus, the Devonian Ichthyostega (fish with legs) is the first amphibian to have been found, though by the end of the Carboniferous about 300 million years ago all the major plant families had appeared except for the flowering plants and cycad palms. However, by the end of the Permian, with Pangea extending virtually from pole to pole, mantle convection caused a plume head to contact the overlying continent and to erupt basaltic lava over an area of about 2.5 million square kilometres to a depth of over 3 kilometres in less than a million years in what is now Siberia. Though the existence of this single continent itself would have had negative climatic and ocean circulation consequences for life, the global impact of the volcanic emissions of dust (sun-light blocking) and sulphur dioxide (acid-rain producing) must have been the overwhelming cause of this third mass extinction, its 90% removal of both land and marine species making it the most catastrophic of all.

The carbon dioxide emissions produced directly by this volcanic event were indirectly augmented by oxidative weathering of the massive coal deposits thrust up by it and by subduction emissions as Pangea was broken-up by seafloor spreading in the Mesozoic (middle life). These carbon dioxide emissions are associated with the global warming which persisted through the age of the dinosaurs which would have found the warmth congenial if cold-blooded and which in the

306

Jurassic, from about 200 million years ago, began to diversify from tens of centimetres high to tens of metres in length, from grazing herbivores to hunting carnivores, and with Archaeopteryx being considered the first bird. In addition, warm-blooded mammals first appear at this time, the heat loss from their smallness being compensated by the subsequent and even warmer Cretaceous Period. However, after existing for about a 100 million years, the northern part of Pangea (North America, Europe and Asia) began to separate from Gondwanaland about 170 million years ago and by the end of the Cretaceous, 120 million years ago, Africa began to separate from South America with the creation of the South Atlantic. As the continents moved apart, the flora and fauna were separated and transported to new climatic zones contributing to extinctions including those of many dinosaurs and to adaptations including that to the flowering plants, while some such as the tuatara of New Zealand remained almost identical to the small reptiles of Mezozoic Gondwanaland.

In turn the Cretaceous came to an end 65 million years ago when a mantle plume rose under the Deccan region as India was rifting away from the Seychelles Bank and initiated an outpouring of lava which lasted for almost a million years, being similar to that which had ended the Permian. This time, however, the effect was compounded by the arrival of a meteorite about 10 kilometres in diameter which impacted near Chicxulub in the Yucatan Peninsula. It has been estimated that this impact was equivalent to the detonation of a megaton bomb on every square kilometre of surface, the resulting crater measuring 180 km in diameter; and that the Earth's crust was shattered and locally melted to a depth of 30 kilometres. The fall-out settled as a layer of iridium-rich clay recognisable in time-sequenced marine sediment cores, iridium being characteristic of meteorites while the associated quartz particles show the fracture patterns of impact. In addition the impact zone having been underlain by gypsum ($CaSO_4$) the resulting sulphur dioxide would have fallen as acid rain. Thus, the combined effect of the volcanic activity and the meteorite impact was the fourth mass extinction, second in severity only to the Permian event. Many marine animals such as ammonites and belemnites became extinct while on land the dinosaurs were wiped out as were all animals of more than about 25 kilograms in weight, though the global cooling which had begun in the Cretaceous may already have removed some of the dinosaurs. In any case, all were now gone, clearing the way for the rise of mammals in the Cainozoic (recent life).

After about a million years the global climate returned to warm equable conditions, though wetter than today. Thus, above the iridium-rich sedimentary band, plankton species and numbers increase while tropical forests extend to middle latitudes and woodlands to the poles. Again, after India had made contact with Asia its coastal margins were uplifted exposing the accumulated remains of marine organisms to oxidative weathering to carbon dioxide associated with temperature increase to the warmest point in the Cenozoic by about 52 million years ago (mid-Eocene). Thereafter, temperature declined again as mountain building in the Himalayas and Andes re-adsorbed this carbon dioxide by the Urey reaction as it has continued to do to the present day. By the Oligocene, 30 million years ago, the climate had become more seasonal, polar forests had gone, higher latitudes were treeless tundra, lower latitudes became drier and there was an ice sheet in Antarctica. In the Miocene, about 20 million years ago, grass made its appearance and extensive savannah grasslands became a feature of the drier mid-latitudes of the Americas and east Africa. As to the mammals, these had begun as the cynodonts of the Triassic about 230 million years ago, had coexisted with the dinosaurs in the Cretaceous, and in the early Eocene had diversified into many of the present day orders including bats, horses, early elephants, whales and our own early ancestors. These last, were rat-sized tree-livers with grasping hands and opposable thumbs, forward-looking eyes and disproportionately large brains similar to modern tarsiers. Thereafter, monkeys developed in the late Eocene, apes and hominids in the Miocene, *Homo habilis* and *Homo erectus* in the Pliocene and *Homo sapiens* in the Pleistocene.

9. 4. 5 Origin of Planets and Satellites

Having reviewed how the results of the scientific method of experimentation elucidated the origin of the universe, the formation and evolution of galaxies, stars and elements, and the evolution of continents, climate and life on Earth, and having noted their absence in Darwinism and in the committee consensus respecting anthropogenic global warming, I now describe their application to elucidation of the origin and evolution of the planets and satellites of the solar system and by extension to the planetary systems of other stars. Here the problem is to explain the composition and distribution of all the bodies in our own solar system, the basic observations being the densities (mass/volume) of these bodies and their distances from the Sun. As to these, were the Sun to be represented by a ball six inches in diameter, the inner planets, Mercury, Venus, Earth and Mars would be pin-head size at respective distances of 7, 13, 18 and 27 yards while Jupiter, Saturn, Uranus and Neptune would be small pea sized bodies at respective distances of about 90, 170, 350 and 540 yards, with Pluto being a speck at about 700 yards.

Now, we know that the Sun condensed from a gas cloud in the company of other stars; that on the basis of the density of such clouds as exemplified by the Orion Nebula, a volume of gas ten million million miles in diameter must have condensed to the Sun's current diameter of one million miles *i.e.* to one ten millionth of the original; and that as a consequence of the dynamic law which causes an ice-skater to spin faster as the outstretched arms are lowered, the rotational speed of the Sun would now be ten million times faster than that of the original gas cloud. Now for such clouds, an initial outer rotation speed of 10-100 cm per second is observed while an increase in equatorial rotation of the Sun to 1000 -10,000 km per second would have caused it to burst like an over-spun flywheel, its actual speed being only about 2 km per second as it is for all stars similar to it. Thus, an external mechanism has to be found to slow gas cloud rotational speed during star condensation and to allow some contraction before it takes effect because Jupiter our largest planet is some 500 million miles from the Sun, much less than the initial diameter of our contracting cloud. Again, stars with surface temperatures < 6000° C have low rotation speeds (that of the Sun being about 5,460° C) while those above 7000° C are usually above 50 km per second, the relevant significance being that whatever the mechanism, it must operate to differing degrees to produce such differences in the final product while having little effect in the early condensation stages.

On the basis of these requirements, it was hypothesised that the condensing spherical cloud would become increasingly oblate and eventually form an outwardly spreading equatorial disc which would slow the rotation as does the raising of a skater's arms outwards to shoulder height. However, were all the material of the present solar system returned to the Sun, its rotational speed though increased from 2 to 100 km per second, would still be insufficient to have formed a disc. Nonetheless, Jupiter and Saturn contain the same proportion of hydrogen as the Sun while Neptune and Uranus are comparatively depleted, suggesting that some of the hydrogen mass which contributed to the disc-forming rotational speed, subsequently escaped. As to estimating how much, we know that the compositions of Sun and disc would have been identical; that carbon, nitrogen, oxygen and neon account for 1% of the Sun's mass; that the combined mass of Neptune and Uranus amounts to 30 times the mass of the Earth; that, therefore, the escaped mass of hydrogen must have been about 3000 Earth-masses; that the total mass of planets amounts to about 450 Earth-masses; that the total mass of escaped hydrogen must thus have exceeded the total mass of the present planets by about sevenfold; that with this missing mass added to the Sun its rotational speed would have been about a 1000 km per second; and that such a rotating mass could have formed a disc when it had condensed to some fifty times the present size of the Sun.

It was now necessary to consider how rotational momentum could be transmitted across the gap which must develop between the inner edge of the disc as it was pushed outwards while the solar condensation continued. From Faraday onwards it has been possible to think of magnetic lines of force as elastic strings and so H. Alfven advanced the analogy of a wheel with its inner hub (the solar condensation) attached to the rim (the separate disc) by spokes. Now, with rigid spokes the rim rotates in the same time as the hub, whereas if the spokes are elastic any tendency for the rim to lag behind the hub will stretch the spokes causing the rim to speed up and the hub to slow down. In fact when the elastic spokes are magnetic lines of force the disc is not so much speeded up as pushed further outwards as required for subsequent planetary condensation in the disc at the distances observed. Again, the field strengths required on the Alfven model are modest compared to those which are known to exist on many stars and are considerably less than those in sunspots. At this point in our knowledge-based reasoning, we have to consider the composition of the inner four planets which have high contents of iron, magnesium and silicon while the solar content of these metals is only about 0.25%. In doing so, we know that the magnetic coupling between the disc and Sun is only possible when the material in the disc is in the gaseous phase; that any condensations to the liquid or solid phases would be left behind as the gases were pushed further from the Sun; and that the composition of these phases would be a function of decreasing temperature from refractory substances such as silicates, iron and other metals closer to the Sun to those of lower boiling points such as hydrocarbons, water and ammonia at increasing distances from it.

Thus, we see that before the disc material reached the distances from the Sun of the great planets the refractory substances would have been separated out; that some water would be associated with silicates as hydrates; that this would account for the stony-metallic nature of the inner planets and the water and possibly some 'oil' on Earth; and that there might be more 'oil' and less water on Venus. As to Jupiter and Saturn, we see that these consist largely of water and ammonia which would have been more abundant than the previously separated refractory substances, thus accounting for the greater volume of these two planets; that their different volumes must be due to the differing extents to which in forming they were able gravitationally to attract uncondensed gases consisting mainly of the hydrogen of the initial disc, the inner regions of which were denuded of such gas before inner planet accretion had advanced sufficiently to exert the necessary gravitational attraction for it. At this point it should be noted that the respective densities of the inner planets are Mercury 4.5-5.0, Venus 4.4, Earth 4.4, and Mars 3.8-4.0 while for the outer they are Jupiter 1.35, Saturn 0.71, Uranus 1.56 and Neptune 2.47; and that Ramsey showed Jupiter and Saturn to contain about 80% hydrogen while water, methane, ammonia and possibly neon could account for the densities of Uranus and Neptune. However, one problem with these two outer planets is to determine the composition of the gas phase which remained at that stage. Thus, they were unable to attract hydrogen as Jupiter and Saturn did while being able to attract water, methane and ammonia suggesting that this must have occurred before the gas phase moved outside their orbits. However the absence of hydrogen may be explained by the Sun having been formed in a cluster of several hundred stars of which the proximity of one might have been sufficient for its heating effect to have driven all residual hydrogen from the outermost regions of the disc in the late stages of planet formation.

Nonetheless, other problems remain, perhaps the principal being the accretion mechanism whereby the disc materials actually formed planets. It has been suggested that ice-slush and oily hydrocarbons may have assisted accretion. Whatever the mechanism, the planetary satellites and the asteroid belt suggest incomplete accretion. Indeed, the planet Pluto, only discovered in 1930 by C. W Tombough at the Lowell Observatory, presents many problems. For a start, though it averages 30% further from the Sun than Neptune, its orbit when nearest to the Sun actually passes inside that of Neptune. Again, while the mass of Pluto, as inferred from slight distortions in the orbit of Neptune, is nearly equal to that of the Earth, its directly observed volume suggests an impossible density of 50 times that of water, though it has been suggested that were Pluto to reflect light as does a polished ball, it would look much smaller than it is. Yet again, its very peculiar orbit caused Lyttleton to suggest that it is an escaped satellite of Neptune. As to satellites in order outwards from the Sun, the Earth is the first to have one, followed by Mars with two, both extremely small compared to our Moon. Again, of the twelve satellites of Jupiter only two have masses greater than our satellite and of the nine of Saturn only one is more massive than ours while none of the five of Uranus compares with it and only one of the two of Neptune does. As to densities, the Moon is less dense than the Earth while Io and Europa (satellites of Jupiter) are similarly dense to Mars, an iron content of about 20% being necessary to explain these three, while otherwise satellite densities decrease as do planet densities with increasing distance from the Sun.

On the other hand, though Earth and Moon were evidently formed quite close to each other, densities compare as 4.4 to 3.33 respectively. Thus, while the Earth contains 30% iron, the Moon can contain none unless its rock is similar to that of the Earth's crust. However,, were it to be of the lighter rocks of the terrestrial continents (density 2.7) the Moon could also contain about 30% iron, whereupon it would have no mantle rock. Again, the absence of volcanic activity suggests that internal radioactivity alone has been insufficient to maintain its internal temperature much above the melting point of iron (1500° C) or of rock (between 900 and 1800° C), and that radioactive heating of the Earth might not be all that significant either. As to the lunar craters, the largest are nearly 100 miles in diameter *i.e.* more than ten times the diameter of any terrestrial volcanic crater, those on the Moon being impact craters caused by the last accretion bodies having impacted at speeds of several miles per second, while those which impacted in the last stages of Earth accretion have been eroded by weathering processes absent on the Moon.

Having suggested that early accretion might have been assisted by adhesive substances until gravitation became influential, questions remain as to how big these later gravitating bodies might have been. As to possible answers, the observed inclination of the axis of spin to the plane of the planetary orbits is according to G. P. Kuiper, Mercury 87° ?, Venus 80° ?, Earth 66.5°, Mars 65°, Jupiter 89°, Saturn 62°, Uranus -7° and Neptune 70° whereas we would expect a 90° orientation as conferred by the spinning disc. Thus, those which deviate substantially from 90 degrees suggest mergence of bodies of substantially comparable size, most notably in the case of Uranus where the deviation from the expected orientation amounts to 97°. As to both composition and accretion, the asteroid belt between Mars and Jupiter appears to delineate the boundary between the rocky-metallic and the gaseous zones with the composition of Jupiter's Io and Europa being that of the inner planets and asteroids and with others such as Ganymede and Callisto being similar to Jupiter itself. Again, while the asteroids, if accreted, would produce a planet with a mass comparable to the Moon, the reasons it did not happen remain unknown.

Thus, though many questions remain unanswered, it seems that the presence of a magnetic field is essential to the above process of planet and satellite formation. Without it, the disc would have continued to grow as solar condensation proceeded to the point where the mass of the disc would have been comparable to the final mass of the correspondingly smaller Sun, whereupon the disc would have accreted to a second star in the evolution of a paired-star system in which one revolved around the other at a distance rather less than the present orbit of the planet Mercury with both rotating at considerable speed, there being no magnetic retardation to slow them down. Such double-star systems known as W Ursa Majoris stars, after the prototype found in the Great Bear constellation, amount to just under 1% of all cases. This, in turn suggests that ordinary slowly rotating stars of which there are about a thousand million in the Milky Way alone, may be expected to have planetary systems.

9. 5 TECHNOLOGY

The foregoing reviews have shown how the Rational Trinity produced craftsmanship and physicochemical science, how the latter assisted the former towards technology and other fields of descriptive and classified knowledge towards new earth and biological sciences and knowledge-based explanations of cosmic, stellar and planetary evolution independent of Rational Duality belief and its pseudo-scientific derivatives. To continue, I now review twentieth-century technology as directly applying the Rational Trinity to enhance our physical welfare independent of Rational Duality belief except where its pseudo-science rejects the above knowledge for alternate belief (c.f. Sections 6.4 and 8.3.4), this phenomenon being further considered here as a prelude to exemplifying its negative effects on social and physical welfare in Chapters 10, 11 and 12.

Again, the neutrality of knowledge is demonstrated by belief-driven war, both hot and cold, having caused the development of some twentieth century technologies subsequently applied to peaceful purposes. Thus, while the release of energy from uranium-235 was implicit in scientific journals by 1939, its use in producing the fission bomb and subsequent fission-generated electricity would not have been so rapid had public funding for the former not been seen as a survival requirement. Again, the need to detect enemy aircraft led to radar and its post-war application to civil aviation and shipping safety, the need to treat infected war-wounds turned Fleming's un-remarked antibiosis into penicillin production and post-war antibiotics development, and the need for military aircraft and rocketry led to post-war civil aviation, space-travel and the moon-landing of 1969 *et seq.* Nonetheless, such incidental benefits of war should not to be seen as unquestionable support for mission-driven public funding. It should be noted that all technological progress is based on stepwise extension and use of existing knowledge and was private-funded (c.f. Section 8.1); that having the mission objective while only believing how to get there, produces activity rather than progress and is invariably public-funded; and that had Alexander wanted a microphone to address the troops, no amount of funding would have enabled Aristotle to give him one.

9. 5. 1 Energy
Given the social and physical benefits of replacing muscle-power with steam-power and of transforming chemical energy to electricity, it might have been expected that nuclear-generated electricity would have been welcomed as removing the inconveniencies of coal mining, transport and use. Alas, the peaceful uses of nuclear-energy were stigmatised by the belief-based Campaign for Nuclear Disarmament which caused the UK, USA and Germany to resist fission-electricity more than did Japan, Taiwan and France, the last supplying more than half its requirements this way by the 1980s. Thus while knowledge-based decisions took more objective account of geopolitical availability and price of fossil fuels, belief-based policy response to the OPEC price increases of 1973 was to turn to solar, tidal, wave, wind, geothermal and nuclear fusion as alternatives to fossil fuels and nuclear fission irrespective of availability and cost considerations, while fossil fuels are now attacked for their alleged influence on global warming irrespective of the astronomical, geological and biological influences reviewed in Sections 9.4.3 and 9.4.4.

Thus, the EEC initiated the EURILIOS solar power plant in Sicily which was connected to the Italian National Grid in 1981 despite the foreseeable inefficiencies of a system in which solar radiation is reflected by sun-tracking mirrors onto a central boiler to drive a steam-turbine. Indeed, in operation it showed that 1% of the total land area of Europe (equal to the existing road system) would be needed to supply its energy requirements by such means. Meanwhile, given that solar heat is more efficiently used for direct heating purposes than for electricity generation, 88% and 10% of direct solar heat collectors in the USA were heating swimming pools and domestic water systems respectively by 1985 while in Israel 30% of buildings had direct solar heating, this being stipulated for all new houses though there is rightly no demand for electricity from solar generated steam. However, the need to provide electricity on satellites had focussed attention (pre-OPEC 1973) on the photovoltaic effect of Bequerel (1839) which converts sunlight directly to electricity. Thus, Chapin, Fuller and Pearson of Bell Laboratories had by 1954 introduced the silicon cell which served this need at 6-10% efficency. Since then efficiencies have risen to 37% with gallium arsenide and gallium antimonide cells being developed by Boeing for the capture of blue and red light respectively. In addition, transparent photovoltaic panels which could replace window glass were patented in 1991. Nonetheless, while cost is not a first order consideration in satellite applications, the cost reductions necessary for mass-market uptake are unlikely to be met immediately, if at all, given the availability of more cost-effective alternatives.

Again, though the medieval tide mill and its power applications have already been described, there are few locations world-wide where the tidal range is larger than the four metre minimum requirement for electricity generation. At one such location on the Rance, Electricite de France built a 750m barrage for this purpose in 1966 while the French preference for the nuclear option appears to have remained intact. On the other hand the construction of such an installation on the Bristol Channel is opposed by belief-based concern for wildlife impacts regardless of whether or not it might be cost-effective. However, such believers advocate the harnessing of wave power which they expect to have low wildlife and visual impacts even though this option is not engineered to the stage of reality-validation already reached by the tidal option. Again, they advocate wind generated electricity despite its reality-evaluation being already negative, the earlier erection of thousands of small windmills for private-domestic use in remote locations having only been acceptable where intermittent operation is better than nothing, the more recent erection of optimally designed wind-turbines to feed electricity into the grid having already been a costly mistake. Indeed, though these continue to be built at disproportionate cost to consumers and taxpayers, they are increasingly described by their advocates as 'demonstrating a commitment to reduce global warming': not as a competitive power-source.

However, regardless of cost, the intermittency of the solar, tide, wave and wind options for electricity generation is incompatible with the requirement for a steadily reliable supply. Thus, the Sun has a diurnal intensity variation which may be further reduced by cloudiness even in daytime, the times of high and low tide and tidal range change from day to day over a monthly cycle and wave-height and wind-speed vary irregularly from flat-calm to storm-force while electricity demand though variable with time of day and season is never zero and must be satisfied at all times. Consequently there must be an on-going standby capacity to meet peak and all other levels of demand with immediate response regardless of reduced sunlight or periods of calm whether short or prolonged. At present there are only two options for providing this standby capacity, these being fossil-fuel combustion and nuclear fission. In any case, steam pressure must be maintained *i.e.* fuel must be consumed continuously for instant generation of electricity when intermittent 'green' sources go off-line to which extent carbon dioxide emissions cannot be avoided without recourse to the nuclear option. Despite these realities, the UK has accepted a requirement by EU Directive to generate 38% of its energy from 'renewables' by 2020: a triumph of belief over knowledge.

312

The first nuclear reactor or "atomic-pile" as he called it, was constructed by Enrico Fermi at the University of Chicago and activated at 3.20 pm on 2 December 1942 to investigate the potential chain reaction on which the practical release of energy would depend. Such a reaction is not sustained in natural uranium because the neutrons from the spontaneous fission of the isotope ^{235}U (present to 0.7%) are absorbed by the preponderant ^{238}U (present to 99.3%) without causing further fission. However, it was found that this unwanted absorption could be reduced if the neutrons were passed through a speed moderator such as 'heavy' water in which the deuterium : hydrogen ratio had been enhanced by selective decomposition of the 'lighter' water molecules by electrolysis, French scientists having escaped in 1940 with all the heavy water they had made. However, in his prototype reactor, Fermi not only had to initiate the desired chain reaction, he also had to control it thereafter, and his solution was to moderate neutron speed by passage through graphite and to control the ensuing chain-reaction by neutron absorption in cadmium. Thus, he machined channels in graphite blocks through which cadmium rods could be slid and surrounded these channelled block-rod units with the natural uranium of his atomic-pile. When this pile was constructed the cadmium rods were slowly withdrawn until the associated instruments registered an increase in neutron production indicating attainment of the critical point for energy generation, whereupon the cadmium rods were thrust back to absorb these neutrons and regain control. On observing the success of this major step towards the Manhattan Project (c.f. Section 9.5.7) Arthur Compton telephoned the president of Harvard, James Conant, to say "the Italian navigator has landed."

However, it was June 1954, before the first reactor to generate electricity came into operation at Obninsk, 80km from Moscow. It generated 5 megawatts using graphite as moderator, enriched uranium as fuel (c.f. Section 9.5.7) and abstraction of heat from the core by exchange with high pressure water in a closed-circuit cooling system. Again, the graphite moderated gas-cooled reactor at Calder Hall was operational by 1956 while the first operational US rector at Shippingport Pennsylvania used heavy water for both moderator and coolant in 1957 as did the Canadian CANDU reactors of the 1950s. Because water is a less efficient absorber of neutrons than is graphite, these US and Canadian reactors have the advantage of a higher 'burn-up' before the uranium fuel elements need to be replaced. Again, if plutonium, ^{239}Pu, is mixed with ^{238}U the neutrons generated by uranium fission produce more fissile plutonium, the first such breeder-reactor producing fuel as it used it having been built at Dounreay, Scotland in 1959 followed by the Phoenix at Marcoule, France.

Again, the continuous geothermal option is available in some locations, hot springs having long been used for central-heating in Reykjavik while natural super-heated steam (>100° C) has generated electricity at Larderello (Italy) since 1905. Such local volcanism has suggested the ubiquitous temperature increase with depth beneath the Earth's surface as a source of thermal energy independent of location. However, injection of surface water through permeable rock to depths of 3000-4000m with surface return has shown that not all rock is sufficiently permeable, that permeability diminishes as pressure increases with depth, and that the low thermal conductivity of rock limits the rate of heat extraction. Accordingly, the feasibility of increasing heat transfer by explosive shattering of rock has been investigated at Los Alamos.

Again, hydrogen fusion being the source of energy in the Sun and hydrogen bomb, efforts are being made to maintain the necessary temperature for controlled release of such energy, a process which would avoid the radioactive by-products of uranium and plutonium fission. For containment of such hydrogen plasma, Lev Andreevich Artsimovich of the then USSR used a toroidal magnetic field (tokamac) in 1963 while in 1993 the Joint European Torus (JET) at Culham, UK, achieved controlled fusion for 2 seconds in a plasma at 220 million degrees K with an energy release of 2 megawatts for an input of 15 megawatts. Though there is still some way to go, a more recent alterative in which pellets of solid hydrogen would be brought to fusion temperature by lasers is under consideration in the UK.

However, such future prospects are irrelevant to the need to replace existing power stations now reaching the ends of their working lives. If electorates wish to limit carbon dioxide production and politicians wish to reduce dependence on overseas oil and gas, both must opt for the nuclear fission option. Otherwise, the current belief-driven debate will be terminated by the reality of 'the lights going out' and much else besides. Thus, of the 55 GW of energy which we currently require, 40% will be lost by 2015 when 6 of our 7 nuclear power stations (10GW) will have been age-decommissioned and nine coal or oil fired stations (13 GW) will have been rendered non-viable by the cost of converting them to compliance with the *Large Combustion Plant Directive* of the EU. Thus, we will have lost 40% of our generating capacity at a time when Westinghouse which incidentally was sold out of UK influence in 2006, already has 19 orders for new nuclear stations each of which take 10 years to build. Thus, many are placing orders where they can, while the UK dithers under the constraint of EU 'state aid' rules and in the knowledge that the building of gas-fired alternatives would place us at the mercy of doubtfully reliable foreign sources of natural gas. Thus, the UK sought to eliminate its imminent power deficit by signing up to 38% reliance on renewable sources by 2020, reality being dismissible in socio-political circles, at least until lights go out and computers crash.

9. 5. 2 Biochemistry and Medicine

In 1906 Paul Ehrlich showed that an arsenic-compound which he called salvarsan was effective against syphilis by being more toxic to *Treponema pallidum* than to human body cells. He also introduced the term chemotherapy for this differential toxicity and expressed his expectation that more 'magic bullets' would be found. Thus, despite Salvarsan being < 100% pathogen specific and having unpleasant and even fatal side-effects, the search was now on for more effective curative agents for this and other diseases. This search became more systematic in 1927 when Gerhard Domagk of I. G. Farbenindustie started to screen all the company's chemical products for possible effectiveness against the causative organisms of septicaemia, meningitis, and pneumonia with animal toxicity testing and clinical trials as indicated. Five years later prontosil rubrum, a red dye for leather, was found effective for streptococcal septicaemia infections in mice and the effective component of the dye was shown by J. Trefouel of the Pasteur Institute in Paris to be replicated by the relatively simple sulphanilamide, from which derivatives known as the sulphonamides such as sulphapyridine and sulphathiazole were effective against a range of pathogens. Meanwhile, in 1928 Alexander Fleming accidentally discovered that the mould *Penicillium notatum* produced an agent effective against *staphylococci*, and though he called it penicillin he did not isolate it or appreciate its significance. However, during a general investigation of antibiosis, it was isolated in 1939 by Howard Florey and Ernst Chain in sufficient purity to reveal the high effectiveness and virtual absence of side-effects which persuaded the US pharmaceutical industry and government to embark on a crash-programme for the supply of penicillin to the armed forces.

In contrast, the diagnostic value of Roentgen's 1898 discovery of X-rays was quickly applied to the examination of broken-bones, the detection of foreign bodies such as bullets, shrapnel *etc* and by the 1930s of pulmonary tuberculosis. Later, their use was extended to give three-dimensional images of scull and brain by computerised axial tomography CAT for which development Godfrey Houndsfield and Allan Cormack received the Nobel Prize in 1979 before the more recent whole body scanner was developed. In the meantime, the absorption of radio-frequency radiation by hydrogen atoms exposed to magnetic fields (nuclear magnetic resonance,

314

NMR) showed frequency shifts diagnostic of chemical locations (chemical-shifts), a phenomenon which became the basis of magnetic resonance imaging, MRI, for the location of abnormalities within the body without the damaging side-effects of X-rays, these being increasingly used to treat tumours by maximising their target intensity and minimising exposure of surrounding issues by rotating the patient or the X-ray beam while similar radiation benefits were achieved by inserting small samples of γ-emitting nuclides into tumours. In addition, knowledge that muscle contractions were associated with measurable electric currents led from early work by A.D. Waller in 1897 through improvements by W. Einthoven in 1903 to the electrocardiograph which monitors pulsations of the whole heart and of each of its four compartments separately. Similarly, early measurements of brain rhythms in dogs by Hans Berger led to his construction in 1929 of the first electroencephalograph. Apart from diagnosis of heart and brain abnormalities, both instruments are now used to monitor patients under general anaesthetic in surgical operations.

Although knowledge of the role of carbohydrates, proteins and fats in the maintenance of a healthy diet had been acquired in the nineteenth century, investigation of what F.G. Hopkins called "accessory food factors" (vitamins) showed that many major diseases were caused by dietary deficiencies rather than by pathogenic microbes. Thus it was learned that beri-beri, scurvy, rickets and pellagra were caused by deficiencies in vitamins B, C, D and nicotinic acid respectively; that some of these were provided directly from a natural balanced diet while some are synthesised by micro-organisms naturally occurring in the gut. Similarly, it was found that deficiencies may also occur with some extremely active molecules (hormones) normally produced adequately by the ductless glands and discharged directly to the bloodstream; and that any vitamin or hormonal deficiencies can in principle be made good by additives to the diet or by medication with the necessary hormones chemically synthesised for this purpose. Again in 1922, Banting, Best and MacLeod discovered that a deficiency in the production of insulin by the pancreas causes diabetes, and that this can be controlled by regular injection of insulin. Later it was found that hormone levels control fertility, and that fertility can be suppressed by ingestion of contraceptives.

Again, though the role of the immune system was welcomed in terms of destroying invasive micro-organisms by producing antibodies (specific proteins) to the antigens (specific proteins) characteristic of the invader, its rejection of transplanted organs had to be suppressed. Thus, over the last fifty years, efforts have been made to avoid organ-rejection by selecting genetically similar donors, by use of immunosuppressive drugs, by artificially engineered organs, or by growing genetically identical organs by cell and tissue culture in the laboratory prior to incorporation and full development in the body. To-date, kidney transplants, pioneered in 1953 by John Merrill in the USA, have been the most successful, many tens of thousands having been performed while the first heart transplant was performed by Christian Barnard of Cape Town in 1967. These techniques have been progressively improved since the early days, though the lack of suitable donors is a limitation particularly with hearts and livers. Again though Xeno-transplantation would remove such limitations, organ rejection and the risk of cross-species infection have hindered this development for over fifty years.

In the meantime, introduction of the artificial kidney by W. Kolff in 1943 enabled periodic correction of renal deficiencies by dialysis. Kolff also introduced the artificial heart in 1957 and in 1976 his colleague R. Jarvik developed a pneumatic version of which some ninety were implanted before the US FDA banned them in 1989. However, the left ventricular assist device LVAD approved by the FDA in 1995 is a heart augmenter (HeartMate) rather than a substitute. It consists of an implanted palm-sized titanium pump with a battery powered controller worn external to the body, the use of which often results in recovery of natural pumping capacity by the heart. Another augmenter is the pace-maker for regulation of heartbeat, introduced in the early 1960s and now implanted in the hundreds of thousands per year. Again, in the 1990s, a number of synthetic polymers were developed whose structure and composition support the growth of tissue from cells harvested from the prospective host or provide a barrier between donated organ and host which limits rejection by the immune system. In addition to providing hybrid organs, this technique has replaced bone, cartilage and other connective tissue. The technique involves growing organs from a few harvested cells of the host on a three-dimensional immunosuppressive polymeric matrix by tissue culture *in vitro* and transferring to the host for full *in vivo* development. This approach, pioneered by V. Yannas, E. Bell and R. S. Langer at MIT and by J.P. Vacanti at Harvard in the 1970s and 80s, enabled A. Atala of the Boston Children's Hospital and Harvard Medical School to pre-culture and implant six beagle bladders with achievement of ten months normal function in 1999.

9. 5. 3 Agriculture

Though world-population has been increasing from Palaeolithic times because of the developments in craftsmanship, science and technology already reviewed, it began to soar in the twentieth century. Now, at a rate of 86 million per year it has increased from 5.7 billion to 6.6 billion between 1994 and 2006 and is estimated to reach between 9.7 billion and 13 billion by 2050. Those who welcomed the "Green Revolution" know that this growth arose from introduction of synthetic pesticides to complement the artificial fertilisers already introduced in the previous century (c.f. Section 8.1.6). Artificial fertilisers enable crops to realise their full growth-potential while pesticides destroy competitive weeds which reduce crop-growth and control fungal diseases and insect predations which destroy crop-values. Those who reject this knowledge and believe fertiliser and pesticide residues to be unavoidably harmful and thus require them to be discontinued in favour of organic farming need to consider how such a reversal of the "Green Revolution" would affect current population levels, even if they choose to ignore those projected.

Anyway, in 1926 F. W. Went discovered that plant growth was stimulated by natural substances first called auxins, and that growth could be inhibited or controlled by compounds now referred to as phyto-hormones thus leading to the development of selective herbicides to destroy weeds without damage to associated crops. The first such 'magic bullet' was ortho di-nitrocrysol patented in France in 1932 as active against dicotyledons to which group most weeds belong while being innocuous to monocotyledons to which all cereals belong. The USA followed with 2-4-dichlorophenoxyacetic acid of which annual production had risen to 10,000 tonnes by 1950. Again, in the 1950s ICI developed the bi-pyridyls such as Paraquat which kill a range of aquatic and grass weeds with spontaneous deactivation at rates sufficient to permit the new crop to be drilled directly without the time and fuel consuming operations of ploughing and harrowing. One of the first chemical fungicides was Bordeaux Mixture (copper sulphate and lime) introduced in 1885 to combat downy mildew of grapevines and still used today in tea, coffee and cocoa plantations. Nowadays, however, a wide range of synthetic organic products are available with new varieties being under continuous development because fungicide resistance progressively develops. Some, such as the dithiocarbamates and phthalimides are sprayed in the earlier manner while others are systemic, being absorbed through the roots to travel through the xylem to attack fungi on stem and leaves. Again, fungal and other diseases such as smut and bunt in cereals can be carried by their seeds, the treatment of which by organo-mercury compounds began in the 1930s, though non-mercury compounds such as Thiram (Du Pont, 1930) have been increasingly used post-1945.

For other pests such as wire-worms, flea-beetles and locusts which cause crop-damage to the point of obliteration, the first antidote was the insecticide DDT discovered by P. H. Muller (Basle, 1939) for which antidote he was awarded the Nobel Prize in 1948, production of DDT having met the war-time need for typhus (louse-borne) control with the success demonstrated in Naples in 1943-44. During the war also, Britain produced another chlorine compound BCH which was effective against wire-worm infestation of soil, flea-beetles in *Brassica* and for locust, mosquito and tsetse fly control. Again, prior to the war, I.G. Farbenindustrie had developed phosphorus-based insecticides such as parathion, the recognised toxicity of which to animals and man was not reduced until the 1950s in Menazon (UK) and Malathion (USA).

However, despite the success of these new products in ensuring maximum growth of plants by controlling competitive weeds and disease agents in crops and stock-animals, and their consequent success in making food more widely, fully and cheaply available, Rachel Carson's *Silent Spring* of 1962 made them mid-wives to the birth of 'environmentalism' by which I mean the self-imposed mission to protect the Earth from all the consequences of human presence which can be imagined and believed to be harmful by the 'environmentalist' to whom knowledge is useful only for selective citation in support of the said beliefs. Such 'environmentalism' seeks to ban rather than to reduce or eliminate by technical means, the negative side-effects of otherwise beneficial technologies while ignoring the environmentalism of craftsmen and technological innovators as practised from earliest times without prompting by agitators (c.f. Sections 11.2.4 and 11.2.5).

Again, the long-standing practice of developing disease-resistance in plants such as potatoes, sugarcane, bananas and strawberries by selective breeding over many generations by layering, grafting and dividing, has been improved in the past 20-30 years by culturing shoots and roots from a tiny fragment of growing-point tissue in a test-tube of nutrient medium for on-growing by conventional means. Thus, it is now possible to produce 200,000 new plants from a single parent in one year and new plant varieties in two years instead of the previous ten, while avoiding the disease-transfer inherent to vegetative propagation. By such means, the Belle de Fontenay potato is widely grown again, though by 1954 it faced extinction by viral infection. Again, the rate of selective-breeding of animals by normal mating was enhanced by artificial insemination for horses in the nineteenth century and was extended to sheep and cattle in the 1920s by I. I. Ivanov. Nonetheless, this process could only be fully applied in the post-war period when the preservation of semen by freezing enabled the genetic material of good sires to be perpetuated long after their deaths to fertilise ova transplanted from the favoured to the less-favoured on the maternal side, a practice which spread from the breeding of 7,500 cows in the USA in 1939 to one million in 1947 and to six million in 1958. Again, while early livestock breeders sought conformity with the characteristics (points) of particular breeds, consumer demand became increasingly influential and led to market-driven preference for leaner animals from the thirties onwards to which breeders responded by halving animal weights. Thus, the role of the traditional herd-book continues to diminish with breeders now satisfying requirements through biotechnology and genetic engineering.

9. 5. 4 Biotechnology and Genetic Engineering

The term biotechnology was first applied in 1919 by Karl Ereky to the use of biological processes to make useful products, though Egyptian and Sumerian production of beer and cheese by such means is recorded as early as 2000 BC. However, during the First World War the Manchester chemist Chaim Weizman (later, first president of Israel) used a fermentation process to augment acetone supplies for manufacture of high-explosives while in 1923 Pfizer (New York) compensated for fluctuations in lemon harvests by fermentation of sugar with the mould *Aspergillus niger* thus introducing the now main source of citric acid. Other important chemicals produced by biological processes include alcohol and more recently the antibiotics of which penicillin was the first. Again following the OPEC crisis of 1973 alcohol was produced as a substitute for petrol by fermenting surplus vegetative material of all kinds (by Brazil) in a process now encouraged by 'environmentalism' to produce bio-diesel instead of food even in regions of food scarcity. However, in contrast, single cell food protein marketed by ICI as 'Pruteen' is produced by applying the bacterium *Methylophilus methylotropus* to methyl alcohol at a plant capacity of 60,000 tonnes per year, while the former USSR was reputedly planning to produce 200,000 tonnes of single cell food protein from paraffins (c.f. Section 9.2.1).

Genetic engineering or modification (GM) is based on our knowledge of the role of DNA (c.f. Section 9.2.5) in the asexual reproduction of single-cell organisms. Thus, DNA double helixes in each cell separate on cell fission to daughter cells and act as templates for the synthesis (from available cell chemicals) of identical double-helixes in each of the daughter cells, the template being the sequence of nitrogen bases in the single helixes, the new double helixes being called recombinant-DNA (rDNA). Now, this natural cloning of bacterial cells through successive generations was first put to use in the comparative testing of potential drugs because any observed differences were attributable to the chemicals, the cells being identical. However, in the course of their investigations, Stanley Cohen of Stanford University and Herbert Boyer of the University of California discovered in 1971 that genetic characteristics could be transferred from one single-cell organism to another species by removing segments of DNA sequence (genes) from the one and 'spicing' them into the DNA sequence of the other. This spicing is the central technique of GM because any spliced-gene replicates through the generations. Thus, the gene which confers the capacity to produce insulin in pigs or cows, say, can be spliced into the readily propagated bacterium *Escherichia coli* to give cultures of this organism which will synthesise insulin just as those of *Penicillium notatum* synthesise penicillin. Another possibility is to confer the nitrogen-fixation of the leguminous plants to cereals to reduce their need for nitrogenous fertilisers. The first rDNA food product, engineered for resistance to softening and rotting in storage was the Flavr Savr tomato, approved by the FDA in 1994 to be followed by the end of that decade by such other GM foods as high-yield oilseed rape and pesticide-resistant soya bean variants.

Although the natural replication of single cells by the splitting and recombination of DNA is referred to as cloning, Hans Spemann suggested in 1938 that the cloning of multi-celled organisms could be achieved by intentional transfer of the entire DNA content of a cell nucleus of a donor organism to a cell of a recipient from which the nuclear material had been removed, followed by normal gestation of the latter. On this basis in 1956, Briggs and King, of the then Institute for Cancer Research in Philadelphia were able to clone a tadpole by replacing the nucleus from a frog embryo cell (recipient) with that from a donor prior to embryonic cell differentiation to skin, nerve *etc*, and in 1966 John Gurdon of Oxford produced cloned adult frogs by nuclear replacement using the intestinal cells of a tadpole as donor to demonstrate post-differentiation 'reprogramming' of cells after transfer. Thereafter, in the 1980s, the splitting of single embryo cells was introduced for livestock-breeders to parallel the natural process of identical twinning and multiple births. In the meantime, a team led by Ian Wilmut at the Roslin Institute, Edinburgh, stopped the multiplication of sheep-udder cells by nutrient deprivation for a few days, fused them with enucleated (nucleus removed) embryonic cells of another adult (six year old) sheep by means of an electric discharge, implanted the resulting embryos in surrogate ewes and after about 300 attempts announced in 1996 the birth of Dolly, the first mammal cloned successfully from an adult cell. In 1998, Dolly gave birth to a healthy lamb after a natural mating and in the same year workers at the University of Hawaii produced more than fifty cloned mice by using an ultra-fine needle to inject the nuclei of naturally dormant cumulus cells (from around the ovaries) into enucleated ova, a technique which did not require starvation for reprogramming and avoided the likelihood of damage by electrical discharge.

Though food processing and preservation techniques had changed little since the nineteenth century other than in scale, some aspects of twentieth century drying might be thought of as biotechnology. Given that the water content of food is high, that of milk being 87% and that of even solid potatoes being 80%, drying was now applied not only for preservation but also for volume reduction. To these ends, milk was caused to run over a hot roller from which the resulting crust was scraped as a powder. Again, milk and eggs were dried by spraying into a rising column of hot air from which the droplets fell out as dry powder. Such techniques were employed during the Second World War, albeit with some alteration in flavour. On the other hand, freeze-drying avoids elevated temperatures and as such was first introduced in Sweden in the 1930s to preserve various biological products such as blood plasma. The process involved placing the pre-frozen material under continuous vacuum to sublime the ice to water vapour for vacuum extraction, and its use was rapidly extended to coffee, soups and vegetables where it was found to preserve flavour. The product is light, highly stable and readily re-constituted by hydration because of its porosity. Again, sterilised ultra high temperature (UHT) milk is now available from a process which subjects milk to about 150° C for a few seconds, and which has been extended to cream, fruit juices and other liquid products. To hikers who wish to carry less weight and to those who wish to transfer elsewhere the two kilowatts consumed by the average domestic freezer, dried products commend themselves.

9. 5. 5 New Materials

Although there are few materials of the twentieth century which weren't already available in the nineteenth, their patterns of use have altered, manufacturing techniques have improved, and new material combinations have been developed, particularly in the post-war period.

As to new uses for metals, mention might be made of sodium vapour street lighting, liquid sodium coolant in nuclear reactors; aluminium and its alloys in transport applications, high tension cables, window-frames and doors, sports equipment *etc*; beryllium and its alloys for their electrical and thermal conductivity properties and in the nuclear power industry; and titanium and its alloys in the aviation and space industries. Some titanium-nickel alloys were found capable of returning to their manufactured shape if heated after deformation and such, so-called shape memory alloys (SMA), now include those of copper-aluminium-nickel, copper-zinc-aluminium and iron-manganese-silicon. Other innovations are the fusing of metals with ceramics to produce the so-called cermets which being machine-workable and highly refractory are used in jet engines, rockets and protective panels on the space shuttle while their piezoelectric properties are used in sensing and recording shock and vibration.

As to glass, Pilkington Brothers introduced the float process in 1952 whereby molten glass is allowed to flow over the surface of molten tin to produce a smooth glaze on the lower surface while continuous fire-polishing by gas-jets produced the same effect on the upper surface to eliminate the need for grinding and polishing by traditional means. In the meantime, Edouard Benedictus had produced (1905) his safety glass by sandwiching a layer of celluloid between two sheets so that, if broken, this Tripex glass cracked without splintering. However, because celluloid turned yellow with age, it was later replaced (1930s) by polyvinyl acetate. Again, low expansion coefficient borosilicate glass was introduced in the post-war period for ovenware and sealed beam headlights for cars, while there were 50,000 km of glass-fibre optical cable in the telecommunications network in Britain alone by 1985 with glass-fibre reinforced plastic now being a major construction material in boat-building, for example.

While most of the plastics and synthetic fibres now used had been available by 1939, post-war mass-production techniques for ever-larger artefacts for ever-widening uses have resulted in polymers now amounting to about 80% of the world's organic chemical production, the versatility of plastics being obvious from their use for insulation on virtually all electric cable; in the manufacture of tubes and pipes, buckets, baths, water-tanks and kitchen utensils; flowerpots, watering-cans and garden tools; paints, especially the water emulsion type; small dinghies, surfboards, sailboards and ropes; food-wrappings, blister-packs and bags. Although the polyamide, Nylon, had appeared in the USA in 1938 and the polyester Terylene had been developed by J. R. Whinfield and J. T. Dickson of the Calico Printers Association in 1941, they only became widely available in the post-war period and still dominate the market to which acrylic fibres have since been added. The advantages of synthetic fibres are that they are resistant to shrinkage and moth damage and can be set in permanent creases and drip-dried quickly. On the other hand, they soften and melt at quite low temperatures though this is the basis of their permanent-creasing. However, new dying processes had to be devised, new fibres had to be made compatible with existing textile machinery and the world of fashion had to be persuaded with respect to texture and appearance. The strategy adopted was to present the new fibres as complementary to those of the traditional cotton, wool and linen and it was found that blends proved successful in combining the best qualities of each. The new fibres have since been accepted by the carpet industry and the motor industry for tyre-walls where cotton was first replaced by rayon and then by nylon. One wonders if the members of the *Club of Rome* predicted their raw material shortages in full knowledge or total ignorance of the extent to which metals have been replaced by plastics (c.f. Section 11.2.4).

Nor did this new technology remain static, early production processes having to be improved in what was a highly competitive market. Thus, in 1953, Karl Ziegler replaced the early high pressure and high temperature production of ethylene with a less energy demanding and thus less costly catalytic process. Again, in 1954 Guilio Natta discovered that propylene could produce fibres more readily than ethylene, since when polypropylene has been widely applied in home furnishings, rope, fishing-nets and bailing-twine. In addition, though the smoothness of synthetic fibres prevents the felting achievable with the rougher fibres of wool and hair in hat and boot making, heating under compression was found to cause fibre fusion at cross-over points to form a firm 'felted' union on cooling, a melting and welding process known as melding. Notwithstanding all of the above benefits, however, there is much adverse comment on the waste disposal problems presented by plastics, these being due to their inherent resistance to the decay which destroys animal and vegetable products. The technical responses to such problems are to note the potential for recycling where this is cost-effective, otherwise to incinerate in combined heat & power systems with due regard to flue gas quality (c.f. Section 11.2.4), and to develop biodegradable plastics for use where durability need be no more than that of paper and cardboard.

9. 5. 6 Computers and Information Technology

Early calculators and machines for information storage and retrieval were still based on mechanical gear trains, punched cards and display dials when Konrad Zuse first became involved in 1934. However, by 1936 he was using the electromagnetic relays already in use in telephone exchanges, his third computer (Z3) relying solely on such relays by 1941 and his Z4 being involved in V2 rocket design. Though such electromechanical devices were an improvement, they were still so cumbersome that the Automatic Sequence Controlled Calculator (ASCO) built in 1944 by IBM and H. H. Aiken of Harvard University, weighed 5 tonnes while the Electronic Numerical Integrator and Calculator (ENIAC) of J. P. Eckert and J. W. Mauchly begun at the University of Pennsylvania in 1943 for the production of gunnery tables, contained 18,000 thermionic valves (tubes), occupied 150 square metres and consumed 100 kilowatts of electricity. In the meantime John von Neuman of Princeton and later of the University of Pennsylvania, proposed use of the base-two instead of the base-ten (c.f. Section 2.3.3) and offered his concept of the stored programme as the logic-base for all future computers, the first of which was built at the University of Manchester in 1948 and named 'Baby'. However, it was the Electronic Delay Storage Automatic Calculator (EDSAC) built by Maurice Wilkes at Cambridge in 1949 which is seen as the first operational stored programme computer put to immediate scientific use, while the Universal Automatic Computer (UNIVAC I) of 1950 intended for the US Census and predictor of Dwight D. Eisenhower's presidential election victory in 1952, is seen as the first operational computer for general business use.

Programme and data storage in 'Baby' was based on a cathode ray tube device by F. C. Williams, whereby dots could be 'written on', and 'read from' the tube screen by a moving electron beam. In the EDSAC this function was supplied by binary pulses emitted by a crystal for transmission and reflection by mercury filled metre-long tubes as suggested by Von Neumann, Eckert and Mauchly. Input to the first stored-programme machines was by strings of binary numbers and later by code-word languages for non-specialists users, these being translated to binary machine code by programmes stored within the computer by specialists. By the 1950s, as in UNIVAC I, punched-cards and punched-tape had been discontinued in favour of the magnetic tape already in use for sound-recording. Again, by the late 1950s, the expensive and energy-inefficient thermionic valve was replaced by the far cheaper, more compact, more reliable and energy-efficient transistor of 1947 of which a few were assembled as valves and a few combined as capacitors on a single support as an integrated circuit by J. St C. Kilby of Texas Instruments in 1958. From there, progress was rapid with hundreds of thousands of electronic components being assembled on a single silicon chip no more than 1cm square and with these in turn being combined to form larger units. Thus, by 1970, Gilbert Hyatt had described an integrated circuit containing all the necessary elements for a computer in registering for a US patent, and in 1971 the Intel Corporation introduced the first commercial microprocessor in which the central processing unit was located on a single chip. Thus, from being released in the early 1970s, microcomputers were adopted by small businesses in the 1980s and for home use in the 1990s and with processing speeds doubling every two years the personal computer of 2001 was 60 million times faster than the UNIVAC I of 1951. Today the gross annual turnover of the chip-based industry exceeds that of the steel industry which dominated the nineteenth century.

The means of storing information improved as processors improved with punched-card and punched-tape methods being superseded by magnetic tape which encoded data as electric charge polarity as in Jay Forrester's ferrite core memory of 1953 and the floppy discs of 1970. Charge polarity was later superseded by optical storage in which lasers write and read data inscribed as a series of tiny surface-pits as read-only-memory on a plastic compact disc (CD-ROM) to a capacity of over 5.25 billion bits (unity or zero) per disc. Again by the late 1990s, efforts were being made to store even greater amounts of data in a three-dimensional matrix on crystal or plastic by holographic means while Michael Noel and Carlos Stroud were using quantum lasers to place charges on electrons for bit storage on single atoms. Again, Japan launched a ten-year programme in 1982 to develop "fifth generation computers" and by 1991 the Institute for New Generation Computer Technology had developed the Parallel Inference Machine (PIM) which operates through logical inference alone, rather than through its numerical representation. This, in turn, led Japan to its "sixth generation computers" based on neural networks intended to simulate our own mental processes of inference, association, emotion, and capacity to learn from experience. It also led a team of US workers to create in 1999 a leech-based biological computer capable of performing simple sums by employing the ability of leech neurons to form new connections and pathways in response to electrical stimuli, the ultimate objective being the creation of self-learning computers which would not need the usual pre-programming and which might be particularly suited to pattern recognition as for identification of face, voice, and hand-writing. In addition, Alan Huang of AT&T introduced a prototype optical computer in 1990 which suggested a potential for computing speeds a thousand times faster than current speeds by using photons instead of electrons for information handling.

Again, printers having been used with computers since 1953, the development of laser printers, word-processors and visual display units (VDUs) took office typing to new levels of efficiency. In addition, desk-top publishing was introduced in the 1980s with development of software for the integration of illustrations with text and of hardware such as scanners and digital photography, while input and output devices other than the key-board and desktop VDU had been introduced by Ivan Sutherland in the form of the first light-pen and the first computer-driven head mounted display (HMD) unit of the 1960s. At the same time, specific computers were being incorporated in everything from light switches and wrist watches, through control of wholesale and retail stock, to the control of automobile engines, machine-tools, oil refineries and power-stations. In turn, these developments led through the 1980s and 90s to the use of computers to generate, graphically visualise and evaluate new engineering concepts structurally and aesthetically before physical creation, and to the fabrication of components directly from the digital file by computer-driven cutting equipment such as milling machines and lasers, or by computer-driven thickness enhancing equipment which applies successive layers of initially molten material. In parallel, it has been possible to simulate operational environments for training purposes, such as the three-dimensional graphic space, mock-cockpit, HMDs and integrated computers of the 1981 Super Cockpit Project of the US Air Force by means of which pilots and aircrew could learn to fly and fight prior to experiencing the reality, while the Virtual Interface Environment Workstation for the training and planning of space-missions was created by NASA. Since the late 1980s, the market for virtual reality (VR), equipment familiarisation and training has grown with simulators becoming simple and cheap enough for the entertainment market.

In 1945, Vannevar Bush outlined a procedure for organising and accessing data by 'associative indexing' in an article in the *Atlantic Monthly* entitled *As We May Think*. However, before this could be realised in practice, the following sequence of events was to transpire. In the 1970s specially adapted television receivers were displaying a wide range of transient information on weather forecasts, sports results, traffic conditions, stock exchange prices, radio and television programmes *etc* on 150 classified pages of the British Teletext System. By 1979 the Prestel Service enabled paying subscribers to key in *via* their telephones to a data-base of tens of thousands of pages supplied by independent contractors. Meanwhile, by 1969 the computers of several universities and government departments had been linked by the Advanced Research Projects Agency of the US Department of Defence into the ARPA net. The next developments were a system for sending electronic mail (email) across a distributed network in 1971; the establishment of an international link between University College London and the Norwegian Royal Radar Establishment in 1973; the establishment of satellite links across two oceans and release of the first public data service, Telenet in 1974; creation by the University of Essex of the first Multi-User Dimension (MUD) which enabled several users to interact simultaneously in a text-based space in 1979; the coining of the word 'internet' to refer to a connected set of networks in 1982; and initiation of World, the first commercial provider of Internet dialup access in 1990. The stage was now set for Tim Berners-Lee of the European Laboratory for Particle Physics to achieve Vannevar Bush's 'associative indexing' with his Hypertext Transfer Protocol (HTTP). This tagged information so that it could be accessed without its location being known, thus enabling the 'browser' interface Mosaic, released by the National Centre for Supercomputing Applications in 1993, to create the world wide web (www) for which the early stage expansion rate was 341,000% per annum.

Meanwhile, telecommunication technology was itself developing with the gradual change in sound signal coding from modulation of electric current in copper wires to laser-generated light pulses in flexible glass filaments. Thus, electronic exchanges initially introduced by Bell Telephones of Illinois in 1960 quickly spread to permit more rapid connections and the automatic logging of calls and charges while the first satellite relay station, Telstar, was launched in 1962, with growth in demand necessitating the laying of eight metallic submarine cables across the Atlantic between 1956 and 1976 to cope with about 4,000 simultaneous calls before the first glass fibre cable was laid in 1988. However, developments in radio and television could only be introduced as other developments permitted and as customers up-dated their equipment. Thus, while the transition from radio signal-carrying by amplitude modulation to frequency modulation had arisen in 1933 from Edwin Armstrong's efforts to reduce 'static', its commercial broadcasting debut was post-war because it was suitable only for very high frequency (VHF) transmissions over limited areas. Again, while transistors became increasingly available from the mid-1950s for the miniaturisation of radios, the dimensions of the cathode ray tube prevented size reduction in television receivers until Matsushita introduced liquid-crystal display in 1979. As to picture quality, the pre-war 405-line picture continued into the 1960s before being replaced by the much sharper 625-line picture and phased alternate line (PAL) signal, while the USA and Japan still retain a 525-line picture and NTSC signal. Yet again, while high definition television (HDTV) has been available since the early 1990s, customer reluctance to up-grade their receivers necessitates the continued broadcasting of low and high resolution signals, though plans are now afoot in several countries for a total transition to HDTV.

9. 5. 7 Military Technology

Though the international scientific community was aware of the prospect of fission energy release at the start of hostilities in 1939, it was a high-level committee set up by the British government and code-named MAUD which concluded that a bomb requiring about 10kg of ^{235}U was feasible. At that time the USA was unfocused as to prospects for electricity generation, ship-propulsion, or weaponry while French preference for the first of these options had to be abandoned in the summer of 1940. Again, while Pyotr Kapitsa had worked under Rutherford prior to 1935, neither Russia nor Germany had resources to spare for such development after the invasion of the former by the latter in 1941. On the other hand, the US response to the Pearl Harbour attack in December 1941 was to devote its unequalled technical-industrial resources to the Manhattan Project which though launched only in June 1942 had tested a uranium bomb by 16 July 1945, had detonated such a device over Hiroshima on 6 August 1945 and three days later a plutonium version over Nagasaki.

Though Fermi had demonstrated the neutron based chain-reaction and its control for natural uranium in his atomic pile of 1942, it was known that the instantaneous energy release needed for a bomb would require enrichment of the ^{235}U content of natural uranium; that such enrichment could only be achieved by physical means, isotopes of any one element being chemically identical; and that such enrichment could not be allowed to reach the critical stage for self-detonation before the intended target was reached. These requirements were ultimately satisfied by preparing uranium hexafluoride, a volatile compound for which the mass difference between ^{235}UF$_6$ and ^{238}UF$_6$ results in a density ratio of 1:1.0086, which according to Graham's Law would result in a differential rate

323

of gas diffusion sufficient to provide progressive enrichment of $^{235}UF_6$ and hence of ^{235}U, were a suitable cascade of diffusion membranes to be available. As to criticality, the rate of neutron escape from a spherical mass is proportional to its surface-area, while the rate of neutron production by fission is proportional to its volume, and because the ratio of surface-area to volume decreases as volume increases, there must be a volume at which neutrons will be produced faster than they can escape, this volume corresponding to the critical mass. For the Hiroshima bomb one sub-critical mass of ^{235}U was fired into a prepared hollow in another sub-critical mass, and for the Nagasaki bomb a hollow sphere of ^{239}Pu (c.f. Section 9.5.1) was rendered critical by a focussed compressive force produced by detonation of a surrounding arrangement of fast and slow explosive charges. Though the first atomic bomb (equivalent to 20,000 tonnes of TNT) was tested in the desert 100km south of its development location at Los Alamos on 16 July 1945, Edward Teller had suggested the possibility of a hydrogen bomb as early as 1942. However, the temperatures required for the fusion of hydrogen to helium (c.f. Section 9.1.4) could only be achieved by prior explosion of a fission bomb, such a combined device being unavailable until the Eniwetok Atoll test of 1 November 1952.

Though the two atomic bombs had been dropped from B-29 bombers and remotely detonated by radio a short distance above the ground, the technology of rocketry had been developing throughout the century. In 1903 Konstantin Tsiolkovsky of the University of Kaluga had extended his observations in the upper atmosphere with his multi-stage principle which minimised weight by discarding empty fuel tanks. Herman Oberth was active in Germany from the 1920s and the German Rocket Society was founded in 1927. From the 1930s the Pennemunde Experimental Station was operational, from where by 1942 Wernher von Braun had produced the liquid-fuelled A-4 with a range of 200 km and a speed of 6,000 km per hour, and by 1944 some 2000 V-2s had been stock-piled before London and Antwerp were attacked. In the meantime, for his meteorological studies, Robert H. Goddard of Clark University Massachusetts had begun to use liquid-fuelled rockets in 1935, after which tactical rocketry produced the US Firebird air-to-air missile (AAM), the British Rapier surface-to-air missile (SAM), the USSR versions used in the Middle East some ten years later in 1973, the French Exocet ship-to-ship missile (SSM) of 1971, and the US Tomahawk cruise missile of the 1970s. As to the serial production of strategic inter-continental ballistic missiles (ICBMs) the SS-6 launched the Sputnik (satellite) in 1957 and sent Yuri Gagarin into space in 1961 and by the mid 1980s the SS-18 could carry multiple megaton war heads over a range of 12,000 km, while the US response was the Thor missile of 1958, the 3000 km range of which was insufficient to reach the USSR from US homeland-bases. However, ten years later, the US Saturn Rocket put the first men on the Moon with its escape velocity of 40,000km per hour.

Meantime, the USSR and Britain had detonated their first atomic bombs in 1949 and 1952 respectively, and their first hydrogen bombs in 1953 and 1956 respectively. Today, the nuclear powers are the USA, Britain, France, Russia, China, India, Pakistan, North Korea (and Israel?). In 1963, faced with the prospect of further nuclear proliferation and increasing access to rocket based means of delivery, the USA, Britain, the USSR and (later) 49 other states signed a Treaty banning the testing of nuclear weapons in the atmosphere, outer space and underwater with a view to reducing the possibility of nuclear war. However, underground tests which contain radioactive fallout were permitted under the Treaty to enable existing nuclear powers to retain a test-capability and to allow for possible civil-engineering applications such as in accessing geothermal energy (c.f. Section 9.5.1). As to ship propulsion, the nuclear option offered freedom of operations without reliance on fuelling ports, fleet refuelling vessels or the resurfacing of submarines for battery re-charging. Accordingly, the USA launched its first nuclear submarine, *Nautilus*, in 1955 and by the
324

1980s the USA and USSR each had over one hundred such submarines while Britain and France had about two dozen which with virtually unlimited cruising ranges could be armed with nuclear missiles such as Polaris and Trident. The USA also built nuclear-powered aircraft carriers and the USSR launched a nuclear-powered ice-breaker, *Lenin*, in 1958.

As to conventional weapons and counter-measures, hydrophones had been developed in the First World War to enable submarines to detect surface ships by engine noise and *vice versa*, which by the 1920s had led to the emission and return of pulsed ultrasonic signals to reveal the position of depth-charge targets, such devices later being used to survey seabed topography and to locate wrecks and shoals of fish. Again, passive detectors were towed at various depths to analyse sounds produced by hostile vessels. On the other hand, the high speed and manoeuvrability of aircraft made them much more difficult to detect and attack successfully, though reflection of radio-waves was implicit in the 1880s work of Heinrich Hertz and their possible detection was implicit in the electromagnetic range-finding patented by Christian Hulsmeyer in 1904, by Marconi's radio-location work at sea in the 1920s and by the incidental detection of radiation-echo from landing aircraft by aerodrome radio-operators. Again, by the 1930s there was parallel discussion of 'death rays' and when the Air Ministry consulted Robert Watson-Watt in 1935 as to the possible use of radio-waves to this end, he proposed using them to detect approaching aircraft, the first such being duly detected at a range of 50km on 11 June 1935. Thus, by 1939-40 Britain had a 20 minute early-warning system capable of detecting incoming aircraft travelling at 500km per hour at a range of 150-160 km. In addition, details of Henri Gutton's magetron radio-wave generator of 1934 were passed from France to wartime Britain where the cavity magnetron was developed as a powerful source of cm-wavelength radiation specifically for radar applications, though such radiation has more recently been used to vibrate food and beverage molecules in the microwave oven.

Since the Second World War, great strides have been made in computers, pattern-recognition, satellite-communication and global-positioning systems all of which have been put to military targeting, guidance and tracking purposes with continuing improvement in the accuracy of missile and bomb attacks. Again, bombs can be dropped on target in conditions of zero visibility, missiles can be remotely guided to targets from increasingly greater distances, and 'stealth' aircraft can fly in high security from radar detection and attack. In addition, tactical missiles can fly close to the surface of sea or land to avoid radar detection and hit their targets with precision while strategic missiles can be precisely targeted at intercontinental ranges. On the defensive side, such missiles can be detected and destroyed even at near-space altitudes long before they would reach their intended targets, a (threatened) defence capability which terminated the cold-war and which if implemented with respect to minor or aspirant nuclear powers, might be similarly dissuasive. Thus, this growing defence capability is of inestimable value in controlling the strategic belligerence of others, while the growing precision of tactical weaponry enables collateral damage to be limited wherever offensive operations against belligerent movements are otherwise unavoidable.

Again, computerised battlefield simulations can immerse real trainee tank crews and infantry in virtual-reality situations involving simulated enemies who respond autonomously, these simulations having been compiled from real battle-data collected from operational sensors in the field such as radar, infrared, GPS and satellite imagery of contested ground, all of which provide experience of action and reaction from the point of view of any of the combatants within it. In addition, the personal status monitor PSM collects, transmits and centrally collates information on location and life-state (heart and respiration rate) of individual soldiers and reports on the location of wounds from the detection of damage to the 'smart' uniform which is part of the PSM package. However, reliance by the military on IT in conducting actual operations opens the possibility of jamming and corrupting enemy IT systems while efforts to secure information superiority over the enemy will not only allow the spread of military disinformation, but also that of civil disinformation on opposing home-fronts. However, it will also enable political establishments to spread disinformation within their electorates in ways not previously available to them.

9. 5. 8 Civil Aviation and Shipping

Though aviation in the First World War and the trans-Atlantic flight of J. Alcock and A. W. Brown in 1919 had established the possibility of commercial air transport, operating costs were high in comparison with traditional rail and ship borne alternatives. However, because of the proven military benefits of aircraft, many governments felt obliged to subsidise civil aircraft operations to provide additional support for manufacturers. In any case, by the time the Dutch KLM was founded in 1919 and the British Imperial Airways in 1924, there were already four US domestic operators of which Pan American was already in competition with Europe. Moreover, a growing market for private flying in fabric covered two-seater aircraft was evidence of an interest which might one day be militarily useful. Thus, over 2000 de Havilland British Moths of 1925 were built for sale at £650 only to be superseded by 10,000 Tiger Moths. In the meantime, duralumin, an aluminium-magnesium-copper alloy previously used for Zeppelin frames, had been used for airframe cladding by Hugo Junkers in the last year of World War I and for his F13, the first commercial civil aircraft in 1919. This cladding was integrally stressed in the 1920s to enhance the strength of wings and fuselage and by the 1930s civil aircraft had comfortably appointed passenger cabins as in the 30-seat DC-3 of 1935 *et seq.* and in the Lockheed XC-35 of 1937 while the Boeing Stratoliner of 1939 had pressurised cabins enabling it to fly at 6000m (twice the height of its predecessors) for improved fuel economy, lower turbulence and greater comfort.

As to power units, the 200kg per horsepower of the first Otto engines of the 1880s had been improved to 6kg per hp for the Wright Brothers' flight of 1903. Thereafter, the best pre-war performance was the 1.5 kg per hp of Laurent Seguin's Gnome while the USA achieved the best performance of the war with the 1 kg per hp of the V-12 Liberty engine, though it took another 25 years for the Wright Cyclone engines of the B-29 bombers of 1944 to reach 0.5 kg per hp. Latterly, piston engines had three cooling options, these being the water-cooled linear engine of motor vehicles and the air-cooled rotary and radial engines of aircraft. In rotary engines, such as the Gnome, the whole engine and propeller rotated about a fixed crank-shaft while in the radial the cylinders were arranged in a circle around the crank-shaft, the latter option being preferable for larger units. This option culminated in the Wright Cyclone engine having 28 cylinders arranged in four circles of seven developing 2,200 horsepower, four of which powered the B-29. Thus immediately post-war, the USA could offer the world's airlines the Lockheed Constellation, the Douglas DC-4 and the Boeing Stratocruiser, all of which were based on the B-29 with Lockheed and Douglas both offering successive stretched-fuselage versions without new design costs.

The first jet-propelled airliner, the de Havilland Comet of 1949, was therefore a response to the earlier US superiority. Unfortunately, this aircraft was dogged by metal-fatigue from 1952 onwards and when re-commissioned in 1958 for trans-Atlantic service by BOAC, it was in competition with the Boeing 707 and Douglas DC-8, the larger capacity, higher speed, and greater range of which rendered it obsolete. Although there was continuing demand for relatively small aircraft for short flights, such as the Vickers 10 successor to the Comet, it was clear by the 1960s that economic considerations favoured large wide-bodied high seat-capacity aircraft such as the Boeing 747. These Jumbo aircraft were made possible by the turbo-fan engine (a hybrid of the jet and turbo-prop) which delivered the thrust necessary for takeoff and safe landing with reduced fuel consumption and less pollution, positive features which were enhanced yet again in the 1990s by the Boeing 777 with two improved engines replacing the previous four, longer range and greater cabin space on smaller external dimensions through use of new light-weight materials. In contrast, though an impressive technical success with its Mach-2 speed the Concorde failed to be fully viable, all its competitors and replacements being based on the large wide-bodied option.

In addition, the twentieth century has produced entirely new transport technologies. Thus, in 1936 Heinrich Focke introduced his prototype helicopter with two counter-rotating propellers to prevent the fuselage from rotating in flight, followed by his six-seat version in 1940. Meanwhile, in the USA Igor Sikorsky who had been involved since 1909 produced his prototype single-rotor helicopter stabilised by the now familiar small tail-rotor, while Juan de la Cierva introduced his autogyro of which several hundred were built without general acceptance being achieved. On the other hand, despite its relatively slow speed, high fuel consumption and maintenance costs the helicopter's unique hovering and manoeuvrability make it indispensable in many civil and military services, such features having been incorporated in the British Jump-Jet by alterable direction of jet thrust. A further extension of fixed-wing flight is the hydrofoil in which the movement of small wings (foils) through water provides lift sufficient to raise a boat's hull out of the water as it gains forward motion to avoid hull friction and enable higher speeds for less fuel consumption, the first commercial hydrofoil service having been on the Rhine in 1937. In addition, Christopher Cockerel's air-cushioned hovercraft achieved its first Channel crossing in 1959 on the 50th anniversary of Bleriot's first aircraft crossing.

Though, passenger liners lost their trade to civil aviation in the post-war period, their use for cruising opened a specialist market for ships of this type, while more than 80% of world freight and 95% of UK-world freight continued to be transported by sea in a wide range of other specialist ships such as roll-on/roll-off ferries, containerships, refrigerated ships, bulk carriers for minerals and tank-ships for crude oil, refinery products, chemicals and pressurised gas. However, such cruising and transportation produces wastes which need proper handling. Thus, the ballast water required for stability of oil tankers on empty passage to the loading port must not be contaminated with oil cargo residues when discharged on arrival. To this end the tanks required for ballast loading are washed with crude oil to re-dissolve all residues including waxes and all such oil and subsequent water washings are transferred to a tank into which the next cargo is loaded on top of the washings for total discharge to the refinery in what is known as the load-on-top (LOT) system. More recently, the potentially deleterious ecological effects of transferring marine organisms from one biological zone to another have been addressed by developing ballast treatment systems which kill them on the ballast passage. Again, the tanks of chemical carriers are water-washed prior to ballast loading or to avoid cross-cargo contamination, the washings being discharged to waste-reception facilities onshore as required by their toxicity levels. Furthermore, oil/water mixtures from machinery-space bilges of all ships can be discharged to the sea only after passage through specially designed oil-water separators, the oil being retained for later discharge to waste-oil reception facilities onshore. Yet again, equipment is installed for onboard treatment of cruise-ship generated sewage and other domestic waste waters, and for grinding and compacting solid domestic wastes to save space prior to discharge to shore-reception. In addition, the sulphur content of heavy fuel oils is regulated and technology is now abating oxides of nitrogen in exhaust emissions, sails are under consideration where winds are voyage-favourable and non-toxic anti-fouling paints have been introduced (c.f. Section 11.2.4).

9. 5. 9 Space Exploration

The thrust of ICBMs eventually became large enough to put an object into orbit round the Earth as was first achieved by the USSR with Sputnik 1 on 4 October 1957, followed by the dog Laika in November 1957, two dogs launched and retrieved in August 1960, and the first cosmonaut Yuri

Gagarin on 12 April 1961. In response, the US Apollo Programme landed Neil Armstrong and Buzz Aldrin on the Moon on 21 July 1969 (Apollo 15) and achieved several hundred lunar man-hours in five more Apollo missions between then and 1972. In all, there were 73 unmanned and manned lunar missions between 1958 and 1975 not all of which were successful and of which 40 were mounted by the USA. Of the successful missions we may note the acquisition of photographs of the far side of the moon by the USSR on 4 October 1959 (2nd anniversary of Sputnik 1), photographs of possible lunar landing sites from Rangers 7, 8 and 9 by the USA in July 1964, the soft landing in the Ocean of Storms by Luna 9 by the USSR in January 1966, the photographs obtained from the US series of Surveyor landings between 1966 and 1968 in planning for the manned landing, the Luna 16 landing by the USSR in the Sea of Fertility on 20 September 1970 which collected lunar samples and returned them to Earth, the delivery by Luna 17 in November 1970 of an eight-wheeled solar-powered remote-controlled vehicle which traversed over 10km while sampling and photographing the lunar surface and measuring cosmic ray intensity, and the delivery by the USA of a similar moon-buggy which travelled nearly four times as far and sent back nearly 10,000 photographs in 1971 prior to the delivery of the manned moon-buggy to extend the range of the two astronauts of Apollo 15 in 1972.

As to unmanned probes to the planets, the US Mariner 2 passed within 35,000km of Venus in June 1963 to photograph an atmosphere of dense cloud and passed within 10,000km of Mars to photograph an arid surface with features somewhat different from the Moon. Again, Mariner 9 had orbited Mars for nearly a year by November 1970 and taken more than 7000 photographs which included the volcano Olympus three times higher than Mount Everest, while on 20 July 1976 (the 7th anniversary of the manned moon landing) Viking 1 after a 12-month journey went into orbit round Mars and released a landing capsule which sent photographs back to Earth and undertook soil analyses, while three months later Viking 2 repeated these operations at a different location. Neither of these landings having obtained evidence for life on Mars, they were followed by a landing of the Sojourner Rover on 4 July 1997 which found evidence for the existence of water between 3 and 4.5 billion years ago while remaining operational for twelve times its designed lifetime of seven days. Again, on October 1975 the USSR landed two units at widely separated locations on Venus to transmit pictures of a barren rock-strewn surface for nearly an hour at atmospheric pressures a hundred times higher than on Earth and temperatures above 100° C.

Meanwhile, in 1974 Mariner 10 had closed with Venus for a 'sling-shot' boost from its gravitational field to send it on to Mercury form where at an altitude of 300km it transmitted thousands of pictures of a surface similar to that of the Moon. Again, in 1990 Magellan reached Venus to transmit extremely detailed topographical data obtained through the cloud cover by radar. Previously in 1973 and 1974, Pioneers 10 and 11 had made close passes of Jupiter to be accelerated by its gravitational field for the former to become the first manmade object to leave the solar system and for the latter to be boosted onwards to survey Saturn. Again, in March and July 1979 two Voyager spacecraft launched in 1977 directly observed the four moons of Jupiter first observed by Galileo and discovered three more. In all, the Voyager missions discovered 22 new moons (satellites) in the solar system including these three for Jupiter, three for Saturn, ten for Uranus and six for Neptune.

Meanwhile the USSR established the first of its Salyut space laboratories in 1971 by which two astronauts had completed a record 139 days in orbit by 1978 whereas the first US Skylab of 1973 reached orbit with damage to its heat-shield, loss of one of its solar panels and a failure of the other to open which required despatch of a two-man crew to repair the damage and restore power. Thereafter this Skylab was manned for a total of only 172 days before it suffered final burn-up on re-entering the Earth's atmosphere. In February 1986 Salyut and Skylab were superseded by MIR 1 to facilitate cooperation between the USA and USSR in making observations from outside our atmosphere and in investigating the effects of weightlessness on physicochemical and physiological processes, for which latter Yuri V. Romanenko completed a record 326 days in space in 1987. Thus, between February 1984 and June 1998 the US Space Shuttle made eleven missions to Mir 1, this Shuttle being a spacecraft/rocket combination of which all the elements other than the liquid fuel tank are reusable. Thus, the boosters are parachuted into the Atlantic for recovery and reuse while the Shuttle itself, after completing its space-mission re-enters the atmosphere to glide back to its base and land like a conventional aircraft at around 300km per hour for re-servicing in about two weeks within a design life of about a hundred round trips. It has accommodation for up to ten persons though the normal crew was seven and a cargo bay nearly 20metres long. Fully laden it weighs 115 tonnes of which 39 tonnes is cargo in contrast to the 6 tonnes total weight of Vostok 1 which immobilised Yuri Gagarin in the tiny cabin of 1961. Aside from manned laboratories various pieces of equipment have been placed in orbit to investigate electromagnetic phenomena beyond the obscuring effects of the atmosphere of which the best known is perhaps the Hubble Space Telescope for studying the evolution of the universe as revealed by the visible, ultraviolet and near infrared spectra from deep space, the initial defects of which were rectified by a Shuttle visit in December 1993.

Japan launched OSUMI its first satellite for scientific purposes in 1970, its first geo-stationary satellite in 1977, and initiated development of its H1 rocket in 1977 for replacement of its N1 by 1986. However, the USA and USSR had by 1984 accounted for about 96% of the 3,000 satellites launched, 80% of which were for scientific purposes and the rest for communications and weather forecasting while the European Space agency's Ariane 1 was only just beginning to show satellite launch performance. For the purposes of maintaining the desired directional requirements of sensors and antennae, satellites were first spun on their axis as a gyroscope while orientation was later maintained by the triple-axial spinning of three flywheels as in the first US geo-stationary satellite ATS-6 of 1974 or by the spinning of a single internal gyroscope. Again, following the tragic Apollo launch of January 1986 in which all seven astronauts died, Shuttle flights were resumed with the re-designed Discovery rocket on 29 September 1988 and the erection of an international space station commenced in 2000 for completion in 2004, this entailing the delivery of some hundred components by some forty-five Shuttle or rocket launches to construct the accommodation necessary for six working crew within overall dimensions of 110 x 88 metres.

In the meantime, observation of the universe from earth had been given a new dimension when Karl Jansky of Bell Telephones detected radio waves from outer space in 1931. Thus, many post-war dish-antennae (radio-telescopes) were erected such as the 80 metre diameter steerable dish built at Jodrell Bank in 1957; the 350 metre diameter immobile Arecibo dish in the bowl of an extinct volcano in Puerto Rico which scans the sky as the earth moves; and the very long baseline array (VLBA) consisting of ten 25 metre parabolic dishes distributed over the 8,000km from Hawaii to the Virgin Islands, the resolving-power of which is a thousand times greater than the most powerful optical telescopes.

9. 6 CONCLUSIONS

It was concluded in Chapters 5 and 6 that craft-like correction of classical beliefs increased in confidence before experimentation reached its then seventeenth century high point in Newton's application of its results to the Earth-Moon system. Thereafter, Chapter 7 concluded that this new scientific method of reality-evaluation of hypotheses by experimentation had by 1900 reduced all material substance to ninety-two elements and transformed all "imponderables" to interchangeable forms of energy; that it extended craft knowledge in the provision of physical welfare to self-sustaining technology to this end; and that it provided descriptive astronomy, earth sciences and biology with deeper knowledge of mechanism at the level of atoms, molecules and cells as described in Chapter 8.

It may now be concluded from Chapter 9 that scientific method from 1900 provided knowledge on particle/energy interaction, particle/wave duality, four-dimensional space-time, atomic and nuclear structure, the chemical bond and its role in organic processes and biological evolution; that this physicochemical knowledge has explained, from the Big Bang plus 10^{-44} seconds, the evolution of galaxies, stars, elements and planets including the Earth with its geological and climatic changes and consequences for life; and that it has continued through technology to satisfy all market demands and opportunities for physical welfare enhancement while taking us to the Moon and sending our equipment to the planets and beyond. Nonetheless, having regard to Sections 2.5, 3.3, Chapter 4 and Section 6.4, it may also be concluded that our knowledge-based success as reviewed in Chapters 6, 7, 8 and 9 remains vulnerable to belief-based disruption of the social cohesion on which these successes depend; that these successes themselves encourage our Ur-belief in rationality to ignore the experimentation underlying Newton's success, to speculate on biological evolution without experimentation and to ignore the concern of craftsmen and technologists for the environment; and that while knowledge suspends belief pending reality-evaluation, belief seeks consensus oxymoronic to knowledge when belief is emotionally preferred.

Thus, we may conclude that our increasing knowledge did not prevent irreconcilable beliefs from causing the Peloponnesian War, the Fall of Rome nor any subsequent eruptions of belief-driven mayhem; that we remain vulnerable to such beliefs whether religious or secular; and that our knowledge has come from belief in essences, spirits and 'the music of the spheres' to the vibration of strings in eleven dimensions without transforming our religious Ur-belief to knowledge but with our Ur-belief in knowledge approaching its intuitive limit. On the other hand, we may conclude that our knowledge is now vastly beyond our initial survival requirements and speculations; that from this vantage we could free ourselves from conflict-inducing beliefs by differentiating science from pseudo-science and knowledge from belief; that as to the former, we need only note the presence or absence of experimentation or the use or non-use of its results, while as to the latter, we need only note where belief has been reality-validated, lacks reality-validation, has been reality-refuted by implementation or needs reality-evaluation prior to implementation; and that we could do so knowing that the reality-evaluation of scientific method is the reality-evaluation of commonsense. As to identifying the remaining obstacles to this replacement of belief with knowledge, I now offer my critique of philosophy.

CHAPTER 10 CRITIQUE OF PHILOSOPHY

Chapters 1-3 showed that the Rational Trinity had produced the craftsmanship and behaviour codes which sustained socio-political systems prior to the Fall of Rome; and that knowledge of the nature of the world was acquired through observation and craft-based mathematics until terminated by the inconvenience of the number-system and by the speculation and belief which did not differentiate knowledge from belief. Chapter 4 then showed that intellectual effort was thus diverted to reinterpretation of Pagan and Christian beliefs through the Rational Duality and to conflicts between orthodoxy and heresy detrimental to socio-political cohesion. Chapters 5 and 6 then showed that despite being undifferentiated from belief, knowledge was increasing through resumption of observation aided by the Hindu number system; that Roman Christianity gave rise to the Reformation and Feudalism to the Age of Revolution in which classical rationality was resurrected in the so-called Enlightenment to oppose religious 'irrationality'; and that three sets of believers were now equally opposed to belief resolution by reality-evaluation despite its success in hypothesis resolution as shown in Chapters 6, 7, 8 and 9 and despite the failure of rationality to resolve differences in socio-political beliefs as shown in Chapter 4 and Section 6.4.

Thus, while the Greeks did not invent rationality, they were certainly not alone then or since in failing to differentiate knowledge from belief, the religious believing their behaviour codes to be God-given, the secular believing them to be irrational belief and neither submitting them or their secular alternatives to reality-evaluation. Again, Chapter 3 showed that the rationality which caused the Greeks to search for Truth from premises which to them could not be otherwise were simply recycling belief rather than acquiring knowledge; that their confidence in rationality arose from their mistaken belief in mathematics as pure rationality; that this caused them to develop the *Rules of Logic* to ensure mathematical certainty for all their premise-derived conclusions; that they thus eschewed as uncertain the (reality-evaluating) sense-perception which had in fact secured the axioms of mathematics though alas not always the premises of their logical arguments; and that despite this aversion to sense-perception, they relied on unacknowledged reality-evaluation in their craftsmanship, their observation-based descriptions of the natural world and the empirical content of their ethics and political philosophy.

However, despite the Rational Trinity having been the source of all progress from time immemorial, adherents of the Rational Duality subdivided philosophy into *Metaphysics* which sought certainty by rationality alone; *Epistemology* (the Theory of Knowledge) which sought to clarify the nature of the knowledge thus acquired; and *Ethics, Philosophy of Politics* and *Philosophy of Religion* all of which sought purely rational justification for behaviour codes, systems of government and religious beliefs and practices. Nonetheless, with reference to my definitions in Chapter 1, this Chapter now shows that metaphysics and epistemology are derivatives of the Ur-beliefs of religion and rationality; that philosophy of religion derives from these though it touches on the reality of human nature; that ethics, political philosophy and political economy should be pursued as science; that philosophers who turn to the social-sciences have to decide whether they are philosophers who produce no knowledge or scientists who could were they to submit their beliefs to reality-evaluation; that those who profess economics are currently too influenced by political belief to be other than pseudo-scientists; that ethicists who turn to psychology are pseudo-scientists unless they adopt reality-evaluation; that without reality-evaluation the designation social-science is no more than an unwarranted allusion to science; and that the sociological definition of science as refutable and variable is a self-revealing definition of pseudo-science as explified in Chapter 11.

However, before reviewing the subdivisions of philosophy in the light of the above, it is useful to review the Rules of Logic which ensure consistency of conclusions with premises, though readers should recall that these rules are inherent to craftsmanship, science and technology which unlike philosophy have the added security of submitting their premises (hypotheses), arguments and conclusions to reality-evaluation. Again, recalling the success of scientific method from the seventeenth century onwards, readers may be astonished at the tardiness with which philosophers rejected reliance on rationality alone, the alacrity with which they resurrected it, the degree to which they now support it with the irrationality of pseudo-science, and their continuing failure to accept logic and mathematics as being only internally consistent and requiring reality-validation for consistency of premise or conclusion with reality. In thus reviewing philosophy, I leave the consequences of reality-rejection to Chapter 11

10. 1 LOGIC

Logic has developed as a distinct discipline over the last 2,500 years, though the so-called Rules of Logic (reasoning) thus codified are as innate as our rationality itself. To the philosopher, however, reasoning is the process which brings us to a true premise and from a true premise to a true conclusion or the process of using evidence to support a conclusion already believed to be true. To the scientist, in contrast, such a logic train will inevitably lead to an erroneous conclusion if the premise, the reasoning or the adduced evidence is wrong, *i.e.* reality-refutable. The discipline of logic is, therefore, that which ensures valid reasoning, whatever else may be wrong and because premises, reasoning and conclusions are expressed in language, logic deals with the relationship between sentences (propositions or assertions) in a process of reasoning (argument) in which the truth of the concluding proposition is inferred from the truth of previous propositions which constitute the evidence for the conclusion. At this point, the similarity to mathematics is clear in that the successive equations of mathematical reasoning are symbolic sentences each stating that one mathematical expression is equal to another, the equality being impossible to dispute, though philosophers never seem to understand this mathematical meaning of 'equality' as I shall show.

Now, inductive and deductive logic must be distinguished. The former establishes conclusive inferences by ensuring that where the reasoning is valid the inference must be valid while the latter attempts to establish the probable validity of inferences for which the evidence is not conclusive. Thus, inductive logic draws particular inferences from general propositions while deductive logic draws general inferences from particular propositions. Clearly if a proposition or assertion can be made of a whole class of things, it can with 100% certainty be made of some of them while a proposition or assertion which can be made of only some of them cannot be made of all of them other than with < 100% certainty. At this point, we see that reality-evaluation argues general conclusions from particular experiences whether in craftsmanship, science, technology or human behaviour codification, all such knowledge being logically deductive, while individual mathematical conclusions from general axioms are logically inductive; and that philosophers from classical times onwards, have been much attracted to the certainty of inductive logic (c.f. Chapter 3) in their pursuit of what they mistakenly refer to as 'absolute truth'.

Indeed, we have already noted Aristotle's contribution to the syllogism in which two propositions or assertions are the premises which if true the third which is the conclusion must be true, the reasoning having progressed from the general to the particular. Thus, for example, the statements that all men are mortal, Socrates is a man, therefore Socrates is mortal, may be used to exemplify the difference between inductive and deductive logic. At first sight, this argument appears to be inductively 100% valid and as with all such arguments from the general to the particular, its conclusive certainty arises from the conclusion having been contained in the premise. However, further consideration reveals that the conclusion in this example is less certain than rigorous inductive logic requires while Socrates or anyone else still lives. It is certain to a very high degree of probability, however, being based on the (reality-validated) observation that all men previously alive are now dead. Yet, the rigorous inductive logician cannot assert that all men now living will die and he would insist that the above conclusion is an example of the deductive logic of science, craftsmanship and technology of which he at least formally disapproves. Indeed it is that which makes him a philosopher and not any of the other three.

However, in proceeding with logic, it should be noted that each of the propositions of the syllogism consists of four parts (words); that each proposition begins with a quantifier, (all, some, one, no, none, nothing); and that each must contain a word as subject (the subject term) about which an assertion is made, a predicate term which designates that which is asserted of the subject and a copula which connects subject to predicate (some form of the verb 'to be'); and that when such is the case the syllogism is in the standard form. Again, though sentences can be in the grammatical forms of proposition, assertion, question, command or wish, logic deals only with propositions or assertions these alone being either valid or invalid in either their affirmation or denial of something or other. Yet again, the quality of a proposition is whether it is affirmative or negative while its quantity refers to whether it is universal, particular or singular *i.e.* whether it refers to all, some or one, singulars being treated as universals because an assertion about an individual is universal for that individual. Again, a term is distributed when it refers to universals, is undistributed when it refers to particulars, every proposition or assertion being either universal or particular and either affirmative or negative. Thus, there are only four possible types of proposition in need of logical analysis with universal affirmative, universal negative, particular affirmative and particular negative being designated A, E, I, O respectively from which it follows that for propositions of type A the subject term is distributed and the predicate term undistributed; for type E both are distributed; for I both are undistributed; and for O the subject term is undistributed and the predicate is distributed. Again, the terms are defined as M (middle) when it appears in both premises, P (major) when it appears as the predicate of the conclusion and subject of the first premise and S (minor) when it is the subject of the second premise and of the conclusion, each of the three appearing twice. In summary, we have all M are P: all S are M: therefore, all S are P.

We are now able to state that if a syllogism complies with all of five rules its conclusion is valid and that if it violates any of these rules it is invalid. The rules of quantity are that the middle term must be distributed at least once and that if a term is not distributed in the premises, it must not be distributed in the conclusion. Again, the rules of quality are that no conclusion can follow from two negative premises, that if either premise is negative the conclusion must be negative, and that a negative conclusion cannot follow from two affirmative premises. In order to apply these rules to ensure that no error of reasoning has occurred or to identify where it has occurred, it is necessary to transcribe the language of everyday speech into the form of the standard A, E, I, O propositions of formal logic for which rules A to I have been formulated.

Thus, rules A to D inclusive are to identify clearly the subject and predicate of the sentence to be transcribed, to supply the missing quantifier, to add the missing complement to an adjective or adjectival phrase to clarify that they refer to noun classes and to supply the implied copula. Thus, 'dogs bark' becomes 'all dogs are barking animals'. Again, rules E to G deal with exclusion, negatives and exceptions. Thus sentences containing 'only' and 'none but' are transcribed by 'all' with interchange of the subject and predicate terms, sentences containing 'nothing', 'none' or 'no one' are given the quantifier 'no' while sentences containing the word 'except' cannot exactly be transcribed into any one of the propositions A, E, I, O. Thus: 'nothing human frightens me' becomes 'no human beings are things which frighten me' and 'everyone except children may attend' becomes either: 'all who are not children may attend' or 'no children may attend', the first being an A proposition and the second an E, any such sentence being valid as one or the other. Again, rule H deals with sentences containing 'anyone', 'anything', 'whoever', 'the', 'if . . . then' or 'whatever' by transcribing them by 'all'. Thus, 'anyone who comes must participate' becomes 'all (persons) who come must participate'. Finally, rule I states that sentences containing 'someone', 'something', 'there is' or 'there are' must be transcribed as 'some'. Thus, 'someone opened the door' would become 'some persons are persons who opened the door'.

However, some arguments cannot be validated according to the rules of the syllogism without writing certain propositions in equivalent form. Thus the argument: that no unwise people are trustworthy: all wise people are un-aggressive: and therefore no trustworthy people are aggressive: has more than the three terms of the syllogism. Indeed it has five: 'unwise people', 'trustworthy people', 'wise people', 'un-aggressive people' and 'aggressive people'. However, noting that the second premise can be written in equivalent form as, 'all aggressive people are unwise' we see that the number of terms is reduced to three and that the resulting syllogism is valid. The rules which enable such equivalent sentences to be written are those of obversion, conversion, and contraposition.

In obversion the quality is changed from affirmative to negative and the predicate is negated (as above), in conversion the subject and predicate are interchanged, and in contraposition the proposition is obverted, converted and inverted again. Thus, for type A 'all men are mortal' obverts to 'no men are non-mortal', for type E 'no men are mortal' obverts to 'all men are immortal', for type I 'some men are mortal' obverts to 'some men are not immortal', and for type O 'some men are not mortal' obverts to 'some men are immortal'. In contrast, however, conversion can only be applied to propositions of types E and I. Thus, 'no cats are dogs' converts to the equivalent 'no dogs are cats' and 'some animals are cats' is equivalent to 'some cats are animals' whereas type O cannot be converted, the proposition that 'some men are not catholic priests' is not equivalent to 'some catholic priests are not men'. Again, while propositions of type A, such as 'all cats are animals' are not equivalent to such as 'all animals are cats', they can be partially converted to the form, 'some animals are cats' by changing the quantity (in conversion by limitation) whereby a valid A type (universal) proposition is converted to a valid type I (particular). As to contraposition, 'all cats are animals' obverts to 'no cats are non-animals' which converts to 'no non-animals are cats' which in turn obverts to 'all non-animals are non-cats'. However, this process can only be applied to propositions of types A and O, there being no contraposition for type I, and only a partial one for type E.

Although invalid reasoning is termed fallacious, there are many more fallacies than those arising from violation of the rules of the syllogism. Indeed, there are more than can be formally identified. Nonetheless, many have been so identified and named, some of which are of ambiguity, of significance, of arguing from authority, of appeal to sentiment, of *argumentum ad ignorantiam*, of *petitio principia*, of division, and of statistics. Thus, I will have occasion to note the ambiguous use of "equality", "brotherhood" and "rights" in discussions of liberal democracy; the arguments from authority, with appeals to sentiment, and from ignorance rather than from knowledge in social

334

policy formulation; and those which beg the question, confuse the whole with the parts and rely on irrelevant statistics in matters of religious and secular belief in general.

From the above, it is clear that logic is closely involved with language. Professional linguists refer to semantics as the study of historical changes in the meaning of words in natural language, the communication of meaning and the removal of barriers to communication including the detection of fallacies. In these contexts extensional meaning is conveyed by the thing itself, while intensional meaning is conveyed by verbal definition. In addition, linguists refer to the grammatical arrangement of the elements of language as syntax. However, in the artificial language of logic the meaning of the symbols have not developed naturally: they are precisely defined. Now, the syllogism is an argument involving a class of things and its referend, in which referring, naming or designating has semantic meaning, while the relationship between these terms is also syntactic regardless of meaning. Thus, in logic, we can say that a syllogism in the form, all M is P, all S is M, therefore all S is P is valid regardless of the meaning attached to the terms while by examining the syntactic arrangement of terms in the argument all P is M, all S is M, therefore all S is P, is seen to be invalid regardless of meaning.

Readers should note, however, that certainty has been achieved by ensuring that the conclusion is contained in the premise and that reasoning has produced no new knowledge, the rules of logic having simply ensured that no error was made along the way. In the same way, the conclusions of mathematical reasoning are contained in the premises, though in this case their restatement is always more useful in particular applications than the premises themselves would have been. As to the relative usefulness of inductive and deductive conclusions, my mathematics teacher used to say that striking a few matches in a box to deduce the uncertain knowledge that all of them will strike when required, is infinitely more useful than having struck all of them in the search for induced certainty. With these introductory remarks I now review the subdivisions of philosophy with respect to the difference between knowledge and belief, between the Rational Trinity and the Rational Duality.

10. 2 METAPHYSICS

It is one thing to avoid the introduction of errors in reasoning or to eliminate them when found. It is another to make any kind of progress. For that purpose reasoning must be applied to something. There must be a point of departure as in the syllogism. As to making such a start, some early Greek metaphysicians either believed that a single proposition of certainty (monism) was a sufficient basis for conclusions to be reached by reasoning, while others believed that more than one would be necessary (pluralism). Again, those who sought explanations for the world in terms of matter and motion are referred to as materialists while those who favoured a mental or spiritual explanation are termed idealists. However, we should note that the spur to progress must have been an awareness of ignorance of both the material and the ideal; that this awareness gave rise to our Ur-beliefs in religion, rationality and knowledge-acquisition, all of which are products of the imagination, whether the derivative beliefs became knowledge though reality-evaluation or not; that no distinction was made between belief and knowledge when even material substance was believed to partake of spirits and essences of the Ideal non-material; and that under these circumstances a metaphysical approach was perhaps inevitable in the first instance, though even metaphysics appears to start from (unacknowledged) sense-experience of reality.

Thus, the first problem tackled metaphysically was that posed by the combination of permanence and alteration as manifest (to the senses) by the constancy of the universe and the transient changes within its physical and biological realms. For Thales, the constant element was the essence of water which underwent observable change from cloud to rain, from rain to river, sea and all other changes which accounted for everything else. For Heraclitus, however, the only permanence was the *Law of Change* itself, while Cratylus went so far as to believe that change was so ubiquitous and active that nothing could endure long enough to be understood. In contrast, Parmenides emphasised permanence to the point of believing that permanent and immutable features of the universe could have no other property than existence; and that nothing of the world of permanent change (flux) could be in the real world of permanent being. From this he concluded that only the permanent can exist; that the changing aspect cannot exist; and that change is therefore illusory and non-existent. Or, as he put it, "Being is: non-being is not". Thus, Zeno's 'paradoxes' were designed to show that attempts to explain change as we experience it in the form of motion for example, lead inevitably to the *reductio ad absurdum* conclusion that either nothing can move or that when moving, infinite time is taken in traversing finite distance.

In case the reader has not resolved Zeno's paradox of Achilles and the Tortoise (c.f. Section 3.1.2) it might be appropriate to do so at this point. In inviting his audience to divide up the distance between Achilles' starting and finishing points and those of the tortoise into ever decreasing fractions for them to run, Zeno fails to notice that when Achilles has run them all, he will only have reached the point the tortoise has reached. So clearly, in the scenario as presented there is no paradox. Achilles, cannot pass the tortoise under the conditions postulated and those conditions do not apply to the real case where there is nothing to prevent Achilles from passing the tortoise thereafter as we know he must. In any case, Archimedes would later show that if anything is sequentially fractioned and the fractions are added in series, the result is the unity thus fractioned (c.f. Section 4. 4).

Again, Democritus sought to resolve the supposed difficulty of permanence or impermanence by suggesting that the unchanging element of the real world was the atom which he believed could not be divided (changed) and which therefore remained permanently distinct from different similarly unchanging atoms except for their perpetual motion through empty space in such a way as to provide permanent impermanence of position. In this way he sought compliance with the permanence believed in by Parmenides and Zeno while allowing for our perception of change in our world of the senses without destroying the unchanging nature of the Ideal world beyond. Thus, we see that imaginative belief about the natural world was the starting point for reasoning about it, and that when the conclusion reached is inconsistent with the world, further beliefs are imagined to deal with the inconsistency. This, of course, contrasts strongly with the reality-evaluation of belief which is craftsmanship and common sense (c.f. Chapters 2, 3 and 5) though for some the absence of reality-evaluation is rendered respectable by calling it philosophy. Similarly, beliefs about God are the starting point for reasoning about God and when the conclusions reached are inconsistent among themselves or with beliefs or knowledge about the natural world, further beliefs are imagined to deal with the inconsistencies and so on (c.f. Chapter 4), the overall consistency of science (knowledge) being beyond attainment by belief alone (c.f. Chapters 6, 7, 8 and 9.

Again, in the *Timaeus*, Plato had expressed the belief that the permanent world is that of Ideas and Forms, while the changing natural world of our experience is but an illusory version of the Ideal; that both worlds are eternal; that the Ideal is the cause of all that happens in the natural world; that the natural world quickly dissipates the received Ideas and Forms to produce its observed transience of order, flux, and chaos; and that the agent of interaction between the two worlds is the *Demiurge* which exists on the interface between them. Platonists, Neo-Platonists, early Christians and even earlier Zoroastrians had or would progressively place man at this
336

interface with a material body in the world of the senses and an immaterial mind capable of knowing the Forms and with a soul capable of directing and of being directed by mind and body, and of ultimately uniting with the eternal and perfect Ideal of Goodness or with the Divine Creator as described in the *Book of Genesis*.

Yet again, Plato's pupil and successor, Aristotle, believed that matter had no qualities and was thus changeless, though having the capacity to be "in-Formed" by the Ideal to assume its various forms in the natural world over time. Thus, the acorn becomes an oak and this belief in 'becoming' caused Aristotle to attribute teleology (purpose and goals) to the natural world. Thus his metaphysical system contends that every object consists of matter having the purpose of acquiring a form or goal proper to itself and with the potential to become Pure Form devoid of matter; that all observed change is to be understood in these terms; that the planets and stars being unchanging apart from their regular motions, are closest of all observable objects to their attainment of Pure Form; that the ultimate goal is the *Unmoved Mover* which being perfect by virtue of being unmoving is the cause of all movement and change in the world of the senses; and that it is these changes which enable objects to achieve the goals proper to themselves by striving for ultimate union with Pure Form, (the *Unmoved Mover*). However, to account for some acorns failing to become oaks and for all such failures to achieve proper goals, Aristotle introduced his belief in "unnatural interference" for such mishaps as an acorn being eaten by a squirrel before becoming an oak.

In the metaphysical system of Epicurus, in contrast, the natural world is believed to be without purpose. This system, based on the atomic theory of Democritus, is most fully described for us by Lucretius in his *De Re Natura*. Thus, Democritus believed that the combination and separation of perpetually moving atoms is a predetermined process in the Ideal beyond; that such predetermination should render it possible to predict future atomic positions in the natural world if their current positions were known; that nonetheless, chance was a permitted element in the world of the senses because of a random swerving of the atomic motions. The world remains purposeless, however, with all happenings at the cosmic and human levels being ultimately dependent on the motion of atoms with the mind and the body being so dependent, the former on a specific soul-atom. In contrast to Aristotle, this is a completely materialistic system in which everything is attributed to the completely purposeless motion of atoms. Stoic metaphysics, on the other hand, believed the fundamental entities to be matter and forceful dynamic reason, the matter continuous and amorphous, the reason conferring characteristics upon the matter by virtue of its force, and imposing change within it by virtue of its dynamism. In addition, reason is severally referred to as the soul of the universe, its rational seeds, the Universal Reason or God. Thus, for the Stoics everything happens for a reason and since this reason is purposeful and goal oriented towards the Good, all that does occur must occur and must be for the best. Thus, in this system as in Epicureanism all is predetermined. Stoicism, however, allowed freedom of thought to brood about our inability to control the future or to be at peace in accepting this inability. In addition, since all accords with the Good of Universal Reason, Stoicism embraces Aristotelian teleology, at least to this extent.

However, at this point, readers may agree that there are as many metaphysical schools of thought as there are ways of posing and responding to a problem with a belief; that while the argument can be rational enough, the conclusion is simply the last step taken rather than a solution to the problem; and that there can be no termination to what is only a stream of speculation (belief) in the absence of reality-evaluation.

The second problem to be tackled metaphysically was that of mind/body interaction, the former being believed non-material (spirit or soul) and the latter material. By the time Descartes addressed this problem, the concept of soul had passed from the 'atomic' formulation of Epicurus through the 'continuous' version of Origen to the individualised soul of Augustine and Aquinas, in the course of which Platonists had been troubled by Christian claims that the Supreme Good or God could act in the world of sense-experience other than through the transfer of Ideas and Forms, and that the Father had been embodied in the Son. However, Descartes must have been aware of the recent fate of Bruno at the hands of the Church in deciding to belittle Galileo as a mere mechanic in contrast to himself the metaphysician.

Thus, for Descartes, God is the creator of mind and matter, the essential property of the former being thought and of the latter extension in space, the former controlled by the Will of God and the latter ordered in compliance with the Laws of God as revealed by our 'mind' investigations. This doesn't take us very far, however. Descartes has simply replaced belief in the blind determinism of the Epicureans and Stoics with the determinism of God while failing to explain how mind affects body. As to this, Descartes refers to the pain experienced in the non-extended immaterial mind when an extended material pin is jabbed into an extended material finger. But, he had set out to explain *how* this happens. In the end, he simply believes that the medium of transfer between material and immaterial is the mind, soul or perhaps the pineal gland (c.f. Section 6.3.3) though he still doesn't say how. It must be concluded, of course, that Descartes failed to explain the mode of interaction of mind and body because the 'mind' does not exist. Thus, the duality addressed by Descartes does not arise with the physicochemical brain interacting through the physicochemical senses with external physicochemical stimuli as the Rational Duality and Trinity. Indeed, we now know that the cosmos and everything in it consists of matter and energy interacting as the particle-wave duality and that this is reality-validated, however counter-intuitive it is.

In contrast to Descartes, Thomas Hobbes believed that the mind was material; that events in the external world produced thoughts (mental events) explicable as various combinations of matter in motion; and that these could produce other such events in our bodies or externally in the world. Others of a less materialist persuasion, believed such physicality to destroy the very idea of thought (belief). Some objectors asked how a train of interacting external and mental events in one brain could be believed to give rise to correct belief by a second brain which believed incorrect another belief in a third brain exposed to the same train of external events. At this point, readers will recall that brains can be sense-stimulated to different imaginative beliefs by the Rational Duality with which others may agree or disagree until reality-evaluation by the Rational Trinity. However, a watered-down version of *Materialism* known as *Epiphenomenalism* was introduced in which material events in the external world were believed to produce more ethereal yet parallel thoughts in the mind by unknown means, as some said, like smoke given off from a fire. Though this is meaningless, other belief options were proposed for resolution of the supposed mind/body problem, belief being unconstrained in the absence of reality-evaluation.

Thus, Nicholas Malebranche, though a follower of Descartes in insisting on the distinction between mind and body denied any interaction between them and believed the mind to be nothing but ideas and the material world to be nothing but extended events, the mind being unable even to know the body, our concept of bodies being only "intelligible extension" and our only evidence for the physical world being the *Book of Genesis* telling us God created it. Again, he believed that when anything happens in either mind or in external matter, God makes a corresponding happening in the other; and that events in either of these realms are not the causes of events in the other: they are the occasions of God's actions in both, a belief referred to as *Occasionalism*. Again, for Gottfried Wilhelm von Leibnitz (1646-1716), every mental or physical entity is a monad, the nature of which is determined by its inherent and fixed properties, these in turn determining its

338

entire fate uninfluenced by any other entity. Thus, Leibnitz believed that there was a pre-established harmony between the monads; that this harmony ensured the parallelism of monad events in the external world with monad events in the minds of those influenced by them; and that this monad harmony was pre-established by God for all eternity. For Baruch Spinoza (1632-1677), however, the separation of mind and body was mistaken, Descartes having left God out of his failed attempt to solve this supposed problem, and Malebranche and Leibnitz having wrongly invoked God's agency in a non-required relationship between them. Thus, Spinoza believed that mind and body were attributes of a single entity named God, Substance or Nature; that there is no interaction between them; that the logicality of mind is identical with the physical order of Nature; and that the mental and physical worlds are but two parallel manifestations of the same thing as it occurs in God or Substance, this belief being called the *Dual-Aspect Proposal*.

The above proposals (beliefs) for resolution of the problem of mind/body interaction with or without Divine agency were not of course the end of the matter. Attention now turned to avoidance of the problem altogether, through proposing (believing) that there is no reality external to the mind and that all occurrences, occur therein. This, so-called *Idealistic Approach* was brought to its highest level of development by Bishop George Berkeley (1685-1753) who believed that the physical objects to which we refer are nothing more than collections of ideas in the mind; that the minds of individuals are finite active agents capable of producing only the limited number of ideas which we have; and that all existence is in the Infinite Mind of God which makes us perceive the particular grouping of ideas which constitute our experience. However, this belief in a world without matter has the implausible consequence that anyone accepting it eliminates all minds other than his own, all objects other than his own beliefs about them, and reduces the universe to a sequence of thoughts occurring in him or her. Is he then God?

This consequence led Johann Gottlieb Fichte to believe that neither Materialism (everything depends on material causes), nor Idealism (everything depends on mental causes) can be proved or disproved, and that one must choose and make ones proposals accordingly. Fichte, having chosen the latter proposed his *Subjective Idealism* in which the universe is believed to be the product of the universal substance (Ego) from which two aspects emerge, the self of which I am aware and the things (Non-Ego) which I regard as other than self. Thus, all awareness of the underlying universe is already in the category of subject (oneself) and object (the external world). Therefore, according to Fichte, the Ego is not the mind of Berkley's self, but the impersonal creative agent of the entire universe from which every personal creative mind is derived. However, to avoid the antagonism of orthodox religion, Fichte often spoke of the traditional concept of God rather than his more impersonal concept of the Ego as the source of all aspects of the universe and of our experience of them.

Again, George Friedrich Wilhelm Hegel (1770-1831) believed that the universe is an *Objective or Absolute Mind* which has been evolving (striving) throughout history towards complete intelligibility. Thus, the Universe began as a chaotic collection of discrete particles incapable of providing any explanation for their existence or interactions in which the *Mind* made itself more intelligible by first synthesising the particles into the discernable pattern of the world's physical system and later into its chemical, biological and human systems in sequence. Thus, Hegel believed that the "march of reason through the world" resulted in an ever fuller expression of this Mind in an ever more consistent explanation of the universe; that the logic of this *Objective* or *Absolute Process* transformed by our experience over time produces a discernible history and that the transformation mechanism is *The Dialectic* by which each attempt to formulate an explanation for the universe (a thesis) is contradicted by another formulation (an antithesis), that the ensuing conflict is resolved in a formulation incorporating the partial truth of both (the synthesis), and that

339

this synthesis is the next thesis to be opposed by another antithesis leading to a further synthesis and so on, Hegel believing that the Absolute is constantly striving towards higher and higher syntheses, a process which will continue until a complete self-realisation of the system is reached in an all-encompassing final synthesis which can be entirely understood.

Thus, Idealism resolved Descartes' dualism of mind/body interaction in favour of mind alone, with Berkley believing everything to be thought and all thought to be in the Divine Mind, with Fichte believing the self and all other things of which the self is aware to emerge from the universal creative Substance or Mind, and with Hegel believing in the universe as Absolute Mind revealing itself outwardly as world history and inwardly as the rational dialectic marching towards full self-realisation and full intelligibility, not just as an objective description of the universe, but as the Absolute intellectually expressed. It is surely apparent that such beliefs do not lend themselves to any conceivable form of reality-evaluation. One can only take them or leave them as beliefs, with a sense of awe at their imaginative ingenuity. However, to take them is to prefer belief to knowledge and unreality to reality.

The third problem to be tackled metaphysically was the existence of free-will in a deterministic universe, though the commonsense view is that we can act freely when not forced by external agencies to act in a particular way. However, the question arose as to whether we are ever free from the force of agencies of which we are unaware. Thus, if we exist in a universe which is fully deterministic, every action has a cause and so our apparently free actions might have hidden causes. We have seen that the materialistic determinism of Stoicism and Epicureanism provided little or no scope for free-will; that Descartes was unable to explain how mind could interact with matter and was thus unable to explain how the mind could exercise free-will on the external world; and that those who believe mind to be paramount appear to transfer all freedom of action to God, even if he is sometimes referred to by some other name. We have also seen that where a difficulty appears to arise, as with the absence of freewill for the stoics, it is always possible to modify a belief or add another. However, this problem of freewill brings us to two critics of metaphysics, Hume and Kant both of whom pre-date Hegel.

David Hume (1711-1776) in his *Enquiry Concerning Human Understanding* went back some two thousand years to the Socratic practice of considering the meaning of such words as justice, courage *etc*. Thus, he asked what meaning was to be attached to substance, the mind/body duality, Idealism and freewill/determinism in the usage of metaphysicians, found that in failing to define their terms properly they had been attempting to solve problems of their own creation, and concluded that their whole endeavour could be dismissed as meaningless. Hume's initial contention was that meaning attaches only to sense impressions or to mathematical concepts whereas the metaphysician's concept of substance as the fundamental element of the universe whether physical, mental or divine is indefinable in terms of sense experience and is simply meaningless. Quite so. Thus, for the metaphysician 'a substance' is something existing by itself apart from and independent of anything else, while Hume's response was that anything conceived by the mind apart from all other conceptions meets this definition of 'substance'. Again, for the metaphysician the existence of our ideas and perceptions needs 'substance', while for Hume we *have* our ideas and perceptions, our impressions *occur*, and it is unnecessary to invoke any other term to explain or support their existence: they just *are*, as far as we can tell.

Similarly, according to Hume, if one eliminates the meaningless/unnecessary concept of two substances, mental and physical and the equally unintelligible idea of a necessary connection between two events in both substances, the mind/body problem reduces to a question of the possibility that certain mental events such as impressions of tastes and smells can be conjoined with physical events involving objects. As to this possibility, Hume contended that this is what we

340

experience when we conjoin the taste with the pear and the sound of middle-C with striking the appropriate piano-key. Thus, while Hume has still not explained how the physical event produces the mental event or *vice versa*, he believed that conjoined events are everywhere in our experience without any causal relationship actually being observed, and that we do not see precisely how the movement of a hammer actually moves a nail forward into wood: it just does. However, this treatment of causality fails to differentiate conjunction from causality (cause and effect) as the latter applies to craftsmanship and experimentation (c.f. Section 6.1 and 6. 3. 2), and leaves Hume more of a metaphysician than he believed himself to be. Again, in his treatment of taste, smell and hearing he fails to acknowledge that these are the result, as is sight, of stimulation of our sense receptors which in turn stimulate or imagination to beliefs whether or not these are reality-evaluated to knowledge through our Rational Trinity or remain beliefs on terminating with the Duality.

Nonetheless, as to the concept of mind in Idealism, Hume finds that we are familiar with the succession of our thoughts without being aware of any mental entity or substance or of its role in the thought process, concludes that the metaphysical concept of mind is just as unclear as that of matter, and refers to his earlier critique on substance. Similarly, with respect to the question of free-will in a deterministic universe, Hume dismissed the problem by applying his belief in causality and conjoined events to the constant conjunction of our motives with our voluntary actions to which extent they become determined. Thus Hume believed that there was as much necessity in human actions as in any other aspect of the universe; and that while liberty was the capacity to act or not according to the determination of the will, actions necessarily follow from motives, from ethics or from social of religious sanctions on behaviour. He might have noted, however, that freewill is no more a problem in us than it is in animals; that in so far as he invokes the explanation "it just does", he could have accepted that all living things have innate capacities by which they survive in their respective habitats by making choices as we know they do (c.f. Chapters 1 and 2); and while the 'mind' does not exist, he should have known that his argument that it doesn't exist because we are unaware of its processes, would equally apply to our brains which do exist.

Though Immanuel Kant (1724-1804) was greatly influenced by Hume, he did not renounce metaphysics as Hume believed himself to have done. Rather, he sought to determine the certainty of metaphysical 'knowledge' and to delineate the means to its acquisition. Though in his *Critique of Pure Reason*, Kant agreed with Hume that experience is the source of all knowledge, he argued that full attainment of this knowledge would be impossible without rational thought. However, while readers will recognise this to be consistent with my route to knowledge through reality-evaluation, Kant the metaphysician was still seeking to establish the nature and extent of a universal and necessary knowledge which he believed we possess independent of experience (of reality-evaluation) and which he called *a priori* knowledge. In my terms, we don't have *a priori* knowledge: we have innate capability. Nonetheless, Kant's task as a metaphysician was to consider whether *a priori* knowledge in which Plato had believed could be shown to exist. To this end, he subdivided knowledge as *analytic* or *synthetic* and showed to his satisfaction that *analytic a priori* knowledge existed in the form of propositions or judgements which are universally and necessarily true solely on the basis of their terms of expression (c.f. Section 10.1). Thus, propositions that "a red rose is red", or "all bodies are extended" are true because what is predicated of the subject is already in its definition, these being examples of *analytic a priori* knowledge.

On the other hand, Kant defined *synthetic a priori* knowledge as arising from the exercise of judgement as to the validity of propositions where the predicate contains information (knowledge)

341

not contained in the subject (c.f. Section 10. 1). However, he noted that such a statement as "this paper is white", though *synthetic*, is not *synthetic a priori* because it can only be judged true or false by experience (reality-evaluation), whereas Kant was looking for propositions the truth of which can be judged without reference to experience, only such truth (knowledge) being *synthetic a priori*. Thus, Kant claimed to demonstrate the existence of such *synthetic a priori* knowledge in a number of ways by arguing, for example, that the proposition $2 + 5 = 7$ is one such, because the predicate of the subject, 7 contains more information than the bare concept of 2 and 5; that all arithmetical statements are thus *synthetic*; and that the agent which makes them *a priori* is intuition. Similarly he argued that the statement 'a straight line is the shortest distance between two points' is *synthetic* because the concept of 'straight' does not include the concept of 'shortest' and being in his belief intuitive is also *a priori*. Again, on this reasoning he believed the statement 'every event has a cause' to be *synthetic a priori*.

It is clear that Kant has introduced the concept of intuition (something of the 'mind', (not of the external world) in an attempt to explain how his *synthetic a priori* judgements are possible without reference to experience. In justification of this introduction he explained that since our experience of the external world is limited to its spatial and temporal features there must additionally be a formal character to everything of which we are aware and upon which we impose forms of intuition. Thus, on the basis of his reasoning, we may expect *a priori* characteristics to be present in any awareness which we may have, such awareness being temporal and geometric and thus amenable to mathematical treatment. Nonetheless, it may be concluded that nothing has been achieved; that in relying on arithmetical equations to sustain his s*ynthetic a priori* category he was failing to acknowledge that being equations they were identical to '(a) red (rose) *is* red' which was the basis of his *analytic a priori* category; and that in any case arithmetic is based on reality-evaluation i.e. experience (c.f. Section 10.3).

No doubt seeing, after such a hopeful start, that his conclusions were a bit thin (actually fallacious), Kant went beyond his forms of intuition to postulate inherent organising and categorising capacities which enable us to make sense of our experiences in an ordered and related manner and to ensure our judgements have quantification and quality (c.f. Section 10.1). Though these last are simply references to the rules of logic (c.f. Section 10.1) Kant believed he had advanced beyond Hume to show to his own satisfaction at least, that we can attain universal and necessary knowledge of the world without reference to the senses, though he agreed with Hume that metaphysics could not produce general and useable knowledge of the world.

At this point readers may agree that Hume did well to see that metaphysical substance is meaningless, though he might have concluded that it was simply unreal, while his use of 'conjoined events' fails to recognise causal relationships as a sub-set of the conjoined with differentiation requiring suitable experimentation (c.f. Section 6.1). Again, to quibble as Hume does as to the relative merits of deductive and inductive logic is sheer pedantry given the futility and uselessness of metaphysics and the overall consistency, predictability and usefulness of craftsmanship, science and technology as already there to be seen even in his day. Readers may also notice that grasping the presence of seven items is not dependent on how they are grouped, as metaphysicians chose to believe. Indeed, in his own terms, Kant failed to recognise mathematics as providing *analytic* inductive knowledge, its conclusions being restatements of its axioms; that these axioms are reality-validated; that *synthetic* knowledge is reality-evaluated which though deductive is the only source of new knowledge; that knowledge is available only through reality-evaluation by sense experience i.e. by direct observation and designed experimentation; and that *a priori* knowledge doesn't exist. Thus, Kant's introduction of 'intuition' and 'forms' are reminiscent of Plato and get him nowhere. Indeed, in his invocation of a capacity to order our

342

experiences and to judge their value we see Kant struggling and failing to demonstrate knowledge-acquisition from metaphysics, Hume having already rejected this claim in an erroneous and convoluted manner. However, while Hume and Kant did not recognise the inability of the Rational Duality to produce knowledge nor the unique capacity of the of the Rational Trinity to do so, they were and are not alone in this failure.

10. 3 EPISTEMOLOGY

The previous section opened with those Greeks who sought knowledge of the world behind appearances and who desired to recognise it as certain when they found it. Here we start with the Sophists who doubted the possibility of being certain about anything and who, in failing to recognise the need for reality-evaluation, were simply stating a fact. However, Gorgias believed that "nothing exists and if it did, no one could know it: and if he did know it, he could not communicate it" while Protagoras believed that "man is the measure of all things". Now, in contrast to the metaphysical preoccupations of their contemporaries as reviewed above, these beliefs could be welcomed as cautionary. However, their proponents were wrong to advise that knowledge by whatever means is unattainable or attainable only as measured against personal desire, and that life should be conducted accordingly. Nonetheless, the Sophists did just this, in training for success by teaching how to speak well, how to convince, how to lead and how in effect to 'get away with it'. Indeed, Socrates expressed concern that those who professed to know nothing could be teaching, and that no-one should 'get away with it' unless he is *right*. This, is a very commendable attitude, though it cannot be implemented without determining knowledge of right and wrong by reality-evaluation, a procedure avoided by philosophers dedicated to rationality alone.

Thus, in his *Dialogues*, Plato set out a purely rational theory of knowledge through the discussions of Socrates. We have seen that he despaired of the world of the senses as a source of knowledge and instead had recourse to his Ideal World of the Forms. We have also seen in the *Memo* that Plato believes we cannot acquire knowledge; that we can only recollect what our pre-existing souls knew of his so-called Forms before we were born; that that which is acquired through the senses (as sensible information) can only be reported as seeming or appearing, while that acquired through accessing the Forms (as intelligible information) can be acquired at different levels, the lowest enabling practical use without understanding, the highest being full awareness and understanding in the mind; and that one can thus know the properties of geometric entities and attain certainty on their relationships without full awareness of the Forms.

Plato's *Allegory of the Cave* presents us with the relationship between actual people and the distorted shadows cast by them on the cave-walls by flickering firelight, asks us to consider what we would know of real people if such shadowy representations were all we had to go on, invites us to conclude that our own world of sense experience stands in the same relationship to the world of the Forms as do the shadows to the actual people whose images they are, and tells us that specified training is required if we are to escape from our world of sense-limited information (the images in the cave) to attainment of knowledge of the world of the Forms (to the reality behind the images). Thus, we need training in reasoning to ponder the meaning of largeness or smallness given that one finger can at the same time be smaller and larger than each of two others; in arithmetic, plane and solid geometry and astronomy to deal with abstraction and contemplation of the most perfect of visible things as a prelude to the Forms which are invisible and only knowable in the mind; in harmonics in order to parallel the audible/inaudible with the visible/invisible; and in the dialectic in order to understand that which underlies mathematics itself and hence to come to knowledge of the Forms and to know that one has arrived at this destination. Overall, we see that Plato rejects the senses and what I call reality-evaluation, without which we know nothing.

In Section 6.3.3, we saw that Descartes' statement "I think, therefore I am" established for him the certainty of his existence. From there he reasoned that such clarity and distinctness must be characteristic of distinguishable truth in general, declaring that "whatever is clearly and distinctly conceived is true". From there he attempted to clarify his meaning through examples such as toothache "of which we have such clarity that we cannot avoid awareness of them, though they are not distinct enough for us to be sure what they are or where they are". He metaphysically thought of awareness (pain) as being in the mind, while concluding that "if we could define an experience so that it could not possibly be confused with anything else, then it would be both clear and distinct". Similarly he concluded that "if we could so define an idea, it would of necessity be *clear* and being so would also be *distinct* from anything else" and thus meet his requirements for truth. Descartes then asserted (the reader may agree with him) that most of his ideas were unclear or indistinct and thus distinguished themselves from what he called "the *innate ideas* which do not arise from experience and cannot be constructed or invented by the imagination". Such ideas according to Descartes are those of mathematical objects (circles, squares *etc.*) and that of a Perfect Being, God, which do not arise from experience and must therefore be implanted by other means.

Having thus, to his satisfaction established two fundamental truths, "I think, therefore I am" and "God exists", Descartes sought further truths and found that he could assert that God does not deceive, and from whence he concluded that a great deal which had been suspect could now be considered reliable including his belief that he himself existed. Thus having considered our rational faculties, Descartes concludes that the judgements which God forces us to make are those regarding clear and distinct ideas and that we are compelled to assent only to such clear and distinct ideas and to regard only such as true. On the other hand we can withhold judgement on matters which are unclear and indistinct, any conclusions which we make regarding such being our responsibility and not God's. In conclusion Descartes states that the faculty of judgement functions reliably in relation to the clear, distinct and innate ideas which God has implanted in us, among which he includes the clear and distinct mathematical ideas which must perforce be true. Thus, the world of *innate ideas* provides absolute certainty, these ideas having been implanted in us by God such that were we to avoid judgements based on unclear and indistinct ideas we would never make mistakes. Again we see Descartes' attachment to belief in the Beyond, the circularity of his reasoning in assuming what he ostensibly sets out to prove, and his blindness to the need for reality-evaluation, all of which lead him to confusion leading to more confusion.

Theories of knowledge like those of Plato and Descartes being essentially metaphysical are classified by philosophers as rational to distinguish them from theories which began by recognising sense-experience, the latter being classified as empirical. I classify them as belief-based and reality-evaluated respectively.

As to the latter, John Locke (1632-1704) in his *Essay Concerning Human Understanding* argued in advance of Hume, that all our knowledge is acquired through sense-experience and subsequent reflection; and that we have no innate ideas, the mind at birth being "void of all characters, without any ideas". He started reminiscent of Galileo, by identifying simple ideas and primary and secondary qualities, a simple idea being the experience of tasting sugar or of smelling a rose, primary qualities being the size and shape of objects and secondary qualities being condition-descriptors of objects such as colour. He went on to suggest that when simple ideas always appear conjoined we assume that they relate to one thing as later would Hume, and that when we experience qualities as conjoined we assume some substrate to be holding them together.
344

On this basis Locke argued that the first kind of knowledge is achieved by comparing two or more ideas to see if they are identical or different; that the second is achieved by noting that two or more ideas belong together; the third by noting that two or more ideas are related in some manner; and the fourth by noting whether or not our ideas relate to real existences outside our minds. Such being the basis of our knowledge, Locke then considered whether varying degrees of certainty might attach to them and concluded that the greatest level of assurance would attach to *intuitive knowledge*. Thus, when we immediately see that something is true about two or more ideas under consideration, "this part of knowledge is irresistible and like bright sunshine forces itself immediately to be perceived as soon as ever the mind turns its view that way and leaves no room for hesitation, doubt or examination, but the mind is presently filled with the clear light of it."

Locke claimed complete certainty for such realisations as that black is not white, a circle is not a square and $3 = 2 + 1$ which he erroneously believed we see intuitively to be so, as later would Hume and Kant (c.f. below). He also claimed that when we do not immediately see a truth about two or more ideas we connect them to other ideas and thus attain what he called *demonstration knowledge*. Though he held each demonstration step to be seen by the mind immediately and intuitively to be certain, he recognised reasoning processes to be liable to error and knowledge thus attained to have a lower level of assurance. With regard to the mind/body problem, however, Locke was still dealing with mind alone. However noting that everyone except philosophers relied on sense perceptions, he took the (empirical) decision to include *'sensitive' knowledge* which assures us of the actual existence of particular things and to which he attributed the lowest level of assurance. Thus, having started well, he prefers intuitive knowledge to empirical (reality-validated) knowledge in the end, thus remaining a philosopher.

However, any reference to the senses rendered a philosophical theory imperfect for George Berkley whose intention was "to demonstrate the reality and perfection of human knowledge, the incorporeal nature of the soul, and the immediate providence of a Deity in opposition to sceptics and atheists" in the belief that the admission of imperfection by such as Locke would lead to doubt in the general population and hence to widespread atheism. In the *Three Dialogues* Berkeley provides his rebuttal in discussion format with his own beliefs being presented by one, Philonous, and those of the opposition by Hylas (matter) in such a way as to detect and exploit internal inconsistencies in Locke's theory. Thus, he argued that even if one agreed with Locke in believing experience of secondary ideas to occur in the mind only, why would such mental experience of primary ideas be evidence of an external material reality when Locke himself provides no reason for these two sets of experience to be different in the mind? After all, Locke only claims a difference between primary and secondary characteristics of objects in an external material world the existence of which he has not yet proved. Again, if we agree with Locke that sensations occur to sentient beings only in the mind and not to inanimate objects, how can we agree with him that we can be aware of such non-sentient inanimate objects even if they do "exist" in an "external material" world?

Thus, Berkeley believes that we can perceive only ideas; that ideas cannot have existence independent of minds; that although everyone believes what is perceived (the idea) to be a real thing it is only our ideas of it which give information about it; and that all things are ideas in the mind of God, our ideas gained through the senses being true knowledge of ideas in God's mind and our science being the order and relationship of ideas in God's mind. Berkeley had to admit, however, that the idea of God could not be derived from sense-experience. Accordingly, he introduced his belief that *notions* distinct from ideas arose in the mind; that the primary *notion* was awareness of ourselves as agents who think, will and act; and that this *notion* being different from our ideas of any other thing gives rise to the *notion* of God, the source of all ideas. Berkeley's arguments with Locke over inconsistencies are characteristic of all disputes between one belief system and another whether theses systems are religious or secular, such disputes being resolvable only by suspension of belief or its submission to reality-evaluation.

David Hume who concluded from his *Enquiry Concerning Human Understanding* of 1739 that it would be more useful to study metaphysicians than metaphysics, had earlier completed *A Treatise of Human Nature* in which he had set out his beliefs on the theory of knowledge revealing himself to be a sceptic who doubted philosophers were capable of revealing the truth about anything whatsoever. Quite so. He started by noting that sciences like physics and the discipline of mathematics were due to human effort and so by attempting to understand the human contribution we might gain some understanding of the nature of the knowledge thus acquired. For Hume our sense-experience gives rise to impressions and ideas of variable force and vivacity while our memory holds ideas in an orderly mental sequence and our imagination arranges them in any order we may want. However, despite this freedom of the imagination our ideas tend to be associated, such that when we think of one idea we think also of a similar idea, one which is contiguous to it in time or space, or one causally related to it. At this point, Hume is with Locke in respect of intuitive knowledge arising from inspection of two or more ideas and of demonstrations of knowledge such as those of arithmetic.

However, while Hume had failed to differentiate causality from contiguity in his critique of metaphysics, he now identified three aspects with regard to events: a present *impression*, an *idea* of another event, and a connection or *inference* from the *impression* to the *idea*. According to this reasoning, Hume believed that we infer a causal connection between two events by building a memory of constant conjunction between them; that though we create a belief in the uniformity and reliability of nature from such conjoined events there is no rational guarantee of any such uniformity or reliability; and that such belief is simply due to custom or habit. As a consequence of such reasoning, he believed that if the constant conjunction had occurred often enough, reoccurrence of one of the conjuncts would automatically bring the other as an idea into the imagination; and that while our imagination is free to think of any idea at this point, only the conjunct idea is thought with sufficient force and vivacity. As to the degree of force and vivacity in relation to events, Hume refers to what he calls normal and abnormal mental habits. The former habits involve believing that $2 + 2 = 4$, that the Sun will rise tomorrow, while the latter habits are the mental quirks by which we derive less well established beliefs, all characteristic of an internal continuity which we call "the self". Again, he tells us that our nature compels us to believe, to choose what to believe and on those choices, subject again to mood, we talk, act and live: and thus, being uncertain of everything, we should be tolerant of the beliefs of others.

On the other hand, I argue that $2 + 2 = 4$ is not a matter of belief, however one classifies belief. We know it to be true by sense experience (reality-evaluation), there being four items present regardless of whether we group them as four, as single units or as $1 + 3$ or $2 + 2$ and while our prediction that the Sun will rise tomorrow is deductive and not inductive, we do not believe it purely out of habit. In any case, Hume appears to be offering a theory of belief rather than of knowledge and one which leaves rather too much as unresolved personal belief to which the only response is mutual tolerance, while my reality-evaluation defines knowledge by differentiating it from belief. As to causality Hume appears to be unclear as to the difference between simple conjunction and true cause and effect, and to miss the relationship between the latter and experimentation. As to the rest, I have shown that our rational and sense-perceptive capacities may be taken as innate; that our Rational Trinity enables us to imagine, believe, and convert some beliefs to knowledge by reality-validation; that our Rational Duality beliefs remain beliefs only in so far as they are retained despite reality-refutation or are beyond the possibility of reality-

346

evaluation; that while tolerance might be appropriate for belief, it doesn't arise with knowledge. Thus, it is unfortunate that even such an anti-metaphysician as Hume 'secured' his rationality on a mistaken reference to arithmetical equations as Locke had done and Kant would do, instead of recognising sense-perception as the only route to knowledge. Again, Hume's distinction between secure and insecure beliefs is spurious, the true distinction being between knowledge (reality-evaluation) and belief (no reality-evaluation). In any case, what did philosophers hope to achieve through rationality alone which could stand comparison with the achievements of reality-evaluation as reviewed herein.

10. 4 ETHICS

Because all (reality-evaluated) guidance such as provided in parts of the *Old and New Testaments* is ignored by philosophers other than as expressions of religious belief, classical ethics is treated as having arisen from attempts to specify *The Good Life* and to advise on how to attain it through rationality alone or as blended with the empiricism of (unreliable) sense-perception. However, following a short period of heightened empiricism and recognition of the futility of rationality alone (c.f. Section 10.8) empiricism was dropped as ethics became the analysis of meaning without definition other than through the classification of ethical theories without reality-evaluation of content. Nonetheless, I now review the empirical content of a subject which touched on reality despite its proprietary rejection by philosophers.

Though for Plato, rediscovery of what he called our prior-knowledge of The Good would automatically produce action consistent with The Good Life, he believed that some might achieve it by accident without understanding it; that those who could not absorb the training for rediscovery would need to imitate and be guided by those who had absorbed and understood it; and that their resulting actions would be virtuous irrespective of understanding. Plato's trainers and role models were the Guardians as described in *The Republic* which clearly shows that he had no concern for happiness as such. For him the Good Life consisted in the rational ability to distinguish right from wrong by reference to the Good and to act always for the best on this basis. Thus, in ethical matters, Plato is classed as absolutist in fundamentally believing that there is only One Good and only one Good Life for all to lead; that there was an absolute distinction between right and wrong with no room for compromise between them; and that Goodness resembled mathematical truth and was not a matter of opinion. This belief within Neo-Platonism was easily carried into authoritarian Christianity, neither having a conscious relationship to reality-evaluation. Again, in appropriating *Old Testament* Judaism, the *Law* and *Commandments* were absorbed without recognising their empiricism, and while Plato believed Goodness be anterior even to God, his concept of it must have originated in empiricism.

Further to empiricism, Aristotle observed that happiness is a common ingredient of all the lifestyles which commonsense considers to be good and *vice versa*. Thus unlike Plato, Aristotle recognised (however unconsciously) that good and bad can only be defined by reference to reality, in his case to the presence or absence of happiness (as reality-evaluated), and that one should always act towards the enhancement of happiness. After striving to clarify the meanings of everyday speech, Aristotle defines happiness in his *Nichomachean Ethics* not as a static destination but as an on-going consequence of a life conducted according to his *Doctrine of the Mean* which in turn amounted to living a life of moderation in reality. Again, in contrast to Plato, Aristotle denies the existence of a mean applicable to all and believes that everyone is capable of the understanding necessary for achieving the good life; that virtue requires understanding; that praise and blame are valid responses to wilful intentions; and that knowledge of right and wrong will automatically lead to virtuous behaviour. In addition, his *Doctrine of Pleasure* rejects the view that pleasure is intrinsically bad, accepts that it is an integral part of the good life, and asserts that "no man can be happy on the rack". It is not surprising that Plato called his former pupil *The Mule* in reference to the mule foal's habit of kicking its mother.

Again, in declaring pleasure to be the defining characteristic of the Good Life, Epicurus counselled moderation for maximum pleasure and minimal pain, and distinguished between activities which can cause pain and those which do not. The latter, such as those associated with friendship and contemplation he called passive, while the former such as sexual activity, gluttony, fame and marriage he called dynamic, and he cautioned that it was better to avoid pain than to seek pleasure. Furthermore, while Eudoxus believed (according to his teacher, Aristotle) that all human activity is innately directed toward pleasure and avoidance of pain, Aristotle and Epicurus knew from experience (reality-validation) that guidance and encouragement are needed whether the tendency is innate or not.

On the other hand, in a manner reminiscent of the Buddha, Diogenes the Cynic saw the good life as requiring rejection of the fruits of civilisation to achieve inner satisfaction through setting aside the sensations of both pleasure and pain. However, Cynicism being essentially asocial and unlikely to inspire a mass movement, contributes no social benefit other than as a reminder to others that consumption is not the be all and end all of human life. On the other hand, Stoicism introduced in the third century BC by Zeno, was more socially acceptable in moderating Cynicism and teaching that while one should not shun the world, one should be indifferent to its influences. His follower Epictetus, being indifferent to life as a slave, tells us in his *Discourse on Progress or Improvement*, that the personal cultivation of indifference ensures our immunity to external agencies and circumstances no matter what their consequences might be for us; that virtue resides in the will; that only the will is good or bad; that we ought to take personal responsibility for our own good behaviour and for our own shortcomings; and that we should view prosperity or misfortune with indifference. Thus, in concluding that self-liberation from desire is conducive to the good life, Epictetus is following the Way of the Buddha while unlike Cynicism, the influence of Stoicism was widespread as shown by *The Meditations* of the Emperor, Marcus Aurelius.

Thus, while Pagan ethics were collectively developed from metaphysical beliefs and from observations of real human behaviour, Christian ethics were believed to have been directly revealed by God through the teachings of Jesus, as the Ten Commandments had previously been to Moses, and as such required adherence with the absolutism of Plato. Nonetheless, the asceticism of the Cynics and the dutifulness of Stoicism can be detected in early Christian ethics, which after incorporation of Neo-Platonism was further influenced by acceptance of Aristotle's Nicomachean Ethics by Thomas Aquinas. Again, the personal responsibility and dedication to duty advocated by Stoicism and discernible in Pelagianism, resurfaced in the personalised relationship between man and God which characterised the Reformation. However, regardless of belief development and reinterpretation, the reality-validated aspects of ethical systems from time immemorial have been transmitted through Pagan, Judaic, Buddhist and other traditions as guidance to the Good Life, whether believed to be revelations from God or not.

Indeed, it may be concluded that much of what is believed to be Revelation is in fact reality-validated experience; and that the many differences between respective religions and their respective sects are just expressions of casuistic sectarianism designed to create and maintain intra-group identity and inter-group distinctions, the latter having the potential to disharmony and conflict. Despite these casuistic differences, however, Christianity has been the central influence on European Civilisation, and though it can still be absolutist, levels of authoritarianism vary from

348

sect to sect. As to free will and determinism, Christianity vacillates between the doctrines of original sin as propounded by Augustine and the freedom to choose good or evil as propounded by Origen and Pelagius, the latter pair being the more consistent with the reality-validation which differentiates good from evil in terms of the social cooperation needed for the survival of a group-species and which places responsibility for this survival on each and every individual.

Meanwhile, Baruch Spinoza in his *Ethics* appears to have re-worked the determinism of Democritus by expressing the belief that all things come to pass according to the eternal order and fixed laws of nature; that no man is free to act capriciously or by chance, all actions being determined by his past experience, physical and mental constitution, and relevant laws of nature; and that nothing is good or bad in itself, but is only so in relation to someone. Thus, according to Spinoza one cannot attain the Good Life without rational recognition of the truth that all events are determined and without emotional acceptance of this truth. On the other hand, Frances Hutcheson whose *System of Moral Philosophy* was a foundation of what became known as the Scottish Enlightenment was the first to propose that an action is right to the extent that it produces the greatest benefit for the greatest number. This statement carries the clear implication that good and bad are objectively measurable and it marks a change from the earlier practice of providing guidance to individuals to one of judging the value of individual acts in the social context. The best known exponents of what was to become known as *Utilitarianism*, however, were Jeremy Bentham (who gave no credit to Hutcheson) and John Stuart Mill (c.f. Section 10.5). Again, Hutcheson's recognition that humanity had an innate moral sense contrasted with the negative assessment of Hobbes, (c.f. Section 10.5), with the moderately negative one of Henry Home (later Lord Kames) in his *Sketches of the History Of Man* and with David Hume's emphasis on motivation through self-interest as expressed in his *Treatise of Human Nature* and in his *Essays Political, Literary and Moral*.

Again, Adam Smith (1793-1790) who had been a student at Glasgow under 'the incomparable Hutcheson' saw himself as a moral philosopher and was already admired for *A Theory of Moral Sentiments* before he wrote his famous *Inquiry into the Nature and Causes of the Wealth of Nations*. In both these works, however, Smith maintains Hutcheson's positive view of human nature, though modified by the more negative assessment of Lord Advocate Kames and his disciple David Hume. However, resolution of this difference is never complete and Smith continues to recognise the permanence of the struggle between what human beings ought to be and can be, and what they are and remain. Bentham, however, interpreted the utilitarian principle after the manner of Epicurus as a form of hedonism *i.e.* in terms of the greatest pleasure or happiness for the greatest number. However, from the ethical point of view, the principle in either form implies that the rightness or wrongness of an action is being judged by its consequences and not necessarily by the motives which inspired it.

Again, Immanuel Kant, started his *Theory of Ethics* in Hutcheson's more general way by considering the nature of morality in terms of the difference between a moral action and a non-moral one and of how a man who acts morally differs from one who does not. For Kant, the key lay in distinguishing between acts done from *inclination* and those done from a *sense of obligation*, an obligation being that which *ought* to be done despite any inclination to do otherwise. Up to this point philosophers had held that one could act morally upon one's inclinations, but Kant insisted that one acts morally only when suppressing inclinations to do otherwise *i.e.* when doing what one is obliged to do. Kant then distinguishes between acts which are *in accord with duty* and those done *from duty* and concludes that the former are not necessarily moral, while the latter invariably are. Thus, Kant takes issue with Utilitarianism by claiming that motive trumps consequence in morality and draws a distinction between prudential action and moral action further to clarify his

349

position. Thus, a man who repays a debt out of fear of legal consequences acts *prudentially* while one who feels obliged or duty-bound to do so acts *morally* out of a sense of good will. Finally Kant distinguishes between *hypothetical imperatives* and *The Categorical Imperative*, the former requiring appropriate and specific actions to achieve any particular objective, while the latter enjoins unconditional action without regard to consequences in any situation. The former relates to *prudential* action while the later provides guidance when one is unclear as to what would constitute *moral* action in any given circumstances. Thus the Categorical Imperative is to "act only on that maxim whereby thou canst at the same time will that it should become a universal law". Another formulation is: "so act as to treat humanity, whether in thine own person or in that of any other, in every case as an end withal, never as a means only". For greater clarity this may be expressed as one may not act in a way unacceptable for everyone so to act; or more familiarly, "do onto others as you would have them do to you".

At this point, readers will note that ethics has moved sporadically from metaphysics to observation of natural human traits and from the provision of behavioural advice for individual benefit to ensuring that individual behaviour is beneficial to society as a whole; that in moving from metaphysics to observation it had moved from reliance on belief alone to reliance on knowledge; and that, however unwittingly, it had thus moved from the Rational Duality towards the Rational Trinity, a movement previously discernible in the evolutionary development of man's obligations to God in the *Old Testament* and in the evolution of the gods of Greek mythology to their metaphorical role in Greek law and drama.

10. 5 POLITICAL PHILOSOPHY

Political philosophy has from classical times attempted to define the nature of Ideal Government and later to justify particular forms of government before finally limiting itself to analysing the meanings of words and terms used in political discussion (c.f. Section 10.6). Nonetheless, as might have been expected, political philosophy initially drew heavily from ethics whether empirical or not and whether emphasising the actions of individual or the relationship of the individual to the state.

We have already discussed Plato's conception of Ideal Government and the training requirements for the Governors (Guardians), the specific elements being that a society (state) is nothing but "the individual writ large"; that the Ideal State must be governed by Ideal (perfect) individuals; and that these paragons would have perfect health and knowledge of the Forms. In addition Plato believed that the mind (soul) consisted of three elements, namely, the rational, the spirited, and the appetitive. He meant by the first, the ability to reason, deliberate, argue *etc*; by the second, the possession of courage, tenacity, will *etc*; and by the third, acquisitiveness, greed, self-aggrandisement *etc*. Thus, for perfect mental health, these three elements must be in harmony with reason, supported by the spiritual and in control of the appetitive. In Plato's Ideal State everyone should have equal entry to the process of becoming a Governor through physical, intellectual and moral education for both sexes by the state to age eighteen, followed by selection of prospective rulers from those who become warriors and artisans, by further training for those thus selected, allocation to administrative tasks, evaluation of performance and progressive promotion on merit to ever-more demanding levels with the intention that those who met all requirements would become rulers absolutely, no interference from lesser mortals being permitted, though to prevent corruption by such power they could not have private families or possess private wealth or property.

Again, Thomas Hobbes (1588-1679) states in his *Leviathan* that "the life of man in a state of nature is solitary, poor, nasty, brutish and short" man's nature being selfish and egotistical; and that peace and stability are only secured by a "social contract" involving voluntary renunciation of the freedom thus to act, establishment of laws to control any such tendencies and an enforcing agency of absolute power. Thus, though coming to the same overall conclusion as Plato, Hobbes opted for the King as sole and absolute ruler instead of a governing group selected on ability. Of course, not being able to strip the existing King (Charles I) of family and private possessions to secure his rectitude, he argued that "the King is only as rich as his country" and could not therefore work for his own benefit at the expense of his country. However, even Hobbes sought to limit the power of the sovereign by arguing that having freely entered the contract with the express purpose of protecting their lives, subjects were entitled to refuse to hazard themselves when commanded to do so by the sovereign; and that the sovereign could not breach his covenant with his subjects because they made it with him, not he with them. *Quid pro quo*, however, the subject could not make a new covenant or rebel against the sovereign so long as the latter remained capable of protecting him, dissenting minorities having to acquiesce to the dictates of the sovereign, expressions of opinion being controlled by him, all law and adjudications under the covenant being made by him, and he being free to make war with other nations and levy taxes so to do.

In contrast, John Locke (1632-1704) in his *Second Treatise on Civil Government* likened the Hobbesian "state of nature" to a "state of war" asserting that humanity is not wholly selfish and egotistical; that individuals are generally cooperative and not wholly averse to working for the good of others; that they respect ownership of property by others; that this "state of nature" arises from majority acceptance of the precept that "no one ought to harm another in his life, health, liberty or possessions" and that this is in fact *The Law of Nature*. He further asserted that the difficulties encountered by the majority in controlling the minority who in transgression of this Law killed, stole *etc*, had been the cause which drove individuals in "the state of nature" to form societies voluntarily; that these difficulties arose because each man is otherwise his own judge which may lead to bias; that otherwise there is no adjudicator in cases of dispute; that otherwise adequate force for restraint and punishment may be unavailable even if guilt could be established; and that otherwise there are no means of making the punishment fit the transgression. Locke concludes, therefore, that such considerations lead naturally and voluntarily to the creation of a judiciary to administer the law impartially, an executive to enforce the law, and a legislature to lay down consistent and uniform laws. In addition he asserts that a state of war (Hobbesian state of nature) can only develop in a natural society if someone or some group seeks to gain control over others by force or other absolute means, and that those thus to be dominated have the duty to resist. For Locke, therefore, law not force is the basis of acceptable government, the laws being arrived at through due deliberation by properly chosen representatives of the people and promulgated for the widest possible acquaintance. He also asserts that all men are equal in having rights anterior to those conferred by society; that these cannot be taken away by society; and that of these the right to own property derives from its being "the fruit of one's labours".

However, not everyone who disagrees with the majority is bent on murder, theft *etc*, and so John Stuart Mill (1806-1873) in his essay *On Liberty* sought to defend the individual and minority groups from the "tyranny of the majority" which he considered to be a danger in the society advocated by Locke and being a follower of Hume, he emphasised the liberty/authority dichotomy rather than that of freewill/determinism. Thus, followers of Locke minimise the danger of majority tyranny in democracies ruled by representatives of the people ruled and emphasise the need to avoid regal tyranny, while Mill saw that the rulers are not the people ruled even in democracies and that tyranny could still arise from undue pressure on government to adopt laws against non-conforming or dissenting individuals even when these are harmless. He also saw that the pressure

351

of public opinion even without a legal basis may be strong enough to deprive such individuals of the usual benefits of society, and that there was a need for limits to be placed on the exercise of all such power whether by governments or by pressurising non-governmental organisations (NGOs). Mill also saw that while the first of these dangers might be mitigated by a "declaration of rights" such as the right to free speech, those arising from public opinion (notoriously susceptible to prejudice, superstition and ignorance) presented greater dangers best combated by a general freedom of action unless specifically prevented by law. In advocating individual freedom within society in this way, Mill states that suppression of opinions is an assertion of infallibility, that the suppressed opinion may be true, that when it is neither wholly true nor wholly false it may be clarified by open discussion, that when false it may be corrected by open discussion, and that individual responsibility requires mature and enlightened reflection on all issues facing society.

However, at this point readers may note that such discussion and debate would be needless were opinion to be differentiated as knowledge or belief by reality-evaluation; that the beliefs of Plato, Hobbes, Locke and Mill regarding the nature of government are mixed with knowledge (reality-validations) of human nature to varying degrees which distinguish one from another; that the influence upon them of such knowledge appears to be unconscious; and that adjudication as to the knowledge and belief contents of their respective positions could only be achieved by conscious reality-evaluation with respect to our group species survival needs. Thus, in seeking to adjudicate between opinions (belief options) by debate rather than by reality-evaluation, philosophers remain stuck in the Rational Duality either through ignorance or self-interested recognition that the Rational Trinity would destroy their opportunities to philosophise.

10. 6 POLITICAL ECONOMY

In classical times disposable wealth depended on access to coinage metals. Thus, the cost of building the Athenian fleet which defeated the Persians at Salamis was met by adventitious discovery of silver in the Athenian lead-mines, plunder from foreign wars was largely in bullion and coinage, individual expenditure and lending were the means to socio-political influence, and though there were systems of taxation, often hypothecated, there was no financial system as we know it. Indeed, lending at interest being counter to Christian and Islamic teaching, such business was conducted by Jews until interest-bearing bonds were made respectable by the Medici *en route* to banking as practiced by the Dutch and by the UK after the Glorious Revolution.

In any case, moral philosophy with jurisprudence and economics was central to the Scottish universities' curriculum when Adam Smith (1723-1790) was a student under Hutcheson. Later, as professor of moral philosophy, his own lectures in jurisprudence became so dominated by economics that he started to write a book on 'the nature of public opulence' before he left Glasgow in 1764. Thereafter as tutor to the Duke of Buccleuch on the 'Grand Tour', he met the Physiocrats whose Stoic-derived doctrine of natural law and rights opposed government interference with free-trade (laissez faire) as Smith had done in his university lectures and in his discussions with Glasgow merchants. Thus, shortly after his return from France at the end of 1766 he began *An Enquiry into the Nature and Causes of the Wealth of Nations*.

The prevailing belief was that national wealth depended on the possession of bullion, hence the Spanish preoccupation with the Americas. However, the reality for Adam Smith was that gold and silver became cheaper the more they entered Europe; that their sole use was in producing plate and coinage; that wear in use and the practice of coin-clipping required losses to be made good with intermittent re-coining; and that paper money could be substituted at relatively insignificant cost. Nonetheless, belief in the need to conserve reserves of bullion caused governments to tax imports and subsidise exports with the objective of maintaining a balance of trade favourable to home country reserves, the corollary being that colonies were valued only as providing raw materials and a market for manufactured goods at prices favourable to the home country, to which end colonies were prevented from competitive manufacture and export. Though David Hume had criticised this protectionist policy to some extent, he continued to believe national wealth to be a matter of bullion. However, Adam Smith saw that this belief was the source-error of mercantilism as he now termed such protectionism; that the wealth of nations is their productive labour and consumable goods, not their bullion holdings; that wealth increases as goods and services become cheaper through increased production while anything contributing to scarcity and higher costs produces impoverishment; and that free-trade is thus preferable to mercantilism even for merchants.

Thus, for Smith, wealth increases with the volume of trade between individuals, groups and nations, the increase having started when individuals ceased to do everything for themselves and began the specialisation which he termed the *Division of Labour* (c.f. Chapter 2 and Section 8.1.9). Thus, if a man grows wheat while another bakes bread their cooperation as specialists will produce a greater stock for sale than would their non-specialist involvement in both. In this connection, Smith showed that a pin factory produced 50,000 pins per day by employing ten men on eighteen separate operations, while an unskilled man on his own could not expect to make more than one or two in a day; that the initial impetus to invent and improve the necessary tools for increased production comes from the workers themselves and only later from professional design engineers; and that the latter provide a further example of the division of labour (c.f. Sections 5.7, 8.1 and 9.5). Smith went on to observe that even the modest possessions of an eighteenth century labourer or peasant depended on "the assistance and cooperation of many thousands" and that such cooperation grows spontaneously from the (innate) tendencies of human nature (c.f. Chapters 2 and 3). Thus, his *Invisible Hand* directs the market to the division of labour which enhances the welfare of society without needing 'management' by government in areas where, as exemplified in Chapter 11, it has neither the knowledge nor the organisation required. Thus, the division of labour and Invisible Hand on the Workings of the Market are the causes of the Wealth of Nations.

With regard to market operation, Smith discusses prices and economic value by distinguishing between the real price (value) and nominal price (in money) and argues that "labour is the real measure of the exchangeable value of all commodities" and that fair compensation is due for the "toil and trouble" taken by the worker and avoided by the purchaser. Again, he argues that nominal prices depend on wages, profit and rent; that wages relate to value as defined above; that profit relates to the amount of capital (stock) put in by the owner to provide raw materials, tools and factory, while his organisational and managerial work relate to wages as defined; and that rent is payable for the use of land. Smith then distinguishes between market price and natural price, the former fluctuating with supply, demand and self-interest, the latter being the average about which the fluctuations range. He then argues that this average is related to the average of each of the three factors of cost; and that the natural price is that which will just pay for the natural rates of wages, profit, and rent. Thus, to Smith, a raising of market prices to achieve higher profits encourages more suppliers to enter the market and hence more competition and a lowering of market price to the natural level which maximises benefit to customers, while a market price less than its natural level will not cover the costs of production and hence compensatory reductions in wages, profit or rent will turn workers, factory owners or landowners to other sources of income, whereupon scarcity of supply will raise the price towards its natural level.

As to the bargaining-power of labour, Smith recognises the relationship between the prices of grains, bread and meat to be basic determinants. Thus, if the worker cannot afford to buy food no work can be done. Beyond this, he recognised that wage rates need to compensate for danger, wear and tear on health, and length of training; and that in general the balance of happiness should be more or less equal in all occupations. In this connection he incidentally notes that slavery is less wealth-creating to an owner than are free workers to an employer. He noted also that bargaining-power is always higher in developing economies such as those of eighteenth century Britain and the USA than in stagnant ones such as those of China and Bengal at that time. He also noted that while profit resembles wages in being related to the degree of unpleasantness and risk in running a business, the best indicator of the natural rate of profit is the average rate of bank interest, both being a measure of return on capital while the landlord expects as much as he can get in rent and the tenant pays what he can afford having deducted wages and profit. As to profit disposition, Smith recognised that a producer cannot expect to sell at the rate of production; that he must store his production until he can sell it; that some of the money thus acquired must be spent on immediate consumption while the rest must be divided into fixed and circulating capital; that the first is used for tools, machines, factory building or land improvement; that the latter is used to buy raw materials and to pay wages and rent; and that such utilised stock must be replenished to sustain the business, and more than replenished to expand it. However, Smith also recognised that not all workers contribute to business maintenance through their production, some such as personal domestic servants representing points of consumption to their employer.

As to nations, Smith recognised that wealth increases with production; that production increases with having more productive workers and more efficient tools and machines; that capital expenditure should thus be maximised on productive activities and minimised on non-productive activities. Nonetheless, he recognised that some non-productive consumption was unavoidable. Thus, though he agreed with the Physiocrats that governments should leave well alone in national and global markets, he recognised that government had some unavoidable public duties which could not be left to the private sector, these being defence against external enemies and maintenance of internal law and order; and that taxation could be levied for such purposes, being to this extent an acceptable interference with an otherwise free market. In addition, he recognised the need to raise revenue for public works concerning roads, canals, bridges and harbours, though even here private enterprise would be more cost-effective; for the provision of forts and ambassadors to protect and advance foreign trade; and for education, though his experience at Glasgow and Balliol showed that university teachers took more care over instruction when at least some of their income came *directly* from their students as at Glasgow. As to elementary (pre-university) education, he recommended parish provision and compulsory attendance.

Again, while Adam Smith had identified the (reality-validated) disadvantages of mercantilism, David Ricardo identified the *Comparative Advantage of Free Trade* by which the cheapest possible goods and services are accessible on a global basis, thus further emphasising the need for government interference to be minimal to zero. Nonetheless, Karl Marx (1818-1883) in believing Hegel's *Dialectic* to be a general *Law of History* believed that it was a non-metaphysical and thus 'scientific' explanation more applicable to the social class struggle than to struggle between nation states to which Hegel had *inter alia* applied it; that class struggle was a more reliable pointer to the future than anything offered by Adam Smith and his acolytes; and that communism would terminate the class struggle and the dialectic, there being no synthesis of free-trade and its anti-thesis other than communism and no anti-thesis to the latter.

Thus, by applying Hegel to the class struggle Marx interpreted history as the sequence in which early autocracies broke down through struggle (the dialectic) between kings (thesis) and nobles (antithesis) out of which feudalism was born (synthesis); in which feudalism broke down through the struggle of landed lords and serfs out of which capitalism and the employed were born; and in which
354

capitalism would finally break down through the struggle between employers and employees out of which communism would be born. Marx also argued that the means of production is determined by the class system in any culture; that dispersed cottage-based production was determined by the feudal class structure; and that factory production was determined by the class structure of capitalism. However, while Marx's interpretation of Hegelian belief might be academically acceptable, its real world implementation was likely to be fraught with difficulty. Indeed, its 1917 implementation by Lenin (1870-1924) was only achieved by violent overthrow of a system which had real prospects of achieving social improvement by the wealth creation and distributive mechanisms set forth by Adam Smith. Thus, industrialisation was offering better prospects to rural labour, industrial conditions were being ameliorated by such as Robert Owen (1771-1858) and mass production by such as Henry Ford (1863-1947) was ensuring that his factory workers could buy his model T motorcar of (1908-09) of which 15 million had been produced by 1928 with price reduction by a factor of ~ 4. To set such actual developments aside for Marx's belief-based promise was to terminate the knowledge-based progress of humankind, though the belief was tenacious enough to accept Gulag death-rates as justified by this promise, some being faithful to belief even when reality-refuted by its failure on implementation as further considered in Chapter 11.

Nonetheless, Marx had been confronted with three social classes, one too many for the dialectic. Thus, there were capitalists who owned the means of production and distribution, the workers who were dependent on them and a middle class of small businessmen and professionals. To reduce these to two, Marx rationalised that increase in productivity would increase the wealth of the capitalist class to form a small very wealthy class and a large indigent proletariat, the dialectic revolutionary struggle of which would produce ultimate synthesis to the classless society of communism with the success which had eluded the French Revolution of 1789. Thus, despite all knowledge-based human progress having been due to hierarchical social cohesion, Marx believed it could and should be replaced with 'liberty, equality and brotherhood', and though such belief was to be again reality-refuted, believers are still to be found.

In support of his beliefs, Marx reasoned that the economic value of a commodity is largely the cost of the labour which goes into its production; that its exchange value is its price in the marketplace; that surplus-value is the difference between the economic value which a worker produces and the amount which he actually receives from his employer; that the exchange value is limited by marketplace competition, as Adam Smith would have agreed; that the employer thus seeks to maximise profit by the only way open to him, which is to drive down the wage element of production, with which Smith would have disagreed. Nonetheless, Marx reasoned that employer desire for profit maximisation and worker desire for wage maximisation would make inter-class strife inevitable as marketplace competition constrained the exchange value available to the employer. Though this could be so, it ignores the reality that employers and workers are free to move to more advantageous sources of income as *per* Adam Smith; and that employers are free to ensure production costs are low enough and wages high enough to permit workers to buy the goods they produce as *per* such as Henry Ford. As always, contending beliefs can only be resolved by reality-evaluation though belief is often retained even after its reality-refutation.

Marx believed the collapse of capitalism to be inevitable, not only because of the dialectic, but also because it could not correct the internal defects he believed it to have. Thus, he additionally argued the immorality of capitalism on the belief that it forces men to treat others as means and as tradable commodities; that it produces worker isolation, self-alienation, insecurity and fear of uncontrollable technologies; that its production of possessions in ever-increasing diversity and numbers leads to their worship; and that it thus depersonalises human relationships by treating men as machines and products as idols. At this point it should be recalled (c.f. Chapter 4) that one belief leads to another along whatever route rationality has chosen to follow; that the consequences of capitalism are presented negatively by Marx though they can be presented positively; that assertions one way or the other can only be adjudicated by reality-evaluation; and that true believers are always reluctant to adopt this course of action, even if on rare occasions it occurs to them. However, Marx was right to the extent that communism has never been guilty of 'producing possessions in ever-increasing diversity and numbers'.

However, reality is difficult to dismiss permanently. The communists faced difficulties in this respect from the start and responded with forceful suppression of reality-based dissent, while the capitalist world faced its own difficulties which many believed to be a fulfilment of Marx's prophesies. Thus, when the market failed in the 1920s through a lack of the confidence needed to maintain private investment, there was a consequent slump in stock value, an increase in unemployment and the emergence of two different beliefs as to rectification. Those who followed Marx with varying degrees of enthusiasm opted for central government (state) intervention in various forms while the free-marketers more validly looked to a natural recovery when the cheapness of stock would rekindle private sector confidence to invest in re-growth. However, it had to be admitted that no one knew how long this would take and so Europe went for the permanent state intervention of socialism while the USA went for the New Deal through public investment in major construction projects while retaining confidence in the free market in the longer term. Meanwhile, theorists of political economy went for varying degrees of state intervention under such as Maynard Keynes and John Kenneth Galbraith. Later, when state intervention led to the printing of money to meet ever-increasing wage demands without proportionate productivity increase, the relative inability of such inflated money to buy internal goods and services of increasing scarcity or higher priced imports caused such as Hayek and Freedman to advocate curtailment of money supply in proportion to productivity increase through freeing the private sector from the state's counter-productive interventions.

Thus, while the state intervention of communism succumbed to the reality which it ignored, that of the democracies continues to expand by ignoring Adam Smith's efforts to come to terms with reality through optimal state intervention. Thus, the democracies increasingly suppress the private independence which created the wealth of nations by redistributing it through tax-benefit and public expenditure systems designed to attract the electoral collusion of co-believers to the benefit of political establishments irrespective of party so long as reality permits. However, as to reality, taxation of private industry causes a loss of investment towards further wealth creation while the alternate 'investment' of revenue in public services creates a further loss because these are not only wealth-consuming but also under-productive or loss-making. Indeed, this analysis shows that private enterprise should be encouraged, and that limitation of public expenditure to such unavoidable activities as were recognised by Adam Smith would permit gradual tax reductions to perhaps 50% of current levels accompanied by decreased opportunities to buy belief-based votes and increased regard for knowledge and for the dangers of ignored reality.

Currently, the decreased confidence which periodically afflicts capitalism arises from the bursting of investment bubbles caused by individuals, banks and governments investing in unreality, and in some cases even borrowing to do so beyond the ability to fund their borrowings or to return them on demand. Thus, while governments should not engage in such activities with public money, neither should they encourage lending to become over-stretched with regard to paying on demand, or over-exposed to default by borrowers, while any correcting regulation should be intended to eliminate fraudulent practice rather than private-enterprise itself. Again, electorates should be aware that despite economic theory having become increasingly mathematical, it has none of the predictive ability which would justify its self-proclaimed scientific status, its data

356

collection and use being too subject to political interference for anything more than *post facto* 'explanations' on the basis of one politico-economic belief or another, there being always more than one.

Nonetheless, it should be noted that even in knowledge-based fields individuals are not averse to self-interested involvement in belief-based socio-politics. Thus, while the Board of Longitude (c.f. Section 8.1.4) should have been disbanded when Harrison solved its problem, it remained, under the chairmanship of Sir Humphrey Davy, to press Michael Faraday to study glass properties and compositions in the belief-based hope of improving the performance of optical instruments. Had such a mission-driven committee been self-charged or socio-politically requested to improve artificial lighting, it would doubtless have pressed Faraday to study candle flames, such being the way of government-committees in areas best left to independent scientists and private entrepreneurs (c.f. Chapter 2, and Sections 5.7, 8.1 and 9.5). Indeed, while the Manhattan Project and the Moon Mission were successful applications of existing knowledge, public funding of belief-based missions to new knowledge through committees, councils, agencies *etc*, produce more activity than progress in being more akin to the optical-glass mission of the Longitude Committee than to Faraday's investigation of electricity and magnetism which incidentally improved artificial lighting and much else without the 'assistance' of anything resembling a committee.

Similarly, belief-inspired models of the economy however mathematical will not predict its future state so long as they do not replicate its actual mechanism and so long as the input data do not define its current state (c.f. Section 11.2.4). Thus, for example, so long as belief-inspired political committees decide which factors are to be included in or deleted from calculation of the cost of living index, debt-levels, risk *etc*, so long will economics fail to be a science capable of making reliable predictions, this failure being further evidenced by defensive claims that the current financial crisis was unpredictable. Indeed, economics is so out of touch with the difference between knowledge (reality) and belief (unreality) as to have the Nobel Prize awarded for formulae and procedures believed to dispose of risk or render it harmless despite its continuance and associated liabilities in reality. Thus, economics will remain a pseudo-science no matter how many awards it acquires, so long as it pretends to 'knowledge' while being incapable of making predictions even at the level of commonsense.

Thus it may be concluded, that the arbitrary beliefs of soviet communism failed to provide the welfare levels achieved elsewhere despite its rich endowment in natural resources; and that while the more varied beliefs of current liberal democracies could be reality-evaluated for optimal welfare benefit, they too remain arbitrary and exposed to failure. As to knowledge, Adam Smith unlike Marx did not claim to have discovered a new means to human betterment lacking until 1776, he simply and rightly attributed general wealth creation to innate human enterprise and cautioned against its being restricted even by eighteenth century levels of (belief-driven) intervention. Nonetheless, despite the obvious failure of Marxist-Leninist belief, Smith's description of reality continues to be subverted by increasing levels of belief-driven state intervention. Again, while advances in welfare and wealth creation have always been due to non-political craftsmanship, science and technology, politicians now claim credit for both while reducing the enterprise and personal responsibility on which they depended. Yet again, while promising further advances through state dependency they deny the success achieved by the enterprise and responsibility encouraged by such as Owen and Cadbury in the UK and Ford in the USA. Nonetheless, it is surely not too late to submit contending socio-political beliefs to reality-evaluation lest uncontrolled liberal democrats replicate the catastrophic consequences of communism to the likelihood of which I return in Chapters 11 and 12.

10. 7 PHILOSOPHY OF RELIGION

We have seen (c.f. Section 2.5.4 and Chapters 4 and 5) that religious belief has been widespread since time immemorial; that *Old Testament* prophets and lawgivers together with Zoroaster, Buddha and Confucius predate the Forms and Ideal Good of Plato as later assimilated by Christianity and Islam; that belief in God, one way or another, was central to metaphysics until Hume began to question the nature of metaphysical substance in parallel with science's replacement of essence and spirit by matter and energy. Again, we have seen that despite this replacement having implications for substance and hypostasis with respect to the Holy Trinity, belief in God remains the Ur-belief of religion; and that despite this belief being beyond reality-evaluation, many believers require 'evidence' to sustain their belief and to assist in the conversion of others, while secularists seek 'evidence' to sustain their agnosticism or atheism. Thus, while believers seek to demonstrate the existence of God by reference to the nature of the creation as revealed by scientific method or by reference to philosophical conclusions reached by rationality alone, atheists come to the opposite conclusion on the same 'evidence', believers advancing the *Argument from Design*, the *Cosmological Argument* and the *Ontological Argument* while non-believers counter these as with mirror images. Thus, these arguments will now be considered in reverse order before considering what philosophy has had to say about the nature of God in the belief or disbelief that He exists.

According to Anselm, the Ontological Argument runs as follows. God is that being than which none greater can be conceived. Since I can comprehend this definition of God, I can conceive of God. Moreover, I can conceive of God existing not only as a concept in my own mind but also as existing in reality *i.e.* independently of my ideas. Since it is greater to exist both as an idea and as a real thing than merely to exist as an idea, God must exist both in reality and as an idea. This argument is presented by Spinoza as "God, or substance consisting of infinite attributes, of which each expresses eternal and infinite essentiality, necessarily exists". Again, according to Descartes ". . .there would be no less contradiction in conceiving of a God, that is, of a being supremely perfect, to whom existence was wanting, that is to say, to whom there was wanting any perfection, than in conceiving of a mountain which had no valley." The Cosmological Argument, on the other hand, derives from Aristotle who argued that since all events have causes there must have been a first cause for the cosmos itself, and that the first cause or prime mover must be God. It has also been argued in parallel, that since all events have explanations there must be an ultimate explanation for the cosmos itself and that this requires the existence of God. This Cosmological Argument as set out in the *Summa Theologica* of Thomas Aquinas remains the position of the Roman Catholic Church among others, though it fails to admit the difference in logic between events in the cosmos and the cosmos itself. In contrast the Argument from Design purports to establish from our knowledge of the detailed nature of the mechanical universe, the existence of a *Designer-God*.

These being the so-called proofs of the existence of God, I now turn to what philosophy has rationalised concerning the nature of God. Thus, if we cannot prove that God exists and conversely cannot prove that He does not, we should perhaps consider the nature we could reasonably expect God to have were He to exist. We have seen (c.f. Chapter 4) that Neo-Platonists and Arian Christians had difficulty with the non-Arian belief in God being incarnate in Jesus and living as a man. Thus, while the former could believe Jesus to be a man inspired by God, the latter required Father and Son to be at least similarly Divine. All of this touched on Pagan difficulty with believing the Divine to act other than through human rationality, this difficulty being compounded with the action of the mind on the real world in what was later discussed in metaphysics and epistemology as the mind/body problem, this compound difficulty being further compounded with belief in the Holy Trinity as separate from the world but acting in and on it, taking an interest in individual human lives on earth and offering eternal life thereafter. Meanwhile, from Epicurus onwards, philosophers had to face the contradiction of an all-powerful and just God who seems to violate the Good as humanised in ethics though Plato believed the Good to be anterior even to God. Thus, rational consideration of the religious Ur-belief leads to differing and conflicting derivative beliefs.

However, Deism seeks to avoid the above difficulties by depriving its Separate Power of any direct influence on events occurring in the universe as it now exists. Thus, God having created the universe, wound it up and set it running as would a watchmaker a watch, each successive state of the mechanism is explicable in terms of its previous state with no need or opportunity for subsequent intervention. On the other hand, the Pantheism of Spinoza believed there was no separation, God and Nature being one and the same Divine Substance with everything which exists or occurs being an aspect, modification or attribute of the Divine Substance; that everything is explained or accounted for by showing the manner of its derivation from the Divine Substance, every physical or mental event in the universe being an aspect of the thought or extension of the Divine Substance; and that the proper attitude to the Divine Substance is to appreciate its character through understanding the nature of reality without expecting any specific concern or intervention on behalf of mankind. Nonetheless, despite the paradoxes and contradictions which Deism and Pantheism seek to avoid, the Theistic belief that the gods (polytheism) or God (monotheism) stand in some direct or personal relationship to mankind has remained widespread. However, while the contradictions inherent to Theism either do not arise or are more or less easy to explain away in respect of the limited powers of the individual gods of polytheism, they arise in full strength and cause maximum difficulty with the monotheism of the Judeo-Christian and Islamic traditions because of the mismatch between what we ethically expect of a perfectly good, omniscient and all-powerful God and what we see as the cruelty and injustice of our human world and the amorality of the natural world (c.f. Section 2.1).

Thus, Theistic philosophers seek to minimise this mismatch between specific tenets of particular religions and the central belief of Theism, while adherents of individual religions seek personal congeniality with the selected tenets of their respective sects. However, the contradictions are so pronounced as to provide opponents of these traditions and of the Ur-belief itself with ready tools for their 'demolition' work. Thus, David Hume discounts the Design and Cosmological Arguments in his *Dialogues on Natural Religion* by identifying short-comings in the design which are incompatible with God as Designer, by suggesting that design might be inherent to matter itself, by observing that cause/effect and design/artefact relationships cannot in logic be transposed by analogy from man to God, by identifying shortcomings in the moral order which are incompatible with God as Moralist and by suggesting that the Cosmos might just as well be infinite with no beginning and no end. Again, with respect to the Cosmological Argument, Kant argued in his *Critique of Pure Reason* that causality applies only to the world of sense-experience and cannot be carried over to that which is believed to transcend this experience; that we have no possibility of arriving at a first cause in any cause/effect train, nor any final explanation in any explanation train; and that in general there is no possibility of discussing that which is beyond our world by definition.

Thus, with respect to the religious Ur-belief and its derivatives we are reduced to faith, atheism or agnosticism: to acceptance, rejection or suspension. As to faith we can choose Tertullian (c.f. Section 4.2.5) whose assessment of Christianity could be, so absurd that it can only be believed, or Blaise Pascal who in *Les Pensees* said "Humble yourself, weak reason; be silent, foolish nature; . . . learn . . . what is your true condition, of which you are ignorant. Hear God." Nonetheless, traditional moral codes, ethics and political philosophies have knowledge-contents and beliefs open to reality-evaluation, and though both are treated as belief by both religious and secular, the former has never encouraged us to ignore the reality of our human nature which is more than can be said for secularism.

10. 8 MODERN PHILOSOPHY

The supremacy of empiricism over metaphysics in the philosophy of the USA derived from the influence of John Locke on its formative documents and law and was reinforced by the *Liberal Arts* influence of such notables of the Scottish Enlightenment as Hutcheson (*System of Moral Philosophy*) Kames (*Sketches of the History of Man*) Adam Smith (*A Theory of Moral Sentiments* and *Inquiry into the Nature and Causes of the Wealth of Nations*) and David Hume (*Treatise of Human Nature* and *Essays Political, Literary, and Moral*). Less well known were William Robertson (*History of Scotland* and *History of the Reign of Charles V*), Adam Ferguson (*Essay on the History of Civil Society*), John Millar (*The Origin of the Distinction of Ranks*) and Thomas Reid (*Inquiry into the Human Mind*). Indeed, in some cases the *Scottish School* became directly involved with such as John Witherspoon, Minister of the Kirk in Paisley being invited to become foundation President of Princeton University and Philadelphia attendee at the Continental Congress and Declaration of Independence. Thus, while metaphysics and epistemology had little to show for the European effort of some 2500 years, the UK's practical influence in the USA helped to justify empirical philosophy both academically and governmentally, though the arrival of some Germans after failure of the revolution of 1848 provided a stimulus towards European philosophy with their formation of the *St. Louis Hegelians* whose *Journal of Speculative Philosophy* provided a new medium for philosophical discussion among interested Americans.

One such was Henry James (Senior) of the Harvard Medical School whose interest in the psychology of the intellectual and religious life led to his becoming professor of philosophy at Harvard. His son, William James (1842-1910) in sharing the American aversion to speculation took the pragmatic approach of suggesting that philosophical theories should be instruments for the solution of humanity's problems; and that their instrumental truth should be judged by experience of their success or failure and expressed as their 'cash-value'. Thus, truth is what works, a valid claim in craftsmanship, science and technology, though counter to the philosophical tradition of truth being attainable by rationality alone and independent of human experience. Thus James, unimpressed by theological claims to 'religious truth' or by so-called philosophical or 'scientific' refutations of such claims, sought to determine their 'cash-value'. Accordingly, he argued in *The Varieties of Religious Experience* and in *The Will to Believe* that by disregarding the truth or falsehood of belief and simply observing whether or not it provides increased life-satisfaction for its believers, it can be pragmatically judged true for them.

William James was followed by John Dewey (1859-1952) who took *Pragmatism* to *Instrumentalism* in which our experience is not a known item. It is the encountering of successive situations which require thought towards actions judged appropriate or not by their success or failure when implemented. In his *Reconstruction in Philosophy*, Dewey argued that traditional philosophy was actually a hindrance, its insistence on absolute rational truth preventing solution of the practical problems of society. Thus, he sought to re-direct educational practice from contemplation of the philosophical past to development of problem-solving techniques for the future. As stated, this is more a surrender to scientific method than a basis for reconstructing philosophy. However, educational theorists driven more by the secular beliefs in equality, freedom and rights of liberal democracy than by the knowledge-based policies advocated by Dewey claim nonetheless to be his followers just as many claim to follow Adam Smith while denying him.

In the meantime, back in the old country, renewed efforts were being made by Bertrand Russell (1872-1970) and Alfred North Whitehead (1861-1947) to establish meaning in traditional philosophy by their new discipline of *Mathematical* (or *Symbolic*) *Logic*. In *Principia Mathematica* they presented the mathematical postulates of arithmetic as clarifying the meaning of sentences in natural language. Thus, they reported that complex (molecular) sentences (propositions) always consist of simpler (atomic) propositions connected by words such as 'and', 'or', and 'if . . . then', the rules for the use of which constitute part of the logic-element of this approach, while the other is the analysis of meaning in the separate atomic propositions. As to the latter it was reported that atomic propositions are always of the subject and predicate form, the subject denoting an individual thing and the predicate denoting a characteristic of the thing; that both together denote a fact; that the world consists of such facts; that there are no molecular propositions (no molecular facts) in nature, all such being reducible to the atomic level; that the connecting words in molecular propositions refer to nothing in the world, being syntactic only; that there are no general facts either, all general propositions being reducible to sets of atomic propositions and hence to sets of facts; and that, therefore, the function of philosophy is to inform us about the world of these facts, structured in the form of atomic propositions (c.f. Section 10.1).

On this basis, Russell and Whitehead showed more than a little laboriously, that previous philosophers had mistaken non-existence for existence by failing to realise that grammatical form is not necessarily identical with logical form; and that the transformation of sentences from their grammatical to their logical form according to the procedures of the *Principia* demonstrated whether they had meaning or not. Thus, for example, although the sentence, 'God exists' is grammatically correct having 'God' as subject and 'exists' as predicate, the prescribed transformation shows it to be akin to the sentence, 'The present King of France is wise'. Thus, they showed that such "incomplete symbols" cannot be constituents of atomic propositions; that such sentences do not correspond to facts in the world; and that consequently they have no meaning. There being no present King of France, it is meaningless to describe him in any way. Readers may conclude that reality-evaluation is more straightforward.

Subsequently Ludwig Wittgenstein (1889-1951) in the *Tractatus Logico Philosophicus*, developed *Logical Atomism* to what is now called *Picture Theory* in which the language of the *Principia* pictures the structure of reality as a map pictures the surface of the earth. Thus, for every proper name and related predicate in this language there is a corresponding entity and property in reality, from which it follows that the mistakes of traditional philosophy are eliminated by the analytical procedure of testing whether the sentences of natural language can be re-written in their proper logical form according to the *Principia*; and that though philosophy produces no *new* factual knowledge, it is a genuine activity in being of assistance in avoiding mistaken conclusions. Readers may conclude that reality-evaluation is more straightforward. Nonetheless, the next step in the philosophical identification of meaning was taken by the members of the Vienna Circle such as Moritz Schlick and Rudolf Carnap whose work in developing *Logical Positivism* is perhaps most readily accessible through A. J. Ayer in his *Language, Truth and Logic* of 1946. Thus, Logical Positivism shows that philosophical enquiry cannot produce propositions which are true or false. It merely classifies statements as mathematical or expressions of formal logic, as scientific or as the nonsensical remainder which included most (if not all) of philosophy.

Thus, while statements classified as nonsensical could be described as poetical, emotive, pictorial or motivational at best, they are always non-cognitive. As to the cognitive, these were classed as significant, with mathematical and logical propositions being analytic, and scientific propositions being synthetic (c. f. Kant, Section 10.3). In addition, analytic statements do not refer to the world as such, being true merely by definition or logical form, these being described as trivial, whereas synthetic statements do refer to the world, may be true or false and thus require verification (reality-evaluation), these being described as informative. According to Ayer a sentence will be factually (synthetically) meaningful, if and only if the proposition which it purports to convey can be observed under definable conditions to be either true or false: if not it is meaningless. Again, as Carnap has put it: traditional philosophy purports to tell us something about the world, but because its utterances are in general empirically unverifiable they are either trivially analytic or meaningless. Furthermore in discussing *Verification*, David Rynin explains that to discover what a question means is identical to discovering how one would go about answering it. Thus we can see that the proposition that there is life on Mars is meaningful because it is observationally verifiable or refutable and we know at least in principle how to answer it, while the proposition that there is a God in Heaven is not observationally verifiable or refutable and is therefore meaningless.

Later, Wittgenstein claimed that a perfect language which fully pictured the world could not be realised, and showed by what he called language games how subtle extensions of the use of the terms of ordinary speech led to difficulties in philosophical discussion. Thus, instead of seeking the meaning of certain terms through analysis as Russell and his followers had done, Wittgenstein now sought to indicate significance by showing how such terms are actually used. This approach has led Gilbert Ryle to claim in *The Concept of Mind* that misunderstanding the logic of key terms used to describe mental phenomena such as 'knowing', 'inferring', 'believing' has led to the belief that a non-observable entity referred to as 'the mind' exists, is located separately within the body and feels, thinks, believes and knows, whereas Ryle refers to these activities as dispositions to act, such as those of salt and sugar to dissolve in water. Thus, saying that a person knows something is saying that under certain conditions he is able (has the disposition) to perform in a certain way. Thus, 'knowing' is not a covert activity of an non-observable entity, but the exercise of a capacity (disposition) and hence, 'the ghost in the machine' is a false concept.

To this, I would say that the 'mind' is a superfluous concept beyond reality-evaluation in any case; that the physicochemical brain operates the Rational Duality and Trinity by physicochemical interaction with external physicochemical reality; that beliefs generated by the Duality differ because we are individually different; that beliefs relating to reality can be transformed to knowledge by the reality-evaluation of the Trinity because reality is constant and our capacity to interact with it is species-specific; and that we act accordingly as defined herein.

However, while some philosophers had finally confirmed for themselves that rationality alone cannot produce knowledge, it was not to be expected that all would quietly retire. Indeed, while some had effectively closed-down by declaring philosophy to be solely concerned with clarification of meaning and while I define meaning as reality-validated knowledge and non-meaning as reality-refuted belief, others such as G. E. Moore sought to retain belief. Thus, recalling Hume's belief that moral concepts cannot be derived from scientific premises any more securely than from those of theology or metaphysics because descriptions cannot produce prescriptions in logic, Moore in his Principia Ethica of 1903 asserted that the attempt to define good and bad in terms of descriptive statements about God, metaphysical goodness or human nature, made 'good' synonymous with 'approved by God' and eliminated moral meaning. Thus, having rejected scientific knowledge with an undefined reference to 'premises' and having rejected empiricism despite its reference to reality, modern ethics became the analysis meaning by classifying ethical theories without questioning Hume's belief and without-reference to reality-evaluation.

As to this, I say that good and bad should be defined as either conducive and non-conducive to the survival of *Homo sapiens* as a group-species, just as good and bad are defined as working or not working in craftsmanship, science and technology; that our concepts of good and bad are therefore species-innate; and that by the time ethicists and political philosophers began to consider behaviour codes they were dealing with products reality-evaluated against or survival requirements as a group-species whether consciously or not; that in quoting Hume, Moore was failing to realise this reality; and that to ignore the obvious success of empiricism in ethics and experimentation in science when metaphysicians and epistemologists had recognised the validity of sense-experience in their own terms, is surely perverse.

Nonetheless, those who continue to philosophise continue to ignore reality in following Hume's mistaken belief. Thus, with respect to classification, a subjectivist ethical theory is defined as one in which ethical judgements are neither true nor false or are true or false only in relation to the individual psychology of those who utter them, while an objectivist theory is one which is non-subjectivist. Thus, Hobbes is subjectivist in believing that moral language is just an expression of personal feelings, inclinations and desires, as is Kant to the extent that he turns ethical judgements into commands classified as neither true or false. In contrast, Plato is objectivist because for him moral judgements are either true or false just as mathematical judgements are said to be. However, the above classification focuses on whether moral judgements are akin to 'tastes' or not, being devoid of other significance. Again a naturalistic theory is one according to which moral judgements are true or false and reducible entirely to the 'concepts' of science, usually of psychology and otherwise undefined, while a non-naturalist theory is one in which moral judgements are true or false but are not reducible to any scientific 'concept', this term remaining undefined. Yet again, in a motivist theory moral judgements are not true or false, being merely expressive of the feelings of those who utter them, and evocative of the feelings of those who hear them.

Though the effect of such classification is that ethics is either a branch of philosophy or of science, Moore believed that moral statements are not analogous to scientific statements in that the moral element in them is an expression of feeling and not a statement about anything, this appearing to be the Hobbesian belief shared among modern philosophers by Carnap, Ayer and others. Again, if a motivist theory believes that action depends on the motive from which it was committed, Kant's ethics would be motivist. Yet again Utilitarianism should be an obvious example of a consequence theory, though there are apparently two sub-groups, the hedonistic and the agathistic. In the former the consequences are either pleasurable or painful, in the latter anything other. Finally, there are deontological theories in which rightness or wrongness depends neither on motive nor on consequence, but solely on the nature of the act itself, such being, for example, the keeping of promises with such theories being thus referred to as duty ethics.

Ethics being thus either philosophy or science and with the former being incapable of producing knowledge, one might have expected further enquiry to be 'science-based'. Again with ethics having demoted itself to a process for classifying theories (beliefs) rather than a provider of empirical (reality-evaluated) guidance to behaviour, one has to wonder what a philosopher believes a psychologist to be and *vice versa*, reality-evaluation having been removed from ethics and apparently from psychology as evidenced in Section 11.2.5. Indeed, post-modernism rejects science itself in believing all to be relative belief. Thus, according to philosophy and the social sciences under its influence, not only is God dead, knowledge and morality are too, with everything now being a matter of belief and with socio-political policy needing only to be acceptable to majority belief as shown in Section 11.2.1.

10. 9 CONCLUSIONS

With modern metaphysicians and epistemologists having rejected the Ur-belief in rationality in conceding sense-experience (reality-evaluation) to be our only source of knowledge, and having concluded that religious and philosophical attempts to obtain knowledge beyond sense-experience (reality-evaluation) are futile, there might have been universal agreement that those who remain active in ethics, political philosophy and political economy are bereft of knowledge unless they submit their beliefs to reality-evaluation as scientists; and that those who adhere solely to rationality may be dismissed by the public just as metaphysicians and epistemologists have dismissed themselves. Alas, it must be concluded that continuing reliance on rationality is corrupting psychology to the pseudo-science which generally confuses the public as to the nature of scientific method and the difference between science and pseudo-science.

However, as to the undifferentiated mixture of belief and knowledge which was ethics, it may be concluded that despite Plato's belief in a Good accessible only to rationality, his knowledge of Goodness was his sense-perception of human nature as was Aristotle's behaviour guidance; that the ethics of Zeno and Epictetus (Stoicism) and of Diogenes (Cynicism) reflected their differing sense-perceptions of human response to social disruption; that Epicurus, Hutcheson and Bentham reflected their sense-perceptions of the social implications of human nature; and that Hobbes, Locke and Mill similarly took account of human nature and the social realities of their times. Again, while Spinosa and Kant were more metaphysical and less self-centred than Hume, it may be concluded that all three were influenced by their respective sense-perceptions of the social need for personal responsibility and duty as is reflected by Stoicism, Judeo-Christianity and Islam; and that Hegel used his dialectic to explain social evolution in terms of historical sense-perceptions while Marx rejected reality in favour of belief and while Adam Smith described reality as he observed it to be. Thus, we may conclude that guidance on requirements for living the Good Life within an improving society has always been an amalgam of varying proportions of undifferentiated knowledge and belief; that the belief-content of politico-economic systems renders them variously incompatible with the reality of human nature; and that the reaction of this reality to Marx's 'final' synthesis demonstrated the extent of its incompatibility.

However, it may also concluded that previous ethical and socio-political systems do not define the Good explicitly in terms of the survival requirements of *Homo sapiens*, except perhaps that of Kant with its restatement of the Judaic, Stoic, Christian and Islamic admonition to do unto others as you would have them do to you; that of James who would judge the validity of propositions by whether or not they work in experience (in reality); and that of Dewey who would rationally formulate solutions to problems the validity of which would be judged by experience (reality-evaluation). Thus, it is implicit in these systems that good is synonymous with what works and bad with what does not work. In contrast, Rousseau believed the Good to be whatever the individual wants free from all external restraint, this being a recipe for chaos rather than for social cohesion, while for post-modernist liberal democrats the Good is whatever the majority believes at any time, a Rousseau-like freedom moderated only by the ballot box.

Thus, overall, we may conclude that behaviour codes and socio-political systems have been mixtures of undifferentiated belief and knowledge since time immemorial; that the knowledge-content relating to individual and social survival was acquired by observational sense-perception (reality-evaluation) just as knowledge of tools and artefacts had been acquired for this purpose; that while philosophers eventually recognised the futility of relying on rationality alone, they still failed to differentiate knowledge from belief, right from wrong, and good from bad on reality-evaluation of our group-species survival requirements; and that instead they rejected empiricism and proceeded to reject reality itself.

CHAPTER 11 REJECTION OF REALITY

Though our failure to differentiate belief from knowledge did not prevent knowledge-acquisition and use, it permitted craftsmanship to be ignored, science and technology to be conflated with rationality and empirical ethics to be conflated with religious belief and rejected as such by secular belief. Again, while rejected-reality has overthrown regressive dictatorships, the curtailment of social progress in liberal democracies is obscured by conflation of knowledge with relative belief in continuing rejection of reality.

As to this rejection, Section 11.1 shows that *Academia* defines its *Truth* as rationality, belief thus remaining ubiquitous with only a small minority being engaged in knowledge-acquisition; that technology detaches everyone from reality to varying extents and encourages beliefs counter to our self-knowledge and to technology itself; and that the corrective is reality-evaluation of all such beliefs. Again, Section 11.2 shows that while the advantages of knowledge are obvious, no relativist belief is ever submitted to reality-evaluation; that beliefs in equality, freedom, rights and environment have instead been supported by rejections of commonsense and general knowledge, by selection of 'evidence' and by corruption of specific knowledge and of scientific method; that these misjudgements can be corrected only by exposure of 'Truth' (belief) to reality-evaluation and exposure of all policy failure as reality-refutation of such 'Truth'; that this correction can be maintained only by future beliefs being reality-validated prior to implementation and by future policy being based on knowledge thus enhanced; and that anything less risks social disruption by the reality otherwise ignored or actively rejected.

11. 1 PREFERENCE FOR BELIEF OVER KNOWLEDGE

The current rejection of reality which prefers belief to knowledge is facilitated by our continuing failure to differentiate the one from the other. Thus, even in science-education their differentiation is implicit rather than explicit with science histories conflating knowledge with rationality and doing little or nothing to explain experimentation (c.f. Sections 6.1, 6.3.4 and 12.1) or to exemplify its practice (c.f. Chapters 6, 7, 8 and 9. Again, in the humanities 'Truth' is a matter of rationally comparing and construing what is undifferentiated belief and knowledge though it passes for 'evidence' in jurisprudence, history and literary criticism. Indeed, mistrials frequently arise from judicial inability to separate the undifferentiated mixtures of belief and knowledge presented by self-styled experts. As to preference for belief over knowledge, it is clear that those educated in the humanities disparage the educational value of science and technology and ignore craftsmanship; that scientists fail with everyone else to differentiate belief from knowledge, even failing to explain scientific method in terms of this difference; that the public thus misunderstands scientific method and is unable to differentiate science from pseudo-science; and that none of the job options which attract public attention are conditional on the ability to differentiate knowledge from belief. Indeed, administrative civil servants flaunt their 'generalist ability' to operate without specific knowledge and deal only with the similarly ignorant. As to the few knowledge providers, a science historian of my early acquaintance, Andrew Kent, used to say that creativity was limited to about two minutes on a good day, that the results of a consistent three or four might put one among the 'Immortals' and that the rest was tedium or teaching. I now say that the whole is a confusion of belief within which we all do what we know how, guided at best by commonsense and conditioned reflex.

Indeed in earlier times, belief and knowledge, Ideal and Real were an undifferentiated continuum within which ancient philosophers believed fire and metal working to be god-given and took for granted the craft knowledge which supported their leisure for speculative conjecture. Thus, Aristotle would have been as unaware of reality-evaluation in his observation of nature as his ancestors had been in developing tools and crafts *ab initio* or his contemporaries in producing artefacts by their use. Indeed, they believed the materials of craftsmanship to be manifestations of the four Ideal essences of earth, water, air and fire, while believing animation to be the embodiment of Ideal spirits and souls. Again such beliefs were sequentially discussed in respect of the metaphysical Holy Trinity and mind-body problem. Yet again, it was this lack of belief/knowledge differentiation in Aristotle's writings which opened both to potential rejection by medieval Churchmen. Thus, belief was and is ubiquitous, knowledge the anomaly.

Indeed, the overthrow of Aristotelianism by experimentation was not a loss of belief the Protestant and secular schisms being merely diversification of belief. Indeed, secular attack on the Church's political role in education, welfare and social-planning actually replaced self-knowledge of human nature with secular belief which together with complicity in revolutionary mass murder did nothing to avoid future mayhem. Thus, orthodoxy had spawned two new heresies with attendant loss of knowledge, there being no 'triumph of knowledge over irrationality' as the 'enlightened' are wont to have it. Instead, there was an increase in scope for belief within which a few scientists pursued knowledge by experimentation while inter-religious conflict was compounded with a secular/religious extension in which it was too early to say how freedom to pursue knowledge might fare in a secular future, though as of now it is subject to secular interference in ways never attempted by the religious (c.f. Sections 11.2 and 12.1).

However, unimpeded by the religious, these few scientists created a body of self-consistent knowledge capable of making reliable predictions while secular believers produced inconsistency incapable of predicting anything. Thus, the few addressed the four elements of antiquity (air, water, earth, fire) and showed that air was one of many identifiable gases and was itself a physical mixture of gases; that water (one of many liquids) consisted of two gases in chemical combination; that some earths (solids), when heated converted to different solids with release of gas; and that other solids converted to different solids by combining with the life-sustaining constituent of air. Subsequently, use of the balance showed that substance (matter) was conserved in all its transformations; that these involved reactions of identifiable entities in reproducible proportions by weight to form identifiable compounds of constant composition; that the simplest reacting entities could be referred to as equivalents; and that each equivalent was composed of constant numbers of the same or different types of elemental atoms as free-elements, radicals or compounds. Later, it became possible to determine the weights of the elements relative to hydrogen by determining their number in molecules and radicals by independent means, such as vapour and osmotic pressure measurements. Yet later, these clarifications enabled the entire range of natural materials and all their reactions to be explained in terms of ninety-two identified elements and their respective affinities. In addition, this atomic-molecular knowledge explained and quantified all of the physical properties of solids, liquids and gases, their solutions one in another, the electrical conductance of electrolytes, and the kinetic nature of heat and temperature revealing the inadequacy of believing fire to be the fourth element.

Again, these few scientists turned their attention to light and magnetism, and having shown heat to be a manifestation of the movement of atoms and molecules in otherwise empty space, they now showed light to be a propagation of magnetism and electricity acting in a complementary and alternating manner as waves in this same empty space. Thus, by experimentation and mathematical analysis, they showed that the "imponderables" were forms of energy, interchangeable through application of numerical equivalence factors; and that the physical world consisted only of matter and energy thus defined. Later, Einstein showed that matter and energy were themselves interchangeable with the numerical equivalence factor, c^2. Later still, difficulties in accounting for the interaction of particulate matter with the energy field were resolved on the basis of energy being packaged in quanta, leading de Broglie to show that matter can manifest itself as particles in some reality-evaluations or as electromagnetic waves in others, the vibration frequencies of which were part of the spectrum which includes radio waves, radiant heat, light, X-rays and γ-rays. Thus, sub-atomic particles were shown to be particle/wave dualities in the void within atoms, the atoms themselves being manifestations of the universal void of electromagnetic wave propagation.

Thus, reality, otherwise known as the universe of which we are a constituent part was shown by the self-selected few to merge its matter and energy identities into the electromagnetic wave-particle duality which exists as the void which surrounds, penetrates and supports all the phenomena of which we are aware or can be aware. However, while Einstein and others had hoped for less counter-intuitive knowledge than is currently available, efforts to unify this quantum-duality with his relativity have been unsuccessful for the best part of a century, suggesting ultimate knowledge of reality to be beyond a species which is part of it, and similarly limited as to ultimate knowledge of the physicochemical processes of its own brain. Thus, while our capacity to create hypotheses for reality-validation is tending to its limit and bringing us full-circle to the ignorance we had sought to dispel by religious belief, metaphysical enquiry or scientific method, we must conclude that the predictive power and usefulness of our physicochemical knowledge however incomplete is superior to arbitrary socio-political beliefs which have no predictive power or usefulness; and that current preferment of belief over knowledge can and should be reversed.

In the meantime, however, the levels of physical welfare and disposable wealth created by technology produces a detachment from reality which permits disavowal of our self-knowledge and of technology itself. Thus, by the 1970s, technology had created the prospect of a *Leisure Society* encouraged by five-day production in the three-day weeks of a short-term energy crisis. However, while some of this potential leisure was spent in further wealth creation, more was consumed in reality-rejecting activities in which otherwise leisured men were increasingly joined by women while surrogate productivity became indistinguishable from unemployed leisure other than by income level, such surrogacy being evidenced by quantified product monitoring being replaced by box-ticking supervision of process. Nonetheless, increasing surrogacy did not prevent the training of more scientists, though there were already more alive in the 1950s than had previously lived in total. However, were knowledge to be preferred to belief, such resources could be redeployed on real problems (c.f. below and Sections 11.2 and 12.2)

In the meantime, however, some of these resources are promoting the belief that our social-sciences can ignore our self-knowledge and the experimentation which could expand it; that our technological knowledge is inherently detrimental to the environment; that 'green' alternatives are preferable regardless of relative-cost; and that health, safety and environmental legislation should be enacted regardless of actual cost and of whether or not cause and effect have been identified. Thus, very considerable resources are devoted to substituting belief for knowledge (c.f. Section 11.2) at the behest and with the collusion of pressure-groups, politicians and bureaucrats while the media are mostly reporting and commenting on promises incapable of fulfilment in reality and on pseudo-scientific explanations for their actual failure, all of which is endlessly debated without resolution. However, were the media to recognise policy failure as reality-refutation of belief and to call for knowledge-based alternatives, it would encourage public regard for knowledge, for the dangers of reality-rejection and for politicians willing to deal with the physicochemical world and human nature as they are, rather than with beliefs as to what they should be.

As to preferment of knowledge over belief and of reality over unreality, it may be concluded that current socio-political beliefs should be reality-evaluated against traditional knowledge of human nature or against existing scientific knowledge of the environment; that socio-political policies should no longer be implemented without evaluating their likely outcome against such knowledge; that such precaution is the *sine qua non* of the physicochemical sciences (c.f. Chapters 6, 7, 8 and 9), of those validated by reference to them (c.f. Sections 9.3 and 9.4) and of the technology derived from them (c.f. Section 9.5); that the failure of socio-political policies on implementation should be taken as reality-refutation of belief, as are scientific hypotheses and theories which fail on experimentation (c.f. Sections 6.1, 6.3.4); and that such practice is better than continued reliance on beliefs, the only identifiable characteristic of which is their intention to displace knowledge because of its association with religion or its supposed association with environmental damage. After all, if *Change* is wanted and re-deployable resources are available to achieve it, then Change from belief to knowledge is surely possible and more productive than continual change in elective belief none of which is productive in its rejection of reality.

Furthermore, given that we already have the knowledge-content of the behaviour codes which were the foundation of social cohesion in the first place and of the knowledge-content of the humanities ever since, we should take formal steps to reality-evaluate whatever we consider to be their belief-contents; and given that we have the secular beliefs which disavow this knowledge, we should submit them to the reality-evaluation which would compare their failure to improve social life with their success in making it worse, concerning which there are now more than enough examples on which to make a start. Indeed, it may be concluded that all cultures would benefit from parallel submission of the belief-contents of their behaviour codes to reality-evaluation against our common knowledge of humanity and against our collective need for social cohesion; that this would reduce the influence of divisive beliefs to our collective global benefit by emphasising that which we can hold in common as banner-headlines for all humanity, whatever the fine-print of our respective cultures might be; and that in doing so we would all be recognising the supremacy of knowledge over belief and the dangers of being undone by ignored or rejected reality

11.2 THE CHANGING NATURE OF BELIEF

Having analysed the reasons why secular socio-political belief is preferred to knowledge, having identified the resources now promoting belief over knowledge and having identified the past benefits of preferring knowledge to belief, I now provide further inducement to knowledge preference by contrasting the confusions of belief with the clarity of knowledge (Section 11.2.1); by showing how reality-evaluation would resolve differing beliefs in equality, freedom and rights (Section 11.2.2); and by showing how belief as rationality has diversified to belief as rejection of commonsense and general knowledge (Section 11.2.3), to belief as corruption of specific knowledge (Section 11.2.4), and to belief as corruption of scientific method (Section 11.2.5).

11. 2. 1 Relativism Contrasted with Knowledge
Having shown that religious belief did not prevent the knowledge-acquisition which provides our current welfare and re-distributable wealth, I now show that the denial of reality perversely

encouraged by enjoyment of these benefits does prevent knowledge-acquisition and even knowledge-retention.

Such denial of reality is epitomised by Postmodernism which while failing to notice craft knowledge, asserts scientific knowledge to be belief and the history of science to be its changes of belief. While such changeability well describes belief, pseudo-science and much social-science, I have already shown it to be no part of physicochemical science (c.f. Chapters 6, 7, 8 and 9). However, since such disparagement of science continues to grow, there is need to confirm that knowledge is consistent with reality and as such un-opposable, while belief is always opposed by all who believe otherwise; and that no matter how changeable knowledge may appear to postmodernists, it cannot be voted in or out of fashion as can relative belief. Thus, while postmodernists conflate science with belief and describe it as temporary consensus, its only temporary aspect is hypothesis *en route* to knowledge, transient consensus being synonymous with pseudo-science and oxymoronic to science. However, I now return to the role of suspended belief and hypothesis in science, lest these be the source of relativism's misunderstanding.

Thus, Newton's 'action at a distance' was suspended belief as distinct from hypothesis. When Newton observed the curvilinear motion of the Moon orbiting the Earth, he could only accede to Galileo's suspended belief that bodies move in straight lines in the absence of force, the curvilinear motion of projected cannon balls being due to the presence of force. However, neither he nor Galileo knew how this force acted at a distance on cannon balls or on the Moon. Indeed, neither knew that it existed, its removal being impossible and the effect of its removal being thus unobservable. It is always there . . . if it exists. Thus, they opted to believe that bodies would move in straight lines were it not to exist, though this argument for an otherwise un-observable force is as circular as those for which I reproach Francis Bacon and Descartes. Indeed, Newton was reproached for this circularity and gained acceptance only because his Theory of Gravity enabled the future positions of moving bodies to be *predicted* from knowledge of previous position and momentum, even though the existence of gravity itself could not be reality-validated other than circularly through the predictive power of the Theory. Thus, gravity is suspended belief subject to possible change, though no such change would change the Theory's predictive power in reality.

Again, we have Einstein's Theory of Relativity which, in replacing 'action at a distance' with 'space curvature in the vicinity of mass', accurately predicts motions at speeds and gravitational forces beyond those covered by Newton, though neither of these suspended beliefs has the status of the knowledge provided by reality-validations of their consequences. Again, Einstein's Theory does not cover other phenomena which are separately in the realm of Quantum Theory, the predictions of which are equally in accord with reality-validations in their context. Indeed, it is this duality which sustains the search for a Unified Theory of Relativity and Quanta while the knowledge derived from the Quantum Theory and from those of Newton and Einstein continue to predict observable future events in their respective spheres. Thus, though these theories involve suspended belief, they lead to productive hypotheses when coupled to knowledge, and make predictions capable of reality-validation towards otherwise inaccessible knowledge.

In contrast, Darwin's Theory of Evolution was based on the belief that new species arise from survival of the fittest natural variants of existing species, though this belief was not a hypothesis capable of reality-evaluation, nor was it a suspended belief capable of making valid predictions in association with existing knowledge. Indeed, the only supporting 'evidence' offered was that of analogy, a deficiency which together with its continuous misuse by Darwinists for the socio-political advance of secularism, arguably makes it the source of pseudo-science and postmodernism (c.f. Section 12.1). Thus, while molecular genetics may be expected to elucidate the mechanism of biological evolution, 'survival of the fittest' is cited only in relativist debates on the pros and cons of theism/atheism, left/right politics or some other social belief equally unsupported by experimentation .

A further example of science, is the Law of Conservation of Mass which having been found invariable across all known chemical transformations culminated in the Periodic Table and establishment of the Atomic Theory, both of which are predictive of all associated phenomena in all branches of science and always will be, though just what atoms actually are is already counter-intuitive. However, 'Theory' is not always upgraded to 'Law' by ever-widening consistency with reality, familiarity and habit playing some part in retention of the former term. Indeed, as in the case of Archimedes, the term 'Principle' is retained though no exceptions to either his Principle or to his Law of Flotation will ever be found. Nonetheless, for greater clarity of relative significance, I would suggest 'conjecture' or 'speculation' rather than 'theory' in such as would become Darwin's *Conjecture on Evolutionary Mechanism* (c.f. Section 12.1).

Thus, while scientific method recognises suspended beliefs which lead to hypotheses for reality-evaluation to knowledge, they cannot themselves be reality-evaluated other than by reality-validation of their predictions. When Newton said "I make no hypotheses" he was referring to his belief in action at a distance, not to the hypothesis that given this belief and the reality-validated dynamics of Galileo he could explain and predict the observed orbital motion of the Moon just as his successors would explain and predict all other movements induced by mass interactions at the appropriate speeds and gravitational field strengths. Thus, Newton was implicitly aware of the differences between belief, suspended belief, hypothesis and knowledge while Darwinists and postmodernists are not, thus necessitating explication of these differences to avoid the confusions perpetrated by the latter pair. However, while the public may be unaware *ab initio* of the fundamentals of the scientific-method, professional philosophers, if not pseudo-scientists, really ought to be more careful before claiming that scientists are dealing in belief just as they are, such claims evidencing either innocent ignorance or deliberate misrepresentation to self-serving ends.

What actually happens in science is that knowledge becomes more and more extensively complete in its consistency with reality. In this way Newton is superseded by Einstein in that the latter's theory embraces observations unavailable to Newton in respect of photons of light and of high speed sub-atomic particles in accelerators or in cosmic rays. Thus, Einstein's relativistic dynamics embraces bodies of all masses moving at all speeds while Newton's remain valid for the masses, speeds and gravity forces for which it was valid in the first place, the later theory merging with the earlier at the lower speeds. The Unified Theory, when and if attained, will further widen and deepen our knowledge of reality but no-one need expect fault to be found with the predictive abilities of the Newtonian, Relativistic or Quantum Theories in their respective contexts. Thus, while very substantial progress has been made in our predictive ability on the basis of knowledge, belief-based disparagers of science and their pseudo-scientific fellow travellers cannot predict anything or make any progress, no matter how they change their beliefs.

Nonetheless, such disparagers of scientific knowledge have claimed in justification of their relativism that the Phlogiston Theory (c.f. Section 6.3.4) shows science to be a progression of beliefs. In fact, this theory was a hypothesis that the Ideal spirit or 'substance' of fire was the Real material phlogiston which escaped when a substance combusted. Thus, while the spirit/substance of fire was believed to be imponderable, the hypothecated phlogiston was shown to be of negative weight were it to exist: a *reductio ad absurdum* conclusion which not only displaced phlogiston but also the spirit/substance of fire by showing that combustion involved weight increase by uptake of the atmospheric constituent of respiration, all of which contributed to the Law of Mass Conservation without which chemistry could not have been built. It is truly perverse to cite the reality-refutation of classical belief in the spirit/substance of fire as a change of belief or fashion in science, this refutation of belief being no less significant than Galileo's refutation of Aristotle's belief respecting falling bodies. In any case, non-scientists are never closer to new knowledge than are temporarily puzzled scientists. As soon as a discrepancy is observed between expectation and observation or between the results of two separate lines of experimentation, scientists recognise an opportunity to reach deeper knowledge of reality, phlogiston being but one example of many, one other being the co-existence of the Relativity and Quantum Theories which inspires pursuit of their unification.

It must be concluded that the universal predictive power of knowledge and the inability of belief to predict anything, restates the difference between them which is reality-evaluation; and that postmodernist rejection of reality-evaluation prevents its application to socio-political beliefs and exposes them to continuing failure on implementation, no knowledge ever being attainable by reality rejection.

11. 2. 2 Beliefs as Spectra Resolvable for Reality-Evaluation
Having shown in chapter 2 and 3 that successive socio-political systems were successful to the extent of their (reality-validated) compliance with human nature and having shown in Chapters 4 and 10 that beliefs are limitless and irresolvable when beyond reality-evaluation, I now show that they are just as limitless and irresolvable when reality-evaluation is omitted or its results ignored.

Thus, when feudal interpretations of beliefs in equality, freedom and rights had ceased to comply with innate requirements for social cohesion, belief-based replacements simply added to the mayhem as in Revolutionary France while a succession of interpretations more empirically attuned to these innate requirements led from the earlier British Civil War through the Restoration, Glorious Revolution and subsequent forms of constitutional parliamentary democracy. Again, the interpretations adopted for the American Constitution were empirically designed for enhanced social cohesion. Nonetheless, there are many who still believe the 'French Revolutionary Dawn' to have been 'Enlightened', communism to be 'scientific materialism' and some form of Utopia to be the end-product of postmodernist liberalism. Thus, while revolution and dictatorship have failed more than once, many pursue the same arbitrary objectives through the relativist beliefs of liberal democracy, and while some interpretations happen to succeed while others fail, such are enacted anyway despite their being as replete with contradictions as those of monotheism, though secular liberal democrats quick to point out the latter, remain blind to the former.

However, the range of possible belief interpretations invites their visualisation as spectra extending from absolute equality to absolute inequality, from anarchy to total restriction and from absolute right to absolute duty, and suggests that within all of them the appropriateness of specific interpretations (spectral frequencies) to the realities of family, tribe, city, nation or humanity at large can only be determined reliably by reality-evaluation against human nature or unreliably by periodic majority voting. Again, were we to compare the interpretations exemplified by socio-political systems past and present we would be comparing the social cohesion and productive success achieved in the Athens of Pericles; the UK from the Restoration; the French Republics in succession; the USA from its founding; Germany from the Weimar Republic; the Peoples' Republics of Communism; the dictatorships of Hitler, Mussolini, Petain, Franco, Salazar and the Greek Colonels; the current EU or the projected United States of Europe: and we would have to conclude that if there is one truth there is much heresy and for the same reasons as with religion.

Indeed, dictatorships may be viewed as attempts to eliminate heresy and given that almost all the member states of the current EU have been dictatorships in recent times, it is perhaps no surprise that their current political establishments are averse to referenda on constitutional change while their electorates want them; that only three out of the twenty-seven electorates were
372

permitted referenda on the Lisbon Treaty; that all three gave negative responses which have been ignored; that democratic accountability in everyday affairs is extremely limited; and that EU Directives from Brussels now account for 70 - 80% of all new national legislation without any national parliamentary debate or electoral agreement on a case-by-case basis. Nonetheless, though such aversion to democracy may have its origin in Plato's *Republic* in which the theoretical Guardian Oligarchy was not subject to electorate control, it may be seen that the EU and every other democratic system was or is justified on some or other interpretation of beliefs in equality, freedom and rights, without formal reality-evaluation of any of them, though voting may be allowed now and then, here and there, at the discretion of the prevailing belief-based socio-political establishment.

However, whether voting on the specifics of belief is permitted or not, we know that some interpretations of belief in equality could be reality-validated, while the rest would either be suspended pending reality-evaluation or categorised as reality-refuted. Thus, we know we are all members of the species *Homo sapiens* and are all products of the human genome which confers an intra-species equality, while we also know we exhibit differences: we are not clones. Thus, our brain-body coordination capacities differ and it is a matter of reality-validation that we are not all equal in this respect. After all, some are born with particular genetic diseases of which others are free, some are better craftsmen than others, some are artists and some geniuses. Again, countless millions admire the athletic and entertainment abilities of the few whom they acknowledge to be more adept than themselves. Yet, again, though all have applied differing capacities to life's challenges and opportunities in the same Earthly environment for the same 24 hours per day everyday of our respective lives and collectively through all the generations of humankind, some have more success than others and some social groupings have remained content with stone-age attainments while others have progressed to higher attainments, however these are defined. Thus, though special pleading can be advanced to 'explain' these differences in terms of belief in disallowed equality, lack of freedom or deprivation of rights, the differences in outcomes within families and between families, within cultures and between cultures are real enough and have oscillated often enough to rule out any deficiencies which anyone or any group has the power or obligation to rectify on behalf of another without drawing attention to the fundamental inequality which the thus obliged usually deny.

As to the inequality of ability in general, even informal reality-evaluation shows that individuals from current stone-age groupings can respond to instruction and training in crafts, technologies and sciences new to them at the same rates and to the same extents as those from the groupings responsible for their development in the first place, subject only to those individual differences in ability with which we are all familiar whether we seek to deny them or not. Again, some capable individuals once exposed to the developed world are not slow to exploit their slower brethren in ways which destroy social cohesion more quickly and extensively than anything practiced by the developed world either at home or abroad. More generally, such reality-evaluation shows that this ready if selective knowledge acquisition does not extend to culture-specific beliefs, these being resistant to modification or replacement by other beliefs including those of liberal democracy; that knowledge transfer should nonetheless be equally accessible to all in any given society irrespective of religious or cultural beliefs and practices, while recognising the impossibility of equal outcome even within selected ability streams; and that while conversion of belief should not be expected, differing believers should set examples of cooperative social behaviour which others might emulate irrespective of differences in belief.

Thus, regardless of religion, race or culture, we may conclude that individuals should have equal access to education and training though their ability to benefit from it varies from one individual to another; that the content should be tailored to the learning aptitudes of selected ability streams; and that there should be no obligation on anyone to treat as educationally equal those differences which render streaming meaningful. Similarly, regardless of religion, race or culture we may conclude that individuals should have equal freedom to transfer allegiances among religions and cultures; and that there should be no obligation on anyone to treat as equal those differences which render changes in allegiance meaningful. Again though knowledge is easily transferable, it may be concluded that the secular beliefs of liberal democracy which are antagonistic to the religious beliefs within such democracy are likely to be incompatible with the religious beliefs of other cultures; that co-existence depends on tolerance; that deists, pantheists and polytheists are more tolerant than monotheists in general; that Buddhists are more tolerant than the 'Peoples of the Book'; that those who separate church and state are more tolerant than theocrats who do not; and that if equality of belief-adherence is to be meaningful there must be mutual tolerance with differences in the implications of specific beliefs at the individual and social levels being resolvable by reality-evaluation against the human nature common to all.

In any case, the beliefs of liberalism are not only interpreted differently within individual democracies, they have been interpreted differently within any one society over time. Thus, Locke's 'state of nature' in recognising an equality in cooperativeness while requiring a directing hierarchy is only one example of many in which from time immemorial codes and laws were enacted to harmonise directing and directed and to protect both from the disruptive while recognising the respective contributions of both to the cooperative whole. Thus, social cooperation was maintained through a sequence of hierarchies which runs from theocratic priest-kings to baronial influence on feudal kings, and from separation of church and state to the political parties and widening suffrage of parliamentary liberal democracy, all of which proceeded in different locations at unequal rates and to unequal extents or scarcely at all according to different interpretations of the basic beliefs in equality freedom and rights. Again, John Stuart Mill noted that the people who rule are not those who vote, that majorities can be as dictatorial as kings formerly were, and that motivated minority sub-groupings can act dictatorially within democracies through exercising disproportionate influence on governments elected by individual voters. Thus, we may conclude from such preliminary reality-evaluation that while total equality may be an aspiration of belief, it is impossible to attain in reality, no matter how long debated or how many votes might initially be cast for the aspiration; and that in any case, social cohesion is innate while equality is not, except as in the formerly much used expressions, 'equal in the sight of God' or 'equal before the law'.

Indeed having had more experience of the inequalities of influence sought by pressure groups than Mill ever had, we may now conclude that political parties elected by individual voters, to whom they advertise their dedication to equality, are all too ready to pander to self-appointed sub-groupings in order to gain what are effectively block-votes; that such belief-driven pressure-groups whether they be religious, cultural or secular should be required to act within the civil community without special access to government; that they should rely solely on their individual members to pursue privately the socio-political objectives which they collectively avow; that government should permit what is legal without endorsement or legislative enactment in support of such group interests; that all such groupings and sub-groupings should be encouraged to submit their socio-political beliefs to reality-evaluation and to peer review by other than the belief-committed; and that all assertions of belief should be ignored by government. Indeed political parties, being themselves pressure groups, should adopt this same approach to reality-evaluation. Thus, while liberal democracy is described by some as 'the best in the best of all possible worlds', it may be concluded that its current manifestations are too much in thrall to specific interpretations of beliefs for such a description to be as valid as reality-evaluation would make it. Indeed, it is surely time to recognise that debate and lobbying are evidence of differences in belief and of knowledge being ignored or unsought.

Thus, not only does reality-evaluation show absolute equality to be incapable of producing a viable social system even in the absence of freedom and rights, it also shows the total freedom of anarchy to be as inoperable as any system based on rights alone would be. As to the coexistence of all three, reality-evaluation shows the maintenance of any interpretation of belief-based equality to require corresponding suppression of any freedom or right to believe or behave otherwise; and that systems based on such arbitrary belief eventually succumb to disorder or to temporary dictatorship, neither being able conclusively to suppress the innately hierarchical cooperativeness of our species. For such as Rousseau, the freedom to enjoy his self-conferred rights was to be found in the supposed equality of freedom from Christian restraint enjoyed by the 'Noble Savage' though it entailed consignment of his children to the deprivations of a foundling hospital. For Marx, Lenin, Stalin, Mao and their ilk, communist equality was to be founded on freedom from capitalism through abrogation of the right to own property (the fruits of ones labours) while for Pol Pot equality required a return to 'Year One' by destruction of freedom, rights, property and life itself. Thus, it may be concluded that equality, freedom and rights can never be absolute; that any attempt to achieve these absolutes singly or together is futile; that compromise among them is the only possibility; that compromise will be more durably achieved through reality-evaluations of specific hypotheses than by voting on belief differences; and that the former option would frustrate only those mad enough to prefer belief to knowledge despite the latter's compliance with reality.

Nonetheless, many so-called liberals transfer blame from the above perpetrators of dictatorial excess to their opponents, and portray as iniquitous the knowledge-acquiring social cohesion of the socio-political systems of antiquity, medievalism, industrialism and colonialism when calling for ever-higher levels of so-called liberalism for themselves and for other cultures whether they want them or not. Thus, current liberalism aspires to equal freedom to enjoy rights to do as one pleases, with none being judgemental as to the consequences, and with all honouring the aspiration in the fond belief that these mutually contradictory objectives will be resolved through the ballot box, it being a comfort to believe that the dream was earlier destroyed by dictatorship alone. Nonetheless, the belief interpretations on which communism foundered were counter to the reality on which liberal democracy will founder, all belief-based Utopian aspirations being self-contradictory. More progress would be made were democracies to treat specific beliefs as hypotheses for reality-evaluation to determine the weighted mixtures best suited to the enhancement of human welfare for the individual, the family, the culture and humanity as a whole. Thus, we should reality-evaluate rather than seek conversion through voting or violence.

Again, were the belief advanced as a hypothesis that society would be more socially cohesive were individuals given equal rights to freedom to behave as they like, deterioration rather than improvement would be expected from existing knowledge of human nature as reflected in traditional behaviour codes and cultural literature, though it would have been easy to reality-evaluate this hypothesis more formally before implementing it. The difficulty lies solely in the aversion of social-science to reality-evaluation as evidenced by there having been no investigation of the obvious correlation of antisocial behaviour with just such liberalisation over the last fifty years. Again, despite commonsense and specific knowledge to the contrary, it is still widely believed that state welfare provision as 'of right' does not discourage self-provision despite this 'right' being unnatural in that hunter-gatherers have never expected to eat without doing either. Yet, those who free cetaceans from captivity express surprise at their reluctance to return to the wild despite their continuing to feed them. Even whales avoid self-provision when there is no need.

However, while such interpretations of belief in equality, freedom and rights to the necessities of life are rejections of the reality of existence for all species, the negative effects of their implementation in respect of *Homo sapiens* are obscured by the deployment of one belief in defence of another. Thus, believers in the benefits of encouraging individual freedom do not attribute its negative consequences to its undue exercise, but rather to the deprivation of equality, freedom and rights which society has yet to rectify, thus dismissing the possibility that the belief in question has been reality-refuted by its implementation. Of course, such reasoning absolves believers of error, though it does so by destroying the personal responsibility, conscience and shame which formerly limited behaviour counter to the social cohesion required for our group-species survival and welfare. Moreover, such reasoning defends the belief that freedom is an inalienably equal right; that judgement of its consequences is inappropriate; that fault lies not with the anti-social, but with the adverse social conditions which it is the duty of others to eradicate; that punishment as a corrective is counter to belief; and that imprisonment to reduce victim numbers is counter to belief *etc*. Clearly rationality is a source of unstoppable and hopelessly confused error when and where reality-evaluation is rejected. Surely, reality can only be rejected to this extent when and where technology creates enough re-distributable wealth to maintain the illusion that it can be so rejected.

Thus, it may be concluded that 'joined-up government will not be attainable nor its absence become an embarrassment so long as both governing and governed collude in rejecting reality; and that the practice of defending the failure of one belief by citing others is an absolute barrier to what would otherwise be progress through reality-refutation. On the other hand, were the public to appreciate the extent to which maintenance of these failing beliefs requires rejection of commonsense and acceptance of pseudo-science as exemplified in Sections 11.2.3 to 11.2.5, it would surely opt for knowledge-based progress and find the required reality-evaluations easy to conduct if not already conducted, though the results are as yet ignored.

11. 2. 3 Belief as Rejected Commonsense and General Knowledge

The following examples of the negative consequences of liberal belief thus defined are drawn from recent changes in training and education, from changes in criminal-justice intended to compensate for failures in training, and from changes in performance standards intended to obscure failures in education .

Within hunter-gatherer groups as within animal groups training for socially cooperative survival would have been conducted by parents, and by classical times Aristotle was emphasising the importance of the family for cultural training in manners and behaviour to achieve automatic compliance on the basis of inculcated politeness precluding gratuitous violence. Meanwhile, cultural achievements were being taught in schools to successive generations of potential leaders with literacy and numeracy being extended to potential recruits to middle and lower management as social complexity increased. Later, parish schools were ensuring that all Protestants could read the Bible, the Church having previously provided education for its own maintenance, forward planning and civil service role. Again, self-governing universities were being founded from the fourteenth century onwards in which early medical studies were compatible with the Church's welfare role. In addition, early apprenticeships, articled-clerking positions and on-the-job training in business practice were progressively supported by prior attendance at parish, public, grammar and craft schools, by science and medical teaching in the otherwise humanities-based universities and by the subsequent provision of commercial and technical colleges. Thus, despite the difference between belief and knowledge being implicit only, the emphasis was on bestowing knowledge of how things were done, the able proceeding further than the less able or taking up employment and its training opportunities as soon as possible and proceeding from there. Thus, in the seventeenth century eleven year old boys could self-indenture to the New World, one of whom controlled the Kentucky tobacco crop by the age of twenty-eight before becoming Navy Secretary prior to Samuel Pepys, while in the eighteenth the sons of naval officers could join at age eight, others having to wait till they were twelve.

Though the acquisition of specialist training and of liberal arts education tended to be self-motivated or encouraged by patrons, it harnessed whole societies in cooperative progress over the generations as reviewed herein, with little or no conjecture as to what should be taught and how. Readers will recall that John Dewey's hypotheses were intended to turn liberal arts education towards a greater consideration of reality until corrupted by the belief-based educationalists increasingly 'affordable' by society. Thus, instead of implementing a series of reality-evaluations of hypotheses for improvement at all levels of ability, rationalists devised uniform teaching methods regardless of aptitude-differences on the basis of arbitrary interpretations of belief in the right to equality of outcome and freedom of expression regardless of commonsense. Thus, after the high point of the 1944 Education Act, standards have been falling from the 1960s as evidenced by a decline in literacy and numeracy, an unprecedented need for remedial teaching on university entry, an increase in drop-out rates despite less demanding courses, and a preference for overseas school-leavers and graduates by universities and employers respectively.

Thus, physics, chemistry and biology have been displaced by 'general science' or by 'environmentalism', these providing more scope for belief indoctrination than for knowledge transfer. Again, history was displaced by politically correct treatments of colonialism, slavery, industrialisation, multiculturalism *etc* while language teaching no longer conferred ability to write in foreign languages while a vague grasp of meaning became accepted as translation to English. As to university curricula, qualifications in classics are now obtained without Latin or Greek while numerous courses scarcely require students to meet an academic specialist. Clearly, such changes are driven by the belief that 'all shall have prizes'. Meanwhile, other interpretations of beliefs in equality, freedom and rights have deprived parents and teachers of their traditional entitlement to control children without this disentitlement having any prior reality-evaluation of its potential effects, though the deprivers have found it necessary to attempt to re-establish control by antisocial behaviour orders, community service orders or imprisonment, despite these being *post-facto* and freedom-limiting replacements for traditional practices which were preventive, less freedom-limiting and of greater and more durable effectiveness. Nonetheless, politicians and public have yet to recognise this multi-faceted failure as reality-refutation of the beliefs in which they collude.

Of course, the lowering of school standards to achieve a 50% entry to universities and the lowering of university standards to minimise failure and drop-out ratios are as much a recognition of inequality as was earlier streaming, while an entry target of < 100% seems to be an admission of inequality, however reluctant. Again, the belief in equality which drives the above policy has failed to deliver its stated objective of increasing individual mobility between (unequal) social strata thus providing another ignored reality-refutation of belief by implementation, while prior reality-evaluation would scarcely have been necessary to show that 'academic courses' for all abilities would fail to stretch the academic or the non-academic with craft-based alternatives and thus restrict the upward mobility of both. The leaders of the Industrial Revolution were upwardly mobile only because they were craftsmen and many would not have been, had they been demoralised by an academic course. Fortunately, university graduation was not an entry requirement of the Industrial Revolution while such graduation now does little to maintain what was then built *ab initio,* water and sewage systems now being in a state of incipient collapse, rail and road provision being inadequate and electricity generation being increasingly insecure, though all are subject to belief-driven debate by the undifferentiated products of contemporary education while craftsmen and engineers would be more relevant to infrastructure than management consultants and political advisers.

Meanwhile, belief displaces knowledge even in such a basic task as teaching children to read, with word recognition displacing the phonetic alphabet despite the known benefits of Sumerian phonetic syllables (c. 3000 BC). Again, being aware that the 'white man' communicated by marks on paper, Sequoyah though he spoke no English, had by 1821 reduced the Cherokee language to eighty-six phonetic syllables to which he allocated characters whereby the whole of this very large tribe became literate almost immediately with a newspaper being published in Cherokee and English and with Cherokee translations of books being available by 1828. Even so, increased illiteracy from teaching word-recognition did not effect a return to phonics, though disruptive classrooms can hardly be conducive to learning whatever system is used. Again, the introduction of sex education in schools for the avoidance of pregnancy provides another example of failure to achieve a stated objective, though if the un-stated objective is a free and active sex life for school children in equality with adults regardless of its negative consequences for both, it would have to be judged a success. Either way, increased teenage pregnancy is not taken as reality-refutation of the beliefs underlying such 'education' while it has become the reason for introducing it at ever younger ages, the need for a knowledge-based approach to human nature continuing to be ignored in this as in all other liberal endeavour. As to whether such 'education' contributes to family stability, reality-evaluation shows that births out of wedlock are heading for 50% of the total; that with current divorce rates, children of married parents spend an average of eleven years with both; and that children of un-married parents have only three to four years before parental separation ensues.

Nonetheless, such liberal beliefs continue to transfer traditional roles from family to state-run institutions through policies which strengthen the latter and weaken the former. Thus, governments which formerly recognised the role of the family in providing basic training for life, are now transferring much of this role to schools and even to day-care centres which break the links of children to parents at ever younger ages. Again, though family stability was formerly encouraged by the tax system, such has been withdrawn under an interpretation of equality, freedom and rights which encourages mothers to work and have careers outside the home and to transfer the time formerly available for parent-child interaction to new childcare units, though state-funded facilities for children are already known to be unsatisfactory alternatives to normal parenting. Thus, while earlier suppression of women produced an understandable desire for careers, there is a difference between the freedom to embark on a career and the financial necessity to work outside the home even when one does not desire it, though both are conducive to the liberal state's baleful influence on children.

Indeed, this confusion between tolerant acceptance of career and lifestyle choices and active encouragement and endorsement of particular choices is now extended to a range of preferences and orientations which an alternate interpretation of liberal beliefs would leave to the free choice of individuals and their acceptance of consequences without any endorsement of right or imposition of acceptance on others. However, despite ongoing and seemingly endless debate on all such matters, the resolution of conflicting beliefs can only be reached by reality-evaluation against our requirements for survival and social cohesion which in turn are inextricably linked to the bearing and nurturing of children. Thus, though parental separation or divorce is now freely available and totally devoid of stigma, its consequences extend to the children involved. However, government response is not to encourage commitment but to create a support-agency on the belief that fathers who grudge to support one family can be persuaded to support two or more, though other forms of support short of marital tax reductions, are available for those who exercise their freedom, equality and rights in such ways as to require it.

Thus, the free and easy can ignore reality so long as the state provides necessities through specific interpretations of its liberal beliefs, though other interpretations less concerned with vote garnering would not so provide. Again, the political establishment can similarly ignore reality so long as its belief-based 'solutions' to its belief-created problems provide more sustainable votes than would real solutions to real problems, human gratitude being as it is. Nonetheless, a society in keeping with human realities cannot be created on the votes of the irresponsible and of those anxious to relieve them of responsibility: nor can any real problem be solved by governments motivated by votes in this way. On the other hand, if there is no problem, there is no debate and no votes to be garnered from the belief preferences of voters.

Thus, education maintains a debate among parents of academic children who want education to suit the brightest, others who believe in a range of possible interpretations of equality, freedom and rights, and yet others who feel unhappy at the prospect of their own children being classed non-academic. Again, some believe in the benefits of unrestricted sex even perhaps with minors, some in divorce, some in unrestricted abortion and some in drug-use, while yet others believe the converse to degrees depending on their respective belief interpretations, with all voting according to their preferences. Again, the initiative to reduce crime by stiffer sentencing attracts votes from the tough on crime, while those of the more liberal may be secured if sentences need never be served in full, while neighbourhoods to be adversely affected by prison-building will cast votes for its avoidance. Thus, contradictory beliefs are conducive to the continuous debate which garners votes even if commonsense and general knowledge have to be ignored, modified, neutered or otherwise corrupted to this end.

However, while debate is one thing, solving real problems is another. Indeed, the attempt to list real problems actually solved by government quickly produces a list of failures to meet stated objectives. For example, the current 'war on drugs' has provided no solution, though reality-evaluation of hypotheses derived from earlier control mechanisms and from the alternative of criminalizing their use, could not have produced a greater failure than our current inability to control drugs in prisons, let alone outside. As to extending the list of failures in which commonsense and general knowledge have lost out to vote-garnering on the demographics of belief, readers might wish to add immigration, multiculturalism, abolition of child poverty, child protection, foreign aid, war on terror, spread of democracy, economic management, environmental protection *etc*. Thus, it may be concluded that the costs of such belief-based failure are sustainable only so long as rejected-reality does not overwhelmingly intervene with unsustainable social breakdown, financial crises or failure of electricity supply *etc* (c.f. Chapter 12).

Thus, it may be concluded that social improvement cannot be achieved by pandering to belief-based special interest lobbies and focus groups; that such is sustainable only while voters are content to have their co-believers in office without expecting anything other than fellowship of belief and the possibility of sectional financial advantage; that for real social improvement, interpretations of belief in equality, freedom and rights must be reality-evaluated in their intended areas of implementation, with voters being asked to prioritise knowledge-based policy options instead of having to choose between re-interpretations of beliefs which have already failed on earlier implementations; and that while voters might be losing faith in politicians, they will have to reject their own belief-based policy preferences and insist on knowledge-based (commonsense) alternatives before they can expect any social improvements in reality.

11. 2. 4 Belief as Corruption of Specific Knowledge

Having shown that belief as rejection of commonsense and general knowledge now acts to the detriment of social welfare, I now show that belief as corruption of specific knowledge is now acting to the detriment of our physical welfare by interfering in knowledge-based environmental, health and safety protection on-going since the Bronze Age and in materials recycling on-going since the Palaeolithic, none of which is acknowledged by believers in nonexistent environmental damage even to the detriment of real amenity preservation, let alone to real health, safety and environmental protection.

Thus, while shoreline amenity loss was known to arise from operational discharges of oil from ships and while means to its amelioration were agreed in the *Oil Pollution Convention* of 1954, it was only after the *Torrey Canyon* grounded on the *Seven Stones Reef* in 1967 that the belief in unsustainable ecological damage arose, despite the knowledge that wartime releases from enemy action had not caused observable ecological effects, and that the annual discharge of oil from land-based sources to coastal waters had long exceeded that from peacetime shipping without any long-term ecological effects having been observed. Nonetheless, such large accidental releases close to shore did create commercial losses from disruption of amenity and interference with fishing operations in response to which the *International Convention Relating to Intervention on the High Seas in Cases of Oil Pollution Casualties* and the *International Convention on Civil Liability for Oil Pollution Damage* were duly adopted in 1969 and in force by 1975.

These respective instruments enabled coastal states to do anything necessary to protect against such commercial losses and to ensure the availability of compensation as and when necessary. Meanwhile the tanker owners and the oil industry set up two voluntary schemes to compensate for commercial damage and cleanup-costs in 1969 and 1971 respectively. Again, before the Civil Liability Convention came into force in 1975, the *International Fund for Compensation for Oil Pollution Damage* was adopted in 1971 to increase levels of compensation and to spread liability across ship and cargo owners, the latter coming into force in 1978. Again, though the 1954 Convention was amended in 1962 and 1971, the *MARPOL Convention* of 1973 adopted additional comprehensive annexes on technical procedures and arrangements for the operational handling of oil, bulk-chemicals, packaged goods, sewage and garbage. However, while this was moving towards ratification a series of major incidents in 1976/77 gave rise to a Conference on Tanker Safety and Pollution Prevention in 1978, which adopted a *Protocol to the 1973 Convention* which came into force in 1983 as *MARPOL 73/78*. It is this Convention which now covers all accidental and operational waste releases from ships together with ballast water treatment and atmospheric pollution abatement (cf. Section 9.5.8) and which is now more influenced by 'environmentalist' belief (c.f. Section 9.5.3) than by avoidance of the real commercial damage which merits compensation.

However, in contrast to the comprehensive attention now given to the technical means of preventing operational pollution from ships and to the training necessary to prevent accidents on the part of ship owners and crews (c.f. Section 9.5.8), it is surprising how little has been done in respect of the *quid pro quo* responsibilities of coastal states to mitigate and respond to accidental ship-source pollution when accidents do occur. Indeed, only the UK legislated, as permitted under MARPOL, for discharge of oil to the marine environment to facilitate appropriate experimentation. Thus, without going into details, the resulting R & D programme found that the rapid spread of liquid oils to extremely thin layers promotes their wave-induced dispersion to low concentrations in the underlying seawater and facilitates their natural oxidative decomposition to carbon dioxide and water therein; that while water-in-oil emulsion formation reduces the rate of this dispersion, it still proceeds given enough time; that dispersion rates can be estimated from the physicochemical properties characteristic of each oil; and that the time taken to reach shore under onshore winds and the amount likely to strand can thus be estimated. Again, without going into details, it was also shown that dispersant application reduces the amount of pollutant reaching shore by increasing the rate of natural dispersion by wave-action; that dispersant application also increases the rate of natural dispersion of pollutants from shores by surf-action; and that though collection and removal is the better option for higher viscosity and hence more persistent pollutants, it additionally requires emulsion-breaking, oil/water separation and recycling or disposal of the recovered oil, all of which were also covered by the R & D. In addition, this programme identified, evaluated and published the optimal design parameters for the equipment and techniques necessary for dispersion and recovery from water surfaces and from all types of shorelines to guide optimal selection of equipment from the range commercially available by the end of the programme and thereafter, sufficient of which had been designed or approved within it to cover the full range of requirements in conformity with the realities of response.

Thus, the programme showed that slick thickness limited the encounter rate and hence the recovery rate of a 1m wide response unit moving at ≤ 1 knot, to ~ 0.2 m^3 (tonnes) per hour and *pro rata*, the speed being limited to avoid oil loss with the water passing beneath the unit, while the effective recovery rate is limited by wave-height and by viscosity-dependent pump rate; that aircraft suitably equipped for dispersant spraying with *pro-rata* encounter rate had a treatment rate dependent on flying speed, load-capacity and distance between operational and loading locations, and an effectiveness directly dependent on oil : dispersant application ratio, and inversely dependent on pollutant viscosity; that shoreline encounter rates were proportional to stranded layer thickness; and that with such spillage response capacities on sea and shore being variously compatible with the 2-3000 tonnes to be expected from damage to a single tank, it was essential to remove cargo and bunker oils from casualties to avoid being overwhelmed by further releases due to subsequent weather-related damage to additional tanks.

However, despite the above knowledge on the inherent limitations of spillage response and on the need to move casualties to shelter as soon as possible, and despite the existence of the Convention on Casualty Intervention, national contingency plans rarely amount to more than arranging for all interested parties to share responsibility for belief-based decisions day-to-day. Thus, despite the toxicity of dispersants being too low to measure at the concentrations resulting from spraying operations, interested 'environmentalists' manage to prevent their use time and again, while the known limitations of sea-going pollution recovery never displaces their belief-based preference for it, the ensuing shoreline pollution assisting their anti-shipping campaign. Yet again, 'environmentalists' oppose intervention for sheltered removal of cargo and bunkers while states prefer to leave casualties at the accident site to avoid transfer of liability from owners to the state, or to send them seawards despite further release being minimised in shelter and maximised on exposure. Indeed, sheltered cargo-bunker transfer was accepted as UK intervention policy only after the *Sea Empress* incident of 1996 had turned the usual small initial release to one of 70,000 tonnes.

As to whether marine oil pollution incidents are more than commercially damaging, it may be noted that their biological impacts are invariably transient; that in expressing concern for extinction of species, 'environmentalists' do not compare incident-related deaths with natural death and regeneration rates for the species affected; that they do not distinguish the vulnerability of swimming birds which are subject to surface oiling and flying species which leave the area when the oil slick obscures their view of fish targeted from the air; and that no publicity is given to the absence of such flying-hunters in polluted areas. Again, though the number of dead birds on shorelines in winter was offered as evidence of damage from operational oil discharges from passing ships, the absence of such carcases in summer was ignored, as was knowledge that natural mortality was higher in winter than in summer and *post-mortem* winter-oiling was thus irrelevant. In any case, despite the number of incidents since 1967 there has been no lasting damage to bird species, while shorelines denuded of marine organisms by oil and boat-slipways cleared of organisms for pedestrian safety are re-colonised as are weeded gardens, and while 'environmentalism' prevents mitigation of impacts from initial release and intervention to limit further release.

Further to knowledge-based environment, health, safety and amenity responses as distinct from belief-driven agitation, readers will recall that process modifications have always been introduced when real need is identified, as for example when earlier metallurgical processes were brought to industrial scale (c.f. Section 8.1.9) and when new processes such as for the gas industry were introduced (c.f. Section 8.1.11). Again, health and safety benefits arose from raw sewage treatment and water purification in what became the water industry (c.f. Section 8.1.12) while amenity benefits were conferred when motor transport eliminated horse-droppings (c.f. Section 8.1.2). Yet again, centralised electricity-generation eliminated pollution from local coal-fired power units (c.f. Section 8.1.3) and provided pollution-free electricity at the point of use (c.f. Section 8.1.12) while ever-more efficient aero-engines became correspondingly less polluting (c.f. Section 9.5.8). In continuity of this progress, I show below that developments in existing processes and replacements for outdated ones still confer health, safety and environmental benefits either intentionally or incidentally; that technical solutions to all identified problems can be developed where needs indicate or as cost-effective opportunities arise; and that progress is hindered by the intervention of belief-driven activists and vote/revenue garnering politicians.

Thus, while belief-driven legislative control of scientific-technical activities has done little to encourage progress, it has the potential to stop or reverse it, and to eliminate recognised benefits for no reality-validated need. Indeed some 'environmentalists' demand restrictive legislation on 'the precautionary principle' despite the impossibility of proving a negative, such aversion to progress appearing profound enough to forgo all modern conveniences for Palaeolithic gathering, hunting being incompatible with 'animal rights' and agriculture being accepted only in the belief that it had no effect on pre-existing forest.

Again, the demand for recycling arises from the belief that we will run out of raw materials, such predictions being based on projected rates of consumption and sizes of known mineral deposits. Though many 'predicted' termination dates for specific materials have already passed without acknowledgement by believers, such beliefs reveal an aversion to business activity which is stronger than knowledge of our need or desire for it (c.f. Section 9.5) while known deposits provide no information on future prospects, these being proven only as need dictates. Again, scarcity increases market price which permits access to sources previously too expensive to work, or alternatives are introduced which reduce calls on the scarcer choice which is further conserved by cost (c.f. Section 9.5.5).

Thus, tin having provided corrosion resistance to mild steel cans used for food containment, the response to decreasing availability would be either a technological effort to maintain corrosion resistance with thinner coatings or to provide cheaper alternatives. In general, new materials such as aluminium or plastics are introduced by economic necessity without the need for interventions by self-appointed doomsayers, the world being unlikely to come to a sudden standstill so long as governments permit due regard for reality. Nonetheless, belief to the contrary has not succumbed to the realities of science, technology or market economics. Instead, it has led to demands for recycling with apparent unawareness that this has been practised for robust economic reasons ever since metals were first used by man, such recycling having been achieved by melting and re-working (c.f. Section 2.4.5), and by adding scrap to new production as in the Siemens Process where up to half the new steel has been recycled (c.f. Section 8.1.9). Even those who stole lead from roofs had long known of the metal recycling market. Again, recycling of the wastes from coke production gave birth to the new gas and chemical industries, and the internal combustion engine used the wastes from coke production and from the early oil industry (c.f. Sections 8.1.2 and 8.1.11). Indeed, having killed animals for food, early man recycled bone, horn, sinew, skin, fur and feather for tools and useful artefacts (c.f. Section 2.1). Thus, those demanding legislation to encourage recycling are unaware of its antiquity, its continuity or its limits.

As to its limits, it is essential to recall that the term 'waste' properly defines that which cannot be recycled economically. To illustrate the significance of this definition let us recall that in mineral processing ore is first separated from the gangue which having no use has no economic value. Even the most proselytising recycler might be induced to accept that gangue is waste by definition. However, because of the nature of metal extraction from the ore (c.f. Section 2.4.4) the overall process would be non-cost-effective if all of the metal and associated non-metal had to be used. Even so, sulphur and phosphorus residues are recycled for sulphuric acid and fertilizer production (c.f. Section 8.1.9). Thus, it follows that only economically useless residue is waste by definition, and that only a fanatic would require a use to be found for everything, given that such a requirement would eliminate the use of metal itself on grounds of cost.

Let us now consider our tin can as a candidate for recycling and ask ourselves why it was disposable as waste in the first place. Those who still believe everything to be recyclable will be surprised to learn that the tin can was *designed* to be disposable. Thus, it was designed not only to satisfy its requirements as a container, but also to ensure that it had insufficient value to cover the cost of recycling at the end of its useful life as a container, thus rendering it disposable as waste by definition. If for reasons of metal scarcity such a container came to embody recyclable potential through an increase in its intrinsic value, cheaper construction materials would be used to maintain disposability as the most cost-effective option. In contrast, motorcars, railway locomotives and ships have residual intrinsic value at the end of their useful lives, cannot otherwise be designed to serve their functions, and so have always been recycled. To emphasise that some items are recyclable while others are inherently disposable without loss of value, readers might like to compare platinum crucibles with polystyrene cups. Thus, value can be recycled and non-value cannot, that which has no recoverable value being waste. No scientific, technological or economic ingenuity can recycle value from an item which has been designed scientifically, technologically and economically to have no value at the end of its useful life, however many regulations purport to enforce it. Again, in contrast to tin cans, glass bottles were formerly recycled by collection and re-use, this being cost-effective because of the comparatively high cost of glass production and the cost-sharing regularity of supply and re-collection of milk bottles in particular, though even this was discontinued in favour of waxed-cardboard cartons when washing-plant costs became too high for reuse to be viable against alternatives at costs consistent with disposal. Glass containers or anything else can only be economically recycled when the value recovered is greater than the recovery cost.

Thus, all costs such as those of separation, accumulation and transport, washing and wash-water treatment, intermediate-treatment such as the de-inking of printed paper, and the reprocessing of each potentially recyclable component must be included in assessing the market value of the reclaimed material for comparison with that of fresh material before recycling can be judged economically viable or not. Any material thus judged non-viable is a waste for disposal, the options for this being similarly prioritised in terms of cost. In this way metals, glass, paper and plastics may be recycled depending on current costs of fresh material and the cost implications of their state of presentation in the waste-stream. Organic and comestible wastes may be composted and other combustible materials may be incinerated with combined heat and power recovery being a recycling of energy, though certain chemical wastes may need specific treatment of incinerator emissions or may be decomposed in specialist land-fill sites incorporating liquid effluent treatment, and incineration of vaporous emissions as necessary. Incineration or disposal is preferable when it is impossible to recover recycling costs, though sensible decisions cannot be made when belief-driven demands prevail over knowledge. Needless to say, 'environmentalists' oppose combined heat and power in the belief that incinerator emissions cannot be adequately treated and thus ignore an annual energy equivalent of 10 million tonnes of coal and the virtual elimination of landfill.

However, where recovered value is high enough to pay for recycling with a positive financial return, it should be unnecessary to ban disposal to land-fill or to discourage its use by legislating its cost above the level imposed by scarcity. Indeed, were recycling schemes meeting their implied objectives in value saved, competitive bids could be invited from contractors desirous of accessing such value, thus relieving householders of the need to pay for its collection after having been legislated to segregate it in their own time and even to deliver it to a recycling centre at their own expense in some cases. On the other hand, if licence-paid contracting is not possible because economically recoverable values do not actually exist, then officialdom should admit that householders are having to pay for segregation and collection, for loses inherent to the recycling of definitive waste, and for the now artificially inflated charges for land-fill still necessarily used. Though recycling programmes are designated 'green', it is never made clear whether this term denotes environmental benefits as yet un-quantified or the naivety of compliant householders. Clarity will only be achieved when the net recycled value of domestic waste is reported to householders on a commodity-specific basis and council taxes reduced accordingly. Private contractors are always content to supply loss-making services so long as taxpayers are legislated to make them profitable.

As to protection from putative environmental impacts, it is similarly necessary to distinguish cost-effective benefits from those pursued regardless of cost and in some cases even without establishing cause and effect. Identification of putative cause has never been too difficult in the workplace where the effect is quickly observed and confirmed when changes in practice eliminate both together, such knowledge having often been applied to the wider environment. Thus, the distressing effects of breathing sulphur dioxide must have been quickly associated with the roasting of sulphides to oxides in metal extraction at the outset of metal working (c.f. Section 2.4.4) a longstanding experience which insured the removal of sulphur from coal-gas before supply to the consumer (c.f. Section 8.1.11). Later, it was found that atmospheric dispersion of chimney emissions of sulphur dioxide from coal-burning in urban domestic grates was insufficient to avoid breathing difficulties in the wider environment under the atmospheric temperature inversions associated with fogs. Even so, only the most sensitive complained while others regarded visibility reduction as an inconvenience of fog *per se*. Be that as it may, documentation of excess pulmonary deaths in London in the winter of 1952 led to the *Clean Air Act of 1954* which made the prior treatment of coal for domestic consumption a requirement and the burning of anything other than these 'smokeless' fuels on domestic grates an offence. However, implementation of the Clean Air Act led to the search for other dragons to slay though these were increasingly difficult to find, while the cost-benefit of their slaying became correspondingly questionable or even adverse.

One such quest was directed at the sulphur dioxide emissions from coal-fired electricity generation. Though the previous policy of high-stack dispersal and atmospheric dilution of emissions had been successful in protecting the human population from bronchial problems, it was

384

now attacked for causing damage to tree foliage and to aquatic life in ponds and lakes. While this causal relationship was more a matter of belief than knowledge, Norway followed by others began to claim that the high-stack policy of the UK was transporting the (alleged) detrimental effects of our sulphur dioxide across the North Sea, while Ireland later made similar trans-Atlantic claims which were even more difficult to square with reality. Firstly, the relationship between the emissions and their alleged effects was much less clear than that between London fog and excess winter deaths, no-one ever having blamed power stations for breathing difficulties. Secondly, the cited tree damage, being species-specific and extremely patchy over relatively small areas, suggested unidentified local causes. Thirdly, small ponds exhibit natural changes during their transient lives among which are the acidification changes cited, and it became increasingly difficult to sustain these claims for larger bodies of water. Fourthly, concentrations of sulphur dioxide even close to the points of emission were simply not high enough to have the effects complained of at the distances cited given their turbulent dilution in the very much larger volumes of intervening atmosphere.

Nonetheless, the belief-driven pressure to do something, forced consideration of the feasibility of removing sulphur dioxide from power-station emissions by water scrubbing and neutralisation to calcium sulphate in such a way as to release carbon dioxide to the atmosphere instead of sulphur dioxide, though the calcium sulphate (Plaster of Paris) thus produced would have been far in excess of any conceivable requirements, necessitating its classification as a waste requiring disposal to land-fill. Thus, while sulphur dioxide had previously dispersed in the atmosphere at virtually no additional cost to electricity-generation and with only disputable (even imaginary) consequences, it was being proposed to concentrate it into solid calcium sulphate at the capital and operating costs of an entirely new industrial-scale process with its own indisputable problems of disposal and associated costs. However, the socio-political insecurity of coal-supply and the feasibility of its ready replacement by oil and increasingly available natural gas, terminated all belief-driven agitation over 'acid rain' and avoided the economically absurd removal of sulphur dioxide from power station emissions, though the burning of natural gas in power stations was itself known to be unwise economically and strategically.

The next concerns were emissions of unburned hydrocarbons and oxides of nitrogen from heat-engines, and releases of volatile hydrocarbons from paint-drying and from the venting of tanks involved in the transportation and storage of petroleum and its products, all of which, whether significant or not, have since been dealt with by technical innovations. Thus, the efficiency of aero, automotive and marine engines has been increased, while unburned hydrocarbon exhaust emissions have been reduced by engine-control systems with remaining residues being combusted over automotive platinum catalysts. Again, emissions of nitrogen oxides have been decreased by lowering combustion temperatures by various means or by creating reducing mixtures, while volatile hydrocarbon-based paints were replaced by water-based varieties and control of tank-filling vapour release is achieved by vapour return-lines and pressure control.

However, 'environmentalists' are not content with minimisation or elimination of the effects of known causes, nor are they content to accept reality-refutations of specific belief-based concerns even where such would prevent the misuse of otherwise productive resources. Indeed, there are some so opposed to the free-enterprise system which sustains our current and projected lifestyles as to be discomfited when it solves the problems which they raise to thwart it. Again, there are those who use their 'environmentalist' beliefs to redirect resources from productive to non-productive ends to confound the system of which they disapprove. Again, current agitation to reduce the sulphur content of the otherwise waste product which is heavy marine fuel oil ignores both the additional costs and wider environmental damage of doing so while that to eliminate anthropogenic emissions of carbon dioxide from fossil fuel combustion has no regard for the global economic damage which will ensue from even attempting to do so.

Thus, such agitators reveal a partiality which requires explanation in that they have shifted their focus from emissions of minor constituents of fuel (e.g. the ~1% sulphur in coal) to the total carbon-content of all fossil fuels while ignoring natural factors in global temperature variation, suggesting warmth to be more deleterious to life than cold, and ignoring the sea level rises which have already removed all earlier migratory land bridges (c.f. Sections 2.2.2 and 9.4.3). Indeed, if reduction in fossil fuel combustion in electricity-generation is as necessary as 'environmentalists' claim, their associated aversion to nuclear power when other available alternatives are either inadequate or comparatively expensive (c.f. Section 9.5.1) is perverse to say the least. As to pressurised sequestration of fossil fuel emissions of carbon dioxide in subterranean strata at volumes orders of magnitude greater than those of the sulphur dioxide content, the necessary procedures are as yet untried, would add significantly to costs, could not be applied to all fossil fuel emissions, and have not been proven necessary. Thus, attempts to stop current practice regardless of all such considerations, raises questions as to motive, though the associated debate could simply be a vote and revenue garnering exercise in which claims to be saving the planet by decorating it with windmills are 'balanced' by passing taxation of fossil fuel use and carbon trading costs to consumers selectively compensated by revenue redistribution in the usual way, so long as reality can be ignored.

However, it may be concluded that we should focus on real problems rather than on 'environmentalist' beliefs; that technological solutions to real environmental problems are always either available or in prospect; that real solutions should not be rejected by 'environmentalist' belief; that the most cost-effective and environmentally benign options should always be chosen; that while the nuclear route to power-generation can replace fossil fuel, the latter should not be made more expensive till anthropogenic carbon dioxide is proved detrimental; that it is nonsensical to act on belief in knowledge-based fields; that global warming and cooling are natural phenomena; and that given governmental propensity to promise rather than to deliver, it is comforting not to be facing the start of the next Ice Age . . . at least not yet.

11. 2. 5 Belief as Corruption of Scientific Method

Having shown that belief rejects commonsense and general knowledge to the detriment of social welfare and corrupts specific knowledge by selective 'evidence' in scientific/technical fields to the detriment of physical welfare, I now provide examples of its corruption of scientific method by misused mathematical modelling and statistical analysis in what would otherwise be physicochemical science, and by misused terminology in what could otherwise be the human-sciences.

Because scientific method requires the cause and effect relationship under investigation to be isolated from all others (c.f. Sections 6.1 and 6.3.4) progress was more rapid in the physicochemical sciences where this is easier to arrange than in biological systems where the effect of a cause is often unobservable because of homeostatic maintenance of the physiological balances on which life depends (c.f. Section 8.2.7). However, there are non-biological systems which exhibit just such internally interactive (multi-parameter) complexity, one such being the global atmosphere. Indeed, it is this feature which makes weather forecasting so difficult even when the most powerful computers are used with the intention of disentangling its mutually interactive cause and effect relationships. Nonetheless, increasing computer-power encouraged early investigation of mechanism in the more stable features of the atmosphere such as the trade-wind and monsoon systems by means of mathematical modelling.

Such modelling embodies mathematical expression of physicochemical knowledge and of hypotheses as to the mechanism by which the feature under investigation actually comes about. Thus, the objective is to compare the computed description of the feature with its reality as directly observed and to achieve ever-higher levels of agreement between the two by reiterative adjustment of the hypothetical components of the model, these adjustments being suggested by the convergence or divergence previously achieved, ever closer convergence being indicative of new knowledge of the target mechanism and hence of the atmosphere in general. Readers will recall that mathematical models have been similarly used to investigate the mechanism of galaxy condensation and stellar accretion from hypothetical levels of heterogeneity in the hydrogen density of the early universe (c.f. Section 9.3.1) and the mechanism of tectonic plate movement from hypothetical levels of mantle convection (c.f. Section 9.4.2). However, it is intrinsic to modelling that agreement between modelled description and the phenomenon as observed might be fortuitous; and that independent reality-validated confirmation of any agreement is essential, such as from experimentation-based knowledge of nuclear reactions and of stellar evolution (c.f. Sections 9.1.4 and 9.3.1) or of mantle viscosity deduced from crust relaxation on ice removal (c.f. section 9.4.2).

Thus, given the interactive multi-parameter reality under investigation and the hypothetical nature of the cause-effect relationships on which further knowledge is being sought, it must be recognised that any agreement between computed output and observed reality is guidance only as to the appropriateness of the hypotheses being evaluated; that such outputs are clearly not predictions in the scientific sense of the term, though they are often loosely so-called, scientific predictions being based on fully known cause and effect relationships previously reality-validated in mathematical terms as in Boyle's Law, for example. Again, even when investigative mathematical modelling provides outputs more or less consistent with the observed monsoon and trade wind features of the atmosphere, such levels of consistency would not be sufficient to predict the date of monsoon onset in any given year, or the latitude and longitude of trade wind pick-up on any given voyage, though such predictive power might be attained were the underlying cause and effect mechanisms ever to be known in their full complexity. Again we recall that weather forecasting is still not weather prediction, though the continuing effort to improve forecasting provides knowledge of the processes involved and may improve forecasts given enough time.

As to predicting global temperatures as a function of future emissions of anthropogenic carbon dioxide, the difficulties of atmospheric mathematical modelling are compounded by the difficulties of accounting mathematically for the geological contributions of carbon dioxide to the atmosphere from tectonic plate movement which themselves vary with time (c.f. Section 9.4.2) and for the geological and oceanic re-absorption processes of mountain weathering and photosynthesis which together with subduction, cycle the carbon dioxide from its gaseous to its sequestered states and back to the gaseous, also to unpredictable extents over varying periods of time (c.f. Sections 9.4.2 - 9.4.4). Thus, when computed outputs of global temperature as a function of atmospheric greenhouse gas concentration are compared with actual measurements in due course, they may agree or disagree, fortuitously. In the meantime, however, it may be concluded that present outputs cannot be accepted as predictions in the scientific sense, and that formulating potentially damaging policy upon them is irresponsible. In addition, since adjustment of hypotheses towards ever closer agreement between output and reality is the whole point of mathematical modelling when properly practiced, one is forced to question whether adjustment in this case is not so much for this legitimate purpose as for the illegitimate one of ensuring that 'predicted' temperature rises are small enough to be credible, yet large enough to cause concern. In any case, no agreement between 'predicted' and actual has been achieved thus far.

Thus, we are as likely to experience a gradual temperature rise towards the warmest point of our current glacial period as we are to experience another inter-stadial warming or cooling as has recurred frequently since *Homo neanderthalensis* and *sapiens* evolved. By now, we could have been hoping for prolongation of the current warm period on the not unreasonable grounds that temperate or tropical conditions at any latitude are preferable to Ice Age conditions. It is also worth recalling that at the coldest period of our current Ice Age, the ice-sheet over Britain was several kilometres thick; that there were elephants and hippopotami in the south of England during one of its inter-stadials around 115,000 years ago; and that sea-level has been rising since before the English Channel/southern North Sea were last passable on foot.

Before considering the corruption of scientific method which uses statistical analysis to suggest cause and effect relationships where none exists or is insignificant even if it does, I now refer to a physiological cause and effect relationship which cannot be doubted. Thus, the eighteenth century Navy knew that scurvy would kill entire ships' crews were they deprived of fresh vegetables and fruit for long enough; and that access to them in coastal voyaging entirely prevented it. Cause and effect thus established, it was shown by experimentation with limejuice that scurvy was 100% avoidable by provision of what is now known as vitamin C, no matter how long the deprivation of fresh vegetables and fruit. Had statistical analysis as now practiced, been necessary to show a marginal effect of a putative cause, the eighteenth century Admiralty would not have supplied limejuice. In contrast, marginal results are now integral to drug testing (c.f. Section 9.5.2) in which effectiveness and unwanted side-effects are sought by comparing the drug with a neutral control (the placebo) intended to eliminate any extraneous effects of the procedure which itself is conducted on the double-blind system with neither the test subject nor the tester knowing whether the drug or the placebo has been administered. Such care suggests the effects sought are small enough to be virtually undetectable whereas no placebo/double-blind testing was necessary to reality-validate the efficacy of limejuice.

Again, the earlier practice of taking so-called remedies in the belief that they would do some good now extends to a wide range of nutritional supplements and self-medications, all of which are adequately available from a balanced diet, the only real problem now being how to avoid eating too much food. However, this belief-driven enthusiasm for preventive treatment now fuels the search for medical conditions even before symptoms are presentably noticeable, the rationale being the earlier the diagnosis the surer the cure. In this connection we might usefully look at the statistics of mass-screening through the example of a hypothetical disease which is present to 1% of the age group screened and for which the effectiveness of detection is < 100%, say 90%. Thus, for a screening sample of 1000 individuals 10 would actually have the disease of whom 9 would test positive and 1 negative, while of the 990 not having the disease only 891 would test negative, the remaining 99 testing positive. Thus, of the 108 testing positive only 9 would actually have the disease, one with it would be missed, and 99 would be needlessly alarmed. In general, no diagnostic test will ever be 100% effective for the detection of marginally sub-clinical conditions and as such will not detect all with the disease, though it will produce 'false-positive' results for many without it. It follows that those detected should not automatically fear the worst and that care is needed in assessing the cure rates attributed to early diagnosis, only 8.3 % of those detected (9 out of 108) actually having the disease in the above example.

Nonetheless, in addition to population screening for marginal conditions, the search is more or less continuous for environmental causes of disease where none are evident. Such belief-driven fears and concerns arise, for example, in respect of the nuclear industry, municipal waste incinerators, heat-engines, power-cables, mobile phones, pesticide residues, GM crops, passive smoking *etc*, all of which are subject to statistical analysis of the results of mass-surveys. In contrast, burns due to radiation, behavioural changes in hatters from mercury vapour, breathing discomfort from sulphur dioxide in Bronze Age metal extractors *etc* were observed without much searching, were sufficiently obvious for the causes to be identified, and were eliminated by removal of cause through preventive action. However, where a putative source causes no identifiable effect it is impossible to reality-validate concerned belief and equally impossible to undertake preventive action. Yet such considerations deter neither the belief-driven 'investigator' nor his fund provider in their search for correlations, let alone cause and effect relationships. Nor does failure to find either deter calls for those believed responsible to prove there is no effect, while the logically indefensible 'precautionary principle' is invoked as reason to have the targeted practice banned by legislators equally content with this belief-driven nonsense. Meanwhile concern is perpetuated by reports that the effect sought has been found to this or that level of statistical significance, while reports averring in similar statistical terms that it has not been found never dispel concern. It may confidently be concluded, however, that such closely-contested statistical arguments show that the cause and effect relationship under consideration has no significance, even supposing it exists (c.f. Section 6.1).

However, in psychology and related subjects, action is taken on the bases of beliefs which cannot, even in principle, be subjected to reality-evaluation, such beliefs being given spurious credence by a mere change in terminology. Thus, Sigmund Freud (1856-1939) claimed to have acquired knowledge of the subconscious by creating pseudo-technical jargon to obscure the impossibility of reality-evaluating the said subconscious in himself, let alone in others. Similarly, Munchausen's Syndrome by Proxy is a circularity impossible of reality-evaluation. Again, the transmission of *ideas* (beliefs) has been given a pseudo-scientific explanation by calling them *memes* by analogy with genes, the latter having been previously described as selfish in yet another airing of Darwinism. While there are other such examples of asserting one thing to be another to confer a spurious credence upon it, the one I have chosen for more detailed exemplification is the recent attempt by psychologists to convert self-esteem from an undefined descriptor to an entity capable of external influence for the improvement of observable behaviour.

Thus, from the 1980s the belief has grown among psychologists that raising the self-esteem of the young would reduce crime, teenage pregnancy, drug abuse, violence, educational underachievement and even casual environmental pollution, no attention being given to the converse possibility that self-responsibility in shunning such activities would produce self-esteem or that those wishing to promote the latter should encourage the former and observe the consequent behaviour changes. Thus, reports on this topic were written without considering whether self-esteem might be cause or effect, what the term might actually mean, how it might be measured or what hypotheses might be submitted to reality-evaluation with respect to its further elucidation. Nonetheless, despite such considerations having been ignored, some 15,000 reports on self-esteem had been produced by 2005, at which point a team of reviewers selected about 200 of them on the expedient of deciding whether objective (good) rather than subjective (bad) criteria had been used to assess self-esteem in each investigation. Thus, for example, the reviewers noted that self-reported (subjective) levels of self-esteem correlated with self-assessment of physical attractiveness, but not with (objective) panel assessments of this characteristic; and that self-reported high self-esteem correlated with self-reported high optimism about everything in life and *vice versa*, though the reviewers judged panel assessment to be unreliable in respect of assessing optimism or pessimism. Be that as it may, panel assessments of self-esteem itself cannot be more reliable than those of optimism or of pessimism. Indeed, correlations are not evidence of cause and effect either way while high self-esteem/optimism and low self-esteem/pessimism may not even be correlates: they could be synonyms in the absence of defined meaning.

Nonetheless, with respect to their 200 selected reports, the reviewers sought to correlate self-esteem with academic achievement, the ability to form relationships, sexual activity, unwanted pregnancies, alcohol and illicit drug abuse, aggression, financial satisfaction, life satisfaction and happiness, though levels of satisfaction and happiness must surely be self-reported rather than objectively assessable. Indeed, there is an identity between self-esteem and self-satisfaction which amounts to their being synonyms. In any case, correlation does not establish causality and in none of the above reports, some surveying 20,000-25,000 people, was there any evidence that external enhancement of self-esteem would confer any of the benefits, the expectation of which had inspired these reports in the first place, the benefits never having been quantified against putative cause in any of them. However, it may be concluded that reportage in peer reviewed journals is sufficient in itself to maintain the belief among practitioners that psychology is a science like any other (c.f. Sections 10.8 and 10.9).

11.3 CONCLUSIONS

Despite having shown that the Rational Duality produces only belief and that the Rational Trinity has produced all of our knowledge of craftsmanship, science, technology and behaviour codes, it has nonetheless to be concluded that belief as rejection of commonsense and general knowledge is now usurping the knowledge-contents of traditional behaviour codes to the detriment of social-science and social welfare; and that belief as rejection of specific knowledge and scientific method is now usurping physicochemical and environmental knowledge to the detriment of technology and physical welfare. It may also be concluded that these detriments will worsen so long as electorates and political establishments are content to accept arbitrary beliefs in equality, freedom, rights and 'environmentalism' as 'knowledge'; that this acceptance will not be reversed until electorates differentiate knowledge from belief, recognise policy failure on implementation as reality-refutation of belief, and insist on reality-evaluation of future policy before implementation; and that this differentiation and insistence are necessary if we are to avoid being overwhelmed by reality directly, or indirectly by socio-political systems with more respect for reality than for liberal democracies which reject it (c.f. Section 2.5.3).

CHAPTER 12 SUMMARY AND CONCLUSIONS

In summary, it should be recalled that the innate capacities of *Homo sapiens* evolved from his animal and hominid precursors; that through his Rational Duality he initially believed Real and Beyond to be a continuum from which he later produced self-knowledge and craftsmanship by his Rational Trinity and mythical and metaphorical deities reflecting his self-knowledge by a combination of both; that his religion accepted all useful and otherwise demonstrable knowledge of the world, conflicting only with counter-orthodox heresies and speculations; and that belief, whether religious or secular, continues to be the source of conflict even when resolvable by the Rational Trinity or by suspension of belief inaccessible to it. In addition, it should be recalled that Rational Trinity resolution is available for conflict over traditional behaviour codes and recent alternatives; and that while religion is in contact with reality through such codes and while philosophy was in contact with it through empiricism, secularism has no contact with reality when relying on rationality alone or in alliance with pseudo-science.

Thus, Sections 12.1 and 12.2 conclude that all pseudo-scientific justifications of socio-political belief should be set aside; that specific beliefs should be reality-evaluated as hypotheses against our natural needs for survival and welfare as a group-species; and that our re-deployable resources should be directed to the solution of real problems on the basis of existing and future knowledge. In addition, Sections 12.3 and 12.4 conclude that the likelihood of making this three-fold *Change* increases with the continuing failure of belief-based policy and the lameness of the excuses offered when rationality and pseudo-science are overwhelmed by reality; and that further incentives to this three-fold Change will arise as the benefits of differentiating knowledge from belief become obvious and its practice becomes routine.

12.1 HARMONISATION OF SECULARISM AND RELIGION

Before attempting this harmonisation we need to understand the origin and nature of the disharmony. Thus, we should recall that the spurious debating advantage over religion which secularism gained by conflating its rationality with science was reduced by religion's acceptance of science and would have been eliminated altogether had science made explicit reference to its synonymous experimentation. Thus, to reduce religion's acceptance of science and its own danger from it, secularism opposed the *Genesis* myth with Darwin's Mechanism Conjecture (c.f. Section 8.3.4) to make religion adopt an anti-science stance and thus make scientists less likely to weaken the anti-religious stance by referring to its lack of experimentation. Indeed, the disharmony thus created was belief-based and as such endlessly debatable, neither religious belief, atheism nor the Conjecture being accessible to reality-evaluation in any form. Thus, while knowledge of the fossil record has no need to debate with belief, Darwinism's sole purpose is debate to supplant religious belief with secular belief in the name of rationality. However in rejecting religious belief, Darwinism also rejected its associated knowledge of human nature, a rejection which coupled to its promotion of rationality over experimentation has turned social-science to the pseudo-scientific promotion of secular belief over knowledge to the detriment of social cohesion and welfare. Nonetheless, this disharmony between the secular and religious could be resolved and its negative consequences removed were they to adopt a mutual regard for knowledge and for the Unknowable.

As to this harmonisation we should recall that while the disharmony arose from differences in belief beyond reality-evaluation, it is now more about differences in behaviour codes which can be reality-evaluated. Thus, the former could be mutually accepted or rejected as belief or suspended as metaphor depending on the emotional benefit thus conferred, while the latter could be mutually evaluated as to satisfaction of the requirements for humanity's survival and social welfare as a group-species. As to the former, nothing more can be said and certainly nothing calling for life or death conflict, while as to the latter, reality-evaluation could show, for example, that pregnancy-avoidance is closer to individual welfare than termination by abortion; that anything less than replacement birth-rate is incompatible with group-survival while higher rates which out-run food-supply are incompatible with welfare; that constancy and commitment are more nurturing to the next generation than promiscuity and selfishness; that parental nurturing is more beneficial than consignment to child-minders, music and dance teachers, weekend and summer camp organisers or whatever supposed alternatives there are to parenting; and that official encouragement to abortion on demand and to engendering children to an unknown future by donation of ova and sperm do little in themselves to encourage nurturing in general.

In any case, recalling that the spectra of belief in equality freedom and rights are intelligible to all, and that some interpretations were reality-validated to the knowledge-content of traditional behaviour codes, it should be possible to agree that social policies based on interpretations incompatible with requirements for group-species survival and welfare should be rejected by all; that new hypotheses which might satisfy these requirements should be reality-evaluated as to their success or failure in doing so; and that some beliefs have already been reality-refuted by their failure to meet stated objectives on implementation. Again, while some dismiss traditional empiricism as a basis of individual and social control, others would agree that control is innately acceptable to our group-species survival and welfare; and that there is no reason to reject our bequeathed cultural empiricism without reality-evaluation of the need to do so, nor is there any reason to accept the arbitrary beliefs of self-appointed secularists with only interim endorsement by co-believing marginal majorities. Similarly, recalling that environmentalism is a belief spectrum from which hypotheses have been reality-validated in our technological development, and from which yet others defined as 'environmentalist' should be rejected as belief only, I now differentiate knowledge-rejecting 'secularism' from secularism to harmonise the latter with religious empiricism in a mutual regard for reality, mediated by differentiation of behavioural knowledge from emotionally beneficial belief.

Thus, the secular and religious could mutually recall that social, economic and environmental policies based on belief unrelated to reality cannot be deliverable in reality; that socio-political systems justified by rationality alone exist only so long as their policy failures can be obscured by changes from one set of party-political promises to another; that political establishments are not damaged by such changes only so long as electorates fail to differentiate belief from knowledge in terms of non-compliance or compliance with reality; and that non-compliance can eventually become wide enough for reality to overwhelm political establishments and indeed socio-political systems themselves. Thus, by recalling the non-compliance with reality which overthrew feudalism and was causing trouble for communism, and the compliance with reality which had sustained craftsmanship, science and technology from time immemorial to the twentieth century, both the secular and religious could conclude that proposals to extend wartime central planning and public funding to peace-time economic management should have been submitted to reality-evaluation before the UK government of 1945 implemented its policy of 'public ownership of the means of production and distribution';

392

and that the non-compliance of this policy with reality has been only partially hidden by the recycling of party-political government ever since.

Thus, the secular and religious could conclude that while nationalised industries failed, nationalised social services prone to soviet-style waste continue to consume > 40% of GNP; that while attempts were made to enhance private sector efficiency through direct funding of National Laboratories, slogans such as 'winning the peace as we won the war' and 'the white heat of technology' achieved nothing not otherwise achievable more efficiently in the private sector; and that while reality-denial has weakened to the extent of requiring surrogate measures of performance in the public sector, national efficiency and international competitiveness will remain limited so long as substantial fractions of the electorate receive or seek public funds one way or another. Indeed, with government contracts being prized for their profitability, it is not to be expected that the Public-Private Finance Initiative will exhibit private sector efficiency, the inducement to participate being the avoidance of normal commercial risk. Again, both secular and religious may conclude that while disregard for reality permits political establishments and colluding client groups to waste money, they fear nothing other than parliamentary reshuffles despite the possibility of reality-induced demise of the system itself; that in supposed postponement of this fate, colluding client groups may be expected to receive government help when reality overcomes their mutual beliefs; and that the collusion of such groups with the governmental vote-garnering debt-accumulation which caused the current financial crisis and its need for yet further borrowing, demonstrates the instability of the current system and its need to be conducted by those who can tell the difference between knowledge and belief.

Meanwhile, the secular and religious may mutually recall that disregard for reality in social, economic and environmental affairs continues because of its multi-fold opportunities for vote garnering from advice given, promises made and actions taken even when these conflict among themselves, let alone with reality. Thus, for example, it may recalled that governments advise against buying goods and services said to pollute and to consume irrecoverable resources, while promising to preserve employment in the provision of these same goods and services, and to counter the price rises which conserve these same resources; that they advise against alcohol consumption while introducing 24-hour licensing, advise against flying while planning to double airport capacity, promise to reduce drug-dependence while relaxing regulation and policing, avoid taxing aviation-fuel to preserve cheap holiday flights while justifying high taxation of road use and automotive fuel as planet protection, talk of freedom while extending regulation for its own sake, talk of doing while thwarting doers, and talk of prudence while permitting unsustainable debt accrual.

Thus, while a democratic system of revenue collection, vote garnering and revenue disbursement could be sustainable on a knowledge-base, it must be concluded that our system is currently belief-based on 'secular' opposition to hitherto sustaining behaviour codes, on the recycling of unsustainable politico-economic beliefs regardless of reality, and on 'environmentalist' opposition to hitherto sustaining technology; that such a belief-based system is sustainable only by commonsense and knowledge external to itself; and that when the influence of this residual commonsense and knowledge is overwhelmed by the consequences of the system's beliefs, reality will terminate it as it always does. On the other hand, it may also be concluded that the system could become knowledge-based by harmonising secularism with religious empiricism, by a new knowledge-based economics and by harmonising environmentalism with technology.

12.2 RESOURCE DEPLOYMENT ON REAL PROBLEMS

Having recalled that our current resource consumption on self-created socio-political problems arises from our knowledge-rejection and disregard for reality, it may be concluded that such consumption could be avoided were knowledge to replace belief; and that such resources could be redeployed to the solution of real problems so far obscured by belief. Thus, the new knowledge-based economics could manage resource deployment on real problems by optimising distribution between private and public sectors through realty-evaluation of hypotheses to this end; by re-establishing the harmonisation of technology with the environmentalism which hitherto operated to our physical welfare enhancement; by harmonising secularism with the religious empiricism which hitherto underpinned our social cohesion; and by redressing the previous lack of social-science hypotheses for reality-evaluation towards improving our social welfare by the scientific method which has proved its worth in physicochemical science.

As to formulation of the necessary social hypotheses, we should compare the advantages of our former acceptance of religious empiricism with the disadvantages of its recent rejection and have regard to our group-species survival requirements. Thus, both the secular and religious may recall that from earliest times religious empiricism inculcated personal responsibility for socially acceptable behaviour from childhood onwards by preventive guidance and corrective rehabilitation within family, kin and tribe; that law was held in reserve against upbringing failure, to compensate victims, impose fines, imprison or execute in proportion to severity of offence and need to prevent recurrence, punishment *per se* being left to the hereafter and rehabilitation to offender and offended; and that in contrast, the empiricism which formerly guided upbringing and created law is now overridden by arbitrary beliefs which, in the name of rationality, confer equal freedom and right to do as one pleases in expectation of obverting former misdemeanours and crimes. However, it may also be recalled that response arrangements continue to be made in expectation and experience of their continuity; that traditional means of prevention and rehabilitation within family, neighbourhood and school have been criminalized together with the misdemeanours previously controlled at this level and thus transferred to the former reserve level of law; that endless debate has ensued as to whether criminals should be rehabilitated or punished while these options are now too late to be as preventive as they were at the earlier level of misdemeanour; and that responsibility for criminality is now transferred from the individual to the shortcomings of society which it is the self-imposed role of government to rectify according to the beliefs which anathematised traditional codes and practices with acclamations of liberal rationality at the outset.

Thus, recalling that such rationalists should not be running anything, and that the above beliefs as hypotheses could have been reality-refuted by existing knowledge without needing confirmation by failure on implementation, the secular and empirical religious could campaign for the political establishment to accept that social cohesion requires individuals to take personal responsibility for it; that the freedom of families, neighbourhoods and schools to inculcate such responsibility by traditional means should be restored to them because no penal system can correct for its absence; that law should be limited to its previous reserve role; that restitution of these respective roles requires redrafting of recent civil rights and criminal justice legislation to encourage commonsense and traditional empiricism supplemented by fresh hypotheses for reality-evaluation as necessary; and that future policy should be based on knowledge rather than on belief, and certainly not on reality-refuted belief. Again, the political establishment should likewise be pressed to accept that the self-esteem associated with acceptance of personal responsibly is now being destroyed for many by beliefs which encourage them to ignore or deny their own nature; that subsequent attempts to protect them from the consequences of so doing are reality-refutations of the supposed benefits of such beliefs; and that while the self-imposed government role of managing society requires low levels of personal responsibility and high levels of dependency, failure to take responsible for self and family is detrimental to social cohesion and welfare in ways which cannot be rectified by the indirect methods to which government and law are inherently limited.

Thus, it may be concluded that while the political establishment should have recognised the knowledge-content of our traditional behaviour codes as preventative and rehabilitative of anti-social behaviour and should have secured them against demolition by the 'secular', it chose to join in the demolition; that it now has no alternative but to contribute to its reconstruction through the harmonisation of secularism with religious empiricism; and that because the objective of this harmonisation is to correct the current lack of personal responsibility and independency at all levels, the state could best assist by not diminishing them further by over-protection of the young which prevents the development of self-responsibility through experiential learning and by over-provision of adult support which cultivates yet more dependency.

Again, recalling that rationalists should not be running anything, the secular and empirical religious should campaign in respect of defence and cultural interaction for establishment acceptance that while the threats posed by nuclear-weapons and by terrorism remain ever present and ill-defined, neither are diminished by belief-based debates on unilateral disarmament or by arbitrary interpretations of beliefs in the equality, freedom and rights of those doing the threatening; and that while cultural integration has always been successful with the knowledge-based willing, it cannot be forced on the belief-based unwilling. Again, in respect of world trade and population projections indicative of the need for another revolution in agricultural production, the secular and empirical religious should campaign for establishment acceptance that it would best assist by distancing itself from belief-based organic farming, bio-fuel cultivation instead of food, 'set-aside' and conversion of agricultural land to nature reserves; and by promoting knowledge-based use of pesticides, fertilisers and genetic modification.

Thus, all may conclude that solutions to the real problems of improving internal security, economic prosperity, international and intercultural relations, national defence, global food production and world trade, should be facilitated by political establishments acting in accordance with the Adam Smith analysis; that likewise all action should be in the private sector which previously produced the knowledge-based welfare we have enjoyed thus far; that all future socio-economic policies must be knowledge- rather than belief-based; that resources should be redeployed accordingly; that many current problems would evaporate were the beliefs which created them rejected; and that the best way to secure our future both socially and physically is to build our behaviour codes on our nature and requirements as a group-species and to encourage individual self-reliance and enterprise instead of mollycoddling both to extinction while ignoring the reality with which we must all deal to survive and prosper both individually and collectively.

12.3 PROSPECTS FOR KNOWLEDGE-BASED POLICY ADOPTION

It should be possible to convince debaters that differences in beliefs respecting equality, freedom, rights, environmentalism and private/public resource distribution are only resolvable by reality-evaluation; that consensus of belief is still belief and almost certainly interim; that belief is not a basis for progress unless reality-evaluated; and that the Change as yet undefined by those seeking it, must be from belief to knowledge as advocated herein. Again, it should be possible to convince the public that the present credit crisis was created by believing the 'feel good factor' to be sustainable when its required debt levels were reality-defying; that the mathematical models which 'proved' such levels to be risk-free were spurious; and that whether the risk was recognised or not by self-styled experts, 'the boom was busted' by reality as all belief-based policy eventually is. Indeed, the raising of 'environmental' taxes to pay for an ever-growing and ever-wasteful public sector is already encountering limits to voter tolerance and a reluctance to support a social agenda based on promises undeliverable in reality whatever the cost.

Thus, the political establishment is becoming aware of public reluctance to accept the cost implications of current 'secular' and 'environmentalist' policy and is hoping ambivalence will be a multi-fold deliverer of votes and revenue pending another confrontation with reality. Thus, while taxing aviation fuel at the rates applying to road vehicles would reduce air-traffic at a stroke, policy-makers content themselves with advising the public not to fly while they consider the rates of taxation it would be willing to pay to continue flying in compliance with the planned airport expansion, a policy which reveals a higher concern for vote and revenue collection than for environmental damage whether real or imagined and which parallels current policies on petrol and road tax and on alcohol duty. However, the political establishment is beginning to recognise that 'environmentalism' is less a taxation bonanza and more an obstacle to reliable electricity generation than it first believed, while electorates are beginning to recognise that the costs of emissions curtailment and carbon trading will be passed to consumers with emissions being paid for rather than curtailed and carbon being recycled rather than sequestered. Again, both political establishment and public are becoming aware that even if global warming were anthropogenic, the effect of a total UK shut-down would quickly be cancelled by the current rate of coal-fired power-station building in China alone; and that the aspiration of the entire globe is for development and not for shut-down as the concern expressed over the current economic recession amply demonstrates.

Thus, with the incompatibility of one belief with another and of all with reality becoming evermore obvious, both electorates and political establishments should be persuadable of the need to pursue knowledge-based solutions to real problems through the market as practiced hitherto, and of the futility of belief-based administrative initiatives which ignore reality. Thus, for example, both will have to recognise that resource deployment on local consequences of natural climate change where required, is absolutely preferable to attempting the cessation of carbon dioxide emissions which in any case have not been disentangled from the natural carbon cycle of the planet and which are likely to be incidentally reduced by on-going and more cost-effective technical developments; and that economic reality also requires the freeing of global markets to the self-help which will widen investment in research and development towards the solution of real problems. Thus, after years of promising to eradicate poverty at home by redistribution of wealth and public-funded employment rather than by self-help within the wealth-creating private-sector, and of promising to alleviate it overseas by foreign-aid rather than by private sector globalisation, India and China are now self-developing and altering the financial environment of those who still believe the donation of public money to be the answer to everything at home and abroad..

Thus, it may be concluded that electorates and political establishments will have to take knowledge-based decisions on the distribution of public/private involvement and corresponding resource deployment best suited to respond to real problems of human behaviour, population growth, optimisation of energy generation and use, provision of food and fresh water, access to raw materials, market globalisation and national and international security. However, they will also have to accept and provide training and education according to ability if they are to have a wealth-generating role in providing real solutions to real problems now and in future. Thus, with real
396

problems enough to distract us from the unreal, it may be concluded that the prospects for knowledge-based policy adoption are good and will continue to improve as the benefits of differentiating knowledge from belief and science from pseudo-science become increasingly obvious as the practice becomes routine.

12.4 FURTHER INCENTIVES TO KNOWLEDGE-BASED POLICY ADOPTION

Recalling that some 75% of domestic legislation now comes direct from a belief-driven Brussels intent on creating a Federal Europe against the known wishes of electorates, there is further incentive to adjudicate future policy on knowledge rather than on central assertions of belief. As to reality-rejection, the countries of post-war western Europe indulged themselves in belief-based criticism of the USA and belief-based sympathy for the aims of communism while leaving their freedom from its domination to the greater realism of the USA despite having a larger population than either the USA or the USSR. As to reality-acceptance, there can be no doubt that the productivity-based influence of the USA has been due to the high levels of self-motivation, self-reliance and self-responsibility of its citizenry within a socio-political system which encourages such self-sufficiency in contrast to the European systems which suppress it in creating dependency. Thus, while knowledge and belief are as undifferentiated in the New World as they are in the Old, the latter now needs this differentiation to reinvigorate itself and the former needs it to reinforce the vigour it is now losing.

As to the world beyond Europe and the USA and their relationships with it, the desire for knowledge-based development is strong while belief-based cultural differences continue to create apprehension and conflict. However, were Europe and the USA to reduce their own internal and external conflicts by differentiating knowledge from belief as advocated herein, they could commend this process for resolution of intra- and inter-cultural conflict everywhere. Indeed, in recognising their own needs in this respect, they could immediately and credibly invite other cultures to move with them to the common position which would unite all peoples in their humanity whatever their individual achievements, aspirations or positions of contentment might be. In any case, all cultures now have the independent incentive to turn from the conflict-inducing beliefs of the Rational Duality on which none can rely in the face of reality, to the constancy of the Rational Trinity knowledge on which all can rely in compliance with reality.

INDEX

Arianism 79, 80, 81, 82
Arians 36, 84, 358
Arimium (Rimini), Council of 81, 91
Aristarchus of Samos 56, 59, 94
Aristophanes 46, 47, 48, 49
Aristotelianism 367
Aristotle 42, 52-54, 55, 80, 248, 253, 333, 347-348, 358, 364
    and metaphysics 337
    and the Middle Ages 104, 110, 118-119, 120, 121, 123
    and rejection of reality 367, 372, 376
    and the Renaissance 148, 152, 156
    translations of works 106, 107, 117, 118
Arithmetic 111, 117
Arithmetica Infinitorum 157
Arius 78, 79, 82
Arkwright, Richard 225
Arles, Council of 91
armour, early 34
Armour, P. D. 224
armour from Dark Ages to 1700 135
Armstrong, Edwin 323
Armstrong, Neil 328
Arnald of Villanova 121, 122
Arp, H. C. 287-288
ARPA net 322
Arrhenius 198, 199, 200
art, birth of 10-11, 12
artefacts, birth of 10-11, 12
Artsimovich, Lev Andreevich 313
Aryabhata 107, 113
Aryans 36, 84, 358
Arzachel 114-115
Asclepiades of Bithynia 64
asepsis 250
Ash-Wednesday Supper, The 141
asses as pack animals 19
Assyria 14
Assyrian Empire 36
Assyrian ships 24
Assyrians 22, 35
Aston 269, 270
astrolabes 61, 129
astrology 104-105
astronomy
    1600-1700 146-147, 148, 149, 151

1700-1900 217
Alexandrian advances in 60, 61-62
Dark Age advances in 122, 141
development of 44-45, 46, 48, 49, 51, 52- 53, 55, 56, 58-59
Islamic developments in Middle Ages 114-115
planets and satellites, origin of 308-311
relationship with physics and chemistry 241-244
20th-century 285-297
    advances 328-329
    atomic structure 297-298
    Big Bang 293-296, 298
    black holes 297-298
    Chandrasekhar's Limit 288, 289, 290, 291
    cosmic rays 292
    creation, continuous 293-295
    distance measurement 291-293
    expansion 293-295
    Grand Unified Theory 297, 298
    Hertzsprung-Russell Diagram 286-288, 289, 291, 292, 294
    Hubble Constant 293, 294
    radio-sources 292-293
    RR Lyrae stars 288, 289, 292
    Standard Model 297
    star formation and evolution 286,-290
    Steady State Hypothesis 294
    String Theory 298
    super novae 290-291, 294
    Super String Theory 298
    union of, with experimentation 158-159
Aswan (Syene) 58
AT&T 322
Atala, A. 316
Athanasius 82
Athenian fleet 352
Athenian thinking: 500 BC-300 BC 46-54
Athenians 37
    Civil Law 41

Cromford, Derbyshire 225
Cronos, son of Ouranus 47
Cronstedt 232
Crookes 207, 208
crop cultivation, early 12-13
Cross, Charles Frederick 225, 235
crossbows, early 34
Crossley Brothers 215
Croton 45
crows 8
Crusade, First 105
crusaders 133
crystals 191-192
Cugnot, Nicolas 219
Culham, UK 313-314
Cullen, W. 190
cuneiform, Sumerian 16
Curie, Marie 208, 267, 270
Curie-Joliot, Irene 270-271
Cuthbert 92
Cuvier, Georges 246, 247, 252, 254, 255
cycle development 241
Cynicism 348, 364
Cyprian, Bishop of Carthage 73, 74, 87-88
Cyril, Bishop of Alexandria 86-87
Cyrus of Persia 37, 71

da Luzzi, Mondino 121
Daguerre, Louis-Jacques-Mande 240
Daimler, Gottlieb 215, 216
dairy products 26, 224-225
Dal Riadha 92
Dalton, John 169, 170-171, 172, 176, 190, 205, 245
Dalton's Hypothesis 172, 173
Dalton's Law of Partial Pressure 171, 187
Damasus, Bishop 88
dams, early 18
Daniel, Ralph 226
Danube Valley 37
Darby, Abraham 220, 228, 233
Darius, Emperor 19, 37
Dark Ages *see* Middle Ages
Darwin, Charles Robert 254, 255, 256-257, 258, 306
Darwin's Conjecture on Evolutionary Mechanism 371, 391
Darwin's Theory of Evolution 258, 259, 370

Darwin, Erasmus 256
Darwinism 308, 389, 391
Darwinists 258, 259, 370, 371
date-palm, early cultivation of 14
Dated Creed 81, 82, 84
Davis, John 129, 292
Davy, Sir Humphrey 180, 198, 207, 224, 227, 253, 357
DDT 317
De Aquis Urbis Romae 64
De Doctrina Christiana 85, 89
De Fide 82, 119
de Havilland Comet 326
de Havilland Moth/Tiger Moth 326
De Medicina Statica 150
De Principiis 75-76
De Re Metallica 140
De Re Natura 65, 337
De Revolutionibus 141
De Trinitate 82
dead, reluctance to abandon 41
Debierne 268
Debye 199
Decius 76
defence, frontier 35
Deism/Deists 359, 374
deities, Greek 42-43, 47-48 *see also* gods, Greek
deity, concept of 54
Delaware River 218
Delhi 107
Demiurge 336
Democedes 45
Democritus 44, 54, 55, 110, 153, 170, 171, 336, 337, 349
Dempster 269, 270
Descartes 142, 150, 151-152, 156-157, 158, 159, 344, 358, 370
        and metaphysics 337-338, 339, 340
Descent of Man 257
Description of The Marvellous Canon of Logarithms 142-143
Desormes, J. B. 235
Dewar, James 190-191
Dewey, John 360-361, 364, 377
Dewi 92
Dialectic 354

measurement of, relationship with
physics and chemistry 244-245
Roman advances in studies of 63
Earth sciences, 20th-century 298-311
climatic consequences of plate
tectonics 303-305
crust thickness 300-302
Earth, age of 299
geology 299
life on Earth, origin, evolution and
extinctions of 305-307
magnetic anomalies 300-301
ocean depth 299-301
planets and satellites, origin of 308-311
311
plate tectonics 299, 301-302
climatic and biological
consequences 303-305, 306
Earth studies, in Dark Ages 140-141
Eastman, George P. 226, 240
Ebers Papyrus 14
Eckert, J. P. 320-321
eclipses, solar, Saronic cycle 43
economy, political 352-357
belief-based socio-politics 357
communism 355-356, 357
free trade, comparative advantage 354
labour, bargaining power of 353-354
labour, division of 353
market operation 353
and Marx 354-356
mass production 355
mercantilism 353
and Smith 352-354, 355, 356, 357
state intervention 356
taxation 356
wealth of nations 354
Edgar 179
Edicts, Imperial 81, 83, 85, 87, 93
Edinburgh, Roslin Institute 318
Edison, Thomas 227, 239-240
Education Act (1944) 377
educational standards, decline since 1960s 377
Edward I, King 133
EEC (European Economic Community) 311
eels, spawning of 53
Egbert, King 104
Egypt 106

brought within Roman Empire 38
building, early 20
community bakeries 26
conquests 36
Coptic Church 87
crops 14
fortifications 35
land surveys 43-44, 46
metals, use of 28, 31
New Kingdom 36
Old Kingdom 36
weaving 26
Egyptian calendar 18
Egyptian hieroglyphs 16, 124
Egyptian ships 23
Egyptians, empirical relationships identified 43
Egyptians and calculation of pi 97
Egyptians and urban water supplies 18
Ehrlich, Paul 250, 314
Eightfold Path 39
Einstein, Albert 262, 264, 265-266, 271, 296, 298, 367
298, 367
Einstein's Theory of Special Relativity 264-266, 370, 371
266, 370, 371
Einstein's Theory of General Relativity 264-266, 296, 298, 370, 371
266, 296, 298, 370, 371
Einthoven, W. 315
Eisenhower, Dwight D. 321
El Cid 111
Elbing 127
Elburz mountains 13
electric motors 202, 237
electric traction 221
Electricite de France 312
electricity
Ampere 198
conductivity of solutions 200
electrolysis 198-199
generation 216-217
Ohm 198
Volta 197-198
storage 216-217
supply technology 236-237
understanding the nature of 197-201
unity with magnetism and light 204-207
207
electrocardiograph, development of 315
electro-deposition of metals 232-233

electroencephalograph, development of 315
electrolysis 198-199
Electrolysis, Laws of 198, 199, 201, 208
Electrolytic Dissociation, Theory of 199
electromagnetic spectrum 208-209
Electromagnetic Spectrum, Equations of the 258
electron 208
Electronic Theory of Atomic Structure 182
electronic theory of valence 274-275
element, first use of word 180
Elementa Physiologiae 252
Elementary Treatise on Chemistry 168
Elements 117
elements, classification of 181-184
elements, spectra of 273-274
elements in compounds, weights of, constancy of combining 166-169
Elements of Agricultural Chemistry 180, 224
elements of all things, proposals for 44, 45, 46, 54-55
Elements of Chemistry 166
Elements of Geometry 56
Elixir of Life 139-140
Elkingtons of Birmingham 233
Ely Cathedral 131
Empedocles of Agrigentum 46
empires, early, rise and fall 36-38
empiricism (self-knowledge) 2
Enclosure Acts 223
Encyclopaedists 65
Encyclopedie ou Dictionnaire des Science, des Arts et des Metiers 230
Endeavour 254
energy, 20th-century 311-314
    geothermal 313
    hydrogen fusion 313-314
    nuclear 311, 313
    solar 311-312
    tidal 312
    wind 312
energy (non-matter), understanding the nature of 184-207
    electricity *see* electricity,
    understanding the nature of
        heat 185-186
        associated with bonding of
        atoms in molecules 192-193
        mechanical equivalence of 204-207
        as motion of atoms and molecules 186-192
    light 203-204
    magnetism 201-202
    temperature 185-186
    unity of electricity, magnetism and light 204-207
    the void 193-197
        diffusion 196
        osmosis 196-197, 199
        solubility 193-194
        solutions, freezing of 194-196
energy (non-matter) and matter, further elucidation 207-209
    cathode rays 207-208
    electromagnetic spectrum 208-209
    electron 208
    radioactivity 208-209
    X-rays 208
Enfield, Royal Small Arms Factory 231
Engelhardt 232
engines, aircraft 326
engines, internal combustion 214-216
England 104, 302
    Norman Conquest 132-133
'English, King's' for writing 104
English Channel and ice age 11
Enlightenment 162, 163
Enquiry Concerning Human Understanding 340
Enterprise 218
entertainment technology, 1700-1900 239-240
Entrecasteaux, J. A. Bruni d' 245
environmental causes of disease, search for 388-389
environmental impacts 384-385
'environmentalism' 317, 318, 392
'environmentalists' 381, 384, 385-386
enzyme term introduced 251
Ephesus, Councils of 86, 87
Epic of Gilgamesh 11
Epictetus 348, 364
Epicurean system of metaphysics 337, 338
Epicureanism 110, 153, 340
Epicureans 55, 338
Epicurus of Samos 55, 348, 359, 364

Grosseteste, Robert 118, 119, 138
Grotthus 198
group-living, capacity for 7
Guardians (Greek governing elite) 51, 347, 350
Guericke, Otto von 153
Guglielmimi, D. 191
Guide to the Perplexed 116
Gulf Stream 305
gun-powder 109
        development of 133-134
        and mining 227
Gurdon, John 318
Gurney, Sir Goldsworthy 219
Gutenberg, Johan 125
Guthrie, T. 195
Gutton, Henri 325
Guye and Pintza's Volumetric Method 175

habitat related migration in Palaeolithic age 11-12
Haddock 293
Hadley, George 245
Hadrian 38
Hadrian's Wall 35
Hales, Rev. Stephen 155, 166
Hall, Charles M. 231
Hall, Marshall 252-253, 292
Haller, Albrecht von 252, 255
Halley, Edmund 153, 160, 242, 243, 244, 245, 246
Hallstatt culture 33-34
Hambledon Hill, Wiltshire 20
Hamilcar 37
Hammurabi, King of Babylon 15-16, 36
Hampson 190
Hancock, Thomas 219
Handbook of Physiology 252
Hannibal 35, 37
Harappan 15
Hargreaves, James 225
Harlech Castle 133
harmonisation of secularism and religion 391-393
Harrapans 36
Harrington, Sir John 237
Harrison, John 218, 244, 357
Hartley 196
Harvard University 316, 320

Harvey, William 150
Hasdai ben Shaprut 116
Hauy 191
Hawaii, University of 318-319
Hayek 356
heart, artificial 315
heart augmenters 315-316
heat
        associated with bonding of atoms in molecules 192-193
        of combustion 193
        of formation 193
        mechanical equivalence of 204-207
        as motion of atoms and molecules 186-192
        of reaction 192-193
        specific 173-174, 177, 185, 186
        understanding 185-186
Hebrew Scriptures 88, 89
Hector 101
Heezen, Bruce C. 300
Hegel, George Friedrich Wilhelm 339-340, 354, 355, 364
Heisenberg, Werner 263, 264, 276
Heisenberg's Uncertainty Principle 263-264
Heitler, Walther 276
helicopters 327
helium 209
Helmholtz, Hermann 205-206
Helmont, Jan Baptist van 138, 152
hemp, early use of 14, 26
Henderson, Thomas 244
Henry Grace a Dieu 127
Henry the Navigator, Prince 126-127
Hensen, Victor 254
Henyey 293
Heracataeus 44
Heracleides of Pontus 56
Heracleitus 44, 50, 336
Heraclius 106
herbal treatments, early 14
herbicides 316
Hercataeus of Miletus 44
Herman 294
Herman the Cripple 118
Hero of Alexandria 22, 23, 60-61, 214
        translations 106
Herod Antipas 76

Herodotus of Halicarnassus 21, 44
Herophilus of Chalcedon 56
Heroult, Paul Louis Tousaint 231
Herschel, Frederick William 242, 243, 244, 293
Hertz, Heinrich 207, 239, 325
Hertzsprung-Russell Diagram 286-288, 289, 291, 292, 294
Hesiod 122
Hess, G. M. 193
Hess's Law 193
hieroglyphs, Egyptian 16
Hilary of Poitiers 82
Hiltner 292
Himalayas 302
Hindu caste system 38
Hindu mathematics 107-109, 110, 111-112, 113
Hindu number system 17, 142, 164, 331
Hinduism 39
Hipparchus of Nicaea 60, 96, 122
Hippo 90-91
Hippocrates of Chios 49, 57
Hippocrates of Cos 48-49, 104, 117, 123
       translations 106
Hippocratic Oath 64
Hiroshima 323, 324
Hispellum 79
histology 250
History and Present State of Electricity 197
History of Scotland 360
History of the Reign of Charles V 360
Hittites 30, 31, 36
Hittorf 207
Hitzig, Eduard 252
Hobbes, Thomas 338, 349, 350-351, 363, 364
Hodgkin, Dorothy M. C. 285
Hoe, Richard 238
Hoff, J. H. Van't 196, 199, 200
Hoffman's Method 175
Hohenheim, Aureolus Philippus Theophrastus Bombastus von (Paracelsus) 139-140, 232
Hoke, Leonore 301
Holland 23
Hollywood, John 122
Holmes, Arthur 299
Holy Spirit, concept of 82, 85
Home, Henry (Lord Kames) 349, 360

Homer 39, 42, 43, 122
hominid behaviour, divergence of 7-8
hominids, early, craftsmanship of 8
Homo erectus 6, 307
Homo habilis 6, 9, 307
Homo heidelbergensis 7
Homo neanderthalensis 7, 11, 41, 257
Homo sapiens 93, 307
      belief in reincarnation 41
      brain size 7
      capacities, inherited and unchanging 8-9
      earliest finds 7
      hunter-gatherer lifestyle 9, 303
      innate capacities of 391
      innate selfishness and cooperativeness 39
      migration, habitat related 11-12
      structure 7
      and tools 9-10
      Unknown and Unknowable, addresses 41
Homoean Christianity/Christians 83, 90-91
Homoean Creed 82, 84
homoousis (of identical substance) 79, 80-81, 82, 87
Homs, Lake of 18
Honain Ibn Ishaq 107
Honorius 84, 90
Hooft, 't 297
Hooke, Robert 153, 154, 155-156, 184, 255
Hooker, Joseph Dalton 254, 255
Hopkins, F. G. 315
hoplites (Greek armoured infantry) 34
hormonal deficiencies 315
Horologium 158
Horologium Oscillatorium 158
Horse-Hoeing Husbandry 223
Houdry, Eugene 236
Houndsfield, Godfrey 314
hovercraft 327
Howd, Samuel 217
Hoyle, Fred 293-294
HTTP (Hypertext Transfer Protocol) 322-323
Huang, Alan 322
Huang-ti, Emperor, wife of 26
Hubble 293, 296
Hubble Constant 293, 294

Cosmic Background Explorer satellite
COBE) 294, 295
Virtual Interface Environment
Workstation 322
National Centre for Supercomputing
Applications 323
Natta, Guilio 320
Natterer 190
Natural History 65, 104, 123, 231, 255
Natural Questions 65, 117
Nature, Law of 351
Nautilus 324
naval warfare from Dark Ages to 1700 135
navigation, advances in, 1700-1900 217
navigation from Dark Ages to 1700 126, 128-129
Nearchus, admiral 54
Nebuchadnedzar 35
Neckham, Alexander 128
Need, Samuel 225
Needham, Joseph 248
Neo-Platonism 68-69, 82, 94, 110, 347
Neo-Platonists 336-337, 358
Neptunists 246
Nero 76
nervous system 252-253
Nestorian Church 105-106
Nestorianism/Nestorians 86, 87, 91, 118
Nestorius, Bishop of Constantinople 86
Neumann, John von 321
New Astronomy with Commentaries on the Motions of Mars 147
New Chemical Nomenclature, A 168
New Generation Computer Technology, Institute for 321
New Hall, Staffordshire 226
New Haven, Connecticut 239
New Testament 72, 93, 347
New York Elevated Railway 221
Newark copper mine (USA) 213
Newcomen, Thomas 212-213, 215
Newlands, J. A. R. 182
Newton, Sir Isaac 157, 158, 159, 160, 161, 162, 163, 206, 209, 286, 329
   and the new experimentation 147, 149
   and physics entering new era 262, 265, 266

and relationship of physics to other sciences 242, 245
and relativism contrasted with knowledge 370, 371
and understanding the nature of matter 166, 171
and understanding the nature of non-matter (energy) 185, 203, 204
Newton's Calculus 57
Newton's Law of Cooling 185, 186
Newton's Law of Gravity 243
Newton's Laws of Motion 187, 257
Newton's Theory of Gravity 257, 295, 370
Niagara Falls hydroelectric plant 217, 231
Nicaea, Council of 79, 80
Nicaea, Imperial Palace 79
Nicaean Edict 84
Niccoli, Niccolo 123
Nicene Creed 76, 79, 80, 81, 82, 83, 84, 86
Nicenes 85
Nicholas V, Pope 123
Nichomachean Ethics 53, 55, 120, 347, 348
Nicias 46
nickel technology, 1700-1900 231, 232, 233
Nicolas de Cusa 138, 141, 145, 148, 152
Niepce, Joseph 208, 240
Nile, River 18, 23
Nile Valley 13, 14, 15, 36, 43
Nimes, Pont du Gard 18
Nineveh 23, 35, 36, 37
Ninian 91
Nipkow, Paul 239
Nippur 99
nitrogen in plants 250-251
nitrogen oxides 169
nitrous oxide 253
Nixon, John 227
Nobel, Alfred 227
Nobel brothers 236
Noel, Michael 321
non-matter, understanding the nature of *see* energy, understanding the nature of
Normandy, Duchy of 105
Normans 132-133
Norsemen 105, 126, 127, 132
Northumbrians 92
Norway 385
Norwegian Royal Radar Establishment 322

428

organ transplants 315
organs, artificial 315
organs, hybrid 316
Origen 75-76, 85, 88, 90, 338, 349
Origin of Forms and Qualities 154
Origin of Species by Means of Natural Selection,... 257
Origin of the Distinction of Ranks, The 360
Orontes Valley, Syria 18
Oseberg ship 126
osmium 232
osmosis 196-197, 199
Ostia 21
OSUMI satellite 329
Oswy 92
Otto, Nikolaus August 214-215, 326
Otto cycle 215, 216
Otto-Langen atmospheric gas engine 215
Ouranus (the sky) 47
Ovdat 18
Ovid 122
Owen, Richard 254
Owen, Robert 355, 357
Oxford university 105, 120
oxides 169
oxygen, discovery of 167, 168

Pacific Ocean 300
paddle-wheel propulsion 218-219
Paganism, eradication of 87, 88, 90
Palaeolithic age, craftsmanship in 9-11 *see also* craftsmanship in creation of agricultural and urban living
Palaeolithic age, migration in 11-12
palaeontology, relationship with physics and chemistry 246, 247
palaeontology term introduced 254
palladium 232
Palladius, Bishop of Ratiaria 85, 92
Pallaiuolo, Antonio 139
Pan American 326
Panama, Isthmus of 305
Panama Canal 219, 227
Pangea 299, 306, 307
Pantheism/Pantheists 359, 374
Pantheon 21
papermaking 124-126
Papin, Denis 212

Papplewick 225
parabalani 86
Paracelsus 139-140, 232
Parallel Inference Machine (PIM) 321
Paris
    Abbey of St Denis 131
    Academie des Sciences 216, 234, 244, 245
    Ecole Central 216
    Le Grand Café 240
    St Cloud pottery 226
    University of 105, 120
        Faculty of Arts 119
Paris Exhibition (1867) 232
Paris Exhibition (1889) 215
Parkestone, Suffolk 6-7
Parmenides of Elea 49, 150, 336
Parsons, Charles 214, 219
Parthenon 21
Parthians 34
partnerships, male/female, evolution of 7-8
Pascal, Blaise 153, 157, 360
Pascal's Triangle 113-114
Paschen Series 273
Pasteur, Louis 13, 238, 249-250, 283
Pasteur Institute 314
pathogens, treatment against 314
Patrick 92
Paul 70, 71-72, 73, 75, 88
Paul, Epistles of 70, 72, 73, 74
Paula 88
Pauli 273
Pauling, Linus 285
Pavlov, Ivan Petrovitch 253
Pearl Harbour 323
Pearson 312
Peenemunde Experimental Station 324
Pelagianism 90, 348
Pelagius 90, 91, 92, 162, 349
Peloponnesian War 43, 46
Pen-y-Daran ironworks 220
pendulum experiments 158, 244-245
penicillin 311, 314, 318
Pennsylvania, University of 320-321
pentagrams 45
pentene 277
Pepi I, statue of 31
peptides 278-279

Sol Invictus cult 77, 78
solar eclipses, Saronic cycle 43
solar energy 311-312
Solomon ibn Gabirol 111
Solon (the Law-giver) 42, 43, 49-50
solubility 193-194
solutions, freezing of 194-196
Solvay brothers process 234-235
Somering, Samuel T. von 238
Somme valley 257
Sommellier, Germain 222
Sophists 343
Sophocles 46, 47, 48, 122
soul, forms of, and Aristotle 52
Soul, World 68
Soumis mines 31
sound-recording device, first 239-240
South Metropolitan Gas Company 234
space exploration 324, 327-329
Space Shuttle 329
Spain 30, 117, 124
Spallanzani, Lazzaro 248
spectrum, electromagnetic 209
Spemann, Hans 318
spinning, development of 26
Spinoza, Baruch 339, 349, 358, 359, 364
Spithead Naval Review (1897) 214
Split, Diocletian's Palace 21
Spode, Josiah 226
Spontaneous Disintegration, Theory of 267
Sprague, Frank Julian 221
Sputnik 1 satellite 324, 327
square roots 94-96, 98-99, 100
square roots, development of 142
square roots and Binomial Theorem 114
stabilisations 3
Stahl, Georg 154, 155, 167
staining techniques in histology 250
Standard Oil of Indiana 236
Stanford Linear Accelerator 297
Stanhope, Lord 238
Stanley brothers 'Steamer' 220
stannite (tin pyrites) 29
star formation and evolution 286-290
starch 279
Starley, James 241
Stas, J. S. 178, 179
statistical analysis, misused 386, 388

Steady State Hypothesis 294
steam power 212-214, 219-220
    in agriculture 223
    propulsion of ships 218-219
steam rotating sphere 61, 214
steam turbines 214, 219
steel making, early 30, 31
steel technology, 1700-1900 228-230
Steno, Niels 246
Stephen, Bishop of Rome 74-75, 87-88
Stephenson, George 220, 221
stereo-isomerism 249-250
sterile medical equipment and procedures 250
Stevens, Thomas 241
Stevin, Simon 142
Stirling 133
Stockton to Darlington railway 220
Stoicism 337, 340, 348, 364
Stoics 54-55, 57, 337, 338
stone buildings, development of 20, 21
Stourbridge Lion 221
Strabo of Amasia 30, 63, 123
Strassman, Hans 270
Stratigraphical System of Organised Fossils 246
Strato of Thrace 54
Street, Robert 214
String Theory 298
Stroud, Carlos 321
Strowger, Almon B. 239
structure, chemical determination, in carbon chemistry 281-283
structures, chemically determined, confirmation of, in carbon chemistry 283-285
Strutt, Jedediah 225
Strutt, R. J. 299
Struve, F. G. W. 244
Sturmey-Archer 241
submarines, nuclear 324-325
Suez Canal 219
sulphanomides 314
sulphur dioxide emissions 384-385
sulphuric acid manufacturing 235
Sumeria 19, 26, 36
Sumerian numeral system 16
Sumerian phonetic syllables 378
Sumerian wedge syllables (cuneiform) 16
Sumerians 36

Breinigsville, PA USA
29 March 2010

235133BV00002B/43/P